To
Brenda, Kateri, and Kristina

Printed in the United States of America.

Library of Congress Catalog Card Number 94–78775

Text Only:
    ISBN 1–878975–54–4
Text + Student Resource Manual:
    ISBN 1–878975–46–3

Kolb Publishing Company
6395 Gunpark Drive, Suite N, Boulder, CO 80301
(303) 530-7778   FAX (303) 530-7773

Preface

The Fourth Edition of *Investments* builds on the strength of the first three editions, and it features a number of important refinements. As with the first three editions, *Investments* provides a comprehensive analytical survey of the investments field, including portfolio theory and security analysis. Furthermore, it incorporates an integrated treatment of financial derivatives, with chapters on futures, options, swaps, and financial engineering. The text has been thoroughly revised and updated, and its readability has been improved throughout. As a learning vehicle, this new edition of *Investments* continues the comprehensive approach adopted in the Third Edition. As an integral part of the entire package, *Investments* includes:

- the text
- a Student Resource Manual and Software Guide
- an extensive selection of computer programs and exercises designed to enhance the learning of investments.

These elements are fully integrated, and they are designed to be mutually supportive.

The Text

The *Investments* text has many distinctive features. Capital Market Theory is kept in view throughout. The text is quantitative enough to support analytical rigor, but advanced topics are generally presented without an overly mathematical treatment. For example, *Investments* takes an intuitive approach to such topics as market anomalies, the joint character of tests of the Efficient Markets Hypothesis and the Capital Asset Pricing Model, Roll's critique of the CAPM, and the Arbitrage Pricing Theory.

Every chapter includes a section of questions and problems (to be used with the Instructor's Manual) and a list of Suggested Readings relevant to the chapter. In the Fourth Edition, these student exercises have been greatly strengthened in two ways. First, the text includes more than 100 questions and problems that have been drawn from recent examinations for the Chartered Financial Analyst (CFA) designation. These are reprinted by permission of the Association for Investment Management and Research (AIMR). They are clearly labeled and emphasize to the student that the material covered in the text has a strong and obvious practical relevance. Second, the end–of–chapter questions and problems include a number of exercises using real–world data that reinforce the material covered in the chapter.

Consistent with changing finance curriculums, this new edition of *Investments* has a higher proportion of international topics than virtually any other text in the market. Most chapters include a treatment of international topics as an integrated feature of the chapter development.

Investments is organized into five parts. Since the book makes no assumptions about previous study or knowledge of investments, Part One examines market fundamentals and organization. After introducing the concepts of risk and return in Chapter 1, the two most prevalent kinds of securities—stocks and bonds—are discussed. Chapter 2 deals with the debt market, and Chapter 3 focuses on the stock market. Chapter 4 examines security issuance, and Chapter 5 lists sources of investment information. Part One closes with a detailed look at regulation and taxation in Chapter 6. While much of this material is descriptive and institutional in character, it provides the necessary background for understanding risks, returns, and their trade–offs.

Part Two explores investing in fixed income securities. Bond pricing and bond portfolio management are examined. In Chapter 7, general principles of bond prices and price behavior are developed and duration is explained. In addition, Chapter 7 includes a discussion of convexity. Chapter 8 discusses bond portfolio management and considers the term structure of interest rates, the risk structure of interest rates, portfolio maturity strategies, and immunization techniques.

Part Three focuses on investing in equities. Traditional fundamental stock analysis is presented by looking at the decision rules for investing in stocks. Chapter 9 develops stock pricing principles through the Dividend Valuation Model. The three traditional phases of stock analysis are then presented in three respective chapters: Chapter 10 covers analysis of the economy, Chapter 11 covers industry analysis, and Chapter 12 focuses on company analysis. Concepts explored in these three chapters include leading economic indicators and forecasting results, demographic factors and social change, and the Fundamental Analyst's Model with the factors that determine the justified P/E ratio.

In a complex and varied security market, the investor must evaluate many different securities and types of securities. It is across these many instruments that the investor must allocate investment funds. The study of the best way to apportion funds to existing investment opportunities is treated in Part Four, portfolio management. Diversification and portfolio formation are treated in Chapter 13. In Chapter 14, the market price of risk is developed through analysis of the capital market line and the security market line. The effect of the efficient markets hypothesis on the performance standard set up in the capital asset pricing model (CAPM) is explored in Chapter 15, as are challenges to the CAPM. Chapter 16 looks at mutual funds, an entire industry which has grown up around the concept of diversification.

Part Five explores financial derivatives, and it consists of separate chapters on futures, options, swaps, and financial engineering. Chapter 17 examines the role of futures contracts in controlling risk in portfolio management, and Chapter 18 does the same for options. Chapter 19 provides an introduction to the swap market. Chapter 20, on financial engineering, shows how futures, options, and swaps can be used together to create new products with special risk and return characteristics.

The Student Resource Manual

This 500–page book is an integral part of the *Investments* learning package. For each chapter, the Manual includes a detailed outline of the chapter contents, numerous multiple–choice study questions, and a review of the chapter's key terms and concepts. In addition, there are study questions and problems with answers and solutions for all of chapters.

Software

As an integral part of the entire learning package, *Investments* includes three different types of software. Most finance texts do not include software. Of those texts accompanied by software, the software is generally an afterthought. In many instances, the software is not specific to the text and it lacks instructions.

Investments is different; it includes three dramatically different computer and software resources to aid in learning investments. The Fourth Edition of *Investments* includes *REALDATA*—a comprehensive resource of real–world data and more than 100 computer exercises that employ the data. Second, the book contains the latest version of the *Investmaster* software that accompanied earlier editions. The third program is *STUDY!*, which is essentially a study guide and self–testing program on a disk. Each of these programs is discussed fully in the software instructions portion of the Student Resource Manual.

REALDATA. REALDATA consists of approximately 700 time series of real–world financial and economic data. The types of data range from money supply figures, to interest rate series, to stock returns data, to mutual fund indexes, to price indexes, and beyond. These data are contained in 36 spreadsheet files. The instructions in the *Student Resource Manual* present definitions of each series so that students can find a particular variable easily. The *Student Resource Manual* also contains more than 100 computer exercises using the data provided. For example, one exercise might ask a student to find and interpret the beta of Apple Computer. Another exercise might ask students to compute and explain the correlations among alternative stock market indexes. These exercises are keyed to particular chapters of *Investments* so that students may solve the exercises to build their knowledge of particular concepts they are studying. I have used *REALDATA* in my investment classes, and I have found it to be a powerful tool for helping students extend their understanding.

Investmaster. Investmaster, which accompanied earlier editions of this text, has been revised to accompany the Fourth Edition. The program contains ten modules that cover the gamut of the investments course, including: coupon bond analysis, the dividend valuation model, the Black–Scholes option pricing model, portfolio diversification, regression analysis, and statistical analysis.

Where appropriate, each module includes a graphics feature. For example, it is very easy to use *Investmaster* to explore how changing the correlation between the returns of two securities will affect the risk of a two–asset portfolio. *Investmaster* can graph this changing relationship with ease. The user can save and recall data sets for further analysis. *Investmaster* can save its graphs to a PCX file for printing by most standard word processing programs. In sum, *Investmaster* has become a proven software support item, and this new version includes a number of important improvements and enhancements.

STUDY!. The program *STUDY!* includes a bank of multiple–choice questions created specifically for *Investments*. The student begins the program by selecting any combination of chapters for study. The program loads all available questions for those chapters in a random order and begins to present them to the student. If the student answers correctly, the program updates the student's score on screen and moves to the next question. If the student's answer is wrong, the program gives the correct answer and updates the score. By using the *STUDY!* program, students can cover all of the essential conceptual issues in any set of chapters that they choose.

The Instructor's Package

Investments is supplemented by a complete instructional package. I believe it is the best package to accompany any text. It includes four elements.

- ♦ Instructor's Manual and Test Bank
- ♦ Computerized Test Bank
- ♦ Transparency Masters of tables and figures
- ♦ Lecture Notes presented as transparency masters

The Instructor's Manual and Test Bank contains answers and solutions to all end–of–chapter questions and problems, including the CFA questions and solutions to all *REALDATA* exercises. It also contains a multiple–choice test bank. The Computerized Test Bank is prepared for IBM–PC type computers. It consists of files of multiple–choice questions for each chapter. (These are the same questions printed in the Instructor's Manual and Test Bank.) The Test Bank questions are presented in WordPerfect files. This approach allows the instructor to use his or her familiar word processing software and avoids the need for learning a specialized test–generating software package.

The Instructor's Package also includes a comprehensive set of Transparency Masters of tables and figures from the text. In addition, the Instructor's Package provides a comprehensive set of Lecture Notes to cover all of the key topics in the text. These are presented in large type, so they can be used as easy–to–see lecture notes, or they can be used as transparency masters for outlines of lecture topics.

Acknowledgments

This text required the sustained efforts of many people. A number of colleagues from different universities have contributed to this book through reading and commenting on earlier editions. I would specifically like to thank the following colleagues:

Raj Aggarwal	John Carroll University
Omar M. Benkato	Ball State University
Richard Boebel	Tulane University
Genna Brown	University of Miami
Thor W. Bruce	University of Miami
Thomas Burrows	California State University at Dominguez Hills
Idupeep S. Chhachhi	Western Kentucky University
Pat Clarke	University of Massachusetts
Francis Colella	Simpson College
Martin Engelken	Trinity College
Randy Ferrer	University of Miami
Richard Followill	Radford University
Julian E. Gaspar	Texas A & M University
Gaylon E. Greer	Memphis State University
Jae Ha Lee	University of Oklahoma
Patrick A. Hays	Western Carolina University
Kendall P. Hill	University of Alabama
Eugene Istchenko	University of Miami
Robert K. Jabs	California Baptist College
Steven L. Jones	University of Georgia
Alan Jung	San Francisco State University
Ronie Karanjia	Fordham University
Daniel J. Kaufman	Wright State University
Suk H. Kim	University of Detroit Mercy
Malek K. Lashgari	University of Hartford
Ricardo Leal	Georgetown University
Herman Manakyan	Western Kentucky University
Bala Maniam	Texas A & M International
Robert W. McLeod	University of Alabama
Stuart Michelson	Eastern Illinois University
David B. Milton	Bentley College
Michael Muoghalu	Pittsburgh State University
Akorlie Nyatepe–Coo	University of Wisconsin at La Crosse
Richard T. Nyerges	Southern Illinois University
James E. Owers	Georgia State University
Spuma M. Rao	University of Southwestern Louisiana
Ricardo Rodriguez	University of Miami
Kevin Stephenson	Middlebury College
Max Zavanelli	Stetson University

Here at Kolb Publishing I would like to thank Adam Carlin, who worked long and hard to improve the *Student Resource Manual*, the *Instructor's Manual*, and the accuracy of the text. Randy Ferrer and Eugene Istchenko independently solved all of the *REALDATA* exercises to ensure the accuracy of the solutions in the *Instructor's Manual*. Kateri Davis managed the production process, and Ami Corbett assisted in the typesetting of the ancillaries. Evelyn Gosnell prepared the computer–drawn graphics for the entire text. Andrea Coens edited the text and all of the ancillaries, and Sandi Schroeder prepared the index. Joe Rodriguez designed the cover. Brian Wilson of Ryder Systems prepared much of the *REALDATA* material.

Sharyn Ladner of Richter Library at the University of Miami provided access to materials. The cover photograph shows a detail of a totem pole in Vancouver, British Columbia.

As the long list of acknowledgments indicates, preparing a package such as *Investments* involves many steps and the efforts of many contributors. I am indebted to all of them, for without their efforts this new edition would never have seen the light of day.

Robert W. Kolb
University of Miami

Contents

CHAPTER TWO

The Debt Market   28

CHAPTER THREE

The Stock Market: An Overview   85

The Primary Market and Investment Banking   **138**

Sources of Investment Information   **161**

CHAPTER SIX

The Security Market: Regulation and Taxation   182

PART TWO
Investing in Debt Instruments   197

CHAPTER SEVEN

Bond Pricing Principles   *199*

CHAPTER EIGHT

Bond Portfolio Management   *244*

PART THREE
Investing in Equities   291

CHAPTER NINE

Preferred and Common Stock Valuation   *293*

CHAPTER TEN

Economic Analysis and the Stock Market   **320**

CHAPTER ELEVEN

Industry Analysis   **350**

CHAPTER TWELVE

Company Analysis   *381*

PART FOUR
Portfolio Management

CHAPTER THIRTEEN

Diversification and Portfolio Formation 407

The Market Price of Risk 445

Efficient Markets and the Capital Asset Pricing Model 489

Investment Companies and Performance Evaluation 540

PART FIVE
Financial Derivatives and Risk Management   565

CHAPTER SEVENTEEN

The Futures Market   *567*

CHAPTER EIGHTEEN

The Options Market   603

CHAPTER NINETEEN

The Swap Market 644

CHAPTER TWENTY

Financial Engineering 670

Appendix   *697*

Index   *699*

Market Fundamentals and Organization

Part One of this book consists of the first six chapters. These chapters acquaint the reader with the overall structure of securities markets and introduce some of the basic concepts that are necessary to successful investing.

Chapter 1 presents some of the key measures of profitability for investments and shows that the riskiness of an investment is a key element in the investor's decision. Basically, the greater amount of risk that an investment involves, the higher must be the reward to the investor. Chapter 1 also introduces some of the key measures of risk.

Chapters 2 and 3 discuss the organization of the bond market and the stock market. These markets are extremely well developed in the United States, and offer the investor a wide variety of different investment options. A knowledge of the different markets and instruments is important for the success of any investor. Chapter 4 discusses the primary market—the market for the creation and original issuance of securities. The primary market is extremely important to firms because corporations raise the new capital necessary for the conduct of their businesses by issuing securities in the primary market.

Investors are almost always in search of new information. Because of this, a familiarity with the various sources of information is essential. Chapter 5 introduces many of the most important sources of investment information and explains how they are used. It also presents samples of many of the most important investor publications. While investors may seek information, they cannot avoid regulation and taxes. These topics are covered in Chapter 6. The securities markets are regulated by several different federal organizations, and their overlapping jurisdictions are important to understand. A knowledge of the principles of taxation is also crucial to investment success. By being aware of some clear rules for the control of taxes, investors can greatly enhance the after-tax returns from their investments.

Introduction

Overview

There are many kinds of investments, and this text deals with one very important kind—investment in financial claims, such as stocks and bonds. This chapter begins by distinguishing among the kinds of investments discussed in this book and then explains the goals of investing in securities. Like all investments, investment in financial claims requires the reduction of consumption in the present in the hope of increasing consumption opportunities in the future. The increase in consumption in later periods is the return on the investment, and it is the anticipation of this return that motivates the investor to reduce current consumption.

Like all other kinds of investments, investing in financial claims involves the choice of some level of risk. The investor can choose investments that have virtually no risk or investments that have a great deal of risk. For the present, think of risk as the chance that the investment will have an undesirable result—such as the loss of the invested funds. Later in this chapter, we learn to measure risk quantitatively.

The basic problem confronting any investor is to secure the desired return while avoiding undesired risk. The quick answer to this dilemma is to invest where there is high return and low risk. However, investment opportunities with high expected return are almost invariably accompanied by high risk. This basic fact makes the study of investments exciting and important, because the investor must find an answer to the following question: How can I find those investments with the best combination of risk and return? There is a trade–off between the good (high returns) and the bad (high risk), and the investor must know how to measure both returns and risk, and how to choose the investment with the most favorable combination. This chapter introduces the basic ideas of risk and return and the unavoidable trade–off between them, and it shows how to measure them. The chapter concludes with a survey of the organization of the book.

Securities Investment

This book is an introduction to the world of investing in securities, examining only a special portion of the different kinds of investments that can take place. When Robinson Crusoe refrained from eating an ear of corn in order to use the corn for seed, he made a very important investment. He might have put the corn under his mattress to eat the next day, but that would not have been investment. Investment requires foregoing consumption today in order to have a greater expected amount of a particular good in the future. By using the corn for seed, he sacrificed the immediate consumption of the corn in exchange for the hope of a more plentiful supply of corn in the future. While this was certainly a case of investment, Robinson Crusoe did not invest in securities. A **security** is a financial claim, usually evidenced by a piece of paper, on some other good. For example, a share of stock represents a fractional ownership in all of the real assets and productive resources of a corporation. If you own a share of the common stock of General Motors, you own a fraction of the real assets of General Motors, such as its plants and equipment, land, inventory, and all of the other goods owned by the corporation. Securities often represent a title to some set of real assets, but that is not always the case. The U.S. Treasury issues bonds to help finance the national debt, and Treasury obligations are securities. But a Treasury bond gives its owner the right to expect periodic cash payments from the government and nothing more. It does not represent an ownership interest in the land, weapons, buildings, and other physical assets owned by the government. In short, securities may represent title to real assets or they may be strictly financial claims, calling for payment by another financial asset under specific circumstances.

The restriction of our discussion to securities investment is an important one, one that does not really consider the decision to acquire physical assets as investments (for example, collectibles such as stamps, coins, art works, or even real estate). Finance theory treats the decision to acquire physical assets in corporate finance as a capital budgeting decision. As explained later, the principles that govern securities investment are very close in spirit to those that govern capital budgeting decisions, but there is an important difference in the goods that are acquired by the two investment processes.

The Goals of Investment

At one level, it is fairly easy to state the goal of investing in securities—the goal is to make money! To make money by investing in securities requires that the investor choose some level of risk. With the realization that you must choose a risk level, the goal of investing becomes more difficult to specify.

In this book, we make several simplifying assumptions about the typical investor. First, we assume the investor is interested only in the monetary benefits of investing. The investor is not, for example, interested in the pleasures that might be obtained from tracking an investment portfolio on a daily basis. Second, we assume the investor prefers more wealth to less, other things being equal. Finally, we assume the investor is risk–averse; that is, the investor prefers to avoid risk where possible. This does not mean that the investor will refuse to undertake risk. Rather, it means that he or she will demand compensation, in the form of a greater anticipated investment profit, for the bearing of risk.

These last two assumptions, which seem to describe most people quite realistically, point out the essential tension that characterizes securities investment. The investment opportunities that seem to offer the greatest increase in wealth tend also to be the riskiest. The investor will typically face a situation in which a benefit—higher return on the investment—has to be traded off against an undesired element—the greater riskiness of the investment. If it were not for the conflict between the desirability of large profits on the investment and the riskiness that seeking such large profits entails, it would be quite simple to state the goal of securities investments.

Given the fact that the investor constantly tries to secure high investment profits, while controlling exposure to risk, the goal of investing can be stated as follows:

- for a given level of risk, to secure the highest expected return possible, or,

- for a particular required rate of return, to secure the return with the lowest risk possible

This definition of the goal of investing makes clear the nature of the trade–off between risk and return. However, the key words in the definition ("risk" and "return") are not specified with sufficient precision. Also, the definition is not very helpful in one way. While it makes clear that there is a trade–off between risk and return, it says nothing about how an investor should make the trade–off. We will address both of these questions in turn. Actually, most of this book is about how to make the trade–off between risk and return. This problem is considered in different contexts in many of the subsequent chapters, and Chapters 14 and 15 analyze this problem.

The Measurement of Return

Different techniques exist for measuring the return on an investment. In the investment community, a variety of these measures are used, so it is important to know several. This section introduces some useful measures of the return on an investment.

The Wealth Relative (WR)

One of the most useful measures of an investment's return is the **wealth relative**, or **WR**, and it can be defined very simply:

$$WR = \frac{\text{Current Value of Investment}}{\text{Original Value of Investment}} \qquad \textbf{1.1}$$

We can illustrate this measure with an example. Assume an investor purchases one share of stock in firm XYZ on April 1 for $88.00. Three months later, on July 1, the stock price is $94.50. In this case, the holding period was three months, extending from April 1 to July 1. Thus we define the **holding period** as the length of time an investment is held. According to the formula given above, the wealth relative for this investment would be:

$$WR = \frac{94.50}{88.00} = 1.0739$$

There are several important features and limitations of the wealth relative as a measure of investment performance. One good point about the WR is its ease of computation. Also, the WR tends to have a value around 1.0. If there is a profit on an investment during a given holding period, the WR will be greater than 1.0. A loss means that the WR would be less than 1.0. No profit or loss would be indicated by a WR equal to 1.0. Note also that there cannot be a negative WR. The worst case occurs when you invest money and lose it all. In such a situation, the WR is zero, but it will never be negative.

Returns and Yields

While the WR is a convenient measure of an investment's performance, and one that is used extensively throughout this text, the WR has certain limitations. The WR given earlier must be converted into a **return** or **yield** to be stated in percentage terms. We use return and yield interchangeably throughout the text to refer to a percentage change in the value of an investment. The relationship between the WR and the return or yield is very straightforward:

$$\text{Return} = WR - 1 \qquad \textbf{1.2}$$

In the preceding example, the return is .0739 or 7.39 percent:

$$\text{Return} = 1.0739 - 1 = .0739 = 7.39\%$$

Now we have distinguished WRs, which have typical values about 1.0, and returns, with typical values around zero. In the investment community, one often hears talk of "10 percent returns" and so on. In other words, "return" is often used to refer to the percentage change in the value of an asset.

To say that this particular investment had a WR of 1.0739 or a return of 7.39 percent does not tell everything that we might want to know about the performance of this investment. In particular, the investment covered only three months, so it would be difficult to compare this investment's performance with another investment with a different time frame. To solve that problem, it is customary to report returns and yields on an annualized basis. So WRs and returns typically need to be annualized. If all investment returns are expressed as the return per annum, then it is much easier to compare the performance of several investments.

Annualized WRs and Returns

In the preceding example, the investment earned a return of 7.39 percent in only three months. This simple return can be converted to an annual basis by using the simple WR and applying the following formula:

$$\text{Annualized WR} = \text{WR}^{(1/n)} \qquad \qquad \textbf{1.3}$$

where n = number of years the investment is held.

In terms of the example, the investment had a WR of 1.0739 and was held for three months (or one–quarter of a year). The annualized WR can be calculated using Equation 1.3 as follows:

$$\text{Annualized WR} = 1.0739^{(1/.25)} = 1.0739^4 = 1.33$$

The annualized return bears the same relationship to the annualized WR as the simple return does to the simple WR:

$$\text{Annualized Return} = \text{Annualized WR} - 1 \qquad \qquad \textbf{1.4}$$

In the example, the annualized return can be calculated to be 33 percent:

$$\text{Annualized Return} = 1.33 - 1 = .33 = 33\%$$

If an investment has a return of 7.39 percent in one–quarter of a year, it is tempting to think that an annual rate of earnings would be four times as great, or at a rate of 29.56 percent. If an investment really has a gain of 7.39 percent in three months, then the profit is available for reinvestment, and the potential for compounding needs to be considered.

The method shown in Equation 1.3 implicitly assumes that the earnings on the investment can be compounded at an interval equal to the period over which the WR was originally measured, in this case quarterly. In other words, it assumes that the investment will earn a return of 7.39 percent every quarter, and that the funds invested from quarter to quarter will include the gains (or losses) of the previous quarters. By contrast, just multiplying the first quarter's return of 7.39 percent by four in order to approximate the return for the year would be assuming implicitly that there was no compounding whatsoever.

These differences are important to consider and even play a significant role in politics from time to time, especially when politicians speak about inflation. Assume that in January the inflation rate is 2 percent. If we want to extrapolate January's inflation rate to the whole year, we have at least two choices. The anti–administration forces would have a natural tendency to employ an assumption of compounding, since taking account of compounding always produces a greater calculated change. These politicians might say that the 2 percent inflation rate of January was at an annual rate of 26.82 percent. Such a claim would, in fact, be reasonable, since the politician would be assuming that every month there would be a 2 percent price rise over the price level in effect at the beginning of the month. Such a calculation would be:

$$\text{Annual Inflation Rate} = 1.02^{12} - 1 = 1.2682 - 1 = 26.82\%$$

Raising 1.02 to the twelfth power reflects the assumption that there will be a monthly increase of 2 percent, which will be an increase on the preceding month's change as well. This is exactly the same kind of calculation used in the preceding example to calculate an annualized return.

The administration, needing to defend a 2 percent inflation rate in January, would have a natural tendency to minimize the bad news. Administration spokespeople might say that the inflation rate was at an annual rate of 24 percent (i.e., 2 percent times 12 months). Either way, the inflation rate is bad enough, but it is probably more accurate in this case to consider the compounding.

All such return calculations implicitly employ some assumption about the compounding interval. The important point is to be aware that some assumption is being made and to make sure to use comparable assumptions when trying to compare returns on two or more investments.

The Measurement of Mean Return

There are two different kinds of mean (or average) returns that need to be distinguished. For a single investment, with returns measured for a number of periods, there is a mean return per period. On the other hand, for a group of investments measured over the same time period, there can also be a mean return for the various investments that comprise the group. The method for calculating these is different, so it is important to keep the ideas separate.

Measuring Mean Return for a Single Investment

Investors often hold a security for a number of periods and have information about the return on the investment for each of the periods. Calculating the mean return

Table 1.1

━━━━━━━━━━━━━━━

Investment Returns for a Single Investment

Year	Year–End Price	WR	Return
1991	$11.50	—	—
1992	14.75	1.2826	28.26%
1993	12.30	.8339	−16.61
1994	15.60	1.2683	26.83

for a single investment can be illustrated best by an example. Consider the information given on such an investment in Table 1.1. Over the entire period, from year–end 1991 to year–end 1994, the WR was 1.3565 (15.60/11.50) and the annualized WR was 1.1070, which equals $1.3565^{.33}$.

The mean return on a single investment over several time periods should have a special property. If the mean return were earned in each of the time periods, the wealth at the end of the entire holding period should equal the wealth that was actually achieved. In terms of this example, an initial investment of $11.50 that earned a mean return for three successive periods should give a final wealth of $15.60. The use of WRs gives an easy way to find such a mean return.

For investment over successive time periods, the mean return can be found by multiplying together the WRs from the successive periods and taking the nth root of the product, where n equals the number of time periods. Such a mean is known as a **geometric mean**. In this example:

$$\text{Mean WR} = [(\text{WR}_{1992})\,(\text{WR}_{1993})\,(\text{WR}_{1994})]^{.33}$$

$$= [(1.2826)\,(.8339)\,(1.2683)]^{.33}$$

$$= 1.1070$$

If this mean WR of 1.1070 had been earned in each of the three periods, the final wealth would have been equal to $15.60, as the following equation shows:

$$\text{Final Wealth} = \$15.60 = (\$11.50)\,(1.1070)^3$$

At first it seems awkward to use this method of multiplying all WRs together. Instead, it seems more intuitive to take the simple arithmetic average of the WRs to find the mean. Doing that gives an arithmetic mean WR of 1.1283.

While this may be more intuitive to calculate, it has the disadvantage of being misleading. If the investment had a WR of 1.1283 in each of three years, the final terminal wealth would have been $16.52, not the $15.60 that was actually achieved.

Using the geometric mean gives a mean WR that is more informative for measuring the mean return on an investment over successive time periods, and for that reason it will be used throughout this book.

Once we have found the mean WR, the mean return follows immediately, because:

$$\text{Mean return} = \text{Mean WR} - 1$$

Measuring the Mean Return for a Group of Investments

When managing a group of investments (for example, a portfolio of a number of stocks), it is often important to know what the mean return was across the whole set of investments. In such a situation, there are still two different cases to consider. First, there could be an equal investment in all of the different assets. Alternatively, there might be different amounts invested in the various assets. The calculation of the mean return for both cases can use the same basic formula:

$$\text{Mean WR} = \sum_{t=1}^{N} w_i \, \text{WR}_i \qquad \textbf{1.5}$$

where:

w_i = the percent of funds committed to Asset i
WR_i = the WR for Asset i
N = the number of assets in the portfolio

The calculation of the mean WR for a group of assets can be illustrated using the data in Table 1.2, and this shows how to interpret the Greek letter Σ (*sigma*) in Equation 1.5. The mean return for all of these investments taken as a group is given by an application of Equation 1.5:

$$
\begin{aligned}
\text{Mean WR} \ &= \ (.10)\,(1.15) + (.65)\,(1.04) + (.25)\,(.93) \\
&= \ .115 + .676 + .2325 \\
&= \ 1.0235
\end{aligned}
$$

Table 1.2

Returns on a Group of Assets

Asset	Amount Invested	Percentage	WR
A	$100	.10	1.15
B	650	.65	1.04
C	250	.25	.93

The mean WR, taking into account the different amounts of money committed to each of the assets, is 1.0235. In the special case where equal amounts are committed to all of the assets, the term w_i simply drops out of Equation 1.5, since all of the assets are alike in the proportion of funds they receive.

These two different mean WRs, one for a single investment over time and one for a group of investments over the same time period, need to be kept distinct. Notice especially that both are called **mean WRs**. In the actual investment world, there are no special terms to keep these ideas separate, so the individual must determine which measure of the mean WR is appropriate for the particular case at hand.

The Measurement of Risk

There are many ways of talking about risk, and most of them are misleading to one degree or another. For example, people in the investment community often talk about "downside risk and upside potential." For the sake of convenience, it is useful to have a standardized way of measuring risk that is also precise.

The best way of measuring risk for investments is to focus on the variance σ^2 and standard deviation σ of the WR or return. One convenient feature of these risk measures is that they have a definite relationship. The standard deviation is the square root of the variance. The decision to measure risk by the variance or standard deviation implies that the investor is interested in the dispersion of WRs or returns from their means. The greater the chance of getting a result far away from the mean, the greater the risk of a particular investment. Figure 1.1 illustrates this difference in risk by showing the probability distribution of returns for two hypothetical assets.

The mean WRs for these two assets are both 1.0. No matter which asset is chosen, an investor would expect to earn the same WR. The difference between the two lies in the amount of risk that each involves. Since the returns on both securities are normally distributed, it is necessarily the case that about 67 percent of the total area under the curve lies within one standard deviation of the mean.[1] For Asset A, the standard deviation of returns is .15, but for Asset B, the standard deviation is .30.

For Asset A, there is a .67 probability of getting a return that falls in the range from .85 to 1.15. For Asset B, there is a .67 probability of getting a return that falls in the range from .70 to 1.30. This means that the chance of getting very large or very small returns from Asset B is higher than the chance of getting such returns from Asset A. When considering risk, most investors are interested in avoiding the probability of extremely low returns. Because Assets A and B are assumed to have returns that are normally distributed, we can say exactly what those probabilities are. With Asset A, for example, there is only about a 2.5 percent chance of getting

---

[1]For more on probability distributions, see J. Kmenta, *Elements of Econometrics*, 2e, New York: Macmillan, 1986, Chapter 3.

Figure 1.1

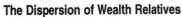

The Dispersion of Wealth Relatives

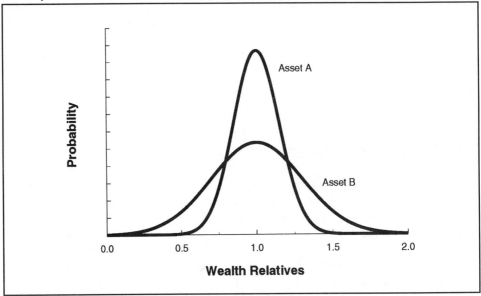

a WR less than .7. This is so because a WR of .7 is two standard deviations below the mean return. Since Asset A's returns are distributed normally, we know that there is only a 2.5 percent chance of a return that is two standard deviations below the mean return. But with Asset B, there is a 16.5 percent chance of a WR as low as .7. For Asset B, a WR of .7 is only one standard deviation below the WR. With normally distributed returns, the chance for a return one standard deviation below the mean is about 16.5 percent. Obviously, Asset B is much riskier than Asset A, because Asset B has a much greater chance of a low WR.

Our discussion thus far has been only an intuitive way of explaining the idea of risk that is measured by the variance or standard deviation. It is not always convenient or meaningful to make risk comparisons in such a way, so it is valuable to have a more precise measure, which is provided by the variance or standard deviation. The variance of the WR is defined by the following equation:

$$\sigma^2_{WR} = \sum_{t=1}^{T} \frac{(WR_1 - \text{Mean WR})^2}{T} \qquad \textbf{1.6}$$

where:

T = the number of individual WRs being used to make the calculation
Mean WR = the arithmetic mean WR

Table 1.3

Calculation of the Standard Deviation and Variance

t	WR_t	WR_t – Mean WR	$(WR_t$ – Mean WR$)^2$
1	1.14	.12	.0144
2	1.07	.05	.0025
3	1.03	.01	.0001
4	.84	−.18	.0324
			Sum = .0494

Arithmetic mean WR = 1.02.

The calculation of the variance and standard deviation can be illustrated in an example using the data of Table 1.3. The table uses four time periods of data to compute the variance of the WR. Over these four periods, the WRs diverged quite significantly. At best there was a 14 percent positive return and at worst a loss of 16 percent. These raw data are shown in the column labeled "WR_t," from which the arithmetic mean WR of 1.02 was calculated. The next step is to subtract the arithmetic mean return from each of the individual returns, as shown in Column 3. The entries in Column 3 are called deviations. The next step, the results of which are shown in Column 4, is to square each of the deviations. The sum of the squared deviations is .0494, as shown at the foot of Column 4. The variance equals the sum of the squared deviations divided by the number of periods of data used in the calculation. In this case:

$$\sigma^2_{WR} = .0494/4 = .01235$$

$$\sigma = \sqrt{\sigma^2} = \sqrt{.01235} = .1111$$

The variance and standard deviation can be compared with those of other assets to provide a comparison of the risk levels. Of the two risk measures, the standard deviation is probably the more useful, since its units have the same magnitude as the variable being measured. In this case, the standard deviation was .1111 or 11.11 percent. Based on the data in Table 1.3, there is about a 67 percent chance that the WRs for the asset in question will fall in the range of .9089 to 1.1311.[2]

---

[2]This assumes that the probability returns distribution is normally distributed and stationary. These assumptions are not always exactly appropriate, but they are sufficiently rigorous for present purposes.

Historical Returns and Risk

To this point, we have seen how to measure WRs and returns, along with the risk of investments. We now consider the historical performance of broad asset classes to emphasize these concepts. To do this, we consider the period from the end of 1925 to the end of 1993—a period of 68 years—and we focus on three broad asset classes: common stocks, Treasury bills (T–bills), and long–term Treasury bonds (T–bonds). (As the next chapter explains in more detail, Treasury bills are debt obligations of the U.S. Treasury issued to allow the government to borrow for a period of one year or less. Treasury bonds are long–term borrowings of the U.S. Treasury.)

Figure 1.2 shows how an investment in each of these asset classes would have performed from year–end 1925 to year–end 1993, by focusing on a $1 investment in each asset class. The analysis assumes that any proceeds from the investment are

Figure 1.2

Wealth Indexes for Common Stocks, T–Bonds, and T–Bills
1926–1993

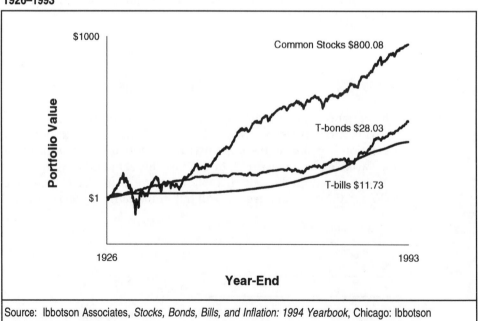

Source: Ibbotson Associates, *Stocks, Bonds, Bills, and Inflation: 1994 Yearbook*, Chicago: Ibbotson Associates, Inc., 1994.

reinvested in the same asset class. A dollar invested in common stocks would have grown to $800.08.[3] A dollar invested in Treasury bonds would have grown to $28.03, and a dollar invested in Treasury bills would have grown to $11.73. Obviously, a policy of investing in common stocks over this period would have paid much better than lending to the U.S. government by buying Treasury bills or bonds.

There is another side to the story, however. Investment in the different asset classes involves substantially different risks. For the 68 years from 1926–1993, the standard deviation of returns has been greatest for stocks, second for T–bonds, and lowest for T–bills:

Asset Class	Annualized Standard Deviation
Stocks	.205
T–bonds	.087
T–bills	.033

Table 1.4 summarizes the performance of stocks, bills, and bonds. Taking stocks as an example, the annualized WR over the entire period was 1.101, so the annualized return was 10.1 percent. The arithmetic mean WR was 1.121 and the standard deviation of the WRs was 20.8 percent. These statistics give a convenient way of summarizing a great deal of information. Knowing that the standard deviation of returns was 20.8 percent tells you that there is a 67 percent chance of an investment made in common stocks at the beginning of a year being worth somewhere in the range of 89.3 percent to 130.9 percent of its original value at

Table 1.4

■■■■■■■■■■

Investment Performance for Different Asset Classes
1926–1993

Asset Class	Annualized Mean Wealth Relatives		Annual Standard Deviation
	Geometric	Arithmetic	
Large Common Stocks	1.103	1.123	20.5%
Treasury Bills	1.037	1.037	3.3
Treasury Bonds	1.500	1.504	8.7

Source: Ibbotson Associates, *Stocks, Bonds, Bills, and Inflation: 1994 Yearbook*, Chicago: Ibbotson Associates, Inc., 1994, p. 31.

---

[3]These common stocks results are for larger companies. Small company stocks actually performed much better over this long period.

year's end. It also lets the potential investor know that there is a fairly large chance (about 33 percent) of gains or losses in a year in excess of 20.8 percent. The mean return and standard deviation of returns are two of the most important measures in all of contemporary investment thought. They will be used repeatedly throughout this text, both as measures to be considered for their own importance and as tools to explain other ideas.

Measuring Returns on Foreign Investments

One of the major themes of this text is the growing internationalization of the world of securities investing. Investing in foreign securities generally involves investing in an asset with cash flows denominated in a foreign currency. For example, German stocks pay dividends in German marks and Japanese bonds pay interest in Japanese yen. Each investor has a domestic currency in which she has the greatest interest. For example, the U.S. investor may invest abroad, but she is most interested in the dollar outcome of that investment.

Measuring return in a foreign investment requires that we consider not only the return on the foreign security, but that we also evaluate the effect of the exchange rate between the domestic and the foreign currency. The **exchange rate** is the price of one currency in terms of another. For example, if the exchange rate between the U.S. dollar and the German mark is $.55, this means that the dollar value of one mark is $.55. (By the same token, the mark value of one dollar is just the inverse of this amount $1/.55 = 1.8182$, meaning that one dollar is worth 1.8182 marks.)

To make this more concrete, let us assume that a U.S. investor buys a German stock for DM 100 and sells it in six months for DM 115. For this investment, the WR is $115/100 = 1.15$. However, from the point of view of the U.S. investor, it is also important to consider the effect of the exchange rate, because changes in the value of the dollar relative to the mark can have a very important effect on the dollar outcome of the investment.

For this same stock investment, let us assume that the exchange rate at the time the stock is purchased is .55, so one mark is worth $.55. Therefore, the dollar cost of the stock is $55 = (DM 100)($.55 per mark). At the end of the six–month holding period, let us assume that the mark is worth only $.52. In this case, the dollar proceeds from selling the German stock for DM 115 will be only $59.80 = (DM115)($.52 per mark).

We have already seen that the WR for the investment in the stock was 1.15, measured in marks. However, we also want to know the WR from the point of view of the U.S. investor. The U.S. investor committed $55 to the stock and received proceeds of only $59.80, which implies a WR of $1.0873 = $59.80/$55$. The falling value of the mark caused the WR to drop from 1.15 to 1.0873. Had the mark risen in value, the change in the exchange rate could have increased the WR measured in dollars. For example, if the mark had risen in value over the six months from $.55 to $.62, the dollar proceeds would have been $71.30 = (DM 115)($.62 per mark).

With this increase in the value of the mark, the WR measured in dollars would have been 1.2964 = $71.30/$55.

From this example, we can see that there are two ways to take the effect of changing exchange rates into account as we measure WRs. First, we can express all cash flows in the domestic currency, which would be dollars for our U.S. investor. If the investor buys a German stock for a net outlay of $55 and receives proceeds of $59.80 after the currency conversion, then the WR is simply $59.80/$55 = 1.0873. Second, we can find the WR measured in the domestic currency as follows:

$$WR_d = WR_f \left(\frac{FX_t}{FX_i} \right)$$

where:
WR_d = the WR measured in the domestic currency
WR_f = the WR measured in the foreign currency
FX_t = the exchange rate at the termination of the holding period
FX_i = the exchange rate at the initiation of the holding period

Applying this equation to our initial example, we noted that the holding period measured in German marks (WR_f) was 1.15. The exchange rate at the beginning of the investment (FX_i) was $.55 per mark and the terminal exchange rate (FX_t) was $.52. Therefore:

$$WR_d = 1.15 \left(\frac{\$.52}{\$.55} \right) = 1.0873$$

This is the same answer that we obtained before.

Risk and Expected Return: The Keys to Investment

This chapter has placed a great deal of emphasis on return and risk, because the correct understanding of these two concepts, and the relationship between them, is absolutely critical to a successful investor. Almost all investors prefer high expected returns and low risk. Unfortunately, investments with these characteristics are difficult to find. Certainly, all investors are competing to discover the high expected return/low risk investments.

This implies that there is a risk/expected return trade–off. The investor who demands high expected returns must be willing to bear high risk. This is the first key to successful investing. We must be aware of the existence of the risk/expected return trade–off and understand the nature of the trade–off in order to develop a successful investment strategy.

The second key is to understand that "there is no free lunch." This is a favorite saying of economists, who are fond of odd sayings. In this case, they mean that you cannot have something desirable without paying for it in one way or another. In the case of securities investment, the lunch is high expected return, and the price that is paid for it is the bearing of risk. Consequently, this second key is closely allied to the first, but it also means something more. In an important sense, investors are paid an equilibrium price for bearing risk. Understanding how that price of risk is determined and measured gives a potential investor or investment manager a much greater insight into the risks and potential rewards of securities investment.

The third key is to understand performance measurement correctly. There is probably no one of adult age in the United States who has not heard the tale of someone's fantastic profits in the stock market. From such stories, it is tempting to assume that the investor telling the (truthful?) story has done quite well. However, if there is a risk/expected return trade–off and there is no free lunch in the securities market, performance measurement becomes much more complicated.

We cannot measure performance simply by the profits reaped in a given trading period. Instead, to measure performance, we need to know how an investor's returns compare to the risk that was being borne. This implies that stories of great success in investing are almost totally meaningless as evidence of superior performance. To measure performance rationally, we must fit it into the web of risk and expected return. For example, a man recently won $40 million in a state–sponsored lottery. If this is all we know of the story, it sounds like an attractive opportunity. However, from this fact alone, we know nothing of the odds that this "investor" faced. To know whether participating in such a lottery is a good idea, we would also need to know the chances that we could win the same amount versus the risk that we would lose the price of the lottery ticket.

In conclusion, the careful reader of this book should be able to take possession of these three keys to successful investment:

1. There is a risk/expected return trade–off in the securities market.
2. There is no high return to be anticipated without the bearing of a high degree of risk.
3. The success or failure of any investment performance can only be measured by considering both the return that was earned and the degree of risk that was borne.

The chapters that follow are directed toward explaining these ideas and showing their relevance to investment management.

Organization of the Text

The book is organized into five parts, as follows:

I. Market Fundamentals and Organization
II. Investing in Debt Instruments
III. Investing in Equities

IV. Portfolio Management

V. Financial Derivatives and Portfolio Risk Management

In the chapters that make up each of these parts, more specialized topics are considered. One of the special features of the book is the emphasis on the international dimension of securities investments. Almost every chapter relates the chapter topic to the situation in countries outside the United States.

Each of the chapters that follow concludes with questions for you to consider. Most of these questions act to summarize the main ideas of the chapter, but some of them require more thought. Because securities investment necessarily involves an analytical approach in planning and measuring results, many chapters conclude with problems and exercises to help you sharpen developing skills.

Market Fundamentals and Organization

Since the book makes no assumptions about previous study or knowledge of investments, the first part of the book examines market fundamentals and the way they are organized. You might have looked at a copy of *The Wall Street Journal* at some time and been struck by the bewildering variety of numerical data presented and the special terminology employed. Almost all of this information is about securities or investing in securities.

One of the main goals of the first part of the text is to organize much of that information for you and help you to feel comfortable with the special vocabulary and ideas of investments. As a first step toward that goal, Part I, Market Fundamentals and Organization, discusses the two most prevalent kinds of securities—stocks and bonds—and the markets in which they are traded.

Many stocks and bonds have a very active life, passing from owner to owner. For most investors, this active life of a security is familiar. However, relatively little is known about how stocks and bonds came into existence. The familiar securities exchanges, such as the New York Stock Exchange and the American Stock Exchange, form an important part of the secondary market for securities. A **secondary market** is a market for already existing securities. A **primary market** is the market for the original issuance of securities. Because all stocks and bonds are created in this primary market, it is of crucial importance. Also, many of the most prestigious and highly paid jobs are to be found in **investment banking**—the segment of the securities industry that deals with the original distribution of securities in the primary market.

The government plays an important role in the working of the securities market through regulation and through taxation. These governmental activities need to be understood in order to profit from securities investment. Regulation affects all of the securities markets and has a great impact on the safety of investments and the kinds of profits that investors can make. For example, many observers believe that a lack of government regulation of the securities markets helped to bring about the stock market crash in October 1929, which ushered in the Great Depression.[4] Many also believe that lax governmental regulation helped to foment the Crash of 1987. Yet today, there is a strong movement by the government to deregulate areas of the economy such as transportation, health services, and the financial sector.

Perhaps even more important than government regulation is taxation. Many investment decisions are directly affected by tax laws and rules. The impact of taxation can often be the deciding factor in the decision to buy or sell a given security. Thanks to the tax laws, specialized firms have been developed to help investors avoid the effects of taxes. Taxation has even changed the very structure of the securities industry. For example, a significant portion of the securities markets is devoted to issues that have special tax–sheltering features.

These important general topics—security issuance and trading, the organization and scope of the basic markets, and the role of regulation and taxation—prepare you for the parts of the book that follow. While much of the material of Part I is descriptive and institutional in character, it provides the necessary background for understanding the risks and returns—and the trade–offs between them—that are most important for the securities investor.

Investing in Debt Instruments

Part II, Investing in Debt Instruments, introduces and explores the world of bonds. Generally speaking, any security that promises a fixed periodic payment is a bond. As we will also see, things are somewhat more complicated, since some bonds do not promise a fixed payment. Most bonds, however, have certain payments that are scheduled to be made at specific times.

Because bonds have similar features in terms of their payments, it is possible to develop general principles about bond prices and their behavior. This provides a way for the potential investor to determine which bonds are worthy of investment and which are not. With the 1985 failure of the Washington Public Power Supply Service to make its scheduled bond payments, the 1991 bankruptcy of Bridgeport, Connecticut, and with the continuing debt crisis in many Third World countries, it is clear that an understanding of the relationship of bond prices to such factors as the risk of the bonds is very important to the investor. In fact, as will become clear in almost every chapter, the relationship between a security's price and its level of risk is a very close one.

Investing in Equities

The stock market is probably the most familiar segment of the securities market. Part III, Investing in Equities, examines the decision rules for investing in stocks and the basic pricing principles for stocks. As mentioned earlier, shares of stocks represent title to the productive assets of corporations. As such, they represent an

---

[4]For a famous example, see John Kenneth Galbraith, *The Great Crash, Nineteen Twenty–Nine*, Boston: Houghton Mifflin, 1979.

ownership, or equity, position in the firms. Stocks offer no promised or fixed payments to the stockholders. Instead, the stockholders hold a residual position—they own what is left after others (bondholders, suppliers, employees, and so on) are paid. For this reason, stocks tend to be relatively riskier than bonds. For many people, this makes stocks more exciting since returns can be either much higher or lower than those from bonds.

For professional investors and their advisors, there is much hard work and analysis in addition to the excitement. The process of security analysis is traditionally divided into three phases: analysis of the economy, analysis of the industry, and analysis of the firm. For most stocks, the movement of the stock market is one of the most important factors in determining what happens to the value of the stock. Stock market movements have been compared to the movement of the tide which carries along with it the individual stock. Very few investors would try to select stocks for investment without giving close consideration to the big picture, namely, what they expect to happen to the stock market as a whole.

Additionally, it is wise to consider the industry context as a background for the firm. Even if the general market conditions are good and you have selected a good firm, that is not enough for success, particularly if the industry in which the firm is competing is heading for hard times. So industry analysis, for most professional stock market analysts, is an important function. They strive, in this phase of their analysis, to understand the conditions that will influence the fortunes of different industry groups.

Only after the investor is satisfied with the market and industry analyses is it really appropriate to turn full attention to the firm itself. In examining the company, the analyst is concerned with the position of the firm within the industry, its market position, its competitive position, and the quality of its management.

Portfolio Management

In a complex and varied security market setting, such as that in the United States, the investor must evaluate many different securities and types of securities, and it is across these many instruments that the investor must allocate investment funds. The study of the best way to apportion funds to existing investment opportunities is treated in Part IV, Portfolio Management. A **portfolio** is the collection of securities held by an investor and may include a variety of stocks, bonds, and other instruments. The way in which funds are allocated to the many investment opportunities determines the riskiness and the expected profitability of the investment.

One of the most important concepts of portfolio management is diversification. Almost all investors hold a portfolio that is diversified in some way. **Diversification**, or the allocation of funds to a variety of securities with different characteristics, is one of the most successful ways of controlling risk in securities investment.

In fact, diversification has given rise to an entire industry. **Mutual funds** are financial organizations that accept funds from hundreds or thousands of investors, pool those funds, and use the collected funds to invest in a portfolio of securities.

Each of the investors owns a fraction of all of the securities in the portfolio. This provides even very small investors with an opportunity to hold many different securities, thereby achieving a high degree of diversification. It is not an exaggeration to say that the main contribution of mutual funds is that they provide investors with ready–made diversification at a low cost.

With so many investment opportunities and professional investment management companies, such as mutual funds, it is important to be able to compare the performance of various portfolios. A casual survey of *The Wall Street Journal* on any given day will show a number of claims for successful investment performance by companies soliciting new investment funds. Over the last 20 years, experts in finance have worked hard to define a standard of portfolio performance. With this standard, it is possible to measure the performance of other investments.

The key idea behind a performance standard is the consideration of both risk and return. Some securities have more risk than others, and investment in the riskier securities should give a higher return than safe investments. This higher return is necessary to compensate investors for the greater risk they bear. Therefore, it is impossible to evaluate investment performance by considering differences in profitability without considering risk.

The concept of an efficient market has helped shape this performance standard. An **efficient market** is one in which the prices reflect a given body of information. A market is said to be efficient relative to some specified set of information, and this definition has one very important consequence.[5] If a market is efficient with respect to a given body of information, the information set cannot be used to beat the performance standard except by chance.

During the last 20 years, financial researchers have explored the efficiency of security markets in great depth. To most students of investments, the conclusions of this research are startling. A strong body of evidence shows that much of the information used by investors to guide their investment decisions is already reflected in security prices. This evidence for efficiency means that studying certain sets of information, where that information is already reflected in market prices, cannot be expected to improve investment performance.

Financial Derivatives and Portfolio Risk Management

Another important recent development in investments is the explosion of new markets for derivative instruments. A **derivative instrument** is a financial obligation that has value depending on the value or performance of some more basic financial security. For example, a stock option is a financial instrument that allows its owner to buy or sell a given share of stock at a specified price. Thus, an investor might own an option on IBM that allows her to purchase a share of IBM at $100 no matter what the price of IBM is. The value of the stock option depends on the value of the

---

[5]This conception of efficiency was first defined and elaborated by Eugene F. Fama in "Efficient Capital Markets: A Review of Theory and Empirical Work," *Journal of Finance*, 1970, pp. 383–417.

underlying share of IBM. Thus, the stock option is a derivative instrument—its value depends on the value of a more fundamental security.

There are three basic types of derivative instruments: futures, options, and swaps. The markets for these instruments have grown explosively in recent years as portfolio managers have come to understand the powerful tools that these derivative instruments provide for controlling risk. This section includes a chapter on each of futures, options, and swaps.

Futures contracts have existed for well over 100 years, and futures contracts exist on physical goods as well as financial instruments. The last decade has brought an explosion in the different kinds of futures contracts available. Buying a futures contract on wheat, for example, involves the commitment to pay a certain price for a quantity of wheat at a specific time in the future and to accept delivery of the wheat in exchange for the payment. By trading a futures contract for wheat, a farmer could guarantee the sale price for a crop of wheat many months before the actual harvest. The essential point of a futures contract is that the price for the good is set now, but the delivery of the good and the payment for the good occur later.

Futures contracts provide an opportunity for much exciting speculation. It is easy to make and lose large sums of money in futures trading; however, futures contracts have an important role in portfolio management as well. As mentioned earlier, one of the most important aspects of portfolio management is the control of the risk position of the portfolio, relative to the expected return on the portfolio. With the birth of futures contracts on foreign currencies, interest rates, and stock indexes, futures markets have become an extremely useful tool to the portfolio manager.

The same is true of options. **Options** are a kind of security representing what is known as a contingent claim. A **contingent claim** is one that has a payoff only in certain conditions that are specified at the outset of the investment. Options occur in everyday life, as well as in financial markets. Of the many options that occur in finance and economics, stock options have received the most attention, probably because of the emergence of an organized stock options exchange.

Options trading has become a significant financial tool for at least two reasons. First, options provide investors with the chance to make a dramatic change in the value of their portfolios in a very short time. (One drawback of this feature is that the change in value can be either positive or negative.) Second, options are a useful tool in portfolio management. Every sign today points to the increasing importance of options. As a further complication, there are now option contracts on futures.

The newest type of derivative instrument to emerge on the financial scene is a swap. The key feature of a **swap** is the exchange (or swap) of one sequence of cash flows for another. For example, one portfolio manager may hold German bonds that will pay their interest in German marks. The portfolio manager may desire to swap these future cash flows in marks for a sequence of cash flows in dollars. To engage in this transaction, the portfolio manager needs to find a trading partner who will accept the German mark cash flows and pay for them with a suitable sequence of dollar cash flows. With an active swap market, portfolio managers can carefully craft the exact payment streams that will come from their existing portfolio. Currently, the swap market is experiencing explosive growth, with portfolio managers actively swapping cash flows in foreign currencies and cash flows from debt securities.

Futures, options, and swaps have become very important in the management of portfolio risk and return. In building a portfolio, the investor must strive to avoid unnecessary risk by wise diversification. Some risk is unavoidable, of course, so the investor must select the level of risk that is appropriate to his or her financial circumstances and personality, and futures and options can play an important role in this process.

Techniques of portfolio risk management have become so important that they have given rise to the specialized risk management branch of finance known as **financial engineering**—the construction of specialized financial arrangements from the simpler building blocks of futures, options, and swaps. Through financial engineering, finance specialists carefully shape the exact payoff and risk characteristics of portfolios to meet specialized needs. The chapter on financial engineering introduces this emerging and exciting branch of investment management.

A Final Note on Risk and Return

Mastery of the material covered in this book will give the reader a good foundation to go forward, either as an investor or as a student of more complicated techniques. Throughout the book, emphasis is placed on laying a firm foundation for managing risk and expected return and for avoiding market myth. Only by beginning correctly can further study and experience help to develop our understanding of the complex phenomena encountered in securities investment.

It must also be remembered, however, that the risk and expected return combination selected depends upon the character of the individual investor, as the following story indicates. The great financier Bernard Baruch was confronted by an investor with a problem. Concerned with the risk of his securities investments, the investor was unable to sleep for fear of losing his money. Baruch's alleged advice was: "Sell down to the sleeping point." Even after the best portfolio for an individual is constructed, the investor must have reasonable expectations and be able to evaluate the performance of the portfolio in a judicious manner. This can be accomplished only by a thorough understanding of the concepts of risk and expected return and the trade–off between them.

Summary

This chapter outlined the scope and organization of the book and introduced the key concepts of risk and return. This text focuses on investment in financial claims, or securities, as opposed to physical capital. In investing, the investor sacrifices current consumption in the hope of increased future consumption opportunities. In undertaking such investment, there is necessarily exposure to risk. Consequently, the key decision facing the investor in a market with many investment opportunities is how to pursue high returns while minimizing risk. This trade–off between risk and expected return is the key problem facing the investor.

Because these concepts of risk and return are so important, this chapter developed quantitative measures of both risk and return, and these measures will be employed in many of the chapters that follow. As the discussion of the organization of the text indicates, Part I presents the institutional background of securities markets, and Parts II and III focus on investing in bonds and stocks. Part IV develops the techniques for combining numerous securities into portfolios that have the desired risk and return characteristics. Finally, Part V discusses derivative instruments and how to use them to manage portfolio risk. The book concludes by introducing the techniques of financial engineering, a specialty that may lead to the more exact management of risk in the pursuit of investment returns.

Questions and Problems

1. What is the difference between financial and real investment? If a student foregoes current consumption in order to attend a university, is the investment in education financial or real investment?

2. In this book, we generally assume that investors dislike risk. If a particular investor liked both risk and high expected returns, what kinds of opportunities could be found in the financial marketplace?

3. In terms of risk and return, what are the goals of investing?

4. Your uncle claims to have doubled his money in the stock market this year, even without the benefits of ever having studied investments. How should you evaluate his claim?

5. The variance is affected by outcomes both above and below the mean. One might argue that this makes it a poor measure of investment risk, because the only risk concerning an investor is the risk that returns might be below the mean. How can you respond to this criticism?

6. Why do investors diversify?

7. Over three years, an investor earns the following returns: 8 percent, 11 percent, and 15 percent. What is the arithmetic mean annual return for these returns over the three–year period? What is the annual mean geometric wealth relative and return for this investment?

8. An investor invests in a series of one–year investments starting with $700. After the first year, the investment is worth $784.00; after two years, it is worth $878.10; after three years, it is worth $983.40; and after four years, it is worth $1,101.50. Calculate the annual arithmetic and geometric mean returns. Are they the same? Why or why not? (Hint: What is the variance of the individual arithmetic returns?)

9. Two banks offer savings plans. The first, Compound National, offers to pay 1 percent per month, that is, all earnings will be compounded monthly. Simple National Bank will pay 12.5 percent per year without compounding. Which bank should an investor prefer? Why?

10. For a five–year period, a stock portfolio had the following returns: –15 percent, 23 percent, 11 percent, –3 percent, and 37 percent. What was the arithmetic mean return and the variance of the returns?

11. Mr. Diversey held a portfolio with three stocks. He invested 20 percent of his funds in Stock A, 45 percent in Stock B, and 35 percent in Stock C. The return for Stock A was 13 percent; for Stock B, the return was –5 percent; for Stock C, the return was 9 percent. What was the return for the entire portfolio?

CFA Questions

A. The difference between an arithmetic average and a geometric average of returns:
   a. increases as the variability of the returns increases.
   b. increases as the variability of the returns decreases.
   c. is always negative.
   d. depends on the specific returns being averaged, but is not necessarily sensitive to their variability.

B. What are the mean, median, and mode, respectively, of the following data series: 1,2,3,5,8,8,15?
   a. 6,5,8
   b. 6,8,5
   c. 8,5,6
   d. 5,8,6

C. An investment of $232 will increase in value to $268 in 3 years. What is the annual compound growth rate?
   a. 3.0%
   b. 4.0%
   c. 5.0%
   d. 6.0%

Use the following data in answering Questions D through F. The annual rate of return for JSI's common stock has been:

	1989	1990	1991	1992
Return	14%	19%	–10%	14%

D. What is the arithmetic mean of the rate of return for JSI's common stock over the four years?

   a. 8.62%
   b. 9.25%
   c. 14.25%
   d. None of the above

E. What is the geometric mean of the rate of return for JSI's common stock over the four years?

   a. 8.62%
   b. 9.25%
   c. 14.21%
   d. Cannot be calculated due to the negative return in 1991

F. What are the median and mode of the rate of return for JSI's common stock?

	Median	Mode
a.	9.25%	14.5%
b.	14.0%	undefined
c.	14.0%	14.0%
d.	14.5%	14.0%

Suggested REALDATA Exercises

The following *REALDATA* exercises explore the concepts developed in this chapter: Exercises 41, 45, 66, 67, 68.

Suggested Readings

Brealey, R. A., *An Introduction to Risk and Return from Common Stocks*, Cambridge, MA: MIT Press, 1983.

Leibowitz, M. L. and W. S. Krasker, "The Persistence of Risk Stocks versus Bonds over the Long Term," *Financial Analysts Journal*, 44:6, November/December 1988, pp. 40–47.

Malkiel, B., *A Random Walk Down Wall Street*, New York: W. W. Norton, 1981.

CHAPTER TWO

The Debt Market

Overview

This chapter begins the exploration of the institutional features of the debt market. The prices of all debt instruments depend on the payments that are promised by the issuer and market conditions which determine the value of those promised payments. This chapter introduces the bond pricing formula, which expresses the relationship among yields, prices, and promised payments on bonds—relationships that hold for all debt instruments.

Although the bond pricing formula applies to all debt instruments, it is traditional to divide the debt market into two segments—the money market and the bond market. The money market is comprised of those debt instruments that are issued with a maturity of one year or less. All debt instruments originally issued with maturities greater than one year are considered to be bonds. While this distinction is somewhat arbitrary, it is quite useful, because money market instruments exhibit important family resemblances, as do instruments in the bond market. This chapter discusses both the bond market and the money market.

Debt instruments exhibit many peculiarities, which often play a vital role in determining their value. Wide differences in contractual obligations provide variety to the debt market and challenge the investor to become aware of a host of important distinctions. Nonetheless, all prices of debt instruments depend on the relationship expressed in the **bond pricing formula**.

After a discussion of the basic bond pricing principles, the chapter briefly examines the size and structure of the world market for long–term debt. This helps to set the U.S. bond market in the proper prospective, which is typically divided into three distinct segments: the U.S. government debt market, the corporate bond market, and the municipal bond market. Each of these market segments has its own special features, which are explored in turn. For completeness, a brief discussion of the mortgage market is also included.

In the corporate and the municipal markets, the peculiarities in lending terms among the many different issuers often play a great role in determining the value of bonds. These features are delineated in the bond contract, or indenture, which specifies the obligations of the bond issuer to the bond holder. These provisions range from promises about the assets reserved to pay off the bondholders to stipulations about the exact time and manner of the retirement of the bonds. These differences are of particular importance because they determine the risk and expected return associated with each issue.

For money market instruments, the general bond pricing principles all hold. However, the money market employs some special methods for calculating yields of various types, such as the **discount yield** and the **bond equivalent yield**. These are explored in the chapter which concludes with a survey of the more important types of money market instruments. In the money market, as in the bond market, different instruments have different levels of risk, and these risk differences are reflected in the expected returns offered by the different instruments.

The Bond Pricing Formula

Chapter 1 introduced the basic concepts of risk and return. This section elaborates on the idea of return on investment in the context of the pricing of debt instruments. Debt instruments can be categorized as pure discount instruments or as coupon bonds. This section explores the algebra of bond pricing by examining the simpler case of pure discount instruments, which are quite common in the money market, and then focuses on coupon bonds.

Pure Discount Instruments

To illustrate the idea of the pricing relationship, consider a straightforward type of debt security called a **pure discount bond**. This bond promises a certain single payment at a specified time in the future and is sold for less than this promised future payment. This type of security is simple in structure, yet it is important in the debt market. For example, many money market instruments, such as Treasury bills, are pure discount bonds. Normally, the promised future payment is the **par value** or **face value** of the bond—the final promised payment on a bond. The difference between the par value and the selling price is the **bond discount**. Such a security is a **pure discount bond**, because there is no payment between the original issue of the bond and the maturity of the bond when it pays its face value.

The price of a pure discount bond can be expressed as a function of the par value, the yield on the security, and the time until it matures:

$$P = \frac{C_m}{(1 + r)^t} \qquad \text{2.1}$$

where:

P = the price of the instrument
C_m = the cash flow to be paid when the bond matures at time m

r = the annualized yield to maturity on the bond
t = the time in years until the bond matures

As an example, consider a pure discount bond that matures in five years and has a face value of $1,000. If the bond has a yield to maturity of 12 percent,[1] its price must be $567.43:

$$P = \frac{\$1,000}{(1.12)^5} = \$567.43$$

In this simplest kind of bond, the basic features of bond pricing are all present. The promised cash flow, the price, and the yield are all inter–related. The yield to maturity is the yield that will be realized if the promised payment is made. The riskier the promised payment, the higher the promised yield or expected return must be in order to induce investors to hold such bonds.

Coupon Bonds

In the money market, many instruments have the structure of pure discount bonds, but that is not normally the case for longer maturity debt instruments. It is much more typical for there to be multiple payments associated with a bond. Most bonds issued today have a par value that is paid to the owner of the bond at a specified date in the future when the bond matures. Bonds typically make regularly scheduled payments between the original date of issue and the maturity date as well, and these intervening payments are called **coupons**. In most cases, the coupon payments are made semiannually. For such bonds, the bond pricing formula becomes more complicated:

$$P = \sum_{t=1}^{m} \frac{C_t}{(1 + r)^t} \qquad \text{2.2}$$

where:
C_t = the cash flow received by the bondholder at time t

Although more complex, this formula is very similar to Equation 2.1, but there are just more payments from the bond to consider. As a straightforward example, consider a coupon bond that has a face value of $1,000, a yield of 13 percent, pays a semiannual coupon of $60, and matures in one year. Normally, the last coupon payment is made at maturity, so on the maturity date, the bond will

---

[1]The yield to maturity is the annualized return that would be earned over the life of the bond if all interim cash flows are reinvested at that same yield to maturity.

pay the face value amount plus the last coupon payment. With this information, the bond pricing formula can be applied to this bond in the following way:

$$P = \frac{\$60}{1 + .13/2} + \frac{\$1,060}{(1 + .13/2)^2}$$

$$= \$56.34 + \$934.56 = \$990.90$$

There are two important points to notice about this application of the bond pricing formula. First, the coupon rate is 12 percent applied to a $1,000 par value bond. Therefore, the total annual coupon is $120, but it is divided into the two semiannual coupon payments of $60 each. Second, because the cash flows occur semiannually, we must account for the semiannual compounding that this implies. Therefore, the stated yield of 13 percent is divided by 2, because there are two payments from the bond per year. In the computation, the present value of the bond, which equals its price, is based on a 6.5 percent semiannual rate of interest. Bond tables and bond price calculations are always based on this kind of computation.

Par, Premium, and Discount Bonds

In this example of the calculation of the yield to maturity, there is a slight difference between the market price and the face value. However, the market price of a bond often differs from its face value and this difference can be quite large. When the market price exceeds the face value, the bond is a **premium bond**. If the market price equals the face value, the bond is a **par bond**. When the price is less than the face value, the bond is a **discount bond**. Notice that there is a difference, however, between a discount bond and a pure discount bond. Bonds with coupons can have prices less than their face values, and are then discount bonds. Pure discount bonds will always have market prices less than the par values, except at the point of maturity. The unique feature of pure discount bonds is that they pay no coupons.

Yield Approximations

Often bonds are issued with original maturities of 30 years. Semiannual payments means that there will be 60 payments promised by the bond. Without a computer, calculating the price of such a bond, even when the yield is known, is a tedious process. Even if we know the value and timing of all the payments and the price of the bond, it is more difficult to calculate the yield, because the calculation must be recursive. If we calculate the yield by hand, there is no alternative to using trial and error. We discount the cash flows at a particular yield and compare the resulting calculated price with the market price. If the calculated price exceeds the market price, the yield used for the calculation was too low. We must adjust the yield and discount the cash flows again, repeating this process until the calculated price matches the market price. Only then have we found the correct yield to maturity.

A Yield Approximation Formula

Fortunately, there are alternatives to making yield calculations by hand, some of which are exact and one of which makes an approximation. If one does not know the exact yield of a bond and is willing to be satisfied with a close estimate, the yield approximation formula shown in Equation 2.3 gives a good estimate.[2]

$$\text{Approximate Yield to Maturity} = \frac{C + (FV - P)/n}{(FV + P)/2} \qquad 2.3$$

where:
   C = the annual coupon payment
   FV = the bond's face value
   P = the bond's market price
   n = the number of years until the bond matures

The idea behind this approximation formula is quite straightforward—dividing an estimate of the annual profit from the bond by the average investment over the bond's life.

   In this yield approximation formula, the numerator estimates the annual income to be received from the bond, which consists of two parts. First, the bondholder receives the annual coupon payment. But as a bond approaches its maturity date, its price must converge toward its par value, since it is the par value of the bond that will be paid to the bondholder. The second part of the numerator, $(FV - P)/n$, is an estimate of the change in the bond's price toward its par value in a given year. The denominator, $(FV + P)/2$, gives the average investment in the bond over its life from the present, when one pays P for it, until the maturity date, when one receives the face value, FV.

   To see the performance of this yield approximation formula, consider a bond maturing in five years and paying a 10 percent annual coupon with a face value of $1,000. If the bond were priced at $1,059.12, it would have a yield to maturity of 8.5 percent as shown by the following calculation:

---

[2]Other ways of obtaining bond yields are by using calculators with financial functions, computer programs, and bond yield books. For more on bond yield books, see Chapter 7.

$$P = \frac{100}{(1.085)} + \frac{100}{(1.085)^2} + \frac{100}{(1.085)^3} + \frac{100}{(1.085)^4} + \frac{1100}{(1.085)^5}$$

$$= \$1059.12$$

Using this yield approximation formula gives a close estimate:

$$\text{Approximate Yield to Maturity} = \frac{100 + (1000 - 1059.12)/5}{(1000 + 1059.12)/2} = .0856$$

Yield approximations have had a long history, with continuing efforts to create an improved formula.[3] One recent contribution uses some advanced mathematics to derive a formula that is superior to the traditional yield approximation given earlier.[4] This improved formula is:

$$\text{Approximate Yield to Maturity} = \frac{C + (FV - P)/n}{(FV + 2P)/3} \qquad \textbf{2.4}$$

For our example, this new formula gives:

$$\text{Approximate Yield to Maturity} = \frac{100 + (1000 - 1059.12)/5}{[1000 + (2)(1059.12)]/3} = .0848$$

This second result is closer to the true yield of 8.5 percent. Figure 2.1 shows the size of errors from the two methods for a bond with a face value of $1,000, a coupon rate of 10 percent, and a true yield of 8 percent. The percentage errors in the yield approximations are shown on the vertical axis, with varying maturities being represented on the horizontal axis. For the entire range of maturities, Equation 2.4 gives closer estimates of the true yield.

Accrued Interest

One peculiarity of the bond market that awaits the unwary investor is the unusual method used to quote bond prices. For most bonds, the bond price does not reflect

---

[3]See G. A. Hawawini and A. Vora, "Yield Approximations: A Historical Perspective," *Journal of Finance*, 37:1, March 1982, pp. 145–56.

[4]See Ricardo J. Rodriguez, "Estimating the Yield to Maturity of a Bond: A Generalized Treatment," Working paper, University of Miami, 1987.

Figure 2.1

Errors in Yield Approximation Formulas

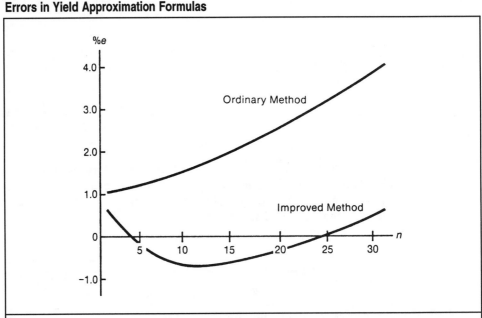

Source: Ricardo J. Rodriguez, "The Quadratic Approximation to the Yield to Maturity," *Journal of Financial Education*, 17, 1988, pp. 19–25.

the actual price that must be paid. Instead, one must pay the stated price plus the **accrued interest**—the portion of the next coupon payment that has been earned by the bondholder, but which the bondholder has not yet received. As an example, consider the five–year bond just discussed. At maturity the bond will pay $1,100, consisting of the final coupon payment plus the face value. Immediately prior to maturity, the bond must have a total value just slightly less than the promised payment of $1,100. However, its quoted price will be $1,000, but it will have $100 of accrued interest. The purchaser of a bond must pay the quoted price plus the accrued interest. The accrued interest is easily calculated using the following formula:

$$\text{Accrued Interest} = (\text{Coupon Payment}) \left(\frac{\text{days since last coupon payment}}{\text{days between coupon payments}} \right)$$

2.5

These basic pricing formulas apply to all bonds and will be used throughout our discussion of bond pricing, particularly in Chapters 7 and 8.

Figure 2.2

Net Federal Debt Outstanding

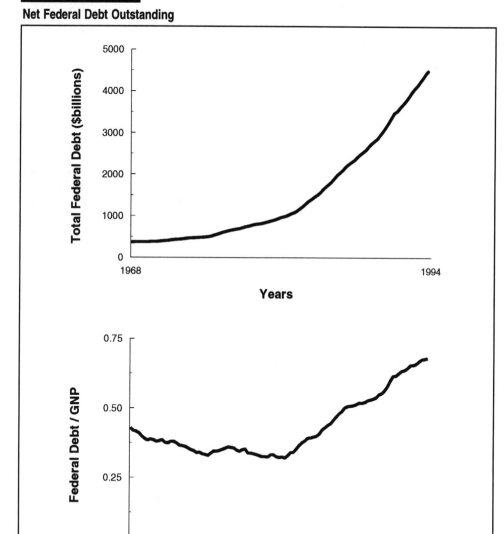

Source: *Federal Reserve Bulletin*, various issues.

The Bond Market in the United States

The U.S. bond market can be divided into three major categories by issuer—the U.S. government, corporations, and municipalities.[5] Each of these types of issuers has special characteristics that make its bonds different from those issued by a member of the other groups. These characteristics include maturity, tax status, and risk level. Consequently, it is easiest to focus, in turn, on each of the different segments of the market.

The Market for U.S. Government Bonds

The U.S. government is the world's single largest debtor, with new federal borrowing exceeding $358 billion in 1993. The borrowing by the U.S. government can be divided between debt issued by the U.S. Treasury, such as Treasury bills (T–bills), notes (T–notes), and bonds (T–bonds), and debt issued by agencies of the U.S. Government, such as the Government National Mortgage Association (GNMA), the Federal Housing Administration (FHA), and the Tennessee Valley Authority (TVA). Together, they are responsible for a tremendous amount of outstanding debt, as shown in Figure 2.2. The total outstanding federal debt now exceeds $3.4 trillion, the consequence of a very rapid increase that began in 1975. Of this outstanding debt, the most important part is U.S. Treasury debt.

Treasury debt.   The three principal kinds of U.S. Treasury obligations are Treasury bills, notes, and bonds. Treasury bills are debt instruments with an initial maturity of one year or less. The focus here will be on the longer Treasury maturity issues, the notes and bonds, while Treasury bills are discussed later in this chapter with other money market instruments. Treasury notes and bonds have similar payment streams, and differ only in their maturity. Officially, a Treasury note is an instrument having an original maturity lying in the range of 1 to 10 years, and a Treasury bond has a maturity when issued in excess of 10 years. In practice, Treasury bonds are issued for much longer maturities, usually for 30 years.

Table 2.1 shows the amount of outstanding Treasury obligations and the portion represented by bills, notes, and bonds. The current large portion of notes differs from the composition of Treasury debt in earlier years as a result of a shift from the longer–term bonds to the medium–maturity notes. Quotations for various federal issues are carried daily in *The Wall Street Journal* and other major newspapers, as shown in Figure 2.3. The first three columns of the quotations identify the instrument. The first column indicates the annual coupon rate, as a percent of par. A rate of 10 percent on a bond with a par value of $10,000 means that the bond would pay annual interest payments of $1,000. The "s" following the rate is

---

[5]Mortgages are also considered in this chapter, but they are not normally regarded as bonds.

Table 2.1

Treasury Bonds, Bills, and Notes Outstanding on December 31, 1993

Treasury Issue	Amount Outstanding (billions)	Percentage (%)
Bills	2,989.5	54.67
Notes	714.6	13.07
Bonds	1,764.0	32.26

Source: *Federal Reserve Bulletin*, April 1994, Table 1.41.

included only for ease of pronunciation. Usually, this annual coupon amount will be paid in two equal semiannual installments.[6] The next two columns indicate the year and month the bond matures. Since these instruments will always make the last semiannual coupon payment on the maturity date, one knows the cash flows that will come from the bonds from the first three columns. A particular bond, such as one identified as "10s 1997 May," would be referred to as "the tens of ninety–seven." Since notes and bonds have the same structure, the quotations are mixed. Those securities originally issued as notes are identified by an "n" following the bond identifier.

Some of the bonds show two maturity dates. For example, if a bond shows a maturity such as 1997–2002, the second is the actual maturity date. The first indicates the first date at which the bond might be called. A bond is called when it is retired early at the discretion of the issuer. In the normal event, bonds will be called only when the prevailing interest rates lie below the coupon rate.[7]

As noted at the top of the listing, the prices shown are mid–afternoon quotations from the Federal Reserve Bank of New York, based on transactions of at least $1 million in size. These are not necessarily prices at which one could have actually traded, but, instead, they indicate the approximate market prices that prevailed at the time. The quotations themselves are expressed as a percentage of the par value of the bond. However, the use of the decimal point is likely to be very misleading. The portion to the right of the decimal indicates the number of 32nds of par. In other words, a price of 97.16 means that the bond is quoted at 97 and 16/32nds of par, or 97.50 percent of par. For a bond with a face value of $10,000, this would translate into a quoted price of $9,750. As in all markets, there

---

[6]Some people think that the "s" means that the bond pays a semiannual coupon. As a matter of fact, most of these bonds do pay their coupons semiannually, but that is not indicated by the "s."

[7]For a more detailed discussion of callable bonds, see the section on "The Bond Contract" later in this chapter.

Figure 2.3

Quotations for Treasury Notes and Bonds

TREASURY BONDS, NOTES & BILLS

Thursday, June 23, 1994

Representative Over-the-Counter quotations based on transactions of $1 million or more.

Treasury bond, note and bill quotes are as of mid-afternoon. Colons in bid-and-asked quotes represent 32nds; 101:01 means 101 1/32. Net changes in 32nds. n-Treasury note. Treasury bill quotes in hundredths, quoted on terms of a rate of discount. Days to maturity calculated from settlement date. All yields are to maturity and based on the asked quote. Latest 13-week and 26-week bills are boldfaced. For bonds callable prior to maturity, yields are computed to the earliest call date for issues quoted above par and to the maturity date for issues below par. *-When issued.

Source: Federal Reserve Bank of New York.

U.S. Treasury strips as of 3 p.m. Eastern time, also based on transactions of $1 million or more. Colons in bid-and-asked quotes represent 32nds; 101:01 means 101 1/32. Net changes in 32nds. Yields calculated on the asked quotation. ci-stripped coupon interest. bp-Treasury bond, stripped principal. np-Treasury note, stripped principal. For bonds callable prior to maturity, yields are computed to the earliest call date for issues quoted above par and to the maturity date for issues below par.

Source: Bear, Stearns & Co. via Street Software Technology Inc.

GOVT. BONDS & NOTES

Rate	Maturity Mo/Yr	Bid	Asked	Chg.	Ask Yld.
5	Jun 94n	100:00	100:02	....	0.00
8 1/2	Jun 94n	100:01	100:03	− 1	0.00
8	Jul 94n	100:07	100:09	....	2.26
4 1/4	Jul 94n	100:00	100:02	....	3.52
6 7/8	Aug 94n	100:12	100:14	....	3.54
8 5/8	Aug 94n	100:19	100:21	− 1	3.64
8 3/4	Aug 94	100:20	100:22	....	3.53
12 5/8	Aug 94n	101:05	101:07	− 1	3.42
4 1/4	Aug 94n	99:31	100:01	....	4.02
4	Sep 94n	99:29	99:31	+ 1	4.08
8 1/2	Sep 94n	101:02	101:04	....	4.04
9 1/2	Oct 94n	101:15	101:17	+ 1	4.26
4 1/4	Oct 94n	99:28	99:30	....	4.41
6	Nov 94n	100:15	100:17	....	4.56
8 1/4	Nov 94n	101:11	101:13	....	4.47
10 1/8	Nov 94	102:02	102:04	....	4.43
11 5/8	Nov 94n	102:20	102:22	....	4.43
4 5/8	Nov 94n	99:31	100:01	....	4.53
4 5/8	Dec 94n	99:27	99:29	....	4.81

Rate	Maturity Mo/Yr	Bid	Asked	Chg.	Ask Yld.
6 3/8	Jul 99n	98:21	98:23	+ 6	6.68
8	Aug 99n	105:16	105:18	+ 4	6.70
6	Oct 99n	96:25	96:27	+ 6	6.72
7 7/8	Nov 99n	105:03	105:05	+ 6	6.72
6 3/8	Jan 00n	98:09	98:11	+ 5	6.74
7 7/8	Feb 95-00	101:15	101:19	− 1	5.30
8 1/2	Feb 00n	108:03	108:05	+ 5	6.74
5 1/2	Apr 00n	94:04	94:06	+ 5	6.73
8 7/8	May 00n	110:04	110:06	+ 4	6.75
8 3/8	Aug 95-00	102:27	102:31	+ 1	5.64
8 3/4	Aug 00n	109:15	109:17	+ 4	6.82
8 1/2	Nov 00n	108:11	108:13	+ 4	6.85
7 3/4	Feb 01n	104:19	104:21	+ 5	6.86
11 3/4	Feb 01	125:30	126:02	+ 6	6.80
8	May 01n	105:31	106:01	+ 6	6.89
13 1/8	May 01	133:30	134:02	+ 7	6.84
7 7/8	Aug 01n	105:08	105:10	+ 5	6.92
8	Aug 96-01	103:15	103:19	+ 6	6.18
13 3/8	Aug 01	136:03	136:07	+ 6	6.87
7 1/2	Nov 01n	103:03	103:05	+ 7	6.95

Source: *The Wall Street Journal*, June 24, 1994, p. C18. Reprinted by permission of *The Wall Street Journal*,

is both a bid and an asked price, both of which are quoted here.[8] The "Bid Chg." column indicates the change in the bid price since the previous day's quotation.[9]

---

[8]The **bid price** is the price that prospective purchasers offer for the good, while the **asked price** is the price demanded by the owner of the instrument.

[9]Securities dealers make a market in a particular security by offering to buy it at one price (the bid price) and trying to sell it at a higher price (the asked price). The difference between the two prices is the **bid–asked spread**, and this difference constitutes the dealers' gross profit margin. We explore the concept of the bid–asked spread more fully for the stock market in Chapter 3.

The "Yld." column indicates the bond's yield to maturity. In spite of the fact that all of the bonds have the same issuer, and one of impeccable creditworthiness, there are important differences in yields among the different issues, even though they are of the same risk level.

In the past 65 years, investments in Treasury securities have been similar in their returns, but very different in their risk levels, as measured by the standard deviation or variance of returns. Over the period from 1926–1993, Treasury bills have returned about 1.6 percent less than Treasury bonds, but T–bill returns have been much less risky. Figure 2.4 presents the year–by–year returns for both bills and bonds. The investor in Treasury bills has never had an actual loss in any given year because Treasury bills all mature in one year or less, and they have always been paid as promised. The investor in Treasury bonds has been stung on occasion, however. Even though all payments on Treasury bonds have been made as promised, an investor in Treasury bonds could still have a loss in a given year. The dollar return on holding a Treasury bond for a given year consists of the coupon payments received plus any price change in the bond itself. In the years of losses, the fall in the bond price exceeded the coupon income, giving a net loss on the holding of the Treasury bond.

Table 2.2 summarizes the returns for investment in both T–bills and T–bonds for the period from 1926 to 1993. On an inflation–adjusted basis, the real return (total return less the effect of inflation) is quite small. This is shown by the change in the purchasing power for an initial investment of $1,000. If one had invested $1,000 in T–bills and kept it in T–bills, one would have earned only a 0.5 percent increase in purchasing power over these years. The persistent Treasury bond investor would have had about a 1.8 percent increase in purchasing power. Clearly, over this period, the rate of return on Treasury securities was only slightly higher than the inflation rate.

Table 2.2

■■■■■■■

Returns for Investment in Treasury Bills and Bonds, 1926–1993

	Bills	Bonds
Arithmetic Mean Return	3.7%	5.3%
Standard Deviation of Returns	3.3	8.7
Geometric Mean Return	3.7	5.0
Real Geometric Mean Return	0.5	1.8
For a $1,000 Investment in 1926:		
Terminal Value	$11,728	$28,034
Terminal Purchasing Power	1,442	3,447

Source: *Stocks, Bonds, Bills, and Inflation: 1994 Yearbook*, Chicago: Ibbotson Associates, 1994.

Figure 2.4

Annual Returns on Bonds and Bills, 1926–1993

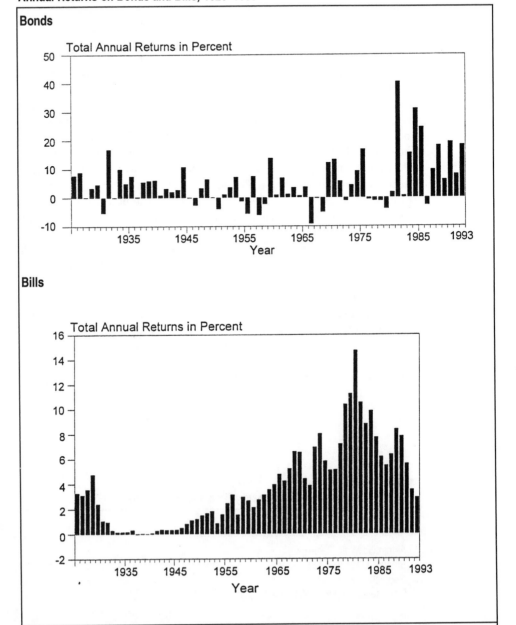

Source: Ibbotson Associates, *Stocks, Bonds, Bills, and Inflation: 1994 Yearbook*, Chicago: Ibbotson Associates, 1994, p. 53, 60.

Average Maturity of Treasury Debt. As we have seen, Treasury debt consists of bills, notes, and bonds, which differ in their maturity at time of issue. The overall maturity structure of the Treasury's debt depends upon the mix of these three instruments and the previous issuance of bonds and notes that still have time remaining until maturity. Over time, this maturity mix has changed quite dramatically. Over the last 50 years, the average maturity of Treasury debt has been as long as 10 years and as short as 2.5 years, as Figure 2.5 shows. Immediately following World War II, the average maturity was quite long, and it declined for the next 30 years, hitting a minimum in late 1975. In the last 20 years, the average maturity has increased to about six years.

As we will explore in more detail in Chapters 7 and 8, bonds that have different maturities often have different yields. The schedule showing the relationship between the maturity of bonds in the same risk class and the yields on those bonds is known as the **yield curve**. Often long–maturity bonds have a higher interest rate than shorter–maturity bonds. The Treasury has the job of financing the federal government at the lowest possible interest rate, so it seeks to offer securities at lower yields. As the yield curve changes and governmental financing needs

Figure 2.5

Average Maturity of the Marketable Debt

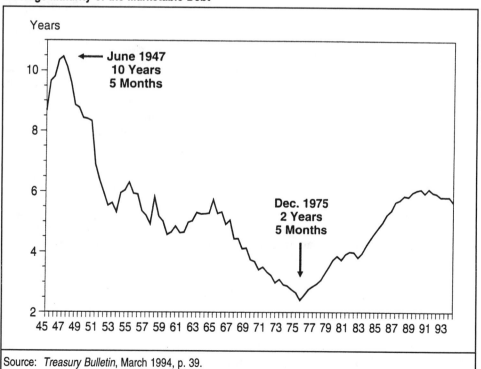

Source: *Treasury Bulletin*, March 1994, p. 39.

change, the Treasury changes the mix of bills, notes, and bonds to pursue the lowest cost financing mix. This leads to changes in the average maturity of the Treasury debt, as shown in Figure 2.5.

Zero Coupons and STRIPS. A Treasury note or bond consists of a stream of coupon payments and a final payment that returns the face value to the investor. **Coupon stripping** is the act of removing the individual interest coupons from the bond and treating each payment as a separate security. The resulting instruments are zero coupon bonds, because each represents a single payment due on a particular date. For example, a 20–year bond with a face value of $100,000 and a coupon rate of 10 percent could be stripped into 41 zero coupon instruments. One instrument has a face value of $100,000 and is due in 20 years. The other 40 instruments consist of the individual coupon payments of $5,000, and each would be due on the specified coupon payment date over then next 40 semiannual periods.

The market for stripped securities began in 1982 when Merrill Lynch stripped securities and marketed them under the name "TIGR," Treasury Investment Growth Certificates. Salomon Brothers, a competing firm, introduced a similar instrument called a CATS, Certificates of Accrual on Treasury Securities. LIONS (by Lehman Brothers) soon followed CATS, making a total of three name–brand stripped Treasury–based products. In February 1985, the Treasury itself introduced its own version of a stripped bond, and called it a STRIPS, Separate Trading of Registered Interest and Principal of Securities. By 1991, the total value of STRIPS outstanding exceeded $250 million, with the Treasury's STRIPS having largely crowded out the feline products.[10]

Treasury Auctions. Each week, the U.S. Treasury auctions Treasury bills in the money market. Some weeks the auction includes the sale of Treasury notes and bonds as well. Purchasers bid for the new securities by offering either competitive or non–competitive bids through one of the 12 Federal Reserve Banks. In a competitive bid, the bidder specifies the amount of bills desired and the yield at which it is willing to accept them. Investors may also submit non-competitive bids. In a non–competitive bid, the securities are awarded at a yield that equals the average of the competitive bids. Large bond trading firms and bond dealers typically make competitive bids, while individual investors almost always specify non–competitive bids.

The Federal Reserve transmits the collected bids to the Treasury Department, which takes account of the noncompetitive amount of securities desired. The Treasury then awards the securities to the competitive bidders offering the lowest yield (highest price). The noncompetitive bidders receive their securities at the average of the accepted competitive bids, and competitive bids are honored until the Treasury exhausts the amount it wishes to sell.

---

[10] This account relies largely on the Federal Reserve Bank of New York's pamphlet, "Zero Coupons and STRIPS."

Individuals can submit their own bids directly to a Federal Reserve Bank or through a regular securities broker. The largest amount that can be awarded to any single noncompetitive bidder is $1 million face value.

Death and Taxes: Flower Bonds. A **flower bond** is a specially designated U.S. Treasury bond that is redeemable at its owner's death for its face value plus accrued interest in payment of federal estate taxes. Thus, a bond that has a market price of 90.00 can be redeemed for 100.00 in payment of estate taxes. Obviously these bonds are attractive if you plan to die soon. These bonds were issued before 1966 and they typically have very low coupon rates, generally in the range of 2–4 percent. Nonetheless, they are attractive for a small clientele of investors. Because of their special tax provisions, flower bonds generally sell at a higher price and lower yield than otherwise similar bonds. In fact, it is possible to analyze a flower bond as a combination of a regular Treasury bond plus a life insurance policy.[11]

Federal Agency Debt. In addition to the Treasury, there are many federal agencies and federally sponsored agencies that also issue debt. A **federal agency** is a direct arm of the U.S. government. These federal agencies do not issue debt on their own, but their financing needs are met through issues of the Federal Financing Bank. These federal agencies include the Defense Department, the Export–Import Bank, the Federal Housing Administration, and several other agencies. By contrast, a **federally sponsored agency** is a privately owned entity that raises funds in the market. Examples of these sponsored agencies include the Federal Home Loan Banks, Farm Credit Banks, Federal Home Loan Mortgage Corporation, and the Resolution Funding Corporation (established in 1989 to deal with the Savings and Loan crisis). Table 2.3 lists these federal agencies and federally sponsored agencies and shows their current levels of debt, which together exceeded $550 billion by 1994.

With the exception of the Farm Credit Financial Assistance Corporation, there is no federal guarantee of these agency securities. Nonetheless, there is a perception that the federal government will not allow these securities to default. As a result, the yields on these agency issues are slightly higher than the yields on comparable Treasury issues, but slightly lower than the yields on comparable debt of corporations.

Figure 2.6 shows the quotations for federal agency debt issues. The system of quotation is very similar to that for Treasury issues. Note, however, that the coupon rates are expressed as decimals. Again, bid and asked prices are expressed as points and 32nds of par, just as they are for Treasury issues. Yields on Treasury issues are based on the actual number of days between coupon payments, but agency issue yields are based on the assumption that every month has 30 days.

---

[11]For the treatment of a flower bond as a combined Treasury bond and life insurance policy, see D. Mayers and C. W. Smith, Jr., "Death and Taxes: The Market for Flower Bonds," *Journal of Finance*, 42:3, July 1987, pp. 685–702. These last flower bonds are quickly approaching their maturity date.

Table 2.3

Federal and Federally Sponsored Credit Agencies

Millions of dollars, end of period

Agency	1989	1990	1991	1992	1993 Sept.	1993 Oct.	1993 Nov.	1993 Dec.	1994 Jan.
1 Federal and federally sponsored agencies	411,805	434,668	442,772	483,970	0	0	0	0	0
2 Federal agencies	35,664	42,159	41,035	41,829	43,753	43,796	44,055	45,193[r]	44,988
3 Defense Department[1]	7	7	7	7	7	7	7	6[r]	6
4 Export-Import Bank[2,3]	10,985	11,376	9,809	7,208	5,801	5,801	5,801	5,315	5,315
5 Federal Housing Administration[4]	328	393	397	374	213	243	255	255	80
6 Government National Mortgage Association certificates of participation[5]	0	0	0	0	0	0	0	0	0
7 Postal Service[6]	6,445	6,948	8,421	10,660	9,732	9,732	9,732	9,732	9,732
8 Tennessee Valley Authority	17,899	23,435	22,401	23,580	28,000	28,016	28,260	29,885	29,855
9 United States Railway Association[6]	0	0	0	0	0	0	0	0	0
10 Federally sponsored agencies[7]	375,428	392,509	401,737	442,141	0	0	0	0	0
11 Federal Home Loan Banks	136,108	117,895	107,543	114,733	132,651	133,365	139,364	141,577	139,241
12 Federal Home Loan Mortgage Corporation	26,148	30,941	30,262	29,631	52,702	63,427	56,809	49,993	61,245
13 Federal National Mortgage Association	116,064	123,403	133,937	166,300	195,786	193,925	195,165	201,112	203,013
14 Farm Credit Banks[8]	54,864	53,590	52,199	51,910	51,636	51,759	51,861	53,123	52,621
15 Student Loan Marketing Association[9]	28,705	34,194	38,319	39,650	38,795	38,790	40,840	39,784	0
16 Financing Corporation[10]	8,170	8,170	8,170	8,170	8,170	8,170	8,170	8,170	0
17 Farm Credit Financial Assistance Corporation[11]	847	1,261	1,261	1,261	1,261	1,261	1,261	1,261	0
18 Resolution Funding Corporation[12]	4,522	23,055	29,996	29,996	29,996	29,996	29,996	29,996	0
MEMO									
19 Federal Financing Bank debt[13]	134,873	179,083	185,576	154,994	129,329	127,348	126,490	128,187	125,182
Lending to federal and federally sponsored agencies									
20 Export-Import Bank[3]	10,979	11,370	9,803	7,202	5,795	5,795	5,795	5,309	5,309
21 Postal Service[6]	6,195	6,698	8,201	10,440	9,732	9,732	9,732	9,732	9,732
22 Student Loan Marketing Association	4,880	4,850	4,820	4,790	4,790	4,760	4,760	4,760	2,760
23 Tennessee Valley Authority	16,519	14,055	10,725	6,975	6,325	6,325	6,325	6,325	6,075
24 United States Railway Association[6]	0	0	0	0	0	0	0	0	0
Other lending[14]									
25 Farmers Home Administration	53,311	52,324	48,534	42,979	38,619	38,619	38,619	38,619	38,619
26 Rural Electrification Administration	19,265	18,890	18,562	18,172	17,653	17,561	17,561	17,578	17,511
27 Other	23,724	70,896	84,931	64,436	46,415	44,556	44,556	43,698	45,176

1. Consists of mortgages assumed by the Defense Department between 1957 and 1963 under family housing and homeowners assistance programs.
2. Includes participation certificates reclassified as debt beginning Oct. 1, 1976.
3. On-budget since Sept. 30, 1976.
4. Consists of debentures issued in payment of Federal Housing Administration insurance claims. Once issued, these securities may be sold privately on the securities market.
5. Certificates of participation issued before fiscal year 1969 by the Government National Mortgage Association acting as trustee for the Farmers Home Administration, the Department of Health, Education, and Welfare, the Department of Housing and Urban Development, the Small Business Administration, and the Veterans Administration.
6. Off-budget.
7. Includes outstanding noncontingent liabilities: notes, bonds, and debentures. Some data are estimated.
8. Excludes borrowing by the Farm Credit Financial Assistance Corporation, shown on line 17.
9. Before late 1982, the Association obtained financing through the Federal Financing Bank (FFB). Borrowing excludes that obtained from the FFB, which is shown on line 22.

10. The Financing Corporation, established in August 1987 to recapitalize the Federal Savings and Loan Insurance Corporation, undertook its first borrowing in October 1987.
11. The Farm Credit Financial Assistance Corporation, established in January 1988 to provide assistance to the Farm Credit System, undertook its first borrowing in July 1988.
12. The Resolution Funding Corporation, established by the Financial Institutions Reform, Recovery and Enforcement Act of 1989, undertook its first borrowing in October 1989.
13. The FFB, which began operations in 1974, is authorized to purchase or sell obligations issued, sold, or guaranteed by other federal agencies. Because FFB incurs debt solely for the purpose of lending to other agencies, its debt is not included in the main portion of the table in order to avoid double counting.
14. Includes FFB purchases of agency assets and guaranteed loans; the latter are loans guaranteed by numerous agencies, with the amounts guaranteed by any one agency generally being small. The Farmers Home Administration entry consists exclusively of agency assets, whereas the Rural Electrification Administration entry consists of both agency assets and guaranteed loans.

Source: *Federal Reserve Bulletin*, Table 1.44, June 1994, p. A33.

Ownership of U.S. Government Securities and the Burden of Federal Debt

One of the developing public issues of the 1990s that promises to be of great importance is the continuing growth of the federal deficit and the burden that it creates. This section takes a brief look at the size of that burden and the owners of the securities that comprise the federal debt. Figure 2.7 shows how private holdings of Treasury marketable debt (bills, notes, and bonds) have grown in the last decade. By the end of 1994, this portion of the federal debt was nearing $3 trillion. In addition, there is a total of about $1.5 trillion in non–marketable debt, for a total of

Figure 2.6

Quotations for Agency Issues

GOVERNMENT AGENCY & SIMILAR ISSUES

Thursday, June 23, 1994

Over-the-Counter mid-afternoon quotations based on large transactions, usually $1 million or more. Colons in bid-and-asked quotes represent 32nds; 101:01 means 101 1/32.

All yields are calculated to maturity, and based on the asked quote. * -- Callable issue, maturity date shown. For issues callable prior to maturity, yields are computed to the earliest call date for issues quoted above par, or 100, and to the maturity date for issues below par.

Source: Bear, Stearns & Co. via Street Software Technology Inc.

FNMA Issues

Rate	Mat.	Bid	Asked	Yld.
7.45	7-94	100:04	100:08	0.99
8.90	8-94	100:17	100:21	3.27
10.10	10-94	101:19	101:23	4.00
9.25	11-94	101:17	101:21	4.63
5.50	12-94	100:06	100:10	4.82
9.00	1-95	102:03	102:07	4.73
11.95	1-95	103:19	103:23	4.79
11.50	2-95	103:28	104:00	4.82
8.85	3-95	102:18	102:22	4.88
11.70	5-95	105:01	105:05	5.51
11.15	6-95	105:00	105:04	5.57
4.75	8-95	98:24	98:28	5.77
10.50	9-95	105:08	105:12	5.80
8.80	11-95	103:23	103:27	5.83
10.60	11-95	106:02	106:06	5.82
9.20	1-96	104:19	104:25	5.89
7.00	2-96	101:12	101:18	5.97
9.35	2-96	104:26	105:00	6.06
8.50	6-96	104:09	104:15	6.04
8.75	6-96	104:24	104:30	6.03
8.00	7-96	103:13	103:19	6.09
7.90	8-96	103:08	103:14	6.14
8.15	8-96	103:23	103:29	6.15
8.20	8-96*	100:14	100:20	3.09
7.70	9-96	102:30	103:04	6.15
8.63	9-96	104:27	105:01	6.14
7.05	10-96	101:20	101:26	6.18
8.45	10-96	104:22	104:28	6.15
6.90	11-96*	100:16	100:22	4.99
7.70	12-96	102:30	103:04	6.30
8.20	12-96	104:14	104:20	6.17
6.20	1-97*	99:05	99:11	6.48
7.60	1-97	102:31	103:05	6.23
7.05	3-97*	101:02	101:08	5.19
7.00	4-97*	101:04	101:10	5.26
6.75	4-97	100:27	101:01	6.34
9.20	6-97	107:10	107:16	6.37
8.95	7-97	106:19	106:25	6.45
8.80	7-97	106:08	106:14	6.46
9.15	9-97*	100:29	101:03	3.62
9.55	9-97	107:05	107:13	6.71
5.70	9-97*	96:29	97:03	6.72
5.35	10-97*	96:00	96:06	6.56
6.05	10-97*	97:24	97:30	6.75
6.05	11-97	98:04	98:10	6.61
9.55	11-97	108:12	108:18	6.67
7.10	12-97*	101:05	101:11	6.66
8.60	12-97*	101:24	101:30	6.42
9.55	12-97	108:16	108:22	6.69
6.30	12-97*	98:13	98:19	6.76
6.05	1-98	97:28	98:02	6.67
8.65	2-98	106:00	106:06	6.69
8.20	3-98	104:09	104:15	6.81
5.30	3-98*	94:27	95:01	6.84
5.25	3-98	94:27	95:01	6.77
9.15	4-98	107:18	107:24	6.79
8.38	4-98*	102:09	102:15	5.26
8.15	5-98	104:19	104:25	6.72
5.25	5-98*	94:03	94:09	6.96
5.40	5-98*	94:11	94:17	7.02
5.38	6-98	94:28	95:02	6.82
5.10	7-98*	93:08	93:14	6.98
8.20	8-98*	102:15	102:21	5.70
5.35	8-98*	94:14	94:20	6.87
4.70	9-98*	92:00	92:06	6.87
7.85	9-98	103:29	104:03	6.71
4.95	9-98*	92:22	92:28	6.91
4.88	10-98*	92:03	92:09	6.98
5.05	11-98	93:16	93:22	6.74
5.30	12-98*	93:24	93:30	6.90
7.05	12-98*	100:26	101:00	6.78
7.05	12-98*	99:21	99:27	7.09
5.55	2-99*	94:16	94:24	6.89
7.50	3-99*	100:24	101:00	6.86
9.55	3-99	110:12	110:20	6.86
8.70	6-99	107:18	107:26	6.81
8.45	7-99	106:01	106:09	6.95
8.65	7-99*	100:03	100:11	0.38
6.35	8-99	97:10	97:18	6.92
8.55	8-99	106:23	106:31	6.92
9.00	10-99*	101:02	101:10	4.32
8.35	11-99	105:22	105:30	7.00
8.65	12-99*	101:24	102:00	4.13
6.10	2-00	95:30	96:06	6.93
9.30	2-00*	102:10	102:18	5.01
9.05	4-00	109:09	109:17	7.01
9.80	5-00*	103:16	103:24	5.31
8.90	6-00	109:01	109:09	6.97
9.20	9-00	111:04	111:12	6.91
8.25	12-00	106:00	106:08	7.03
8.63	4-01*	103:17	103:25	6.34
8.70	6-01*	103:24	104:00	6.49
8.88	7-01*	104:16	104:24	6.35
7.80	12-01*	100:24	101:00	5.44
7.20	1-02*	97:27	98:03	8.04
7.50	2-02	101:21	101:29	7.17
7.90	4-02*	101:03	101:11	7.35
7.55	4-02	101:14	101:22	7.26
7.80	6-02*	99:01	99:09	7.92
7.30	7-02*	97:01	97:09	7.76
7.00	8-02*	96:09	96:17	7.58
6.93	8-02*	95:16	95:24	7.64
6.95	9-02*	96:22	96:30	7.45
7.30	10-02*	97:31	98:07	7.59
6.80	10-02*	94:30	95:06	7.59
7.05	11-02	98:04	98:12	7.31
6.80	1-03	96:16	96:24	7.32
6.40	3-03*	92:06	92:14	7.60
6.63	4-03*	93:19	93:27	7.60
6.45	6-03*	92:13	92:21	7.59
6.20	7-03*	90:27	91:03	7.58
6.25	8-03*	91:00	91:08	7.59
5.45	10-03	87:04	87:12	7.35
6.20	11-03*	90:10	90:18	7.63
5.80	12-03	89:12	89:20	7.34
6.40	1-04*	91:22	91:30	7.60
6.90	3-04*	94:17	94:25	7.67
6.85	4-04	96:09	96:17	7.35
7.60	4-04*	98:14	98:22	7.79
7.65	4-04*	98:25	99:01	7.79
7.55	6-04*	98:26	99:02	7.69
7.40	7-04	100:13	100:21	7.31
0.00	7-14	20:00	20:08	8.14
10.35	12-15	128:05	128:13	7.64
8.20	3-16	104:06	104:14	7.77
8.95	2-18	113:17	113:25	7.68
8.10	8-19	103:10	103:18	7.77
0.00	10-19	13:21	13:29	7.96
9.65	8-20*	103:10	103:18	9.28
9.50	11-20*	103:00	103:08	9.17

Federal Home Loan Bank

Rate	Mat.	Bid	Asked	Yld.
8.30	7-94	100:10	100:14	2.57
6.70	8-94	100:11	100:15	3.69
8.60	8-94	100:21	100:25	3.62
6.58	9-94	100:16	100:20	3.86
8.30	10-94	101:07	101:11	4.09
4.75	11-94	99:28	100:00	4.73
5.89	11-94	100:11	100:15	4.70
8.20	11-94	101:09	101:13	4.68
8.05	12-94	101:16	101:20	4.70
5.45	1-95	100:06	100:10	4.89
8.40	1-95	101:27	101:31	4.89
5.94	2-95	100:17	100:21	4.91
8.60	2-95	102:08	102:12	4.92
6.45	3-95	100:20	100:24	5.40
7.88	3-95	101:22	101:26	5.36
9.00	3-95	102:16	102:20	5.36
6.04	4-95	100:10	100:14	5.48
8.88	6-95	103:02	103:06	5.54
10.00	6-95	104:12	104:16	5.31
10.30	7-95	104:20	104:24	5.68
4.60	8-95	98:16	98:20	5.84
4.50	9-95	98:06	98:10	5.92
5.00	10-95	98:25	98:29	5.86
5.38	11-95	99:09	99:13	5.81
9.50	12-95	104:31	105:03	5.89
8.10	3-96	103:06	103:12	6.02
9.80	3-96	105:31	106:05	6.02
6.68	4-96	100:29	101:03	6.03
4.36	4-96*	96:28	97:02	6.08
7.75	4-96	102:29	103:03	5.93
8.25	5-96	103:24	103:30	6.04
8.25	6-96	104:00	104:06	5.99
4.41	7-96*	96:13	96:19	6.22
8.00	7-96	103:15	103:21	6.10
7.70	8-96	103:00	103:06	6.10
8.25	9-96	104:04	104:10	6.16
7.10	10-96	101:27	102:01	6.14
8.25	11-96	104:15	104:21	6.14
6.85	2-97	101:00	101:06	6.35
7.65	3-97	103:03	103:09	6.32
9.15	3-97	106:25	106:31	6.34
6.99	4-97	101:15	101:21	6.34
6.34	6-97	99:28	100:02	6.32
9.20	8-97	107:08	107:14	6.55
5.26	4-98*	94:10	94:16	6.91
9.25	11-98	108:27	109:01	6.84
9.30	1-99	109:04	109:12	6.88
5.43	2-99	94:03	94:11	6.87
8.60	6-99	106:21	106:29	6.94
8.45	7-99	106:07	106:15	6.92
8.60	8-99	106:30	107:06	6.92
8.38	10-99	105:25	106:01	7.00
8.60	1-00	107:04	107:12	6.98
9.50	2-04	113:21	113:29	7.45

Federal Farm Credit Bank

Rate	Mat.	Bid	Asked	Yld.
3.32	7-94	100:00	100:04	0.00
3.60	7-94	100:00	100:04	0.00
3.65	7-94	100:00	100:04	0.00
3.26	8-94	99:28	100:00	3.22
3.64	8-94	99:29	100:01	3.26
4.19	8-94	99:31	100:03	3.17
3.40	9-94	99:25	99:29	3.89
3.77	9-94	99:27	99:31	3.90
4.31	9-94	99:30	100:02	3.90
4.48	9-94	100:00	100:04	3.76
8.63	9-94	100:23	100:27	3.74
13.00	9-94	101:17	101:21	3.48
3.43	10-94	99:16	99:20	4.82
4.00	10-94	99:24	99:28	4.43
4.45	10-94	100:00	100:04	3.98
3.48	11-94	99:20	99:24	4.19
4.63	11-94	100:00	100:04	4.23
3.62	12-94	99:12	99:16	4.80
4.94	12-94	99:30	100:02	4.77
11.45	12-94	102:22	102:26	4.70
3.61	1-95	99:09	99:13	4.79
4.84	1-95	100:00	100:04	4.59
8.30	1-95	101:24	101:28	4.86
3.53	2-95	99:02	99:06	4.93
6.38	4-95	100:19	100:23	5.39
4.43	4-95	99:08	99:12	5.26
5.16	5-95	99:25	99:29	5.27
5.47	6-95	100:02	100:06	5.26
5.50	12-95	99:12	99:16	5.86
5.08	1-96	98:15	98:21	6.00
6.65	5-96	100:30	101:04	5.99
4.55	2-97*	95:16	95:22	6.37
5.12	3-97*	96:21	96:27	6.41
11.90	10-97	115:19	115:25	6.52
5.27	2-99*	93:15	93:23	6.89
5.79	3-99*	95:07	95:15	6.94
8.65	10-99	107:08	107:16	6.92
7.95	4-02*	98:21	98:29	8.14

Student Loan Marketing

Rate	Mat.	Bid	Asked	Yld.
8.50	7-94	100:00	100:04	0.00
7.50	7-94	100:05	100:09	0.26
8.10	7-94	100:08	100:12	1.89
8.30	9-94	100:28	101:00	3.89
7.54	10-94	100:28	101:00	3.97
0.00	11-94	99:28	99:29	4.05
8.55	2-95	102:00	102:04	4.86
5.28	2-95	100:03	100:07	4.89
7.63	3-95	101:23	101:27	4.93
9.50	9-97*	100:29	101:03	3.95
8.75	8-00*	100:13	100:21	4.30
9.80	9-00*	105:13	105:21	4.99

Figure 2.7

Growth in Marketable Treasury Debt

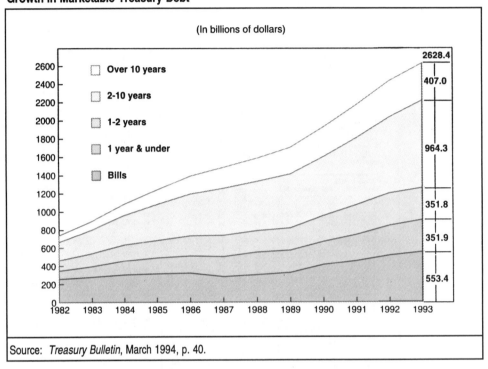

(In billions of dollars)

Source: *Treasury Bulletin*, March 1994, p. 40.

$4.5 trillion of debt on which the federal government pays interest. About $1 trillion of this debt is held by the Federal Reserve and other arms of the government itself.

This still leaves about $3.5 trillion in private hands. The major owners of federal securities are private nonbank financial and nonfinancial holders. The nonbank financial holders have grown much in importance. This group includes pension funds, savings and loan associations, and various financial investment companies, such as money market mutual funds.[12] The private domestic nonfinancial holders consist mainly of various corporations and households.

Financing of the federal debt places a large burden on the taxpayer and consumes a significant portion of the annual budget of the federal government each year. Figure 2.8 shows the growth in the annual interest payments required to service the debt. By 1994, this annual interest cost had grown to more than $200 billion. Today, many people are concerned that this mushrooming debt and the associated interest costs create a tremendous obligation that is being passed to

---

[12]**Mutual funds** are portfolios of securities that are owned in common by a group of investors. A money market mutual fund is one that invests in money market instruments.

Figure 2.8

Growth in Interest Cost of the Federal Debt

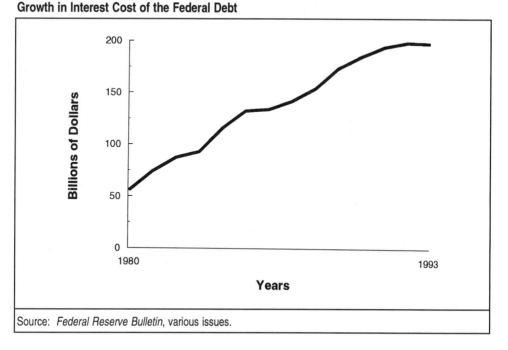

Source: *Federal Reserve Bulletin*, various issues.

future generations. Failure of current taxpayers to fund the current expenses of the government means that subsequent citizens must pay for what we spend today.

The Corporate Bond Market

It is important to see corporate bonds in relationship to other nonfederal long–term debt. Figure 2.9 presents the major categories of long–term borrowings for issuers other than the Federal government. As the graph indicates, corporate bond issuances exceed mortgage borrowing and tax–exempt debt. The issues of state and local governments make up the municipal bond market and will be examined in the next section, followed by a discussion of the mortgage market.

Corporate Bond Quotations

One of the best readily available sources for quotations on corporate bonds is *The Wall Street Journal*, where New York Exchange Bonds are quoted, as shown in Figure 2.10. In most respects, the quotations are similar to those of Treasury bonds, but there are some important differences. The identifier is essentially the same as in the Treasury bond market. The next column shows the **current yield**, which

Figure 2.9

Annual Long–Term Nonfederal Borrowings

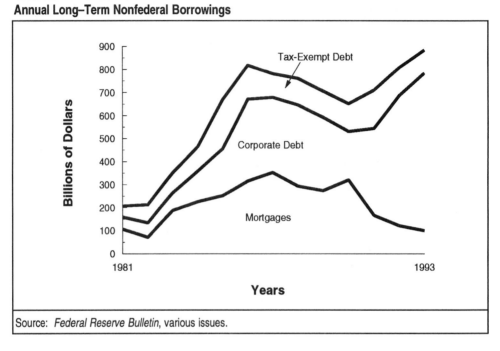

Source: *Federal Reserve Bulletin*, various issues.

equals the annual dollar coupon amount divided by the current market price in dollars:

$$\text{Current Yield} = \frac{\text{Annual Coupon Payment}}{\text{Bond's Current Market Price}} \qquad \textbf{2.6}$$

In some cases, the current yield column carries the designation "cv," which indicates that the bond is a **convertible bond**, a bond that may be converted into another security, usually common stock, at the option of the bond's owner. (Convertible securities are discussed in more detail later in this chapter and in Chapter 18.) In rare cases, the current yield column may show an "f," which indicates that the bond is traded **flat**. For a bond traded flat, the purchaser need not pay the accrued interest in addition to the bond price. This system of pricing is used when a bond is in default or when the next coupon payment is particularly uncertain.

The next column shows the day's trading volume expressed as the number of bonds. Since almost all corporate bonds have a face value of $1,000, the volume figure gives a quick guide to the face amount volume that was traded in a particular issue on a given day. The next three columns give the high, low, and closing prices for the trading in a particular bond. The price quotations are

Figure 2.10

Corporate Bond Quotations

NEW YORK EXCHANGE BONDS

CORPORATION BONDS
Volume, $20,385,000

Bonds	Cur Yld	Vol	Close	Net Chg.
AMR 9s16	9.4	60	95⅝	...
AMR 8.10s98	8.0	220	101¾	+ ¼
ATT 7½06	7.5	138	99¾	+ ½
ATT 4¾98	5.1	125	93	− ⅛
ATT 4⅜96	4.6	15	96	...
ATT 4⅜99	4.9	6	89½	+ ½
ATT 6s00	6.3	34	94½	+ ¼
ATT 5⅛01	5.7	22	89¼	− ¼
ATT 8⅝31	8.4	7	103	...
ATT 7⅛02	7.1	53	99⅞	+ ⅝
ATT 8⅛22	8.1	256	100	...
ATT 8⅛24	8.1	15	100⅛	+ ⅜
ATT 4½96	4.6	99	97½	− ⅛
ATT 6¾04	7.1	85	95⅜	...
Actava 9½98	10.0	10	95	...
Advst 9s08	cv	10	96	− 1
AirbF 6¾01	cv	5	108½	− 1½
AlskAr 6⅞14	cv	80	81½	+ ¾
AlskAr zr06	...	26	40¼	...
AlbnyInt 5s02	cv	9	88¾	− ¾
AlldC zr98	...	3	75	− 1⅜
Allwst 7¼14	cv	15	92	− 1
AMAX 14½94	14.0	3	103 23/32	+ 5/16
ACyan 8⅜06	8.3	100	100⅝	− ⅜
Ametek 9¾04	9.5	10	102⅜	+ ½
Ancp 13⅞02f	cv	5	109	− 1
Anhr 8⅝16	8.4	23	102¾	− ¼
AnnTaylr 8¾00	8.9	252	98	+ ⅛
Arml 9.2s00	9.5	45	96¾	...
AshO 6¾14	cv	5	97	− ¼
Atchsn 4s95	4.2	15	96	...
ARch 10⅜95	9.9	35	104½	− ⅛
AutDt zr12	...	19	40	...
BkrHgh zr03	...	8	54	− 1½
Bally 10s06f	cv	10	87	− 1
BkNY 7½01	cv	1	149½	− 6¾
Barnt 8½99	8.1	500	105½	+ ¾
Barnet 9⅞01	8.9	10	111⅜	+ 3⅛
BellPa 8⅛17	8.1	2	99¾	+ ¼
BellsoT 8¼32	8.2	15	100⅜	− ⅛
BellsoT 7⅞32	8.1	41	96¾	...
BellsoT 6½00	6.6	25	97¾	+ ⅜
BellsoT 7s05	7.2	49	97	− ¼
BellsoT 7½33	8.1	15	92¾	+ ⅝
Bellso 5⅞09	6.9	96	85	+ ¾
BstBy 9s97	8.9	14	101	...
BstBuy 8⅝00	8.8	18	98⅜	+ ⅛
BethSt 9s00	9.0	14	100	...
BethSt 8.45s05	8.8	73	96	− ⅜
BethSt 8⅜01	8.6	1	97¾	+ 1¼
Bevrly 7⅝03	cv	16	99½	...
Boeing 8⅜96	8.1	100	103¾	+ ¼
BoisC 7s16	cv	7	87	...

Quotations as of 4 p.m. Eastern Time
Thursday, June 23, 1994

Volume $20,539,000

	Domestic Thu.	Domestic Wed.	All Issues Thu.	All Issues Wed.
Issues traded	334	344	337	347
Advances	129	139	129	141
Declines	134	126	137	126
Unchanged	71	79	71	80
New highs	3	2	3	2
New lows	24	17	24	17

SALES SINCE JANUARY 1
(000 omitted)

1994	1993	1992
$3,870,740	$5,303,964	$6,050,038

Dow Jones Bond Averages

−1993− High	−1993− Low	−1994− High	−1994− Low		−1994− Close	−1994− Chg.	−1994− %Yld	−1993− Close	−1993− Chg.
109.77	103.49	105.61	96.43	20 Bonds	98.14	−0.02	7.43	107.47	+ 0.07
105.59	102.30	103.43	93.48	10 Utilities	94.83	−0.12	7.86	104.75	− 0.10
114.51	104.58	107.93	98.76	10 Industrials	101.45	+0.07	7.017	110.20	+ 0.24

Bonds	Cur Yld	Vol	Close	Net Chg.
Litton 12⅝05	11.6	1	109	− ⅜
LglsLt 9⅝24	9.9	5	97½	− 4
LglsLt 7.3s99	7.8	130	94⅛	− ⅛
LglsLt 8.9s19	10.5	285	85	− ¼
LslsLt 9s22	10.5	52	85¾	− ⅛
LglsLt 7½07	9.1	80	82¾	− ¾
LglsLt 8.2s23	10.3	50	79½	+ ⅛
MACOM 9¼06	cv	20	92	+ ¾
MGM Grd 11¾99	10.8	18	108½	...
MGM Grd 12s02	10.9	50	110⅜	− ½
Malan 9½04	cv	10	100	− 2
MarO 8.5s06	8.7	11	98	+ ½
MarO 7s02	7.5	96	93⅜	+ ⅞
Masco 5¼12	cv	20	91½	...
Mascotch 03	cv	10	74¾	+ 1¼
Maxus 8½08	9.8	19	87	...
McDnlDg 8⅝97	8.2	20	104¾	+ ¼
McDnlDg 9¾12	8.9	15	109½	...
Mead 6¾12	cv	5	101½	− ½
Medplx 11¾02	11.0	22	106½	+ ¼
Mediplx 03	cv	25	116½	...
Medusa 6s03	cv	20	97½	+ 3½
Melln 7¼99	6.3	1	115	+ 1½
MerLyGlbl 98	...	50	95¼	+ ½
MichB 7¾11	7.8	17	99	+ ⅛
TucEP 7.65s03	8.5	10	90½	...
Tyco 10⅛02	11.3	235	90	− 5½
UNC 7½06	cv	33	90½	− ½
UNC 9⅛03	9.1	10	100	− 2
US West zr11	...	83	30⅛	...
USA Wst 8½02	cv	5	103	− 1
USAir 12⅞00	14.3	84	90¼	− ⅜
USLICO 8½14	cv	10	103	+ ½
USX 4⅝96	4.8	7	97⅜	...
USX 5¾01	cv	19	85⅛	+ ⅝
USX 7s17	cv	84	88½	− ¼
USX zr05	cv	161	42⅜	− ½
Unisy na15s97	...	54	111⅜	+ 1⅛
Unisys 8¼00	cv	106	106	− ½
Vencor 6s02	cv	28	102½	− ¼
Waban 6½02	cv	55	90	...
Watrhse 03	cv	56	73	+ ⅜
Webb 9¾03	10.2	18	95⅞	+ ½
Wendys 7s06	cv	6	142	− ¼
WstDig 9s14	cv	123	101	− 2¾
WhlPit 9⅜03	9.8	192	95¾	+ ¾
WisBl 7¼07	7.5	25	96¾	...
Xerox 13¼14	12.3	20	108	− ⅛
Zenith 6¼11	cv	70	69¼	− ⅜

Source: *The Wall Street Journal*, June 24, 1994, p. C16. Reprinted by permission of *The Wall Street Journal*,

expressed as a percentage of par. For example, on a bond with a $1,000 face value and a price quoted of 80 3/8, the actual dollar price would be 80.375 percent of the $1,000 par value, or $803.75. To actually acquire a bond with this quoted price, one would also have to pay the accrued interest as well. The final column shows the change in the price from the preceding day's close to the current day's close.

Although this page in *The Wall Street Journal* is the most readily available source of daily quotations, it is limited in many respects. In spite of the fact that the

Table 2.4

New York Stock Exchange Bond Trading

Year	Annual Volume $mil	Average Daily Volume $mil	Number of Trades	Avg. Trade Size No. of Bonds
1984	6,982.3	27.6	620,547	11.25
1985	9,046.5	35.9	726,279	12.46
1986	10,464.1	41.4	774,890	13.50
1987	9,727.1	38.4	659,231	14.76
1988	7,702.1	30.4	522,173	14.00
1989	8,836.3	35.1	492,920	16.90
1990	10,892.7	43.1	516,328	20.30
1991	12,698.1	50.2	611,794	20.20
1992	11,629.0	45.8	550,526	21.121
1993	9,743	38.5	439,478	22.17

Source: *New York Stock Exchange Fact Book*, 1994, p. 105.

dollar volume on the New York Stock Exchange often exceeds $30 million a day, relatively few bonds are traded over this exchange. This becomes clear if one examines the size of the day's trading for many of the issues. Seldom does the day's trading show more than 100 bonds of one type being traded.[13] Table 2.4 shows bond trading statistics for the NYSE. In fact, the NYSE trades relatively few bonds, relative to the over–the–counter market.

The Corporate Bond Over–the–Counter Market

The **over–the–counter market** (OTC) is a loose organization of traders without a centralized physical location. Rather, the OTC participants communicate with each other electronically from their own offices.[14] While, there are few reliable statistics on the actual trading volume in the bond market, it is possible to observe the

[13] The American Stock Exchange also has a bond exchange associated with it. In both the bond market and the stock market, the New York Exchange dwarfs the American.

[14] The structure of the over–the–counter market is described in much more detail in Chapter 3.

annual issuance of bonds. By 1994, the total amount of corporate bonds issued was approaching $500 billion.[15]

When it issues a bond, a corporation promises to make a series of payments of a certain amount on pre–specified dates. For the purchaser of the bond, the best thing that could happen is that the issuer keeps his promise. There is no question of hoping for payments above those that were promised. As a result, for many bond investors, the chance that the promise will be kept becomes extremely important. To aid bond investors in making their assessment about the future payment prospects of a particular bond, there are services that rate the quality of various bonds. The ratings are designed to measure default risk—the chance that one or more payments on the bond will be deferred or missed altogether. Table 2.5 presents the categories of the two principal rating services. In general, these two ratings systems follow each other very closely. Figure 2.11 shows the explanations of its ratings provided by Standard & Poor's. Moody's has a similar explanation for its rankings. Bond returns depend on other factors besides whether the promised payments are made. If one holds a bond until it matures and the issuer makes all payments as promised, one will earn the yield to maturity on the bond at the time of purchase. For shorter holding periods, bond returns are uncertain. Bond prices can change as a result of changes in interest rates and changes in the prospects of the issuing firm.

Table 2.5

Bond Rating Categories

	Moody's	Standard & Poor's
Investment Grade	Aaa Aa A Baa	AAA AA A BBB
Below Investment Grade	Ba B Caa Ca C	BB B CCC–CC C DDD–D

[15] Chapter 4 considers the process by which firms issue new securities.

Figure 2.11

Standard & Poor's Bond Ratings

DEBT

A Standard & Poor's corporate or municipal debt rating is a current assessment of the creditworthiness of an obligor with respect to a specific obligation. This assessment may take into consideration obligors such as guarantors, insurers, or lessees.

The debt rating is not a recommendation to purchase, sell or hold a security, inasmuch as it does not comment as to market price or suitability for a particular investor.

The ratings are based on current information furnished by the issuer or obtained by Standard & Poor's from other sources it considers reliable. Standard & Poor's does not perform any audit in connection with any rating and may, on occasion, rely on unaudited financial information. The ratings may be changed, suspended or withdrawn as a result of changes in, or unavailability of, such information, or for other circumstances.

The ratings are based, in varying degrees, on the following considerations:

I.   Likelihood of default-capacity and willingness of the obligor as to the timely payment of interest and repayment of principal in accordance with the terms of the obligation;
II. Nature of and provisions of the obligation;
III. Protection afforded by, and relative position of, the obligation in the event of bankruptcy, reorganization or other arrangement under the laws of bankruptcy and other laws affecting creditor's rights.

AAA Debt rated 'AAA' has the highest rating assigned by Standard & Poor's. Capacity to pay interest and repay principal is extremely strong.

AA Debt rated 'AA' has a very strong capacity to pay interest and repay principal and differs from the higher rated issues only in small degree.

A Debt rated 'A' has a strong capacity to pay interest and repay principal although it is somewhat more susceptible to the adverse effects of changes in circumstances and economic conditions than debt in higher rated categories.

BBB Debt rated 'BBB' is regarded as having an adequate capacity to pay interest and repay principal. Whereas it normally exhibits adequate protection parameters, adverse economic conditions or changing circumstances are more likely to lead to a weakened capacity to pay interest and repay principal for debt in this category than in higher rated categories.

BB, B, CCC, CC, C Debt rated 'BB', 'B', 'CCC', 'CC' and 'C' is regarded, on balance, as predominantly speculative with respect to capacity to pay interest and repay principal in accordance with the terms of the obligation. 'BB' indicates the lowest degree of speculation and 'C' the highest degree of speculation. While such debt will likely have some quality and protective characteristics, these are outweighed by large uncertainties or major risk exposures to adverse conditions.

BB Debt rated 'BB' has less near-term vulnerability to default than other speculative issues. However, it faces major ongoing uncertainties or exposure to adverse business, financial, or economic conditions which could lead to inadequate capacity to meet timely interest and principal payments. The 'BB'

rating category is also used for debt subordinated to senior debt that is assigned an acutal or implied 'BBB – ' rating.

B Debt rated 'B' has a greater vulnerability to default but currently has the capacity to meet interest payments and principal repayments. Adverse business, financial, or economic conditions will likely impair capacity or willingness to pay interest and repay principal. The 'B' rating category is also used for debt subordinated to senior debt that is assigned an acutal or implied 'BB' or 'BB – ' rating.

CCC Debt rated 'CCC' has a currently identifiable vulnerability to default, and is dependent upon favorable business, financial, and economic conditions to meet timely payment of interest and repayment of principal. In the event of adverse business, financial, or economic conditions, it is not likely to have the capacity to pay interest and repay principal. The 'CCC' rating category is also used for debt subordinated to senior debt that is assigned an actual or implied 'B' or 'B – ' rating.

CC the rating 'CC' is typically applied to debt subordinated to senior debt that is assigned an actual or implied 'CCC' rating.

C The rating 'C' is typically applied to debt subordinated to senior debt which is assigned an actual or implied 'CCC – ' debt rating. The 'C' rating may be used to cover a situation where a bankruptcy petition has been filed, but debt service payments are continued.

CI The rating 'CI' is reserved for income bonds on which no interest is being paid.

D Debt rated 'D' is in payment default. The 'D' rating category is used when interest payments or principal payments are not made on the date due even if the applicable grace period has not expired, unless S&P believes that such payments will be made during such grace period. The 'D' rating also will be used upon the filing of a bankruptcy petition if debt service payments are jeopardized.

Plus (+) or Minus (–): The ratings from 'AA to 'CCC' may be modified by the addition of a plus or minus sign to show relative standing within the major categories.

NR indicates that no public rating has been requested, that there is insufficient information on which to base a rating, or that S&P does not rate a particular type of obligation as a matter of policy.

Debt Obligations of issuers outside the United States and its territories are rated on the same basis as domestic corporate and municipal issues. The ratings measure the creditworthiness of the obligor but do not take into account currency exchange and related uncertainties.

Bond Investment Quality Standards: Under present commercial bank regulations issued by the Comptroller of the Currency, bonds rated in the top four categories ('AAA,' 'AA,' 'A,' 'BBB,' commonly known as "Investment Grade" ratings) are generally regarded as eligible for bank investment. In addition, the Legal Investment Laws of various states may impose certain rating or other standards for obligations eligible for investment by savings banks, trust companies, insurance companies and fiduciaries generally.

Source: Standard & Poor's Corporation, *Bond Guide*, August 1991, p. 10.

History of Corporate Bond Returns

Figure 2.12 presents the returns for a portfolio of high–quality long–term corporate bonds for 1926 to 1993. Over this period, these bonds returned an annual rate of 5.6 percent. After subtracting inflation, the annualized real return was only 2.4 percent. As another guide to the returns, $1 invested in corporate bonds in 1926 would have grown to $40.34, and purchasing power would have increased from $1 in 1926 to $4.96 by year–end 1993.

These returns for top–quality bonds do not tell the entire story. There are many other types of bonds with different yields as well, with the differences in yields due largely to differences in risk. Figure 2.13 shows the yield relationship between top–quality and lower quality corporate bonds. The difference in yields between bonds of different quality rankings, or levels of default risk, appears to widen when interest rates are high and also when the economy is in recession. This

Figure 2.12

Returns on High–Quality Corporate Bonds, 1926–1993

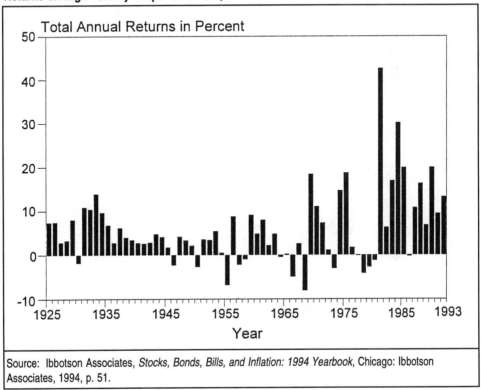

Source: Ibbotson Associates, *Stocks, Bonds, Bills, and Inflation: 1994 Yearbook*, Chicago: Ibbotson Associates, 1994, p. 51.

is likely to be the case because the probability of default for weaker bonds rises more rapidly in recessions than it does for top–rated bonds.[16]

High–Yield Corporate Bonds

The high–yield corporate bond market developed into special prominence in the 1980s. These bonds are lower rated or speculative grade bonds and are commonly referred to as **junk bonds** (S&P BB or lower, and Moody's Ba or lower). As Figure 2.11 shows, Standard & Poor's regards BB and lower grade bonds as "predominantly speculative with respect to capacity to pay interest and repay principal in accordance with the terms of the obligation." Before the late 1970s, virtually all publicly traded bonds were issued with an investment grade rating (S&P BBB or better or Moody's Baa or better). There were lower grade bonds trading in the

---

[16]For more on default risk and the yield differences it creates, see Chapter 7.

Figure 2.13

Yield Differentials for Different Quality Corporate Bonds

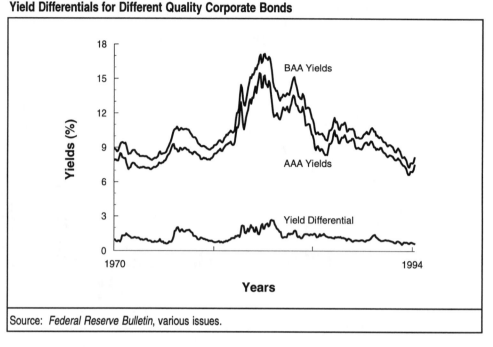

Source: *Federal Reserve Bulletin*, various issues.

marketplace, but these bonds had been issued as investment grade and had been subsequently downgraded as "fallen angels." About this time, some firms began to issue debt rated BB or Ba and lower under the leadership of the investment banking firm Drexel Burnham Lambert. Between 1977 and 1989, the amount of outstanding junk bonds increased from about $1.1 billion to $24.2 billion, and by 1989 about $205 billion in junk bonds were outstanding.[17] Much of this debt was issued in the waves of mergers and corporate restructurings that characterized the 1980s.[18] While the amount of outstanding junk bonds is still higher today, the rate of growth has diminished considerably.

The bond ratings of S&P and Moody's aim to measure **default risk**, the chance that one or more promised payments will not be made as promised. For an

---

[17] For more on junk bonds, see M. E. Blume, D. B. Keim, and S. A. Patel, "Returns and Volatility of Low–Grade Bonds, 1977–1989," *Journal of Finance*, 46:1, March 1991, pp. 49–74. This account of junk bonds relies largely on this article.

[18] For example, a firm desiring to acquire a target company might issue junk bonds to obtain the necessary cash for the acquisition. Similarly, firms that were taken private by a management buyout of other shareholders (a leveraged buyout or LBO) would often obtain financing for the buyout by issuing junk bonds.

Figure 2.14

Realized Returns and Standard Deviation for Major Asset Classes 1977–1989

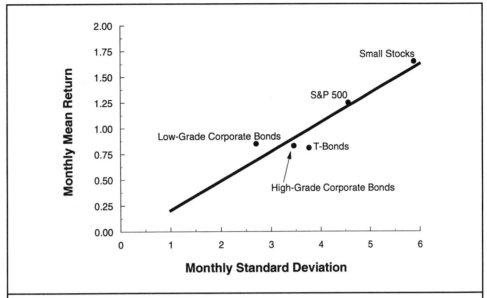

Source: Blume, M. E., D. B. Keim, and S. A. Patel, "Returns and Volatility of Low–Grade Bonds, 1977–1989," *Journal of Finance*, 46:1, March 1991, pp. 49–74.

investor concerned with the risk/expected return trade–off, default risk is just one consideration. If junk bonds have a sufficiently high expected return, it might compensate for the greater chance that junk bonds would default. A variety of studies have sought to measure the default experience of corporate bonds, with the rough consensus being that bond portfolios might lose 1–2 percent of their value each year through default.[19] However, if yields are high enough to compensate for this loss through default, junk bonds could still be an attractive investment.

Figure 2.14 shows the results of one study of risk and return for junk bonds that covered the 1977–1989 period. Compared with other major asset classes, junk

[19]See Howard S. Marks, "High Yield Bond Portfolios," in F. J. Fabozzi, T. D. Fabozzi, and I. M. Pollack, *The Handbook of Fixed Income Securities*, Homewood, IL: Business One Irwin, 1991, pp. 972-988 for a discussion of the issue of default losses.

bonds offered a fairly attractive combination of returns and risk over this period.[20] However, these results may not be indicative of future returns and risk.

The Municipal Bond Market

A **municipal bond** is a debt security issued by a government or a quasi–governmental agency, other than those associated with the federal government. Prime among these issuers are states, cities, and their political sub–divisions. These securities form a distinct segment of the bond market due to the special character of their issuers and their tax status. Most municipal bonds are exempt from federal income taxation. This key feature distinguishes municipal bonds from the rest of the bond market.

Because of their tax exemption, municipal bonds are of greater relative value to investors with high marginal tax rates. Such investors can obtain the same after–tax return from a relatively low–yielding municipal bond or a higher yielding taxable bond. As Equation 2.7 shows, the difference can be important.

$$\text{Equivalent Tax-Exempt Yield} = (1 - \text{Marginal Tax Rate}) (\text{Taxable Yield})$$

2.7

For example, consider an investor with a 35 percent marginal tax rate, faced with a choice between a taxable bond yielding 10 percent and a tax–exempt bond yielding 7 percent. For bonds of like risk and maturity, the rational investor should prefer the bond that gives the higher after–tax return. The taxable bond yielding 10 percent has an equivalent after–tax yield equal to a tax–exempt yield of only 6.5 percent:

$$.065 = (1 - .35).10$$

Assuming that the bonds were equally risky and suitable in other respects, the investor should prefer the lower yielding tax–exempt bond, which will return an after–tax yield of 7 percent. Table 2.6 presents taxable yields and their equivalent tax–exempt yields for investors in different tax brackets. As the table shows, the higher the tax rate, the greater should be the preference for tax–exempt securities.

---

[20] See M. E. Blume, D. B. Keim, and S. A. Patel, "Returns and Volatility of Low–Grade Bonds, 1977–1989," *Journal of Finance*, 46:1, March 1991, pp. 49–74. These results are largely confirmed by E. I. Altman, and M. L. Heine, "How 1989 Changed the Hierarchy of Fixed Income Security Performance," *Financial Analysts Journal*, 46:3, May/June 1990, pp. 9–12. David J. Ward and Gary L. Griepentrog, "Risk and Return in Defaulted Bonds," *Financial Analysts Journal*, May/June 1993, pp. 61–65, find that defaulted bonds actually had the highest monthly return compared to other asset classes during the 1972 to 1991 period.

Table 2.6
$\blacksquare\blacksquare\blacksquare\blacksquare\blacksquare\blacksquare$

Taxable and Tax–Exempt Equivalent Yields

		Marginal Tax Rate (%)			
		20	30	40	50
	8	6.4	5.6	4.8	4.0
	10	8.0	7.0	6.0	5.0
Taxable Yield	12	9.6	8.4	7.2	6.0
(%)	14	11.2	9.2	8.8	7.0
	16	12.8	11.2	9.6	8.0

Equivalent tax–exempt yields are shown in the interior of the table.

Given the after–tax equivalences shown in Table 2.6, it is not surprising that market yields for tax–exempt securities are lower than those of risk–equivalent taxable securities. Figure 2.15 shows the historical yield relationships between AAA tax–exempt and AAA taxable securities. Although the rating systems for tax–exempt

Figure 2.15
$\blacksquare\blacksquare\blacksquare\blacksquare\blacksquare\blacksquare$

Yield Differentials for U.S. High Grade Corporate and Municipal Bonds

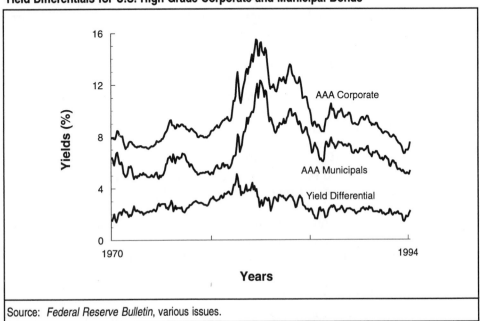

Source: *Federal Reserve Bulletin*, various issues.

Figure 2.16

Municipal Bond Quotations

TAX-EXEMPT BONDS

Representative prices for several active tax-exempt revenue and refunding bonds, based on institutional trades. Changes rounded to the nearest one-eighth. Yield is to maturity. n-New. Source: The Bond Buyer.

ISSUE	COUPON	MAT	PRICE	CHG	BID YLD	ISSUE	COUPON	MAT	PRICE	CHG	BID YLD
Anne Arundel Md Ser94	6.000	04-01-24	94⅛	+ ⅛	6.44	NYC Indus Dev Agcy-n	6.125	01-01-24	94⅛	+ ⅜	6.58
Calif Health Fac	5.550	08-15-25	85⅜	+ ⅛	6.64	NYC Lcl Govt Asst Cp	5.500	04-01-18	87¾	+ ⅛	6.51
Fla Mun Pwr Agy Ser93	5.100	10-01-25	82⅛	...	6.43	NYC Muni Water Fin	5.500	06-15-23	88	+ ¼	6.41
Florida St Bd Ed	5.125	06-01-22	83⅜	+ ⅛	6.40	NYS Environmental	5.875	06-15-14	94¼	+ ⅛	6.38
Florida St Bd Ed	5.800	06-01-24	92⅜	+ ⅛	6.35	NYS Med Care Fac	6.125	02-15-14	96⅞	+ ⅛	6.40
Fulton Co Sch Dist Ga	5.625	01-01-21	90⅜	+ ⅛	6.37	NYS Med Care Facil	5.250	08-15-14	86⅝	...	6.43
Ga Muni Elec Auth	6.500	01-01-26	100¼	...	6.48	Orange Co Fla	6.000	10-01-24	95¾	...	6.32
Hawaii Dept Budgt&Fin	5.450	11-01-23	86⅜	...	6.49	P R Elec Pwr Auth	6.375	07-01-24	98½	...	6.49
Hawaii Hsng Fin & Dev	6.000	07-01-26	91⅞	+ ¼	6.61	PuertoRico pub im go 94	6.450	07-01-17	100⅜	+ ⅛	6.42
humphreys idb tenn swdi	6.700	05-01-24	100	...	6.70	PuertoRico pub im go 94	6.500	07-01-23	100¼	+ ⅛	6.48
Ill Hlth Fac Auth Rev-n	6.000	08-15-24	92¼	− ⅛	6.60	Reedy Creed Fla	5.000	10-01-14	84⅞	+ ⅛	6.32
Ill Regional TA	6.250	06-01-24	96⅜	...	-6.52	S.F. Cal. Sewr Ref Rev	5.375	10-01-22	86⅛	+ ¼	6.44
Kansas City Util Sys	6.375	09-01-23	100	+ ⅛	6.37	Salam Co Poll Ctrl -n	6.250	06-01-31	97⅛	− ⅛	6.45
L.A. Co. Pub Wks Fin Au	6.000	10-01-15	95¼	...	6.41	Salem Co Pol Ctrl	5.450	02-01-32	83½	...	6.65
LA Calif Wstwtr Sys-n	5.875	06-01-24	92⅞	...	6.41	Salt Riv Proj Ariz	5.000	01-01-16	83½	...	6.41
Mass Bay T A	5.900	03-01-24	92¼	+ ⅛	6.49	Santa Clara Wtr Calif-n	6.000	02-01-24	94¾	+ ⅛	6.40
Metro Wash Arpt Auth-n	5.875	10-01-15	93⅜	− ⅜	6.42	TBTA NY	5.000	01-01-24	80¼	+ ⅛	6.51
Mo Hlth & Ed Facs	5.250	05-15-21	83⅜	+ ⅜	6.55	Univ of Calif	6.375	09-01-19	99¼	+ ⅛	6.43
N.J. Econ Dev Auth PCR	6.400	05-01-32	97¼	...	6.60	Univ of Calif	6.375	09-01-24	99	+ ⅛	6.45
NYC Indus Dev Agcy-n	6.000	01-01-15	94¼	+ ¼	6.50	Valdez Al Marine Term	5.650	12-01-28	86	...	6.69

and taxable bonds are slightly different, AAA ratings are the highest for both categories, so they are approximately equal in risk. The yield spread between the two kinds of bonds reflects the eagerness of investors for opportunities to escape taxation.

In addition to exemption from federal taxation, some municipal bonds are also exempt from income taxation by the state and municipality in which they were issued. A bond exempt from federal, state, and municipal taxation is said to be **triple tax–exempt**. Such bonds are popular in states such as California and New York which have locations that tax income at all three levels.

Although the municipal bond market is huge in total size, it is not a very liquid market.[21] Many municipal issues are not very large, and some investors want to hold on to issues once acquired. Consequently, it is somewhat difficult to acquire good information on the current prices of some issues. Two good sources are *The Wall Street Journal* and the Blue List of Standard & Poor's. Figure 2.16 presents a typical listing from *The Wall Street Journal*. Only the most closely followed issues are reported there, and the prices are only given in bid/asked form. The listing is not necessarily a listing of transaction prices.

---

[21]A **liquid market** is one in which an asset can be sold easily for a price that approximates its true value.

Figure 2.17

Issuance of Municipal Bonds

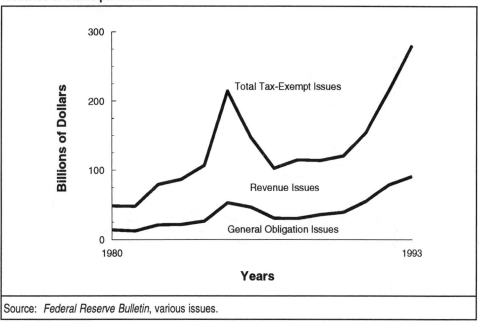

Source: *Federal Reserve Bulletin*, various issues.

Issues in the municipal bond market can be divided into **general obligation bonds** and **revenue bonds**. General obligation bonds are bonds backed by the issuer's taxing power, such as a state or local government. By contrast, revenue bonds are backed only by the revenue from some specific project. The administrators of port authorities, airports, turnpikes, and hospitals are typical issuers of revenue bonds. For revenue bonds, all bond payments must come from the revenue of the particular project. For example, a revenue bond issued by a hospital would have to be paid for by the profits earned by the hospital. Without question, the revenue bonds have a certain risk element since the enterprise must be a success if the bondholders are to be repaid. For general obligation bonds, the issuer at least has taxing power to rely on to secure the necessary funds to repay the bondholders. Figure 2.17 shows the recent issuances of municipal bonds. By 1994, the annual issuance approached $300 billion.

The Mortgage Market

One of the largest components of debt is the **mortgage**, or the debt owed on real estate. In speaking of the mortgage market, it is important to distinguish between real estate mortgages and mortgages as a type of collateral for a debt obligation. In one sense, we mortgage a car to secure a car loan. Any time an asset is pledged to

Figure 2.18

Monthly Mortgage Payments: Percentage Paying Principal and Interest

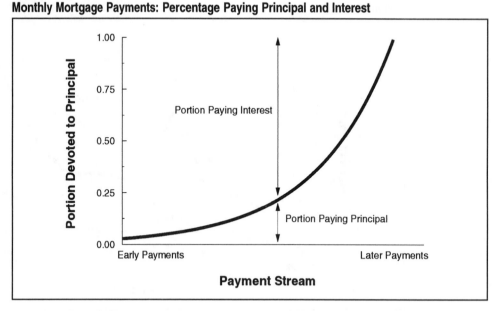

secure a loan, a mortgage is created. Since real estate loans are so typically secured by a pledge of real estate, such loans are themselves called mortgages. This section focuses on real estate mortgages. As Figure 2.9 indicated, mortgage borrowing is comparable in amount to corporate borrowing and exceeds municipal borrowing.

Most mortgages are for residential properties. The initial maturities for these mortgages range up to 30 years and often carry a fixed rate of interest for the entire period. Recently, so–called creative financing plans (including **variable–rate mortgages** and **balloon mortgages**) have become popular. A variable–rate mortgage allows the interest rate to vary with economic conditions. For example, the rate on the mortgage might be tied to the rate on Treasury bills and adjusted every six months. A balloon mortgage is structured so that the final payment, which might occur three to seven years after the mortgage is initiated, is much larger than the ordinary monthly payments.

The traditional 30–year fixed–rate mortgage is different from the typical bond with its coupon payments and return of principal upon maturity. The main difference in the structure of these instruments stems from the fact that a mortgage is typically an **amortized loan**. In an amortized loan, the payment remains the same over the life of the loan, with part of the payment going to pay interest and part going to pay the principal of the loan. Over time, the portion devoted to paying interest and the portion repaying principal change. As an example, consider a 30–year 10 percent mortgage with an initial principal amount of $100,000. For this mortgage, the monthly payment would be $877.57. Of this payment, $833.33, or 95 percent, would go toward paying the interest in the first month of the mortgage.

Figure 2.18 shows how the proportion of the payment going to principal and interest changes over the life of the mortgage. For the illustration, we assume a 30–year mortgage at 10 percent. Of the first payment, 94.9 percent goes to repay interest, leaving only 5.1 percent of the payment to reduce principal. By the end of the mortgage, that relationship has reversed, with almost all of the final payment paying off the last bit of principal.

Mortgage Pass–Through Securities

After a mortgage is granted by a financial institution, the institution may itself continue to own the mortgage, or it can sell the mortgage in the market for mortgage obligations. Currently, it has become very common to create a **mortgage pool**—a collection of individual mortgages that can be treated as a unit. Once the pool is created, securities are created based on the mortgages in the pool. Thus, investors can buy a participation in the entire pool of mortgages, instead of investing in a single, particular mortgage.

These securities are a **mortgage pass–through security** because the original lender continues to collect payments from the borrower and passes them through to the investors in the mortgage pool. Each security holder receives a payment based on the investment made in the pool. The investors in the pool have a diversified mortgage investment, owning a portion of many mortgages. This provides diversification against default and the risk that the principal on an individual mortgage might be paid early.

Three federally sponsored agencies facilitate the development of mortgage pass-through securities in order to stimulate the mortgage market. They do this by issuing a guarantee that the payments will be made on the mortgages as promised. In effect, this substitutes the creditworthiness of the agency for the owner of the individual properties covered in the mortgage pool. These agencies are the Government National Mortgage Association (GNMA, pronounced "Ginnie Mae"), the Federal National Mortgage Association (FNMA, pronounced "Fannie Mae"), and the Federal Home Loan Mortgage Corporation (FHLMC, pronounced "Freddie Mac"). Table 2.3 shows their recent financing activities.

These agency–guaranteed mortgage pass–throughs provide an attractive means for individual investors or managers of bond portfolios to invest in residential mortgages. Because they are guaranteed by federally sponsored agencies, these mortgages tend to be quite safe from default risk, but they have a higher yield than Treasury issues. Nonetheless, these pass-throughs are subject to other risks that make them quite complicated. Principal among these risks is the chance that individual property owners will pay their mortgages early if interest rates fall. If this happens, the pass–through investor receives a return of principal that must face reinvestment at the new lower rates.

The Bond Contract

The **bond contract**, or **bond indenture**, is a legal document stating in precise terms the promises made by the issuer of a bond and the rights of the bondholders. For all corporate bonds issued in interstate commerce and having an issue size exceeding $5 million, the Trust Indentures Act requires that a trustee be established. The trustee for a bond issue is responsible for protecting the rights of the bondholders and monitoring the performance of the issuer to assure that its promises are kept. The trustee will usually be a bank that is financially independent from the issuer. The bond indenture will be made out to the trustee, who acts as an agent for the bondholders in enforcing the terms of the bond contract.

In addition to specifying the amount and timing of payments to be made to the bondholders, the bond indenture also contains numerous covenants. Among the most important of these are the portions defining the security that the issuer is offering for the bond and the specification of how the bond is to be retired.

Bondholders naturally desire the greatest security possible for their investment, other things being equal. This leads some issuers to offer bonds backed by mortgages on specific corporate assets. For example, an issuer could offer a fleet of vehicles or a production plant as security for a bond issue. In the event of default, the trustee would be empowered to seize the specified assets in order to recoup the investment of the bondholders. Such a bond may be either a **first mortgage bond** or have some inferior status, such as a second or third mortgage. A first mortgage bond gives the bondholders first claim on the assets specified in the mortgage. In the event of a serious default or bankruptcy, those assets are earmarked to be used to repay the bondholders, so the first mortgage is the best kind of collateral available to bondholders.

In addition to mortgage bonds, some firms offer security under slightly different arrangements. For firms that do not have sufficient physical assets to offer as collateral, it is customary to pledge securities. Bonds secured by financial assets are known as **collateral trust bonds**. In the railroad industry, the railroad cars or rolling stock of the railroad have often been pledged as collateral. This type of security is called an **equipment trust certificate**. Under this form of security, the bond issuer does not actually own the equipment until the bond issue is paid off, which makes it easier for the bondholders to seize and dispose of the assets in the event of default. Although originated in the railroad industry, this type of collateral is used by a variety of transportation firms, such as airlines and shippers.

Most bonds issued by corporations have no security pledged to the bonds. This type of bond is known as a **debenture**. Debentures are often used by financially strong corporations that have no mortgage bonds outstanding. Sometimes, however, the debentures are issued after mortgage bonds are already outstanding. In such cases, the debentures have an inferior claim on the assets of the corporation. In addition to straight debentures, there are also **subordinated debentures**, which are unsecured bonds that have an inferior claim to other outstanding debentures. The subordinated debentures are said to be junior to the more senior, original debentures. Figure 2.19 presents the priority of claims among

Figure 2.19

Priority of Claims by Security Type

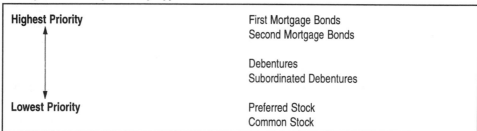

the outstanding securities of corporations. First mortgage bondholders have the strongest position on the assets, while common stockholders have the weakest.

Without any specific security pledged to them, debentures may seem to be a very risky kind of investment. To offset that risk, bond contracts for debentures, as well as for mortgage bonds, often have certain restrictive covenants that protect the bondholders by restricting the behavior of the issuer. For example, a restrictive covenant might require a firm to maintain a certain level of current assets relative to its current liabilities, or the firm may be prohibited from issuing additional debt until the outstanding debt is retired. Still another type of restrictive covenant might constrain the amount of dividends that could be paid to common stockholders. All restrictions are designed to enhance the safety of the bond investment. The trustee has the responsibility for ensuring that the issuer complies with the restrictions.

The bond contract also specifies how the bond is to be retired, and there are many different ways of paying off a bond. Many corporate bonds, as well as many U.S. Treasury bonds, are callable bonds. For a **callable bond**, the issuer has the right to call the bonds in before maturity and pay them off at a certain price stipulated in the bond contract. Issuers have an incentive to call their existing bonds in if the prevailing interest rate is lower than the coupon rate being paid on the bond. Usually the issuer is not permitted to call the bond for a certain period of time after issue. Also, the price the issuer must pay to call the bond, the **call price**, usually gives a premium over the par value to the bondholder. This call price is usually above the par value of the bond and declines toward the par value as the bond approaches maturity. Often, only a portion of a bond issue is called, and the particular bonds to be called are selected at random, with the selected bonds being published by serial number in the financial press.

Callable bonds are often retired by the use of a **sinking fund**. The sinking fund provision of a bond contract provides for the orderly retirement of bonds prior to the maturity date. The sinking fund may operate in two basic ways. The trustee may use the resources of the sinking fund to purchase bonds in the open market or the sinking fund may provide for retirement of a certain portion of the bonds on a redemption date. In such a case, specific bonds are called to be surrendered on a certain date.

Sometimes bonds are scheduled for retirement with a certain principal amount becoming due at predetermined dates. Such a bond is called a **serial bond**. This gives the investor an opportunity to select the maturity date that best suits the investment plan.

Another method of retiring bonds is through conversion. The bondholder of a **convertible bond** has the option of surrendering the bond and receiving in return a specified number of shares of common stock, thereby converting the bond into stock. The number of shares to be received for each bond is known as the **conversion ratio**. The **conversion price** is the price paid for each share of stock, assuming that the bond is converted, and equals the market price of the convertible bond divided by the conversion ratio. The **conversion premium** is the additional amount per share of stock that one pays to obtain the share by converting the bond rather than by buying the stock in the marketplace.

These terms may best be illustrated by an example. Consider a convertible bond with a par value of $1,000 and a market price of $940. The common stock of the issuing company is currently selling for $40. The bond contract allows the bondholder to convert the bond into 20 shares of common stock. In this case, the conversion ratio is 20. If the bond is converted, a bond worth $940 is surrendered for $800 worth of stock (20 shares each worth $40). Since a $940 bond is being surrendered for 20 shares of stock, the conversion price of a share of stock equals $940/20 or $47. The price to acquire the stock through conversion exceeds the price of the stock by $7, the conversion price minus the market price of the stock. This $7 is known as the conversion premium.

The option to convert the bond into stock is a valuable right. The bondholder receives continuing interest payments but has the chance to convert the bond into stock if it becomes attractive. It is not always easy to say when the conversion should take place, but sometimes the right strategy is clear. In the previous example, assume that the market price of the bond stayed at $940, but the stock price went to $50. If this were ever to happen, the following strategy would guarantee a riskless profit without investment—an arbitrage opportunity.[22] One could buy the bond in the market for $940, convert it into 20 shares of stock with a total value of $1,000, sell the stock, and pocket $1,000. This would generate an immediate profit of $60, ignoring transaction costs.

For reasons to be explored in more detail later in this book, one cannot expect to find arbitrage opportunities. The example does illustrate one important point, however. The price of the convertible bond and the stock are interrelated. If the stock price is $50, the price of the convertible bond must be at least $1,000. Otherwise, there would be the arbitrage opportunity just mentioned, and the existence of arbitrage opportunities is equivalent to money being left on the street without anyone bothering to pick it up. One cannot expect to find money lying on

---

[22]**Arbitrage** is the opportunity to earn a return without risk or investment. As will become clear in later discussions, the existence of arbitrage opportunities violates the basic idea of the risk/return trade–off.

the street waiting to be picked up by a chance passerby—especially not on Wall Street.[23]

The Money Market

As mentioned in the chapter overview, it is customary in the debt market to distinguish between the money market and the bond market. The rest of this chapter covers the **money market**, the market for debt instruments with a maturity of one year or less at the time of issuance. Some money market instruments are available only to certain kinds of financial institutions, but many are widely available to all types of investors. For the most part, instruments of the money market share many family resemblances. Their yields tend to move together and the method of price quotation is common to many of the instruments. After discussing yield quotations common to the money market, this chapter considers some of the most important money market instruments.

Money Market Yield Concepts

In the money market, **interest–bearing instruments** are issued with a given par value and a stated coupon rate. Interest is earned based on that par value and coupon rate. **Discount paper** is a money market instrument that is issued with a stated par value and no coupon rate. Discount paper is sold at a discount below its par value, and because these instruments have no coupons, they are short–term zero coupon bonds, in effect. Discount paper includes Treasury bills, bankers' acceptances, and commercial paper. Certificates of deposits and Eurodollar certificates of deposit are interest–bearing instruments. Conventions for yield quotations and pricing differ between the two types of instruments, so the distinction is quite important.

The Discount Yield.   Compared to the previous discussion of yields for debt instruments in general, the method of yield calculation and price quotation widely used in the money market is quite different. Many money market securities are quoted in terms of the **discount yield**. The price quotation is expressed in terms of this discount yield, but from this, one must calculate the actual dollar price of the instrument. The formula for the discount yield, d, is quite straightforward:

$$d = \left(\frac{360}{t} \right) \left(\frac{DISC}{FV} \right) \qquad\qquad \textbf{2.8}$$

[23] For more on convertible bonds, particularly their characteristics as options, see Chapter 18.

where:

DISC = the dollar discount from the face value

FV = the face value of the instrument

t = the number of days until the instrument matures

The actual dollar price, P, depends on the face value and the amount of the dollar discount, DISC:

$$P = FV - DISC = FV \left(1 - \frac{(d)\ (t)}{360}\right) \qquad \textbf{2.9}$$

As an example of the way this system works, consider a 90–day money market instrument with a face value of \$1,000,000 that has a discount yield of 11 percent. The dollar discount, DISC, for this instrument would be:

$$DISC = (\$1,000,000) \left(\frac{(.11)\ (90)}{360}\right) = \$27,500$$

and the actual dollar price would be:

$$P = FV - DISC = \$1,000,000 - \$27,500 = \$972,500$$

One feature of the discount yield is its assumption that the year has 360 days. Other yield measures use a year of 365 days. Even if the 360–day year assumption is acceptable, the discount yield still differs considerably from the yield given by the bond pricing formula. For this particular example, the difference is large, and typical. Using the bond pricing formula of Equation 2.1, a 90–day pure discount instrument with a face value of \$1,000,000 and a price of \$972,500, would be yielding 11.31 percent:

$$\$972,500 = \frac{\$1,000,000}{(1 + .1131/4)}$$

The Bond Equivalent Yield. To compare the yields on money market instruments with other kinds of bonds, it is necessary to get all of the instruments onto the same yield basis. To make discount instruments comparable to bonds, there is a **bond equivalent yield**. For the bond equivalent yield, the idea is to compute a yield that reflects the opportunity that bond market investors have to receive and reinvest semiannual coupon payments. For an instrument with a discount yield maturing in less than six months, the equivalent bond yield, EBY, can be given by the following formula:

Table 2.7
_____

Discount Yields Versus Equivalent Bond Yields

Discount Yields	Equivalent Bond Yields (%)		
	30–day maturity	182–day maturity	364–day maturity
6	6.114	6.274	6.375
8	8.116	8.453	8.639
10	10.227	10.679	10.979
12	12.290	12.952	13.399
14	14.362	15.256	15.904

Source: Marcia Stigum, _The Money Market_, 3e, Homewood, IL: Dow Jones–Irwin, 1990, p. 49.

$$EBY = \frac{(365)\,(d)}{360 - (d)\,(t)} \qquad \textbf{2.10}$$

For the 90–day instrument used as an example above, the EBY would be:

$$EBY = \frac{(365)\,(.11)}{360 - (.11)\,(90)} = .11468$$

For maturities in excess of six months, the EBY is difficult to calculate, but Table 2.7 shows the way in which the discount yield and EBY differ.

The differences between the discount yield and the bond equivalent yield are larger the higher the interest rate and the longer the time until maturity. In some cases, the difference between the two yields can approach 2 percent, as is the case for a discount yield of 14 percent and a 364–day maturity.

Major Money Market Instruments

Treasury Bills. One of the most important kinds of securities in the money market that is based on a discount yield is the **Treasury bill**. T–bills are obligations of the U.S. Treasury which are issued weekly with a maturity of 91 and 182 days. T–bills with a 52–week maturity are offered monthly. There are occasional additional offerings. Normally, auctions are held on Mondays, with bids being submitted before 1:30 p.m. Delivery normally takes place on the following Thursday. The bills

Figure 2.20

Normal Yield Relationships in the Money Market

Very Short Maturity Instruments	
higher yields	Fed Funds
lower yields	Repurchase agreements
Longer Maturity Instruments	
higher yields	Eurodollar CDs
	Domestic CDs
	Bankers' acceptances
	Commercial paper
lower yields	Treasury bills

have a minimum denomination of $10,000 and go up from that minimum in increments of $5,000.[24]

Currently, there are more than $525 billion worth of T–bills outstanding, with daily trading volume exceeding $32 billion. As such, T–bills represent one of the most important instruments of the money market. Further, since they are instruments issued by the U.S. Treasury, they also have the lowest yields, as Figure 2.20 indicates.

Figure 2.21 presents the quotations from *The Wall Street Journal*, which reports trading for the preceding business day. The bills are arranged in order of ascending maturity in the first column. The next two columns present the quotations, which are given as discount yields. Since these are yields, the bid quotation is greater than the asked quotation, but the bid price is naturally less than the asked price. One might read the bid quotation as an offer to pay an amount that will give a certain discount yield. In addition to the bid and asked yield quotations, the last column gives the bond equivalent yield. It is computed according to Equation 2.10, using the asked discount yield.

Commercial Paper.   Another important money market instrument is **commercial paper**, which also uses the discount yield method of quotation. Commercial paper consists of short–term debt obligations of industrial and financial firms. To escape the requirement of registering with the Securities and Exchange Commission (SEC), the maturity cannot exceed 270 days. The issuer of commercial paper promises to

---

[24] For more details on T–bills and the full range of money market securities, there are two excellent sources: Timothy Q. Cook and Bruce J. Summers, *Instruments of the Money Market*, 6e, Richmond, VA: Federal Reserve Bank of Richmond, 1986, and Marcia Stigum, *The Money Market*, 3e, Homewood, IL: Dow Jones–Irwin, 1990, p. 49.

Figure 2.21

Quotations for Treasury Bills

TREASURY BILLS

Maturity	Days to Mat.	Bid	Asked	Chg.	Ask Yld.
Jul 07 '94	0	3.57	3.47	+0.13	0.00
Jul 14 '94	7	3.65	3.55	+0.07	3.60
Jul 21 '94	14	3.60	3.50	+0.13	3.55
Jul 28 '94	21	3.81	3.71	+0.23	3.77
Aug 04 '94	28	3.68	3.58	+0.12	3.64
Aug 11 '94	35	3.88	3.84	+0.13	3.91
Aug 18 '94	42	3.91	3.87	+0.05	3.94
Aug 25 '94	49	3.90	3.86	....	3.93
Sep 01 '94	56	3.96	3.92	−0.02	4.00
Sep 08 '94	63	4.06	4.04	−0.02	4.13
Sep 15 '94	70	4.09	4.07	−0.02	4.16
Sep 22 '94	77	4.19	4.17	....	4.27
Sep 29 '94	**84**	**4.21**	**4.19**	**+0.01**	**4.29**
Oct 06 '94	91	4.31	4.29	+0.04	4.40
Oct 13 '94	98	4.33	4.31	+0.01	4.42
Oct 20 '94	105	4.35	4.33	....	4.45
Oct 27 '94	112	4.37	4.35	....	4.47
Nov 03 '94	119	4.40	4.38	−0.01	4.51
Nov 10 '94	126	4.46	4.44	+0.01	4.57
Nov 17 '94	133	4.49	4.47	−0.01	4.61
Nov 25 '94	141	4.54	4.52	....	4.67
Dec 01 '94	147	4.58	4.56	−0.01	4.71
Dec 08 '94	154	4.64	4.62	−0.01	4.78
Dec 15 '94	161	4.65	4.63	−0.01	4.79
Dec 22 '94	168	4.69	4.67	....	4.84
Dec 29 '94	**175**	**4.66**	**4.64**	**+0.01**	**4.81**
Jan 12 '95	189	4.77	4.75	+0.02	4.93
Feb 09 '95	217	4.84	4.82	−0.01	5.01
Mar 09 '95	245	4.92	4.90	−0.01	5.11
Apr 06 '95	273	5.02	5.00	−0.03	5.22
May 04 '95	301	5.13	5.11	−0.02	5.36
Jun 01 '95	329	5.17	5.15	−0.02	5.41
Jun 29 '95	357	5.18	5.16	−0.03	5.44

Source: *The Wall Street Journal*, July 6, 1994. Reprinted by permission of *The Wall Street Journal*,

pay the holder a given fixed amount on a certain day in the future. The commercial paper is sold at a discount from that promised future payment. The issuer offers no collateral, except the firm's good faith and credit. Figure 2.22 shows the explosive growth in the commercial paper market over the past few years. By the end of 1993, more than $550 billion of commercial paper was outstanding. Most of the commercial paper continues to be issued by financial companies. Some of the particularly big issuers of commercial paper are the finance subsidiaries of American automakers (e.g., General Motors Acceptance Corporation) and the major money center banks of New York (e.g., Citibank).

One good source for yield quotations on commercial paper, as well as for other money market instruments, is the daily column in *The Wall Street Journal* entitled "Money Rates" (see Figure 2.23). After the debacle of Penn Central's default on its commercial paper in the early 1970s, the market was receptive to only very good credit risks for quite a while. In recent years, less creditworthy issuers have gained access to the market, with these issues referred to as high-yield commercial paper. Figure 2.24 shows the yield differential between commercial paper and T-bills, reflecting the difference in creditworthiness and riskiness between the

Figure 2.22

Growth of the Commercial Paper Market

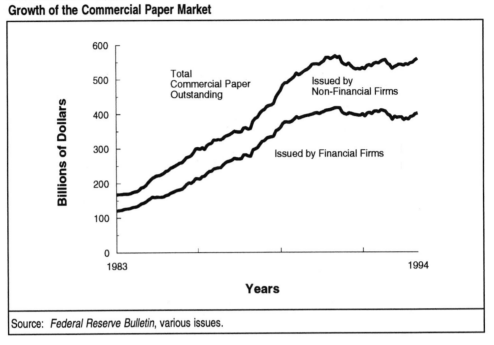

Source: *Federal Reserve Bulletin*, various issues.

Treasury and the issuers of commercial paper. Also, instruments of different maturities have somewhat different yields.[25]

Bankers' Acceptances. The **bankers' acceptance** is a money market instrument, priced on a discount yield basis, and used almost exclusively to finance international trade. A bankers' acceptance is a draft against a bank ordering the bank to pay a specified amount at a future date. When the bank accepts that obligation and stamps the draft **accepted**, it creates a bankers' acceptance. The bank will undertake this obligation because the drawer of the draft (analogous to the writer of a check) has arranged for the bank to provide the service. Once the acceptance is created, it may be sold in a secondary market.

In international trade, few firms are willing to ship goods on open account, as is often done domestically. Since firms in two different countries may not know the other so well, and may not have strong measures of recourse against those who default on their obligations, it is useful to involve banks in the process. It is much easier for a foreign supplier to trust the name of a respected American bank than

[25]The tendency for different maturities of the same kind of security to have different yields reflects the importance of the term structure of interest rates or the yield curve. The yield curve is discussed at length in Chapter 7.

Figure 2.23

Money Market Rate Quotations

MONEY RATES

Thursday, June 23, 1994

The key U.S. and foreign annual interest rates below are a guide to general levels but don't always represent actual transactions.

PRIME RATE: $7\frac{1}{4}$%. The base rate on corporate loans posted by at least 75% of the nation's 30 largest banks.

FEDERAL FUNDS: $4\frac{1}{4}$% high, 4 1/16% low, 4 1/16% near closing bid, $4\frac{1}{8}$% offered. Reserves traded among commercial banks for overnight use in amounts of $1 million or more. Source: Prebon Yamane (U.S.A.) Inc.

DISCOUNT RATE: $3\frac{1}{2}$%. The charge on loans to depository institutions by the Federal Reserve Banks.

CALL MONEY: 6%. The charge on loans to brokers on stock exchange collateral. Source: Dow Jones Telerate Inc.

COMMERCIAL PAPER placed directly by General Electric Capital Corp.: 4.27% 30 to 44 days; 4.32% 45 to 59 days; 4.35% 60 to 89 days; 4.45% 90 to 119 days; 4.55% 120 to 149 days; 4.65% 150 to 179 days; 4.75% 180 to 224 days; 4.85% 225 to 259 days; 5% 260 to 270 days.

COMMERCIAL PAPER: High-grade unsecured notes sold through dealers by major corporations: 4.36% 30 days; 4.46% 60 days; 4.56% 90 days.

CERTIFICATES OF DEPOSIT: 3.69% one month; 3.78% two months; 3.96% three months; 4.33% six months; 4.85% one year. Average of top rates paid by major New York banks on primary new issues of negotiable C.D.s, usually on amounts of $1 million and more. The minimum unit is $100,000. Typical rates in the secondary market: 4.30% one month; 4.43% three months; 4.75% six months.

BANKERS ACCEPTANCES: 4.27% 30 days; 4.35% 60 days; 4.40% 90 days; 4.50% 120 days; 4.60% 150 days; 4.65% 180 days. Offered rates of negotiable, bank-backed business credit instruments typically financing an import order.

LONDON LATE EURODOLLARS: $4\frac{3}{8}$% - $4\frac{1}{4}$% one month; $4\frac{1}{2}$% - $4\frac{3}{8}$% two months; $4\frac{5}{8}$% - $4\frac{1}{2}$% three months; $4\frac{3}{4}$% - $4\frac{5}{8}$% four months; $4\frac{7}{8}$% - $4\frac{3}{4}$% five months; 5% - $4\frac{7}{8}$% six months.

LONDON INTERBANK OFFERED RATES (LIBOR): $4\frac{3}{8}$% one month; $4\frac{5}{8}$% three months; 5% six months; 5 9/16% one year. The average of interbank offered rates for dollar deposits in the London market based on quotations at five major banks. Effective rate for contracts entered into two days from date appearing at top of this column.

FOREIGN PRIME RATES: Canada 8%; Germany 5.01%; Japan 3%; Switzerland 7.50%; Britain 5.25%. These rate indications aren't directly comparable; lending practices vary widely by location.

TREASURY BILLS: Results of the Monday, June 20, 1994, auction of short-term U.S. government bills, sold at a discount from face value in units of $10,000 to $1 million: 4.18% 13 weeks; 4.55% 26 weeks.

FEDERAL HOME LOAN MORTGAGE CORP. (Freddie Mac): Posted yields on 30-year mortgage commitments. Delivery within 30 days 8.43%, 60 days 8.50%, standard conventional fixed-rate mortgages; 5.625%, 2% rate capped one-year adjustable rate mortgages. Source: Dow Jones Telerate Inc.

FEDERAL NATIONAL MORTGAGE ASSOCIATION (Fannie Mae): Posted yields on 30 year mortgage commitments (priced at par) for delivery within 30 days 8.42%, 60 days 8.51%, standard conventional fixed rate-mortgages; 6.60%, 6/2 rate capped one-year adjustable rate mortgages. Source: Dow Jones Telerate Inc.

MERRILL LYNCH READY ASSETS TRUST: 3.58%. Annualized average rate of return after expenses for the past 30 days; not a forecast of future returns.

Source: *The Wall Street Journal*, June 24, 1994, p. C16. Reprinted by permission of *The Wall Street Journal*,

Figure 2.24

Yield Differentials Between Commercial Paper and Treasury Bills

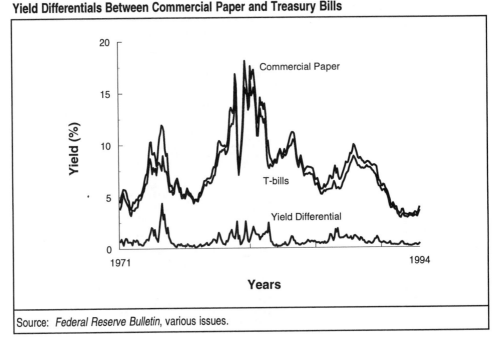

Source: *Federal Reserve Bulletin*, various issues.

a small importing firm. The creation of a bankers' acceptance means that the bank is committed to making the specified payment even if the importing firm, for whom the acceptance was created, defaults. This gives the foreign supplier an added measure of safety. The original obligation of the American firm still remains, so bankers' acceptances are normally **two–name paper**—the bank and the original firm for whom the acceptance was created are both obligated to make the payment.

Banks profit from these transactions by charging an interest rate on any funds advanced, and by charging an acceptance fee of one–fourth to two full percentage points additional interest. Acceptances of differing maturities have different rates, as is the case with all debt instruments. In recent years, the bankers' acceptances market has been contracting, due to the growing popularity of other financing vehicles. At the end of 1993, there were about $32 billion of bankers' acceptances outstanding.

Certificates of Deposit. Banks acquire funds by accepting deposits and by borrowing money in other ways. One of the most important forms of bank borrowing is through **certificates of deposit**, or CDs. CDs may be either negotiable or non–negotiable. Small CDs are often held by individual investors, and these are typically non–negotiable. Large CDs, $100,000 or more, are negotiable and form an important part of the money market, exceeding even T–bills in market size.

Unlike the discount yield instruments discussed so far (T–bills, commercial paper, and bankers' acceptances), CDs are interest–bearing instruments, with the interest being added to a given principal amount. So, for example, the purchase price of a $1,000,000 three–month CD would be $1,000,000, with the issuing bank owing interest plus principal three months later.

Eurodollars.   A **Eurodollar** is a dollar–denominated bank deposit held in a bank outside the United States. A **Eurodollar CD** is a dollar–denominated CD issued by a bank outside the United States. In addition to Eurodollars, one sometimes hears mention of Asian dollars and Petro dollars. As defined here, these would be components of the Eurodollar market as well. Asian dollars are dollar–denominated deposits held in Asian–based banks, while Petro dollars are dollar–denominated deposits generated by oil–producing countries. The most important part of the Eurodollar market is the CD sector, which is about 50 to 60 percent as large as the domestic CD market. Many foreign banks issued Eurodollar CDs to attract dollar–denominated funds. Many investors prefer Eurodollar CDs to domestic CDs since, being somewhat riskier, Eurodollar CDs pay a somewhat higher rate.

The greater risk for Eurodollar CDs arises from the fact that the issuing banks are not as tightly regulated as U.S. banks. Accordingly, the issuing banks must pay more for their funds. Since they escape the cost of tighter regulation, they are also able to pay the higher rate the market demands.

To a large extent, the Eurodollar market was created by U.S. banking regulation. Virtually all bank deposits in the U.S. are insured by the Federal Deposit Insurance Corporation (FDIC), an agency of the U.S. government. The charge for this insurance must be paid by the insured bank. For banks outside the United States, the insurance requirements are normally less stringent, so foreign banks can escape some of this cost.

Another feature of U.S. banking regulation that helps to keep the Eurodollar market in business is the imposition of reserve requirements. Banks in the United States must keep a certain percentage of their assets on deposit in the form of noninterest–earning assets, such as vault cash. If there were no reserve requirements, banks could create an infinite amount of loans from any deposit base. The higher the reserve requirement, as a percentage of deposits, the more restricted the bank is in the amount it can lend. Reserve requirements for U.S. banks tend to be far more stringent than those imposed on banks in other countries. Consequently, the cost of operating many foreign banks is lower than it would be for a U.S. bank.

These regulatory differences create important cost differences between U.S. banks and their foreign competitors, but they also create significant risk differences. Due to the differences in their risk levels and cost structures, banks taking Eurodollar deposits must pay, and are able to pay, a higher interest rate than would

Figure 2.25

Yield Differentials Between Domestic and Eurodollar CDs

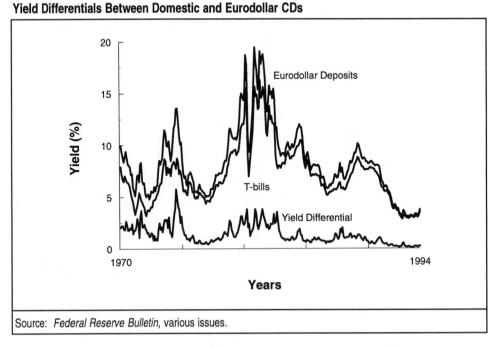

Source: *Federal Reserve Bulletin*, various issues.

be paid by a domestic U.S. bank. Figure 2.25 shows the rate relationship between domestic and Eurodollar CDs.[26]

Repurchase Agreements. A **repurchase agreement**, or **repo**, arises when one party sells a security to another party with an agreement to buy it back at a specified time and at a specified price. The difference between the sale and repurchase price defines the interest rate. In effect, a repurchase agreement involves the sale and purchase of the same security for different prices at different settlement dates.

Repos are useful mainly for short–term financing. In fact, the vast majority of repo agreements are for just one day. Because of this, they are often called **overnight repos**. Repurchase agreements for longer periods are called **term repos**. Many corporations find themselves with excess cash from time to time that can be invested for a very short period until it is needed. By buying a security with a commitment to resell it the next day at a slightly higher price, a corporation can put its excess cash to work. The desire for this kind of transaction has led to the

[26]For more on Eurodollar CDs and the importance of U.S. banking regulation in the creation of that market, see Joseph F. Sinkey, Jr., *Commercial Bank Financial Management*, New York: Macmillan, 1986.

creation of the repo market, with a current size exceeding $750 billion. Most of the securities used as collateral in the repo market are U.S. government securities.

Federal Funds. Another example of a short–term market is the market for **Federal funds,** or **Fed funds**. As mentioned earlier, the Federal Reserve Board requires that commercial banks keep a certain amount of reserve balances (such as vault cash) on hand. These reserve balances yield no return, so banks naturally try to minimize their excess reserves, which are reserves above the required limit. Because of this, some banks find themselves temporarily needing additional reserves, while other banks find themselves with excess reserves to lend out.

This regulatory structure helped to give rise to a market in Fed Funds. The vast majority of market participants for Fed Funds is composed of the more than 13,000 commercial banks in the United States. Like repos, most Fed Funds are loaned on an overnight basis, with average daily volume exceeding $130 billion. Participation in the market is limited, however. Since banks are prohibited from paying interest on overnight deposits received from nonbank institutions, the market is restricted in scope. For this reason, and because Fed Funds are unsecured, their interest rate exceeds the rate on repurchase agreements.

Yield Relationships in the Money Market

Even though the money market is defined as consisting of those securities issued with original maturities of one year or less, there is a considerable difference in yields within the market. As we have seen, Figure 2.20 summarizes these relationships. For the very short (overnight) maturities, the repo rate typically lies below the Fed funds rate.

For those instruments with longer maturities, the T–bill offers the lowest rate. This is reasonable, since it has the best backing of all instruments, the promise of the U.S. Treasury. Commercial paper and bankers' acceptances typically have rates that are very close, with commercial paper issued by top industrial corporations having a perhaps slightly lower yield. Both commercial paper and bankers' acceptances lie below the yield of CDs. The difference between the commercial paper and CD rates reflects the greater creditworthiness of the best industrial corporations in relation to the banks. A bankers' acceptance can offer a lower return than a CD because it is two–name paper, which gives the lender an added margin of security. Finally, Eurodollar CDs must pay a greater rate than domestic CDs because of their greater risk.

While the relationships shown in Figure 2.20 are the norm, we must recognize that there may exist occasional exceptions to these relationships. Also, within each of the categories of money market instruments, there are yield differentials that reflect the varying creditworthiness of the particular issuers.

The remainder of the book will focus on longer–term investment media. Most investment managers direct their funds more toward longer–term instruments because they tend to have higher returns. This is not to say that the money market is not important for investment management. In fact, virtually every investment institution makes continual use of the money market. Every investment manager

Figure 2.26

Issues of Straight International Bonds, 1993

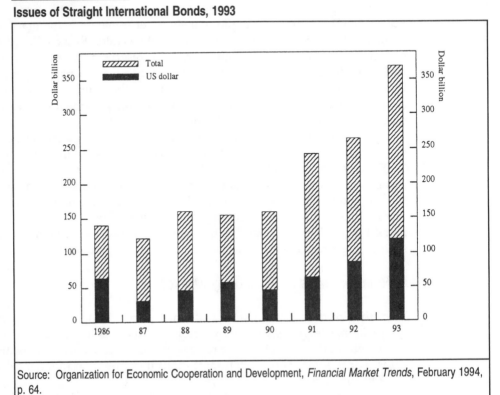

Source: Organization for Economic Cooperation and Development, *Financial Market Trends*, February 1994, p. 64.

needs to be concerned about the liquidity of the investment portfolio, and every pool of money available for securities investment has funds that cannot be immediately put into longer–term securities. Participation in the money market is a way of putting to work excess funds or funds needed to maintain liquidity. It is in this sense that the money market is not the prime objective of securities investment for most participants. In spite of that fact, it is one of the most widely used of all markets.

The International Bond Market

An **international bond** is a bond available for sale outside the country of its issuer. For example, if a U.S. firm issues a bond that is available for sale both in the United States and abroad, it is an international bond. Similarly, if a U.S. firm issues a bond denominated in a foreign currency for sale exclusively in the country of the foreign currency, the bond is a **foreign bond**. An example of a foreign bond would be a bond issued by General Motors, denominated in Italian lira, and sold in Italy. An

external bond is either an international bond or a foreign bond. In 1993, $481 billion of bonds were issued on the international market. There are a number of different types of bonds issued on the international market including straight bonds, floating rate bonds, equity–related bonds, and Eurobonds. We consider each of the major types of international debt issues in turn.

Straight Bonds

A **straight bond** is a bond with a fixed payment schedule with no special features, such as convertibility into stock or a floating interest rate. In essence, a straight bond is similar to the corporate bonds we considered previously. By far, straight bonds constitute the largest component of the international debt market, with total issues of about $370 billion in 1993. Figure 2.26 shows the recent issues of straight international bonds. About 32 percent of the straight bonds issued in 1993 were denominated in U.S. dollars.

Floating Rate Notes

A **floating rate note** (FRN) is a bond that pays a different coupon rate over time as the general level of interest rates fluctuates. Compared to the U.S. domestic bond market, floating rate notes are much more important in the international bond market. In 1993, there were $69 billion of FRNs issued, with U.S. dollar denominated bonds accounting for about 45 percent of that total.

Equity–Related Bonds

Equity–related bonds include both convertible bonds and bonds with equity warrants. We have considered convertible bonds earlier in this chapter. An **equity warrant** is a security that gives the holder the right to acquire a newly issued share of common stock from a company for the payment of a stated price. Equity warrants are often attached to bonds as a way of enticing prospective bond investors. For example, an equity warrant might be issued that gives the holder the right to buy a share for $100 within the next seven years. The value of this warrant depends on a number of factors, including the price of the share that can be bought and the length of time until the warrant expires. In most essential respects, warrants are similar to stock options that we discuss in Chapter 18. In 1993, about $20 billion of bonds with equity warrants were issued, along with about $18 billion of convertible bonds.

Eurodollar Bonds

A **Eurodollar bond** or a **Eurobond** is a bond issued by a borrower in one country, denominated in the borrower's currency, and sold outside the borrower's country. For example, a British steel company might issue a bond denominated in British pounds and sell it in the world market outside of Britain. A Eurobond can be a straight bond, a FRN, or an equity–related bond. In 1993, there were $148 billion of Eurobonds issued, accounting for about 30 percent of all external bonds issued in 1993. More than half of these Eurobonds were straight bonds.

Composition of the International Bond Market

We now consider the composition of the international bond market by the type of bond issued and by the currency in which the bond was denominated. Table 2.8 summarizes the composition of new international bond issues in 1993. Of these bonds, fully 77 percent were issued as straight bonds. Equity–related bonds made up the next largest category, with FRNs being relatively scarce. Table 2.9 shows the currency of issue for external bond issues in 1993, with 35.9 percent of the bonds being denominated in U.S. dollars. Note that a very small proportion of bonds were denominated in the European Currency Unit (ECU). The **ECU** is a special composite currency of the European Economic Community (the common market). It consists of a basket of the currencies of its member nations, such as Germany, France, and Britain. Problems in the common market seem to be responsible for the ECU's fall from favor.

The International Money Market

In our discussion of the international money market, we include a variety of short–term and medium–term forms of lending. In this section, we consider the different types of loans that dominate the short–term and medium–term international markets, and we consider the size and constitution of the market as well. Syndicated loans and other types of lending in the international market bend our rule that the money market is limited to original maturities of one year or less. While the one–year rule may hold for the U.S. market, many forms of international lending have original maturities longer than one year, yet these loans cannot be regarded as belonging to the bond market.

Syndicated Loans

One of the dominant forms of credit in the international market is a form of bank lending called a **syndicated loan**—a loan made by a consortium of banks to a single borrower. By far, syndicated loans dominate the short–term end of the international debt market. In 1993, there were syndicated loans granted totaling $130 billion. Syndicated loans are priced as a spread above **LIBOR—London Interbank Offered Rate**. LIBOR is the rate that banks participating in the international debt market charge each other for short–term loans. Thus, most syndicated loans are floating rate loans, with the interest rate being reset periodically to reflect the current LIBOR. In general, syndicated loans are not securitized; that is, the lender cannot sell the loan to another investor. Even though these loans are not securities, they merit our attention because of their crucial importance in international lending.

Table 2.8

New International Bond Issues, 1993

Instrument	Dollar Value (billions)	Percentage of Total
Straight Bonds	369.1	77.0
Floating Rate Notes	69.8	14.6
Convertibles	18.1	3.7
With Equity Warrants	20.6	4.3
Zero Coupon Bonds	1.8	0.4

Source: Organization for Economic Cooperation and Development, *Financial Market Trends*, February 1994, p. 54.

Table 2.9

Currency of Issue for External Bond Offerings in 1993

Currency	Percentage of Total Issues
U.S. dollar	35.9
Deutschemark	11.8
British sterling	10.8
Japanese yen	9.6
French franc	8.7
Canadian dollar	6.4
Swiss franc	6.1
Italian lira	3.1
Dutch guilder	2.6
European Currency Unit (ECU)	1.6
Other	3.4

Source: Organization for Economic Cooperation and Development, *Financial Market Trends*, February 1994, p. 58.

In 1993, average spreads for syndicated loans were 85 basis points above LIBOR. A **basis point** is 1/100 of 1 percent. Average maturities on new issues were about six years. In addition to the spread above LIBOR, the lenders typically charge a facilities fee. This fee compensates the lenders for processing the loan and for holding funds available to meet the terms of the financing commitment over the life of the loan.

For lenders, syndicated loans have important advantages because this form of lending allows them to participate in a loan without having to commit too large a portion of their capital. In effect, lenders achieve diversification through syndicated lending. For borrowers, syndicated lending allows a larger loan size than would be possible from a single lender.

Corporations are major borrowers in the syndicated loan market, as are the governments of developing countries. Recently, Eastern European governments have become major borrowers via syndicated loans. Most syndicated loans are denominated in U.S. dollars. The majority of these loans continue to be granted in U.S. dollars.

Euro–Commercial Paper (ECP)

We have already explored the importance of commercial paper in the U.S. market, and we have observed the rapid growth of commercial paper in the United States. **Euro–commercial paper** is commercial paper traded in the international market, usually denominated in dollars. In 1993, approximately $37 billion of Euro–commercial paper was issued. To a large extent, Euro–commercial paper has been crowding out syndicated lending because industrial firms have credit ratings equaling or exceeding those of banks. Thus, these firms can float their own direct obligations on the market and save by circumventing bank lending.

Note–Issuance Facilities

A **note–issuance facility** (NIF) is a form of medium–term lending through a variety of instruments, usually floating rate notes. The borrower makes an arrangement with a syndicate of commercial banks that commits the banks to buy the borrower's notes or to lend funds to the borrower. Usually, the term of the facility is three to ten years. The banks charge an annual fee for providing the borrowing facility even if it is not used. In 1993, only $1.5 billion was borrowed through NIFs, down substantially from the 1987–1988 range of $20 billion and the peak of $40 billion in 1985. The diminution of NIFs is largely due to the perceived increase in bank risk. Also, firms gaining direct access to capital markets place less reliance on NIFs guaranteed by banks.

Committed versus Back–Up Facilities

For the most part, NIFs represent a **committed facility**—the banks issuing the facility commit themselves to making the loans as promised to the borrower. In effect, an NIF is a committed back–up facility. It is also possible for a syndicate of lenders to offer an **uncommitted back–up facility**—an expressed intention, but no commitment, to lend under specified circumstances. These facilities are of dubious worth, because the funds may not be available to meet the borrower's requirements. These uncommitted facilities are fairly unimportant in the international lending scene.

Summary

This chapter discussed the institutional background of the debt market as it exists in the United States and abroad. The chapter began with a discussion of the bond pricing equation, a general expression for the value of any debt instrument. Other related yield measures were also discussed.

The chapter discussed the magnitude of the bond and money markets and described the different issuers in each of the segments of the market. With many different kinds of issuers, there are many different kinds of debt instruments. The expected return for these different kinds of instruments is determined largely by differences in the creditworthiness or riskiness of the issuer. Not surprisingly, the greater the risk of a given issue, the higher the yield to maturity promised by the issuer.

Questions and Problems

1. What are the three principal classes of bond issuers?
2. What are the three principal kinds of U.S. Treasury debt?
3. Compared to the rest of the world, what is the relative size of the United States in the bond and equity markets?
4. In spite of the fact that T–bills and T–bonds have experienced virtually identical returns over the recent past, T–bonds seem to have had a greater variance of returns. Does this violate the basic idea of a trade–off between expected return and risk? Why or why not?
5. What do the bond ratings provided by firms such as Standard & Poor's and Moody's attempt to measure?
6. Why do municipal bonds tend to attract investors with high incomes? For an investor in Florida, which has no state income tax, would a municipal bond that is triple tax exempt in New York City be attractive? Why or why not?
7. The contract between a corporation and its bondholders often restricts the dividends that the firm can pay to stockholders. What is the purpose of this kind of provision?
8. Why do firms issue callable and convertible bonds? Other factors being equal, which kind of bond should have a higher yield? Why?
9. What is the difference between a foreign bond and a Eurobond?
10. Why has the Eurodollar market flourished?

11. The money market reflects a relationship among yields on different types of instruments. What explains these yield differences?

12. Even within a given class of securities, such as certificates of deposit, there are well–established yield relationships. Assume that Bank A has traditionally had a yield on its CDs one–half of a percentage point lower than the yield on those of Bank B. If that difference became smaller, how would you interpret the change?

13. A bond is available with a price of $975 that promises to pay $1,000 one year from now with no intervening payments. What kind of a bond is this and what is its yield to maturity?

14. For a pure discount bond with a face value of $100, what will its price be if it matures in one year and has a yield to maturity of 12.5 percent?

15. A bond matures in two years, has a par value of $1,000, has a coupon rate of 11 percent paid semiannually, and yields 14 percent. What is its price? Is this a pure discount, par, discount, or premium bond? Why? Answer the preceding questions assuming that the same bond yields 8 percent.

16. For the preceding bond, what is the approximate yield under both the assumption of a 14 percent and an 8 percent yield to maturity? (Hint: Do you need to know the yield to maturity to compute the approximate yield?)

17. Assume that a year has 360 days and that a bond with a coupon rate of 12 percent and a face value of $1,000 pays its coupon semiannually. If the bond last paid its coupon 60 days ago, what is the accrued interest on the bond? If the bond matures in 120 days, what is the full cash price that one must pay for the bond?

18. A bond has a coupon rate of 8.75 percent and is currently selling for $775 on a par value of $1,000. What is its current yield?

19. A $10,000 T–bill matures in 47 days and is currently selling for $9,750. What is its discount yield? What is its bond–equivalent yield? What is its yield to maturity, based on the bond pricing formula?

CFA Questions

All CFA examination questions are reprinted, with permission, from the Level I *1992-1994, CFA Candidate Study and Examination Program Review*. Copyright 1992-1994, Association for Investment Management and Research, Charlottesville, Va. All rights reserved.

A. Which of the following are advantages of mortgage–backed securities (MBS)?
   I. MBS yields are above those of similarly rated corporate and U.S. Treasury bonds.
   II. MBS have high quality ratings, usually AAA, with some backed by the full faith and credit of the U.S. Government.
   III. MBS have no call provision, thus protecting the investor from having to make a reinvestment decision before maturity.

    a. I and II only
    b. II and III only
    c. I and III only
    d. I, II, and III

B. Find the yield–to–maturity of a 20–year zero coupon that is selling for $372.50 (assume the issue has a maturity value of $1,000).
    a. 5.1%
    b. 8.8%
    c. 10.1%
    d. 13.4%

C. An analyst finds that the semiannual interest rate that equates the present value of the bond's cash flow to its current market price is 3.85%. It follows, therefore, that:
    I.   the bond equivalent yield on this security is 7.70%.
    II. the effective annual yield on the bond is 7.85%.
    III. the bond's yield–to–maturity is 7.70%.
    IV. the bond's horizon return is 8.35%.
    a. I and II only
    b. II, III, and IV only
    c. I, II, and III only
    d. III only

D. Empirical evidence from the past 60 years indicates there is a high positive correlation between the returns on 30–day U.S. Treasury bills and the:
    a. return on long–term U.S. Treasury bonds.
    b. inflation rate in the United States.
    c. return on U.S. common stock.
    d. return on U.S. corporate bonds.

E. A 5 1/2%, 20–year municipal bond is currently priced to yield 7.2%. For a taxpayer in the 33% tax bracket, this bond would offer an equivalent taxable yield of:
    a. 8.20%
    b. 10.75%
    c. 11.49%
    d. none of the above

F. A municipal bond carries a coupon of 6 3/4% and is trading at par; to a taxpayer in the 34% tax bracket, this bond would provide a taxable equivalent yield of:
    a. 4.5%
    b. 10.2%
    c. 13.4%
    d. 19.9%

G. Which *one* of the following yields is used to value a bond?
    a. Current yield
    b. Nominal yield
    c. Effective yield
    d. Yield–to–maturity

Suggested REALDATA Exercises

The following *REALDATA* exercises explore the concepts developed in this chapter: Exercises 5, 12, 54, 55, 56, 58, 60.

Suggested Readings

Boehmer, E. and W. Megginson, "Determinants of Secondary Market Prices for Developing Country Syndicated Loans," *Journal of Finance*, 45:5, December 1990, pp. 1517–1540.

Cook, T. Q. and T. D. Rowe, eds., Federal Reserve Bank of Richmond, *Instruments of the Money Market*, 6e, 1986.

Fabozzi, F. J. and T. D. Fabozzi, "Treasury and Stripped Treasury Securities," *The Handbook of Fixed Income Securities*, 3e, Homewood, IL: Business Irwin One, 1991.

Fabozzi, F. J. and D. Z. Nirenberg, "Federal Income Tax Treatment of Fixed Income Securities," *The Handbook of Fixed Income Securities*, 3e, Homewood, IL: Business Irwin One, 1991.

Fabozzi, F. J., R. S. Wilson, H. C. Sauvain, and J. C. Ritchie, Jr., "Corporate Bonds," *The Handbook of Fixed Income Securities*, 3e, Homewood, IL: Business Irwin One, 1991.

Feldstein, S. G. and F. J. Fabozzi, "Municipal Bonds," *The Handbook of Fixed Income Securities*, 3e, Homewood, IL: Business Irwin One, 1991.

Fons, J. S. and A. E. Kimball, "Corporate Bond Defaults and Default Rates 1970–1990," *The Journal of Fixed Income*, 1:1, June 1991, pp. 36–47.

Goodman, L. S., J. Jonson, and A. Silver, "Federally Sponsored Agency Securities," *The Handbook of Fixed Income Securities*, 3e, Homewood, IL: Business Irwin One, 1991.

Howe, J. T., "Credit Considerations in Evaluating High–Yield Bonds," *The Handbook of Fixed Income Securities*, 3e, Homewood, IL: Business Irwin One, 1991.

Ibbotson, R. G. and L. B. Siegel, "The World Bond Market: Market Values, Yields, and Returns," *The Journal of Fixed Income*, 1:1, June 1991, pp. 90–99.

Long, R. D., "High–Yield Bonds," *The Handbook of Fixed Income Securities*, 3e, Homewood, IL: Business Irwin One, 1991.

Lowell, L., "Mortgage Pass–Through Securities," *The Handbook of Fixed Income Securities*, 3e, Homewood, IL: Business Irwin One, 1991.

Marr, W. and J. Trimble, "The Persistent Borrowing Advantage in Eurodollar Bonds: A Plausible Explanation," *Journal of Applied Corporate Finance*, 1:2, Summer 1988, pp. 65–70.

Pavel, C. and J. N. McElravey, "Globalization in the Financial Services Industry," Federal Reserve Bank of Chicago *Economic Perspectives*, 14:3, May/June 1990, pp. 3–18.

Senft, D. and F. J. Fabozzi, "Mortgages," *The Handbook of Fixed Income Securities*, 3e, Homewood, IL: Business Irwin One, 1991.

Stigum, M., *The Money Market*, Homewood, IL: Dow–Jones Irwin, 1990.

Strongin, S., "International Credit Market Connections," Federal Reserve Bank of Chicago *Economic Perspectives*, 14:4, July/August 1990, pp. 2–10.

Tran, H. Q., L. Anderson, and E. L. Drayss, "Eurocapital Markets," *The Handbook of Fixed Income Securities*, 3e, Homewood, IL: Business Irwin One, 1991.

Wilson, R. S. and F. J. Fabozzi, *The New Corporate Bond Market*, Chicago: Probus Publishing, 1990.

Yago, G., *Junk Bonds: How High Yield Securities Restructured Corporate America*, New York: Oxford University Press, 1991.

CHAPTER THREE

The Stock Market: An Overview

Overview

This chapter introduces the rights and obligations associated with common stock ownership and explores the institutional features of the stock market in the United States. The chapter focuses on the market for already existing shares, such as the most familiar stock market, the New York Stock Exchange. The chapter also considers the structure of the brokerage industry. For most people, the stock market represents the focus of the securities markets. The nightly news frequently reports the day's developments in the stock market, but features no other security reports on a regular basis. In addition to having the widest recognition in the popular culture, the stock market receives the most attention from professional researchers. As a result, the stock market is probably the best understood of all security markets.

With thousands of different stocks being listed for trading in the United States, summary measures of stock market price trends and activities are very useful. The summary measures, or market indexes, give the public a convenient way of following general stock market activity. Since these indexes are so widely quoted in the media, this chapter also briefly examines some of the most important indexes.

The organization of the U.S. stock market has changed radically in the last fifteen years and gives every sign of further evolution. The market's recent history has been one of greater fragmentation in some respects, accompanied by greater integration in others. For example, major market movements beyond the major exchanges have diminished the power of major institutions such as the New York Stock Exchange and have spread the trading of stocks across a broader spectrum of competing exchanges. Advances in electronic communication and computer technology have contributed toward integration. As the technology has advanced, it has become increasingly easy to secure rapid and accurate communication, pulling the market toward more nearly complete integration. The development of foreign markets, particularly in Japan, now threatens to overshadow U.S. stock markets. These developments are also covered in this chapter, which begins with a discussion of the features of common stock itself.

Common Stock Rights and Responsibilities

Common stock represents an ownership interest in a corporation. The management of the firm is charged with advancing the interests of the common stock owners, implying that management should maximize the price of a share of common stock. This outlook essentially identifies the interests of the shareholders with their wealth position in the stock. According to this view, the firm's managers act as agents of the shareholders, operating the firm as the shareholders would if they were the managers themselves. Problems arise in this relationship because the interests of the agent–managers are not always the same as those of the principal shareholders. For example, managers may overspend on fancy office furnishings—paid for out of the pockets of the shareholders—but the benefits are enjoyed only by the managers.[1]

As owners of the corporation, the shareholders have certain privileges and responsibilities that are conferred upon them by owning the common stock. Because it represents ownership, common stock constitutes a **residual claim** on the assets and proceeds of the firm, that is, a claim on the value of the firm after other claimants have been satisfied. For example, owners of bonds issued by the corporation are entitled to receive their promised payments before the stockholders receive payments on their investments. In this sense, stockholders are the last in line to enforce their claims against the firm.

By the same token, the residual claim is very important. The stockholders may be last in line to enforce their claims, but they can justifiably claim everything in the firm once the other claimants have been satisfied. The investor in common stock hopes that this residual amount will grow—that the excess over the claims due to others (bondholders, employees, suppliers, etc.) will be a growing amount.

In this sense, common stock is the riskiest claim against a firm. As will become increasingly clear, the hope of large returns normally goes with the acceptance of greater risk. In spite of the riskiness of common stock, stock has important risk–limiting features. In the United States, common stock ownership confers a limited liability to its owners. In a sole proprietorship, claims against a business can be pursued to capture the personal assets of the owner. For example, a shop owner without liability insurance conceivably could lose his house and personal automobile if a customer injured on the shop premises sues for damages. There is essentially no limitation on the liability of the owner in a sole proprietorship.

In a corporation, however, the owners cannot lose more than the value of their initial investment. The worst that could happen for a common stock investor would be for the stock to become worthless. In such an event, the entire purchase

---

[1]The conflict between principals and agents can be of much more momentous importance than the question of the budget for office furniture. See, for example, Michael Jensen and William Meckling, "Theory of the Firm: Managerial Behavior, Agency Costs and Ownership Structure," *Journal of Financial Economics*, 3, October 1976, pp. 305–360.

price of the common stock is lost, but the investor cannot lose more. For example, victims of a chemical spill for which a corporation was responsible might be able to acquire all of the assets of the firm. They could not, however, proceed against the stockholders to make them pay additional compensation out of their other resources.

Holders of common stock commit their funds and assume the last place claim on the value of the firm in hopes of securing substantial profits. Payoffs to shareholders come in two forms. The price of the shares could increase, generating a capital gain. Alternatively, the firm could pay a cash dividend. Consequently, the wealth relative (WR) for an investor in common stock can be calculated as follows:

$$WR = \frac{\text{Current Stock Price} + \text{Cash Dividends Received}}{\text{Original Stock Price}} \qquad 3.1$$

While the stock is owned, the only cash flow from the shares is the cash dividend. Many firms, particularly new ones and those in financial distress, pay no dividends. Most firms that pay dividends do so on a quarterly basis, although that is not always the case.[2]

In addition to having the right to receive cash dividends, owners of common stock have the right to vote on major matters pertaining to the operation of the firm. These voting rights are usually exercised at the time of the annual meeting. For the most part, this is not an important right, at least in major corporations with numerous shareholders. Typically, shareholders vote on issues that have been carefully defined by management with an eye toward securing the desired outcome. As an example, shareholders are often asked to vote on new directors for the corporation, with a slate of nominees having been picked by management. On occasion, however, the right to vote can be very important, perhaps on the issue of selecting new key management for the firm.

In the normal event, management directs the course of most corporate elections. One important tool for doing so is the use of the **proxy**. Since the votes are normally taken at the firm's annual meeting, it is impossible for most shareholders to actually appear at the meeting to cast their votes. Instead, they can empower some other party to vote for them by giving them a proxy. Management can solicit these proxies from indifferent shareholders or those shareholders who cannot attend the meeting. This situation enables management to acquire a great deal of voting power. In some firms, management has an even more effective means of amassing voting power. Shareholders who fail to return their proxy forms may be considered to have conferred their proxies to management. Given the normal inertia of many shareholders, this arrangement virtually guarantees effective control of the voting by the current management.

---

[2] Wrigley, Inc., largely owned by Mr. Wrigley, has the distinction of being one of the very few firms to pay dividends monthly. Dividends are so crucial for common stock that they play a key role in determining the value of a share of stock, as will be explained in Chapter 9.

On occasion, real disputes arise that cause serious dissension and make the voting issue important. Dissident shareholders might try to unseat management or try to change fundamental managerial policies. To do so, the dissident shareholders need to acquire voting rights themselves by gaining proxies. This leads to a **proxy fight**, the struggle to gain voting rights from shareholders who will not be attending the annual meeting.

In some firms, common stock is classified, usually as either Class A or Class B. While this situation is unusual, it does exist. Usually the difference between the two classes of stock is simply the difference in voting rights. Normally, the Class A stock will have voting rights and the Class B stock will not. This difference in voting rights can generate a slight price differential between shares of the two classes, with the voting stock having a slightly higher price.[3]

Owners of common stock occasionally receive **stock dividends** or **stock splits**. These occurrences generate no cash flows for the owners of the stock, so they are substantially less important than cash dividends. A stock dividend occurs when additional shares are created by the firm and given to the current shareholders. A stock split is basically similar. This kind of distribution is called a **stock dividend** when the amount of increase in the number of shares is 25 percent or less. The distribution of shares is a **stock split** when the percentage increase is more than 25 percent. Stock splits occurred as early as 1682 when the East India Company declared a stock split of 2–for–1.[4]

To see how this works, assume that an investor owns 100 shares of a stock trading at $80, and the corporation decides on a 20 percent stock dividend. After the stock dividend, the stockholder would have 120 shares. The question then becomes how much those shares will be worth. Other things being equal, this decision to have a stock dividend generates no cash flow for the firm. As such, it should have no impact on the value of the firm, which means that the shares should fall in value by an amount proportional to the stock dividend. The original market value of the 100 shares was $8,000. After the stock dividend, there are 120 shares. Since, by assumption, nothing has happened to make the firm's cash flows different, the wealth of the stockholder should be unchanged. This means that the 120 shares should have a total value of $8,000, or a price of $66.67 per share.

The decision to have a stock dividend or a stock split, by itself, cannot change the basic operations or the future cash flows of the firm, so it should not

---

[3] American Maize Products, Inc., listed on the American Stock Exchange, has two classes of stock that fit this pattern, with a typical price difference between the two classes of shares of about 25 cents per share.

[4] J. Lakonishok and B. Lev, "Stock Splits and Stock Dividends: Why, Who, and When," *Journal of Finance*, 42:4, September 1987, pp. 913–932.

Figure 3.1

Frequency of Stock Splits

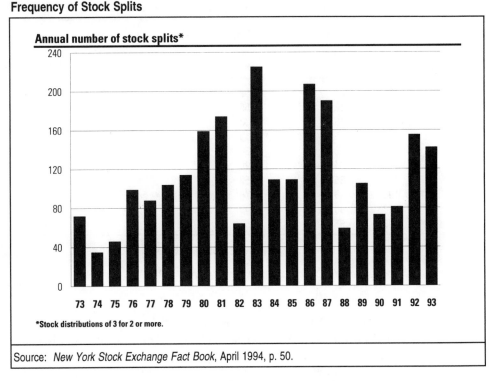

Annual number of stock splits*

*Stock distributions of 3 for 2 or more.

Source: *New York Stock Exchange Fact Book*, April 1994, p. 50.

have any impact on the value of the firm.[5] Stock splits are usually spoken of as being a "2–for–1" split (the investor receives two shares to replace each original share held) or a "5–for–4" split and so on. Many firms have a practice of regular small stock dividends in the range of 2 to 5 percent.

Notice that a stock dividend or stock split with the cash dividend per share held constant implies an increased cash dividend. This is clear from the preceding example of a 5–for–4 stock dividend on a 100–share position with an initial share value of $80. Assume that the original cash dividend was 20 cents per share. This means that the annual dividend originally received was $20 per year. If that cash dividend is maintained at 20 cents per share, but the number of shares is increased to 120, then the annual cash dividend will be increased to $24 on the holding.

---

[5] The classic study of the impact of stock splits on share prices, "The Adjustment of Stock Prices to New Information," by E. Fama, L. Fisher, M. Jensen, and R. Roll, *International Economic Review*, 10, 1969, pp. 1–20, concludes that stock splits have no effect on the value of the underlying shares.

Table 3.1

The Size of Stock Dividends and Splits (1984–1993)

Year	Less than 25%	25% to 49%	50% to 99%	2–for–1 to 2–1/2–for–1	3–for–1 to 3–1/2–for–1	4–for–1	Over 4–for–1	Total
1993	21	18	52	87	3	—	—	181
1992	18	9	55	87	10	2	1	182
1991	18	8	33	46	1	—	1	107
1990	25	7	19	49	2	—	3	105
1989	28	9	34	66	2	2	1	142
1988	34	11	29	25	4	1	—	104
1987	36	18	59	118	10	1	2	244
1986	43	22	78	118	9	1	1	272
1985	40	17	43	60	6	—	—	166
1984	57	12	50	51	6	1	1	178

Note: Includes common and preferred issues. Data based on effective dates.

Source: *New York Stock Exchange Fact Book*, April 1994, p. 50.

Figure 3.1 presents a summary of the recent history of stock splits for firms listed on the New York Stock Exchange. The number of splits seems to fluctuate dramatically, with relatively few splits occurring in poor market years such as 1974. Table 3.1 shows the size of stock dividends and stock splits for recent years, illustrating the tendency for firms to have very small stock dividends. However, the number of stock dividends appears to be decreasing steadily.

It is not clear why stock splits and stock dividends continue to be so popular, but several explanations are possible. First, some corporate managers either do not read or do not believe the research that has been conducted in this area. When a stock pays a dividend, the stock price must adjust in increments of 12½ cents. This may make it impossible for the share price to adjust exactly. Because of this and other market imperfections, it may be that share prices do not fully adjust to the stock dividend.[6] There is still a widespread tendency for firms to try to improve

---

[6] For example, see J. Randall Woolridge, "Ex–Date Stock Price Adjustment to Stock Dividends: A Note," *Journal of Finance*, March 1983, pp. 247–255. In this paper, Woolridge finds that the stock price does not adjust completely for the stock dividend, particularly for very small dividends, such as those less than 6 percent. Other papers suggest that stock splits lead to increased price volatility, such as J. Ohlson and S. Penman, "Volatility Increases Subsequent to Stock Splits: An Empirical Aberration," *Journal of Financial Economics*, 14, 1985, pp. 251–266. D. A. Dubofsky, "Volatility Increases Subsequent to NYSE and AMEX Stock Splits," *Journal of Finance*, 46:1, March 1991, pp. 421–431, finds that the volatility increase is greater on the New York Stock Exchange than on the American Stock Exchange. Finally, C. G. Lamoureux and P. Poon, "The Market Reaction to Stock Splits," *Journal of Finance*, 42:5,

their stock prices by stock splits or dividends. Second, some proponents of stock distributions believe that investors perceive the additional stock as some kind of benefit. In fact, this may not be any benefit at all. Stock transaction costs are cheapest, as will be discussed in more detail later, for a **round lot**—a block of stock of 100 shares or some multiple of 100. If a stock dividend or split leaves an investor with an **odd lot**, a holding not evenly divisible by 100, then the transaction costs can be higher on a percentage basis. In this situation, the stock dividend or split could cost the investor by raising transaction costs. Third, and finally, stock splits may be a useful way of bringing the stock price into a popular trading range. Recent research indicates that this may be the most important motivation.[7] Some market observers believe that stock prices in the $20 to $40 range are most favored by investors. If a stock split moves the share price into this favored range, the increased popularity of the shares could make them more valuable. Unfortunately, there is no firm evidence in support of this view.[8]

General Organization of the Stock Market

As mentioned in the overview, the stock market has developed several important new dimensions in recent years. This chapter deals with the **secondary market**, the market for already existing securities. There is also a **primary market**, a market for the sale of new securities, which is examined in Chapter 4. While this division is clear enough, some market developments have led to the existence of a third market and a fourth market. The secondary market consists of organized stock exchanges, such as the New York Stock Exchange (NYSE), the American Stock Exchange (AMEX), and a dealer market (the over–the–counter or OTC market). The third and fourth markets are informal trading arrangements used mainly by the very largest traders. Each division of the stock market will be discussed in turn.

Organized Exchanges

For many people, the stock market simply is the New York Stock Exchange, which does dominate the market in certain respects. However, there are a number of

---

December 1987, pp. 1347–1370, argue that the increased volatility gives tax breaks to stock traders by allowing them to manage their tax–reported gains and losses and that this opportunity explains why stock prices increase after stock splits.

[7]See J. Lakonishok and B. Lev, "Stock Splits and Stock Dividends: Why, Who, and When," *Journal of Finance*, 42:4, September 1987, pp. 913–932.

[8]If the stock split lowers the price so that more investors can trade round lots, it might have the effect of reducing their transaction costs, thereby increasing the popularity of the shares and raising the price. Again, there is no persuasive evidence to support this hypothesis.

organized stock exchanges in the United States and many foreign stock exchanges as well. An organized stock exchange is a stock market with a centralized trading floor, where all stock trading takes place under rules created by the exchange and the U.S. government. In the United States, the organized exchanges share many organizational features, largely because the smaller exchanges have patterned themselves after the NYSE. This makes it possible to discuss their common organizational features together. This section begins by examining those common principles of organization, and goes on to examine the two largest U.S. stock exchanges in greater detail. The section concludes by tracing the flow of an order from the public to the floor of the exchange and with a survey of the different types of orders that one might place.

General Organizational Features. A **stock exchange** is a voluntary organization formed by a group of individuals to provide an institutional setting in which common stock, and other securities, can be bought and sold. Usually, the stock exchange is a non–profit corporation, which exists to further the financial interest of its members. Members of stock exchanges own memberships or **seats** on the exchange. The exchange formulates rules to govern trading activity on the exchange and enforces these rules on its membership. Only members of the exchange or their representatives are allowed to trade on the exchange. In that sense, the members have a monopoly position, because all orders to buy or sell securities on a given exchange must flow through an exchange member.

One of the key regulations imposed by the exchange concerns restrictions on the place and time at which trading may occur. Each stock exchange allows trading only on the floor of the exchange and only during approved trading hours. The floor of an exchange is an actual physical location to which orders are transmitted for execution. The floor of the exchange is equipped with a vast array of electronic communications equipment, which is used to convey orders to the floor and to confirm to the initiator of the order that the order has been executed. In addition, it is important for participants on the floor of the exchange to have a regular flow of information from the outside world. Since new information of all types might affect share prices, the people on the floor need access to regular news about world and national events, but they also need special information about business developments. These informational needs are served by the regular wire services, such as the Associated Press (AP), and by special business news wire services, such as Reuters and Dow Jones.

People working on the floor of the exchange fall into several groups. First, the exchange employs a number of people on the floor. These workers oversee the trading activity and report the outcomes of trades to the public on a continuous basis. The exchange operates the electronic communications system for reporting trading activity. A second group of people on the floor consists of exchange members, who trade for their own account. That is, these traders invest their own capital in the pursuit of profit. The key privilege of membership on an exchange is the right to trade on that exchange. Brokers form a third group. A broker receives orders from the public outside the exchange and executes the order (to either buy or sell a given quantity of a specified security) and charges a commission for this service. As such, a broker does not trade for his own account, but executes the orders of others. Two of the largest brokerage firms are Merrill Lynch and PaineWebber.[9] A fourth group of floor participants consists of the specialists for each security. A specialist is assigned to each security traded on an exchange and stands ready to trade at least 100 shares of that stock. In addition, the specialist keeps a record of all orders awaiting execution in the stock. These key functions of the specialist require more examination.

The Specialist.   The **specialist**, who always holds a seat on the exchange, makes a market in an assigned security. This means that every share of stock traded on an exchange passes under the scrutiny of the specialist. As we will see, the specialist has a privileged position, and accompanying obligations. The specialist has two basic functions. First, the specialist acts as a broker on some transactions for other trading parties. In this brokerage function, the specialist facilitates transactions for others and charges a fee. Second, the specialist may act as a dealer, buying and selling for his or her own account. Exchange rules and laws regulate how the specialist may perform these two functions. We consider first the role of the specialist as a dealer, and then turn to the specialist's brokerage function. We then review the rules that govern the specialist's behavior.

The Specialist as a Dealer.   The specialist stands ready to buy or sell securities on order from other members of the exchange or to the public. This requires considerable capital investment in the shares held in inventory and it also involves taking a risk position in the stock. As compensation for the capital investment and the assumption of risk, the specialist attempts to make a profit on each share of stock traded. As a dealer, the specialist acts as a market maker and acts as either the buyer or the seller in the transaction. In 1993, the specialist was the buyer or seller in 17.1 percent of the share volume on the NYSE.

Acting as a dealer or **market maker**, the specialist maintains a **bid–asked spread**—the difference between the price at which she is willing to buy and to sell a share. The specialist offers to buy shares at the lower bid price and to sell them at the asked price. For example, assume that the specialist believes that a share is worth exactly $100. The specialist can make money by buying shares for slightly less than the "true" price of $100 and by selling shares for slightly more than $100. For this example, the bid price might be $99.875 and the asked price might be $100.125. Thus, the bid–asked spread is $.25, and this difference represents the gross profit that the specialist tries to capture by trading.

As a pure market maker, the specialist might merely try to set bid and asked prices so that the number of buy orders exactly balanced the number of sell orders. This would leave the specialist's inventory at a constant level, and the specialist would make a gross profit equal to the bid–asked spread on the purchase and subsequent sale of each security.

---

[9]The operation of the brokerage industry is explained in a later section entitled "The Brokerage Industry."

However, the life of the specialist is not so easy. New information reaches the market on a random basis and influences stock prices. A specialist who does not respond to the new information, and who leaves the bid and asked prices as they were, will soon receive orders only on one side of the market. If the news is favorable for a given stock, and the specialist does not adjust the bid and asked prices upward to reflect the new information, there will be more buy orders than sell orders. This order flow would soon deplete the inventory of the specialist, who would then be unable to fulfill the function of market–making. Further, the specialist would suffer a loss by selling shares out of the inventory for less than they are worth. The specialist must be ready to change the level of the bid and asked prices in response to new information. For even the most conservative specialist, one merely seeking to make the bid–asked spread on each transaction, there is still a great deal of finesse required in order to create an even number of buy and sell orders in the face of changing market conditions.

The spread between the bid and asked prices represents the gross profit margin for the specialist; therefore, the wider the bid–asked spread, the greater the specialist's profits, other things being equal. The exchange, however, monitors the performance of the specialist to ensure that the bid–asked spread remains within a reasonably narrow range. Even so, the specialist has a certain degree of latitude in setting both the level of prices and in setting the bid–asked spread. In times of great uncertainty in the stock market, due either to general market conditions or to developments affecting the specialist's particular security, the specialist may respond by widening the bid–asked spread.

At times, traders outside the exchange may know more about the future of the stock price for a given share than the specialist. Traders with this kind of special knowledge are called **informed traders**. They contrast with **liquidity traders**—traders who buy because they have funds to invest or who sell because they need cash. If the specialist confronts an informed trader, the specialist runs the risk of losing on trades due to a lack of information. Consequently, the specialist's first reaction to unusual trading activity will often be to widen the bid–asked spread. A wider spread provides a larger safety margin for the specialist because it increases the profit margin.

Compared to most traders for a particular stock, however, the specialist normally has a great deal of information. One of the richest sources of information comes from the fact that the specialist maintains the limit order book in which all limit orders awaiting execution are recorded. A **limit order** is an order to be executed only at a certain price, if that price becomes available. Maintaining this book provides the specialist with privileged access to information regarding supply and demand for the shares, and this information can become quite valuable. For example, imagine a situation in which a given share trades at $30 per share and the limit order book shows a large number of orders to sell shares at $30.50. The specialist then knows that the large contingent sell order will help to keep prices on the shares from going up very much. This tells the specialist not to increase inventory in hopes of a big price rise in the stock.

Another important decision facing the specialist concerns how large an inventory to hold. The specialist always needs to maintain at least some shares in inventory to meet immediate demand. However, if the specialist believes that share prices will rise in the near future, then he or she should increase the inventory. This could be accomplished by a slight adjustment in the level of prices quoted or by adjusting the bid–asked spread. The chance to make speculative profits, based on privileged information, is an important potential source of income for the specialist, one that cannot be ignored.

The Specialist as Broker.   So far, we have seen that the specialist tries to make money by capturing the bid–asked spread on each transaction in which the specialist buys or sells. However, specialists do not trade for their own accounts in most stock transactions. In 1993, the specialists were neither buyers nor sellers in 82.9 percent of the volume. In these transactions, the specialists function as brokers helping to execute transactions for other parties. In fact, exchange rules regulate the specialist's trading.

In the limit order book, the specialist holds a record of customers' willingness to buy and sell in a particular stock. Typically, there will be a number of orders to buy and a number of orders to sell, both at various prices. To make the analysis concrete, assume that the stock has just traded at $40 per share, and the specialist holds limit orders to sell at $40.25 and $41 and limit orders to buy at $39.75 and $39. The specialist herself is willing to trade for her own account with a bid–asked spread of $39.50 to buy and $40.50 to sell. Thus, the specialist does not offer the highest bid price nor the lowest asked price. For a potential customer, the specialist is obligated to reveal the highest bid price and the lowest asked price, which would be $40.25 asked and $39.75 bid. In this situation, a customer can buy at $40.25 or sell at $39.75, and the specialist would act only as a broker. Thus, to participate as a buyer or seller in the transaction, the specialist must bid more than any limit order to buy in the limit order book, or must ask less than any limit order to sell in the limit order book.

Another rule that often keeps the specialist from acting as a buyer or seller is the rule that gives public orders at the same price precedence over the specialist's desire to buy or sell. As an example of this rule, consider a limit order to buy a particular stock at $40. This order, as we have seen, would be reflected in the specialist's limit order book. While such an order is in the book, the specialist cannot buy at $40 for his own account. Instead, the specialist must give precedence to the outside order. In this situation, the specialist would allow the customer's limit order to be filled and would collect a brokerage commission for facilitating the transaction. (This brokerage fee for the specialist is typically about two cents per share.) A similar rule applies to customer limit orders to sell.

Obligations of the Specialist.   As we have seen, the specialist has significant trading advantages that are conferred upon her by the exchange. With these advantages come certain responsibilities. First, the specialist is obligated to make a market in the stock and to trade with the public in 100 share lots. The specialist cannot always simply sit on the sidelines. If there are not complementary orders available from the public, the specialist must trade.

As a second obligation, the specialist must maintain price continuity. For example, if the last trade in a stock was at $50 and the current bid–asked spread from public orders is $45 bid/$55 asked, the exchange would expect the specialist to trade at a narrower bid–asked spread. For frequently traded stocks, the bid–asked spread is $.125 to $.25. A third obligation of the specialist is to stabilize prices. If orders from the public are running heavily on the sell side, the specialist is expected to act as a buyer to keep the prices from falling too much.

Summary. In sum, the specialist occupies a unique position in a stock exchange. All transactions are funneled through the specialist, who acts as either a broker or as a principal in each transaction. Keeping the limit order book gives the specialist privileged information about the market, and this information has considerable value. By the same token, the specialist faces informed traders who have superior information, and the specialist can lose substantial sums by trading against those informed traders. In return for the monopoly position granted by the exchange, the specialist is required to make a market in the stock, to keep the bid–asked spread reasonably small, and to trade to stabilize prices.

The Floor Broker.   While all orders must eventually reach the specialist to be executed, the floor broker plays an important role as well. Typically, floor brokers facilitate the execution of larger orders. The floor broker may be an employee of a large brokerage firm, such as Merrill Lynch. Alternatively, the order may be handled by a free–lance floor broker, who makes a living by helping to execute orders that come to the floor of the exchange. In either case, the floor broker conveys the order to the specialist and has it executed.

The floor broker is much more than a messenger, however. Because floor brokers work larger orders, they generally have the discretion to **work an order**—to try to fill the order at the best price. If the order is a large buy order, for example, it may not be wise to try to execute the order all at once the moment it reaches the floor. The floor broker may be able to get a lower price per share by filling a portion of the order now and the rest in a few minutes.

Because floor brokers are paid based on shares traded, they have an incentive to trade as quickly as possible. However, they know that the brokerage firm that gave them the order could have given the order to someone else, so the floor broker also has an incentive to do the best job in filling the order.

Order Flow.   We now consider how orders flow from the customer to the floor, how they are executed, and how the trade is reported to the customer. Orders can be initiated from virtually anywhere. Consider, for example, an individual in Miami, Florida wishing to purchase a share of IBM, which is listed on the New York Stock Exchange. Since the individual is not a member of the NYSE, he or she must trade through a member, such as a brokerage firm.

Opening an Account. Many brokerage firms, such as PaineWebber or Merrill Lynch, have offices in all major cities. Before an individual can trade through a brokerage firm, it is necessary to have a brokerage account. There are usually no special requirements, other than filling out a few forms to open an account, although certain types of accounts may require some proof of financial capacity and a deposit with the brokerage firm. When the account is opened, a local account representative is assigned to service the account. The account representative will be the main contact person for the customer. The account representative is also called a broker, but the account representative's function is not at all like the floor broker's discussed earlier.

Placing and Transmitting an Order. Once the account is opened, the customer may contact the broker by telephone and place an order. Let us assume that the order is to buy 100 shares of IBM. The customer's account representative enters the order in the brokerage firm's communication system and the order is transmitted to the brokerage firm's representatives on the floor of the exchange.

Execution of the Order. Once an order reaches the exchange, it may be completed in one of two fundamentally different ways. First, if the order is large or requires special treatment, it will be given to a floor broker for execution, as we described above. Second, if the order is small and requires no special treatment, it may be handled electronically through SuperDOT (Designated Order Turnaround). In this case, the order is electronically transmitted to the specialist, and the order is executed immediately without any effort by a floor broker. Our example of a 100 share order to buy IBM is a small order for a highly active stock, so it will almost certainly be handled through SuperDOT. In both cases, the order arrives at the specialist's physical location on the floor of the exchange.

Exchanges arrange their trading floors with particular physical locations, or **trading posts** for each security. The specialist is located at the trading post for that particular security. The trading post is the nerve center for the entire set of communications that might occur for the sale or purchase of a given security. All orders to buy or sell a given security must ultimately come to the trading post for the particular stock.

Reporting the Trade. Once the trade is executed, the transaction must be reported to the customer, the customer's brokerage firm, and the public at large. If the order was executed by a floor broker, the broker records the price and other relevant information on a card and returns this to the brokerage firm's booth on the floor of the exchange. If the order was handled through SuperDOT, the specialist confirms the trade to the brokerage firm's computer. In either case, the brokerage firm records all of the information for its own records and reports the trade to the account representative. The account representative reports the order to the customer. In our example, the account representative in Miami would receive confirmation of the purchase of IBM and would call the customer to report the price at which the shares were purchased.

The transaction is also reported to the public by officials of the exchange. An exchange clerk enters the trade into the computer which transmits an electronic ticker tape to subscribers all over the world. Within one minute of execution, the

Figure 3.2

Order Flow for Stock Exchange Transactions

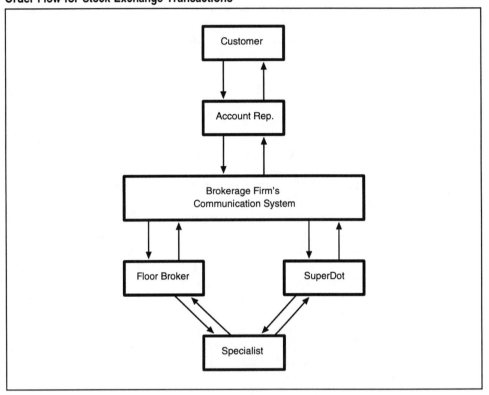

report of the trade has appeared on the tape, letting all interested parties know of the transaction.

Summary. The entire transaction described above takes only a few minutes. Usually, the customer can place the order and receive confirmation of the order during the same two–minute phone call. Figure 3.2 summarizes the flow of the order and its confirmation to the customer.

Final settlement for stock transactions occurs five business days after the transaction is made, and the customer is expected to have the necessary funds on deposit with the broker by that time, including the commission that must be paid to the brokerage firm for executing the transaction.

The New York Stock Exchange

By far, the New York Stock Exchange dominates the stock exchanges in the United States and matches any exchange in the world. Domestically, the NYSE accounts for

Figure 3.3

Monthly Trading Volume of the New York Stock Exchange

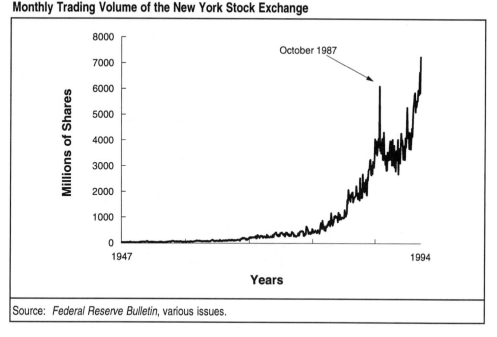

Source: *Federal Reserve Bulletin*, various issues.

about 50 percent of share volume and about 64 percent of dollar volume, due to the higher average price of NYSE shares. If we focus only on domestic organized exchanges and exclude the OTC market, the NYSE accounts for over 80 percent of share volume and 86 percent of dollar volume.

The NYSE traces its origins to May 17, 1792, when 24 brokers formed the first organized stock market in the United States. This meeting took place under a buttonwood tree at what is now 68 Wall Street. In 1817 the name "New York Stock and Exchange Board" was adopted, with the current name taking effect in 1863.

From quite humble early beginnings, the NYSE has grown to mighty proportions. This is reflected in the trading volume on the exchange. On March 16, 1830, the dullest day in the history of the exchange, 31 shares were traded. In spite of such times of lethargy, the NYSE has shown marked increases in volume. Now it is normal for the day's trading volume to be more than 100 million shares. In January 1987, the NYSE share volume went over the 300 million share mark on a single day for the first time. In light of that fact, it may be surprising to notice that share volume for a single day of trading did not exceed 50 million shares until 1978, and did not ever top 100 million shares until 1982. Figure 3.3 shows the monthly

Table 3.2

Initial Listing Requirements for the New York Stock Exchange

1. Current annual earnings (pre–tax) of $2.5 million.
2. Earnings in the preceding two years of $2 million.
3. Net tangible assets of $18 million.
4. Market value of outstanding shares of $18 million.
5. 1.1 million shares held publicly.
6. At least 2,000 shareholders owning 100 shares or more each, or 2,200 shareholders together with an average monthly trade of 100,000 shares.

Source: *New York Stock Exchange Fact Book*, April 1994, p. 26.

volume of trading on the NYSE, with a typical monthly volume of about 5.8 billion shares.[10]

Not every firm can be listed on the NYSE; only those firms meeting certain minimum requirements are eligible. The exchange imposes requirements in the form of earning power, total value of outstanding stock, and number of shareholders. Table 3.2 presents the current minimum listing requirements for initial listing on the NYSE.

Many shares listed on the NYSE are also listed on other exchanges. Transactions for all NYSE–listed securities are shown on one reporting system, called the **consolidated tape**, no matter where the transaction actually took place. Other organizations participating in the consolidated tape listing are: the American, Pacific, Midwest, Philadelphia, Boston, and Cincinnati stock exchanges; the National Association of Securities Dealers; and Instinet. (The last two organizations are part of the over–the–counter market.)[11] The NYSE consistently accounts for about 80–85 percent of the total consolidated tape volume, followed by the Midwest and Pacific Stock Exchanges. The American Stock Exchange (AMEX) has little role in the consolidated tape reporting system since very few firms are listed on both the NYSE and the AMEX. Table 3.3 shows the distribution of the consolidated tape volume for the recent past.

Exchange membership confers valuable rights to the owner of the seat. In the case of the specialist member, the specialist obtains a monopoly access to the potentially valuable information in the limit order book. A member brokerage firm obtains the right to execute orders for the public and to charge them commissions for the service. Because of this, exchange memberships are valuable capital assets which are traded openly in a market.

---

[10]As Figure 3.3 shows, October 1987 was the month with the highest trade volume ever. On October 19, 1987, Black Monday, the market crashed, leading to a tremendous volume for that day and several succeeding days. We discuss the Crash of 1987 in Chapter 17.

[11]See the discussion of the over–the–counter market later in this chapter.

Table 3.3

Distribution of Consolidated Tape Volume by Market (1984–1993)

Year	NYSE* (%)	AMEX (%)	PSE (%)	CHX (%)	PHLX (%)	BSE (%)	CSE (%)	NASD (%)	INST (%)	Total (%)
1993	81.94	0.00	2.54	4.08	1.47	1.31	1.28	7.38	0.01	100.00
1992	82.26	0.00	2.98	4.45	1.65	1.49	1.03	6.57	0.12	100.00
1991	82.85	0.00	3.29	4.51	1.59	1.69	0.70	5.82	0.14	100.00
1990	82.85	0.00	3.04	4.88	1.90	1.69	0.65	4.82	0.16	100.00
1989	84.13	0.00	3.09	5.59	1.83	1.57	0.46	3.20	0.14	100.00
1988	86.20	0.00	2.81	5.56	1.33	1.25	0.53	2.18	0.14	100.00
1987	86.17	0.00	3.02	5.71	1.40	1.29	0.42	1.90	0.09	100.00
1986	84.00	0.00	3.63	6.26	1.65	1.41	0.39	2.55	0.12	100.00
1985	83.39	0.00	3.52	6.95	1.56	1.28	0.16	2.88	0.25	100.00
1984	84.03	0.00	3.23	6.79	1.70	0.97	0.19	2.91	0.18	100.00

*Data after 1988 includes rights and warrants.

Participating Markets:
NYSE, New York; AMEX, American; PSE, Pacific; CHX, Chicago; PHLX, Philadelphia; BSE, Boston; CSE, Cincinnati; NASD, National Association of Securities Dealers; INST, Instinet.

Source: *New York Stock Exchange Fact Book*, April 1994, p. 26.

The day's transactions for NYSE securities are reported widely in the financial press. *The Wall Street Journal* presents the consolidated tape quotations as the "NYSE–Composite Transactions" shown in Figure 3.4. Prices are quoted in dollars per share, with the smallest fraction of a dollar being 1/8, or 12½ cents. The first two columns of figures show the high and low share prices for a stock over the last year. The annual cash dividend is shown in dollars, based on the current dividend declaration of the firm. The column labeled "Yld %" is the dividend yield on the shares, which is given by the following equation:

$$\text{Dividend Yield} = \frac{\text{Current Annual Dividend}}{\text{Current Stock Price}} \qquad \textbf{3.2}$$

The next column shows the P–E Ratio, or the **Price–Earnings Ratio**.[12]

$$\text{P–E Ratio} = \frac{\text{Current Stock Price}}{\text{Current Annual Earnings}} \qquad \textbf{3.3}$$

---

[12]Chapters 11–13 discuss the meaning and interpretation of the dividend yield and the P–E ratio.

Figure 3.4

New York Stock Exchange Composite Transactions

NEW YORK STOCK EXCHANGE COMPOSITE TRANSACTIONS

	52 Weeks Hi	52 Weeks Lo	Stock	Sym	Div	Yld %	PE	Vol 100s	Hi	Lo	Close	Net Chg
	1 13/16	¾	AllncEntn wtB			...	...	200	15/16	⅞	15/16	+ 1/16
	10½	8⅞	AllncGlblEnv	AEF		...	...	74	9½	9⅜	9½	...
n	16¼	12	AllianceWrld II	AWF	1.42a	11.5	...	2367	12⅝	12¼	12⅜	– ⅛
	22½	12¾	AllianceWrld	AWG	1.68a	12.7	...	671	13⅜	13⅛	13¼	...
	30	21¾	AlliantTech	ATK		...	9	121	29½	29⅛	29⅛	– ⅛
	27⅝	21⅝	AlldIrishBk	AIB	1.06e	4.9	...	36	22	21⅝	21¾	– ½
	29¼	25½	AlldIrishBk pf		2.97e	10.8	...	81	27¾	27⅜	27⅜	– ¼
	17⅜	9½	AlliedPdts	ADP		..	10	274	15	14¾	14¾	– ⅛
s	40⅝	32⅛	AlliedSgnl	ALD	.67	1.9	15	2299	36⅝	36⅛	36⅛	– ⅛
s	22⅛	15	AllmrPC	APY	.16	.9	9	46	17½	17¼	17½	+ ⅛
	12¼	10	Allmerica	ALM	.84a	7.7	...	89	10⅞	10¾	10⅞	...
▼	10¾	9⅝	AllmonTr	GSO	.48e	5.0	...	216	9⅝	9½	9⅝	...
	34¼	22⅝	Allstate	ALL	.72	3.0	15	2878	24½	24¼	24¼	...
s	31¼	24	ALLTEL	AT	.88	3.4	18	1035	26¼	26	26⅛	...
	6⅛	3⅞	Allwaste	ALW		...	23	319	5⅞	5⅝	5⅞	+ ⅛
n	27¾	16¾	Alumax	AMX		...	...	551	26⅛	25⅝	26	+ ⅜
	82	64¼	Alcoa	AA	1.60a	2.1	dd	3164	75⅜	74½	74¾	+ ¼
	30¾	19¼	Alza	AZA		...	53	1599	25¼	24⅝	24⅞	– ⅜
	10½	6	AmaxGold	AU	.06j	...	dd	1501	8	7¾	7⅞	– ⅛
	49¾	35¾	Ambac	ABK	.48	1.2	8	261	40⅝	39½	39½	–1
	25⅞	16⅝	AmcastInd	AIZ	.48	2.4	13	97	21	20⅝	20⅝	– ⅝
	54¾	42⅜	AmerHess	AHC	.60	1.2	dd	1911	51⅞	50⅝	50⅞	– ⅞
n	25½	20⅞	Amerco pfA		2.13	9.3	...	32	23¼	22¾	23	+ ⅛
	10	8⅞	AmAdjTerm95	ADJ	.43e	4.8	...	249	9⅛	8⅞	8⅞	– ⅛
	9¾	8¼	AmAdjTerm96	BDJ	.50e	5.9	...	255	8⅝	8½	8½	...
	9¾	8	AmAdjTerm97	CDJ	.56e	6.8	...	425	8⅜	8¼	8¼	– ⅛
	9¾	7⅞	AmAdjTerm98	DDJ	.58e	7.0	...	627	8⅜	8¼	8¼	...
	9¾	7⅞	AmAdjTerm99	EDJ	.59e	7.4	...	349	8⅛	8	8	– ⅛
	11	7⅞	AmAnnuity	AAG	.05e	.5	8	188	9⅝	9¼	9½	+ ⅛
	31	20⅜	AmBarrick	ABX	.10f	.4	31	6166	24⅝	24⅛	24½	+ ¼
	35⅞	29⅜	AmBrand	AMB	2.00f	6.2	12	3114	33¼	32¼	32½	– ⅝
	28¾	18¾	AmBusnPdts	ABP	.80	3.9	13	39	20⅝	20½	20½	– ⅛
	21¼	17⅜	AmCapBdFd	ACB	1.54	8.6	...	165	17⅞	17½	17⅞	+ ¼
	24	19¾	AmCapCvSec	ACS	1.08a	5.3	...	1	20⅜	20⅜	20⅜	– ⅛
	8⅜	6⅝	AmCapIncTr	ACD	.65	9.1	...	169	7⅛	7	7⅛	...
	56⅞	42¼	AmCyanmd	ACY	1.85f	3.4	dd	4811	54⅝	53	54⅛	+1⅞
n	11	9¾	AmEagle	FLI	.03p	...	...	25	10¼	10	10	– ⅛
	40⅜	27¼	AmElecPwr	AEP	2.40	8.5	13	1589	28⅜	28⅛	28⅛	– ⅛
s	32⅛	23⅛	AmExpress	AXP	1.00	3.7	9	10249	26⅞	26⅜	26¾	...
n	45¼	36¾	AmExpressDECS	AXD	2.30	5.6	...	283	41¼	40⅞	41¼	+ ⅜
	36½	24⅞	AmGenerl	AGC	1.16	4.1	23	2647	29⅛	28½	28½	– ⅝
	9⅞	6⅝	AmGvIncFd	AGF	.77a	10.6	...	313	7¼	7	7¼	+ ¼
	12¼	8¼	AmGvIncoP	AAF	.96a	10.8	...	299	8⅞	8¾	8⅞	...
	10¾	8½	AmGvTermTr	AGT	.78	8.3	...	55	9⅜	9¼	9⅜	...
	29	24¼	AmHlthProp	AHE	2.27e	9.1	15	391	25	24¾	24⅞	– ⅛
	25⅛	16¾	AmHeritgLf	AHL	.66	3.7	11	11	17¾	17⅝	17¾	– ⅛
	66⅛	55⅜	AmHomePdts	AHP	2.92	5.1	12	3356	57¾	57⅜	57⅜	– ⅜
	28¼	22⅛	AmIncHldg	AIH	.32	1.2	12	39	27⅛	27	27	+ ⅛
	3¼	1⅝	AmIndProp	IND	.12j	...	...	100	1¾	1¾	1¾	...
s	100¼	81¾	AmIntGroup	AIG	.46f	.5	15	2327	93⅜	92⅛	92½	– ⅜
	26⅝	**10¼**	**AmMedHldg**	**AMI**		...	**24**	**4661**	**25½**	**23¾**	**24**	**–1⅝**
	29¼	19	AmMedRespns	EMT		...	31	366	25½	25⅛	25⅛	...
	15⅝	11⅜	AmMuniInco	XAA	.87	6.8	...	42	12⅞	12¾	12⅞	+ ⅛
	11¼	9⅝	AmMunTermTr2	BXT	.62	6.0	...	41	10¼	10	10¼	+ ⅛
	10⅝	9⅜	AmMunTermTr3	CXT	.57	5.8	...	31	9⅞	9⅞	9⅞	+ ⅛
	11¾	9¾	AmMunTermTr	AXT	.65	6.2	...	107	10½	10⅜	10½	+ ⅛
	14¼	9⅛	AmOil&Gas	AOG		...	49	1070	10⅜	10¼	10¼	– ⅛
	11⅞	8⅛	AmOpIncoFd	OIF	1.00a	11.1	...	400	9	8⅞	9	...
	8¼	5¾	AmPrecInd	APR	.25f	3.5	21	16	7⅛	7	7⅛	+ ⅛
	39¾	23⅜	AmPremier	APZ	.88	3.3	9	1171	27	26⅞	27	...
s	34	19	AmPresidnt	APS	.40	1.9	8	805	21¼	21	21¼	– ⅝
	37½	23½	AmerRe	ARN		...	17	174	30⅝	30⅛	30⅛	– ⅝
	9½	7	AmRE Ptnrs	ACP	.36j	...	6	107	7⅞	7⅞	7⅞	– ⅛
	15⅝	8⅞	AmRltyTr	ARB		...	dd	13	12⅛	12⅛	12⅛	– ⅛
n	15⅛	11	AmSelctPort	SLA	1.13	9.5	...	95	12	11¾	11⅞	...
s	27⅛	19⅞	AmStores	ASC	.48	1.9	14	3664	25⅛	24¾	24⅞	– ¼
▼	28¼	19⅛	BkrsLife	BLH	.60	3.2	8	495	19⅛	18⅜	18½	– ⅝
	84⅝	64½	BankTrst	BT	3.60	5.2	6	1455	69⅜	68¼	68⅝	– ½
n	25⅝	24¾	BkTrst dep pfO		.27p	...	...	1029	25⅛	24 61/64	24 61/64	...
	27¼	23⅝	BankTrst un		2.14	8.6	...	39	25¼	25	25	...
	6¼	3⅞	BannerAero	BAR		...	dd	67	4¾	4¾	4¾	– ⅛
	1½	9/16	BanyanMtgInv	VMG		...	17	151	¾	11/16	11/16	...
	39	27¼	Barclays	BCS	1.13e	3.5	...	108	33¼	32½	32¾	– ½
	27¾	25½	Barclays pr		2.78	10.5	...	181	26½	26¼	26⅜	+ ⅛
	27¾	25¼	Barclays prB		2.72	10.5	...	34	26⅛	26	26	...
	31	26⅝	Barclays pfD		2.88	10.3	...	61	28	27½	27⅞	+ ¼
	27	21¼	Barclays prE		2.00	8.7	...	98	22⅞	22¾	22⅞	+ ⅜
	30¾	26⅜	Barclays pfC		2.81	10.3	...	48	27⅝	27¼	27⅜	+ ⅛
	30½	20½	Bard CR	BCR	.56	2.3	22	1009	24⅝	23¾	24⅝	+ ⅞
n	34	20	BarnesNoble	BKS		...	...	856	23¾	23½	23⅝	– ¼
	37¾	29½	BarnesGp	B	1.40	3.8	26	44	36¾	36⅝	36⅝	– ⅛
	48⅞	37⅜	BarnettBks	BBI	1.64f	3.7	10	1620	45	44⅝	44¾	– ¼
	99	80¾	BarnettBks pfA		4.50	5.2	...	361	87⅜	87	87	...
	72½	61½	BarnettBks pfC		4.00	6.1	...	18	66	65½	65½	– ¼
	18½	13½	Bass	BAS	.78e	5.0	...	3	15⅝	15⅝	15⅝	– ⅛
	12⅝	7¼	BattleMtn	BMG	.05	.5	dd	3353	10⅝	10⅜	10½	+ ⅛
	70½	53⅝	BattleMtn pf		3.25	5.1	...	507	63½	63¼	63¼	– ¼
	53⅞	37½	BauschLomb	BOL	.98f	2.6	14	5845	38⅜	37¾	37¾	– ⅛
	29	20	BaxterInt	BAX	1.00	3.9	dd	6221	26⅜	25½	25½	–1
n	22¾	20	BayApartmt	BYA		...	...	354	21¼	20¾	20¾	– ½
	32	23⅝	BayStGas	BGC	1.46f	6.0	14	39	24¾	24⅜	24½	– ⅛
n	18½	17¼	BeaconProp	BCN		...	...	528	17½	17¼	17¼	– ⅛
	24¾	16⅞	BearStearns	BSC	.60b	3.4	5	5249	17½	17⅛	17½	+ ½
	26⅝	21⅞	BearStearns pfB		1.97	8.3	...	2021	24¼	23¾	23¾	– ⅜
n	25½	21⅝	BearStearns pfC		1.90	8.0	...	30	23⅞	23⅝	23⅞	+ ⅛
n	24¾	20¾	BearStnEPICS pfA		2.00	9.0	...	333	22⅜	22⅛	22⅛	– ⅛
	37½	21⅛	BearingsInc	BER	.64	2.0	22	85	32	31½	31⅝	...
n	18¾	13¾	BeazerHm	BZH		...	...	139	15⅛	14¾	14¾	– ¼
	28¾	19⅝	BeckmanInstr	BEC	.40	1.6	dd	392	26	25⅝	25⅝	– ¼
	40¾	34	BectonDksn	BDX	.74	1.9	14	2345	40¼	39¾	39¾	– ¼
	7¼	4⅛	BedfdPrpty	BED	.30e	4.4	9	27	6⅞	6¾	6¾	– ⅛
n	20¼	14¼	Belden	BWC	.10e	.6	...	384	17⅞	17½	17⅝	+ ⅛
	69⅛	49	BellAtlantic	BEL	2.76f	5.0	16	3613	56⅜	55	55⅜	+ ⅛
	19¾	12⅝	BellIndus	BI	.40b	2.3	14	55	17⅛	17	17⅛	...
	63⅞	53	BellSouth	BLS	2.76	4.6	25	3029	60⅞	60¼	60⅜	– ⅜
	55	44	Belo AH A	BLC	.60	1.3	20	299	47⅜	46¾	46¾	– ⅝
	25⅛	19⅞	Bemis	BMS	.54	2.3	24	679	23¼	22¾	23	+ ⅛
s	40⅞	34½	Beneficial	BNL	1.52	4.0	10	504	37⅞	37⅝	37⅞	...
	67¾	59	Beneficial pfA		4.50	7.5	...	1	59¾	59¾	59¾	– ⅛
	69	57¼	Beneficial pfB		4.30	7.2	...	6	60⅜	60	60	– ¼
	36⅞	23⅜	Benetton	BNG	.47e	1.5	...	14	31½	31½	31½	+ ⅛
	1⅜	13/16	Benguet	BE		...	...	100	15/16	⅞	⅞	...
	19⅞	14⅛	BergnBruns	BBC	.48	2.9	23	628	17	16⅝	16⅝	– ⅜
	17800	14000	BerkHathwy	BRK		...	25	z60	16350	16350	16350	+50
	12¾	10	BrkshreRlty	BRI	.86	7.9	52	104	10⅞	10¾	10⅞	...
	14⅞	12	Berlitz	BTZ		...	dd	1	13⅝	13⅝	13⅝	+ ⅛
	13⅜	8	BerryPete	BRY	.40	4.0	dd	44	10⅜	10⅛	10⅛	...
s	37¾	10¾	BestBuy	BBY		...	26	12494	28	26⅞	27¼	– ⅝
	24¼	12⅞	BethSteel	BS	j	...	dd	2366	19¾	19¼	19⅜	– ¼
	57⅜	50¼	BethSteel pf		5.00	9.3	...	14	53⅞	53½	53½	– ⅜
	53⅝	40	BetzLab	BTL	1.44f	3.3	21	577	43⅛	43	43	...
	16⅛	9¼	BeverlyEnt	BEV		...	27	4297	13	12¾	12¾	...
n	67	48½	BeverlyEnt pf		2.75	4.8	...	32	57⅜	57	57	– ½
	33⅝	26½	BIC Cp	BIC	.80	2.8	15	46	28¾	28½	28½	– ⅛
	37⅝	13⅞	BiocraftLabs	BCL	.10	.7	23	156	15⅝	15⅛	15¼	– ½
	7⅞	**5**	**BioWhit**	**BWI**		...	**27**	**137**	**6⅝**	**6⅝**	**6⅝**	**– ⅜**
	32⅝	20¾	BirmghamStl	BIR	.40	1.4	44	715	29	28½	28⅝	– ⅜
	22⅞	17½	BlackDeck	BDK	.40	2.3	18	4933	18	17⅝	17¾	+ ¼
	27⅛	19⅜	BlackHills	BKH	1.32	6.6	12	221	20¼	19¾	20	+ ¼
	10¾	8½	BlackRockAdv	BAT	.73	7.9	...	87	9⅜	9¼	9¼	...
	15⅞	13⅛	BlkrkCal2008	BFC	.86	6.3	...	229	13⅞	13⅝	13⅝	– ¼
	15¾	13⅞	BlkrkFla2008	BRF	.86	5.9	...	52	14⅝	14½	14⅝	+ ⅛
▲	24⅞	18	Bowater	BOW	.60	2.4	dd	1205	25⅝	24½	25¼	+ ¾
n	25¾	21	Bowater dep pfB		1.65	6.8	...	39	24¼	24	24¼	+ ⅜
n	25⅜	22	Bowater dep pfC		2.10	9.4	...	8	22⅜	22⅜	22⅜	...
n▲	**26**	**12**	**BoydGaming**	**BYD**		...	...	**581**	**12⅛**	**10¾**	**11⅜**	**– ⅝**
	16⅝	11	Bradlees	BLE	.60	4.2	11	116	14⅜	14¼	14⅜	...
	31¾	15⅞	BrazilFd	BZF	1.01e	4.6	...	521	22¾	22⅛	22⅛	– ¼
	26¼	11½	BrazEqtyFd	BZL	.08e	.5	...	419	18¼	17¾	17¾	– ½
	44	10¾	BreedTech	BDT		...	24	1306	29½	28	28¼	– ⅞
	90¼	63⅛	BriggsStrat	BGG	1.84	2.7	11	532	69¾	68	68⅞	– ¾
	23⅝	9⅜	BrillAuto	CBA	.08	.6	...	189	12⅝	12¼	12⅝	...
s	33⅝	21⅜	BrinkerInt	EAT		...	26	8880	22⅜	21½	21⅞	– ⅝
	62¼	50	BrisMyrsSqb	BMY	2.92	5.3	14	5062	55⅛	54¾	54¾	– ⅛
	74⅛	44	BritAir	BAB	.59e	1.0	...	557	61¼	60⅞	61	– ¼
	54¼	39	BritGas	BRG	2.76e	6.9	...	597	40¾	40	40	– ½
	75⅛	51⅜	BritPetrol	BP	1.96e	2.6	39	5829	74⅝	73⅞	74	+ ⅛
	23⅛	12⅞	BritSteel	BST	.28e	1.3	...	566	21	20¾	20¾	...
n	49½	35⅞	BritishTele 2nd	BTYP		...	...	442	38¾	38⅜	38½	+ ¼
	74⅞	53⅞	BritishTele	BTY	3.01e	5.3	...	825	57	56½	56⅝	+ ⅛
	16⅜	8¼	BrdwyStore	BWY		...	dd	1421	9¼	8¾	8⅞	– ¼
▼	**5⅝**	**2⅛**	**BrdwyStore wt**			...	...	**108**	**2**	**1¾**	**1⅞**	**– ¼**
	56	37¼	BrokenHill	BHP	1.18e	2.1	..	70	56	55⅛	55⅜	+ ⅜
s	6	1¼	BrookeGp	BGL		...	dd	77	1⅝	1½	1⅝	+ ⅛
s	28⅞	22⅛	BklynUnGas	BU	1.35	5.4	15	234	25⅛	24⅞	25⅛	+ ⅛
	38⅞	29¾	BrownGp	BG	1.60	4.2	dd	109	38¼	38	38⅛	+ ⅛
s	30⅛	23⅛	BrownFormn A	BFA	.95	3.4	14	29	28⅜	28	28	+ ⅛
s	30½	24¼	BrownFormn B	BFB	.95	3.3	14	604	28¾	28⅜	28⅜	+ ⅛
	7⅝	6½	BrownFormn pf		.40	5.7	...	44	7	7	7	+ ⅛
	32¼	20⅞	BrownFer	BFI	.68	2.2	25	4569	30¾	30½	30¾	...
	25⅜	12½	Brunswick	BC	.44	1.9	38	2109	23¾	23⅝	23⅝	– ¼
	18⅝	11⅜	BrushWell	BW	.20	1.2	24	130	16½	16¼	16¼	– ⅛
	41⅝	32⅝	BuckeyePtr	BPL	2.80	7.5	10	52	37¾	37½	37½	...
	49¼	22½	BuenosAires	BAE	.46p	...	...	140	33¼	32⅝	32¾	– ½
n	54¾	22½	BufetInd	GBI		...	...	124	29⅛	29	29⅛	+ ⅛
	17⅜	14⅛	BurgerKgInv	BKP	1.56f	9.5	19	48	16¾	16½	16½	– ¼
s	28⅜	13⅛	BurlgtnCoat	BCF		...	13	622	18¾	18¼	18½	– ¼
	17⅛	12⅝	BurlgtnInd	BUR		...	13	536	13½	13¼	13⅜	+ ⅛
	66⅝	48⅝	BurlgtnNthn	BNI	1.20	2.2	18	2164	55	54⅛	54¼	– ⅛
	75	60½	BurlgtnNthn pfA		3.13	4.9	...	59	64¼	63⅞	64	...
	26½	19¾	BurlngtnRes	BRU	2.30e	10.7	...	261	21½	21⅜	21½	+ ⅛
	53⅞	40¼	BurlgtnRes	BR	.55	1.3	22	2273	43¼	42⅜	42⅝	– ⅝
	20⅞	16⅛	BurnhmPacif	BPP	1.40	7.9	21	227	17¾	17½	17¾	...
n▲	17	15¼	BushBoake	BOA		...	...	1490	17¾	17¼	17⅜	+ ⅜
			-C-C-C-									
	35⅞	23⅝	CBI Ind	CBH	.48	1.8	dd	980	28	27⅜	27⅜	– ⅛
n	21	17⅝	CBL Assoc	CBL	1.50	7.2	...	709	20⅞	20⅝	20⅞	+ ⅜
	326½	214	CBS	CBS	2.00	.8	12	684	260	257	257½	–1⅜
	32⅝	18⅞	CCP Insur	CCP	.08	.4	6	368	21¾	21¼	21¼	– ⅜
	15	7⅝	CDI	CDI		...	25	94	14	13⅞	13⅞	– ⅛
	73¾	56½	CIGNA	CI	3.04	4.3	17	2364	71½	71	71⅜	+ ⅜
	9¼	7½	CIGNA High	HIS	.90a	11.8	...	795	7⅝	7½	7⅝	+ ⅛
	33¾	25½	CIPSCO	CIP	2.00f	7.7	11	375	26	25⅝	26	+ ¼
	35⅛	23¼	CMAC	CMT	.20	.8	9	298	26½	25¾	25¾	– ⅝
s	32⅜	12¾	CML	CML	.08	.6	10	1208	13¼	13⅛	13⅛	...
	27½	20¼	CMS Engy	CMS	.72	3.6	11	1086	20½	20¼	20¼	– ¼
	96¾	61¾	CNA Fnl	CNA		...	dd	49	62⅝	62⅛	62⅝	+ ¼
	13	10¼	CNA IncShrs	CNN	1.08	9.5	...	16	11½	11⅜	11⅜	– ⅛
	51⅞	39⅞	CPCInt	CPC	1.36	2.7	17	2635	51⅜	50¾	50⅞	...
	18⅜	13¾	CPI Cp	CPY	.56	3.6	21	382	16⅜	15¾	15¾	– ⅜
	9⅞	5⅜	CRI Liq	CFR	3.20e	59.5	...	86	5½	5⅜	5⅜	– ¼
	13¼	8¼	CRSS	CRX	.12	1.1	28	133	10⅝	10⅝	10⅝	– ⅛
s	21¼	16½	CSS Ind	CSS		...	8	8	16⅝	16⅝	16⅝	– ⅛
	92⅜	67⅞	CSX	CSX	1.76	2.3	18	2955	78⅜	76⅞	77¾	+ ⅞
	26⅛	19⅛	CTS	CTS	.40	1.6	65	42	24⅞	24¾	24⅞	...
	39¾	25	CUC Int	CU		...	33	2224	28⅛	27	27⅛	–1¼
	11½	9	CV REIT	CVI	1.08	10.7	10	28	10¼	10⅛	10⅛	+ ⅛

Source: *The Wall Street Journal*, June 24, 1994, p. C3. Reprinted by permission of *The Wall Street Journal*, © (1994) Dow Jones & Company, Inc. All rights reserved worldwide.

The next column shows the number of shares (in hundreds) traded on the day being reported. The next three columns, labeled "High," "Low," and "Close," show the respective prices for that day's trading. The final column, "Net Chg," shows the difference from the previous day's close to the close of the day being reported. As shown in Equation 3.1, the WR on a share of common stock depends on the change in price on the share plus the payment of the cash dividend, if any.

Table 3.4

Growth in Share Volume Across Selected Markets (1981–1993)

Year	Companies			Issues			Share Volume (in millions)		
	NASDAQ	NYSE	AMEX	NASDAQ	NYSE	AMEX	NASDAQ	NYSE	AMEX
1993	4,611	2,361	869	5,393	2,904	1,010	66,540	66,923	4,582
1992	4,113	2,088	814	4,764	2,658	942	48,455	51,376	3,600
1991	4,094	1,885	860	4,684	2,426	1,058	41,311	45,266	3,367
1990	4,132	1,769	859	4,706	2,284	1,063	33,380	39,665	3,329
1989	4,293	1,719	859	4,963	2,241	1,069	33,530	41,699	3,125
1988	4,451	1,681	896	5,144	2,234	1,101	31,070	40,850	2,515
1987	4,706	1,647	869	5,537	2,244	1,077	37,890	47,801	3,506
1986	4,417	1,573	796	5,189	2,257	957	28,737	35,680	2,979
1985	4,136	1,540	783	4,784	2,298	940	20,699	27,511	2,101
1984	4,097	1,543	792	4,728	2,319	930	15,159	23,071	1,545
1983	3,901	1,550	822	4,467	2,307	948	15,909	21,590	2,081
1982	3,264	1,562	834	3,664	2,225	945	8,432	16,458	1,338
1981	3,353	1,565	867	3,687	2,220	959	7,823	11,854	1,343

Source: National Association of Securities Dealers, *Fact Book*, April 1994, p. 33.

The American Stock Exchange and the Regional Exchanges

Of the other organized exchanges, the American Stock Exchange is clearly the largest. What is not apparent, however, is the falling importance of the AMEX. In 1973, the AMEX accounted for 53.13 percent of the non–NYSE share volume on organized exchanges, and for 33.02 percent of the market value of such trading. Relative to the other exchanges, it has clearly fallen in size over the recent past. Among the organized exchanges, it is also clear that the NYSE has gained market share at the expense of the smaller exchanges. Table 3.4 summarizes the growth rates in share volume and market value of shares traded for the NYSE and the AMEX. The NYSE is growing faster than the AMEX, but the real growth is happening in the over–the–counter market.

The Secondary Market:
The Over–the–Counter Market

Relative to the organized exchanges, particularly the NYSE, the over–the–counter (OTC) market receives relatively little attention. This is really an oversight. Trading on the OTC market has been growing faster than trading on organized exchanges, even the NYSE. Further, recent and future advances in computer technology will probably benefit the OTC market more than the organized exchanges because of the structural differences between the two types of markets.

General Organizational Features

The over–the–counter market differs from organized exchanges in a number of ways, but two important differences stand out. First, the OTC market does not rely on a central trading place. Instead, the market is made up of many people in diverse locations. Second, the OTC market does not use specialists. Instead, there are a number of **market makers**, firms and individuals making a market in particular stocks.

In a sense, these differences are embodied metaphorically in the name over–the–counter. This nickname comes from the fact that participants in the market were originally thought to be like retailers who kept a supply of shares and sold them to buyers across the counter, just as one might buy a bolt of cloth in a general store. In important respects, this system continues in effect today, with a number of market makers for each security.

The privilege of trading in the OTC market is granted by the National Association of Securities Dealers (NASD), based on financial soundness and qualification examinations. This industry group plays a role analogous to the exchange as a regulator of market entry. In addition, the NASD plays an important self–regulatory role. The differences between the OTC market and the organized exchanges become clear when considering the flow of orders to buy or sell stock.

Flow of Orders

Only a member of the NASD is allowed to trade in the over–the–counter market. Buying or selling shares traded on the OTC market necessitates the use of a broker along with a brokerage account. Usually, opening a single account ensures that one can trade on both the organized exchanges and the OTC.

Having established an account, one may decide to place an order to buy 100 shares of Apple Computer, one of the leading securities traded on the OTC. The broker, trying to execute this order, does not have a centralized trading floor where these shares are traded. Instead, the broker needs to find a market maker who is willing to sell the Apple Computer shares out of inventory.

For all practical purposes, this is as easy as placing an order on the NYSE. Brokers and other traders in the OTC market use the National Association of Securities Dealers Automated Quotation (NASDAQ) system. The broker obtains a quotation by using the brokerage firm's computer connection to NASDAQ and can normally complete the transaction within one or two minutes. Since there are a number of market makers for each stock (instead of a single specialist, as on the organized exchanges), the broker needs to find the best price for the customer. Before the introduction of NASDAQ in 1971, this search was conducted by telephone and teletype. Now the computer terminal in the broker's office

Figure 3.5

Wealth Relatives for Large and Small Companies' Stocks

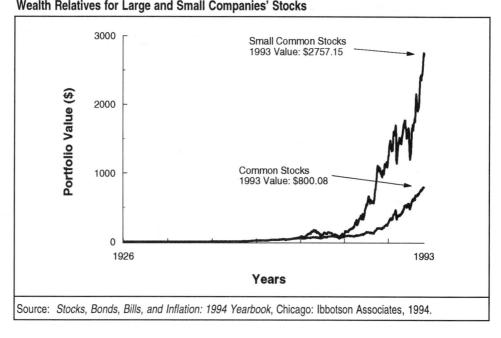

Source: *Stocks, Bonds, Bills, and Inflation: 1994 Yearbook*, Chicago: Ibbotson Associates, 1994.

automatically shows the best available bid and asked prices.[13] The broker then contacts the dealer offering the best price for the shares and consummates the transaction. For small orders of frequently traded stocks, the Small Order Executive System (SOES) automatically routes an order to the market maker with the best price.

Stock Trading on the OTC Market

Firms traded OTC tend to be quite a bit smaller than their NYSE counterparts. Historically, smaller firms tend to have greater returns than larger firms, as well as more risk. This tendency of small firms to outperform large firms can be seen in several ways. First, within the NYSE itself, small firms tend to do better. Figure 3.5

---

[13] There are actually three kinds of terminals connected with NASDAQ. The Level 1 terminals simply show the best prices available, and this kind of terminal is typically used by brokers serving the public. Level 2 terminals show bid and asked prices for a variety of dealers. These are used by brokers and institutional investors, such as pension funds. Level 3 terminals allow direct trading via computer with other dealers, and they are available only to dealers. At year–end 1993, there were 236,727 terminals worldwide. This number includes 193,603 Level 1 terminals in the United States, and 27,903 Level 1 terminals abroad.

Table 3.5

NASDAQ and NYSE Index Changes

	Percentage Change in	
Year	NASDAQ	NYSE
1973	−31.1	−19.6
1974	−35.1	−30.3
1975	29.8	31.9
1976	26.1	21.5
1977	7.3	−9.3
1978	12.3	2.1
1979	28.1	15.5
1980	33.9	25.7
1981	−3.2	−8.7
1982	18.7	14.0
1983	19.9	17.5
1984	−11.2	1.3
1985	31.4	26.1
1986	7.4	14.0
1987	−5.3	−.3
1988	15.4	13.0
1989	19.3	24.8
1990	−17.8	−7.5
1991	56.8	27.1
1992	15.5	4.7
1993	14.8	7.9

Source: *New York Stock Exchange Fact Book*, April 1994, and National Association of Securities Dealers, *Fact Book*, 1994.

shows how $1 invested at year–end 1925 would have grown by year–end 1993, depending on whether it was invested in typical NYSE securities or in the smallest 20 percent of NYSE securities. As shown in the figure, $1 invested in the typical larger firm would have grown to $800.08 by the end of 1993, while $1 put into the smaller firms would have grown to $2,757.15.[14]

This difference in performance by size is emphasized by considering the performance of NYSE–listed securities versus those making up the NASDAQ index.

---

[14] The large stocks were made up of the Standard & Poor's Composite Index. Until 1957, these were 90 of the largest stocks. After that time, it was made up of 500 of the largest firms.

Table 3.5 shows the changes in the NASDAQ and NYSE indexes. Both indexes measure changes in stock prices only, leaving dividends out of the computation.[15] The OTC market includes about 15,000 securities, yet many of these have only a local market, such as the stock of local banks. Only the larger, more important firms are carried on NASDAQ. NASDAQ has quotations for about 4,000 stocks, compared with about 1,800 listed on the NYSE. Also, following a mandate of Congress passed in 1975, the SEC has helped the NASD formulate a National Market System, in which prominent OTC stocks are reported. There are about 3,400 securities now quoted in the National Market System, a change that may stimulate the OTC market.

The National Market System

The purpose of the National Market System (NMS) is to provide more timely information on developments in the securities markets for the more important OTC stocks. For non–NMS NASDAQ securities, for example, a dealer only enters his bid and asked prices into the NASDAQ computer. For NMS securities, dealers must also report the price of any security traded within 90 seconds after the trade is made. For non–NMS securities, the dealers report the total transactions in each security at the end of the day. For NMS securities, dealers report the size of each trade along with the price report following each trade. This provides much better information to other traders and erodes the privileged position of the market maker. Table 3.6 shows the qualification standards for inclusion in the NMS. As the table indicates, the SEC requires some firms to be included, while others are eligible for voluntary inclusion.

Quotations for OTC securities appear each day in *The Wall Street Journal*, as shown in Figure 3.6. The quotations are similar in structure to those for the NYSE. Other quotations, aside from NMS securities, also appear in *The Wall Street Journal*. These typically show only a bid–asked price due to their small volume. For stocks of primarily local interest, quotations can often be found in the local newspaper but are unlikely to appear in *The Wall Street Journal*. Table 3.7 shows the ten most active NMS issues in 1993 and the annual share volume for each firm.

Contrasts with Organized Exchanges

There has been a long–standing debate over the best structure for a stock market. The system used by the organized exchanges gives the specialist a monopoly power, with a privileged trading position and access to the limit order book. Presumably, the holder of a monopoly uses that power for profit. In a dealer market, there are a number of competing market makers. However, when markets are inactive and it is difficult to reach the various market makers for quotations, one can have a trade at an unfair price, due to lack of information. This criticism of the

---

[15]Since NASDAQ securities are smaller than those on the NYSE, they tend to pay smaller dividends as well. This may bias the return comparison of Table 3.5 to a slight degree.

dealer market used in the OTC market is now much weaker than before NASDAQ and the NMS. In the major OTC stocks, the trader has information about current stock prices that is just as good as the information available to the trader on an organized exchange.

Sophisticated computer equipment allows instant access to the best prices available in the market. The requirement in NMS securities that transaction prices be reported virtually immediately helps market participants be sure they are receiving fair prices. Further developments in computer technology can be expected to extend the reporting requirements now in place for NMS securities to other smaller security issues.

Trading Procedures and Practices

In this section, we consider three basic types of trading procedures and practices. First, we consider the types of orders that traders can place. Thus far in our discussion of trading and order execution, we have focused primarily on market orders, with a brief mention of limit orders. This section discusses the principal

Table 3.6

Inclusion Criteria for the NASDAQ National Market System

	Initial NASDAQ/NMS Inclusion		Continued Inclusion
Standard	**Alternative 1**	**Alternative 2**	**Inclusion**
Registration under the Securities Exchange Act of 1934 or equivalent	Yes	Yes	Yes
Net Tangible Assets	$4 million	$12 million	$2–4 million
Net Income	$400,000	—	—
Pretax Income	$750,000	—	—
Public Float (Shares)	500,000	1 million	200,000
Operating History	—	3 years	—
Market Value of Float	$3 million	$15 million	$1 million
Minimum Bid	$5	—	—
Shareholders of Record	400–800	400	400
Number of Market Makers	2	2	2

*Domestic common stocks only.

Source: National Association of Securities Dealers, *Fact Book*, 1994, p. 43.

Figure 3.6

OTC–Traded Price Quotations

NASDAQ NATIONAL MARKET ISSUES

	52 Weeks Hi	Lo	Stock	Sym	Div	Yld %	PE	Vol 100s	Hi	Lo	Close	Net Chg
	27¾	19¾	AnchrBcpWis	ABCW	.24	.9	9	46	27½	27¼	27¼	...
n	**17⅛**	**10¾**	**AnchorGaming**	SLOT		...	...	**352**	12¼	11¼	11¼	−1
	7½	3¾	AndersnGp	ANDR		...	dd	10	6¼	6¼	6¼	+ ½
	21¾	12¼	AndovrBcp	ANDB	.40	1.9	12	259	21⅜	20⅞	21⅛	+ ⅛
s	39½	17 53/64	AndrewCp	ANDW		...	27	1107	36½	35¼	35½	− ¾
	21¼	13	Andros	ANDY		...	9	1102	17½	16	17⅛	+ ⅜
	8½	3¼	Anergen	ANRG		...	...	365	5	4½	4¾	...
n	30¼	18½	ANTEC Cp	ANTC		...	...	298	23¾	23¼	23¼	− ¼
	4 3/16	2⅜	ApertusTech	APTS		...	dd	889	4 1/16	3 15/16	4	...
	27¾	12¾	Aphton	APHT		...	...	11	13½	13¼	13¼	− ¼
	17¾	**11¼**	**ApogeeEnt**	**APOG**	**.30**	**2.1**	**39**	**1612**	**14¼**	**13¼**	**14¼**	**+1**
n	18¼	16	Apogee	APGG		...	...	26	16¾	16½	16½	− ¼
	41¾	22	AppleCptr	AAPL	.48	1.9	dd	18205	26¼	24⅞	25⅛	−1⅛
s	18½	8 35/64	AppleSouth	APSO	.02	.1	40	2075	14¾	13¾	14¼	...
s	**25¼**	**10 21/32**	**Applebee**	**APPB**	**.06**	**.5**	**26**	**3374**	**13½**	**11⅞**	**12¼**	**−1**
	15½	7¾	ApplncRecyc	ARCI		...	dd	62	9¾	9¼	9¾	...
	7⅜	3⅞	AppldBiosci	APBI		...	dd	1769	6¼	5⅞	6	+ ⅛
n	**25**	**13¾**	**AppldDigital**	**ADAX**		...	...	**1346**	**19**	**16½**	**16½**	**−1½**
	7⅞	3¾	AppldExtr	AETC		...	dd	138	7¼	7	7¼	+ ¼
	21⅜	6½	AppldlmuSci	AISX		...	...	655	8½	7¾	8½	+ ⅜
s	33	8⅞	Appldlnnovt	AINN		...	36	256	23¼	21½	21½	−1
s	52	25⅛	AppldMatl	AMAT		...	21	11468	40¾	39	39	−1¼
	6½	**3⅜**	**AppldMicbio**	**AMBI**		...	**48**	**72**	**4⅛**	**3⅞**	**3⅞**	**− ¼**
n	11½	4¾	AppldSciTech	ASTX		...	...	82	5¾	5⅜	5¾	+ ¼
	7¾	**4¼**	**AppldSignal**	**APSG**		...	**15**	**182**	**4¾**	**4½**	**4½**	**− ¾**
	4⅛	**1¾**	**ArabShld**	**ARSD**		...	...	**635**	**2⅜**	**2**	**2**	**− ⅛**
	21½	15½	ArborDrug	ARBR	.24	1.3	cc	213	19	18¼	19	+ ¾
n	**25**	**12¾**	**ArborHlth**	**AHCC**		...	...	**225**	**22**	**20½**	**20½**	**−1½**
	20¾	10 11/16	ArborNtl	ARBH		...	11	2191	19¾	18½	19⅝	− ⅛
	19	**10½**	**ArchComm**	**APGR**		...	**dd**	**1361**	**17**	**15½**	**15½**	**−1⅛**
s	2⅝	1 13/16	ArchPete	ARCH		...	cc	31	2 5/16	2¼	2 5/16	− 1/16
	30½	18¾	Arctco	ACAT	.28	1.0	19	265	27	26½	26⅞	+ ⅜
n	16	10¼	ArdenIndlPdt	AFAS		...	...	46	10½	10¼	10¼	− ⅜
n	16⅜	9½	Arethusa	ARTHF		...	cc	72	11⅜	11 5/16	11 5/16	+ 1/16
	35½	26¼	ArgonautGp	AGII	1.16f	4.3	8	90	27½	27	27¼	+ ¼
	33¼	12½	ArgosyGaming	ARGY		...	38	186	14	13¼	13¼	− ¼
	6½	**3½**	**ArgusPharm**	**ARGS**		...	...	**10**	**4¼**	**4¼**	**4¼**	**+ ¾**
n	9¾	8½	ARIAD Pharm	un		...	...	1617	9	8½	8½	...
	15¾	8⅛	ArkansBest	ABFS	.04	.3	11	392	12¼	12	12	− ⅛
	22	16¼	ArmorAll	ARMR	.64	3.1	19	322	21¾	20¾	20¾	− ¾
s	22¾	15⅜	Arnoldlnd	AIND	.40	2.1	16	150	19¾	19¼	19¼	− ⅜
n	7½	4	ArrisPharm	ARRS		...	...	166	6½	6	6⅛	+ ⅛

	52 Weeks Hi	Lo	Stock	Sym	Div	Yld %	PE	Vol 100s	Hi	Lo	Close	Net Chg
	5¼	1½	BodyDrama	BDRM		...	dd	16	1½	1½	1½	...
n	14½	9	Bollingrlnd	BOLL		...	...	3	9¾	9¾	9¾	...
	10	5¼	BonTonStr	BONT		...	10	103	8⅝	8¼	8½	+ ¼
	25¾	17½	BooksMillion	BAMM		...	32	265	23⅝	22⅝	22⅝	− ⅞
	30¾	22½	BooleBg	BOOL		...	15	8	29¼	27¾	28¾	+1
	28¼	13	Boomtown	BMTN		...	31	738	16	15¼	15⅝	− ⅜
	26⅜	15¾	Boral	BORAY	1.08e	5.5	...	16	19¾	19¾	19¾	− ⅛
	23¼	8½	Borland	BORL		...	dd	2447	8¾	8½	8½	...
n	**12¾**	**7¾**	**BorrorCp**	**BORR**		...	...	**185**	**9**	**8½**	**8½**	**− ¾**
	20¼	13½	BostnAc	BOSA	.40	2.7	13	5	14¾	14¾	14¾	− ¼
	41½	29	BostnBcp	SBOS	.76	2.4	6	425	33½	32	32	−1½
n	51	34	BostonChick	BOST		...	...	1824	38	36	36¼	−1
	14¾	6⅜	BostonTech	BSTN		...	27	5361	8⅝	8¼	8¼	− ⅛
	14⅛	9¼	BoxEngy B	BOXXB		...	...	915	9¾	9½	9½	− ⅛
n	11½	10¼	BoydBros	BOYD		...	...	540	11½	11	11	− ¼
	4 9/16	1⅞	BradPharm	BPRXA		...	10	151	3	2⅞	2 15/16	− 1/16
	3 3/16	½	BradPharm	wtA		...	...	30	1⅞	1¾	1¾	− ⅛
	1¼	¼	BradPharm	wtB		...	...	10	¾	¾	¾	+ 1/32
	48	34½	BradyWH	BRCOA	.68	1.5	18	49	46¼	45	45½	− ½
	17½	9	BrantreeSvg	BTSB	.20	1.2	11	165	16½	16	16½	+ ¾
	1 3/16	⅛	BranfdSvg	BSBC		...	dd	30	5/16	5/16	5/16	+ 1/16
	11⅝	**3¾**	**BraunFash**	**BFCI**		...	**12**	**251**	**4⅝**	**4¼**	**4⅝**	**+ 5/16**
	¼	1/16	BrkwatrR g	BWRLF		...	...	8	3/32	3/32	3/32	...
	15	**8¼**	**Brenco**	**BREN**	**.20**	**1.7**	**27**	**289**	**12¾**	**12**	**12**	**− ⅝**
	2⅛	⅜	vjBrendls	BRDLQ		...	...	1	1⅝	1⅝	1⅝	− ¼
s	20	17	BrentnBk	BRBK	.44	2.3	11	9	19¼	19¼	19¼	+ ¼
	14¾	8½	BridFood	BRID	.20	2.3	14	18	9	8¾	8¾	...
	15¾	**4¼**	**BriteVoice**	**BVSI**		...	**dd**	**423**	**9⅞**	**8⅞**	**9**	**− ¾**
	8	5¾	BroadNtl	BNBC	.04e	.6	11	1	7⅛	7⅛	7⅛	+ ⅛
n	52¼	11	BroadbndTch	BBTK		...	dd	4491	20¼	18¾	19¼	+ ¼
	6	3	Bdcstlnt	BRIN		...	dd	18	3¼	3⅛	3⅛	+ ⅛
n	19	10¼	BdcstgPtnr A	BPIX		...	...	99	12¾	12	12	− ½
	15¾	6¾	BroadSeymr	BSIS		...	...	238	11¼	10½	10¾	+ ⅛
	16¼	7¼	BrockCandy A	BRCK	.16	1.9	12	86	8½	8	8½	+ ⅜
	25	10	BrockCntrl	BROC		...	30	189	19¼	18½	19¼	+ ¾
	59¼	**31½**	**BrodrSftwr**	**BROD**		...	**44**	**8926**	**43¼**	**40¾**	**41¾**	**+2½**
n	35½	33¾	BrooklynBcp	BRKB		...	...	20	34½	34½	34½	− ¼
	18½	12	Brookstone	BKST		...	20	13	15	14¾	14¾	− ½
	18¼	5¾	Brooktree	BTRE		...	5	132	7¾	7½	7 9/16	+ 5/16
	15¾	**9½**	**Brooktrout**	**BRKT**		...	**24**	**206**	**12¾**	**12**	**12**	**− ¾**
n	21¾	9¾	BrosCoffees	BEAN		...	...	134	12	11½	11½	...
	17½	10½	BrownTom	TMBR		...	cc	1291	14⅞	14⅜	14¾	+ ⅜

Source: *The Wall Street Journal*, June 24, 1994, p. C7. Reprinted by permission of *The Wall Street Journal*,

types of orders that the market allows. Second, we consider the rules that govern trading on margin. In margin trading, a trader pays for only part of the price of the stock and borrows funds from a broker to make up the difference. Third, we consider the basic rules that govern short selling—selling stock that one does not own.

Table 3.7
▬▬▬▬▬▬▬

Ten Most Active NMS Stocks, 1993

Company	1993 Share Volume (000s)
Intel Corporation	1,049,801
Novell, Inc.	835,712
Tele–Communications, Inc.	702,218
MCI Communications Corp.	549,109
Cisco Systems, Inc.	527,391
Spectrum Information Technologies, Inc.	523,643
Microsoft Corp.	507,276
Apple Computer, Inc.	504,138
Amgen, Inc.	500,015
Oracle Systems Corporation	449,654

Source: National Association of Securities Dealers, *Fact Book*, 1994.

Types of Orders

There are different ways to initiate an order when trading stocks. Whether one deals through an organized exchange or via the OTC market, the process is similar in most respects, so the following description assumes that trading is conducted over an organized exchange. In the description of trading to this point, only the most straightforward kind of order, called a **market order**, has been considered. A market order instructs the broker to buy or sell a security at whatever price prevails on the market floor at that time. A market order is an order for immediate execution.

A **limit order** is an order to transact only if certain conditions are met, rather than being an order for immediate execution. For example, a limit order to buy a stock at a share price of $70 means that the stock will be purchased if and only if it becomes available for a price of $70 or less. As a consequence, it is possible that limit orders might never be executed. A limit order to sell at $80 will be executed if the stock can be sold for $80 or more.

A **not held order** can be either a limit order or a market order. Marking an order as "not held" gives the floor broker the freedom to seek a better price. For example, a not held market order tells the broker to transact promptly, but instructs the broker to work the order to obtain the best price. This can be important if the order size is very large and attempting to transact the entire amount immediately might cause the price to move. In a not held limit order, the broker has the freedom to work the order for the best price, but the limit portion of the order instructs the broker not to exceed the limit. Thus, in a not held limit order to sell at $70, the broker is free to work the order to obtain the best price above $70, but the broker cannot sell for a price below $70.

A **percentage order** instructs the broker to make a transaction only as a certain percentage of the order flow in a given stock. For example, a 50 percent order to buy 1,000 shares at $40 instructs the broker to convert 100 shares of the percentage order into a limit order any time 100 shares of the stock trade below $40. A trader uses a percentage order to avoid initiating new, and perhaps unfavorable, trading prices. This can be important for large orders. If the order is very large, attempting to execute it all at once in its entirety may result in adverse price impacts.

A **stop order** is an order that becomes active when a certain price condition is met. It can be either a stop market order or a stop limit order. For example, let us assume that a share trades at $50. A trader might place a stop market order to buy at $48. If any transaction takes place at $48 with another trader, the stop market order becomes a market order to buy, and the order is executed at the current market price. This does not guarantee that the price obtained will be $48. For example, the stock might just have one trade at $48 that triggers the stop order, and the price might immediately bounce higher than $48. The stop market order would then be executed at that slightly higher price. The trader might have placed a similar order as a stop limit order to buy at $48, limit $48. This order is also activated when a trade occurs at $48, but the stop limit order now becomes a limit order to buy at $48. This specification ensures that the maximum price that the trader will pay is $48.

Traders can use stop orders to protect gains. For example, assume a trader bought a stock at $25, and the price has now risen to $40. The trader would like to hold out for additional gains but does not want to risk losing the $15 paper profit. The trader could place a stop market order to sell at $35. This order would be activated as a market order if the price touches $35, and the trader would be out of the market with a sale at (or very close to) $35. If the price continued to rise from its current level of $40, the stop order would never be activated and the trader could continue to profit. In this case, the stop order helps the trader protect a gain.

In addition to specifying the conditions under which orders will be executed, the trader can also control the time dimension of stop or limit orders or the portion of an order that can be filled. A **day order** is in effect just for the current trading day. If market conditions do not allow the order to be executed today, then the order is canceled. A **good until canceled order (GTC)** is an order that is left in effect until it is canceled, so it can stay in effect virtually forever. An **at the opening** order instructs that the order be executed only at the opening of the trading session. Any portion of the order that cannot be filled at the opening is canceled. A **fill or kill order** instructs the broker to fill the entire order at a particular price immediately or cancel the order. An **immediate or cancel** order instructs the broker to fill the entire order, or any part, at a particular price immediately or cancel the order. An **all or none** order instructs the broker to fill the entire order or not to transact. A **market–on–close** order is an order to transact at the market price as close to the close of trading as possible. A **limit or market–on–close** order is a limit order left in effect during the trading day. If the order is not executed during the day, it becomes a market order at the close of trading.[16]

Margin Trading

As with almost every good in today's economy, it is also possible to purchase shares on credit. If one wishes to invest in stocks in an amount that exceeds the cash available to pay for them, one can buy the shares through **margin trading**. In this situation, one borrows some of the share price from the brokerage firm, which itself borrows money at the **broker's call rate**, the rate charged by banks for loans to brokerage houses on loans secured with securities. Combining the investor's own funds and the loan from the broker provides enough money to pay for the shares. The broker holds the shares as collateral for the loan. Since the Great Depression, the percentage that one can borrow has been regulated by the Federal Reserve Board Regulation T. The proportion of the share value that the investor must invest out of personal funds is called the **initial margin**. Currently, the maximum percentage of the shares' value that one may borrow is 50 percent. The initial margin has been set at 50 percent since January 3, 1974. Before then, it was sometimes higher, but since World War II, it has never been lower.

The advantage, and potential disadvantage, of margin trading is the greater leverage that it gives the investor. Assuming the investor borrows 50 percent of the invested funds from the broker, the investor realizes the full gain or loss on the shares, even though only one–half of the share value was invested. To make this more concrete, consider a simple example in which an individual buys 1,000 shares (at $100 per share) by investing $50,000 of his own funds and borrowing the other $50,000 from the broker at 10 percent interest. Assume that the share price has risen after one year to $115, so the value of the entire block of shares is $115,000. The investor could then sell the shares and pay the broker $55,000 principal and interest. This would leave a profit of $10,000 on the original investment of $50,000, or a 20 percent return. Without margin trading, the investor would have earned only 15 percent.

Note also that any fall in share prices also has a greater impact on the investor's fortunes. In this example, no matter what happens to the share price, the investor will owe the broker $55,000 after one year. For instance, suppose that the share price fell from $100 to $80. After one year, the value of the 1,000 shares would be $80,000. If the broker is paid $55,000, this leaves only $25,000 for the investor. In this case, a 20 percent drop in the share price causes a 50 percent loss for the investor. Without margin trading, the investor would have lost only 20 percent.

In addition to the initial margin, stipulated by the Federal Reserve Board, the broker also imposes a **maintenance margin** requirement. When share prices fall, the value of the shares, which serve as the collateral for the broker, deteriorates. The

---

[16]This account of the types of orders relies on Robert A. Schwartz, *Equity Markets: Structure, Trading, and Performance*, New York: Harper & Row, 1988. Schwartz provides an extensive and insightful discussion of many aspects of stock trading.

broker can require additional cash funds from the investor in such a situation. This demand for more cash is known as a **margin call**. The investor must then pay the broker the new funds or the broker will sell the shares, retain the money owed to the brokerage firm, and return the excess to the investor.

In October of 1929, there were no restrictions on margins whatsoever, and it was customary for investors to borrow 100 percent of the share value from brokers. This allowed investors of very limited resources to assume enormous positions in the market. This practice was wonderful in a time of consistently rising prices, which existed in 1929. However, because of the extreme percentage of borrowed funds, any drop in prices would quickly cause margin calls from the broker. It was impossible for overextended investors to meet the margin calls. The broker would then sell the shares at whatever price the market would bear.

Under a fully leveraged system, as existed prior to 1929, a large drop in share prices could develop into a deadly spiral. The drop in share prices would generate margin calls, which many investors could not meet. Failure to meet the margin calls would bring many more shares on the market as brokers sold off shares to recoup their losses, which further depressed prices. The further drop in prices, of course, led to new margin calls. This spiral of falling stock prices and margin calls played an important role in the Great Crash of 1929 and was largely responsible for the onset of the Great Depression. In response to this danger, the Federal Reserve Board received authorization to regulate initial margin.

Short Sales

Normally, we think of stock transactions as following a pattern of buying shares and eventually selling them, with the difference in purchase and sales price constituting the profit or loss on the transaction. It is also possible, however, to sell shares that one does not currently own, a practice known as **selling short** or **short selling**. In a **short sale**, a trader begins by selling shares that he does not own, with the intention of buying them back later at a lower price. For example, simple financial advice has always been to "buy low and sell high." Short selling reverses this advice to "sell high and buy low." In both cases, one tries to find a situation where the sales price exceeds the purchase price.

In some situations, selling what you do not own can lead to a jail term. In the stock market, however, it is a recognized and legitimate form of trading to profit from an anticipated drop in the price of a stock. To execute a short sale, the trader has the broker borrow shares from another investor and sell them in the market. Brokers have a ready supply of shares to borrow for most stocks, since they hold shares for many customers in **street name**. That is, customers simply leave their shares in the custody of their brokers. The broker is specifically authorized to loan these shares by the agreement which opens the brokerage account.

Figure 3.7 shows the flow of shares and funds in the short sale of 100 shares with an initial price of $30 per share. The figure assumes that the short seller receives 50 percent of the funds when the sale is initiated. The broker borrows shares for the short seller, and then sells them in the market for $3,000. After the purchaser pays for the shares, the broker retains 50 percent of the proceeds and

Figure 3.7

Flow of Shares and Funds in Short Selling

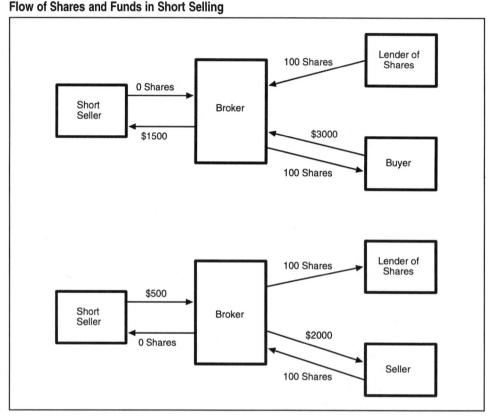

passes the other half to the short seller, so the short seller receives $1,500 upon initiating the transaction. (This is consistent with a 50 percent margin requirement for short sales.)

We assume that the price of the shares later drops to $20 per share and the short seller decides to cover the sale. The broker places a buy order and acquires the 100 shares, paying the seller $2,000. The $2,000 comes from the $1,500 that the broker retained when the short sale began, plus an additional $500 that the short seller must provide to the broker to close the transaction. The broker returns the shares to the original lender, and the short seller's total profit is $1,000—the initial $3,000 sale price less the $2,000 purchase price to reacquire the shares and return them to the lender.

It should be recognized that short selling essentially involves trading on margin, since the short seller takes a position in the market without putting up the full value of the transaction. Also, the short seller must make any dividend payments to the lender of the shares. Finally, our example ignores the transaction costs involved in initiating and completing the short sale. These complications make it clear that one must have a thorough understanding of these intricacies and a clear agreement with one's broker before engaging in short sales.

The Third and Fourth Markets

Transaction sizes may vary from a single share to a huge number of shares. Trading odd lots can sometimes be more expensive, since one may have to have an order executed through an odd–lot broker. At the other end of the range, some stock transactions are for a very large number of shares. Transactions for 10,000 or more shares of stock are called **block trades**. These block trades involve millions, sometimes billions, of dollars and are executed on behalf of large institutional traders, such as pension funds, mutual funds, and charitable foundations. Block trading is an important activity for the organized exchanges, particularly for the NYSE. In 1993, 53.8 percent of the entire share volume was through block trades, with almost 6,000 block trades occurring per day on average. The total number of shares involved in block trades during the year exceeded 35 billion. The largest block trade of the year was for 14.1 million shares.

While block trading accounts for about half of the share volume on the NYSE, it is less important than it has been. In 1993, block trading on the NYSE set a record. The NYSE competes with the third and fourth markets for these large and lucrative block trades. The third and fourth markets are so named because they arose after the primary market (the market for new issues) and the secondary market (the organized exchanges and the OTC market).

The **third market** is a market for large blocks of shares that operates outside the confines of the organized exchanges and the OTC market. The major traders in the market are large institutions who have a frequent need to move large blocks of shares. In the third market, brokers assist the institutions by bringing buyers and sellers together. In fact, virtually the only transactors in the third market, and the fourth market as well, are institutional investors. These institutions have played an increasingly dominant role in the market over the last 20 years.

The third market arose in the 1960s and early 1970s, due in large part to the commission structure of the organized exchanges, particularly the NYSE. The NYSE had a fixed commission schedule that all members were obliged to follow. For trades in round lots, the schedule required proportional commissions. For example, the commission on a trade of 50,000 shares would be 500 times as large as the commission on a trade of 100 shares. This meant that large trades would incur enormous commission charges. Further, the amount of effort to consummate a trade of 50,000 shares was not nearly 500 times the effort to trade 100 shares. In an effort to avoid the high commissions charged by the NYSE, larger institutions began to execute their trades in the third market, effectively bypassing the NYSE and saving on commission charges.

A further refinement of this practice was the development of the **fourth market**. Like the third market, the fourth market consists mainly of institutional traders seeking to economize on transaction costs. The difference is that in the fourth market, the institutions trade among themselves without the intervention of any brokers.

To an important extent, these two markets were brought into being by the fixed commission structure of the NYSE. The policy of fixed commission rates was brought to an end by the intervention of the SEC, which forced the exchange to allow its members to charge whatever they wished for commissions. This new policy went into effect on May 1, 1975, known as **Mayday** in the industry. Brokers willing to negotiate commissions on block trades have attracted much of this business back to the NYSE, as is evidenced by the fact that block trading has increased on the NYSE every year since 1975. Another important result of the freeing of commissions from the fixed schedule was a revolution in the brokerage industry.

The Brokerage Industry

The brokerage industry today continues to evolve rapidly. Many of the traditional restrictions against commercial bank activity in the securities industry are being lifted, and barriers against brokerage–firm activity in traditional banking activities are being lowered. As a result, one finds commercial banks with subsidiary discount brokerage houses and brokerage firms offering accounts that provide the services of a checking account.

The key function of a brokerage firm is the execution of customers' orders for securities purchases and sales. Traditionally, brokerage firms have also offered research on the quality and investment prospects of different securities. Until recently, it was customary for virtually every brokerage firm to provide research reports to clients free of charge. Many still do, and providing research is one of the main competitive tools that brokerage firms use. For many investors, research continues to be an important service.

Not all investors consider research to be an important service of their brokerage firms. Some investors believe that other sources of research are preferable, or that research is not really useful. In an effort to capture this different clientele, the brokerage industry has become segmented. After May 1, 1975, when commissions were freed from any restrictions by the NYSE, a number of **discount brokers** started business. Their aim was to offer cheaper commissions and to capture the portion of the market not desiring research. Today, the brokerage industry can be partitioned into full–line brokerage houses and discount brokers. Full–line brokerage firms continue to supply research reports and a much higher level of service. The discount brokers focus on executing customers' orders. The broker at a full–line firm functions largely as a salesman, drumming up orders from a client list. Discount brokers work much less intensively, waiting for calls from clients. In a full–line brokerage firm, the broker often has a congenial, perhaps even personal, relationship with his clients. In a discount brokerage firm, the investor may not even know the name of the broker executing an order. These differences in service and philosophy can lead to sizeable differences in commission costs, which can be an important factor in the profitability of the investment.

Transaction Costs and Portfolio Management

The cost of trading a share of stock includes the brokerage commission, but there are other important costs that the trader must pay, and sometimes these are less visible. We have already discussed the bid–asked spread, which every trader faces on every transaction. In this section, we briefly consider commissions and the factors that affect the bid–asked spread. In addition to commissions and the bid–asked spread, large traders face a third type of cost, a **price impact**—a change in the price of a share due to the making of a transaction. However, we also discuss estimates of the total cost of transacting, and we consider the long–term impact of trading on the value of a portfolio.

Commissions

Table 3.8 shows some sample commissions for full–line brokerage houses and discount brokers. The commission charged usually depends on both the number of shares and on the share price. Merrill Lynch and PaineWebber are two well–known full–line brokerage firms. Schwab is the largest and one of the best–known discount brokerage firms, while OVEST and Discount Brokerage are smaller discount brokers. As we discuss later, commission costs appear to be the largest component of the transaction costs facing traders.

As Table 3.8 shows, the transaction cost per share drops dramatically for larger orders. For Discount Broker E, for example, the $200 commission to trade 2,000 shares worth $50 per share is only .2 percent of the value of the shares. This implies a dollar commission of $.10 per share. However, for very large transactions, the commission cost may be as low as $.02 per share. For a $50 share, this $.02 would be .04 percent of the share's value.

Table 3.8

Full–Line vs. Discount Commission Structures

Shares/Price	Full–Line Brokerages		Discount Brokerages		
	A	B	C	D	E
200/$15	$ 86.00	$ 86.00	$ 54.00	$ 35.00	$ 35.00
500/$25	235.00	235.00	94.50	72.00	65.00
1000/$25	419.00	414.00	132.00	127.00	102.50
2000/$50	900.00	890.00	225.00	200.00	200.00

The Bid–Asked Spread

As we have seen, specialists on organized exchanges and market makers on the OTC maintain an inventory of stocks and sell from these stocks to accommodate market orders. In this section, we consider the size of the bid–asked spread. It is also possible to decompose the bid–asked spread into three elements: order processing costs, inventory holding costs, and adverse information costs.[17] Thus, we go on to consider the decomposition of the bid–asked spread into these elements.

Size of the Bid–Asked Spread.   A variety of factors affect the size of the bid–asked spread. In general, bid–asked spreads are smaller for active stocks. With higher activity, the specialist or market maker has economies of scale, so the bid–asked spread can be smaller in percentage terms. If the stock is volatile, the dealer has a greater risk exposure from holding an inventory. To offset this risk, the specialist or market maker widens the bid–asked spread. The specialist or market maker knows that other parties may have superior information about future price movements in the stock. To protect against these informed traders, the dealer must widen the bid–asked spread. In general, if market activity signals that new information may be arriving, the dealer will widen the bid–asked spread. For market makers, there is also competition. The greater the number of market makers, the smaller will be the spread. This factor is related to volume of trading or activity, because highly active stocks attract more market makers.

These factors (activity, volatility, informational effects, and competition) can all vary across different stocks. Not surprisingly, therefore, estimates of the bid–asked spread vary, depending on the stock and the market being examined. For example, Fortin, Grube, and Joy conclude that spreads for exchange–listed stocks tend to be lower than those for OTC stocks.[18] They find that the average bid–asked spread for OTC stocks is about 7 percent of the value of the stock. By contrast, Stoll finds an average spread of about 2.5 percent for National Market System stocks.[19] Spreads on the NYSE appear to be smaller, at about .65 percent according to Stoll. Loeb finds that spreads on active and highly liquid stocks are about .60 percent.[20]

---

[17] This analysis follows H. Stoll, "Inferring the Components of the Bid–Ask Spread: Theory and Empirical Tests," *Journal of Finance*, 44:1, March 1989, pp. 115–134.

[18] See R. D. Fortin, R. C. Grube, and O. M. Joy, "Bid–Ask Spreads for OTC NASDAQ Firms," *Financial Analysts Journal*, May–June 1990, pp. 76–79.

[19] H. Stoll, "Inferring the Components of the Bid–Ask Spread: Theory and Empirical Tests," *Journal of Finance*, 44:1, March 1989, pp. 115–134. See especially pp. 128–129.

[20] T. F. Loeb, "Trading Cost: The Critical Link Between Investment Information and Results," in W. H. Wagner, *The Complete Guide to Securities Transactions*, New York: Wiley, 1989, pp. 125-135.

Traders face the bid–asked spread on every transaction. However, if the market maker places the bid and asked equal amounts away from the estimated true value of the stock, a one–way transaction will incur only half of the bid–asked spread. Thus, the full bid–asked spread is a direct estimate of the round–trip (purchase and sale) transaction costs due to the bid–asked spread.

Components of the Bid–Asked Spread. Studies have sought to decompose the specialist's or market maker's bid–asked spread into its relevant components, as we mentioned above. By considering these elements, we can gain a better understanding of how a specialist or market maker functions.

Order Processing Costs. Order processing costs are the costs that a specialist or market maker charges simply for filling an order. These include compensation for the market maker's time and represent a fee for performing the paperwork necessary to consummate the transaction.

Inventory Holding Costs. A specialist holds inventory of a stock at all times. Assume that a specialist currently holds the optimal inventory of her stock and assume that she now receives a buy order that she fills from this inventory. If the specialist held an initial inventory that was optimal, her inventory is now too low. This gives her an incentive to change the quoted bid–asked spread to attract stock so that she can rebuild her inventory to the desired level. Thus, the specialist subtly shifts the quoted bid–asked spread to maintain the optimal inventory. The holding cost component of the spread compensates the specialist for sacrificing diversification; it does not compensate the specialist for the time value of money or the risk inherent in holding the stock. Compensation for the time value and the risk of the stock are earned by holding the security.[21]

Adverse Information Costs. We have seen that the specialist holds a privileged informational position by knowing the contents of the limit order book. We also noted that traders other than specialists and market makers sometimes have their own informational advantage. For example, an insider in a firm might know non–public information that will affect the price of the stock. **Adverse information** is information unknown to the specialist or market maker that may affect the price of the security. The specialist or market maker must set the bid–asked spread to protect against these informed traders, who possess adverse information. Because the adverse information may be positive or negative for the price of the stock, the adverse information cost implies that the specialist or market maker must widen the bid–asked spread.

---

[21]As we will see in later chapters, stocks should be priced to fairly compensate their owners for the time value of money and the risk inherent in holding the stocks that cannot be avoided through diversification.

Summary. Thus, we have seen that the bid–asked spread can be decomposed into three elements: the order processing cost, the inventory holding cost, and the adverse information cost. Stoll estimates that the bid–asked spread can be decomposed into these three elements according to the following percentages:

Order Processing Cost	47%
Inventory Holding Cost	10%
Adverse Information Cost	43%

Price Impacts

Consider a firm with a relatively low market value and shares that trade inactively. An attempt to buy 10,000 shares of such a firm can cause the price of the shares to rise. If the order is placed as a market order, the sudden surge in demand for the shares may outstrip the available supply. The excess demand for the shares and the price prevailing when the order is initiated can cause the price to rise. In this case, the very act of attempting to buy the shares can have a significant price impact.

Price impacts are likely to arise only for large traders. Individual traders are unlikely to generate price impacts. Large institutions carefully manage their orders in order to minimize or avoid price impacts. For example, they might place a number of small orders over time to make up the total order that they want to trade. Alternatively, institutions might shop among other institutions to find a single party willing to sell the shares at a single price close to the prevailing market.

Transaction Costs and Trading

We now want to consider the impact that transaction costs have on portfolio management and portfolio returns. We assume that there is no price impact, either because the transaction is small or the transaction is being managed to avoid price impacts. Let us also assume that commissions and one half of the bid–asked spread together cost .5 percent of the value of a share. This is a one–way transaction cost, so buying and selling a share would cost 1 percent of the share's value. Based on the various estimates that we considered above, we can see that this is a very low transaction cost that would be available only to very large traders. Individual traders face much higher transaction costs.

Buying and selling together constitute a round–trip transaction, and this round–trip is also known as the **turnover** of a share. For large portfolios, it is common to measure the **turnover ratio** for the entire portfolio. Thus, if the entire portfolio value is exchanged during a year, the annual turnover ratio would be 100 percent. The frequency of trading, or the turnover ratio, becomes very important in assessing transaction costs.

In line with our earlier estimates and assumptions, if buying and selling a stock costs 1 percent of the stock's value, it becomes clear that frequent trading is very costly. With annual stock market returns of 10 percent on a buy–and–hold strategy, a 200 percent turnover ratio would cost 20 percent of the year's expected return, even with our very low transaction costs. Very large professionally managed portfolios frequently have a 100 percent annual turnover ratio. Based on our estimates, it appears that such a portfolio loses 1 percent of its total value to transaction costs. For such a practice to be worthwhile, the portfolio must make an additional 1 percent from the new stocks that are acquired.

Market Indexes

Market indexes provide a useful tool to summarize and to conceptualize the vast array of information generated by the continuous buying and selling of securities. At the same time, the use of market indexes presents new problems. First, many different indexes compete for attention. Second, indexes differ in construction and can differ widely in interpretation. There are indexes for almost all kinds of instruments. However, indexes for bonds, options, futures, and other instruments besides stocks are not well known or widely followed. Consequently, this section focuses exclusively on stock market indexes. The most widely quoted stock market indexes for the United States are the Dow Jones Industrial Average, the S&P 500, and the NYSE Composite Index. We consider each in turn.

Dow Jones Industrial Average (DJIA).   Without doubt, the most widely cited market index of any type is the Dow Jones Industrial Average. The national television network news programs report changes in the Dow each day, and when people say, "The market was up 12 points," they mean the Dow Jones index increased 12 points. Yet, as a gauge of the stock market, the Dow Jones Industrial Average is extremely limited. It reflects price movements of only 30 of the very largest industrial concerns listed on the NYSE. These are the mammoth firms, such as Exxon and IBM. The firms included in the Dow Jones Industrial Average vary as the economy changes, but they are always 30 of the largest, most powerful, industrial firms, often called **blue chip stocks**.

  The Dow is computed by adding the prices of the 30 stocks in the index and dividing by a special divisor:

$$\text{DJIA} = \frac{\sum_{n=1}^{30} P_n}{\text{Divisor}} \qquad \textbf{3.4}$$

where:
$$P_n = \text{the price of stock } n$$
$$\text{Divisor} = \text{the special DJIA divisor}$$

Because the prices are all added, the DJIA is a **price–weighted** index. Each stock contributes to the index value in proportion to its price. Because the index depends on the number of dollars from summing all the prices, the DJIA does not reflect the percentage change in the price of a share. For example, consider a stock that doubles from $1 to $2, and contrast this price change with a stock that moves from $100 to $101. In the first case, a stock has increased 100 percent, while in the latter case, a stock has increased just 1 percent. For the DJIA, both stock price changes have the same effect on the index, because the index depends on the sum of the prices, not the percentage price changes of the individual stocks.

For the index to reflect the level of prices in the market accurately, simply substituting one stock for another should not change the index. The same principle holds for stock dividends and stock splits. Therefore, the divisor must change to accommodate the change in stocks or the stock dividend or the stock split. To see how the divisor functions, assume that the current sum of all of the stock prices is $1689.375 and the current divisor is 0.889. This implies a DJIA value of $1689.375/ 0.889 = 1,900.31. Now we assume that Dow Jones decides to delete a stock priced at $6 and replace it with a stock that trades at $47. If the substitution is made, the new total of prices is $1,730.375. If the divisor is not changed, the new index value will be 1,946.43. Thus, the substitution of one stock for another, with no change in the divisor, manufactures a jump in the DJIA of 46 points. Obviously, this cannot be permitted or the index will become meaningless as a barometer of stock prices.

In this example of substituting one stock for another, the divisor must change to maintain a constant index value of 1,900.31 with the new total of prices of $1,730.375. Therefore, the new divisor must satisfy the following equation:

$$1900.31 = \frac{1730.375}{\text{New Divisor}}$$

$$\text{New Divisor} = \frac{1730.375}{1900.31} = .9106$$

Thus, to keep the index value unchanged, the new divisor must be .9106. Generalizing from this example, we see that Equation 3.5 gives the value for the new divisor:

$$\text{New Divisor} = \frac{\text{New Sum of Prices}}{\text{Index Value}} \qquad \textbf{3.5}$$

To find the new divisor, compute the new sum of prices that results from substituting one firm for another. Then divide this sum by the original index value.

One of the most attractive features of the Dow Jones index is its availability. In addition to being widely quoted, *The Wall Street Journal* features it every day, as Figure 3.8 shows. After all, Dow Jones and Company, Inc., publishes *The Wall Street Journal*. For each day of trading, a vertical line shows the high and low reached for the index that day. The horizontal tick mark indicates where the index closed. Current values of the Dow Jones index exceed 3,000, compared to some other indexes to be examined, which have values around 200. The level of the index signifies nothing important by itself; only relative movements matter.

Figure 3.8

The Dow Jones Averages

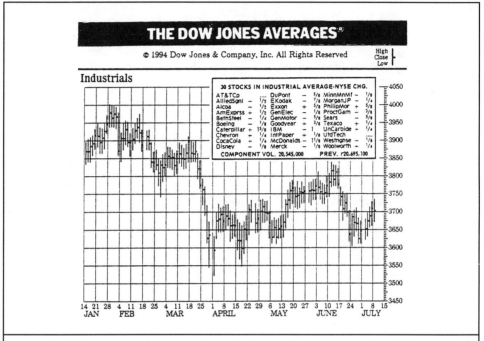

Source: *The Wall Street Journal*, June 24, 1994, p. C1. Reprinted by permission of *The Wall Street Journal*, © (1994) Dow Jones & Company, Inc. All rights reserved worldwide.

S&P 500. The Standard and Poor's (S&P) 500 Index is a broader market index than the Dow. As the name implies, the S&P index consists of 500 stocks drawn from various industries. The stocks included in the S&P 500 account for more than 80 percent of the market value of all stocks listed on the NYSE, although a few OTC–traded firms are included among the 500. Another feature of the S&P 500 is that each stock in the index is weighted according to the market value of its outstanding shares, so this index is a **value–weighted index**. For example, IBM receives a weight of almost 4 percent in the index, while General Cinema Corporation has a weight of about .05 percent. This reflects the fact that the market value of IBM's shares is about 80 times as large as those of General Cinema.

The value of the S&P 500 index is reported relative to the average value during the period of 1941–1943, which was assigned an index value of 10. As a simplified example of the way the index is computed, assume that the index consists of only three securities, ABC, DEF, and GHI. Table 3.9 shows how the value of the three firms would be weighted to calculate the index. For each stock, the total market value of the outstanding shares is computed. In the table, the three firms' shares have a total value of $19,000. If the value in the 1941–1943 period had

Table 3.9

Calculation of S&P 500

	Outstanding Shares		Price		Value
Company ABC	100	×	$50	=	$ 5,000
Company DEF	300	×	40	=	12,000
Company GHI	200	×	10	=	2,000
			Current Market Valuation	=	$19,000

If the 1941–43 value were $2,000, then $19,000 is to $2,000 as X is to 10.

$$\frac{\text{Current Market Valuation}}{\text{1941–43 Market Valuation}} \quad \frac{\$19,000}{\$2,000} = \frac{X}{10}$$

$$\$190,000 = \$2,000X$$
$$95.00 = X$$

Source: Chicago Mercantile Exchange, "Inside S&P 500 Stock Index Futures."

---

been $2,000, the current level of the index would be calculated as shown in the table, where "X" is the current index level with a value of 95.00. Mathematically, the calculation of the index is given by:

$$\text{S\&P Index} = \left(\frac{\sum_{i=1}^{500} N_i P_i}{\text{O.V.}} \right) 10 \qquad \textbf{3.6}$$

where:
O.V. = original valuation in 1941–43
N_i = number of shares outstanding for Firm i
P_i = price of shares for Firm i

The weights of each firm change as their prices rise and fall relative to other firms represented in the index. Firms such as Exxon, AT&T, and IBM represent large shares of the index, while other firms have only a minuscule impact. The index is computed on a continuous basis during the trading day and reported to the public.

The New York Stock Exchange Composite. The New York Stock Exchange Composite Index is broader than the S&P 500, since it includes all stocks listed on the New York Stock Exchange. At the end of 1993, there were 2,361 issues traded on the NYSE and, therefore, included in the index. The largest 50 companies account for about 39 percent of the value of the NYSE capitalization, with the smallest 1,670 making up the remaining 61 percent.

The weight of each stock in the index is proportional to its value, just as is the case with the S&P 500 index. Therefore, the NYSE index is a value–weighted index. The NYSE and S&P 500 indexes are calculated using a similar method. However, the NYSE Composite index takes its base date as December 31, 1965. At any subsequent point in time, the value of the NYSE index is given by:

$$\text{NYSE Index} = \left(\frac{\sum\limits_{i=1}^{1774} N_i\, P_i}{\text{O.V.}} \right) 50.0 \qquad \textbf{3.7}$$

where:
   O.V. = original value of all shares on the NYSE as of December 31, 1965

Equation 3.7 says that the value of the NYSE index equals the current value of all shares listed on the NYSE divided by the December 1965 base value, with the result being multiplied by 50 as a simple scaling device. This gives an initial value of 50.00 for the index. By late 1974, the index stood at 32.89, was as high as 81.02 in 1980, and exceeded 170.00 in early 1987. It closed at a value of 259.08 at the end of 1993.

Other Indexes.   There are many other indexes for the stock market in addition to those discussed in this section. For example, the AMEX has its own index as does the NASDAQ. These are not as closely followed as those discussed here. All of the indexes mentioned in this section are reported on a daily basis in *The Wall Street Journal* in the "Stock Market Data Bank" column, as shown in Figure 3.9.

Comparison of the Indexes

In this section, we briefly compare the three major stock market indexes. Figure 3.10 shows the history of the three indexes over the 1981–1994 period. As the graph shows, the indexes tended to move in a similar manner. However, there are important differences in the volatility and the correlations among the indexes.
   For 1981–1994, the standard deviation of the monthly percentage changes in the indexes was as follows:

DJIA	.0351
S&P 500	.0342
NYSE	.0341

As we might expect, the more stocks in the index, the less volatile the percentage price change. Also, because big firms tend to be more stable than small firms, we would expect a value–weighted index to be less volatile than a price–weighted index.

Figure 3.9

Stock Market Data Bank

STOCK MARKET DATA BANK								6/23/94

MAJOR INDEXES

HIGH	LOW (†365 DAY)		CLOSE	NET CHG	% CHG	†365 DAY CHG	% CHG	FROM 12/31	% CHG
DOW JONES AVERAGES									
3978.36	3449.93	30 Industrials	3699.09	− 25.68	− 0.69	+ 208.48	+ 5.97	− 55.00	− 1.47
1862.29	1495.72	20 Transportation	1625.48	+ 4.64	+ 0.29	+ 110.22	+ 7.27	− 136.84	− 7.76
256.46	177.76	15 Utilities	178.29	− 1.51	− 0.84	− 64.59	− 26.59	− 51.01	− 22.25
1447.06	1263.56	65 Composite	1292.23	− 4.93	− 0.38	+ 15.17	+ 1.19	− 88.80	− 6.43
456.27	416.31	Equity Mkt. Index	424.91	− 3.43	− 0.80	+ 1.42	+ 0.34	− 17.28	− 3.91
NEW YORK STOCK EXCHANGE									
267.71	243.14	Composite	248.29	− 1.68	− 0.67	+ 1.69	+ 0.69	− 10.79	− 4.16
327.93	292.06	Industrials	305.56	− 2.28	− 0.74	+ 9.40	+ 3.17	− 9.70	− 3.08
246.95	199.04	Utilities	203.80	− 0.89	− 0.43	− 24.94	− 10.90	− 26.12	− 11.36
285.03	231.21	Transportation	244.85	− 1.45	− 0.59	+ 11.77	+ 5.05	− 25.63	− 9.48
233.33	200.75	Finance	212.09	− 1.22	− 0.57	− 1.13	− 0.53	− 4.73	− 2.18
STANDARD & POOR'S INDEXES									
482.00	438.92	500 Index	449.63	− 3.46	− 0.76	+ 3.01	+ 0.67	− 16.82	− 3.61
560.59	501.83	Industrials	522.83	− 4.41	− 0.84	+ 11.80	+ 2.31	− 17.36	− 3.21
453.63	365.22	Transportation	390.77	− 0.54	− 0.14	+ 18.32	+ 4.92	− 34.83	− 8.18
189.49	148.69	Utilities	154.53	− 0.40	− 0.26	− 18.49	− 10.69	− 18.05	− 10.46
48.40	41.39	Financials	44.92	− 0.38	− 0.84	+ 0.57	+ 1.29	+ 0.65	+ 1.47
184.79	164.09	400 MidCap	164.55	− 1.98	− 1.19	+ 0.46	+ 0.28	− 14.83	− 8.27
NASDAQ									
803.93	688.72	Composite	700.85	− 11.89	− 1.67	+ 12.13	+ 1.76	− 75.95	− 9.78
851.80	707.76	Industrials	712.64	− 11.93	− 1.65	+ 0.01	− 0.00	− 93.20	− 11.57
956.91	836.03	Insurance	899.80	− 3.85	− 0.43	+ 62.87	+ 7.51	− 20.79	− 2.26
762.08	600.73	Banks	752.80	− 0.70	− 0.09	+ 152.07	+ 25.31	+ 63.37	+ 9.19
356.61	304.38	Nat. Mkt. Comp.	310.66	− 5.42	− 1.71	+ 6.28	+ 2.06	− 32.95	− 9.59
342.72	282.86	Nat. Mkt. Indus.	286.58	− 4.97	− 1.70	+ 1.78	+ 0.62	− 36.18	− 11.21
OTHERS									
487.89	427.60	Amex	431.25	− 1.97	− 0.45	+ 0.26	+ 0.06	− 45.90	− 9.62
305.87	274.21	Value-Line(geom.)	277.62	− 2.38	− 0.85	+ 3.41	+ 1.24	− 17.66	− 5.98
271.08	228.33	Russell 2000	242.50	− 2.78	− 1.13	+ 14.17	+ 6.21	− 16.09	− 6.22
4804.31	4383.10	Wilshire 5000	4438.93	− 37.86	− 0.85	+ 45.91	+ 1.05	− 218.90	− 4.70

†-Based on comparable trading day in preceding year.

Source: *The Wall Street Journal*, August 24, 1994, p. C2. Reprinted by permission of *The Wall Street Journal*, © (1994) Dow Jones & Company, Inc. All rights reserved worldwide.

In spite of the small differences in volatility, the correlations among all of these indexes are high, typically exceeding 95 percent. We might expect these results, because each index is based on a diversified portfolio. As the S&P 500 index represents about 80 percent of the value of NYSE stocks, there is an extremely high correlation between the S&P 500 and NYSE Composite indexes. The correlation

Figure 3.10

The DJIA, S&P 500, and NYSE Composite, 1970–1994

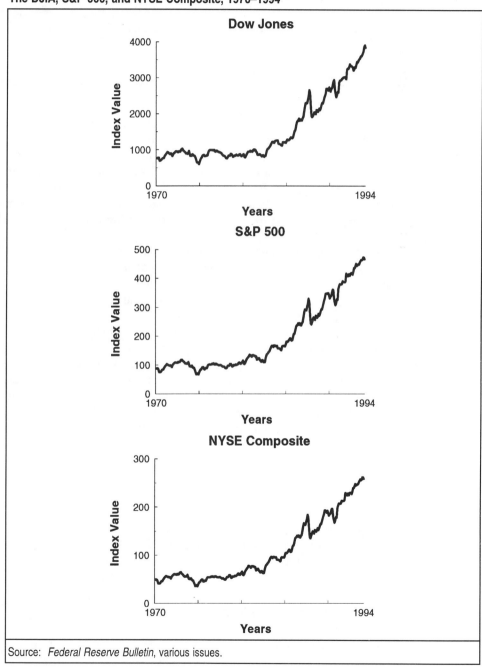

Source: *Federal Reserve Bulletin*, various issues.

Table 3.10

Correlations Among Three Stock Indexes, 1981–1994

	DJIA	S&P 500	NYSE Composite
DJIA	1.0000		
S&P 500	0.9573	1.0000	
NYSE Composite	0.9545	0.9965	1.0000

between the DJIA and the other two indexes is somewhat lower, reflecting the less diversified character of the Dow. Table 3.10 presents a correlation matrix for the three indexes during 1981–1994. The correlations are based on monthly percentage changes in the index values. In every case, the correlation is greater than 95 percent. The S&P 500 and NYSE are the most closely correlated. This is due to the large number of identical stocks and the great diversification represented by these portfolios, in addition to the fact that both of these indexes are value–weighted indexes.

Another important point to bear in mind is that these are all stock price indexes. They are normally reported without including dividends. As such, they typically do not provide a good indication of the total returns earned on the stocks in the index. To use the indexes accurately, one needs to be conscious of whether the dividends should be included or not.

In general, each index gives a measure of performance for some segment of the stock market. On any given day, they tend to move up or down together. Further, for reasons to be explored later, individual stocks tend to move in the same direction as the market indexes. Because of this, following the major indexes can give a good guide to general stock market activity. If you hold a portfolio of stocks, and the Dow Jones Industrial Average increases by 12 points on a given day, you can be almost certain that your portfolio increased in value. The indexes provide a very convenient way of summarizing this activity.

The Worldwide Stock Market

For many years after World War II, the U.S. stock market enjoyed a dominant position among world markets with a market value about as large as the rest of the world's through the 1970s. In the 1980s, this position changed dramatically. This section explores the growing importance of non–U.S. stock markets.

Alternative Trading Procedures

The U.S. stock market is a **continuous market**, a market in which a good is available for trading throughout the trading session. By contrast, some markets use an entirely different system. In a **call market**, each security is called for trading at a specific time and it can be traded only at that time. For example, Zurich and Frankfurt are call markets. A call market works as follows. An exchange employee calls a price for the share currently available for trading. Demand and supply of the shares are measured at the called price. Let us assume that the current price results in excess demand for the shares, with more shares wanted at the price than other participants are willing to supply. In this event, the exchange official will call a higher price and survey the supply and demand at the new price. This process continues until an equilibrium price is found. Then all transactions occur at that established price.

Markets may use several calls per day for each stock. By trading only one stock at a time, as some markets do, all attention focuses on a particular stock. This process concentrates the market's available liquidity on the stock being called, and may lead to more efficient pricing. This can be important in a market with low liquidity. Trading procedures are radically different at exchanges around the world with many exchanges using some variant of the call system.

Computerized trading is also surging in popularity. In the United States, the OTC market is essentially a computerized trading environment. Some exchanges have developed the computerization more fully. For example, the Toronto Exchange developed the Computer Assisted Trading System (CATS) and this system has been adopted by other exchanges in other countries.[22]

World Equity Market Capitalization

This section briefly considers the comparative capitalization of stock markets around the world. We begin by considering the largest stock markets in the world, those of Japan, the United States, Britain, Germany, and France. We then consider the smaller European exchanges, and we conclude by discussing some markets in emerging nations. As we will see, the market value of the top few major markets far exceeds the combined value of all other markets.

The World's Largest Stock Markets. For decades, the United States stock market has had the greatest value of any market. That is no longer true. Table 3.11 presents the market capitalization of the five largest markets and shows their annual growth rate over the 1983–1992 period. The United States has the largest market capitalization by far. However, this has not been true for the entire period. In 1989, for example, the market capitalization of Japan was the largest in the world. In the early 1990s, Japan lost almost half of its market value. Other countries in Table 3.11 have a higher growth rate than the United States, so the relative dominance of the United States equity markets is likely to decrease over time. Table 3.11 also shows the number of shares listed in these major markets.

---

[22] Bruno Solnik, *International Investments*, 2e, Reading, MA: Addison–Wesley, 1991, pp. 110–111.

Table 3.11

Market Capitalization of the World's Largest Markets

Country	Market Capitalization ($ billions)	Annualized Growth 1982–1992	Number of Domestic Firms Listed
United States	$4,757.9	9.63%	7,014
Japan	2,399.0	15.55	2,118
Britain	838.6	14.02	1,874
France	350.9	24.86	786
Germany	348.1	15.47	665

Source: International Finance Corporation, *Emerging Stock Markets Factbook 1993*.

Smaller European Stock Markets. Virtually every European country has its own stock market. Table 3.12 shows the market capitalization of selected European stock exchanges at the end of 1992, along with the rate of growth and the number of firms listed in these markets.

Stock Markets in Emerging Nations. Table 3.13 shows data on selected stock markets in emerging nations, presenting information on market capitalization, growth in market capitalization, and the number of shares listed. Some of these markets have recorded very rapid growth in the last decade. Nonetheless, market capitalization remains small, as does the volume of shares traded. In the coming years, it is likely

Table 3.12

Market Capitalization of the Smaller European Stock Markets

Country	Market Capitalization ($ billions)	Annualized Growth 1982–1992	Number of Domestic Firms Listed
Holland	$171.4	17.66%	314
Italy	115.3	18.91	228
Spain	99.0	24.68	399
Sweden	76.6	9.76	118
Belgium	64.2	19.51	171
Denmark	39.5	14.04	268
Austria	21.8	30.66	112
Luxembourg	12.0	7.49	59

Source: International Finance Corporation, *Emerging Stock Markets Factbook 1993*.

Table 3.13

Market Capitalization of Selected Emerging Stock Markets

Country	Market Capitalization ($ billions)	Annualized Growth 1982–1992	Number of Domestic Firms Listed
Mexico	$139.1	46.74%	195
Korea	107.4	37.69	688
Taiwan	101.1	29.54	256
Malaysia	94.0	15.22	366
India	65.1	24.67	6,700
Thailand	58.3	44.30	305
Brazil	45.3	11.60	565
Chile	29.6	27.56	245
China	18.3	N/A	53

Source: International Finance Corporation, *Emerging Stock Markets Factbook 1993.*

that the fledgling Chinese market will develop rapidly. Currently, the newly formed nations that comprised the Soviet Union are developing their economic plans and struggling to create viable financial markets. Considered from a global point of view, most of the growth in equity markets will come from smaller developed markets and these emerging markets. Consequently, the markets of the developed world will become less dominant over time. This change is likely to be slow. Using the classification of the International Finance Corporation of developed and emerging markets, the developed markets held 97.5 percent of all equity market capitalization in the world in 1983. In 1993, the developed markets still held 93 percent of the world's equity capital. For investors in countries with developed markets, investment in smaller and emerging markets can be a valuable tool in diversification.

Dual Listing and American Depositary Receipts

Some stocks are listed on several exchanges in different countries. For example, multinational pharmaceutical and oil firms may be traded on many different exchanges around the world. As we have seen for the NYSE, exchanges impose listing requirements before they accept a firm's shares for trading. Rules for listing differ markedly in different countries, with U.S. requirements being among the most restrictive. For example, a foreign firm wanting to list on a U.S. exchange must register with the Securities Exchange Commission and provide detailed financial reports that conform with U.S. accounting practices. In addition, the firm must disclose relevant information in conformity with U.S. laws. Many countries require far less disclosure than the United States, so these firms may be quite unwilling to reveal so much proprietary information merely to have their shares listed on U.S. exchanges.

To avoid these restrictions on trading in the United States, the American Depositary Receipt was created. An **American Depositary Receipt (ADR)** is a document showing that shares of stock have been deposited with a bank that acts as a depositary for the shares. The bank holds the foreign shares and trades ADRs that represent title to those shares it holds on deposit. In effect, the bank owns the shares, and trades claims against those shares. The purchaser of an ADR holds a claim for a certain number of shares deposited with the bank. The company whose stocks are held by the depositary pays dividends to the bank, and these dividends are paid in the currency of the issuing firm. The depositary exchanges the foreign funds into U.S. dollars and pays the American investor a dollar dividend.

In 1993, more than 800 foreign stocks were traded as ADRs in the United States. Some of these are listed on the NYSE and through NASDAQ. NYSE ADR volume was 3.647 billion shares (worth about $142 billion), while NASDAQ volume was 4.4 billion shares (worth about $73 billion). For the U.S. investor, ADRs provide an important vehicle for gaining investment access to foreign shares.

Foreign Stock Market Indexes

Virtually every stock market has some stock market index designed to summarize trading results. For the U.S., we have already seen that the major indexes are the S&P 500, the Dow Jones Industrial Average, and the NYSE Composite. Table 3.14 describes the indexes on major non–U.S. exchanges. These have received increasing attention in recent years and are likely to become more important. The Financial Times Stock Exchange (FTSE) from London and the Nikkei from Tokyo are reported daily in *The Wall Street Journal*. With the Dow having values of about 3,000, a jump

Table 3.14
———

Market Indexes for Major non–U.S. Exchanges

Country	Principal Exchange	Market Index
Great Britain	London Stock Exchange	FTSE 100 (Financial Times Stock Exchange)—100 stocks
Japan	Tokyo Stock Exchange	Nikkei Stock Average—225 stocks
France	Paris	CAC (Compagnie des Agents de Change)—249 stocks
Germany	Frankfurt	FAZ (Frankfurter Allgemeine Zeitung)—100 stocks
Hong Kong	Hong Kong	Hang Seng Index—33 stocks
Canada	Toronto	TSE 300 Composite Index (Toronto Stock Exchange)—300 stocks

of 50 points still attracts considerable attention. By contrast, the Nikkei index has values in the 25,000 range. Accordingly, jumps of 200–400 points are not so unusual for the Nikkei.

The Europe, Australia, Far East Index (EAFE) is compiled and reported by Morgan Stanley Capital International (MSCI). This index summarizes stock activity from 22 countries and is widely reported. A similar index, the FT–Actuaries, is published by the *Financial Times*, the British counterpart of *The Wall Street Journal*. There are different versions of the FT–Actuaries, some focusing on particular regions. Together, the FT–Actuaries cover about 2,500 stocks.

Summary

This chapter considered the rights and responsibilities of the stockholder and examined the organization of the stock market. The owner of a share of stock owns a fraction of the issuing corporation. As an owner, the shareholder has the right to participate in making key decisions and to share in the profits that the firm earns. As an owner, the shareholder has a claim on the value of the firm after the firm's obligations have been met. If the firm loses money continually and goes bankrupt, the law protects shareholders from losing more than their original investment.

The stock market consists of a number of organized stock exchanges and an active dealer market called the over–the–counter market. The stock exchanges, such as the New York Stock Exchange, are better known and are characterized by having a central physical location for trading. By contrast, the over–the–counter market matches buyers and sellers through the use of electronic communications.

In addition to the stock exchanges and the over–the–counter market, there are also important markets called the third and fourth markets. In the third market, large institutions work through brokers to consummate large block trades. By using this market, the institutions were able to avoid the high fixed commissions of the exchanges before discount brokerage was allowed, and currently they use these markets to keep their transactions private. In the fourth market, large institutions make block trades of stock, but without the assistance of intermediating brokers.

Recent years have witnessed dramatic changes in the stock market in the United States. The fixed commission system of the organized exchanges has been abandoned, and the over–the–counter market has moved toward a higher degree of efficiency through advances in electronics. Currently, the federal government has mandated that there will eventually be a single stock market, and the future promises more sweeping changes in the operation and organization of the market.

Questions and Problems

1. The chemical spill in Bhopal, India, at a Union Carbide plant raised fears that the settlement cost could exceed the value of the entire firm and throw Union Carbide into bankruptcy. If Union Carbide's share price had gone to zero, might investors have to contribute additional funds to cover the settlement? Why or why not?

2. Sometimes the interest of the shareholders and the managers of the firm might not agree. Is this ever a problem in practice? Can you give examples of ways in which their interests might disagree?

3. Why is stock ownership a residual claim on the firm?

4. What are the differences in liability for the owners of a corporation and a sole proprietorship?

5. Can a securities market function without a specialist?

6. What are the main differences between the OTC market and an organized securities exchange?

7. If you were a specialist for XYZ Corp. and saw that there were a large number of limit orders to buy at $12, how would adjust your inventory if current trading was at 12 1/4? Why?

8. In a well–functioning securities market, what would happen to a specialist or broker that consistently had the largest bid–asked spread? Why?

9. What informational advantages and disadvantages does the specialist have?

10. You had a limit order to sell Fly–by–Night Airlines at $12. *The Wall Street Journal* quotations show that the high for FBN was $12. Can you be sure that your shares sold? Why? What if the reported high price were 12 1/4?

11. Assume that you place an order to buy 10,000 shares of a thinly traded stock. What might be the effects of this on the share price? What does this suggest about the optimal size of portfolio management firms?

12. Assume that you manage a large portfolio dedicated to investments in the very largest industrial firms in the U.S. Which of the stock market indexes would be most relevant to your task? Which would be the second most suitable?

13. The discussion of foreign stock markets gives information on the risk level and level of returns experienced in these markets. Are these results consistent with the basic idea that higher expected returns tend to be accompanied by higher risk?

14. An investor buys a share of stock for $73 and holds it for three years, at which time the share is sold for $97. During the three years, dividends were received in the amount of $2.80, $2.80, and $3.15. What was the wealth relative for this investment, ignoring any proceeds from re–investing dividends? What was the annualized wealth relative?

15. Assume that you own 130 shares of a stock trading at $14. If the firm has a 4 percent stock dividend, what would you expect to own from the firm after the dividend? How has your wealth changed?

16. For Fly–by–Night Airlines, the current stock price is $12 and the current quarterly dividend is $.10. The most recently reported quarter of earnings was $.23. What is Fly–by–Night's dividend yield and P–E ratio? How does the P–E ratio respond to an increase in the stock price?

17. With FBN Airlines selling at $11, you buy 1,000 shares using the maximum margin of 50 percent. You are able to borrow funds from your broker at 14 percent and you sell FBN at $14 after holding it for one year. What is your wealth relative for this investment? What would it have been if no funds had been borrowed? Answer the same questions assuming that FBN was sold at $12.

CFA Questions

A. A firm's preferred stock often sells at yield below its bond because:
   a. owners of preferred stock have a prior claim on the firm's earnings.
   b. preferred stock generally carries a higher agency rating.
   c. corporations owning stock may exclude from income taxes most of the dividend income they receive.
   d. owners of preferred stock have a prior claim on a firm's assets in the event of liquidation.

B. A securities market characterized by individuals or organizations that buy and sell securities for their own inventories is called:
   a. a primary market.
   b. a secondary market.
   c. an over–the–counter market.
   d. an institutional market.

C. If the market prices of each of the 30 stocks in the Dow Jones Industrial Average (DJIA) all change by the same percentage amount during a given day, which stock will have the greatest impact on the DJIA?
   a. The one whose stock trades at the highest dollar price per share.
   b. The one whose total equity has the highest market value.
   c. The one having the greatest amount of equity in its capital structure.
   d. The one having the lowest volatility.

D. Assume you sell short 100 shares of common stock at $50 per share. With initial margin at 50%, what would be your rate of return if you repurchase the stock at $40 per share? The stock paid no dividends during the period, and you did not remove any money from the account before making the offsetting transaction.

a. 20%
b. 25%
c. 40%
d. 50%

E. Assume you purchase 100 shares of common stock on margin for $50 per share. Also assume the initial margin is 50% and the stock pays no dividend. What would be your rate of return if you sell the stock one year later for $60 per share? Ignore interest on margin and assume you did not remove any money from the account prior to selling the stock.

a. 16.7%
b. 20.0%
c. 33.3%
d. 40.0%

Suggested REALDATA Exercises

The following *REALDATA* exercises explore the concepts developed in this chapter: Exercises 25, 30, 33, 36, 37, 38, 39, 40, 44.

Suggested Readings

Abel, S. S. and E. A. Noser, Jr., "Trader to Broker," *The Complete Guide to Securities Transactions*, New York: Wiley, 1989, pp. 63–77.

Albers, R., "What to Expect From a Dividend Reinvestment Plan," *American Association of Individual Investors*, 13:4, April 1991, pp. 17–19.

Baer, H. L. and D. D. Evanoff, "Payments System Issues in Financial Markets That Never Sleep," Federal Reserve Bank of Chicago *Economic Perspectives*, 14:6, November/December 1990, pp. 2–15.

DeGennaro, R. P., "Settlement Delays and Stock Prices," Federal Reserve Bank of Cleveland *Economic Review*, 25:4, 1989 Quarter 4, pp. 19–28.

Electronic Bulls and Bears: U.S. Securities Markets and Information Technology, Washington, DC: U.S. Government Printing Office, September 1990.

Fortin, R. D., R. Grube, and O. Joy, "Bid–Ask Spreads for OTC NASDAQ Firms," *Financial Analysts Journal*, 46:3, May/June 1990, pp. 76–79.

France, V. G., "The Regulation of Margin Requirements," *Margins and Market Integrity*, Chicago: Probus Publishing, 1991, pp. 1–47.

Hardouvelis, G. and S. Peristiani, "Do Margin Requirements Matter? Evidence from U.S. and Japanese Stock Markets," Federal Reserve Bank of New York *Quarterly Review*, 14:4, Winter 1989–90, pp. 16–35.

Investors' Rights Manual, "Dividends and Interest: Who Gets Payments After a Trade?" *American Association of Individual Investors*, 12:4, April 1990, pp. 8–11.

Schwert, G., "Stock Market Volatility," *Financial Analysts Journal*, 46:3, May/June 1990, pp. 23–34.

Solnik, B., "The Distribution of Daily Stock Returns and Settlement Procedures: The Paris Bourse," *Journal of Finance*, 45:5, December 1990, pp. 1601–1609.

Treynor, J. L., "The Economics of the Dealer Function," *Financial Analysts Journal*, 43:6, November/December 1987, pp. 27–34.

Wagner, W. H., "Broker to Floor," *The Complete Guide to Securities Transactions*, New York: Wiley, 1989, pp. 79–90.

CHAPTER FOUR

The Primary Market and Investment Banking

Overview

When most people think of buying or selling securities, they naturally think first of the large stock exchanges, such as the New York Stock Exchange. These are clearly the most visible institutions in the securities business. However, the securities traded on the New York Stock Exchange are being traded on a **secondary market**—a market for already existing securities.

Before securities reach the secondary market, they must be issued by corporations or governments. This initial offering of securities takes place in the **primary market**, the market for the issuance of new securities. The primary market is much less visible than the secondary market, but it is crucial to the world of investments.

This chapter explores the primary market and the important role played in it by the investment banker. In the United States, investment banking has been kept almost totally distinct from the more familiar commercial banking by a law known as the Glass–Steagall Act. Instead of accepting deposits, as does a commercial bank, the investment banking firm aids corporations and governments in the initial distribution of securities. In doing so, the investment banker typically acts as a consultant to the institution offering the securities, aids in distributing securities, and often bears considerable risk in the process of the initial distribution.

The Primary Market: Size and Scope

New issues in the primary market can be distinguished by the type of issuer and the type of security being issued. The basic issuers of securities are governments and corporations. The securities offered may be either bonds, common stock, or preferred stock. **Preferred stock** is a cross between a bond and common stock. It normally pays a fixed dividend, but the firm is obligated to make the payments only if enough funds are available. Also, the firm need not retire the preferred stock

Table 4.1

New Security Issues of Corporations

Millions of dollars

Type of issue, offering, or issuer	1991	1992	1993	1993 Aug.	Sept.	Oct.	Nov.	Dec.	1994 Jan.^r	Feb.	Mar.
1 All issues¹	465,246	559,827ʳ	765,721	52,955	64,495ʳ	56,143	54,813ʳ	44,394ʳ	57,649	47,918ʳ	53,623
2 Bonds²	389,822	471,502ʳ	642,543	43,688	53,837	45,608	43,214	33,863ʳ	51,612	39,177ʳ	43,030
By type of offering											
3 Public, domestic	286,930	378,058ʳ	487,924ʳ	40,447	49,132	42,645	39,525	32,282ʳ	46,168	31,860ʳ	40,492
4 Private placement, domestic³	74,930	65,853	116,240	n.a.	n.a.	n.a.	n.a.	n.a.	n.a.	n.a.	n.a.
5 Sold abroad	27,962	27,591	38,379ᶜ	3,241	4,705	2,963	3,689	1,582	5,444	7,317ʳ	2,538
By industry group											
6 Manufacturing	86,628	82,058	88,002ʳ	6,132	4,036	3,273	3,334	3,068	4,635	3,511ʳ	1,716
7 Commercial and miscellaneous	36,666	43,111ʳ	60,443ʳ	2,331	2,378	6,306	3,078	2,525	2,869	2,362ʳ	3,419
8 Transportation	13,598	9,979	10,756ʳ	723	288	1,416	648	895	693	100	870
9 Public utility	23,944	48,055	56,272ʳ	3,474	5,163	2,585	1,763	2,336	2,566	1,868ʳ	1,489
10 Communication	9,431	15,394	31,950ᶜ	2,979	2,237	2,991	1,015	2,001	2,495	2,212	2,090
11 Real estate and financial	219,555	272,904ʳ	395,121ʳ	28,049	39,735	29,039	33,376	23,039ʳ	38,354	29,124ʳ	33,447
12 Stocks²	75,424	88,325	123,009	9,267	10,658ʳ	10,535	11,599ʳ	10,531	5,727ʳ	7,702ʳ	9,099ᶜ
By type of offering											
13 Public preferred	17,085	21,339	20,533	3,319	1,358	2,549	1,385	650	1,592	1,318	1,969
14 Common	48,230	57,118	90,559	5,948	9,336	7,987	10,209	9,881	4,135	6,383	7,131
15 Private placement³	10,109	9,867	11,917	n.a.	n.a.	n.a.	n.a.	n.a.	n.a.	n.a.	n.a.
By industry group											
16 Manufacturing	24,111	22,723	22,271	1,961	2,274	2,121	2,169	2,267			
17 Commercial and miscellaneous	19,418	20,231	25,761	1,457	2,242	1,842	3,061	1,970			
18 Transportation	2,439	2,595	2,237	466	153	128	221	162	n.a.	n.a.	n.a.
19 Public utility	3,474	6,532	7,050	582	908	1,103	371	129			
20 Communication	475	2,366	3,439	115	248	18	1,074	1,603			
21 Real estate and financial	25,507	33,879	49,889	4,675	4,666	5,323	4,486	4,381	2,397	3,800	4,360

1. Figures represent gross proceeds of issues maturing in more than one year; they are the principal amount or number of units calculated by multiplying by the offering price. Figures exclude secondary offerings, employee stock plans, investment companies other than closed-end, intracorporate transactions, equities sold abroad, and Yankee bonds. Stock data include ownership securities issued by limited partnerships.

2. Monthly data cover only public offerings.
3. Monthly data are not available.
SOURCES. IDD Information Services, Inc., Securities Data Company, and the Board of Governors of the Federal Reserve System.

Source: *Federal Reserve Bulletin*, July 1994, p. A34.

as it normally does a bond by returning the principal. A security is retired when all promised payments have been made.

Of the three types of securities mentioned—common stock, bonds, and preferred stock—only corporations issue common stock and preferred stock. Since stock, particularly common stock, represents an ownership claim on the issuing entity, it is clear that governments cannot issue stock. Therefore, it is necessary to separate the two kinds of issuers. Table 4.1 presents the recent record of new securities issued by U.S. corporations, with the issues being broken down by broad industrial classifications. For all issues combined—common stock, bonds, and preferred stock—the total has grown steadily over the recent years. Figure 4.1 shows this growth and the changing mix of common stock, preferred stock, and bonds. In 1983, for the first time, the total of the new issues exceeded $100 billion, and it has generally continued to grow since then. As the table shows, corporations issued about $766 billion of securities in 1993.

Figure 4.1

Corporate Security Issues

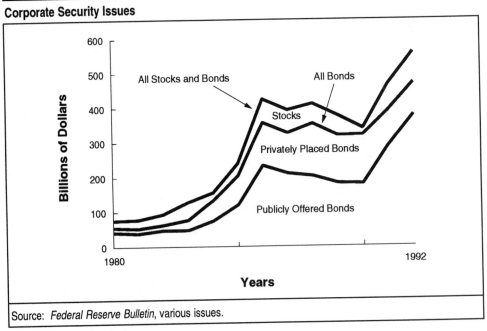

Source: *Federal Reserve Bulletin*, various issues.

Private Placements and Public Offerings

As Table 4.1 shows, there are two types of offerings—public offerings and private placements. In a **public offering**, the issuer offers the security to the public at large, giving any investor the right to purchase the new issue. In a public offering, the entire process of issuance is governed by regulations of the Securities and Exchange Commission (SEC).[1] As an alternative to making a public offering, many companies prefer to make a private placement. In a **private placement**, an entire bond issue is sold to a single buyer, or small consortium of buyers, without the issue ever being made available to the public.

There are several advantages to private placements. If a corporation makes a private placement, the process of issuing the security escapes SEC governance. Because the SEC imposes fairly rigorous and costly rules on the process of publicly issuing securities, it can be cheaper for the firm to engage in a private placement. Another advantage for the issuing firm is the chance to avoid too much public disclosure of its business plans. This disclosure is required by the SEC in any public offering. For a firm engaged in an industry where secrecy is important, particularly

---

[1]Chapter 6 discusses the purpose and function of the Securities and Exchange Commission and other regulatory bodies.

for high technology firms in the computing or defense industries, making a public disclosure can be very undesirable.

In private placements, the buyers of the securities tend to be large cash–rich institutions, such as insurance companies. For these buyers, there are certain advantages to participating in a private placement. Usually bonds that are privately placed pay an interest rate slightly higher than that available in a public offering. For large investors, even a small interest rate differential can be important. For the buyer of a privately placed issue there is also an important disadvantage. The holder of a privately placed security cannot sell the bond, because it has never been scrutinized as required for a public offering. This means that the buyer of a privately placed issue sacrifices liquidity in order to obtain the higher rate of interest paid on private placements. **Liquidity** is a measure of how easily an asset may be converted into cash without loss of value.

As Table 4.1 shows, about 35 percent of the new bond issues are privately placed, with the rest being offered publicly. It is also apparent, particularly from Figure 4.1, that the importance of private placements has been growing in recent years. Some common and preferred stock is also privately placed, but only very small amounts.

Relative Size of Issuers

The vast majority of stock issues are for common stock. In recent years, preferred stock has fallen out of favor as a financing vehicle, in part because corporations must pay preferred stock dividends from after–tax income. This contrasts with bonds, because the interest payments are paid from before–tax income, providing an important tax advantage to corporations that issue bonds rather than preferred stock.[2] Considering the dollar volumes reported in Table 4.1, it is striking to notice that bonds dwarf stocks by a ratio of about five–to–one. As Figure 4.1 shows, this has been true since 1980. In spite of the fact that common stocks generally attract more investor attention than the bond market, the stock market is really quite small compared to the bond market, at least with the primary market. In the secondary market, stocks are traded much more frequently than bonds, so the degree of activity in stock trading is really higher than its size in the primary market would indicate.

The largest issuer of securities in the world is the U.S. government, as shown in Table 4.2, which presents the recent public debt offerings by the U.S. govern-

---

[2] This view would be disputed by some, however. See Merton H. Miller, "Debt and Taxes," *Journal of Finance*, May 1977, pp. 261–276.

Table 4.2

Public Borrowing of the U.S. Government

Year	Amount ($ millions)
1976	82,913
1977	53,516
1978	59,106
1979	33,641
1980	70,515
1981	79,329
1982	134,912
1983	212,425
1984	170,817
1985	197,269
1986	236,187
1987	150,070
1988	166,139
1989	141,806
1990	264,453
1991	276,802
1992	310,918
1993	248,619

Source: *Federal Reserve Bulletin*, various issues, Table 1.38.

ment.[3] The federal government, together with state, county, and municipal governments and agencies, constitutes another vast segment of the primary market.

In addition to the U.S. government, state and local governments issue vast quantities of securities, called **municipals**, or **municipal bonds**. These securities, discussed in Chapter 2, are often exempt from federal and state income taxation. As shown in Table 4.3, this market is also very large, as measured by the dollar volume of new security issues, and has been growing in size relative to the market for corporate securities. When we consider the tendency of corporations to issue bonds in preference to stocks, and add the billions of dollars in bonds issued by governments, it becomes even more apparent how large the bond market is in relation to the stock market.

---

[3] In a certain sense, Table 4.2 understates the magnitude of the U.S. government's role. The figures in Table 4.2 show only the change in the level of the government debt. Each year some debt is repaid and replaced with new debt, however. So the amount of securities issued by the government is really larger than it appears. For example, if we consider Treasury bills (securities issued with original maturities of one year or less) alone, over $300 billion per year is being issued.

Table 4.3

Securities Issued by State and Local Governments

Millions of dollars

Type of issue or issuer, or use	1991	1992	1993	1993					1994		
				Aug.	Sept.	Oct.	Nov.	Dec.	Jan.ʳ	Feb.ʳ	Mar.
1 All issues, new and refunding[1]	154,402	215,191	279,945	24,438	23,504	21,900	18,094	24,520	16,560	14,698	15,461
By type of issue											
2 General obligation	55,100	78,611	90,599	6,414	5,884	7,495	6,422	6,542	4,622	4,365	7,371
3 Revenue	99,302	136,580	189,346	18,024	17,620	14,405	11,672	17,978	11,000	8,553	8,090
By type of issuer											
4 State	24,939	25,295	28,285	2,319	2,758	3,216	885	1,265	1,235	921	3,302
5 Special district or statutory authority[2]	80,614	129,686	164,169	13,769	13,113	9,875	10,992	16,485	10,672	10,263	6,145
6 Municipality, county, or township	48,849	60,210	84,972	8,307	7,476	8,418	4,528	6,770	4,653	3,514	6,014
7 Issues for new capital	116,953	120,272	91,434	8,001	8,759	7,261	6,734	9,543	5,418	8,268	10,114
By use of proceeds											
8 Education	21,121	22,071	17,098	1,883	1,886	547	1,416	1,227	1,573	2,292	1,859
9 Transportation	13,395	17,334	9,571	1,062	789	304	979	429	293	1,223	401
10 Utilities and conservation	21,039	20,058	11,802	1,646	1,255	593	687	1,454	480	243	540
11 Social welfare	25,648	21,796	n.a.	681	2,199	1,764	n.a.	2,171	825	1,660	1,670
12 Industrial aid	8,376	5,424	6,381	212	329	518	673	1,272	392	1,316	470
13 Other purposes	30,275	33,589	29,519	2,544	2,362	3,737	1,820	2,990	5,558	8,774	n.a.

1. Par amounts of long-term issues based on date of sale.
2. Includes school districts.

SOURCES. Securities Data Company beginning January 1993; *Investment Dealer's Digest* before then.

Source: *Federal Reserve Bulletin*, June 1994, p. A34.

The Process of Issuing Securities

This section describes the process by which a corporate issuer brings a new security to market. Developing a good relationship with an investment banker is very important to the financial management of a corporation. Most firms attempt to maintain a close working relationship with one or two investment bankers to whom they can turn when the need arises. Assuming that such a relationship has been established, the corporation and the investment banker would be in regular contact as the financing needs of the firm evolve over time.

The investment banker normally fulfills three functions for the corporation in the process of issuing a new security:

1. consulting,
2. forming a distribution network,
3. bearing risk involved in the issuance of the new security.

As the firm prepares to issue the new security, it must resolve questions such as the timing of the issuance and the pricing of the security. In a public offering, the issuer must meet many regulations of the SEC as well. The investment banker plays a critical role in helping the issuer with all of these matters.

The Investment Banker as Consultant

In the role of consultant to the issuing firm, the investment banker works in three main areas:

1. preparing the necessary registration and informational materials,
2. timing the issuance,
3. setting the price at which the security will be issued.

One of the important SEC requirements for the public offering of new securities is the formal disclosure of the firm's financial condition and future plans. This is done in a **prospectus**, which is a legal document required by the SEC. The investment banker often plays an important advisory role in creating the prospectus.

The prospectus includes a report of the firm's financial condition, the names of the principal officers in the corporation, and an accounting of their holdings in the firm. The document also gives information about the firm's line of business and its plans for future expansion. This information must be detailed and highly accurate. Since the firm offers the securities for sale through the prospectus, any error in the prospectus could make the firm liable for losses sustained by investors. Consequently, the prospectus is usually written by the legal staff in legal prose. The authors of the prospectus usually include top management from the issuing firm, the legal staff of the issuing firm, and legal specialists in prospectus writing. Some of the expertise for the prospectus usually comes from the investment banker.

All firms prefer to issue their securities when they can sell them for a high price. For stocks, the ideal would be to issue securities when the (secondary) stock market peaks. The ideal time to issue bonds occurs when interest rates are very low, helping to ensure a high price for the bonds.[4] Investment bankers often give firms advice on this issue of timing. Another crucial aspect of timing concerns the commercial policy of the firm. Firms, particularly small or relatively new ones, often issue securities after introducing a new product that is expected to be quite successful.

Pricing of the securities is very important as well. Since investment bankers are constantly engaged in the primary market, they should be in a good position to advise on the proper pricing of the new security. The goal of the pricing strategy is to set the highest price that will allow all of the issue to be sold in a fairly short period of time. (An issue that sells out rapidly is said to go **out the window**.) If the price is set too low, the issue will sell out virtually immediately, but it will not bring the firm as much cash as it could have obtained had it been priced properly. On the other hand, an issue that is priced too high will not be sold out promptly. (Such securities are said to be **sticky issues**.)

---

[4]As explained in Chapter 7, bond prices and interest rates are inversely related. Other things being equal, this means that bond prices are at their highest when interest rates are at their lowest.

Figure 4.2

Organization of the Distribution Network

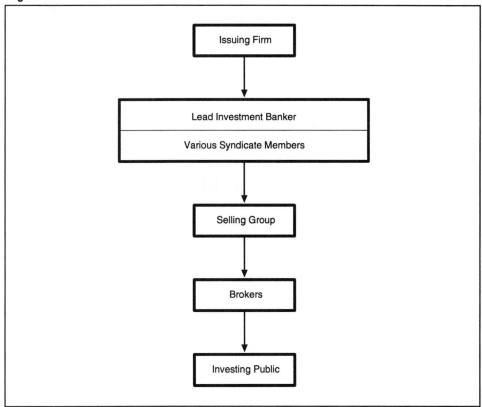

The Distribution Network

Figure 4.2 shows the typical structure of the distribution network. The issuing corporation creates the security, and passes it to the lead bank and the syndicate members. The **lead bank** is the investment bank with primary responsibility for issuing a particular security. The **syndicate members** are other investment banking firms that have committed themselves to assisting in the flotation of a given security. The **flotation** is the initial sale of the security. From the numerous members of the syndicate, the securities are distributed to members of the **selling group**, those investment houses that participate to a smaller degree in the distribution process. Only when the securities reach the brokers is the point of contact with the public achieved. The brokers are in direct contact with their customers, who are the final investors in the securities.

Officially, only the prospectus offers securities for sale. For that matter, only investors who have received a copy of the prospectus are allowed to buy the

Figure 4.3

A Typical Tombstone

This announcement constitutes neither an offer to sell nor a solicitation of an offer to buy these securities. The offering is made only by the Prospectus, copies of which may be obtained in any State from such of the undersigned and others as may lawfully offer these securities in such State.

June 27, 1994

$75,000,000

Surgical Health Corporation

11½% Senior Subordinated Notes Due 2004

Price 100%

(Plus accrued interest, if any, from date of issuance)

Smith Barney Inc.

Donaldson, Lufkin & Jenrette
Securities Corporation

Alex. Brown & Sons
Incorporated

Source: *The Wall Street Journal*, June 27, 1994.

security anyway. Securities are often announced, however, in *The Wall Street Journal* with advertisements such as those shown in Figure 4.3. This kind of advertisement is known as a **tombstone**, due to its size, shape, and color. The tombstone announces the firm making the issue, the price, and the number of securities. It also lists the members of the syndicate. Notice the disclaimer, "This announcement is neither an offer to sell nor a solicitation of an offer to buy any of these securities. The offer is made only by the Prospectus." Because of the strict regulations on

Table 4.4

██████████████

Typical Spreads in a Common Stock Issuance

Price per Share	Received by
$100.00	Corporation
101.25	Lead investment bank
103.00	Other syndicate members
104.50	Selling group members
106.00	Brokers making sales directly to the public

security issuance, an obvious advertisement to sell securities has to say that it is not offering securities for sale.

To illustrate this process of issuing a security, consider a firm making a fairly large size issue ($20 million to $50 million), with the corporation receiving $100 per share of common stock, as shown in Table 4.4. As the security flows through the network of intermediaries, each layer tacks on its profit margin. By the time the security reaches the members of the public, its final price may well be 6 percent or more above the amount received by the corporation. The prices shown in Table 4.4 assume that the security flows through the entire chain, but this will not be true of all of the shares of stock in the issue. For example, the lead bank also markets the shares through its own internal distribution network. The total price difference between the price paid by the final investor and the amount the issuing firm receives is known as the **spread**, and the lead bank keeps a much greater percentage of the spread on securities it sells itself.

The Service and Cost of Risk–Bearing

The forming of the distribution network and the marketing of securities are parts of the retailing function. But the compensation that the investment banker receives is not only for acting as a retailer. The investment banker has two basic ways of distributing securities for the issuer; he may act as an underwriter for the issue, or he may undertake to sell the issue on a best efforts basis. If the investment banker acts as an **underwriter**, the bank actually buys the securities from the issuing firm and then tries to sell them to the public at a profit. In this case, the investment bank bears a great deal of risk, and the spread constitutes the compensation for the investment banker's risk–bearing service as well as the distribution cost. If the investment bank distributes the issue on a **best efforts basis**, it promises to sell the securities at the best price it can obtain. However, the issuing firm continues to own the securities during the distribution process, and the issuer bears the risk associated with price fluctuations.

The services of investment bankers do not come cheaply. The talents of the firm's employees and the risk–bearing service that the firm provides demand a high level of compensation. This section examines the compensation paid, either directly

Table 4.5

Spread Size by Size Type of Issue

	Spread	
Size of Issue ($ millions)	Common Stock	Bonds
Under .5	11.3%	7.4%
.5 – .9	9.7	7.2
1.0 – 1.9	8.6	7.0
2.0 – 4.9	7.4	4.2
5.0 – 9.9	6.7	1.5
10.0 – 19.9	6.2	1.0
20.0 – 49.9	4.9	1.0
50.0 and over	2.3	0.8

Source: Block and Hirt, *Foundations of Financial Management*, Homewood, IL: Richard D. Irwin, 1985, p. 324.

or indirectly, to the investment banker. These costs of issuing securities—known as **flotation costs**—have a strong impact on the cost of acquiring funds and also on the investment desirability of new issues.

Corporations pay their investment bankers in two ways.[5] First, they typically pay out–of–pocket expenses for consulting services, legal fees, and document preparation. Second, the issuer offers securities at a price that allows the investment bankers, and other members of the distribution network, to make a profit. Of these two classes of expense, the second is generally the larger.

When an investment banking syndicate acts as an underwriter, the price the corporation receives must be low enough to allow the syndicate to distribute the securities to the public at a profit. The spread constitutes the gross margin for the distribution network, but in an issue that is underwritten, a large portion of the spread is compensation for bearing risk.

While the prices of Table 4.4 are fairly representative, it should be recognized that the spread depends on the size of the issue and the kind of security that is under consideration. As Table 4.5 shows, spreads are typically lower for debt issues than for issues of common stock. Further, the spread, as a percentage of the proceeds, is smaller the larger the issue size. For very small issues, flotation costs

---

[5]This section focuses only on the process for corporations. Governments and their agencies operate somewhat differently. Many are required by law to offer securities under a process of competitive bidding, rather than through an underwriting system. The U.S. government issues securities through its own special media, including Federal Reserve Banks and U.S. government security dealers.

Table 4.6

■■■■■■■■■■■■■■■■

Spread Size by Size Type of Issue

Size of Issue ($ millions)	Common Stock	Out–of–Pocket	Total
Under .5	11.3%	7.3%	18.6%
.5 – .9	9.7	4.9	14.6
1.0 – 1.9	8.6	3.0	11.6
2.0 – 4.9	7.4	1.7	9.1
5.0 – 9.9	6.7	1.0	7.7
10.0 – 19.9	6.2	.6	6.8
20.0 – 49.9	4.9	.8	5.7
50.0 and over	2.3	.3	2.6

Source: Block and Hirt, *Foundations of Financial Management*, Homewood, IL: Richard D. Irwin, 1985, p. 324.

become prohibitively expensive. In addition to the spread, the issuing firm also pays certain out–of–pocket expenses mentioned earlier. While smaller than the spread, they can add significantly to total flotation costs, as shown in Table 4.6. For small issues, total flotation costs approach 20 percent. For the largest issues, they can be less than 3 percent. The issuing firm must make at least the total flotation cost on the investment being financed by the security issuance in order to break even. This is a sobering fact for the securities investor, because it indicates just how much profit the firm must make before the investor can expect a positive return to be generated on the security.

The Green Shoe Option

For underwritten new issues, the investment banker often has a Green Shoe option. The **Green Shoe option** is the right of the investment banking firm to buy an additional number of securities from the issuer at the original price. The option gets its name because it was first used in an offering by the Green Shoe Company. Usually, the number of securities is limited to some fraction of the total issuance size. The chance to buy additional securities from the issuer at the issue price is a valuable right. So, in effect, the Green Shoe option is a form of compensation that the issuing corporation offers to the investment banker.

As an example of the Green Shoe option, assume that the issue price for a share is $100 and that the issue goes out the window and quickly moves up in price to $110 in the **aftermarket**—the market for the security shortly after its issuance. If the investment bank has a Green Shoe option, it can buy additional shares at $100 and sell them in the open market for $110. The rationale for the Green Shoe option is that it allows the investment banker to meet customer demand if an offer is over–subscribed by interested investors. The option typically remains available to

Table 4.7
━━━━━━━━━

Value of the Green Shoe Option as a Percentage of the Security's Value

Interest Rate (%)	Percentage of Underpricing		
	0	1	2
	Low–Volatility Security		
8	4.67	5.23	5.83
10	4.75	5.32	5.93
12	4.84	5.41	6.03
	Average–Volatility Security		
8	6.25	6.81	7.40
10	6.33	6.90	7.49
12	6.41	6.98	7.58
	High–Volatility Security		
8	7.83	8.39	8.98
10	7.91	8.48	9.07
12	7.99	8.56	9.15

Source: Robert Hansen, "Evaluating the Costs of a New Equity Issue," *Midland Corporate Finance Journal*, 4:1, Spring 1986, pp. 42–55.

the investment bank for about 30 days following the initial issuance. The value of an option depends upon the interest rate and the riskiness of the good on which the option exists.

Generally, the Green Shoe option has considerable value. Table 4.7 presents the typical costs for granting the Green Shoe option in stock issuances. The table categorizes the cost depending upon the level of interest rates, the volatility of the stock being issued, and the percentage the stock is underpriced. These estimates indicate that the Green Shoe option costs the issuer from 4.67 percent to 9.15 percent of the entire value of the stock. This is a very substantial portion of the total cost of issuance.[6]

For example, assume that interest rates are 10 percent, the security is correctly priced (0 percent underpricing in Table 4.7), the stock is of normal volatility, and the Green Shoe option allows the investment bank to purchase up to 15 percent of an initial issuance of $35 million. In Table 4.7 the cost of the option

---

[6]This discussion of the Green Shoe option and this example are drawn from Robert Hansen, "Evaluating the Costs of a New Equity Issue," *Midland Corporate Finance Journal*, 4:1, Spring 1986, pp. 42–55.

in this case is 6.33 percent. For our example, the investment bank can purchase $5,250,000 ($35,000,000 times .15) in shares at the issue price. With the 6.33 percent value of this option, the issuer effectively pays the investment bank $332,325 ($5,250,000 times .0633) in the form of the Green Shoe option.

Investment Bankers and Investing in New Issues

In spite of the high flotation costs just discussed, many new issues do quite well for investors. Pricing of new issues is really an art, rather than a science. A price set too low means that the issuer does not receive full value, while a price set too high means that security purchasers are likely to have low returns. Whether a new issue should have high returns immediately upon issuance depends largely on whether one is an issuer or an investor.

It might appear that investors should seek investment bankers who issue securities that generate large profits. Similarly, firms might choose investment bankers who price securities very aggressively, so that they get the maximum price for their securities. In fact, it seems that an equilibrium can be achieved only when the new issues offer a return comparable with investment opportunities available elsewhere. Otherwise, either investors or the issuing corporations will be displeased and will learn to avoid particular investment bankers. That, of course, would be disastrous for investment bankers, since their role as an intermediary between the corporation and the investors is based on having good relations with both.

Initial Public Offerings

A firm engages in an **initial public offering** (IPO) when it offers securities to the public for the first time. An established firm, such as Exxon, might issue new securities in the primary market, but these issuances would not be an IPO because Exxon has already issued securities before. As an example of an IPO, a partnership might incorporate and sell stock to the public.

Figure 4.4 presents the number of IPOs by month from 1960–1987, and it clearly shows that IPOs occur in waves. A period of intense IPO issuance is called a **hot issue market**. The figure shows that the mid–1980s were very hot, as was the 1968–1969 period. By contrast, 1974–1978 was virtually dead, coinciding with and following the recession of the mid–1970s. For example, there were 780 IPOs in 1969 and only 9 in 1974.[7] Recession struck in 1990, and there were few IPOs, and the top 15 investment banking firms only launched $10 billion of new issues. Through 1994, there has been no dramatic comeback in the primary market.

Figure 4.5 shows the initial return and the returns in the first month of issuance on these IPOs for the same period, 1960–1987. These returns also followed

---

[7]See R. G. Ibbotson, J. L. Sindelar, and J. R. Ritter, "Initial Public Offerings," *Journal of Applied Corporate Finance*, 1:2, Summer 1988, p. 41. Their study did not consider issues for less than $1.5 million and excluded a few other types of special offerings.

Figure 4.4

Number of Offerings by Month for SEC Registered IPOs

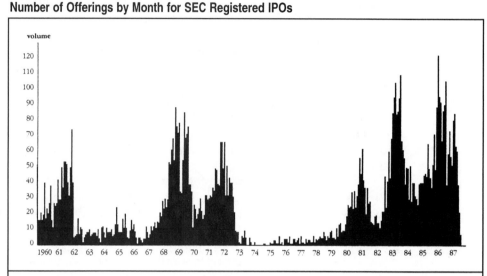

Source: Ibbotson, R. G., J. L. Sindelar, and J. R. Ritter, "Initial Public Offerings," *Journal of Applied Corporate Finance*, 1:2, Summer 1988, p. 40.

a definite pattern, with the largest initial returns preceding the hot issues market by about six months.

Figure 4.5

Average Initial Returns by Month for SEC Registered IPOs

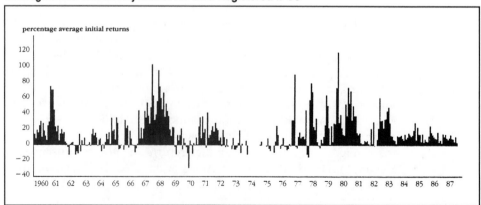

Source: Ibbotson, R. G., J. L. Sindelar, and J. R. Ritter, "Initial Public Offerings," *Journal of Applied Corporate Finance*, 1:2, Summer 1988, p. 40.

Asymmetric Information and the Pricing of IPOs

The returns in Figure 4.5 appear to be extremely high, and numerous researchers have concluded that the returns on IPOs are so high that they violate the normal relationship between risk and return. Thus, other scholars have attempted to explain the high returns. One attractive thesis was advanced by Kevin Rock.[8] Rock points out that potential investors in the security possess **asymmetric information**, a condition that arises when one party has information that is superior to another's. In the case of new issues, some potential investors may better assess the true value of the securities than do other investors. The investors with the good information are said to be **informed investors**. Rock's argument assumes that underwriters sometimes price the securities too high, and sometimes too low. When the underwriter offers an underpriced security, the informed investors will flock to buy as much of the security as possible. Similarly, the informed investors will avoid overpriced issues. This means that the uninformed investors buy little of the underpriced issues, and they buy a great proportion of the overpriced securities.

Underwriters, according to Rock, must price securities in a way that gets them sold. The underwriter must attract both the informed and the uninformed investor. This leads to a systematic underpricing of IPOs in order to sweeten the deal and attract the uninformed investor. In short, IPO underpricing compensates uninformed investors for the risk of trading against superior information.

Are IPOs Underpriced?

It has become widely accepted that IPOs are underpriced, as the very high returns in Figure 4.5 appear to indicate.[9] If we consider the price movement of newly issued shares from the offering date to a time shortly thereafter, it appears that IPOs are offered at a price significantly below the price that is expected to prevail in the aftermarket. In fact, the estimated underpricing ranges from 11 percent to 48 percent for initial public equity offerings.[10] Evidence indicates that new issues of shares and bonds for existing firms are also underpriced, but only by a relatively small amount. A very dramatic example was the 1986 IPO of Microsoft, the personal computer software firm. The preliminary prospectus indicated a price in the range of $16 to $19. The actual issue price was $21. On its first day of trading, the shares closed at $27.75. However, this type of underpricing appears to fluctuate, with the greatest underpricing occurring at the outset of a hot issues market. Later

---

[8]See Kevin F. Rock, "Why New Issues Are Underpriced," *Journal of Financial Economics*, 15, 1986, pp. 187–212.

[9]For a review of this literature, see C. W. Smith, "Investment Banking and the Capital Acquisition Process," *Journal of Financial Economics*, 15, 1986, pp. 3–29.

[10]See Clifford W. Smith, Jr., "Raising Capital: Theory and Evidence," *Midland Corporate Finance Journal*, 4:1, 1986, pp. 6–22.

in the hot issues market, when new issues become very frequent, the magnitude of the underpricing appears to fall or disappear altogether.

Evidence also suggests that prestigious underwriters sponsor issues in which the underpricing is less severe. For the largest potential underpricing, investors might seek issues underwritten by less prestigious firms. The securities underwritten by these less prestigious firms also seem to have a greater variability in their degree of underpricing.[11]

The underpricing appears to be quite short–lived, lasting only a few days or a few weeks. Jay Ritter examined the long–run investment performance and concluded that IPOs underperformed comparable stocks over their first three years.[12] Compared to similar stocks, the e IPOs return only 83 cents on the dollar after three years. Firms that issued at the height of a hot issues market appeared to do the worst. It seems that these firms were attracted to issuing new securities by the high concentration of issues shown in Figure 4.4. Also, Ritter concludes that some firms seem to go public to take advantage of industry–specific fads.

The entire issue of the pricing of IPOs continues to receive scrutiny. Investors can expect that new research will cause a tempering of some of the conclusions discussed in this section.

Shelf Registration

One of the most significant developments in the primary security markets in recent years has been the advent of shelf registration. As we discussed earlier, the process of issuing securities can be quite expensive. These high costs have been deemed necessary by regulators, notably the SEC, to protect the investing public and to maintain a smoothly functioning primary market. Requiring issuers of securities to go through lengthy procedures to guarantee full disclosure and to seek representation by investment bankers for every issue is, undoubtedly, very expensive.

As an experiment to determine whether such costs could be reduced, the SEC, under its Rule 415, first permitted shelf registrations on a temporary basis, and since January 1, 1984, as a permanent technique for issuing a security. **Shelf registration** allows firms to register with the SEC once, and then to offer securities for sale through agents and through the secondary markets for a period of two years following the registration. The rule applies to both stocks and bonds.[13]

---

[11]See R. Carter and S. Manaster, "Initial Public Offerings and Underwriter Reputation," *Journal of Finance*, 45:4, September 1990, pp. 1045–1067.

[12]See J. R. Ritter, "The Long–Run Performance of Initial Public Offerings," *Journal of Finance*, 46:1, March 1991, pp. 3–27.

[13]For more on the exact terms of Rule 415, see John Paul Ketels, "SEC Rule 415—The New Experimental Procedures for Shelf Registration," *Securities Regulation Law Journal*, 10, 1983, pp. 318–338.

There appear to be two chief advantages of this rule for corporations. First, a corporation can reduce its expense of offering securities by registering several securities at one time. Also, shelf registration allows firms to avoid the fixed–commission system of the investment bankers discussed earlier. Not surprisingly, the investment banking community lobbied very hard against the adoption of Rule 415.

The second advantage to corporations arises from the greater flexibility the firm achieves in timing an offering. Before shelf registration, the final "go/no–go" decision on a security issuance had to be made about three to six weeks before the actual offering was to occur. With security markets exhibiting radical fluctuations, the issuing firm can now take advantage of favorable market conditions by issuing quickly under the provisions of shelf registration.

There are also two potential disadvantages to shelf registration. First, the short period required to issue a new security may not provide enough time for the investment banker handling the shelf registration to assure that no misstatements or omissions appear in the registration statement. This requirement for the investment banker to verify the claims made in the registration statement is known as a **due diligence obligation**. Rapid issuing of securities may impair investment bankers' abilities to perform their due diligence obligation.

A second potential problem with shelf registration is that it may lead to higher concentration in the investment banking industry. With rapid issuance of securities under shelf registration, smaller regional investment banking firms may not be able to participate in the syndicate. Also, under time pressure, the larger firms that lead a syndicate might be less willing to include the regional firms. Both factors could lead to higher concentration in investment banking.

In general, the evidence on shelf registration supports the view that shelf registration has led to lower issuing costs for firms that have used it. However, the debate continues with some observers finding little or no benefits to shelf registration.[14]

The Condition of the Investment Banking Industry

In spite of the popularity of shelf registration, the investment banking community has not collapsed. However, recent years have seen a change in the source of investment banking industry profits. This section considers the concentration in the industry and the sources of industry profits.

Firm Size and Concentration in Investment Banking. Table 4.8 shows the size rankings for 1993 according to *Investment Dealers' Digest*. It is interesting to note the extent of concentration in the investment banking industry. Focusing on the top 15 firms,

---

[14]For two recent studies, see F. D. Foster, "Syndicate Size, Spreads, and Market Power During the Introduction of Shelf Registration," *Journal of Finance*, 44:1, March 1989, pp. 195–204; and D. S. Allen, R. E. Lamy, and G. R. Thompson, "The Shelf Registration of Debt and Self Selection Bias," *Journal of Finance*, 45:1, March 1990, pp. 275–287.

Table 4.8

Size Rankings of Major Corporate Underwriters

	Firm	$ Volume (millions)	No. of Issues
1	Merrill Lynch & Co.	$173,783.7	1,007
2	Goldman, Sachs	127,265.4	634
3	Lehman Brothers	115,976.5	681
4	Kidder, Peabody	94,441.1	306
5	Salomon Brothers	91,178.5	504
6	CS First Boston	90,373.8	454
7	Morgan Stanley	67,717.0	413
8	Bear Stearns	56,236.6	288
9	Donaldson, Lufkin & Jenrette	36,911.1	235
10	PaineWebber	29,889.9	179
11	Prudential Securities	28,336.2	161
12	J.P. Morgan and Co., Inc.	22,614.1	149
13	Smith Barney Shearson	14,284.4	171
14	Citicorp Securities	14,139.0	126
15	Nomura Securities Co. Ltd.	13,857.9	40
	Total	1,061,752.3	7,209

Source: *Investment Dealers' Digest*, January 10, 1994, p. 26. Figures show all domestic issues based on full credit to lead manager.

---

which basically constitute the entire industry in size, Table 4.9 shows the percentage of the industry represented by the largest three and the largest five firms. These proportions are known as **industry concentration ratios.**[15] By almost any standard, the investment banking industry is extremely concentrated, with the largest three firms having almost 40 percent of the market, and the largest five garnering 56.8 percent.

The International Primary Market

In this section, we briefly consider the major investment banking firms that are active in the international bond and equity markets. We then turn to a consideration of the investment banking industry in Great Britain and Japan.

---

[15]The use of industry concentration ratios is a common technique in the exploration of industrial structure. For an application of this technique to commercial banking, see A. A. Heggestad and J. J. Mingo, "Prices, Nonprices, and Concentration in Commercial Banking," *Journal of Money, Credit, and Banking*, 8, 1976, pp. 107–117.

Table 4.9

Concentration in the Investment Banking Industry

Largest 3 firms	39.28%
Largest 5 firms	56.76
Remaining Top 12 Firms	60.72
Remaining Top 10 Firms	43.24

Source: *Investment Dealers' Digest*, January 10, 1994, p. 26.

Major Investment Banking Firms in the International Market

Major investment banking firms in the international market come mostly from five countries: Japan, the United States, Great Britain, Switzerland, and Germany. Table 4.10 shows the five leading investment banking firms for international bonds and international equities. Three U.S. investment banks are among the top five for both bonds and equities. (SG Warburg is British; CS First Boston is Swiss; Deutsche Bank is German; Goldman Sachs, Morgan Stanley, and Merrill Lynch are from the United States.)

Investment Banking in Great Britain and Japan

In 1986, Great Britain experienced the **Big Bang**—a major liberalization of regulations governing securities dealing. As part of the deregulation, foreign competition was allowed much more fully than ever before, leading to the merger

Table 4.10

Leading International Investment Banking Firms

Rank	International Bonds	International Equities
1	Goldman Sachs	Goldman Sachs
2	Deutsche Bank	Merrill Lynch
3	Morgan Stanley	SG Warburg Securities
4	CS First Boston	CS First Boston
5	Merrill Lynch	Morgan Stanley

Source: *Euromoney*, April 1994.

Table 4.11

Leading Investment Banking Firms in the British Market

	Bond Issues	Equity Issues
1	GSFB	Samuel Montagu
2	S.G. Warburg	Goldman Sachs
3	Baring Brothers	N.M. Rothschild
4	Salomon Brothers	Scroder Wagg
5	Morgan Grenfell	Lazard Brothers

Source: S. Hayes and P. Hubbard, *Investment Banking*, Boston: Harvard Business School Press, 1990. Data are for 1988.

of many domestic firms and the inclusion of foreign, especially American, firms. Thus, Table 4.11 includes some well–known American firms in its listing of major investment houses in the British market. During the first half of the 1990s, American firms continued to be extremely competitive with native British firms.

In Japan, investment banking has been dominated traditionally by the **Big Four** securities firms: Nomura, Daiwa, Nikko, and Yamaichi. There are other firms, but these four account for a very large percentage of the Japanese market, and they are most active internationally. In the market for new corporate debt and equity, the lead investment bank is almost always a member of the Big Four. In the Japanese financial system, the Ministry of Finance plays a lead role and consults with the investment banks to establish the terms of the offering. Lead manager status rotates among the Big Four, with the other three being named as co–managers. In the 1990s, the reputation of these firms has suffered severely with the revelation of various kickback schemes and questionable connections with members of the Japanese government. These problems, in conjunction with the poor performance of the Japanese economy, have driven these firms from the international prominence they formerly enjoyed. Traditionally, the four firms have ranked from largest to smallest as follows: Nomura, Yamaichi, Nikko, and Daiwa. Among international equity investment banking firms in 1993, only Daiwa made the list of the top 55 investment banking firms.[16]

Summary

This chapter introduced the primary market and explained the function of the investment banker in that market. The United States is the most active country in

---

[16]See *Euromoney*, April 1994.

the world in the flotation of new securities, accounting for approximately one–half of all new securities.

In the process of issuing securities, the investment banker acts as a distribution network for most issues by corporations and municipalities. This is essentially a retailing function. In many cases, the investment banker also underwrites the new issue of security. In an underwriting, an investment banking syndicate buys the issue of securities from the issuer and tries to sell them at a profit. The difference between the amount the issuer receives and the amount the final investor pays is known as the spread. This spread constitutes the gross profit margin and the investment banking syndicate takes this spread as compensation for its retailing and risk–bearing services. In many cases, the risk accepted by the investment banking syndicate is very large.

Questions and Problems

1. Which entity is the largest issuer of securities in the world?
2. What information is found in a prospectus?
3. In Chapter 1, we discussed the relationship between risk and expected return. How might the fees charged by investment bankers for risk bearing be related to the creditworthiness of the issuer, the issuer's general reputation, and the current stability of financial markets?
4. For some popular new issues, a broker might not have enough of the security to satisfy all of the demand among his or her customers. How might the broker allocate the available securities? What does that imply for the choice of a "full service" broker vs. a discount broker that does not participate in any syndicates?
5. Why does the federal government issue only debt and no equity?
6. How much cash does IBM receive if an investor buys a share of IBM on the secondary market?
7. Will a small or a large issue of securities have higher percentage flotation costs? Why?
8. In the United States, which is larger, the bond or the stock market?
9. If you were the president of a software firm trying to raise funds for the introduction of a revolutionary product for personal computers, what considerations would be important to you when choosing between a public offering and a private placement? Why?

CFA Questions

All CFA examination questions are reprinted, with permission, from the Level I *1992–1994, CFA Candidate Study and Examination Program Review.* Copyright 1992–1994, Association for Investment Management and Research, Charlottesville, Va. All rights reserved.

A. "Shelf registration" refers to:
   a. a method by which firms can register securities and gradually issue them for up to two years after the initial registration.
   b. a method by which securities are prepared for listing on an exchange.
   c. the registration of securities that are to be issued as private placements rather than public offerings.
   d. the registration of securities to be sold offshore.

Suggested REALDATA Exercises

The following *REALDATA* exercise explores the concepts developed in this chapter: Exercise 24.

Suggested Readings

Foster, F. D., "Syndicate Size, Spreads, and Market Power During the Introduction of Shelf Registration," *Journal of Finance*, 44:1, March 1989, pp. 195–204.

Hayes III, S. L. and P. M. Hubbard, *Investment Banking: A Tale of Three Cities*, Boston: Harvard Business School Press, 1990.

Ibbotson, R. G., J. L. Sindelar, and J. R. Ritter, "Initial Public Offerings," *Journal of Applied Corporate Finance*, 1:2, Summer 1988, pp. 37–45.

Jog, V. M. and A. L. Riding, "Underpricing in Canadian IPOs," *Financial Analysts Journal*, 43:6, November/December 1987, pp. 48–55.

Kuhn, R. L., *Investment Banking: The Art and Science of High–Stakes Dealmaking*, New York: Harper & Row, Ballinger Division, 1990.

Ritter, J. R., "The Long–Run Performance of Initial Public Offerings," *Journal of Finance*, 46:1, March 1991, pp. 3-27.

Ruud, J. S., "Another View of the Underpricing of Initial Public Offerings," Federal Reserve Bank of New York *Quarterly Review*, 16:1, Spring 1991, pp. 83–85.

Tinic, S. M., "Anatomy of Initial Public Offerings of Common Stock," *Journal of Finance*, 43:4, September 1988, pp. 789–822.

Tucker, J. F., *Buying Treasury Securities at Federal Reserve Banks*, Richmond: Federal Reserve Bank of Richmond, 1983.

Sources of Investment Information

Overview

This chapter explores some of the prominent sources of information for investing in securities, particularly for investing in stocks and bonds. The securities information industry has billions of dollars of sales each year, providing investors with a range of data extending from the worthless to the essential. This chapter focuses on some of the well–regarded sources that can be found in university and local libraries, in addition to those available at the newsstand.

For anyone planning a career in investment management or planning to invest personal funds, being familiar with a variety of information sources is essential. This chapter introduces the world of securities information. As such, it should be a convenient guide for finding specific information about different kinds of economic statistics, reports on general economic trends, and information on particular companies and their securities.

General Business Periodicals

Virtually everyone has ready access to one or more of the periodicals discussed in this section. For most potential investors, the accessibility of these periodicals and the many topics of general interest they cover make them the place to start.

Without doubt, the premier business periodical in the United States is *The Wall Street Journal* published every business day by Dow Jones and Company, Inc. *The Wall Street Journal* contains the most complete source of information on security prices of any daily publication in the country. In addition, it carries news about particular firms and industries, announcements of pending security offerings, international business news, and capsules of national and political news that are likely to be of particular interest to investors and business people. The focus is primarily the news of the day, with relatively little effort to explain the meaning of the events being reported. While it offers the most comprehensive single listing of securities transactions, it does not carry quotations of securities of more local interest, such as the current price of minor bank stocks, for example. Quotations for securities of mainly local interest can be found in most local newspapers on a daily basis.

The *Investor's Business Daily* bills itself as "The Newspaper For Important Decision Makers." Compared to *The Wall Street Journal*, the *Investor's Business Daily* is quite small and new. However, by 1994 the *Business Daily* enjoyed a daily circulation approaching 200,000. The paper contains extensive quotations for securities and focuses on the daily news. It is clearly designed to compete with *The Wall Street Journal*.

The *Commercial and Financial Chronicle* is published weekly and carries exhaustive securities quotations. It is the only publication to carry complete NASDAQ quotations on a weekly basis.

The Wall Street Transcript, published daily, carries very detailed information about business, such as the full text of speeches made by major corporate executives. *Barron's*, the weekly sister publication to *The Wall Street Journal*, carries quotations for securities as of the end of trading for the week, and it features a number of columns and regular features on particular segments of the securities markets.

Business Week, *Fortune*, and *Forbes* are three major business magazines. *Business Week*, published weekly as the name implies, is the most strongly oriented toward news reporting. By contrast, *Fortune* and *Forbes* feature more lengthy reports on particular companies and business personalities. *Forbes* and *Fortune* frequently carry major articles about important trends in the business world as well.

Dun's Review and *Financial World* are similar in many respects to the three better-known publications just described, featuring longer articles with more analysis. *Financial World* often has reports on the stocks of particular industries and reports on different segments of the mutual fund industry.

The world of pension investing is itself a multibillion-dollar industry. Two periodicals, *Institutional Investor* and *Pensions and Investment Age*, are directed toward professionals in this industry. Since the industry is largely concerned with securities investment, there are many worthwhile articles about current trends in the financial markets.

A selection of these publications can form a good general foundation of information about the economy and specific companies. For anyone really interested in the securities markets, *The Wall Street Journal* is an indispensable daily habit. Further, all of these publications take pains to keep the reader's interest. None employs mathematics to any considerable extent, and when they report statistics, they generally do so in a visually appealing way, often with full-color graphs in the magazines.

Indexes to Further Information

The general business periodicals mentioned in the last section are only a few of the most prominent publications. Yet, few people could keep up with even these on a regular basis, never mind the hundreds of other potentially valuable sources of information.

Two printed sources are particularly helpful in managing the overabundance of information about businesses. These are the *Business Periodicals Index* and *The Wall Street Journal Index*. The *Business Periodicals Index* covers hundreds of periodicals that carry items about businesses. It provides a subject index every month. An investor wanting to learn more about a particular company could look up the company's name in the index and get references to news stories about that company. For someone with a particular need for certain information, this is usually a good place to start. *The Wall Street Journal Index* is organized in a similar way, but it focuses only on stories that originally appeared in *The Wall Street Journal*.

There are also some computerized indexes that are used frequently. *Dialog* and *Bibliographical Retrieval Service* are commercial services allowing users to specify key words that might occur in titles or subject descriptions of interest. For example, someone interested in Exxon Corporation could use one of these data bases, specify "Exxon" as a key word, and conduct a search over all of the items in the data base for hundreds of publications. The computer can then provide a reference to the particular article, along with an abstract of the article. Carrying things a step farther, one can even order a printed copy of a selected article. *Dialog* is frequently available through university library reference departments. *Bibliographical Retrieval Service* can be used on a home computer.

Federal Government Publications

One of the most widely available sources of reliable information about the U.S. economy is the U.S. government. The information is followed very closely by the investment community, which attests to its high value. Further, it is generally available free of charge, or at least very cheaply.

The *Federal Reserve Bulletin*, published monthly, carries one or two articles on major economic trends. In addition, it provides regular detailed statistical tables on commercial bank activity, new security issuances, and macroeconomic variables. The *Treasury Bulletin* focuses mainly on the activities of the Treasury Department, including the debt of the United States. One of the most useful regular features of the *Treasury Bulletin* is the yield curve, shown in Figure 5.1.[1] This graph provides a very convenient summary of the yields on Treasury securities of different maturities. These yield relationships are extremely important to investors in bonds.

As the new investor quickly discovers, one of the greatest problems in investment management is information overload. The documents provided by the federal government alone are overwhelming. Consequently, presentations that allow the information to be assimilated quickly are particularly valuable. Graphical presentations are among the easiest to understand and are the specialty of several government publications. The *Survey of Current Business*, published monthly by the

---

[1]The current yield curve is presented in Figure 8.1.

Figure 5.1

The Treasury Yield Curve

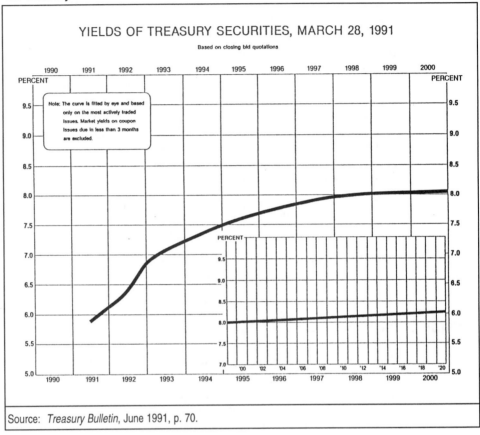

YIELDS OF TREASURY SECURITIES, MARCH 28, 1991

Based on closing bid quotations

Note: The curve is fitted by eye and based only on the most actively traded issues. Market yields on coupon issues due in less than 3 months are excluded.

Source: *Treasury Bulletin*, June 1991, p. 70.

Commerce Department, carries many graphs about general movements in the economy, such as the movement of leading and lagging indicators, capital investment, production, and income.

One of the most closely followed sections is the one on "Cyclical Indicators" presented in Figure 5.2. Some economic variables tend to respond to the economic cycles more quickly than the economy as a whole. These are called **leading indicators**. Others are **coincident indicators** and **lagging indicators**. Many investors pay particular attention to the leading indicators to gather information about likely future economic trends. For example, the *Survey* contains separate indicator series for construction costs and contracts, which indicates how finely it partitions the nation's economic activity. In addition to these disaggregated reports, the *Survey* provides monthly data on the Consumer Price Index (one of the most closely followed measures of inflation), the money supply, interest rates, and many other variables from the financial sector.

Figure 5.2

Cyclical Indicators

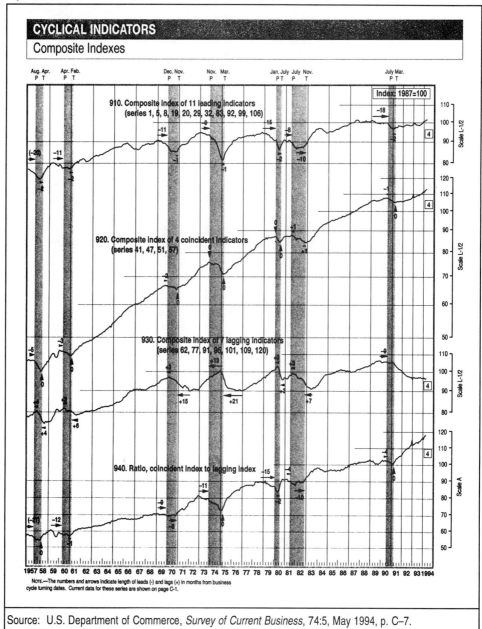

Source: U.S. Department of Commerce, *Survey of Current Business*, 74:5, May 1994, p. C–7.

Another major source of government economic data comes from the banks in the Federal Reserve System. There are 12 Federal Reserve Banks throughout the country, located in Atlanta, Richmond, Boston, New York, Philadelphia, Chicago, Cleveland, St. Louis, Kansas City, Dallas, Minneapolis, and San Francisco. Each of these banks publishes an economic review, appearing either quarterly or monthly. Typically, they contain articles about major economic trends, and often they focus on particular regional economic issues. In addition, the federal banks publish statistical information, such as the "U.S. Financial Data," which the Federal Reserve Bank of St. Louis publishes weekly. It, like most of the Federal Reserve publications, is available free of charge on a subscription basis. It provides a convenient source of weekly information about interest rates and other important economic variables.

The Securities and Exchange Commission oversees much of the activity of the securities markets. As might be expected, it is also a source of considerable information about securities investing. Its two main publications are the "SEC Monthly Statistical Review," published monthly and its "Annual Report." Here the user can find accurate information about virtually all phases of the security business.

Another particularly useful, and highly visual, source of information is the *Federal Reserve Historical Chart Book*, published annually. In fact, many of the figures in the preceding chapters of this book are taken from the *Chart Book*.

The U.S. government offers publications on nearly every economic topic of interest. *Economic Indicators*, published monthly by the Council of Economic Advisers, is prepared for the Congress and contains data on major macroeconomic variables. The *Quarterly Financial Report* of the Federal Trade Commission presents aggregated financial reports, such as balance sheets and income statements, broken down by industry and sub–industry categories. The *Economic Report of the President* is published annually and contains the President's interpretation of recent economic events and an analysis of forthcoming economic concerns. Finally, the *Statistical Abstract of the United States* is also published annually, following a trend started in 1878. Published by the Census Bureau, it contains vital statistics among other statistical information on all phases of the national life in its approximately 1,000 pages.

Information About Specific Industries

In the process of gathering and using information in securities investment, investors need a solid background of general information, such as that which the federal government publications help to provide. However, since funds are committed to individual securities, investors must ultimately narrow their attention to particular firms and their securities. One step along this road is to focus on particular industries. Without question, during any time period, some industries tend to prosper, while others falter. Just by finding the prospering industries, investors can greatly increase the chance of higher returns.

Some of the publications already mentioned provide a great deal of information about particular industries in each issue, such as *Forbes, Business Week,*

Fortune, and *The Wall Street Journal*. Federal government publications, such as the *Survey of Current Business*, provide statistical information about different industries as well. In addition to these sources, there are others that are devoted to specific industries. Virtually every industry has a trade association, such as the American Banker's Association, the American Medical Association, the American Booksellers Association, the Iron and Steel Institute, and so on. While the purpose of these organizations is to promote the interests of their current members, they are also a source of useful information about trends within their industries.

Nearly every industry has one or more trade journals or industry magazines aimed primarily at people working in the industry. Some examples are *Chemical Week*, *Automotive News*, and *Computerworld*. Most of these publications are likely to be of limited usefulness to the potential investor, however. Since their readership is drawn from people already committed to the industry, they are not necessarily helpful to someone trying to make an objective decision about investing in a firm within the particular industry.

Another important source of information about particular industries, and one that contains a higher proportion of analysis, can be the industry reports provided by brokerage houses. Most of the major brokerage houses, particularly full service brokerage houses, make research reports available to their customers. However, these same reports are often available free of charge or obligation by simple request. In fact, the availability of the reports is frequently advertised in *The Wall Street Journal*. (A word of warning: A request for literature is followed quickly by a call from a broker soliciting business.)

Dun and Bradstreet's *Key Business Ratios* is a publication that computes industry specific financial statement ratios for many different industries. For example, it reports the average current ratio for firms in the automobile industry, along with many of the other financial ratios that are used to analyze business firms. This information gives a yardstick for the industry against which specific firms in the industry might be measured. As the investor begins to focus on a particular company in a given industry, it can be useful to know how the liquidity or the debt burden of the firm compares to other firms in the industry. *Key Business Ratios* provides the standard of comparison.

In the industry for investment information, some companies offer an extended product line, such as Moody's and Standard & Poor's, and to a certain extent, Value Line. While the products of each of these firms will be considered in more detail in the discussion of information on individual firms, they are also important for the industry information they provide.

The Standard & Poor's *Industry Surveys* provide basic information on individual industries and their prospects. These reports are often about particular industries and the firms in them. The *Media General Industriscope*, which appears weekly, focuses on the performance of different industries and individual companies. One particularly useful feature of its presentation is the fundamental data it contains. It gives various balance sheet and income statement ratios for assorted industries and for particular companies. The Standard & Poor's *Outlook*, published weekly, gives opinions about which industries and which firms have good prospects.

Figure 5.3

A Value Line Industry Report

April 22, 1994   **FURNITURE/HOME FURNISHINGS INDUSTRY**   **901**

Furniture Industry stocks have not fared well in the past three months. We think, however, that the fundamentals are in place for good earnings gains in 1994. This industry is largely commodity oriented, although manufacturers are seeking ways to differentiate themselves.

INDUSTRY TIMELINESS: 71 (of 96)

A Slow Start This Year

Stocks covered in the Furniture Industry did not generally fare well over the past three months. While the broader market dipped around 4%, the average furniture stock declined over 11%. Indeed, only one company, HON Industries, saw its shares rise over the three-month stretch. We think that part of the drop-off is related to the rise in interest rates, which some investors fear will crimp housing sales. We note, however, that furniture sales usually lag home sales by six to 24 months. Therefore, current-year furniture sales will probably be more affected by last year's housing market than by this year's activity. The recent stock declines may also reflect some weakness in first-quarter earnings due to severe winter storms in the Southeast. The bad weather prevented plants from operating for several days, which left some manufacturers with unfilled orders that will probably be delayed or cancelled by retailers now that the industry is entering a seasonally slow period.

But Momentum Should Build In 1994

We think that business should be relatively good for the residential furniture market in 1994. The furniture industry is likely in a cyclical upturn after undergoing wrenching contraction during the stretch from 1988 to 1991. Because furniture purchases usually can be deferred and because furniture is relatively expensive, consumer demand tends to be strongest once the economy is well along a recovery path. Meanwhile, we think that there is pentup demand from the past few years when consumers were especially tight-fisted.

One marketing difficulty in the furniture industry is that many consumers consider furniture to be overpriced. This perception exists even though manufacturers have been raising prices at a slower rate than inflation. Part of the problem may be due to the fact that furniture is often sold at retail through promotional events that emphasize special price reductions. But this tactic may well give consumers the impression that list prices are too high. Another problem for manufacturers is that styling is similar for a wide range of prices. For instance, a chest of drawers with a veneer wood finish may look very similar to a solid-wood chest, but it will cost substantially less. Consumers have a tendency to look at the two pieces of furniture and wonder why the solid wood chest should be so much more expensive.

One opportunity for improving consumer perceptions is in reducing delivery times. After all, automobile dealers can often deliver a car faster than furniture stores can deliver a couch. Reducing the cycle time has become an important goal for all the manufacturers we cover. This is being accomplished by a combination of computer-aided manufacturing equipment and closer relationships with suppliers. Note that this trend favors larger manufacturers that can afford to invest in expensive new equipment.

Still Largely A Commodity Business

Most consumers looking for a new sofa do not have a particular manufacturer in mind. Instead, they know what type of style they are looking for and what amount they want to spend. We think that this will continue through the decade, but that some manufacturers will be able to develop brand awareness as their sales grow large enough to support direct consumer advertising. In the meantime, many producers are gaining distinction by forming alliances with retailers that agree to dedicate selling space to their furniture lines. Retailers are willing to enter these alliances because they usually receive generous payment terms for inventory, special delivery arrangements, and exclusivity rights. Meanwhile, the manufacturer's products are being displayed in a concentrated area, helping to create brand awareness. This relationship is even more dramatic in the case of whole stores selling one maker's line. Although the operators are usually independent dealers, the store is clearly aligned with the manufacturer in the consumer's mind.

Investment Advice

Even after the recent price decline in Furniture Industry stocks, many of these issues are still trading at above average earnings multiples. Therefore, the solid earnings prospects that we are projecting to 1997-99 for many of these companies are already partially reflected in the price of their shares.

William G. Barr, CFA

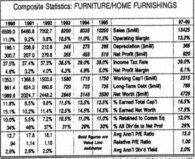

							97-99
1990	1991	1992	1993	1994	1995		
6599.0	6466.8	7002.7	8200	8335	10250	Sales ($mil)	13425
11.0%	9.2%	9.8%	10.5%	11.0%	11.5%	Operating Margin	13.0%
186.1	208.9	212.6	245	275	295	Depreciation ($mil)	365
300.7	207.0	279.8	355	455	510	Net Profit ($mil)	820
37.5%	37.4%	37.3%	38.5%	38.0%	38.0%	Income Tax Rate	38.0%
4.6%	3.2%	4.0%	4.3%	4.9%	5.0%	Net Profit Margin	6.1%
1353.1	1368.5	1503.8	1590	1715	1750	Working Cap'l ($mil)	2315
861.4	824.3	660.6	720	725	735	Long-Term Debt ($mil)	765
1989.8	2024.7	2448.2	2840	3145	3500	Net Worth ($mil)	4725
11.8%	8.5%	9.8%	11.5%	13.5%	13.5%	% Earned Total Cap'l	16.5%
15.1%	10.2%	11.4%	12.5%	14.5%	14.5%	% Earned Net Worth	17.5%
10.0%	5.5%	7.2%	10.5%	11.0%	11.0%	% Retained to Comm Eq	12.0%
34%	46%	37%	31%	29%	30%	% All Div'ds to Net Prof	26%
12.7	17.8	18.1	*Bold figures are Value Line estimates*			Avg Ann'l P/E Ratio	13.0
.94	1.14	1.10				Relative P/E Ratio	1.00
2.6%	2.6%	2.0%				Avg Ann'l Div'd Yield	2.0%

Composite Statistics: FURNITURE/HOME FURNISHINGS

Furniture/Home Furnishings
RELATIVE STRENGTH (Ratio of Industry to Value Line Comp.)
Index: June, 1967 = 100

Factual material is obtained from sources believed to be reliable, but the publisher is not responsible for any errors or omissions contained herein. For the confidential use of subscribers. Reprinting, copying, and distribution by permission only. Copyright 1994 by Value Line Publishing, Inc. ® Reg. TM—Value Line, Inc.   **To subscribe call 1-800-833-0046.**

Source: Value Line Publishing, Inc., *The Value Line Investment Survey*, April 22, 1994, p. 901.

One of the most useful sources of industry analysis and recommendations is provided by the *Value Line Investment Survey*. Each week the survey focuses on about six to ten industries and the stocks within those industries. Each industry in the group for that week is analyzed, and individual firms within the industry are discussed. Figure 5.3 presents a typical industry report. Notice that it presents composite statistics for the industry, allowing comparisons for particular firms against the industry norm. One of the most useful features about all of the *Value Line* products is the willingness to make clear commitments. The industry timeliness ranking tells exactly where they rank the industry out of the 93 that they follow. Further, they recommend certain stocks they believe are likely to perform well, and back up those predictions with a report on the specific firms. A typical report on an individual firm is presented in the following section.

Information Prepared by Individual Companies

The parade of information starts with the information that companies generate about themselves. As discussed in Chapter 4, each new issue of securities requires a prospectus. Potential investors may generally rely on a prospectus as a conservatively stated view of the company's forthcoming prospects.

Every publicly owned firm must also make an annual report available to its shareholders. These are also often available at libraries or can be obtained simply by writing the company and requesting one. In addition, many brokers also keep a file of annual reports. An annual report contains the audited financial reports of the firm, although this information makes up only a small part of the report. Since the annual report is one of the main means by which management communicates with its shareholders, firms do not like to lose the chance to promote themselves. As a result, annual reports often contain ingenious explanations about why the firm did not do so well in the last year and sometimes raise false hopes about the prospects for the coming year. Aside from the audited financial reports, prospective investors should take annual reports with a grain of salt.

Public firms must also file more complete financial data with the Securities and Exchange Commission. This report is called a 10–K and goes beyond the information in the annual report. One of the easiest ways to acquire a 10–K is through Disclosure, Inc., a firm that specializes in duplicating and selling these reports to the public. Also, some libraries keep files of 10–Ks.

Standard & Poor's and Moody's

Standard & Poor's and Moody's are the two dominant firms in the investment information business. They compete across a broad range of products, very nearly duplicating each other in many cases. Standard & Poor's *Corporation Records* and Moody's *Manuals* provide basic information about particular firms. For example, if one wanted to find out the basics about a firm, such as Medtronic, Inc., either source would give fundamental information on the company, such as its major line

Figure 5.4

A Page from the S&P 500 Stock Market Encyclopedia

International Paper 1222

NYSE Symbol IP Options on CBOE In S&P 500

Price	Range	P–E Ratio	Dividend	Yield	S&P Ranking	Beta
Jan. 13'94 71½	1993–4 74⅜–56⅝	31	1.68	2.3%	B+	1.07

Summary

This company is one of the largest U.S. paper and packaging producers and a major producer of lumber and plywood. Approximately one-third of sales are made outside the U.S. Sales and earnings are very sensitive to cyclical economic fluctuations. Earnings from operations in recent periods reflected soft paper markets and product pricing pressures. However, any upturn in industry conditions could propel earnings sharply higher.

Current Outlook

Earnings for 1994 are projected at $3.35 a share, up from $2.34 recorded in 1993.

Dividends are expected to continue at $0.42 quarterly.

Sales for 1994 are expected to rise modestly. Margins should benefit from some improvement in pricing for paper products and cost-reduction efforts, but profitability will continue to be highly dependent on the strength of the general economic recovery. Due to current overcapacity in most paper markets, earnings are not likely to return to peak levels reached in the late 1980's for some time. However, IP is positioned to benefit strongly from any sustained upturn in industry conditions.

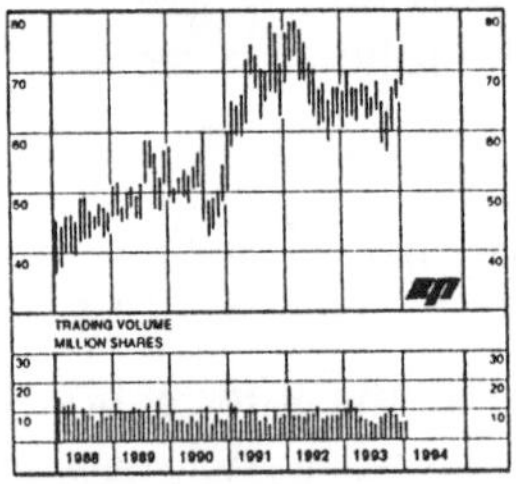

Net Sales (Billion $)

Quarter:	1994	1993	1992	1991
Mar.	---	3.36	3.36	3.10
Jun.	---	3.51	3.39	3.11
Sep.	---	3.40	3.48	3.28
Dec.	---	3.40	3.40	3.22
	---	13.70	13.60	12.70

Sales for 1993 (preliminary) rose fractionally from those of the previous year, as depressed pricing for most printing paper and packaging products largely offset gains in the forest products and distribution segments. In the absence of a $263 million or $2.17 a share after-tax charge for productivity improvements, net income more than doubled, to $2.34 a share from $1.17. Results for 1992 exclude a charge of $0.41 a share related to accounting changes and a $0.05 loss on extinguishment of debt.

Common Share Earnings ($)

Quarter:	1994	1993	1992	1991
Mar.	E0.65	0.52	0.87	1.16
Jun.	E0.85	0.62	0.94	0.91
Sep.	E0.95	0.39	0.82	0.95
Dec.	E0.90	0.81	d1.46	0.59
	E3.35	2.34	1.17	3.61

Important Developments

Jan. '94— IP reported slightly improved activity in its printing papers business in the fourth quarter of 1993, although pulp and paper prices continued to be weak and demand in Europe remained soft. Management added that packaging results during the fourth quarter were about the same as in the third quarter, with a small upturn for packaging exports the only bright spot.

Jul. '93— The company announced an expansion of its paper plant near Selma, Alabama. The expansion, expected to be completed by mid-1995, will add a new white papers machine, two new sheeters, a deinking plant and a gas turbine generator.

Jun. '93— IP, which is the leading supplier of labels to the food industry, opened the world's largest label production facility, a 236,000-square-foot plant in Kentucky.

Next earnings report expected in mid-April.

Per Share Data ($)

Yr. End Dec. 31	1993	1992	1991	1990	[1]1989	1988	1987	[1]1986	1985	1984
Tangible Bk. Val.	NA	44.15	43.68	45.07	43.03	38.40	34.83	33.54	33.34	[2]33.02
Cash Flow	NA	8.17	9.95	11.32	12.74	10.91	7.76	6.60	4.20	3.90
Earnings[3]	2.34	1.17	3.61	5.21	7.72	6.57	3.68	2.90	1.07	0.94
Dividends	1.680	1.680	1.680	1.680	1.530	1.275	1.225	1.200	1.200	1.200
Payout Ratio	72%	145%	47%	32%	20%	19%	33%	41%	110%	128%
Prices—High	69⅞	78½	78¼	59¾	58¼	49⅜	57⅞	40⅛	28⅞	29⅛
Low	56⅝	58½	50½	42¾	45⅛	36½	27	24¼	22⅛	23
P/E Ratio—	30–24	67–50	22–14	11–8	8–6	8–6	16–7	14–8	27–21	32–24

Data as orig. reptd. Adj. for stk. div. of 100% May 1987. 1. Reflects merger or acquisition. 2. Includes intangibles. 3. Bef. spec. items of -0.46 in 1992, -1.95 in 1991, +0.02 in 1985. d-Deficit. E-Estimated. NA-Not Available.

Standard NYSE Stock Reports Vol. 61/No. 14/Sec. 19 — January 20, 1994 — Standard & Poor's 25 Broadway, NY, NY 10004

Copyright © 1994 McGraw-Hill, Inc. All Rights Reserved

1222 International Paper Company

Income Data (Million $)

Year Ended Dec. 31	Revs.	Oper. Inc.	% Oper. Inc. of Revs.	Cap. Exp.	Depr.	Int. Exp.	[3]Net Bef. Taxes	Eff. Tax Rate	[4]Net Inc.	% Net Inc. of Revs.	Cash Flow
1992	13,598	1,701	12.5	1,368	850	[2]289	206	31.1%	142	1.0	992
1991	12,703	1,713	13.5	1,197	700	[2]351	638	37.5%	[5]399	3.1	1,099
1990	12,960	2,088	16.1	1,409	653	[2]303	946	39.9%	569	4.4	1,222
[1]1989	11,378	2,159	19.0	1,345	549	[2]216	1,405	38.5%	864	7.6	1,394
1988	9,533	1,824	19.1	899	485	[2]171	1,222	36.3%	754	7.9	1,218
1987	7,763	1,219	15.7	804	429	195	703	39.0%	407	5.2	816
[1]1986	5,500	819	14.9	1,672	363	143	474	31.4%	[5]305	5.5	647
1985	4,502	446	9.9	794	311	105	166	16.9%	131	2.9	416
1984	4,716	549	11.7	628	295	100	144	16.5%	120	2.5	388
1983	4,357	377	8.7	738	273	95	252	NM	255	5.9	501

Balance Sheet Data (Million $)

Dec. 31	Cash	Curr. Assets	Curr. Liab.	Curr. Ratio	Total Assets	% Ret. on Assets	Long Term Debt	Common Equity	Total Cap.	% LT Debt of Cap.	% Ret. on Equity
1992	225	4,366	4,531	1.0	16,459	0.9	3,096	6,189	10,702	28.9	2.3
1991	238	4,131	3,727	1.1	14,941	2.8	3,351	5,739	10,134	33.1	6.9
1990	256	3,939	3,155	1.2	13,669	4.5	3,096	5,632	9,863	31.4	10.5
1989	102	3,096	2,730	1.1	11,582	8.3	2,324	5,147	8,493	27.4	17.6
1988	122	2,343	1,562	1.5	9,462	8.3	1,853	4,557	7,624	24.3	17.1
1987	233	2,163	1,506	1.4	8,710	4.8	1,937	4,052	6,995	27.7	9.7
1986	200	1,628	1,332	1.2	7,848	4.2	1,764	3,664	6,349	27.8	7.9
1985	271	1,105	755	1.5	6,039	2.3	1,191	3,195	5,127	23.2	3.3
1984	300	1,231	657	1.9	5,795	2.1	1,015	3,298	4,995	20.3	2.8
1983	226	1,201	549	2.2	5,617	4.5	940	3,321	4,961	18.9	7.0

Data as orig. reptd. 1. Reflects merger or acquisition. 2. Net of interest income. 3. Incl. equity in earns. of nonconsol. subs. 4. Bef. spec. items. 5. Reflects accounting change. NM-Not Meaningful.

Business Summary

IP is one of the largest producers of paper, paperboard and packaging products in the world. It is the second largest distributor of paper and office supply products in the U.S. and also produces pulp, lumber, panels and specialty products. Segment contributions in 1992 (profits in millions) were:

	Sales	Profits
Printing papers	29%	–$70
Packaging	26%	338
Distribution	21%	52
Specialty products	14%	63
Forest products	10%	187

Sales outside the U.S., including exports, accounted for 33% of total sales in 1992.

Uncoated papers produced by IP include reprographic and printing papers and premium writing and artist papers. Its coated papers are used in magazines and other publications. Other products include folders, tags, posters, fluff pulp for diapers and sanitary products and paper pulp.

The packaging segment produces linerboard and medium for corrugated boxes and bleached packaging board and packaging for juice, milk, pharmaceuticals, cosmetics, food, cigarettes and chemicals. Other packaging products include kraft paper, multiwall bags and specialty paper.

IP distributes paper, graphic arts equipment and supplies, packaging materials, industrial supplies and office products through about 250 distribution centers, mostly in the U.S. Approximately 20% of the products sold are made by IP.

Specialty products include photosensitive films and papers; natural fibers and nonwoven fabrics; and adhesives, inks and paints. IP is also engaged in oil and gas exploration.

IP controls 6.2 million acres of timberland through its majority interest in IP Timberlands, Ltd. Wood products include lumber, plywood, oriented strand board, siding and panel products.

Dividend Data

Dividends have been paid since 1946. A dividend reinvestment plan is available.

Amt. of Divd. $	Date Decl.	Ex–divd. Date	Stock of Record	Payment Date
0.42	Feb. 9	Feb. 12	Feb. 19	Mar. 15'93
0.42	Apr. 13	May 17	May 21	Jun. 15'93
0.42	Jul. 13	Aug. 16	Aug. 20	Sep. 15'93
0.42	Oct. 13	Nov. 15	Nov. 19	Dec. 15'93

Capitalization

Long Term Debt: $3,249,000,000 (9/93).

Common Stock: 123,570,040 shs. ($1 par).
Institutions hold about 65%.
Shareholders of record: 33,098.

Office—Two Manhattanville Rd., Purchase, NY 10577. **Tel**—(914) 397-1500. **Chrmn**—J. A. Georges. **Sr VP & CFO**—R. C. Butler. **VP-Secy**—A. Wallace. **Investor Contact**—Carol Tutundgy. **Dirs**—W. C. Butcher, F. B. Dent, J. T. Dillon, W. M. Ellinghaus, S. C. Gault, J. A. Georges, T. C. Graham, A. G. Hansen, W. G. Kuhns, D. F. McHenry, P. F. Noonan, J. C. Pfeiffer, S. R. Pierce Jr., E. T. Pratt Jr., R. B. Smith. **Transfer Agent & Registrar**—Chemical Bank, NYC. **Incorporated** in New York in 1941. **Empl**—73,000.

Information has been obtained from sources believed to be reliable, but its accuracy and completeness are not guaranteed. Richard Spiegel

Source: Standard & Poor's Corporation, *Stock Market Encyclopedia*, Standard & Poor's Corporation, Summer 1994, p. 1222. Reprinted by permission of Standard & Poor's, a division of McGraw–Hill, Inc.

of business, its financial structure, and its history. While this background information can be useful, it contains no recommendations or analysis that would be crucial in making an immediate investment decision.

As a source of more timely information on particular companies, two pertinent sources are the S&P *Stock Market Encyclopedia* and Moody's *Handbook of Common Stocks*. Figure 5.4 presents a report from the *Stock Market Encyclopedia*. Moody's *Handbook of Common Stocks* provides an essentially comparable analysis, an example of which is shown in Figure 5.5.

Figure 5.5

A Report From Moody's Handbook of Common Stocks

INTERNATIONAL BUSINESS MACHINES CORPORATION

LISTED	SYM.	LTPS♦	STPS♦	IND. DIV.	REC. PRICE	RANGE (52-WKS.)	YLD.	'93 YR.-END PR.
NYSE	IBM	50.0	69.2	$1.00*	57	60 - 41	1.8%	56½

INVESTMENT GRADE. DEPRESSED SALES OF HIGH-MARGIN MAINFRAME TECHNOLOGY HAVE IMPACTED EARNINGS, ALTHOUGH SALES OF SMALLER COMPUTER SYSTEMS ARE GROWING RAPIDLY.

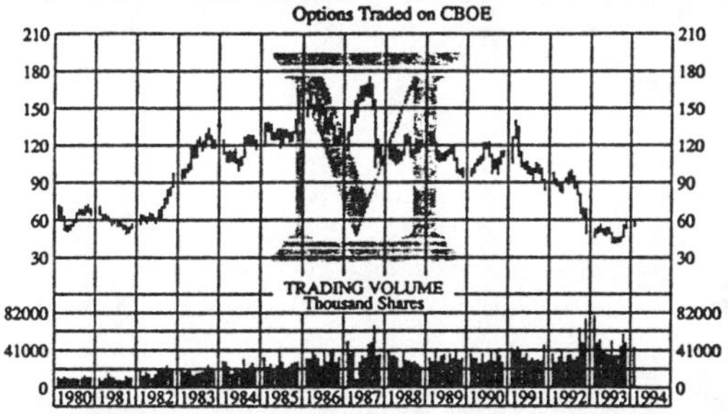

Options Traded on CBOE
210
180
150
120
90
60
30
TRADING VOLUME
Thousand Shares
82000
41000
0
1980 1981 1982 1983 1984 1985 1986 1987 1988 1989 1990 1991 1992 1993 1994

CAPITALIZATION: (12/31/92)

	(000)	(%)
Long-Term Debt	c$12,853,000	30.2
Defer. Inc. Tax	2,030,000	4.8
Com. & Surp.	27,624,000	65.0
Total	$42,507,000	100.0

Shs. ($1.25)-571,435,728

INTERIM EARNINGS:

Qtr.	3/31	6/30	9/30	12/31
1989b	1.61	2.31	1.51	1.04
1990	1.81	2.45	1.95	4.30
1991e	d3.03	0.20	0.30	d2.42
1992f	1.04	1.25	d4.87	d9.57
1993g	d0.50	d14.10	d0.12	0.62

INTERIM DIVIDENDS:

Amt.	Dec.	Ex.	Rec.	Pay.
0.54Q	1/26/93	2/4/93	2/10/93	3/10/93
0.54Q	4/26	5/6	5/12	6/10
0.25Q	7/27	8/5	8/11	9/10
0.25Q	10/26	11/4	11/10	12/10
0.25Q	1/25/94	2/4/94	2/10/94	3/10/94

BACKGROUND:

IBM is the world's largest manufacturer of information processing equipment and systems. Application Business and Solutions Systems manufactures processors and related software and develops solutions for abroad range of industries. Enterprise Systems offers general purpose processors, operating systems and supercomputers. Networking and Pennant Systems provides products to manage networks as well as printers and printing solutions. Personal Systems and Storage products develops personal computers, workstations, tape drives and optical storage devices. Technology products and Programming Systems manufactures logic and memory chips and develops software.

RECENT DEVELOPMENTS:

IBM announced that it would not produce Intel Corp.'s PENTIUM technology in-house, rather that it would focus on its POWERPC technology as its premium microprocessor offered in IBM computers. For the quarter ended 12/31/93, net income recovered to $382 million compared with a loss of $5.46 billion for the comparable period in 1992. Revenues slid 1% to $19.40 billion. High popularity for personal computers helped revenues for PC's and workstations increase significantly as companies continued to turn towards smaller computer systems. This practice contributed to a decrease in sales of mainframe computers.

PROSPECTS:

A strategic shift towards greater marketing emphasis on IBM's personal computers, workstations, and services has succeeded in reviving earnings somewhat, although lower margins associated with these products will be unable to support a full recovery in earnings. Although demand for large computer systems such as mainframes has begun to erode quite rapidly, IBM hopes to slow the departure of 'big iron' customers by offering new, less-expensive versions of traditional mainframes which will be suited for particular tasks.

STATISTICS:

YEAR	GROSS REVS. ($mill.)	OPER. PROFIT MARGIN %	RET. ON EQUITY %	NET INCOME ($mill.)	WORK CAP. ($mill.)	SENIOR CAPITAL ($mill.)	SHARES (000)	EARN. PER SH.$	DIV. PER SH.$	DIV. PAY. %	PRICE RANGE	P/E RATIO	AVG. YIELD %
84	45,937	24.5	24.8	6,582	10,735	3,269	612,686	10.77	4.10	38	128½ - 99.	10.6	3.6
85	50,056	22.4	20.5	6,555	14,637	3,955	615,418	10.67	4.40	41	158½ - 117⅜	12.9	3.2
86	51,250	15.3	13.9	4,789	15,006	4,169	605,923	7.81	4.40	56	161⅞ - 119¼	18.0	3.1
87	54,217	14.3	13.7	5,258	17,643	3,858	597,052	8.72	4.40	50	175⅞ - 102	15.9	3.2
88	59,681	14.7	13.9	a5,491	17,956	8,518	589,741	a9.27	4.40	47	129½ - 104½	12.6	3.8
89	62,710	11.0	9.8	b3,758	14,175	10,825	574,700	b6.47	4.73	73	130⅞ - 93⅜	17.3	4.2
90	69,018	16.0	14.1	6,020	13,644	11,943	571,391	10.51	4.84	46	123⅛ - 94½	10.4	4.4
91	64,792	1.5	d	ed2,827	7,345	13,231	571,018	ed4.95	4.84	N.M.	139¾ - 83½	N.M.	4.3
92	64,523	d	d	fd6,865	2,955	12,853	571,436	fd12.03	4.84	—	100⅜ - 48¾	—	6.5
p93	62,716			gd7,987				gd14.02	1.58	—	59⅞ - 40⅝	—	3.1

♦Long-Term Price Score — Short-Term Price Score; See page 4a. STATISTICS ARE AS ORIGINALLY REPORTED. a-Excludes $315 million ($0.53 per share) credit for an accounting change. b-Includes $2.4 billion ($4.16 a share) charge for restructuring. c-Includes debentures convertible into common stock. e-Includes an acctg. chg. of $2.3 billion ($3.96 a sh.) and a restructuring charge of $3.4 billion. f-Incl. a pre-tax restruct. chg. of $11.6 bill. and excl. an acctg. cr of $1.9 bill. g-Incl. restruct. chg. of $8.9 bill; excl. acctg. chg. of $114 mill.

INCORPORATED:
June 16, 1911 — NY

PRINCIPAL OFFICE:
Old Orchard Road
Armonk, NY 10504
Tel.: (914) 765-7777

ANNUAL MEETING:
Last Mon. in April

NUMBER OF STOCKHOLDERS:
764,630

TRANSFER AGENT(S):
First Chicago Trust Co. of N.Y.
New York, NY

REGISTRAR(S):
First Chicago Trust Co. of N.Y.
New York, NY

INSTITUTIONAL HOLDINGS:
No. of Institutions: 871
Shares Held: 218,343,753

OFFICERS:
Chairman & C.E.O.
L. V. Gerstner, Jr.
Vice Chairman
P. J. Rizzo
Sr. V.P. & C.F.O.
J. B. York
Treasurer
R. Ripp
Secretary
J. E. Hickey

Source: *Moody's Handbook of Common Stocks*, Spring 1994.

Figure 5.6

A Page from Moody's Bond Record

U.S. CORPORATE BONDS — Mark—McGa 51

CUSIP	ISSUE	MOODY'S RATING	INTEREST DATES	CURRENT CALL PRICE	CALL DATE	SINK FUND PROV	CURRENT PRICE	YIELD TO MAT.	1994 HIGH	1994 LOW	AMT. OUTST. MIL. $	ISSUED	PRICE	YLD.
570535AB	Markel Corp. nts. 7.25 2003	Ba1	M&N 1	N.C.	—	No	— bid	—	—	—	75.0	10-26-93	99.30	7.35
571630AS	Marriott Corp. sr.nts. M 9.50 2002	B2 r	M&N 1	N.C.	—	No	99 1/2 bid	9.59	103	94 1/8	200	4-28-92	98.85	
571630AM	sr.nts. I 9.00 1995	B2 r	M&N 24	N.C.	—	No	100 3/4 bid	8.18	102 3/8	99 1/2	99.2	4-26-88	99.02	9.19
571630AC	sr.nts. B 9.625 1996	B2 r	F&A1	100.00	to 2-1-96	No	100 1/8 bid	9.54	102	98 1/2	99.6	1-28-86	99.50	9.70
571630AD	sr.nts. C 8.125 1996	B2 r	J&D 1	N.C.	—	No	99 1/2 bid	8.35	99 1/2	94 1/2	199.4	12-3-86	99.63	8.16
571630AE	sr.nts. D 8.875 1997	B2 r	M&N 1	N.C.	—	No	99 1/2 bid	9.07	100 3/8	95 1/2	99.8	4-30-87	99.81	8.89
571630AG	sr.nts. E 9.875 1997	B2 r	M&N 1	100.00	fr 11-1-94	No	100 1/2 bid	9.69	103	98 7/8	149.8	10-23-87	99.22	9.90
571630AP	nts. 10.25 2001	B2 r	J&J 18	N.C.	—	No	100 1/2 bid	10.14	104 1/2	95 7/8	125	7-11-91	100.00	10.25
571630AF	deb. 9.375 2007	B2 r	J&D 15	N.C.	—	No	100 1/2 bid	9.30	102 1/8	95 1/4	250	6-11-87	99.83	9.40
571630AR	sr.nts. 10.00 2012	B2 r	M&N 1	N.C.	—	No	100 1/2 bid	9.93	104 1/2	94 1/4	200	4-22-92	98.35	10.19
571900AA	Marriott International nts. 6.75 2003	Baa1	J&D 15	N.C.	—	No	91 1/4 bid	8.06	101 5/8	90 1/4	150	12-2-93	99.28	6.85
571834AC	Marshall & Ilsley Corp. sub.nts. 6.375 2003	A2	J&J 15		—		91 bid	7.75	101 1/4	90	100	7-8-93	99.35	6.46
571834AB	nts. 10.50 1995	A1 r	M&N15	100.00	to 11-15-95	No	106 5/8 bid	5.69	106 5/8	102 1/8	60.0	11-14-85	99.72	10.55
573275AM	Martin Marietta Corp. gtd.nts. 6.50 2003	A3	A&O 15	N.C.	—		90 5/8 bid	7.98	102 7/8	88 1/2	400	4-15-93	99.56	6.56
573275AN	deb. 7.375 2013	A3	A&O 15	N.C.	—		90 5/8 bid	8.36	104 5/8	88 1/4	150	4-15-93	99.98	7.47
573275AP	deb. 7.75 2023	A3	A&O 15		—		91 3/8 bid	8.55	105 3/8	88 7/8	150	4-15-93	99.72	7.77
573275AH	nts. 9.50 1995	A3 r	M&N 15	N.C.	—	No	103 bid	6.11	106 5/8	103	125	5-17-88	99.85	9.53
573275AK	nts. 8.50 1996	A3 r	M&S 1	N.C.	—	No	103 1/8 bid	6.53	108	102 7/8	100	3-5-91	99.65	8.59
573275AL	nts. 9.00 2003	A3 r	M&S 1	N.C.	—	No	106 1/4 bid	7.98	119 3/4	104 1/8	100	3-5-91	99.70	9.04
573275AD •	deb. 7.00 2011	A3 r	M&S15	100.00	to 3-15-11	No	90 sale	8.10	96	90	98.63	3-10-81	53.83	13.25
57383QAA	Marvel Holdings, Inc. sr.sec.nt. 0.00 1998	B3	A&O 15		—		—	—	—	—	517.4	4-16-93	57.98	
—	sr.nts. 2003	B3	A&O 15		—		—	—	—	—	251.6	10-13-93	58.66	12.25
573845AA	Marvel Parent Holdings In sr.sec.nt. 1998	B3	A&O 15		—		—	—	—	—	251.7	10-13-93		
574034AA	Maryland Cable Corp. sr.sub.nts. 15.375 1998[1]	Caa r	M&N 1	104.00	to 11-14-94	No	33 bid	—	33	33	161.9	11-17-88	47.72	
574599AL	MASCO CORP. nts. 6.25 1995	Baa1 r	J&D 15	N.C.	—		100 3/8 bid	5.83	102 5/8	100 1/4	200	6-17-92	99.86	6.30
574599AM	nts. 6.625 1999	Baa1 r	M&S 15	N.C.	—	No	96 5/8 bid	7.38	104 7/8	96	200	9-10-92	99.50	6.72
574599AP	nts. 6.125 2003	Baa1	M&S 15	N.C.	—	No	87 7/8 bid	7.99	98 5/8	86 7/8	200	9-8-93	100.00	
574599AN	deb. 7.125 2013	Baa1 r	F&A 15	N.C.	—	No	88 1/4 bid	8.35	100 5/8	87 3/4	200	8-17-93	99.38	7.18
574599AJ	nts. 9.00 1996	Baa1 r	A&O 15	N.C.	—	No	104 1/4 bid	6.52	108 5/8	104 1/8	250	4-16-91	100.00	9.00
574599AC •	deb. 8.875 2001	Baa1 r	J&D 1	100.84	to 5-31-95	Yes	—	—	—	—	5.495	6-4-76	99.50	
574599AK	nts. 9.00 2001	Baa1 r	A&O 1	N.C.	—	No	106 3/8 bid	7.83	118 3/4	105 3/8	175	9-25-91	100.00	9.00
574601AD	MASCO INDUSTRIES, INC. sr.sub.nts. 10.00 1995	Ba3 r	M&S 15	N.C.	—	No	102 bid	7.33	105	101 1/2	300	3-10-88	99.36	10.13
—	MASCOTECH, INC. sr.sub.nts. 10.00 1995	Ba3	M&S 15		—		—	—	—	—	300	3-10-88		
575767AB	Mass. Mut Life Insurance nts. 7.625 2023[2]	Aa3	M&N 15		—		— bid	—	—	—	250	11-12-93	100.00	7.63
575767AD	nts. 7.50 2024[3]	Aa3	M&S 1		—		—	—	—	—	100	2-22-94	99.55	
575634AE	Massachusetts Elec. Co. 1st J 7.125 1998	A1 r	A&O 1	101.10	to 3-31-95	Yes	99 5/8 bid	7.22	101 5/8	99 1/2	15.0	4-17-68	103.48	6.85
575634AH	1st M 7.75 2002	A1 r	A&O 1	102.63	to 9-30-94	Yes	99 1/8 bid	7.88	102 3/4	98 3/4	20.0	10-10-72	101.76	7.60
575634AK	1st O 12.50 2012	A1 r	A&O1	107.14	to 9-30-94	Yes	106 5/8 bid	11.61	107 5/8	106 1/2	2.120	10-13-82	99.00	12.63
575634AL	1st P 9.75 2016	A1 r	J&D 1	106.50	fr 6-1-95	Yes	107 1/2 bid	8.95	107 3/4	104	25.0	6-4-86	100.00	9.75
57564EAA	med.term nts. R 9.75 2019[4]	A1 r	F&A 1	§	—	Yes	—	—	—	—	50.0	Ref. fr. 8-1-94 @ 107.13		
577081AJ	Mattel, Inc. nts. 6.875 1997	Baa2 r	F&A 1	N.C.	—	No	96 1/8 bid	8.29	—	—	100	7-31-92	99.29	7.05
577081AK	nts. 6.75 2000	Baa2	M&N 15	N.C.	—	No	95 3/4 bid	7.63	104 3/8	95	100	5-19-93	100.00	6.75
577341AA	Maui Electric Co., Ltd. gtd.nts. 5.15 1996[5]	Baa1	J&D 16	N.C.	—		—	—	—	—	10.0	12-16-93	100.00	5.15
577730AH	Maxus Energy Corp. nts. 9.875 2002	B1 r	A&O 15	100.00	fr 10-15-99	No	92 7/8 bid	11.20	101 3/4	92 1/2	250	9-21-92	100.00	9.88
577730AK	nts. 9.50 2003	B1 r	F&A 1	100.00	fr 2-15-00	No	92 1/8 bid	10.92	101	91 1/4	100	1-19-93	99.25	9.62
577730AL	nts. 9.375 2003	B1 r	M&N 1	N.C.	—	No	91 1/2 bid	10.83	100 1/4	91	200	10-20-93	100.00	9.38
577730AM	nts. B 9.375 2003	B1	J&J 18		—		—	—	—	—	60.0	1-10-94		
577730AC •	s.f.deb. 8.50 2008	B1	A&O 1	101.98	to 3-31-95	Yes	76 bid	12.12	98 1/4	85	97.7	3-22-78	99.25	
577730AF	s.f.deb. 11.25 2013	B1 r	M&N 1	104.74	to 4-30-95	Yes	99 3/8 bid	11.33	104 1/2	99 3/8	134.7	5-5-83	99.38	11.28
577730AG	s.f.deb. 11.50 2015	B1 r	M&N15	§106.31	to 11-14-94	Yes	100 3/8 bid	11.45	106 1/8	100	108.8	Ref. fr. 11-15-95 @ 105.17		
577771AF	Maxxam Group, Inc. sr.sec.nt. 11.25 2003	B3 r	F&A 1	105.50	fr 8-1-98	No	95 1/2 bid	12.07	103	95	100	7-27-93	100.00	11.25
577771AE	sr.sec.nt. 12.25 2003	B3 r	F&A 1	106.12	fr 8-1-98	No	—	—	—	—	126.7	7-27-93	55.24	
577913AC	•Maxxam, Inc. sub.deb. 12.50 1999[6]	— r	J&D15	100.00	to 12-15-99	Yes	102 1/8 sale	11.96	105	100	32.3	11-15-79		
577778AV	May Dept. Stores deb. 8.375 2022	A2 r	A&O 1	104.04	fr 10-1-02	Yes	99 7/8 bid	8.38	113 3/8	99 1/8	200	10-1-92	99.71	8.40
577778AK	nts. 9.60 1995	A2 r	J&D 15	N.C.	—	No	103 3/8 bid	6.07	107 3/4	103 3/8	150	6-8-88	100.00	9.60
577778AL	deb. 9.875 2000	A2 r	J&D 15	N.C.	—	No	110 7/8 bid	7.58	121 7/8	110	200	6-8-88	100.00	9.88
577778AQ	nts. 9.875 2002	A2 r	J&D 1	N.C.	—	No	112 3/8 bid	7.84	125 5/8	111 3/8	175	12-6-90	99.50	9.94
577778AP	deb. 10.625 2010	A2 r	M&N 1	N.C.	—	No	123 1/8 bid	8.04	138 1/2	121 5/8	150	11-6-90	99.87	10.64
577778AG	deb. 9.25 2016	A2 r	M&S 1	§105.55	to 2-28-95	Yes	105 5/8 bid	8.65	106 1/4	105 5/8	125	Ref. fr. 3-1-96 @ 104.63		
577778AH	deb. 9.125 2016	A2 r	J&D 1	§105.93	to 11-30-94	Yes	104 bid	8.70	106 1/8	103 1/2	150	Ref. fr. 12-1-96 @ 104.56		
577778AJ	deb. 9.875 2017	A2 r	J&D 1	§106.42	to 5-31-95	Yes	106 5/8 bid	9.17	107 1/4	106 1/2	100	Ref. fr. 6-1-97 @ 104.94		
577778AR	deb. 10.25 2021	A2 r	J&J 1	N.C.	—	No	120 3/8 bid	8.32	136 1/2	119 5/8	100	1-9-91	99.53	10.30
577778AS	deb. 9.75 2021[7]	A2 r	F&A 15	N.C.	—	No	115 3/8 bid	8.30	130 7/8	114 1/2	125	2-12-91	99.52	9.80
577778AT	deb. 9.50 2021[8]	A2 r	A&O 15	N.C.	—	No	112 3/4 bid	8.30	128 1/8	112	150	4-8-91	99.35	9.56
577778AU	deb. 9.875 2021	A2 r	J&D 15	104.56	fr 6-15-01	Yes	114 5/8 bid	8.48	126	113 7/8	100	6-19-91	99.25	9.95
578099AA	Mayfair Super Markets, In sr.sub.nts. 11.75 2003	B3	M&S 30		—		— bid	—	—	—	75.0	3-8-93	100.00	11.75
578592AA	Maytag Corp. nts. 8.875 1997	Baa1 r	J&J 1	N.C.	—	No	104 3/4 bid	7.09	111 1/8	104 5/8	100	6-23-87	99.50	8.88
578592AB	nts. 8.875 1999	Baa1 r	J&J 15	N.C.	—	No	105 5/8 bid	7.51	114 1/8	105	175	7-10-89	99.90	9.89
578592AC	nts. 9.75 2002	Baa1 r	M&N 15	N.C.	—	No	111 1/8 bid	7.83	123	110 1/4	200	5-16-90	99.55	9.81
55262CAC	MBIA, Inc. deb. 8.20 2022	Aa2	A&O 1	103.98	fr 10-1-02	No	98 7/8 bid	8.29	112 1/2	98 1/8	100	10-1-92	99.87	8.22
55262CAA	nts. 9.00 2001	Aa2 r	F&A 15	N.C.	—	No	108 7/8 bid	7.28	119 3/4	108	100	2-8-91	99.35	9.10
55262CAB	nts. 9.375 2011	Aa2	F&A 15	N.C.	—	No	111 bid	8.15	126 1/2	109 1/2	100	2-12-91	99.25	9.46
55262FLN	MBNA American Bank N.A. sub.nts. 7.25 2002	A3 r	M&S 15	N.C.	—	No	96 bid	7.91	106 5/8	95	200	9-14-92	99.40	7.43
55262LAB	MBNA Corp. sr.nts. 6.875 1999	A3 r	A&O 1	N.C.	—		97 bid	7.54	—	—	150	9-22-92	99.88	6.88
579780AB	McCormick & Co. nts. 8.95 2001	A2 r	J&J 1	N.C.	—	No	107 1/8 bid	7.61	117 3/4	106 1/4	75.0	6-27-91	99.49	9.02
579865AQ	McCrory Corp. sr.sub.nts. 7.77 1994[9]	Ca r	JAJ&O15	100.00	to 7-15-94	No	— bid	—	—	—	75.0	7-18-84	100.00	
579865AH •	s.f.sub.deb. 7.75 1995[10]	N.R. r	M&S 15	100.00	to 9-15-95	Yes	15 bid	flat	37	13	14.68	9-1-72		
579865AG •	s.f.sub.deb. 7.625 1997[11]	Ca r	J&D15	100.00	to 12-15-97	Yes	19 sale	flat	36 1/4	17	11.8	9-1-72		
580033AK	McDermott, Inc. nts. 10.25 1995	Baa3 r	J&D 1	N.C.	—	No	103 3/4 bid	6.31	107	103 3/4	150	6-9-88	100.00	10.25
580033AL	nts. 9.375 2002	Baa3 r	M&S 15	N.C.	—	No	104 1/8 bid	8.62	115 3/4	103 1/4	225	3-18-92	99.71	9.42
580135BG	•McDonald's Corp. nts. 7.375 2002	Aa2 r	J&J 15	100.00	fr 7-15-99		98 1/4 bid	7.66	108 1/4	100	150	7-6-92	99.89	7.39
580135AQ •	nts. 11.625 1995	Aa2 r	A&O15	100.00	to 4-15-95	No	101 bid	10.28	—	—	100	4-11-85	99.55	11.70
580135BE •	nts. 9.375 1997	Aa2	M&S 15	100.00	fr 3-15-95	No	102 bid	8.55	105 1/4	102 3/4	100	3-20-90	99.92	9.39
580135AY •	nts. 9.75 1999	Aa2 r	J&J 15	100.00	fr 1-15-96	No	106 sale	8.16	110 1/8	102 1/2	100	1-12-89	99.58	9.82
580135BF •	bonds 8.875 2011	Aa2 r	A&O 1	N.C.	—	No	107 7/8 bid	8.01	117 1/2	114 1/2	100	4-10-91	99.44	8.93
—	McDonald's Mat. & Def Stk nts. 7.67 2004[12]	Aa2	M&S 15	N.C.	—	No	—	—	—	—	200	9-8-89	00.00	
580144AA	nts. B 7.30 2006[13]	Aa2 r	J&D 1	N.C.	—	Yes	—	—	—	—	100	3-22-91	100.00	7.3
580135BH	McDonald's Corp. nts. 6.75 2003	Aa2	F&A 15		—		90 bid	8.39	104 3/8	97 3/4	125	2-12-93	99.50	6.82
580135BJ	deb. 7.375 2033	Aa2	J&J 15		—		87 bid	8.52	101 1/8	90 1/4		7-6-93		
580169AK	•McDonnell Douglas Corp. nts. 8.625 1997	Baa3 r	A&O 1	N.C.	—	No	103 1/2 sale	7.24	108 5/8	102 5/8	250	3-26-92	99.56	8.73
580169AN •	nts. 8.25 2000	Baa3	J&J 15	N.C.	—	No	100 7/8 bid	8.06	105 1/4	100 1/4	200	6-23-93	100.00	8.25
580169AL •	nts. 9.25 2002	Baa3 r	A&O 1	N.C.	—	No	106 5/8 sale	8.09	116	102 1/8	350	3-26-92	99.40	9.34
580169AM •	bonds 9.75 2012	Baa3 r	A&O 1	N.C.	—	No	108 3/4 sale	8.77	122 7/8	107	350	3-26-92	99.00	9.86
—	McGaw Inc. flt.rt.nts. 0.00 1997[14]	Ba2	A&O 1	000.00	—		—	—	100	100	60.0	4-1-92	100.00	

[1]Discount. Co. in Chapter 11. [2]Private placement. [3]Private Placement [4]Secured, 1st Mtge. Cl. 89-1. [5]Gtd. by Hawaiian Electric Co., Inc. [6]Exchange offer. Form. MCO Holdings. [7]Amortizing deb. [8]Amortized Deb. [9]Exch. var. rt., Co. filed for Chap. 11. [10]Iss. in exch. for com. stk. [11]Iss. 1972-Exch. Co. filed for Chap. 11. [12]Gtd. by McDonald's Corp. [13]Gtd. ESOP Nt., Ser. B. Gtd by McDonald Corp. [14]Sr. Sec.

Notes: Moody's ratings are subject to change. Because of the possible time lapse between Moody's assignment or change of a rating and your use of this monthly publication, we suggest you verify the current rating of any security or issuer in which you are interested. For standard abbreviations and symbols, see page 5.

Source: *Moody's Bond Record*, June 1994.

Figure 5.7

A Page from Standard & Poor's Bond Guide

104 INT-IOW Standard & Poor's

Title-Industry Code & Co. Finances (In Italics) / Individual Issue Statistics / Exchange	Ind / Interest Dates	Fixed Charge Coverage 1990 / S&P Debt Rating	1991 / Date of Last Rating Change	1992 / Prior Rating	Eligible	Year End / Bond Form	Million $ Cash & Equiv. / Redemption Provisions: Regular Price	Curr. Assets / Regular (Begins) Thru	Curr. Liab. / Sinking Fund Price	Balance Sheet Date / Sinking Fund (Begins) Thru	L. Term Debt (Mil $) / Refund/Other Restriction Price	Refund/Other Restriction (Begins) Thru	Capitalization (Mil $) / Outst'g (Mil $)	Total Debt % Capital / Underwriting Firm	Underwriting Year	Price Range 1994 High	Price Range 1994 Low	Mo. End Price Sale(s) or Bid	Curr. Yield	Yield to Mat.
Int'l Lease Finance (Cont.)																				
Nts 5¾s '99	Jj15	A+			X	R	NC	....	....	....	....	....	150	S1	'94	100⅞	98⅜	98½	5.84	6.11
Nts 6½s '99	fA15	A+			X	R	NC	....	....	....	....	....	100	M2	'92	103¾	100½	100⅝	6.46	6.36
Nts 6.20s 2000	Mn	A+			X	R	NC	....	....	....	....	....	100	M6	'93	102	98⅜	98⅝	6.29	6.47
Nts 8⅞s 2001	Ao15	A+			X	R	NC	....	....	....	....	....	150	M2	'91	114⅝	112⅜	113⅝	7.81	6.46
F/R[1]Nts 3.5625s '97	[2]	A+			X	R	NC	....	....	....	....	....	100	L4	'93	100	99¾	100	3.56	....
Int'l Minerals & Chem	*14*	*Now IMCERA Group, see*																		
SF Deb 9⅞s 2011	Ms15	BBB+	11/92	BBB	X	R	100	(3-15-01)	100	(3-15-02)	....	....	134	L2	'86	120½	114¾	115⅝	8.56	8.19
International Paper	*50*	*3.89*	*2.72*	*2.94*		*Dc*	*287.0*	*4603*	*4527*	*9-30-93*	*★3649*		*11785*	*48.1*						
• Deb 5⅛s 2012	mN15	A−	10/86	A+	X	R	100	....	....	....	....	....	[3]149	G1	'82	83	78	s78	6.57	7.30
Deb[4] 7⅝s 2023	Ms	A−			X	BE	103.43	(3-1-03)	....	....	....	....	200	F2	'93	105⅜	98⅞	99½	7.66	7.67
Deb 6⅞s 2023	mN	A−			X	R	NC	....	....	....	....	....	200	K3	'93	97¼	91	91⅜	7.50	7.59
Nts[5] 9⅝s '95	aO15	A−			X	R	NC	....	....	....	....	....	150	F2	'90	109	107½	107½	8.95	4.78
Nts[5] 9.70s 2000	Ms15	A−			X	R	NC	....	....	....	....	....	150	F2	'90	119⅞	115⅝	115⅞	8.37	6.48
Nts[5] 9.40s 2002	Jd	A−			X	R	NC	....	....	....	....	....	100	F2	'90	118¼	115⅝	117¾	7.98	6.58
Nts[4] 6⅛s 2003	mN	A−			X	BE	NC	....	....	....	....	....	200	C4	'93	99⅞	96	96⅜	6.36	6.64
Nts[5] 7⅝s 2007	Jj15	A−			X	R	NC	....	....	....	....	....	200	K3	'92	113⅞	108⅜	108¾	7.01	6.60
International Shipholding	*64*	*1.85*	*1.90*	*1.94*		*Dc*	*45.50*	*98.00*	*63.90*	*9-30-93*	*265.0*		*421.0*	*68.4*						
• Sr Nts[6] 9s 2003	jJ	BB−			Y	R	103.375	(7-1-98)	....	....	....	....	100	B10	'93	103½	101⅝	100½	8.96	8.92
Int'l Technology	*53*	*2.91*	*2.35*	*1.59*		*Mr*	*37.80*	*176.0*	*90.30*	*9-30-93*	*129.0*		*301.0*	*44.5*						
• Sr Nts 9⅝s '96	jJ	B+	8/93	B	Y	R	100	....	....	....	....	....	50.0	H3	'86	100¾	99¾	s100	9.38	9.36
Int'l Telephone & Tel	*17*	*Now ITT Corp,see*																		
Deb 6½s 2001	jJ	A+	6/90	A	X	R	100	....	....	....	....	....	[3]150	L4	'81	99¾	98¾	99	6.57	6.67
Deb 7½s 2011	jJ	A+	6/90	A	X	R	100	....	....	....	....	....	[3]150	L4	'81	99½	96⅝	97⅛	7.72	7.80
InterNorth,Inc	*73e*	*Now Enron Corp,see*																		
Nts 9⅝s 2006	Ms15	BBB	8/89	BBB−	X	R	NC	....	....	....	....	....	192	G1	'86	129⅛	123⅛	123½	7.79	6.74
Interstate Power Co.	*75*	*3.78*	*3.68*	*2.69*		*Dc*	*2.03*	*68.30*	*60.30*	*9-30-93*	*203.0*		*427.0*	*47.5*						
1st 4⅝s '95	Mn	A+	10/82	A	X	CR	100	....	100	....	....	....	14.0	H1	'65	99⅞	99½	99⅞	4.63	4.73
1st 6⅛s '97	Mn	A+	10/82	A	X	CR	100.67	4-30-94	100.09	4-30-94	....	....	17.0	H1	'67	100½	100½	100½	6.09	5.95
1st 8s 2007	Fa15	A+			X	R	NC	....	100	....	....	....	25.0	S1	'92	117⅛	111½	111⅞	7.15	6.62
1st 8⅝s 2021	mS15	A+			X	R	108.03	9-14-94	100	....	®105.65	9-14-01	25.0	S1	'91	107½	107½	107½	8.02	7.95
1st 7⅝s 2023	Mn15	A+			X	R	105.751	5-14-94	Z100	....	®104.31	5-14-03	94.0	S1	'93	105¼	99⅞	100⅝	7.58	7.57
Investment Prop. Assoc.	*38*	....	....	....		*Dc*	*No Recent Fin'ls*													
Jr Mtg 9s '94	jD	NR				R	100	....	100	....	....	....	[3]27.0	W5	'69	99¾	99⅝	99¾	9.02	9.31
[7]Investors Savings Corp	*10b*	*1.65*	*3.14*	*2.97*		*Dc*				*9-30-93*	*321.0*		*366.0*	*87.7*						
Sub Nts[8] 9¼s 2002	[9]dec	NR				R	100	(12-15-95)	....	....	....	....	23.0		'92	102¾	102	102¾	9.00	8.79
Iowa Elec Lt & Pwr[10]	*75*	*2.26*	*2.32*	*2.37*		*Dc*	*0.75*	*69.20*	*184.0*	*9-30-93*	*436.0*		*844.0*	*53.6*						
1st J 6¼s '96	mS	A	8/77	A−	X	R	100.56	8-31-94	Z100.36	8-31-94	....	....	15.0	M2	'66	100⅜	100⅜	100⅜	6.23	6.09
1st L 7⅞s 2000	jD	A	8/77	A−	X	R	101.63	11-30-94	Z100	....	....	....	15.0	S1	'70	101⅜	101⅜	101⅜	7.77	7.61
1st M 7⅝s 2002	Mn	A	8/77	A−	X	R	102.10	4-30-94	Z100	....	....	....	30.0	E3	'72	101¾	101¾	101¾	7.49	7.33
1st Y 8⅝s 2001	Mn15	A			X	R	NC	....	Z100	....	....	....	60.0	M2	'91	117⅛	112½	112¾	7.65	6.39

Uniform Footnote Explanations-See Page 1. Other: [1] Int to 4-20-94,adj qtrly aft. [2] Due 10-15-97:Int pd qtrly on 3rd Wed Jan,etc. [3] Incl disc. [4] (HRO)On Chge of Ctrl at 100. [5] (HRO)At 100 for certain events. [6] (HRO)On Chge of Ctrl at 101. [7] Now Investors Bank Corp. [8] Death red benefit,ltd,as defined. [9] Due 12-15-02:int pd 1st day of ea month. [10] Subsid of IE Industries.

Source: Standard & Poor's Corporation, *Bond Guide*, March 1994, p. 104. Reprinted by permission of Standard & Poor's, a division of McGraw–Hill, Inc.

In comparison with stocks, both Standard & Poor's and Moody's give less attention to bonds, perhaps because much information about stock investing is pertinent to bond investing as well. They are not forgotten, however. Standard & Poor's publishes its *Bond Guide* while Moody's has its *Bond Record* and *Bond Survey*, both published monthly. Figure 5.6 presents a typical page from Moody's *Bond Record* containing basic information about the bonds issued by each company, such as their ratings, whether they have a sinking fund, and their payment dates. In addition to straight bonds, the *Bond Record* also covers convertible securities, commercial paper ratings, and preferred stock ratings. Standard & Poor's *Bond Guide* and Moody's *Bond Survey* are roughly comparable. A page from Standard & Poor's *Bond Guide* appears as Figure 5.7. It gives basic information about the bond, such as its rating and legal status, but it also provides information about the company's financial status, particularly those measures that might be of particular interest to bondholders. Also in the bond area, Standard & Poor's publishes its *Municipal Bond Selector*.

Figure 5.8

A Page from Standard & Poor's Stock Guide

108 **INT-INT** Standard & Poor's

¶ S&P 500 / # MidCap 400 / • Options Index	Ticker Symbol	Name of Issue (Call Price of Pfd. Stocks)	Market	Com. Rank. & Pfd. Rating	Par Val.	Inst. Hold Cos	Inst. Hold Shs. (000)	Principal Business	Price Range 1971-92 High	1971-92 Low	1993 High	1993 Low	1994 High	1994 Low	Apr. Sales in 100s	April, 1994 Last Sale Or Bid High	Low	Last	%Div Yield	P-E Ratio
1	IPR	✓Inter-City Products	AS	NR	No	19	5378	Mfr heat/cooling equip,pipe	8¼	2¼	6¾	2⅜	3⅛	2½	482	3	2⅝	2¾	...	d
2	Pr	8% cm Cv Cl C Pref(25)	AS	NR	No	1	62		24½	14¼	21¾	14½	18¼	15	....	....	....	14½B	...	..
3	INNN	Interactive Network	NMS	NR	No	25	1981	Dvlp stgn: interactive TV sys	14⅞	3¼	15¼	4⅜	11	6⅛	13961	7½	6⅛	6⅞	...	d
4	IIC	InterCapital Cal Ins Muni Inc	NY,Ch	NR	1¢	3	.1	Closed-end muni bond fund	....	....	16⅛	13¾	15½	12⅝	2846	14	13⅛	13⅝	6.5	..
5	IQC	InterCapital Cal Qual Muni Sec	NY,Ch	NR	1¢	..	...	Closed-end muni bond fund	....	....	15⅛	13⅞	14⅜	11	2861	12¾	11½	11¾	7.0	..
6	ICB	InterCapital Inc Sec	NY,Ch	NR	1	12	16	Closed-end inv:fixed income	25⅞	13⅞	22	18¼	20½	18¼	1174	19⅛	18¼	18⅞	8.2	..
7	ICS	InterCapital Ins Cal Muni Sec	NY,Ch	NR	1¢	..	...	Closed-end muni bond fund	....	....	....	....	15⅛	14⅛	366	14⅞	14⅛	14¼	5.1	..
8	IMB	InterCapital Ins Muni Bd Fd	NY,Ph	NR	1¢	8	41	Closed-end muni bond fund	18½	14½	18	16	17⅞	14¾	1148	15¾	14¾	15¾	⊙•7.1	..
9	IIM	InterCapital Ins Muni Income	NY,Ch	NR	1¢	9	33	Closed-end muni bond fund	....	....	15⅞	13⅝	15	11¾	9619	13⅛	11¾	12⅞	7.0	..
10	IMS	InterCapital Ins Muni Sec	NY,Ch	NR	1¢	..	...	Closed-end muni bond fund	....	....	....	....	15⅜	14¼	2224	15	14¼	14¼	5.3	..
11	IMT	InterCapital Ins Muni Tr	NY,Ph	NR	1¢	7	38	Closed-end muni bond fund	15⅞	14	16⅞	15	16¾	13⅞	4812	14⅞	13⅞	14½	6.9	..
12	ION	InterCapital N.Y.Qual Muni Sec	NY,Ch	NR	1¢	..	...	Closed-end muni bond fund	....	....	15¾	14½	14⅝	11⅛	1508	12	11⅛	11⅜	7.0	..
13	IQI	InterCapital Qual Muni Income	NY,Ph	NR	1¢	10	36	Closed-end muni bond fund	15½	14¼	16	14¼	15⅞	13¼	8948	14	13¼	13½	⊙7.3	..
14	IQT	InterCapital Qual Muni Inv	NY,Ph	NR	1¢	9	43	Closed-end muni bond fund	16	14¼	16¾	15⅛	16½	13¾	3418	14¾	13¾	14⅝	7.4	..
15	IQM	InterCapital Qual Muni Sec	NY,Ph	NR	1¢	5	16	Closed-end muni bond fund	....	....	15⅛	14¼	14⅜	10⅞	9181	11⅞	10⅞	11½	7.5	..
16	ICAR	✓Intercargo Corp	NMS	B+	1	25	2042	Underwriters specialized insur	17	3¼	14½	10	12¼	7½	1341	11	8¾	10	1.7	35
17	ISB	✓Interchange Finl Svcs	AS	A–	No	13	382	Commercial banking,New Jersey	21¾	1⅞	18	13	16½	14	299	15½	14¼	15⅛	4.6	9
18	ISS	✓INTERCO Inc(New)	NY,Ph	NR	No	60	46180	Mfr furniture & footwear	9⅝	6⅝	15¾	9⅜	15¾	12⅝	2795	14⅛	12⅝	13⅜	...	15
19•[1]	IDC	✓Interdigital Communications	AS,Ph	C	1¢	32	3653	Wireless digital communic prd	20⅝	2⅜	11⅜	4⅜	5⅝	3⅜	38756	5⅜	3⅜	5⅛	...	d
20	IFSIA	✓Interface Inc'A'	NMS	A–	10¢	73	11110	Mfr carpet tile,comm'l use	19¾	3¼	15½	9¾	17	12⅛	32212	14	12⅛	13¾	1.8	18
¶21•[2]	INGR	✓Intergraph Corp	NMS	B–	10¢	162	22311	Computer graphics systems	40½	3⅞	13½	8½	11¼	8¾	35821	10¼	8¾	9½	...	d
22	IGHC	✓Intergroup Healthcare	NMS	NR	.001	62	3392	Managed hlth care svc, Arizona	30	11	50	21¼	57¼	36¾	11533	48¼	36¾	44⅞	...	22
23	INTM	✓Interim Services	NMS	NR	1¢	5	1394	Temprary help services	....	....	....	....	28¼	20	16518	26¼	23⅞	24½	...	27
24	IK	✓Interlake Corp	NY,B,Ch,P	NR	1	57	12372	Diversified ind'l mfg co	61¾	2¾	4¾	2⅜	3¾	2⅜	3126	3¼	2¾	2¾	...	d
25	LEAF	✓Interleaf Inc	NMS	B–	1¢	43	6811	Computer aids for publishing	24⅛	2½	13⅝	4⅛	8¼	6⅛	13495	7½	6¼	6⅞	...	d
26	INLQ	✓INTERLINQ Software	NMS	NR	1¢	20	1810	Dvlp mtge lending software	....	....	9¼	6	9	6½	5133	8¼	6½	7¾	...	14
27	IMG	✓Intermagnetics Gen'l	AS	B	10¢	20	763	Mfr superconductive mtls	21⅜	2⅞	22¼	6⅛	18⅞	12¼	10651	18⅞	14¼	17⅞	s...	..
28	INMT	✓Intermet Corp	NMS	C	10¢	65	11109	Iron foundry-auto indus	19	3⅜	12	6	10½	7¾	4920	9½	7¾	8	...	d
29	IMET	✓Intermetrics Inc	NMS	†B	1¢	15	713	Computer software prod & svc	20¾	2¼	4⅝	3½	5¾	4⅜	1941	5¾	4½	5⅜	3.0	8
30	IAL	✓Intl Aluminum	NY,B,Ch,P	B+	1	26	1901	Mfr & sale aluminum prod	30¾	1	24½	20⅝	28	23⅜	369	26¾	24⅞	25	4.0	25
¶31•[3]	IBM	✓Intl Bus. Machines	[4]NY,B,C,Ch,P,Ph	B–	1¼	967	233930	Lgst mfr business machines	175⅞	37⅝	59⅞	40⅝	60	51⅜	533971	59½	51⅜	57½	1.8	d
32	TUNE	✓Intl Cablecasting Tech	NMS	C	1¢	60	9191	Cable audio program'g svcs	9⅛	1⅝	7⅛	3	4¾	2⅞	31320	4⅛	3⅛	3⅝	...	d
33•[2]	KCN	✓Intl Colin Energy	NY,Ch	NR	No	44	4830	Oil&gas explor,dev,prod'n	13⅜	2¾	21⅜	10⅜	15½	11⅝	4228	13½	11⅝	12⅜	...	11
34	ICSI	✓Intl Container Sys	NMS	B	1¢	5	70	Mfrs plastic beverage cases	15⅞	2	4½	2⅜	3⅛	2⅛	49	2¼	2⅛	2¼B	...	19
#35	INDQA	✓Intl Dairy Queen 'A'	NMS	B+	1¢	71	9550	Lmtd menu stores: franch'g	25¾	1/16	21	15½	18½	15¾	6295	18½	17½	18¼	...	15
36•[5]	FAM	✓Intl Family Entert'nt 'B'	NY,Ph	NR	1¢	93	12993	Oper cable TV'Family Channel'	15⅜	9⅛	25⅛	13⅝	22¼	15¾	5437	17½	15¾	16⅛	...	33
¶37•[6]	IFF	✓Intl Flavors/Fragr	NY,B,C,Ch,P,Ph	A+	12½¢	440	76664	Dev&mfr flavor&fragr prod	38¼	5½	39⅞	33	39⅜	35⅝	27986	37⅜	35⅜	36½	2.9	21
#38•[7]	IGT	✓Intl Game Technology	NY,Ch,Ph	B	.000625	330	85457	Coin oper video/reel games	26⅜	7/16	41⅜	23¾	34	22⅝	212232	28¼	22⅝	26	0.5	26
39	IMAK	✓Intl Imaging Materials	NMS	NR	1¢	43	3371	Mfr thermal transfer ribbons	....	....	20½	14	20¼	15	4512	17¼	15	15⅜	...	24
40	IJIN	✓Intl Jensen	NMS	NR	1¢	19	1314	Mfr loudspeakers & compon'ts	16	7¾	10½	6	9	6¾	320	7¾	6¾	6¾	...	d
41	ILI	Intl Lottery	AS	NR	1¢	..	...	Mfr instant lottery machines	....	....	....	....	13⅛	11	5921	13⅛	11	11	...	32
42	IMV	✓Intl Movie Group	AS,Ch	NR	1¢	3	79	Foreign distributor of films	3¼	⅝	1 3/16	¼	⅜	3/16	2553	⅜	3/16	¼	...	d
#43	IMC	✓Intl Multifoods	NY,Ch,P	B+	10¢	119	11558	Diversified food prod/svcs	31½	3¾	27½	17¼	19⅛	15⅛	7851	16¾	15⅛	15¾	5.1	d
44•[8]	MXX	✓Intl Murex Technologies	AS,Ch,Ph	NR	No	15	691	Mfr medical diagnostic prod	17⅜	3⅜	7¾	2⅞	6½	4⅜	4049	5¼	4¾	5⅛	...	31
45	WS	Wrrts(2wrrts:pur 1 com at $9.50).	[9]AS	NR	No	1	.9		8½	⅛	1 11/16	5/16	⅜	1/16	....	....	....	....	...	..
¶46•[3]	IP	✓Intl Paper	NY,B,C,Ch,P,Ph,Mo	B+	1	610	83681	Mfr paper,pulp&wood prod	78½	14¼	69⅞	56⅝	77⅞	60⅝	106672	67½	60⅝	65¼	2.6	27
47	POST	Intl Post Ltd	NMS	NR	1¢	..	...	Post TV production svcs	....	....	....	....	12	9	2188	10¼	9	9¼	...	10
48	PWR	✓Intl Pwr Machines	AS	C	10¢	8	238	Uninterruptible power sys	22½	¼	4½	1 11/16	3⅞	2	1787	2¾	2	2¼	...	7
49	INT	✓Intl Recovery	NY,Ch,Ph	NR	1¢	46	2355	Aviat'n fuel'g svc/oil recy'g	26	1⅝	16	9¾	16⅛	12½	1666	14⅝	12⅞	14½	...	12
50•[10]	IRF	✓Intl Rectifier	NY,B,Ch,P	B–	1	63	9996	Power semiconductors	25¼	1	15	9⅜	19⅛	13	21010	16½	13	15⅞	...	31
51	IRI	✓Intl Remote Image'g	AS	B–	1¢	10	128	Mfr urinalysis workstation	50	⅝	7¾	3⅛	6⅛	3⅞	2318	5⅛	4	5¼	...	19

Uniform Footnote Explanations-See Page 1. Other: [1]P:Cycle 3. [2]ASE:Cycle 1. [3]CBOE:Cycle 1. [4]Mo,To [5]NY:Cycle 2. [6]CBOE:Cycle 2. [7]ASE,CBOE:Cycle 1. [8]ASE:Cycle 2. [9]To [10]CBOE:Cycle 3. [51]Δ$30.15,'90. [52]©$0.005,'93. [53]©$0.01,'93. [54]©$0.03,'93. [55]Pfd in M$. [56]Special divd. [57]Stk dstr of Pembina Ltd. [58]Fiscal June'92 & prior. [59]Fiscal Mar'90 & prior. [60]12 Mo Dec,'90. [61]®$1.12,'92. [62]®$0.90,'93. [63]Accum on pfd. [64]®$0.24,'93.

Source: Standard & Poor's Corporation, *Stock Guide*, May 1994, p. 108. Reprinted by permission of Standard & Poor's, a division of McGraw–Hill, Inc.

For stocks, Standard & Poor's publishes its *Stock Guide*, which is roughly comparable to Moody's *Stock Survey* (both appear monthly). Figure 5.8 shows a typical presentation from the S&P *Stock Guide* containing basic information about the recent price performance of the shares, the financial position and earnings of the firm, recent dividend history, and similar information.

Brokerage Firm Reports

Most of the full–line brokerage houses have active research departments. Customers of the firm can easily acquire some of these reports from their brokers. One problem with actually using these reports is that they tend to appear in different formats over time, making it difficult to compare one recommendation with another. This may be particularly problematic when the reports are from different firms.

Also, many of the reports are somewhat ambiguous. When one gets through reading a recommendation, it is sometimes not clear whether to buy or sell the security. Of the reports prepared by brokerage firms, the overwhelming majority are positive. Part of the reason for this is political. Brokerage house analysts acquire much of their information from the firms themselves, so they are reluctant to develop reputations for nastiness. In addition, the corporations being analyzed may sometimes be customers of the brokerage firm.

These comments are not intended to condemn all brokerage firm research, the vast majority of which no particular individual could possibly review. Rather, these comments are intended as a warning. Investors should remember that the research is often purchased through the payment of relatively high commission rates compared to those available from discount brokers, who provide little or no research to their customers.

Value Line

One of the best sources of information about particular firms that might help an investor make an actual and immediate decision about investing in a particular common stock is the *Value Line Investment Survey.* As mentioned earlier, each week the *Survey* focuses on certain industries and the firms within those industries. One of the particularly good features of Value Line's approach is that it has a systematized procedure for providing definite advice one way or the other about particular firms (see Figure 5.9).

Each report discusses the firm's position, and supports its appraisal. The appraisal of the firm's prospects is made concrete in its ranking system for "timeliness" and "safety." A ranking of 1 is the highest, on a scale of 1 to 5. This simple system tells the investor how Value Line regards the prospects for each firm. Part of the Value Line service is its weekly "Selection and Opinion" report, in which Value Line features a particular stock recommended to perform extremely well. Compared with many recommendations that one might read, which are often "wishy–washy," Value Line makes definite and unambiguous recommendations. Further, there does seem to be some evidence that their rankings have value. In addition, Value Line publishes reports on options and convertible securities and on OTC special situations.

Chart Services

One popular way of predicting future stock price movements is to extrapolate from past movements. Some investors believe that the past stock price movements provide a reliable guide to future movements. To employ this mode of analysis, it is useful to have commercially prepared charts. These charts are available from a wide variety of vendors who advertise frequently in *Barron's*, for instance. A sample chart is presented in Figure 5.10. The analyst who believes in these methods should

Figure 5.9

A Value Line Company Report

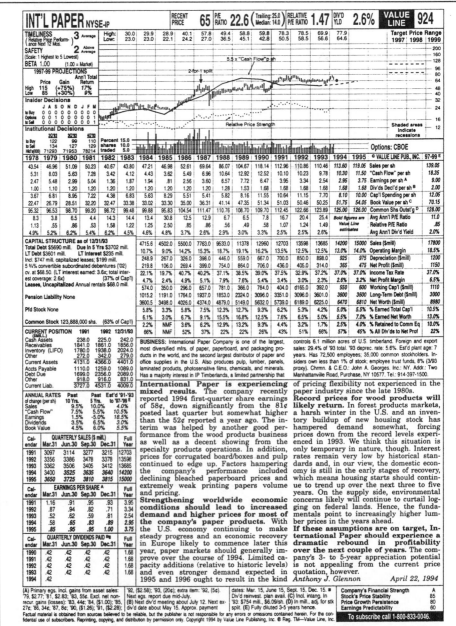

Source: Value Line Publishing, Inc., *The Value Line Investment Survey*, April 22, 1994, p. 924.

Figure 5.10

A Price History Chart

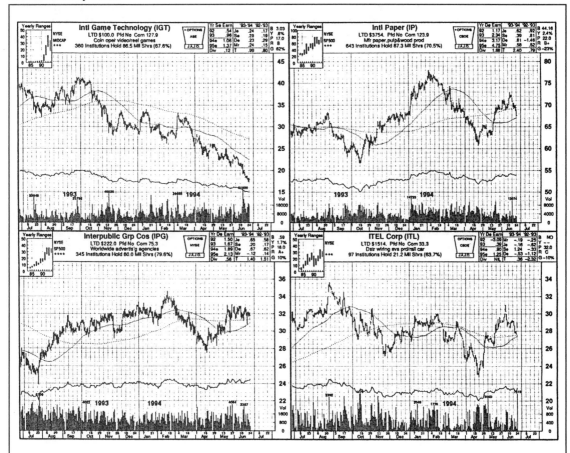

Source: Standard & Poor's Corporation, *Trendline*, June 24, 1994, p. 96. Reprinted by permission of Standard & Poor's, a division of McGraw–Hill, Inc.

be able to use such a chart to make predictions about the future of the stock in question. Even for the nonbeliever, it is sometimes interesting to see the stock's performance in the recent past.

Academic Journals

For the investor willing to make a considerable investment in understanding pricing relationships in the security markets, academic finance journals provide the key resource. Information in these journals is not likely to make one rich immediately, but for developing an understanding of security markets, they are unsurpassed.

The most respected journals in the field make full use of fairly sophisticated mathematics and statistics. Consequently, they are not for everyone. The *Journal of Finance*, the journal of the American Finance Association, leads the field. It is followed closely by the *Journal of Financial Economics*, the *Review of Financial Studies*, and the *Journal of Financial and Quantitative Analysis*. Each journal has its own character, but each contains carefully researched, responsible analyses. Somewhat less mathematical, with a more practical orientation, is *Financial Management*, the journal of the Financial Management Association. This journal is more oriented to the financial management of corporations. It also includes a number of articles relevant to security investing. Each of these journals is published quarterly, except for the *Journal of Finance*, which has five issues per year.

There are two journals that are quite readable, yet still give a flavor of the kinds of research being undertaken by the academic community. The *Financial Analysts Journal* is published specifically for financial analysts. As such, it is directed toward practicing professionals. The mathematical level of *Financial Analysts Journal* is tractable for most readers, and it often has readable articles on interesting and relevant topics. The *Journal of Portfolio Management* is similar in many respects. It features many short articles per issue, all of them focusing mainly on securities investment. Both of these are published quarterly and may provide the best starting point for finding out what academic research is all about.[2]

The American Association of Individual Investors (AAII) serves the interest of individual investors and publishes the *AAII Journal*, which contains many interesting and accessible articles about all aspects of investing. While not strictly an academic journal, many articles are written by academics for the intelligent lay investor. This allows academics to convey the latest academic thinking (if any!) without mathematics. The journal also includes timely and informative articles about the mechanics of securities transactions.

Computerized Data Bases

Computerized data bases have been important to finance. That trend toward using them is now extremely strong, and it will continue to grow in importance. Standard & Poor's offers *Compustat*, which comes in different parts to focus on different industries and provides data on both a quarterly and annual basis. The essential feature of the data base is that it contains financial statements from many companies over many years. For example, one computer tape might have annual reports for several hundred companies for each of the last 20 years.

---

[2]There are many other academic journals of merit as well, such as: *Journal of Financial Research; The Financial Review; Housing Finance Review; Journal of Economics and Business; Journal of Money, Credit, and Banking; Journal of Banking and Finance*, and others. In addition, there are many economics journals that often have articles on investments.

The Center for Research in Security Prices (CRSP) sells its data base, generally called the **CRSP tapes**. The most prominent feature of this data base is that it includes data on the common stock returns of more than a thousand companies on a daily basis. Daily data are now available as far back as 1962, and monthly data extend back to 1926. It also includes information on dividends. Another data base available from CRSP consists of monthly data on all U.S. Treasury securities. Compustat and the CRSP tapes are the standard data sources in their areas for academic research, and they are also used by many corporations. Because of their cost, however, their use is mainly limited to institutions.

For the individual investor, the availability of computerized data bases is constantly improving. There are two important information sources available to home computer users that offer a wide range of services—*Compuserve* and *The Source*. A subscriber to one of these services may call a local telephone number with a computer communication device (a modem) and read data bases with security quotations updated at least daily. Dow Jones offers a similar service called *Dow Jones News Retrieval*. In fact, it is already possible to trade securities by using a home computer.

Value Line also produces Value Screen II, a product that is ideal for home computers. It contains balance sheet and income statement data for about 1,700 companies. In addition, the software also includes Value Line's projections for future appreciation and earnings growth.

International Securities Information

Information about investing in foreign securities is much scarcer than the information available for domestic firms. There are, however, some valuable sources. Foreign newspapers, of course, are important, and many countries have firms that specialize in providing investment information. However, this discussion focuses only on English–language publications that should be readily available in university libraries.

In the category of general news, two daily newspapers stand out. For Great Britain, and good coverage of the European continent, the *Financial Times* is very important. It is essentially the British answer to *The Wall Street Journal*. In the Orient, there is another edition of *The Wall Street Journal* called the *Asian Wall Street Journal*.

Euromoney is an exceptionally useful monthly magazine published in England. As its name implies, it focuses principally on the European markets, but it has articles on the Orient, particularly developments in Japan, Hong Kong, and Singapore. Regular columns focus on activities in the Eurobond market and international bank lending, and it often features developments in foreign currency exchange markets as well. For a source of readable, informative, timely articles, it is one of the best business magazines.

The Economist, a British weekly publication, is another excellent source for following world business. It often features brief tutorials that make difficult and highly mathematical topics easy to understand. Compared to most U.S. magazines, its coverage and understanding of international finance is superb. In addition, it is an excellent general news magazine with an international focus.

Statistical information about foreign security markets is available from some of the major international organizations, such as the World Bank, the United Nations, the International Monetary Fund, and the Organization for Economic Co–Operation and Development (OECD), along with some publications of the U.S. government. One of the most comprehensive sources is *International Financial Statistics*, published monthly by the International Monetary Fund. It covers exchange rates, interest rates, industrial production, imports and exports, and commodity prices with reports on specific countries from Afghanistan to Zimbabwe. Each edition is more than 450 pages long in an 8½–by–11–inch format, so it can really be quite inclusive. *International Financial Statistics* is also published on a computer tape in order to facilitate more sophisticated analyses. The Fund also publishes *Balance of Payment Statistics* and *Direction of Trade Statistics* on a monthly basis. Annual publications include the *Government Finance Statistics Yearbook* and an annual edition of *International Financial Statistics*. In addition, the Fund publishes *Staff Papers*, which are research papers on specific topics prepared by staff economists. The United Nations publishes the *Monthly Bulletin of Statistics*, which carries data on industrial production and trade.

The U.S. Department of Commerce publishes *International Economic Indicators* quarterly. This publication focuses on the role of the United States in the world economy, providing considerable information on imports and exports. It also examines free–world imports and exports and the performance of the Common Market countries as a group. The *International Letter*, published every two weeks by the Federal Reserve Bank of Chicago, contains brief articles about important trends in international finance. Also, it carries useful information on exchange rates for many countries.

Many other publications of the U.S. government carry some international information, even if they are not devoted to the international scene exclusively. For example, the *Quarterly Review* of the Federal Reserve Bank of New York features a number of articles each year on international issues. These are valuable because they deal with timely topics in a readable way. The *Treasury Bulletin* contains a section on international statistics, and the *Federal Reserve Bulletin* also carries international data.

In the international arena, no companies provide the wide range of services that Standard & Poor's and Moody's do for the U.S. market. However, one source of information about foreign companies is *The World Directory of Multinational Enterprises*, featuring short reports on major multinational corporations. All of the academic journals mentioned are likely to carry articles from time to time that are pertinent to international investing. The *Columbia Journal of World Business* and *The Journal of International Business Studies* carry articles related to finance in virtually every issue. Both are fairly accessible to the general reader, but one cannot expect to find articles about investing in international securities in each quarterly issue.

Summary

This survey is woefully incomplete—any survey is. The wealth of information available is truly staggering, so this chapter seeks only to provide an introduction to some of the more popular sources. Anyone interested in securities investment needs to make an investment in learning how to find relevant information. There is no substitute in this process for browsing in the library. The reader who seeks out some of the items mentioned in this chapter is sure to find other items of value as well.

Questions and Problems

1. Where can you find the level of GNP for the United States for the first quarter of 1984? For Great Britain?
2. Where is the inflation rate for the United States (as measured by the CPI) for the first half of 1985 reported?
3. Where is the level of the Dow Jones Industrial Index at the end of 1974 reported?
4. What source or sources should an investor examine to learn about current developments in money market rates?
5. Explain how you would go about learning about the chemical leak in Bhopal, India, and its impact on Union Carbide.
6. The specialty steel industry in the United States might be a potential candidate for investment. How could you learn more about the industry and its prospects? To what source or sources could you turn for information about the particular firms within the industry?
7. Assume that your uncle has held some shares of Medtronic, Inc., since 1981, but that he has not been receiving his dividends properly. Where could you go to find the amount of the missing dividends and the right party to write to in order to receive the dividends?
8. American Maize Products trades on the American Stock Exchange, but has two classes of stocks listed. How could you find out about the differences between these two classes of stock?
9. How could you learn the quarterly earnings of Exxon for 1984?
10. Many Latin American countries currently have a great problem with their bank debt to foreign banks. Payment on that foreign debt depends crucially on the ability of these countries to export. How could you find information on the U.S. dollar value of annual exports for Brazil and Argentina?
11. Preferred stock, as mentioned in the previous chapter, seems to have features of both stocks and bonds. Where would you look for a detailed analysis of the character of preferred stock?

CHAPTER SIX

The Security Market: Regulation and Taxation

Overview

This chapter concentrates on securities market regulation and the taxation of security returns in the United States. Most of the important regulations of securities markets now in force in the United States stem from the 1930s. As a response to the financial collapse of 1929 and the ensuing Great Depression, which were largely the result of poor controls over securities dealings, several important laws were passed bringing many phases of securities flotation, selling, and investing under the control of the federal government. With some changes, this movement has continued since the 1930s. This chapter presents these regulations chronologically, emphasizing the way in which the web of regulation has been extended to catch an ever–growing percentage of security market activity.

Taxation is one of the most complicated and rapidly changing subjects in business. It is also one of the most important, because its impact on all dimensions of business is staggering. Taxation's effect on securities investment is equally important. The Tax Reform Act of 1986 revolutionized the tax treatment of securities investing, and the second major part of this chapter focuses on this new tax environment.

The Legislation of Regulation

This section provides a chronological discussion of the major laws regulating the securities market. As we will see, these laws formed the basis for contemporary markets, with much of the regulation growing out of the crisis of the Great Depression. Various laws defined the separation between commercial banking and investment banking, specified the conditions under which firms could issue new securities, and brought the operation of securities exchanges under federal regulation.

Glass–Steagall Act or the Banking Act of 1933

As the movement to regulate the securities market gained force in the early 1930s, one of the very first pieces of legislation passed was the **Glass–Steagall Act**, or the Banking Act of 1933. As the second name implies, it is directed at banking as well as the securities industry. The essential provision of the act prohibits commercial banks from acting as security underwriters for initial security offerings. At the time, it was believed that the ability to operate in both commercial and investment banking concentrated too much power in too few hands.

This separation of the commercial banking and investment banking functions is unique to the United States. In Germany and Japan, for instance, all of the major investment banking concerns are commercial banks. In the United States, many observers believe that the Glass–Steagall Act has had an injurious effect on commercial banks, claiming it prohibits them from diversifying their operations into an area where they already have some expertise and which they might use to help control their risk exposure.

Now the Glass–Steagall Act is starting to erode rapidly. In July 1988, the Supreme Court ruled that commercial banks may underwrite commercial paper, municipal revenue bonds, mortgage–backed securities, and securities collateralized by consumer debt. The grounds for this decision were that banks would not be "engaged principally" in underwriting, and this principal involvement was the activity that was banned by the Glass–Steagall Act. These underwriting activities must be conducted by a nonbank subsidiary of a bank holding company, and these activities may not produce more than 5 percent of the subsidiary's revenues. The Federal Reserve Board must grant approval for a bank to engage in this business. Early actions show that the Board will be tough in granting permissions, and that it is intent on keeping weak banks out of the new business. In 1989, the Federal Reserve extended this trend by allowing J.P. Morgan and Co. to underwrite corporate debt through its securities trading firm. While these new rules are promising for commercial banks, they have moved slowly to exert their new powers. After all, there are sophisticated investment banking firms with firmly entrenched positions waiting to exploit any missteps by the new kids on the block.

Securities Act of 1933

The **Securities Act of 1933** was the first major piece of legislation directed specifically toward the securities market itself, and it is basically a "truth in securities" law. The law states that issuers of new securities must provide truthful information about the securities to potential investors, and it prohibits fraud in security sales. It is this law which requires that a potential investor be given a prospectus before investing and specifies the kinds of information that must be contained in the prospectus. As discussed in Chapter 4, the prospectus must contain information about the firm, its officers, the purpose of the issue, the financial position of the firm, and any legal actions pending against the firm.

Another major provision of the law requires that the prospective issuer file a registration statement with the Securities Exchange Commission (SEC). False statements in the SEC registration statement are subject to criminal penalties. Additionally, any purchaser of securities sold under a misleading registration statement may sue the issuer to recover lost funds.

The law is intended to cover long–term securities, such as stocks and bonds. As such, it specifically excludes certain securities from the requirement of registering and providing a prospectus. For instance, short–term debt obligations with original maturities of 270 days or less are excluded, as are government securities and many debt obligations issued by commercial banks. On the basis of their size, securities offerings of less than $500,000 are also excluded.

Rule 144a

Rule 144a of the Securities Act of 1933 governs private placements and stipulates that a security originally issued as a privately placed security cannot be sold for two years from the date of issue. The purpose of this rule was to protect unwary investors from securities that had not gone through the registration process. In 1990, the SEC adopted Rule 144a, which alters this restriction in fundamental ways.

In essence, Rule 144a permits the immediate resale of privately placed securities to a Qualified Institutional Buyer (QIB). A QIB is an institution, other than a bank or savings and loan association, that engages in transactions of more than $100 million of securities per year. For banks and savings and loans to be QIBs, they must meet the minimal trading requirement and they must have $25 million in net worth. In addition, brokers and dealers may qualify as QIBs, making an estimated total of more than 4,000 potential buyers in the U.S.

This change in the law is potentially very important for non–U.S. issuers of securities. As we saw in Chapter 4, many foreign firms avoid the U.S. market because of the relatively strict financial regulation. Rule 144a may offer a way for sophisticated financial institutions in the United States and abroad to trade in this new market niche. Under this new program, there is no requirement to register with the SEC under the Securities Act of 1933. Non–U.S. issuers will not have to present financial statements that comply with U.S. rules, and they will not be forced to disclose confidential information.

In the early days of Rule 144a, the market has developed slowly. While Rule 144a makes privately placed instruments more liquid, liquidity may not be as important in the private placement market. (The overwhelming bulk of privately placed issues are bought by insurance companies, who generally hold until the instruments mature.) It remains to be seen whether this innovation leads to fundamental change in the international securities market.

Securities Exchange Act of 1934

While the Securities Act of 1933 brought the primary market under federal regulation, the **Securities Exchange Act of 1934** extended federal regulation to the secondary market, or at least the organized exchanges operating in that market. The other main contribution of this act was the establishment of the Securities and Exchange Commission.

The law specifically requires that securities exchanges register with the SEC and that they agree to comply with the laws governing them. Further, each exchange must organize its own procedures, consistent with the guidelines prepared by the SEC, for the proper conduct of business. These exchange guidelines specify fair and unfair practices and include procedures for disciplining or expelling exchange members who transgress. The SEC has the power to enforce the laws in those cases where exchange self–regulation is lax. As a consequence, the exchanges have a strong incentive to maintain a clean house, both in order to assure public confidence and to escape the grasp of the SEC.

Today the SEC has a staff of more than 1,500. Five members, appointed by the President for terms of five years, constitute the commission. While this may seem like a large organization, it is certainly too small to oversee all phases of the securities business carefully. For this reason, self–regulation is crucial to the entire network of control over securities markets. To a large extent, the interests of the exchanges and other participants in the securities markets coincide. The entire securities industry requires public confidence if it is to operate. As a result, the exchanges generally prosper when they regulate themselves in conformity with the desires of the SEC.

One of the most critical issues in the entire field of securities regulation is the control of corporate insiders, because this concern goes to the heart of investor confidence. The act defines a **corporate insider** as an employee or officer of the corporation who has access to non–public information about the firm. If such parties could use that information to generate trading profits, then members of the public would be reluctant to invest in the securities of the firm. Outside investors could justifiably believe that they are competing at a disadvantage in the investment process with other parties who have a superior position because of their special knowledge about the firm.

To deal with this potentially damaging situation, the act prohibits insiders from making speculative profits on the shares of the company about which they have inside information. Further, every shareholder with more than 10 percent of the outstanding shares of the firm, as well as the officers and directors of the firm, must report their transactions in the shares of the firm. These reports of insider activity are made public through *The Wall Street Journal* and the SEC's "Report of Insider Activity." Also, insiders may not engage in short sales of their firm's stock. This restriction helps curtail various cases of price manipulation. Nonetheless, violations of these rules continue to be a major problem, as a later section on insider trading will explain.

The Securities Exchange Act of 1934 also established margin requirements. As discussed previously, the practice of allowing investors to borrow 100 percent of the funds necessary to invest in securities contributed to the great crash of October 1929. The law gives the Federal Reserve Board the authority to regulate margin.

Public Utility Holding Company Act of 1935

Physical limitations make it extremely difficult to have a competitive market for the products of public utility firms, such as gas and electricity. As a result, public utilities hold one of the world's largest monopolies. Believing that this monopoly power was not being used in the public interest, the **Public Utility Holding Company Act of 1935** brought major parts of the financial dealings of such firms under the jurisdiction of the SEC.

The SEC was empowered to examine and control the corporate structure of the firms in this industry, to regulate their accounting practices, and to determine the proper kinds of securities the companies could issue. This act helped to control a situation in which the companies had created a maze of corporate relationships, which served the interest of a small group at the expense of the public.

Maloney Act (1939)

The Maloney Act amended the Securities Exchange Act of 1934, the original terms of which gave authority over organized exchanges to the SEC. The essential purpose of the **Maloney Act** was to extend similar control to the over–the–counter market. In doing so, it created the legal basis upon which the National Association of Securities Dealers (NASD) was founded in 1939.

As discussed in Chapter 3, the NASD functions as a self–regulating trade association for participants in the OTC market. Its incentives for controlling the avarice of its members are essentially parallel to those of the organized exchanges. Since the SEC predates the NASD, it has had control over that organization since its inception. All rules adopted by the NASD must be reported to the SEC. These rules cover fair practices, fraud, misrepresentation, and penalties for infractions. The SEC has the authority to revoke the rights of NASD to function as an industry association. This ultimate sanction gives the SEC a loud voice in the day–to–day operations of the NASD.

Trust Indenture Act of 1939

In bond issues, it is normal for a trustee to be appointed to protect the rights of the bondholders. Prior to the passage of the Trust Indenture Act, there was no legal safeguard to make sure that the trustee could act independently and strongly on behalf of the bondholders. If the trustee is dependent on the corporation issuing the bonds, then the issuer may be able to break the terms of the indenture agreement, leaving the bondholders without any effective remedy.

The **Trust Indenture Act** requires that the trustee maintain its financial independence from the issuing firm, so that it is free to enforce the terms of the indenture. Further, the act specified more closely the kinds of information that must be included in the indenture agreement and stipulated that the issuer must provide a list of the bondholders and semiannual financial reports to the trustee.

Investment Advisors Act of 1940

Investment advisors, those who give investment advice for compensation, were brought under the regulation of the SEC by the **Investment Advisors Act of 1940**. The act prohibits fraud and deception and requires advisors to keep records, which can be inspected by the SEC. In addition, the act controls some advertising practices. For example, many investment advisors advertise their successful history of recommendations, but they include the warning that past success is no guarantee of future success.

The law, however, does not require any proof of competence on the part of the advisor as a condition of registering with the SEC. The claim that someone is a Registered Investment Advisor is really only a claim that he or she has complied with this law, not a claim of any knowledge or ability as an investment advisor.

Securities Investor Protection Act of 1970

The **Securities Investor Protection Act of 1970** established the Securities Investor Protection Corporation (SIPC). The SIPC is a government corporation that acts as an insurance company to protect investors against failing brokers and securities dealers. The act requires securities firms to participate in the SIPC and to contribute fees to the fund.

Without the existence of such a fund, investors have a very risky position should a broker fail. For example, a brokerage firm might go bankrupt when it is discovered that the securities left in its charge have been sold and the proceeds spent. Without the SIPC, the customers of the brokerage firm might never recover their funds. While it is intended that the fund will be fully supported by assessments made against brokerage firms, back–up government pledges of funds are available should the fund ever be depleted.

Employee Retirement Income Security Act of 1974

The **Employee Retirement Income Security Act** (ERISA) of 1974 brought pension funds under federal regulation. Pension funds have grown to be the most important part of retirement planning for many workers. Also, the payouts from pension funds are so far in the future for most workers that some control over the behavior of pension fund managers is needed to be sure that the funds will really be available when workers come to retirement age.

This act charges pension fund managers with the preservation of capital and with a responsibility to make prudent investments to contribute to the growth of capital as well. This **prudent manager rule** requires that pension fund managers behave prudently when making investment decisions. One immediate result of this rule is that pension fund managers must take steps to prove that they acted prudently. For example, a prudent manager would not place all of the pension funds in extremely speculative securities. Likewise, a prudent manager would not invest all of the company's pension funds in the stock of the same company. While this rule is somewhat vague, it gives a sound principal to specify the appropriate conduct of pension managers.

One problem with the prudent manager rule is that pension fund managers must devote their energies to amassing evidence of their prudence. This can impair their efficiency and the performance of the pension fund. The authors of the act presumably viewed this as a reasonable cost to gain control over potential abuses.

Securities Act Amendments of 1975

In 1975, Congress amended the Securities Act of 1933. One of the more important features of the act was the requirement that the SEC move toward establishing a single nationwide securities market. This has prompted the composite reporting of securities transactions from different exchanges and the development of the National Market System by the NASD.

The act also outlawed fixed commission rates, but it allowed the New York Stock Exchange to continue to require its members to trade all NYSE–listed securities only on the NYSE. The act also directed the SEC to establish minimum capital requirements for brokers.

Insider Trading

The Securities Exchange Act of 1934 limited the trading of corporate insiders and required reports of insiders for transactions in the firm's shares. The prohibition against insider trading applies both to principals of the firm involved and to others who happen to learn of material, non–public, information. The case of Texas Gulf Sulphur illustrates trading by corporate insiders, while trading on inside information by a non–employee is illustrated by a case involving a writer of a *Wall Street Journal* column.

Insider Trading by Corporate Employees

Texas Gulf Sulphur Company (TGS) had conducted aerial mineral exploration for a number of years and located a promising site in Timmins, Ontario.[1] The first core sample was very rich in copper, zinc, and silver. Diversionary drilling was conducted in other locations, while additional land around Timmins was purchased. By March 31, 1964, the land acquisition program was sufficiently advanced to permit more test drilling in the Timmins field. These samples were also extremely promising, and the April 11, 1964, editions of several major newspapers contained rumors of the successful drilling.

---

[1] This account of the Texas Gulf Sulphur case relies on H. Lusk, C. Hewitt, J. Donnel, and A. Barnes, *Business Law and the Regulatory Environment*, 5e, Homewood, IL: Richard D. Irwin, 1982, pp. 545–549.

On April 13, 1964, TGS issued a press release stating that nothing of special value had been discovered, saying: "Recent drilling on one property near Timmins has led to preliminary indications that more drilling would be required for proper evaluation of this prospect. The drilling done to date has not been conclusive." On April 16, 1964, TGS held a press conference announcing that the Timmins property would yield 25 million tons of ore.

Between the first discovery of the site and the April 16 press conference, some TGS executives bought shares of the firm, knowing about the rich find. During the entire period from November 1963 to May 1964, TGS stock rose from $18 to $54 per share. The SEC went to court, claiming the insider trading and the release of false information in the April 13 press release were in violation of the Securities Exchange Act of 1934. The court upheld the SEC's position. Part of the judge's ruling read as follows:

> Thus, anyone in possession of material inside information must either disclose it to the investing public, or if he is disabled from disclosing it in order to protect a corporate confidence, or he chooses not to do so, must abstain from trading in or recommending the securities concerned while such inside information remains undisclosed. So, it is here no justification for insider activity that disclosure was forbidden by the legitimate corporate objective of acquiring options to purchase the land surrounding the exploration site: if the information was, as the SEC contends, material, its possessors should have kept out of the market until disclosure was accomplished.[2]

Insider Trading by a Non-Employee

Occasionally, someone who is not a director, officer, or employee of a firm may gain access to information about a firm's prospects that is material to making an investment decision. If that information has not been made public, it is illegal to use that information as a basis for trading. As an example, assume in the TGS case that an independent pilot being used by TGS for its aerial exploration learned about the rich ore deposits. The law would prohibit the pilot from trading on that information. The same applies to independent lawyers and accountants who might have access to special information about a company.

The prohibition against insider trading is even broader than these examples imply, as the case of *The Wall Street Journal* column, "Heard on the Street" reveals. "Heard on the Street" is a daily column in *The Wall Street Journal* that is like a finance gossip column. Each column might mention several firms, focusing the financial community's attention on particularly good or bad prospects for each of the firms. One market analyst said of "Heard on the Street" that "when a company is written up in that column, if there are a lot of positive comments, the stock

---

[2] Quoted in H. Lusk, C. Hewitt, J. Donnel, and A. Barnes, *Business Law and the Regulatory Environment*, 5e, Homewood, IL: Richard D. Irwin, 1982, p. 546.

always goes up. If there are a lot of negative comments, the stock goes down. If you knew what that column was going to say, you could trade on that information."[3]

A columnist for "Heard on the Street," R. Foster Winans, was fired by *The Wall Street Journal* for conspiring with a group of traders to use the advance knowledge of what was going to appear in the column. The traders would use that advance information to take a position in the stocks that were to be featured in the column. When the stories ran, the stock price would respond accordingly, leaving the trading group with a nice profit. The SEC reported that it was investigating 21 such incidents involving the "Heard on the Street" column, most of which were written by Winans. Winans apparently admitted these charges and later denied them, but was finally convicted.

Increases in Insider Trading and Increasing SEC Activity

The "Heard on the Street" case occurred at a time of apparently increasing insider trading activity, according to a completely separate *Wall Street Journal* report.[4] Apparently, one area of highest abuse concerns mergers. On news that a firm is the target of a takeover attempt, it is not unusual for the price of shares of the target firm to increase dramatically. Some people know of the pending takeover before it is publicly known, and this inside information is very valuable. As a response to this increase in alleged insider activity, or perhaps as the reason insider activity has received more attention, the SEC enforcement actions have escalated dramatically in recent years. In spite of the recent dramatic increase in the number of SEC actions, the number is pathetically small in comparison to the range of insider trading that is probably taking place. This is due to a relatively small staff at the SEC and the great difficulty in tracking and proving insider trading violations.

Taxation

The Tax Reform Act of 1986 instituted sweeping changes in the structure of tax rates and dramatically altered the taxation of income from securities investing. Changes introduced under the Clinton administration mainly raised the income tax rates for those taxpayers with higher incomes. It is impossible to consider all of the major aspects of taxation in this chapter. Consequently, this section focuses only on federal income taxes for corporations and individuals arising from security transactions. This is still a very broad topic, so the following discussion is intended only to indicate the major features of the system. The discussion first considers the definition of taxable income, and then it discusses how interest and dividends are taxed. Capital gains and losses receive special treatment.

---

[3] *Miami Herald*, March 30, 1984, p. 1.

[4] See *The Wall Street Journal*, March 2, 1984, p. 1, and related stories.

Taxable Income Derived from Securities Investing

In the United States, incomes of both corporations and individuals are subject to federal income tax.[5] Investing in securities gives rise to taxable income from two major sources:

1. cash flows from owning the securities (dividends or interest payments),
2. changes in the value of the securities (capital gains or losses).

Historically, these two kinds of incomes have been treated quite differently. One of the most important features of the 1986 law is the elimination of the distinction between capital gains and dividends or interest.

Taxation of Interest and Dividends

Interest received by individuals or corporations, whether it be interest on long–term bonds, money market accounts, or bank accounts, is all taxable income. An important exception is the interest paid on tax–exempt municipal debt obligations, which is free of federal income taxation. Both individuals and corporations simply add 100 percent of any interest income to other taxable income. For individuals receiving dividends, the full amount is taxable. For corporations that own securities and receive dividends, 80 percent of all dividends received are tax–exempt. The remaining 20 percent is added to other taxable income.

Capital Gains and Losses

Changes in the value of a security give rise to tax obligations and benefits. An increase in the price of a security during the time it is held is known as a **capital gain**, while a decrease in price is known as a **capital loss**. Capital gains and losses may be either realized or unrealized. In most cases, a capital gain or loss is realized when an investor sells a security and receives the cash flow associated with a gain or suffers a cash outflow associated with a loss. Also, for the most part, only realized capital gains and losses give rise to tax consequences, although there are some exceptions. Under the 1986 act, capital gains are added to taxable income while capital losses are subtracted from taxable income. This means that taxable investment income in a given year equals the sum of all dividends and interest received plus all realized capital gains minus all realized capital losses.

Capital gains and losses are classified as either short–term or long–term. Short–term gains are gains realized from the purchase and sale of an asset within one year. Thus, capital gains contrast with ordinary income, such as income earned as wages. In general, short–term gains are taxed at the same rate as ordinary

---

[5] Taxation of options and futures contracts is considered in the chapters on options and futures.

Table 6.1

▰▰▰▰▰▰

Personal Federal Income Tax Schedule 1994 and Subsequent Years

Individual's Taxable Income	Tax
Up to $22,750	$0 + 15%
$22,750 to $55,100	$3,412.50 + 28% of all amounts over $22,750
$55,100 to 115,000	$12,470.50 + 31% of all amounts over $55,100
$115,000 to $250,000	$31,039.50 + 36% of all amounts over $115,000
$250,000 and above	$79,639.50 + 39.6% of all amounts over $250,000

Married Couples Filing Jointly Taxable Income	Tax
Up to $38,000	$0 + 15%
$38,000 to $91,850	$5,700 + 28% of all amounts over $38,000
$91,850 to $140,000	$20,778 + 31% of all amounts over $91,850
$140,000 to $250,000	$35,704.50 + 36% of all amounts over $140,000
$250,000 and up	$75,304.50 + 39.6% of all amounts over $250,000

income. Long–term gains are taxed at the same rate as ordinary income, except they are subject to a maximum rate of 28 percent.

Personal Tax Rates

Once the taxable income is calculated, the taxpayer must still calculate the tax to be paid. Table 6.1 presents the tax rates applied to individuals and couples for 1994 and subsequent years. Taxable personal income consists of all income, including wages and investment income, adjusted for many factors. For instance, interest paid on a home and certain allowances for dependents are subtracted from income in the computation of taxable income.

Once the taxable income is computed, the tax rates shown in Table 6.1 can be used to compute the tax due. For example, assume that a couple is filing jointly and has a taxable income of $60,000. Using the table, we can see that the tax would be $5,700 plus 28 percent of all income above $38,000. The tax computation would be:

$$\text{Tax} = \$5,700 + .28(\$60,000 - \$38,000)$$
$$= \$5,700 + \$6,160$$
$$= \$11,860$$

For this couple, the tax paid on each additional dollar of income, or the **marginal tax rate**, equals 28 percent. As the table shows, the highest marginal tax rate for

Table 6.2

Federal Tax Rates for Corporations for 1994

Taxable Income		Tax Rate (%)	Starting Tax ($)
From ($)	To ($)		
0	50,000	15	0.00
50,000	75,000	25	7,500.00
75,000	100,000	34	13,750.00
100,000	335,000	39	22,250.00
335,000	10,000,000	34	113,900.00
10,000,000	15,000,000	35	3,374,500.00
15,000,000	18,333,333	38	5,124,500.00
18,333,333		35	6,391,167.00

personal taxes is 39.6 percent. State or local income tax would be in addition to this federal tax.

Corporate Tax Rates

Table 6.2 presents the federal income tax schedule for corporations. As for individuals, corporate income is subject to many adjustments in figuring taxable income. Some of the most important of these are the adjustments for interest expenses and depreciation. Until recently, the highest marginal tax rate was 46 percent, but under present law the highest marginal rate is 39 percent. For large corporations, the effective marginal tax rate is 35 percent.

Double Taxation of Dividends

The tax laws are famous for some of their peculiarities. One which has attracted a great deal of attention is the **double taxation** of dividends. Corporations paying dividends must pay them out of their after–tax earnings. Dividends paid to individuals are then taxed as regular income. The double taxation arises because these funds are taxed at the corporate level and at the individual level.

To see the effect of this double taxation, consider a corporation in the 34 percent marginal tax bracket paying dividends to an individual in the 28 percent marginal tax bracket. Assume that the corporation has $100 of pre–tax income available to pay as a dividend to the shareholder of this example. The $100 of pre–tax income will be only $47.52 by the time it reaches the shareholder's pocket, as the following calculation shows.

$100.00	Pre–Tax Income
– 34.00	Corporate Income Tax at the 34% rate
$ 66.00	Dividend Paid Out by Corporation
– 18.48	Individual Income Tax at the 28% rate
$ 47.52	Spendable Proceeds for Shareholder

Summary

The current web of regulation of the securities markets and the securities industries grew out of a response to perceived abuses. To many observers, the financial collapse of the securities market and many bank failures during the Great Depression were the result of improper or excessively risky practices. The system of regulation now in place aims to control the permissible risk exposure of certain investors and to protect the investing public from dishonest practices. By doing so, the financial system and the entire economy should be strengthened.

With the passage of the Tax Reform Act of 1986, the tax system in the United States has been simplified. One of the most important simplifications has been the decision to treat earned income, such as wages and investment income, in the same way. Nonetheless, for the securities investor, proper tax management is very important in maximizing after–tax proceeds. This requires close attention to the choice of dividend, interest, and the realization of capital gains and losses as the form of reward for the investor.

Questions and Problems

1. What is the relationship between commercial banking and investment banking in the United States? What law stipulated that relationship?
2. What is currently developing in the relationship between commercial and investment banking? Give examples.
3. What kinds of securities are regulated by the Securities Act of 1933? How have banks responded to this act in the structuring of the kinds of securities they offer?
4. What is the difference between a registration statement and a prospectus?
5. Which act regulates the primary market, and which regulates the secondary market?
6. Does a securities exchange determine its own rules, or must it follow a detailed set of rules stipulated by the Securities Exchange Commission? What do you think about this system? Why do you think that the system is organized in this manner?
7. Sitting in a Wall Street deli enjoying a pastrami sandwich, you hear a conversation about a pending takeover of Apple Computer by IBM. What restrictions does the law place on your use of this information?

8. Why are there special laws regulating the financial practices of public utility firms?

9. While the law clearly places organized security exchanges under regulatory supervision, is the same true of the over–the–counter (OTC) market? If so, which law provides for supervision of the OTC market?

10. A manufacturing corporation might issue bonds and seek a trustee for the bond issue that it can control in order to avoid making the full payments to the bondholders. If it did so, what kinds of securities laws would be likely to be broken in the process?

11. Discount brokers offer reduced services at reduced prices in comparison to full–line brokerage houses. Are securities left in trust with both kinds of brokers equally protected? What laws are relevant here?

12. Which law stipulates a "prudent man" rule? What are the advantages and disadvantages of such a rule?

13. Different nations have different rules regarding the taxation of securities profits and losses. How can these be important for economic activity?

14. Assume you have held a security for 170 days and have a paper loss of $2,000 on it. Considering tax consequences alone, what action might you be wise to take? What if there were a $2,000 gain instead?

Suggested Readings

Electronic Bulls and Bears: U.S. Securities Markets and Information Technology, Washington, DC: U.S. Government Printing Office, September 1990.

France, V. G., "The Regulation of Margin Requirements," *Margins and Market Integrity*, Chicago: Probus Publishing, 1991, pp. 1–47.

Hardouvelis, G. and S. Peristiani, "Do Margin Requirements Matter? Evidence from U.S. and Japanese Stock Markets," Federal Reserve Bank of New York *Quarterly Review*, 14:4, Winter 1989–90, pp. 16–35.

Hsieh, D. A. and M. H. Miller, "Margin Regulation and Stock Market Volatility," *Journal of Finance*, 45:1, March 1990, pp. 3–29.

Kopcke, R. W., "Tax Reform and Stock Prices," Federal Reserve Bank of Boston *New England Economic Review*, March/April 1988, pp. 3–22.

Investing in Debt Instruments

Part Two of this book presents the basic concepts of bond valuation and bond portfolio management. A bond is essentially a fixed income obligation, because most bonds promise a set of payments at specific dates over the future. The valuation of a bond depends on the probability that the promised payments will be made and on general economic conditions that affect interest rates.

Chapter 7 introduces the basic principles of bond valuation. It explains why bond prices tend to fall when interest rates rise. It also explains why the prices of bonds with longer periods before maturity tend to be more sensitive to changes in interest rates. A thorough understanding of these principles is crucial to successful bond investing.

Chapter 8 explores some of the basic ideas of bond portfolio management—the management of a carefully chosen collection of bonds. It is not sufficient merely to choose one bond that the investor expects to perform well. Instead, for most applications, it is better to have a portfolio of bonds. As a result, bond investing usually involves the selection of individual bonds, but it also requires the selection of bonds that will contribute to the desirable characteristics of the portfolio. Among these desirable characteristics are the correct risk level and the best maturity mix. Individual bonds will differ in these characteristics, so the investor needs to know how to combine these different bonds to construct the best portfolio.

Bond Pricing Principles

Overview

This chapter builds on the institutional discussion of the bond and money markets presented in Chapter 2. Successful investing in bonds depends on a thorough knowledge of the pricing principles for bonds. Even a typical corporate bond with fixed coupon payments and repayment of principal at maturity still has important pricing relationships that require analysis. For example, assume an investor anticipates rising interest rates. Would this belief make the bond market more or less attractive? What implication does the anticipation of higher interest rates have for the choice between long– and short–maturity bonds? What do rising interest rates imply for the choice between bonds with large and small coupons? These are crucial issues for any bond investor. This chapter develops the basic principles of bond pricing and the movement of bond prices in response to changing market conditions.

Fortunately, well–established principles explain and predict the movement of bond prices as a result of changes in market rates of interest. As explained later, the change in the price of a bond for a given change in interest rates depends on the time remaining until the bond matures, the bond's coupon rate, and the level of interest rates. Only by understanding the price relationships between interest rates and bonds of different descriptions can one develop the skills necessary for good bond investing. Consequently, this chapter explores the relationships among the key variables of bond pricing: the maturity, the coupon rate, and the market rate of interest.

Although the principles of bond price movement are well understood, they remain somewhat unwieldy by themselves. This is because it is difficult to assess the different, but simultaneous, influences of coupon rate, maturity, and changing interest rates. However, it is possible to develop a single measure of a bond's price sensitivity to changing interest rates. This measure is called **duration**, and this chapter extends the basic bond pricing principles to include this summary measure of sensitivity. In addition, we discuss the idea of **convexity**, a related measure of bond price sensitivity.

For bond investors, changes in interest rates are the decisive factors in the success or failure of an investment program. After analyzing how bond prices react to changes in interest rates, this chapter provides an introduction to the factors that determine the level of interest rates. Not surprisingly, expected inflation plays a critical role.

When managing a bond investment, the investor often has a particular horizon in view and would like to work to maximize the value of the bond investment at some future date. To measure performance toward this goal, a new yield concept is needed in addition to those discussed in Chapter 2. It is called the **realized compound yield to maturity** (RCYTM).[1] All of these concepts are applicable to the investment in a single bond. As such, the ideas developed in this chapter pave the way for Chapter 8, which discusses bond portfolio management—the management of a carefully chosen collection of bonds.

The Effect of Time on Bond Price Movements

Bond prices change merely as the result of the passage of time. For example, the typical corporate bond pays its face value of $1,000 upon maturity. As a result, no matter what the purchase price of the bond, the bond will have a price of $1,000 at maturity. This means that the bond's price must converge to $1,000 over its life, even if interest rates do not change at all.

As mentioned in Chapter 2, all bonds can be classified as premium, par, or discount bonds, depending on whether their prices exceed, equal, or fall below the principal amount. At maturity, the price of the bond equals the principal amount to be returned. Consequently, for premium bonds prior to maturity, the bond's price will generally fall over its life, even if interest rates do not change. By the same token, if a bond sells at a discount, its price must rise, reaching the principal amount by the maturity date. To illustrate the time path of bond prices, assume interest rates are constant at 10 percent. Figure 7.1 shows the paths that the prices of five bonds will follow over time. All of the bonds are issued with 30–year maturities, but they differ with respect to their coupon payments, according to the following schedule.

> Bond A: 30–year, 14% coupon
> Bond B: 30–year, 12% coupon
> Bond C: 30–year, 10% coupon
> Bond D: 30–year, 8% coupon
> Bond E: 30–year, 6% coupon

Since we assume that interest rates are constant at 10 percent, Bonds A and B will be premium bonds. Whenever the coupon rate exceeds the bond's yield, the

[1]This name was first used for this idea by S. Homer and M. Liebowitz, *Inside the Yield Book*, Englewood Cliffs, NJ: Prentice Hall, 1972.

Figure 7.1

Price Paths Over Time for Four Bonds with a Constant Yield of 10%

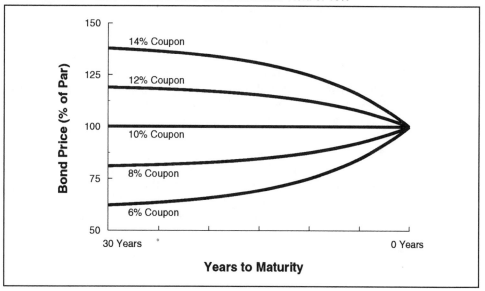

bond must sell at a premium. Notice that the prices of Bonds A and B fall over time. At maturity, the premium is gone and the prices of both bonds equal the par value. Bond C will always be priced at its par value of 100.00, as long as yields remain at 10 percent. Bonds D and E, with coupon rates below the yield to maturity, sell at a discount. Therefore, their prices must rise toward the par value, reaching the par value at maturity. Again, notice that these price changes occur when interest rates are constant. Figure 7.1 is drawn under the assumption that interest rates are constant at 10 percent over the entire 30–year life of these bonds. Bond C, with its 10 percent coupon rate, would have a price of 100.00 over the entire period. Its price path would have followed the line for a 10 percent coupon in Figure 7.1.

When we consider that rates fluctuate, we see that price movements become more complex. Recall that we also must consider accrued interest, as explained in Chapter 2, and that quoted bond prices normally do not reflect accrued interest. Thus, for the bond with the coupon rate equal to the yield to maturity, the quoted price will always equal the par value. The accrued interest must be added to the quoted price, however, to determine the actual sales price of the bond.

The Effect of Interest Rates on Bond Price Movements

In bond pricing, it is essential to understand the ways in which the prices of bonds with different characteristics respond to changes in the market rates of interest. The effect of a given change in interest rates on the price of a bond depends upon three key variables:

1. the maturity of the bond,
2. the coupon rate,
3. the level of interest rates at the time of the change in interest rates.

This section develops five well–recognized principles of bond pricing which explain how the price of a given bond changes in response to a sudden change in interest rates. These principles demonstrate the different effects of a change in interest rates as a function of the three key variables. Throughout this section, we assume interest rates change instantaneously from one level to another and then examine the resulting bond price change.

The starting point is the basic valuation equation of finance, as it is applied to bonds. Equation 7.1 simply states that the price of a bond (P) equals the present value of all promised cash flows from the bond (C_t) when those cash flows are discounted to the present at the bond's yield to maturity, (r).

$$P = \sum_{t=1}^{M} \frac{C_t}{(1 + r)^t} \qquad\qquad \textbf{7.1}$$

The cash flows include both coupon payments and the return of the bond's principal at maturity.

The Bond Pricing Principles

The five bond pricing principles discussed in this section were proven rigorously by Burton Malkiel in a now famous article.[2] Here the principles are illustrated rather than proven. Each principle is illustrated using bond prices that can be computed or found in a book of bond tables. A bond table gives prices for bonds of different maturities, different coupon rates, and different yields. Table 7.1 presents selected portions from a bond yield book. A bond yield book shows the value of corporate bonds as a percentage of the bond's par value for different coupon rates, different maturities, and different yields. For example, consider a bond with 20 years remaining until maturity and having a 12 percent coupon rate. If this bond yields 10 percent, its price will be 117.16, as shown in Table 7.1. This quoted price of 117.16 means that the bond's price will be 117.16 percent of the par value of the bond. For a bond with a par value of $1,000, for example, its price would be $1,171.60.

---

[2]See Burton G. Malkiel, "Expectations, Bond Prices, and the Term Structure of Interest Rates," *Quarterly Journal of Economics*, May 1962, pp. 197–218.

Table 7.1

▬▬▬▬▬▬▬

Selected Portions from a Bond Yield Book

Yield	6% Coupon Rate Maturity (Years)				12% Coupon Rate Maturity (Years)			
	5	10	20	30	5	10	20	30
0.0400	108.98	116.35	127.36	134.76	135.93	165.41	209.42	239.04
0.0450	106.65	111.97	119.65	124.56	133.25	159.86	198.23	222.81
0.0500	104.38	107.79	112.55	115.45	130.63	154.56	187.86	208.18
0.0550	102.16	103.81	106.02	107.31	128.08	149.49	178.25	194.97
0.0600	100.00	100.00	100.00	100.00	125.59	144.63	169.34	183.03
0.0650	97.89	96.37	94.45	93.44	123.16	139.98	161.07	172.20
0.0700	95.84	92.89	89.32	87.53	120.79	135.53	153.39	162.36
0.0750	93.84	89.58	84.59	82.20	118.48	131.27	146.24	153.41
0.0800	91.89	86.41	80.21	77.38	116.22	127.18	139.59	145.25
0.0850	89.99	83.38	76.15	73.01	114.02	123.27	133.39	137.79
0.0900	88.13	80.49	72.40	69.04	111.87	119.51	127.60	130.96
0.0950	86.32	77.72	68.91	65.43	109.77	115.91	122.20	124.69
0.1000	84.56	75.08	65.68	62.14	107.72	112.46	117.16	118.93
0.1050	82.84	72.54	62.68	59.13	105.72	109.15	112.44	113.62
0.1100	81.16	70.12	59.88	56.38	103.77	105.98	108.02	108.72
0.1150	79.52	67.81	57.28	53.84	101.86	102.93	103.88	104.20
0.1200	77.92	65.59	54.86	51.52	100.00	100.00	100.00	100.00
0.1250	76.36	63.47	52.60	49.37	98.18	97.19	96.35	96.11
0.1300	74.84	61.44	50.49	47.38	96.41	94.49	92.93	92.48
0.1350	73.35	59.49	48.52	45.55	94.67	91.90	89.70	89.11
0.1400	71.91	57.62	46.67	43.84	92.98	89.41	86.67	85.96
0.1450	70.49	55.84	44.95	42.26	91.32	87.01	83.81	83.02
0.1500	69.11	54.12	43.33	40.78	89.70	84.71	81.11	80.26
0.1550	67.76	52.48	41.80	39.41	88.12	82.49	78.56	77.68
0.1600	66.45	50.91	40.38	38.12	86.58	80.36	76.15	75.25

Principle 1
Bond prices move inversely with interest rates.

In Equation 7.1, the present value of a single payment depends upon the value of the denominator, which depends on both the amount of time until the payment is to be received and the rate of discount being applied to the payment. The higher the rate of interest in Equation 7.1, the larger the denominator and the smaller the present value of the cash flow.

This principle can be illustrated using Bond C, a 30–year, 10 percent coupon bond. In Figure 7.1, we saw that the price of this bond would be 100.00 over its whole life, if interest rates remained at 10 percent. If interest rates change suddenly from 10 percent to 8 percent, the new price of the bond will be 122.62. Conversely,

Figure 7.2

The Price of Bond C for Various Yields
(Bond C: 30–Year, 10% Coupon)

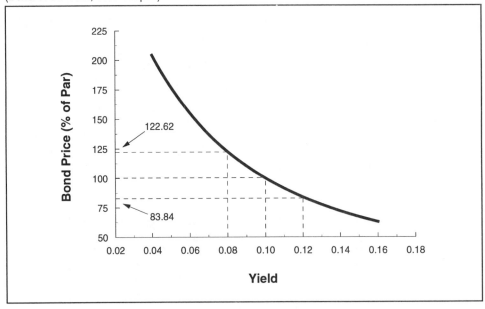

if interest rates suddenly rise from 10 to 12 percent, the bond will trade for 83.84, as summarized below.

Bond C: 30–year, 10% coupon

If $r_C = 12\%$, then $P_C = 83.84$.
If $r_C = 10\%$, then $P_C = 100.00$.
If $r_C = 8\%$, then $P_C = 122.62$.

This illustrates the first principle. Conversely, a decrease in interest rates creates an increase in the price of the bond. Figure 7.2 shows the price of Bond C for a variety of yields. We will refer to this kind of graph as a price/yield graph, because it shows how the bond price is related to the yield on the bond. Notice the degree of curvature in the graph. For yields that are very low relative to the bond's coupon rate, the slope of the curve approaches the vertical, starting to become parallel with the Y–axis. Similarly, for yields that are very high relative to the coupon rate, the slope of the curve flattens, starting to become parallel with the X–axis.

While an increase in interest rates causes the price of any bond to fall, the amount of the fall depends on particular features of the bond. Principle 2 states the relationship between maturity and the amount of a change in the price of a bond.

Principle 2
The longer the maturity of a bond, the more sensitive is its price to a change in interest rates, holding other factors constant.

To illustrate the greater sensitivity of longer maturity bonds to changes in interest rates, consider again Bond C, which has a maturity of 30 years and a coupon rate of 10 percent. For comparison, we introduce Bond F, which has a maturity of five years and a coupon rate of 10 percent. Thus, Bonds C and F have the same coupon rate, but Bond C has a longer maturity than Bond F. According to Principle 2, Bond C should be more sensitive to changes in interest rates than Bond F, because Bond C has the longer maturity. To illustrate this relationship, consider an initial position for both bonds in which they yield 10 percent and then observe the price change on each bond when the interest rate drops from 10 to 8 percent or rises from 10 to 12 percent.

Bond C: 30–year, 10% coupon
Bond F: 5–year, 10% coupon

	Interest Rates			Percentage Price Change	
	$r = 8\%$	$r = 10\%$	$r = 12\%$	Yield Falls	Yield Rises
P_C	122.62	100.00	83.84	+22.62	−16.16
P_F	108.11	100.00	92.64	+8.11	−7.36

Bonds C and F differ only in their maturities, with their coupon rates and initial yields being the same. When interest rates fall from 10 to 8 percent, both bond prices increase, in accordance with Principle 1. However, the price of Bond C increases by 22.62 percent, while the price of Bond F increases by only 8.11 percent. Notice that the price change, measured in dollars, is greater for Bond C than for Bond F. That need not be the case according to this principle. Principle 2 means that a bond with a longer maturity has a greater percentage price change than a bond of a shorter maturity for any given change in interest rates. Figure 7.3 shows how the prices of Bonds C and F differ for various yields. The figure shows that both bonds are priced at 100.00 for a yield of 10 percent. For lower yields, both bond prices are greater than 100.00, and for higher yields, both bond prices are below 100.00. The main difference between the curves for the two bonds is the relative steepness of the curve for Bond C, which shows its greater sensitivity to changes in yields. This is exactly the point of Principle 2; the longer the maturity, the greater the sensitivity of the bond price to a change in yields.

Principle 2 has immediate practical applications. Considering our two bonds, if interest rates rise on both bonds, both prices will drop. Assume that interest rates rise by 2 percent on both bonds. The price of Bond C will drop more, on a percentage basis, than the price of Bond F. If an investor fears rising interest rates, it would be important to know that Bond F is not so sensitive to the change in

Figure 7.3

Prices for Bonds C and F for Various Yields
(Bond C: 30–Year, 10% Coupon; Bond F: 5–Year, 10% Coupon)

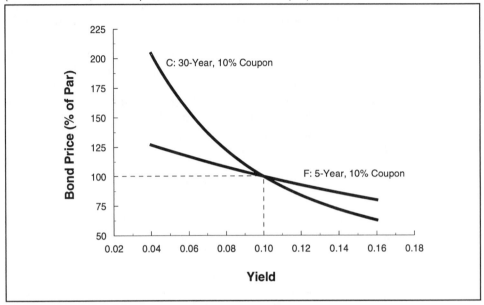

rates. Conversely, if an investor anticipates falling yields, there is reason to prefer Bond C, because its price would rise more, on a percentage basis, than the price of Bond F.

Principle 3
The price sensitivity of bonds increases with maturity, but at a decreasing rate.

Principle 2 makes clear that a 30–year bond should have more sensitivity to changing interest rates than a 5–year bond. However, according to Principle 3, the difference in sensitivity between a 15–year and a 10–year bond will be smaller than the difference in sensitivity between a 10–year bond and a 5–year bond, because the sensitivity increases at a decreasing rate.

To illustrate this principle, consider Bond C and two new bonds, Bond G, which has 20 years to maturity and a 10 percent coupon rate, and Bond H, with 10 years until maturity and a 10 percent coupon rate.

Bond C: 30–year, 10% coupon
Bond G: 20–year, 10% coupon
Bond H: 10–year, 10% coupon

	Interest Rates		Percentage Price Change	Difference in the % Price Change
	$r = 10\%$	$r = 8\%$		
P_C	100.00	122.62	22.62	
				2.83
P_G	100.00	119.79	19.79	
				6.20
P_H	100.00	113.59	13.59	

The difference in maturity between all adjacent bonds is ten years, and the bonds differ only with respect to maturity. However, the difference in the percentage price change between a 10–year and a 20–year bond is 6.20 percent, while the difference between the percentage price change of a 30–year bond and a 20–year bond is only 2.83 percent. In fact, as the table shows, the longer the maturity, the less difference a given maturity difference makes in bond price sensitivity. This implies that the sensitivity difference between a 30–year and a 20–year bond is less important than the sensitivity difference between a 20–year and a 10–year bond. Figure 7.4 emphasizes this relationship by showing how the percentage price change increases with maturity. It uses this same change in interest

Figure 7.4

The Greater Price Sensitivity of Longer Maturity Bonds
(For bonds with a 10% coupon rate and a rate change from 10% to 8%)

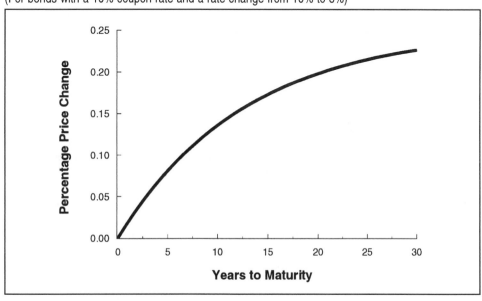

rates from 10 to 8 percent and presents the percentage price change for bonds of many maturities, all with the same coupon rate of 10 percent. As the figure shows, the percentage price change always increases with maturity, but it increases at a decreasing rate.

Principle 4
The lower the coupon rate on a bond, the more sensitive is its price to a change in interest rates, holding other factors constant.

Just as bonds with longer maturities are more sensitive to changes in interest rates, so are low–coupon bonds. This greater sensitivity is due to the fact that bonds with high coupons return more of their value earlier in their lives through payment of a higher coupon rate. To illustrate this principle, consider Bonds A and E. Both bonds have 30 years remaining until maturity. Bond A has a 14 percent coupon rate, while Bond E has a 6 percent coupon rate. We compare how the prices of Bonds A and E change when yields fall from 10 percent to 8 percent on both bonds.

Bond A: 30–year, 14% coupon
Bond E: 30–year, 6% coupon

	Interest Rates		
	$r = 10\%$	$r = 8\%$	**Percentage Price Change**
P_A	137.86	167.87	21.77
P_E	62.14	77.38	24.53

The two bonds have the same maturity and initial yield, but they differ in their coupon rates. The same yield change affected Bond E more strongly because of its lower coupon rate. As expected, the lower the coupon rate, the greater the sensitivity of a bond's price to changes in interest rates. This principle is emphasized in Figure 7.5, which shows the prices of Bonds A and E for various yields. The greater percentage change in the price line for Bond E shows that it is more sensitive to changes in yields than Bond A.

Figure 7.6 illustrates Principle 4 in a slightly different way. It considers many bonds with 30 years to maturity but with widely differing coupon rates. It shows how the prices of those bonds will change when interest rates fall from 10 percent to 8 percent. The most sensitive coupon rate is the zero coupon rate of a pure discount bond. As the graph of Figure 7.6 shows, a drop in yields from 10 percent to 8 percent causes a price increase of 77.51 percent for a 30–year zero coupon bond. For a 30–year 20 percent coupon bond, the yield change causes a price rise of 21.11 percent. Note that the prices of all bonds rise, but the percentage amount of the price rise is lower the larger the coupon rate.

Figure 7.5

The Greater Price Sensitivity of Lower Coupon Bonds
(Bond A: 30–Year, 14% Coupon: Bond E: 30–Year, 6% Coupon)

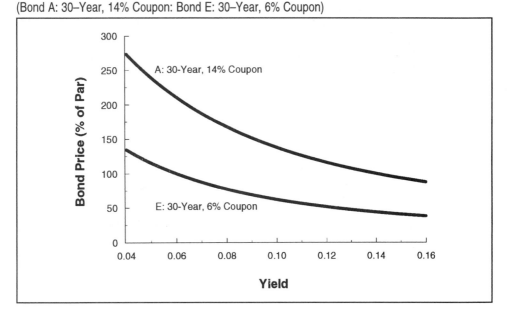

Principle 5
For a given bond, the capital gain caused by a yield decrease exceeds the capital loss caused by a yield increase of the same magnitude.

As noted in Principle 1, bond prices vary inversely with yields. According to Principle 5, a given change in yields, say, a 1 percent change, has a greater effect on the price of the bond when the yield drops, rather than when the yield rises. We can illustrate this principle by considering Bond C again. (Bond C is a 30–year, 10 percent coupon bond.)

Original		Price When Rate		Percentage Price	
Rate	Price	Falls 1%	Rises 1%	Increase	Decrease
8	122.62	137.42	110.32	12.07	10.03
10	100.00	110.32	91.28	10.32	8.72
12	83.84	91.28	77.45	8.87	7.62
14	71.92	77.45	67.10	7.69	6.70

For initial rates from 8 to 14 percent, we show the price for Bond C that corresponds to the rate. The middle portion of the table shows the new prices when rates

Figure 7.6

The Greater Price Sensitivity of Lower Coupon Bonds
(For bonds with a 30–year maturity and a rate change from 10% to 8%)

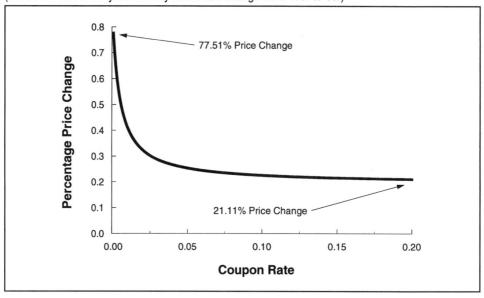

fall or rise by 1 percent. The right side of the table shows the resulting prices. For example, if the initial yield is 12 percent, Bond C is worth 83.84. If interest rates fall by 1 percent, the new price is 91.28, for an 8.87 percent increase. In the same situation, if rates rise 1 percent, the new price is 77.45 for a 7.62 percent decrease. In this situation and for a 1 percent rise or drop in interest rates, the percentage price increase of 8.87 percent exceeds the percentage price decrease of 7.62 percent. In fact, this is true in every instance. For the same change in yields, a falling yield causes a price gain that is larger than the price drop caused by the same–sized increase in yields.

We can also see the same point graphically for Bond C based on Figure 7.7, which shows how the price of Bond C varies with different yields. Consider any point on the graph, such as a 10 percent yield and the corresponding price of 100.00. Consider a yield increase to 11 percent and a yield decrease to 9 percent. The resulting prices are 91.28 and 110.32, as we have already seen. Notice that the price change is larger for the price increase that results from the drop in yields. In Figure 7.7, as we look from left to right, we see that the price of the bond falls as yields increase. However, the price falls at a decreasing rate. That is, a rise in yields from 9 to 10 percent has a larger price effect than a rise in yields from 10 to 11 percent.

Figure 7.7

The Price of Bond C for Various Yields
(Bond C: 30–Year, 10% Coupon)

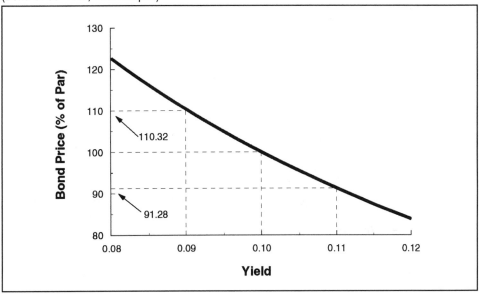

The Need for a Summary Measure

The five principles of bond pricing are all very important for understanding bond investing. However, since each of the principles assumes that all other factors are being held constant, except for the one under examination, it is still difficult to compare the price sensitivity of different bonds. As an example, consider Bonds A and I.

Bond A: 30–year, 14% coupon, yielding 10%; Price 137.86
Bond I: 20–year, 7% coupon, yielding 10%; Price 74.26

Although these bonds have the same yields, their maturities and coupon rates differ. If we consider only the maturity, we would think that Bond A is more sensitive. However, considering only the coupon rate, we would think that Bond I is more sensitive. Merely by inspecting the features of these bonds, we cannot decide which is more sensitive to a change in interest rates. It would be very convenient to have an index of a bond's price sensitivity that allowed direct comparisons between bonds.

For Bonds A and I, Table 7.2 shows that the two bonds have virtually identical price sensitivities. For a drop in yields from 10 to 9 percent, the price of Bond A increases by 9.97 percent, while the price of Bond I rises by 9.88 percent.

Table 7.2

▬▬▬▬▬▬▬▬

Relative Price Changes of Bonds A and I

Bond	Price at 9% (% Change)	Price at 10.0%	Price at 11% (% Change)
A	151.60 (9.97%)	137.86	126.17 (−8.48%)
I	81.60 (9.88%)	74.26	67.91 (−8.55%)

Similarly, if yields rise from 10 to 11 percent, the price of Bond A falls by 8.48 percent and the price of Bond I falls by 8.55 percent.

Here we find that two bonds of very different coupon and maturity can have a price sensitivity that is almost identical. Accordingly, it would be very useful to have some summary measurement of a bond's price sensitivity that reflects all of the factors affecting the sensitivity—the maturity, the coupon rate, and the yield to maturity. Such a measure is called **duration**.

Duration

A concept first developed by Frederick Macaulay, **duration** is a single number for each bond that summarizes three key factors that affect the sensitivity of a bond's price to changes in interest rates.[3] Duration depends on the maturity, the coupon rate, and the yield to maturity. Macaulay's duration (D_m) is given by Equation 7.2.[4]

$$D_m = \frac{\sum\limits_{t=1}^{M} t \left(\dfrac{C_t}{(1+r)^t} \right)}{P} \tag{7.2}$$

where:

P = the bond's price

C_t = the cash flow from the bond occurring at time t

_____

[3]See F. R. Macaulay, *Some Theoretical Problems Suggested by the Movements of Interest Rates, Bond Yields, and Stock Prices in the United States Since 1856*, New York: Columbia University Press, 1938.

[4]A more formal derivation of duration is given in the appendix to this chapter.

r = the yield to maturity
t = the time measured from the present until a payment is made

The Macaulay's duration equation computes the present value of each of the cash flows and weights each by the time until it is received. All of these weighted cash flows are summed, and the sum is divided by the current price of the bond.

How to Calculate Duration

As an example of how to calculate Macaulay's duration, consider a 5–year bond paying an annual coupon of 10 percent, with a yield to maturity of 14 percent and a par value of $1,000. The price of this bond would be $862.69. Table 7.3 sets out the cash flows and shows the calculation of this bond's Macaulay's duration, which is 4.10. This duration calculation gives the duration value in terms of the same periods as the cash flows. In our example, the cash flows were annual, so the duration value is in years. If the bond were a semiannual coupon bond, we would need to convert the duration from semiannual periods to years by dividing the duration figure by 2.0.

Duration as an Elasticity Measure

There is another equation for Macaulay's duration that expresses duration as the negative of elasticity of the bond's price with respect to a change in the discount factor $(1 + r)$.

$$D_m \approx - \frac{\dfrac{\Delta P}{P}}{\dfrac{\Delta (1 + r)}{(1 + r)}}$$

7.3

Table 7.3

The Calculation of Duration

t	C_t	PVC_t	$t(PVC_t)$
1	$100	$87.72	$87.72
2	100	76.95	153.90
3	100	67.50	202.50
4	100	59.21	236.84
5	1100	571.31	2856.55
		862.69	3537.51

Note: PVC_t = present value of C_t

Equation 7.3 shows that duration is essentially an elasticity measure. Macaulay's duration gives a single measure of the way in which a bond's price changes for a change in the discount factor $(1 + r)$. We will see later why Equation 7.3 holds only as an approximation.

The Duration Price Change Formula and Modified Duration

We can rearrange Equation 7.3 to form Equation 7.4.

$$\Delta P \approx -D \, \frac{\Delta (1 + r)}{1 + r} \, P \qquad\qquad \textbf{7.4}$$

As Equation 7.4 shows, to approximate the price change in a bond resulting from a change in interest rates, one needs to know the original level of rates, the original price, the change in rates, and the Macaulay's duration of the bond.

Closely related to Macaulay's duration is the concept of **modified duration (MD)**, which equals Macaulay's duration divided by $1 + r$:

$$MD = \frac{D_M}{1 + r} \qquad\qquad \textbf{7.5}$$

Using the modified duration and recognizing that the change in $1 + r$ equals the change in r, the price change formula of Equation 7.4 becomes:

$$\Delta P \approx - (MD) (\Delta r) (P) \qquad\qquad \textbf{7.6}$$

Equation 7.6 says that the price change of a bond equals the negative of modified duration times the change in yield times the original price before the yield changed. It is equivalent in spirit to Equation 7.4. We will see later why Equation 7.6 holds only as an approximation.

We can now see why Bonds A and I could be so different in maturity and coupon and still have the same percentage price changes—they have virtually the same duration. For Bond A, the duration is 9.63 years and for Bond I, the duration is 9.64 years. While Bond A has the longer maturity, Bond I has the smaller coupon. These two effects are almost exactly offsetting. The result is that Bonds A and I have the same sensitivity to changes in interest rates. Because they have the same duration, the prices of Bonds A and I will change by the same percentage amount for a given change in yields.

Applying Duration

As an example of the price change formula of Equations 7.4 and 7.6, consider again the bond for which the Macaulay's duration was computed. That bond was a 5–year, 10 percent annual coupon bond yielding 14 percent and having a Macaulay's duration of 4.10. With yields at 14 percent, the modified duration is 3.5965 = 4.10/1.14. If yields suddenly drop from 14 percent to 12 percent, the bond's price would adjust upward, and the amount of the adjustment could be found by using Equations 7.4 or 7.6. From Equation 7.4, we have:

$$\Delta P \approx (-4.10) \left(\frac{-.02}{1.14} \right) (862.69) = 62.05$$

Equation 7.6 gives:

$$\Delta P \approx - (3.5965)(-.02)(862.69) = 62.05$$

With this change in price, the new price should be the old price plus the price change.

$$\text{New Price} \approx 862.69 + 62.05 \approx \$924.74$$

We can confirm this price by applying the bond pricing formula to the bond, using the new yield of 12 percent.

$$P = \frac{100}{(1.12)} + \frac{100}{(1.12)^2} + \frac{100}{(1.12)^3} + \frac{100}{(1.12)^4} + \frac{1100}{(1.12)^5} = \$927.90$$

According to the bond pricing equation, the new price is $927.90, not $924.74, as given by Equation 7.4. There are two reasons for this discrepancy. First, any calculation may have some rounding error. Second, Equations 7.4 and 7.6 use concepts derived from calculus, which hold exactly only for infinitesimal changes in variables. In this case, the large change in the yield of 2 percent was responsible for the discrepancy between the two methods.[5]

---

[5] For Bonds F and G, the Macaulay's durations are 8.39 and 8.38, respectively. However, the percentage price changes of Table 7.2 differ due to the slight difference in the durations and the discrete change in yields.

Figure 7.8

The Duration Predicted Price Change for Bond A
(Bond A: 30–Year, 14% Coupon)

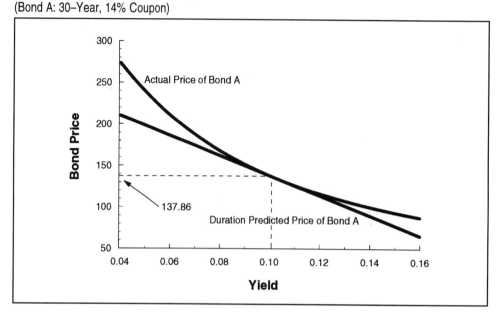

Duration Tracking Errors

To see how discrepancies between actual prices and prices estimated by the duration price change formula arise, consider Figure 7.8 which shows the price of Bond A as a function of the yield. The straight line is drawn tangent to the curve at the point for a yield of 10 percent and a price of 137.86. The tangent line shows the estimated price of the bond for a change in yields, using the duration price change formula of Equations 7.4 or 7.6. Thus, the formula fails to take the curvature of the bond price line into account.[6] This is the principal source of our price estimation errors. As Figure 7.8 shows, these differences can become very substantial for large yield changes. For example, if the yield fell from 10 to 6 percent, the duration price change formula implies a price of 186.14, but the actual price would be 210.70. This is an error of 24.56 or 13.19 percent.

Figure 7.9 shows an enlargement of a portion of Figure 7.8. It focuses on the yield range from 9 to 11 percent. For a decrease in yields from 10 to 9 percent, the modified duration is $8.75 = 9.63/1.10$, and the duration price change formula implies that the price change should be:

---

[6]In terms of calculus, we are taking the derivative of the bond's price at a yield of 10 percent and we are using that derivative to compute the new bond price.

Figure 7.9

The Duration Predicted Price Change for Bond A: Enlarged Portion of Figure 7.8
(Bond A: 30–Year, 14% Coupon)

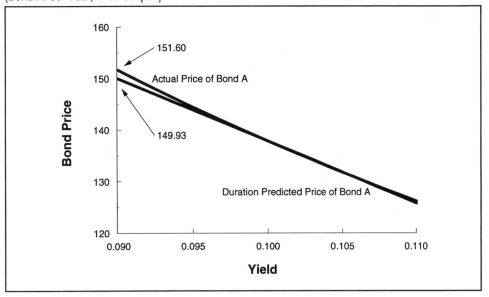

$$\Delta\,\text{Price} \approx -\ MD\ (\Delta r)\ (P) \approx (\,8.75\,)\ (\,-0.01\,)\ (137.86) \approx 12.07$$

The new price should then be 149.93 = 12.07 + 137.86. However, the price of a 30–year bond with a coupon rate of 14 percent and a yield of 9 percent is actually 151.60. Figure 7.9 shows this error, which is 1.1 percent. Figure 7.9 also shows that the error is very small for small changes in yields.

Essentially, the duration price change formula takes into account the curvature of the price/yield line at a given point. It does not take into account how the shape of the curve changes, and how duration changes, away from the initial point at which duration is measured. Figure 7.10 shows how duration changes for Bond A as yields change. Bond A is a 30–year, 14 percent coupon bond. At a yield of 10 percent, we found that the duration of Bond A is 9.63. Figure 7.10 shows the value of the duration of Bond A for yields ranging from 4 to 16 percent. As the figure shows, duration can change dramatically for the same bond with the same maturity and coupon due solely to a change in yields. The following principles summarize how duration changes as the yield, coupon rate, and maturity vary individually:

1. For a given coupon rate and maturity, duration is inversely related to the yield on a bond.

Figure 7.10

Duration Changes for Bond A as a Function of Yield Changes
(Bond A: 30–Year, 14% Coupon)

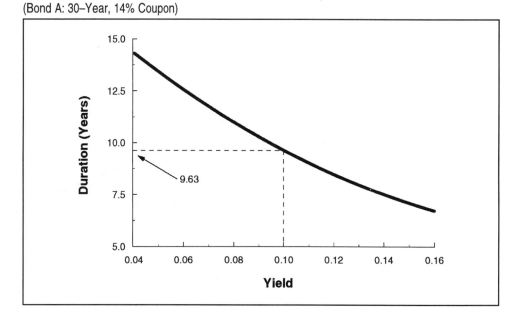

2. For a given yield and maturity, duration is inversely related to the coupon rate.
3. For a given yield and coupon rate, duration is positively related to the bond's maturity.

Convexity

Convexity is an additional measure of the price sensitivity of a bond. In essence, it reflects the way in which duration changes for different yields on the same bond and tries to account for the duration tracking error that we have just discussed. The name refers to the fact that the shape of the price/yield graph is convex. For example, from the viewpoint of the origin in Figure 7.2, the curve depicting the bond prices bulges out toward the viewer. Thus, the graph is convex to the origin. As we will see in this section, the degree of this curvature can be measured with accuracy, and it is an important feature of bond pricing.

We denote convexity as VEX and letting $R = 1 + r$, we define convexity as:

Table 7.4

The Calculation of Convexity

t	$t+1$	C_t	PVC_t	$t(t+1)PVC_t$
1	2	100	87.72	175.44
2	3	100	76.95	461.70
3	4	100	67.50	810.00
4	5	100	59.21	1,184.20
5	6	1100	571.31	17,139.30
			862.69	19,770.64

Note: PVC_t = present value of C_t

$$ \text{VEX} = \frac{1}{P\,R^2} \sum_{t=1}^{M} \frac{t\,(t+1)\,C_t}{R^t} \qquad 7.7 $$

The summation portion of the equation resembles the duration measure, except each term receives an additional weighting given by $(t+1)$.

Computing Convexity

To illustrate the computation of convexity, we find the convexity of the sample bond from Table 7.3. This bond is a five–year bond with a face value of $1,000 that pays a 10 percent annual coupon and yields 14 percent. Table 7.4 shows the calculations.

In Table 7.4, the last column shows the weighted present values of each cash flow. These values are summed and divided by the price of the bond multiplied by 1.14^2. The convexity for this bond is 17.63. Because these cash flows are in years, the convexity measure is expressed in years as well. For a semiannual bond, the convexity measure can be expressed in years by making the computation as shown and dividing the result by 4.0. The appendix to this chapter shows the derivation of convexity and gives details on why it is a sound and useful measure.[7]

---

[7]Recently, some scholars have found closed–form solutions for duration and convexity. These methods allow more rapid calculation of duration and convexity numbers than the summations presented in this chapter. We have focused on the summation approach because it more clearly shows the underlying rationale behind duration and convexity. For closed–form duration measures, see J. H. Chua, "A Closed–Form Formula for Calculating Bond Duration," *Financial Analysts Journal*, May/June 1984, and G. C. Babcock, "Duration as a Weighted Average of Two Factors," *Financial Analysts Journal*, March/April 1985. R. Brooks and M. Livingston develop a closed–form measure for convexity in their paper, "A Closed–Form Equation for Bond Convexity," *Financial Analysts Journal*, November/December 1989, pp. 78–79.

Estimating Price Changes with Duration and Convexity

To use convexity to better approximate the price change for a bond, we use the following equation:

$$\Delta P \approx - MD\ (\Delta R)\ (P) + .5\ \text{VEX}\ (\Delta R)^2\ P \qquad\qquad \textbf{7.8}$$

The first term on the right–hand side is the same that appears in Equation 7.6. It captures the price change in the bond estimated from duration. The second term adds the convexity refinement.

We illustrate this improved formula for estimating the price change by considering Bond A again. Bond A is a 30–year bond with a 14 percent coupon. We have seen that the price of this bond will be 137.86 for an initial yield of 10 percent. In this case, the duration is 9.63, and the modified duration is 8.75. If the yield falls from 10 to 9 percent, we saw that the estimated price change from the duration price change formula is 12.07, for a predicted new price of 149.93 = 137.86 + 12.07. However, the actual price of this bond at a 9 percent yield would be 151.60.

We now consider how to estimate the price change of a bond for a given change in yields by considering both duration and convexity. The convexity of Bond A is 148.27. Applying Equation 7.8, we have:

$$\Delta P \approx - 8.75\ (-.01)\ (137.86) + .5\ (148.27)\ (-.01)^2\ (137.86)$$
$$\approx 12.07 + 1.02$$
$$\approx 13.09$$

With an estimated price change of 13.09, our estimated new price is 150.95 = 137.86 + 12.07 + 1.02. In this equation, 12.07 of the price change is associated with the duration term, and 1.02 of the change is from the second term reflecting convexity. Notice that the convexity term is positive, as it will always be. From Figure 7.8, it is clear that the duration price change formula always undershoots the true change in the bond price, because the duration price change estimate is taken from the line tangent to the price/yield curve. The convexity adjustment gets the estimate closer to the actual price. In our example, the actual price is 151.60, and the estimate taking convexity into account is 150.95, which is within .5 percent of the actual price.

Convexity and Bond Selection

Other factors being equal, investors should prefer greater convexity, as this section illustrates. In a price/yield curve, we have seen that duration essentially measures the slope of a curve at a given point. Convexity, by contrast, reflects the severity of the curve. If a bond had no convexity, its price/yield curve would look like the straight line that is tangent to the price/yield curve in Figure 7.8. For bonds, however, the price/yield graph curves away from that straight line. Figure 7.8 also shows this tendency. If we think of the straight line and the price/yield curve in Figure 7.8 as representing two different bonds, we can see that we would prefer the actual Bond A of that graph to the imaginary bond represented by the straight line. The reason for our preference is clear; for any yield, Bond A is worth more than the corresponding yield point on the straight line.

Essentially, this greater value results from the convexity of Bond A. Convexity is the tendency of the price/yield graph to curve away from the tangent line. The greater the degree of this curvature, the better, because it means the price will be higher for a given yield. Therefore, the more convexity a bond has, the better.

To see this more clearly, consider Figure 7.11, which graphs two bonds that have the same duration but different convexities. The top line is Bond A, a 30–year bond with a 14 percent coupon, while the bottom line is for Bond I, a 20–year, 7 percent coupon. To make the lines in the graph comparable, the graph shows the price of 1.8565 units of Bond I. Bond A's price is greater for both low and high yields. For yields in the middle range, around 10 percent, the prices of the two bonds are virtually indistinguishable.

At a yield of 10 percent, we noted that the duration of Bond A was 9.63 and the duration of Bond I was 9.64. At 10 percent yields, Bond A was worth 137.86 and

Figure 7.11

Price/Yield Graph for Bond A and Bond I
(Bond A: 30–Year, 14% Coupon; Bond I: 20–Year, 7% Coupon)

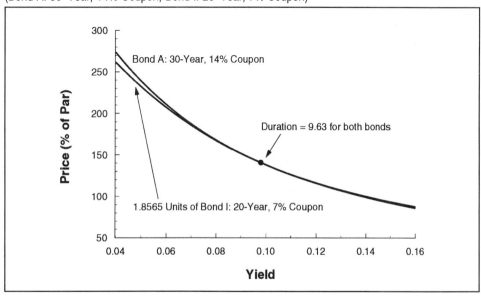

Bond I was worth 74.26. By comparing Bond A with a portfolio of 1.8565 units of Bond I, we have two investments that have the same value for a yield of 10 percent. Also, at 10 percent, the two bonds have the same duration. (Actually, the durations are 9.64 for Bond A and 9.63 for Bond I, a difference that we ignore). However, the two bonds have different convexities. The convexity of Bond A is 148.27, as we have seen, and the convexity of Bond I is 132.08.

In practical terms, this means that Bond A is more attractive than Bond I, under the circumstances of this example. The reason for this is clear. At the current yield of 10 percent, the two investments have the same value. Bond A is worth 137.86, and 1.8565 units of Bond I is worth the same. However, for any yield change, positive or negative, Bond A will be worth more than the Bond I investment. For example, if yields rise, both investments will lose value. Due to its greater convexity, however, Bond A will lose less. Assume yields jump to 16 percent. Then Bond A is worth 87.62 and the 1.8565 units of Bond I are worth 86.03. By contrast, if yields fall, both investments will increase in value, but the increase for Bond A will be greater. For example, if yields fall to 4 percent, Bond A is worth 273.80, but the Bond I investment is worth only 261.82.

Because of its greater convexity, Bond A is better than the same investment in Bond I. Bond traders are, of course, aware of the importance of convexity. In actual markets, bond pricing typically reflects convexity, so one bond will not dominate another as Bond A dominates Bond I in this example. In other words, convexity is a desirable property of a bond and its value is reflected in the market price of bonds.

Duration and Convexity: Some Qualifications

The conclusions we have reached about the benefits of duration and convexity are based on four assumptions. First, we assume that the bonds being analyzed are not callable by the issuer. Second, we have assumed that the yield curve is flat at the time the yield change occurs. Third, we assume that if yields change, they all change by the same amount. Therefore, the yield curve after the change in rates is still flat. Finally, the analysis holds for a single change in yields. We consider the practical implications of each assumption in turn.

Focus on Non–Callable Bonds

Many corporate bonds are callable, so that the issuer can buy the bonds from the bondholder at the call price specified in the bond covenant. If yields fall by a large amount, the price of a non–callable bond would rise along the type of price/yield curve that we have considered in this chapter. However, if the bond is callable, the bondholders know that the issuer may call the bonds and pay them only the call price. Therefore, the price of the bond will not rise as we have assumed if the bondholder is threatened by a call.

As a practical matter, the analysis that we have conducted holds for small changes in yields if the bond is not in imminent danger of being called. For callable bonds, the techniques outlined in this chapter must be applied with caution.[8]

Restriction to Flat Yield Curves

The analysis of this chapter has assumed that the yield curve is flat. As we saw in Chapter 2, the yield curve relates the yield on a bond to the time remaining until the bond matures. In the bond pricing formula, all cash flows are discounted at a single common rate, no matter how far into the future a cash flow is actually received. This assumption was carried over into our duration and convexity measures. By considering only a common yield for all of these payments, we have implicitly assumed that the yield curve is flat. The practical implications of this assumption are not as limiting as they might at first appear.

Restriction to Parallel Shifts in Yield Curves

Our analysis has also focused on a parallel shift in yield curves. Because we are using the same yield to discount all cash flows without regard to the time that they are actually paid, we have seen that the yield curve is assumed to be flat. By the same token, if we consider a change in the one common yield applied to all of the bond's cash flows, we are assuming that the yield curve shifts in a parallel fashion. For example, if yields are at 10 percent, we have assumed a flat yield curve at 10 percent. If we then consider a change in yields to 11 percent, our analysis assumes that the resulting yield curve is flat at 11 percent. Because the yield curves are flat before and after the yield change, they have shifted in a parallel fashion.

These two assumptions, of a flat yield curve and a parallel shift, are potentially very limiting to the practical application of our analysis. After all, yield curves are seldom flat, and changing yields typically result in a yield curve with a new shape. However, researchers have found that these concerns have only very small practical results.[9] As a consequence, it seems permissible to use Macaulay's duration and the accompanying convexity measure with little concern for the effects of changing yield curve shapes.

---

[8]A number of papers focus on the problems of applying duration and convexity to bonds with call features. See for example, B. J. Grantier, "Convexity and Bond Performance: The Benter the Better," *Financial Analysts Journal*, November/December 1988, pp. 79-81; J. A. Schnabel, "Is Benter Better: A Cautionary Note on Maximizing Convexity," *Financial Analysts Journal*, January/February 1990, pp. 78–79; and K. Winkelmann, "Uses and Abuses of Duration and Convexity," *Financial Analysts Journal*, September/October 1989, pp. 72–75.

[9]G. O. Bierwag surveys the practical importance of yield curve shapes on duration models in his book, *Duration Analysis*, Cambridge, MA: Ballinger Publishing Company, 1987. See Chapters 11 and 12 particularly.

Restriction to a Single Change in Yields

In our analysis, we have focused on a single change in yields, but in actual markets, yields change frequently. This can be important, because we have seen that duration and convexity change as yields change, even when time to maturity does not change. This means that strategies that employ duration and convexity will have to be sensitive to changing yields. In the next chapter, we will see that a changing yield environment requires periodic adjustments to a bond portfolio to reflect the changing duration and convexity. In practical portfolio management, the need to rebalance a portfolio is a problem that can be managed quite satisfactorily.

Thus, the assumptions that we have made turn out not to interfere too much with the practical application of duration and convexity to bond investing. In fact, the last decade has seen their use become almost universal among fixed–income portfolio managers.

The Level of Interest Rates

We have seen that the sensitivity of a bond's price depends on the three key variables of maturity, coupon rate, and the level of interest rates. Because so much of bond investing depends on changes in interest rates, the bond investor needs to understand the basic factors that influence the level of interest rates and the changes from one level of rates to another.

In discussing interest rates, it is customary to speak of the overall level of rates, the term structure of interest rates, and the risk structure of interest rates. The term and risk structures of interest rates are important for the choice of individual bonds, but they are even more crucial for managing bond portfolios. Accordingly, Chapter 8 focuses on the term and the risk structures of interest rates and their relationship to bond portfolio management. As a preliminary to considering the full range of issues associated with bond portfolio management, this section focuses strictly on the level of interest rates for bonds that are free of default risk. In practice, this means that the discussion is limited to the determinants of the level of interest rates on U.S. Treasury obligations.

The Nominal Rate of Interest

Yields on debt securities are almost always quoted as a nominal rate of interest. The **nominal rate of interest** reflects only the promised dollar payments without reference to the purchasing power of the payments. For example, a one–year loan of $100 at a rate of 12 percent will return $112. In this case, the nominal rate of interest is 12 percent. When the loan matures and the investor receives the $12 interest payment, the $12 may have a purchasing power that differs from that which was expected. To better understand the determinants of nominal rates of interest, which are, in fact, the market rates of interest, it is customary to identify two components of the nominal rate of interest. Following the work of the great economist Irving Fisher, we express the nominal rate of interest on a default–free security as being composed of the real rate of interest and the expected rate of infla-tion.[10] For any single period, this relationship can be expressed as follows.

For a bond with no default risk:

$$(1 + r) = (1 + r^*) [1 + E(I)] \qquad 7.9$$

where:
r = the nominal rate of interest
r^* = the real rate of interest
$E(I)$ = the expected rate of inflation over the period

For the multi–period case, the same relationship can be expressed as:

$$(1 + r)^t = (1 + r^*)^t [1 + E(I)]^t \qquad 7.10$$

assuming that the rates for the different components are constant over the t periods.

The Real Rate of Interest and the Expected Inflation Rate

The **real rate of interest** has many other names, such as the **pure price of time**, and the **marginal productivity of capital**. All three names point to the same idea. When an investor buys a bond, the inflation rate over the period of the bond's life is uncertain. However, the investor will demand some increase in the purchasing power of funds committed for the bond's life. This leads to a definition of the **real rate of interest**—the expected change in purchasing power necessary to induce investors to postpone consumption.

To continue the previous example of a one–year bond investment with a nominal rate of 12 percent, investors will not be pleased if the inflation rate during that period is 14 percent. The investor who invests $100 in these circumstances will lose purchasing power over the year. The $100 initial investment will increase in value by $12. With an inflation rate of 14 percent, however, what $100 would buy at the outset of the investment will require $114 at year's end. The investor's purchasing power will have fallen over the year from $100 to $98.25, measured in constant dollars. The relative purchasing power of an investment can be found by using Equations 7.9 or 7.10, assuming the rate of inflation and the rate of return for the period are known.

$$\text{Relative Purchasing Power} = \frac{C(1 + r)}{C(1 + I)} = \frac{1 + r}{1 + I} \qquad 7.11$$

---

[10]See his classic work, Irving Fisher, *The Theory of Interest*, New York: A. M. Kelley, Publishers, 1965. The book was originally published in 1930.

where:

    C = the initial investment

    I = the actual inflation rate over the investment period

In our example:

$$\text{Relative Purchasing Power} = \frac{\$100\,(1.12)}{\$100\,(1.14)} = \frac{\$112}{\$114} = .9825$$

The investors' purchasing power after making the investment was only 98.25 percent of the original purchasing power and resulted in a negative real rate of return. This also explains why the real rate is also known as the pure price of time. The **pure price of time** is the change in purchasing power investors demand for postponing their consumption. The price is a pure price because it assumes that no risk is involved in the investment. It is simply a price for postponing consumption, not for bearing default risk.

Having defined the real rate as the expected change in purchasing power necessary to induce investment, the next question becomes: What level of real rates is possible and what do investors demand? As noted, the real rate of return is also called the marginal productivity of capital. If investors demand and receive some real rate of interest, it can only be because some other parties are willing to pay that rate. Rational economic agents will pay a given rate only if the funds obtained at that rate can be employed to generate a higher rate of return.

The **marginal productivity of capital** is the rate of return that can be earned by the next unit of capital to be invested. This is also a real rate, and we can interpret it as the rate at which physical capital can reproduce itself. Additional funds for capital investment will be available only when the capital investment pays a rate of return equal to or greater than the cost of those funds. Because expected inflation affects bond rates and capital investment returns alike, the problem becomes one of balancing the marginal productivity of capital against the real rate of interest. As long as the marginal productivity of capital exceeds the real rate of interest, more funds will be demanded for investment. An equilibrium will be reached when the real rate of interest equals the marginal productivity of capital.

Figure 7.12 presents this situation graphically. It depicts a situation in which the real rate of interest is 3 percent per year. On the horizontal axis, $1 at time = 0 can be transformed into $1.03 of purchasing power at time = 1. The slope of the line running from $1 at time = 0 to $1.03 at time = 1 represents the real rate of interest. A steeper slope would indicate a higher real rate of return. Figure 7.12 also shows the returns for investment in physical capital. The horizontal axis represents the units of physical capital being employed. The vertical axis shows the number of units of physical capital produced by the employment of a given number of units of capital on the horizontal axis.

The curved line in Figure 7.12 shows the changing productivity of investment. When no capital is being utilized, the first unit put to work is extremely

Figure 7.12

▬▬▬▬▬▬▬▬

The Real Rate of Interest and the Marginal Productivity of Capital

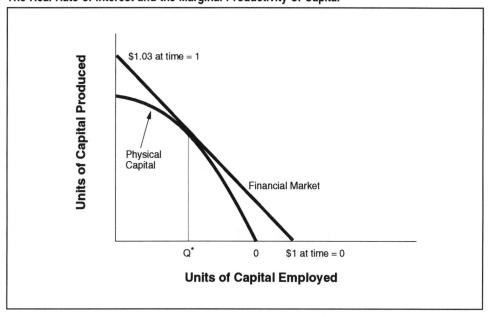

productive. This happens because the capital will be employed first where it has the greatest return, and the graph reflects this high productivity by the very steep slope near the zero level of capital employment. As more and more capital is employed, successive units are less and less valuable, as reflected by the changing slope of the curved line in Figure 7.12. At any point, the slope of the curved line represents the rate of return on the last unit of capital employed.

How much capital will be employed ultimately? The curved line (showing the productivity of capital) is tangent to the straight line (showing the 3 percent real rate of interest) at a single point. Starting with zero capital investment, investment continues so long as the rate of return on capital exceeds the real rate of interest. When the return is less than the real rate, further investment in capital goods is a losing proposition.

Following this line of reasoning, there will be investment in capital along the curved line of Figure 7.12 up to the point where the slope of the curved line equals the slope of the line showing the rate of return in the capital market. At this point, Q^*, the marginal rate of return on capital—the marginal productivity of capital—equals the real rate of interest. Any further investment in capital goods earns a rate of return below the real rate of interest and will be counterproductive because a higher real rate of return could be earned in the bond market.

Strictly speaking, this graphical analysis assumes a world where the real rate of return and the returns to capital investment are both certain.[11] Further complications present themselves when the more complicated situation of uncertainty is considered.

In the securities markets, the investor always faces uncertain future prospects. Given a stated nominal rate on some investment, the investor remains uncertain as to which portion of that nominal rate should be attributed to expected real returns or to expected inflation. Presumably, the expected real return is never negative. If that is a reasonable assumption, investors are often disappointed. There have been numerous cases where the realized real rate of return has been negative. Figure 7.13 presents the returns for the period from 1970 through 1993 for investment in Treasury bills. As the graph shows, this period includes periods of volatile interest rates and high inflation. During this time, real returns were sometimes negative. Assuming that investors only make investments where the expected real return is positive, some investors' expectations were clearly wrong during this period.

It should be noted that this period was very unusual, covering the period of the oil crisis and the subsequent economic adjustments. Also, investors in the early 1980s enjoyed very high real returns, as shown in the bottom panel of Figure 7.13. For a more accurate view, it is useful to consider a long period of time. For the years 1926–1993, the real rate of return on investment in U.S. Treasury securities, whether in bonds or bills, was about 0.5 percent.[12] While experts disagree about the best estimate of the real rate of return, it must be put somewhere in the range from 0 to 2 percent. Given that contemporary interest rates frequently have been above 10 percent, it must be acknowledged that the real rate is not very important in determining interest rates. Instead, the nominal interest rate is mainly composed of the expected inflation rate. This is shown also in Figure 7.13, in which the nominal rate has exceeded the inflation rate for Treasury bills since about 1982.

However, this experience is clearly from the past and reflects actually achieved returns and experienced inflation rates. We must emphasize that the nominal rate of interest depends on the expected rate of inflation, not the actual rate. Quoted interest rates pertain to investment over some future time period. As such, they cannot depend on the actual inflation rate to be sustained during the investment period, since that is not known. Instead, *expected* inflation is the key component.

---

[11]In fact, this analysis follows the introductory portion of an influential analysis of these issues presented in J. Hirschleifer, "Investment Decision Under Uncertainty: Choice—Theoretic Approaches," *The Quarterly Journal of Economics*, 79:4, November 1964, pp. 509–536.

[12]See Ibbotson Associates, *Stocks, Bonds, Bills and Inflation: 1987 Yearbook*, Chicago: Ibbotson Associates, Inc., 1987.

Figure 7.13

Nominal and Real T–Bill Returns, 1970–1993

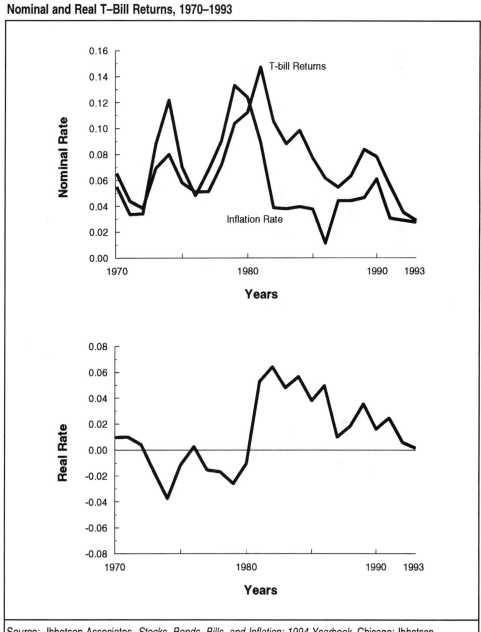

Source: Ibbotson Associates, *Stocks, Bonds, Bills, and Inflation: 1994 Yearbook*, Chicago: Ibbotson Associates, 1994.

Realized Compound Yield to Maturity (RCYTM)

Dramatically fluctuating interest rates can have an important impact on bond investments. For example, consider an investor holding a long–term high–coupon bond. All of the large coupon payments received from the bond must be reinvested at whatever rates prevail when the coupon payments are received. If rates are low when the coupons are received, the investor will have to reinvest the coupons at the new low rate. On the other hand, the holder of a low–coupon bond will have to invest relatively less at the new lower rates. The expectations of future changes in levels of interest rates are very important to bond investors for two reasons. First, as we have seen, changing rates means that bond prices change. Second, the rate earned on reinvested coupons also depends on how interest rates change.

Consequently, this chapter introduces an analytical tool useful for thinking about bond investing—one that takes into account the rates earned on reinvested coupons—the **realized compound yield to maturity (RCYTM)**. Bond investment is often directed toward some specific date in the future. Hence, the rate earned on reinvested coupon payments or on proceeds from maturing bonds is very important in determining the amount of funds available on the target date. For example, a trust fund might be established to mature on the beneficiary's twenty–first birthday. The goal of the investment program would be to secure the greatest amount of wealth possible, subject to acceptable levels of risk, on that date. The rate earned on any funds reinvested before the beneficiary's twenty–first birthday can mean the difference between success and failure in the investment program.

The best measure of progress toward such a goal is the RCYTM because it is a geometric mean growth rate over a given period.

$$RCYTM = \sqrt[n]{\frac{Terminal\ Wealth}{Initial\ Wealth}} - 1 \qquad\qquad \textbf{7.12}$$

where:
Initial Wealth = the value of the funds at the outset of the investment period
Terminal Wealth = the value of the funds at the conclusion of the investment period
n = the number of periods between the outset and the conclusion of the investment period

The RCYTM is simply the geometric mean return on the investment over a given period, which also reflects the rate of return realized on all proceeds from the investment. To see how Equation 7.12 reflects the rate of return on different proceeds from an investment, consider a 5–year, 10 percent annual coupon bond and an investment horizon of five years. If the initial interest rate on this bond is 10 percent, its price will be $1,000, assuming it has a $1,000 face value.

Over the five–year investment horizon, the bond will make four coupon payments of $100 each that will face reinvestment. In order to see how the RCYTM is affected by rates earned on reinvestment of these coupons, consider two cases. In the first case, the coupon payments are merely spent. In the second case, assume that the coupons are reinvested when received at a rate of 12 percent for the rest of the investment period. For both cases, the initial wealth is $1,000, the price of the bond. The difference in the reinvestment rates for the four coupon payments has a drastic affect on the RCYTM.

For the first case, in which the coupons are consumed when received, the terminal wealth will be $1,100. This $1,100 consists of the final coupon payment of $100 and the return of principal of $1,000. For the first case, the RCYTM would be:

$$\text{RCYTM} = \sqrt[5]{\frac{\$1,100}{\$1,000}} - 1 = 1.9\%$$

Starting with a bond earning a yield of 10 percent, consuming the coupons means that the investor has a RCYTM of only 1.9 percent per year. Note that the terminal wealth equals $1,000(1.019)^5$. Any coupon payments that do not have an effect on the wealth at the end of the investment period are not reflected in the RCYTM.

In the second case, in which the coupons are invested at 12 percent upon receipt for the remainder of the investment period, the RCYTM is much higher. The first step is to calculate the value of the terminal wealth, which is a straightforward future value problem:

$$
\begin{aligned}
\text{Terminal Value} &= \$100(1.12)^4 + \$100(1.12)^3 + \$100(1.12)^2 \\
&\quad + \$100(1.12) + \$1,100 \\
&= \$157.35 + \$140.49 + \$125.44 + \$112.00 + \$1,100 \\
&= \$1,635.28
\end{aligned}
$$

The RCYTM is:

$$\text{RCYTM} = \sqrt[5]{\frac{1,635.28}{1,000}} - 1 = 10.34\%$$

In the second case, the RCYTM exceeds the yield to maturity of 10 percent. This gives rise to a general rule about reinvestment rates.

If the reinvestment rate for the interim cash flows exceeds the yield to maturity, the RCYTM is greater than the yield to maturity.

If the reinvestment rate for the interim cash flows equals the yield to maturity, the RCYTM equals the yield to maturity.

If the reinvestment rate for the interim cash flows is less than the yield to maturity, the RCYTM is less than the yield to maturity.

In bond portfolio management, the interim cash flows from the portfolio can often be very large. This means that the successful bond portfolio manager must pay close attention to prospective reinvestment rates in forming and managing a bond portfolio.

Summary

This chapter began by examining how bond prices respond to changes in interest rates. The principles discussed show that:

1. Bond prices move inversely to interest rates.
2. Bonds of longer maturity are more sensitive to interest rate changes than short–term bonds.
3. The sensitivity of bond prices to interest rate changes increases at a decreasing rate with respect to maturity.
4. Bonds with large coupons are less sensitive to interest rate changes than low–coupon bonds.
5. A given drop in interest rates causes a larger capital gain than the capital loss caused by the same size increase in rates.

While these five principles accurately summarize the response of bond prices to interest rate changes, it would be very useful to have a single measure that summarizes these different effects. Macaulay's duration is a single number that allows direct comparison of the sensitivity of different bonds with changes in interest rates. The higher the duration, the more sensitive is a bond to changes in interest rates. We also considered the way in which duration can be used to estimate bond price changes that result from changing yields. We saw that there were some inaccuracies in this estimated price, which led to a consideration of convexity. With the twin tools of duration and convexity, we were able to improve our understanding of the factors that determine bond prices.

The importance of changes in interest rates on bond prices demands that investors understand the basic factors that influence interest rates. Following the analysis of Irving Fisher, we saw that the nominal or market rate of interest for a risk–free bond equals the real rate of interest plus the *expected* rate of inflation. In a riskless world, the real rate of interest equals the rate of return earned by newly employed physical capital.

The chapter also introduced the *realized compound yield to maturity* (RCYTM). This yield measure is particularly useful in measuring bond investment perfor-mance when there is a target date—a common situation in bond investing. When there is a target date for the investment, the goal is to have the most funds available on that target date, subject to a risk constraint. Because the RCYTM focuses on only those cash flows that affect the final proceeds available on the target date, the RCYTM is very useful for measuring success in bond investing when the investment is directed toward a target date.

Questions and Problems

1. Why must the price of a bond converge to its par value at maturity? Is this true of pure discount bonds and coupon bonds? Under what conditions might the price not converge to the par value?
2. Evaluate the following claim: "An investor should never buy a premium bond. A premium bond has a built–in capital loss due to the fact that the bond price must converge to its par value. This means that the return on a premium bond will be adversely affected."
3. What are the three key variables that influence bond pricing?
4. Assume that you are a money manager with a large stock of cash that you will be investing in bonds. You anticipate a strong upward movement in interest rates in general. What do your beliefs imply about the kinds of bonds you will select for investment, particularly with respect to maturity and coupon?
5. Again, assume that you expect sharply rising interest rates and you will buy one of the following two bonds: a 20–year 8 percent coupon bond or a 15–year 9 3/4 percent coupon bond. Does this give you enough information to make a decision? What else might you need to know?
6. Consider three 8 percent coupon bonds with 10–, 15–, and 20–year maturities. Which is the most sensitive to a change in interest rates? What do we mean by saying that one bond is more "sensitive" than another to changes in interest rates? Is the difference in sensitivity between the 10– and 15– year bonds the same as the difference in sensitivity between the 15– and 20–year bonds?
7. Two bonds in your portfolio have computed durations of 4 and 6 years. If interest rates rise by 1 percent, how will the price changes of the two bonds compare? Can you say what the ratio of the price changes for the two bonds will be?
8. What is the relationship between the nominal and market rates of interest?
9. Evaluate the following argument: "Over the past year, inflation has been quite high. Because interest rates depend upon the real rate of interest and the inflation rate, interest rates now should be quite high."
10. What market forces exist to make the real rate of interest equal to the marginal productivity of physical capital in a riskless environment?
11. How would you form an estimate of the market's expectations of future inflation?

12. As an investor, you are trying to decide between two bonds as investments for a 4–year investment horizon. The first has a 12 percent coupon and matures in 3 years. The other is a zero coupon bond maturing in 5 years. Compare and contrast the risks associated with each bond and their suitability for your investment horizon.

13. Why should the nominal rate of interest exceed the expected rate of inflation?

14. As a measure of returns, what is the principal use of the realized compound yield to maturity (RCYTM)?

15. Under what circumstances will the RCYTM equal the YTM? When will the RCYTM exceed the YTM? When will the RCYTM be less than the YTM?

16. Consider a 5–year pure discount bond with a face value of $1,000 that yields 10 percent compounded annually. What is its price? What will its price be if interest rates suddenly rise to 11 percent? What will its price be if interest rates suddenly fall to 9 percent? Are the capital gain and loss the same?

17. What is the price of a 3–year 8 percent annual coupon bond yielding 11 percent and having a face value of $1,000? Assuming annual compounding, what is the duration of the bond?

18. For the bond of Question 17, assume that interest rates suddenly rise to 13 percent. Compute the new price of the bond by discounting the cash flows at the new rate and by using the duration price change formula. Are the two answers the same? Why or why not?

19. What is the duration of a pure discount bond yielding 8 percent and maturing in 3 years and having a face value of $1,000?

20. What is the duration of a 12 percent annual coupon bond maturing in 5 years and yielding 11 percent? Assume a $1,000 face value. (Question: Do you really need to know the face value to make this computation?)

21. Compare the sensitivity of the bonds in the two preceding questions.

22. Today you purchase a $1,000 face value bond paying an 8 percent annual coupon and maturing in 5 years for a purchase price of $930. Assuming that you are able to reinvest all coupons at 11 percent, what is your terminal wealth after 5 years? What is your RCYTM? Make the computations assuming a reinvestment rate of 7 percent.

23. Assume you have an investment horizon of 5 years. You purchase a pure discount bond with a 5–year maturity and a face value of $1,000 for a purchase price of $621. Your friend purchases a 10 percent annual coupon bond with a face value of $1,000 and 5 years to maturity at par. What is the current interest rate on each bond? Assuming that rates do not change, what will be the terminal wealth and RCYTM for each bond, assuming that your friend reinvests all coupons? Assume that immediately after purchase interest rates drop to 8 percent. What will be the terminal wealth and RCYTM for the two investments?

24. Five years ago you invested $100,000 in a portfolio of Treasury bills and kept all proceeds fully invested in the portfolio. Today your portfolio is worth $146,932. What nominal rate of interest have you earned over this period? At the time of purchase the Consumer Price Index (CPI) stood at 133, and today it is at 189. What was the average inflation rate over the period? (Question:

Is this a geometric or arithmetic mean?) How much did your purchasing power increase over this entire period? What was your real return on an annual basis?

CFA Questions

A. An 8%, 30–year corporate bond was recently being priced to yield 10%. The Macaulay duration for this bond is 10.20 years. Given this information, the bond's modified duration would be:
    a. 8.05
    b. 9.44
    c. 9.72
    d. 10.71

B. A certain agency bond has a duration of 8.73 years and a convexity of 122.66. This implies that:
    a. if market yields increase significantly (e.g., rates increase by 250 basis points), the price of the bond will fall by *less* than the amount indicated by duration alone.
    b. if market yields increase significantly, the price of the bond will fall by *more* than the amount indicated by duration alone.
    c. if market yields decrease significantly (e.g., by 250 basis points), the price of the bond will increase by *less* than the amount indicated by the convexity measure alone.
    d. if market yields decrease significantly, the price of the bond will increase by *less* than the amount indicated by duration alone.

C. Using semiannual compounding, a 15–year, zero coupon bond that has a par value of $1,000 and a required return of 8% would be priced at:
    a. $308
    b. $315
    c. $464
    d. $555

D. An 8%, 15–year bond has a yield–to–maturity of 10% and a modified duration of 8.05 years. If the market yield changes by 25 basis points, how much change will there be in the bond's price?
    a. 1.85%
    b. 2.01%
    c. 3.27%
    d. 6.44%

E. Positive convexity on a bond implies that:
  a. the direction of change in yield is directly related to the change in price.
  b. prices increase at a faster rate as yields drop, than they decrease as yields rise.
  c. price changes are the same for both increases and decreases in yields.
  d. prices increase and decrease at a faster rate than the change in yield.
F. The duration of a bond normally increases with an increase in:
  a. term–to–maturity.
  b. yield–to–maturity.
  c. coupon rate.
  d. all of the above.

Use the following data in answering Questions G and H.

Par value	$1,000
Time–to–maturity	20 years
Coupon	10% (with interest paid annually)
Current price	$850
Yield–to–maturity	12%

G. Intuitively and without the use of calculations, if interest payments are reinvested at 10%, the realized compound yield on this bond must be:
  a. 10.0%
  b. 10.9%
  c. 12.0%
  d. 12.4%
H. Given the bond described above, if it paid interest semiannually (rather than annually), but continued to be priced at $850, the resulting yield–to–maturity would be:
  a. less than 12%.
  b. more than 12%.
  c. 12%.
  d. cannot be determined.
I. Consider a five–year bond with a 10% coupon that is currently trading at a yield–to–maturity of 8%. If market interest rates do not change, one year from now the price of this bond will be:
  a. higher.
  b. lower.
  c. the same.
  d. cannot be determined.
J. As compared with bonds selling at par, deep discount bonds will have:
  a. greater reinvestment risk.
  b. greater price volatility.
  c. less call protection.
  d. reinvestment risk.

K. Which *one* of the following is an *incorrect* statement concerning duration?
    a. The higher the yield–to–maturity, the greater the duration.
    b. The higher the coupon, the shorter the duration.
    c. The difference in duration is small between two bonds each maturing in more than 15 years.
    d. The duration is the same as term–to–maturity only in the case of zero coupon bonds.

L. An 8%, 20–year corporate bond is priced to yield 9%. The Macaulay duration for this bond is 8.85 years. Given this information, the bond's modified duration is:
    a. 8.12
    b. 8.47
    c. 8.51
    d. 9.25

M. Yield–to–maturity and current yield on a bond are equal:
    a. when market interest rates begin to level off.
    b. if the bond sells at a price in excess of its par value.
    c. when the expected holding period is greater than one year.
    d. if the coupon and market interest rate are equal.

N. Which bond has the longest duration?
    a. 8–year maturity, 6% coupon
    b. 8–year maturity, 11% coupon
    c. 15–year maturity, 6% coupon
    d. 15–year maturity, 11% coupon

O. A 9–year bond has a yield–to–maturity of 10% and a modified duration of 6.54 years. If the market yield changes by 50 basis points, the bond's expected price change is:
    a. 3.27%
    b. 3.66%
    c. 5.00%
    d. 6.54%

P. When interest rates decline, the duration of a 30–year bond selling at a premium:
    a. increases.
    b. decreases.
    c. remains the same.
    d. increases at first, then declines.

Q. Convexity of bonds is more important when interest rates are:
    a. high.
    b. low.
    c. expected to change very little.
    d. less than the coupon rate on the bond.

R. The semiannual interest rate that equates the present value of the bond's cash flow to its current market price is 4.75%. It follows that the bond's:
   I.   horizon return is 9.35%.
   II. effective annual yield is 9.73%.
   III. yield–to–maturity is 9.50%.
   a. I and II only
   b. I and III only
   c. II and III only
   d. III only

S. An investment in a coupon bond will provide the investor with a return equal to the bond's yield–to–maturity at the time of purchase if:
   a. the bond is not called for redemption at a price that exceeds its par value.
   b. all sinking fund payments are made in a prompt and timely fashion over the life of the issue.
   c. the reinvestment rate is the same as the bond's yield–to–maturity.
   d. all of the above.

T. The interest rate risk of a bond normally is:
   a. greater for shorter maturities.
   b. lower for longer duration.
   c. lower for higher coupons.
   d. none of the above.

U. The yield to maturity on a bond is:
   a. below the coupon rate when the bond sells at a discount and above the coupon rate when the bond sells at a premium.
   b. the interest rate that makes the present value of the payments equal to the bond price.
   c. based on the assumption that all future payments received are reinvested at the coupon rate.
   d. based on the assumption that all future payments received are reinvested at future market rates.

Suggested REALDATA Exercises

The following *REALDATA* exercises explore the concepts developed in this chapter: Exercises 35, 60, 63, 83, 96.

Suggested Readings

Chua, J. H., "A Generalized Formula for Calculating Bond Duration," *Financial Analysts Journal*, 44:5, September/October 1988, pp. 65–67.
Douglas, L. G., *Bond Risk Analysis*, New York: New York Institute of Finance, 1990.
Fabozzi, F. J., *Fixed Income Mathematics*, Chicago: Probus Publishing, 1988.

Fabozzi, F. J., M. Pitts, and R. E. Dattatreya, "Price Volatility Characteristics of Fixed Income Securities," *The Handbook of Fixed Income Securities*, 3e, Homewood, IL: Business Irwin One, 1991.

Hirschleifer, J., "Investment Decision Under Uncertainty: Choice–Theoretic Approaches," *The Quarterly Journal of Economics*, 79:4, November 1964, pp. 509–536.

Ibbotson, R, and R. Sinquefield, *Stocks, Bonds, Bills and Inflation: The Past and the Future*, Charlottesville, VA: The Financial Analysts Research Foundation, 1982.

Malkiel, Burton G., "Expectations, Bond Prices, and the Term Structure of Interest Rates," *Quarterly Journal of Economics*, May 1962, pp. 197–218.

Morrissey, T. F. and C. Huang, "A Nomogram for Estimating Duration," *Financial Analysts Journal*, 43:1, January/February 1987, pp. 65–67.

Rose, A. K., "Is the Real Interest Rate Stable?" *Journal of Finance*, 43:5, December 1988, pp. 1095–1112.

Sullivan, K. H. and T. B. Kiggins, "Convexity: The Name Is New but You Always Knew," *The Institutional Investor Focus on Investment Management*, Cambridge, MA: Ballinger Publishing, 1989, pp. 291–334.

Taylor, R. W., "Bond Duration Analysis: A Pedagogical Note," *Financial Analysts Journal*, 43:4, July/August 1987, pp. 71–72.

Winkelmann, K., "Uses and Abuses of Duration and Convexity," *Financial Analysts Journal*, 45:5, September/October 1989, pp. 72–75.

Yawitz, J. B., "Convexity: An Introduction," *The Institutional Investor Focus on Investment Management*, Cambridge, MA: Ballinger Publishing, 1989, pp. 271–289.

Appendix

This appendix shows the relationship between duration, convexity, and the bond pricing formula. Letting $R = 1 + r$, we can write the bond pricing equation as:

$$P = \sum_{t=1}^{M} \frac{C_t}{R^t} \qquad\qquad \textbf{A7.1}$$

We want to find the derivative of the bond's price with respect to R. For any single payment, we have:

$$\frac{d\left(\dfrac{C_t}{R^t}\right)}{dR} = -\frac{t\,C_t}{R^{t+1}}$$

Therefore, for the bond as a whole, we have:

$$\frac{dP}{dR} = -\sum_{t=1}^{M} \frac{t\,C_t}{R^{t+1}}$$

Multiplying both sides by $-(R/P)$ gives:

$$-\left(\frac{dP}{dR}\right)\left(\frac{R}{P}\right) = \frac{\left(\displaystyle\sum_{t=1}^{M} \frac{t\,C_t}{R^t}\right)}{P} \qquad\qquad \textbf{A7.2}$$

However, the right–hand side is merely the definition of duration. Therefore, duration equals:

$$D = -\left(\frac{dP}{dR}\right)\left(\frac{R}{P}\right)$$

Rearranging these terms gives:

$$D = - \frac{\dfrac{d P}{P}}{\dfrac{d R}{R}} \qquad \text{A7.3}$$

This matches our claim in the chapter text that duration is the negative of the standard elasticity measure. Notice that the equality holds in Equation A7.3, because the dP term is infinitesimal. In Equation 7.3, the changes in yield and price were discrete, introducing the error.

Returning to Equation A7.2 and recalling that modified duration is Macaulay's duration divided by R, we divide Equation A7.2 by R which gives the following result for modified duration:

$$MD = - \frac{\left(\dfrac{d P}{d R} \right)}{P} \qquad \text{A7.4}$$

Isolating the derivative terms in Equation A7.4, we have:

$$\frac{d P}{d R} = - MD\,(P) \qquad \text{A7.5}$$

That is, the derivative of the bond's price with respect to R equals the negative of modified duration times the bond's price. This derivative term gives the slope of the price/yield line for the bond. Notice that MD and P are always positive. Therefore, the slope of the price/yield line is always negative. The duration price change formula follows directly from Equation A7.5 by rearranging terms and allowing for discrete changes in R:

$$\Delta P \approx - MD\,(P)\,\Delta R \qquad \text{A7.6}$$

We now show how the measure of convexity is related to the second derivative of the bond's price with respect to R. For any single cash flow:

$$\frac{d^2 P}{dR^2} = \frac{d\left(- \dfrac{t\,C_t}{R^{t+1}} \right)}{d R} = \frac{t\,(t+1)\,C_t}{R^{t+2}} = \frac{1}{R^2}\left(\frac{t\,(t+1)\,C_t}{R^t} \right) \qquad \text{A7.7}$$

Therefore, for the bond as a whole, the second derivative is:

$$\frac{d^2 P}{dR^2} = \frac{1}{R^2} \sum_{t=1}^{M} \frac{t(t+)C_t}{R^t} \qquad \text{A7.8}$$

Dividing both sides of Equation A7.8 by the bond price gives the following result:

$$\frac{\frac{d^2 P}{dR^2}}{P} = \frac{1}{PR^2} \sum_{t=1}^{M} \frac{t(t+1)C_t}{R^t} \qquad \text{A7.9}$$

The right–hand side of Equation A7.9 is the definition of convexity, VEX, so convexity equals the second derivative of the bond's price divided by the price of the bond:

$$\text{VEX} = \frac{\frac{d^2 P}{dR^2}}{P} \qquad \text{A7.10}$$

Given an initial value for a function, a Taylor series gives a way to approximate the new value of the function. Focusing on our situation in which the price of a bond P is a function of the discount factor R, the Taylor series gives the following rule:

$$\Delta P \approx \frac{\frac{dP}{dR}\Delta R}{1} + \frac{\frac{d^2 P}{dR^2}\Delta R}{2} + \ldots \qquad \text{A7.11}$$

We show only the first two terms, those associated with the first and second derivatives. Under Taylor's rule, it is possible to more closely approximate the change in the value of P by considering higher derivatives. In our case, we consider only the first two. The first derivative is associated with duration, while the second is associated with convexity.

We now divide Equation A7.11 by the bond price, which gives:

$$\frac{\Delta P}{P} \approx \left(\frac{\frac{dP}{dR}}{P}\right) \Delta R \ + \ .5 \left(\frac{\frac{d^2P}{dR^2}}{P}\right) \Delta R \qquad \textbf{A7.12}$$

In the right–hand side of Equation A7.12, the first bracketed expression is the definition of modified duration given in Equation A7.4. Likewise, the second bracketed expression is the definition of convexity from Equation A7.10. Substituting these two definitions and multiplying Equation A7.12 by the price of the bond gives:

$$\Delta P \approx \ - MD \ (\Delta R) \ (P) \ + \ .5 \ (VEX) \ (\Delta R) \ (P)$$
$$\approx [-MD \ + \ .5 \ (VEX)] \ (\Delta R) \ (P) \qquad \textbf{A7.13}$$

Equation A7.13 is exactly the formula for the price change of a bond due to a change in the yield. On the right–hand side, the –MD term is associated with the price change due to duration, while the .5VEX term reflects the price change associated with convexity.

CHAPTER EIGHT

Bond Portfolio Management

Overview

The preceding chapter introduced bond pricing and focused on the principles of bond pricing as applied to a single bond. This chapter builds on that foundation, giving particular emphasis to the issues that confront bond portfolio managers. Chapter 7 concentrated on bonds that were free of default risk. This chapter continues to use that assumption in introducing the term structure of interest rates. Risky bonds are considered later in this chapter.

One of the most basic questions facing a bond manager concerns the proper maturity characteristics of the bonds to hold in a portfolio. We have already observed that yields on bonds can be graphed as a **yield curve**, a graph that shows the relationship between the maturity of a bond and its yield to maturity. Even for a bond portfolio of U.S. Treasury bonds, bond yields vary simply because of differences in maturity.

As discussed in the preceding chapter, longer maturity bonds tend to be more sensitive to interest rate changes and are riskier than short–maturity bonds in the sense that their prices may fluctuate more. However, longer maturity bonds often pay a higher yield than short–maturity bonds, making them enticing for a bond portfolio manager.

To structure a successful bond portfolio, the manager must understand the relationship between maturity and yield in order to determine the appropriate maturity or duration structure of the bond portfolio. By adjusting the maturity or the duration of a bond portfolio, the bond manager determines the sensitivity of the portfolio to changes in interest rates. Making the correct adjustments can have a dramatic influence on the portfolio's returns. As a consequence, the analysis of the yield curve, or the term structure of interest rates, is important for bond portfolio management.

Thus far, we have focused almost exclusively on bonds that are free of default risk. **Default risk** is the risk that one or more of the payments on a bond will not be paid as promised. However, much of the bond market is composed of corporate issues and municipal bonds, all of which have default risk. Differences in default risk give rise to the risk structure of interest rates. The **risk structure of interest rates** is the relationship between the yields of different securities as a function of their level of default risk. Risk levels of various bonds change over time, and the yield differences of bonds from different classes change over time as well. The bond portfolio manager must comprehend those differences and the reasons for their occurrence. In fact, choosing the correct level of default risk is one of the most important decisions the bond portfolio manager must face. By accepting more default risk in the portfolio, the manager secures a greater promised return but increases the danger of missed payments on the bonds.

In practice, choosing the correct maturity composition of the portfolio and selecting the appropriate risk level are two of the prime functions of the bond portfolio manager. However, neither issue would be very important if the manager could forecast interest rates accurately. In fact, if portfolio managers could forecast interest rates with a greater degree of accuracy than the market as a whole, they could reap enormous returns. This chapter also examines the success that can be expected in forecasting interest rates. As the discussion indicates, there is little hope of consistently successful forecasting.

In the face of difficulties with forecasting interest rates, many bond portfolio managers have learned to focus on various kinds of immunization techniques. An **immunization strategy** seeks to make the value of the bond portfolio immune, or insensitive, to changes in interest rates. These management strategies rely on the concept of duration as a key element.

The Term Structure of Interest Rates

In June 1994, short–term Treasury bills had yields lower than 4.0 percent, while long–term Treasury bonds had yields as high as 7.5 percent. At first glance, this is very strange. Both have equal backing by the U.S. Treasury, so they have the same level of default risk. In fact, the only essential difference between these two issues is the length of maturity. This difference in yields, due solely to differences in maturities, is described by the yield curve or the term structure of interest rates. Naturally, this gap of almost 4 percent in yield is of prime importance to the bond portfolio manager. It appears that the portfolio manager should accept the higher yields of the long–term bonds. However, this simple solution is not necessarily correct since it leaves out the important considerations associated with the term structure of interest rates.

The **term structure of interest rates** is the relationship between the term to maturity, or time left until maturity, and the yield to maturity for bonds similar in all respects except their maturities. Since the purpose of yield curve or term structure analysis is to understand the differences in bond yields that arise strictly from differences in maturity, the bonds used in the analysis must be as similar as possible in all other respects. For example, all of the bonds used in a yield curve should be similar in their risk level and should have the same call provisions, sinking–fund characteristics, and tax status.

Figure 8.1

The Treasury Yield Curve

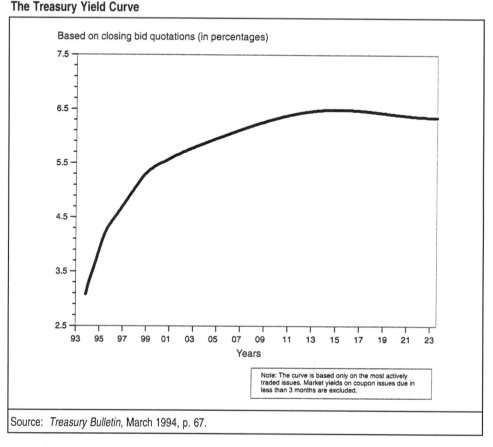

Based on closing bid quotations (in percentages)

Note: The curve is based only on the most actively traded issues. Market yields on coupon issues due in less than 3 months are excluded.

Source: *Treasury Bulletin*, March 1994, p. 67.

These requirements for similarities among bonds used in the yield curve analysis are cumbersome, because it is difficult to find a pool of bonds that meet all of those conditions. For this reason, it is customary to focus on the term structure of Treasury securities. Treasury securities all have the same level of default risk and tend to be alike in their tax status and other features as well. Also, because Treasury securities are lowest in risk, the Treasury yield curve provides the basic yield curve to which the yields of other securities can be related. For these reasons, this section focuses on the Treasury yield curve, shown in Figure 8.1.

In Figure 8.1, the yield curve has a gentle upward slope; that is, the longer maturity instruments have a somewhat higher yield than short–maturity instruments. At other times, the yield curve may take on different shapes. For example, Figure 8.2 shows yield curves for high–grade corporate bonds during this century. Notice the dramatically different shapes. Even within a very short period, violent swings in the shape of the yield curve and in the level of rates can occur. The shape

Figure 8.2

Historical Yield Curves

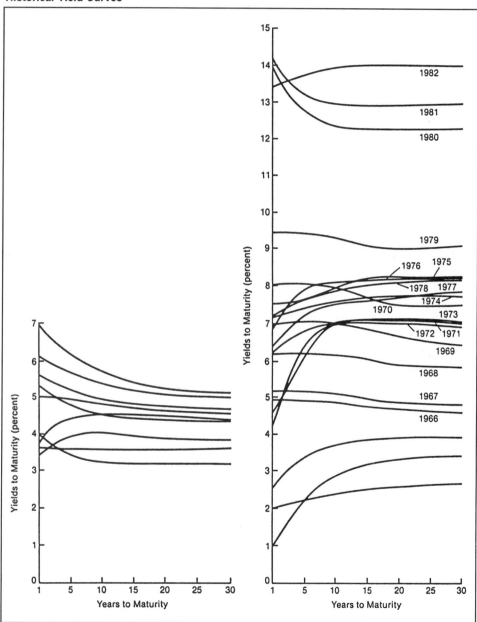

Source: John Wood, "Do Yield Curves Normally Slope Up? The Term Structure of Interest Rates, 1862–1982," *Economic Perspectives*, Federal Reserve Bank of Chicago, July/August 1983, p. 18.

of the yield curve is important because it contains information about the future course of interest rates. Since the future of interest rates is the single most valuable piece of information a bond investor would like to have, understanding the yield curve is extremely important. Developing this understanding of yield curves first requires a knowledge of forward rates.

Forward Rates

Forward rates of interest cover future time periods implied by currently available spot rates. A **spot rate** is a yield prevailing on a bond for immediate purchase. Given a set of spot rates, it is possible to calculate forward rates for any intervening time period.

For convenience, let us introduce the notation that a bond yield expressed as $r_{x,y}$ is the rate to prevail on a bond for the period beginning at time x and maturing at time y. The present is always time = 0, so a bond yield covering any time span beginning at time = 0 is a spot rate. For example, $r_{0,5}$ would be the spot rate for an instrument maturing in five years. If the time covered by a particular rate begins after time = 0, it is a forward rate. The forward rate to cover a period beginning two years from now and extending three years to time = 5 would be expressed as $r_{2,5}$ in our notation. Using this notation, we can now introduce a principle that can be used for the calculation of forward rates.

Principle of Calculation for Forward Rates
Forward rates are calculated on the assumption that returns over a given period of time are all equal, no matter which maturities of bonds are held over that span of time.

Taking a 5–year period as an example, this principle implies that forward rates can be calculated over the five years on the assumption that all of the following strategies would earn the same returns over the 5–year period:

1. Buy the 5–year bond and hold it to maturity.
2. Buy a 1–year bond and when it matures, buy another 1–year bond, following this procedure for the entire five years.
3. Buy a 2–year bond and when it matures, buy a 3–year bond and hold it to maturity.

According to the Principle of Calculation, holding bonds of any maturity over this five–year period would give the same return. Notice that this is not a prediction of returns, but it is an assumption used to calculate forward rates.

In terms of the notation being used in this chapter, we can express these three strategies as follows:

1. Hold one 5–year bond for five years
    Total Return = $(1 + r_{0,5})^5$

2. Hold a sequence of 1–year bonds
    Total Return $= (1 + r_{0,1})(1 + r_{1,2})(1 + r_{2,3})(1 + r_{3,4})(1 + r_{4,5})$
3. Hold a 2–year bond followed by a 3–year bond
    Total Return $= (1 + r_{0,2})^2 (1 + r_{2,5})^3$

We can calculate the forward rates appearing in these strategies by applying the Principle of Calculation, which says that those total returns should all be equal:

$$(1 + r_{0,5})^5 = (1 + r_{0,1})(1 + r_{1,2})(1 + r_{2,3})(1 + r_{3,4})(1 + r_{4,5})$$
$$= (1 + r_{0,2})^2 (1 + r_{2,5})^3$$

To apply the Principle of Calculation, consider a situation in which the following yields obtain for Treasury securities of various maturities.

Spot Rate	Yield	Maturity
$r_{0,1}$	.08	1 year
$r_{0,2}$	.088	2 years
$r_{0,3}$	.09	3 years
$r_{0,4}$	.093	4 years
$r_{0,5}$	.095	5 years

These yields are all spot yields and describe an upward–sloping yield curve, because the yield increases with the maturity of the bond. These spot rates also imply a set of forward rates to cover periods ranging from time = 1 to time = 5. An investor with a 5–year horizon might hold a 5–year bond, with a yield of 9.5 percent. However, there are numerous alternative ways of holding a bond investment over the same time period. As an example of how to calculate forward rates, consider the third strategy in which the investor might hold a 2–year bond followed by holding a 3–year bond. Right now, at time = 0, it is impossible to know what the yield will be on the 3–year bond to cover the time period from time = 2 to time = 5. This rate cannot be known with certainty until time = 2 actually arrives. At time = 0, however, it is possible to calculate a forward rate to cover the time span from time = 2 to time = 5. As shown earlier, the principle of calculation implies:

$$(1 + r_{0,5})^5 = (1 + r_{0,2})^2 (1 + r_{2,5})^3$$

Using the spot rates given above:

$$1.095^5 = 1.088^2 (1 + r_{2,5})^3$$

Now the only unknown is the forward rate, so the equation can be solved for its value:

$$1.5742 = 1.1837(1 + r_{2,5})^3$$

$$1.5742/1.1837 = (1 + r_{2,5})^3$$

$$(1 + r_{2,5}) = \sqrt[3]{\frac{1.5742}{1.1837}} = 1.0997$$

$$r_{2,5} = .0997 = 9.97\%$$

The forward rate, implied by this set of spot rates, to cover the period from year 2 to year 5, is 9.97 percent. Given the relevant spot rates, it is possible to calculate any forward rate. For the five years of this example, all intervening forward rates can be calculated with the data supplied. Notice that nothing has been said so far about how the forward rates are to be interpreted. There are different theories of the term structure that interpret forward rates in somewhat different ways. However, all of the theories that use forward rates to understand the term structure agree that forward rates give important information about the future course of interest rates.

Theories of the Term Structure

Three theories of the term structure have received the greatest attention. They are the pure expectations theory, the liquidity premium theory, and the market segmentation theory. This section considers these theories in detail. The pure expectations theory and the liquidity premium theory both use forward rates as a key element, and both theories can be stated by their interpretation of forward rates.

The Pure Expectations Theory

The **pure expectations theory** states that:

Forward rates are unbiased estimators of future interest rates.

or

Forward Rates = Expected Future Spot Rates

An unbiased estimator is one whose expected value equals the true value of the parameter being estimated. In somewhat more straightforward language, the pure expectations theory claims that today's forward rate equals the expected future spot rate for the period corresponding to the forward rate. In terms of the previous example, where it was calculated that the forward rate for a 3–period bond to cover from time = 2 to time = 5 was 9.97 percent, the pure expectations theory would say that 9.97 percent is a good estimate of the spot rate that will prevail on a 3–year bond beginning two years from now. The actual rate that occurs may be higher or lower than 9.97 percent, but on average, the forward rate will equal the subsequently observed spot rate.

This theory has strong practical implications. If it is true, the observable term structure contains predictions of future interest rates. Why should anyone believe this theory? Its defenders explain it this way. The bond market is well developed and populated with many participants having different wealth levels and different preferences. There are many people in the bond market who do not have any particular preference about the maturity of instruments that they hold. In the absence of any strong maturity preference, these investors seek the best rate of return. So, assume for the moment that the expected total return for a 5–year investment in Treasury securities is greater if one held a 5–year bond for five years, rather than holding a 2–year bond followed by a 3–year bond. These investors, without strong maturity preferences, would prefer the 5–year bond. Anyone holding the 2–year bond would sell it in order to invest the funds in the better–performing 5–year bond.

As the 2–year bonds were sold in order to buy 5–year bonds, there would be strong price effects on both bonds. The price of the 2–year bond would fall and the price of the 5–year bond would rise. These investors would stop switching from the 2–year to the 5–year bond only when the expected returns from the two strategies were equal, eliminating any incentive to switch from one to the other. According to the pure expectations theory, there are many bond investors who will switch their funds to any maturity with a higher yield. However, the willingness of these investors to hold whichever maturity has higher expected returns means that all maturity strategies must have the same expected return in equilibrium. In other words, after all of the maturity switching has stopped and an equilibrium has been achieved, there must be an equal expected return for any investment period, no matter what maturities of instruments are held over that period.

Now we can see how the pure expectations theory ties together forward rates and expected future spot rates. In the previous example, the investor in the 5–year bond yielding 9.5 percent is expecting to earn 9.5 percent per year over the 5–year period. According to the pure expectations theory, an investor with a 5–year horizon holding a 2–year bond and planning to follow that by holding a 3–year bond must expect to earn the same 9.5 percent annual return over the entire period. However, the yield to maturity on the 2–year bond is only 8.8 percent. The investor who earns 8.8 percent for the first two years of a 5–year holding period must earn much more in the last three years to have a 9.5 percent rate of return over the whole period.

One dollar invested for five years at 9.5 percent will be worth $1.57 at the end of the period. If the investor planning to hold the 2–year bond at 8.8 percent followed by a 3–year bond wants to earn the same rate of return, he or she must experience a higher yield on the 3–year bond. In fact, the expected rate of return on the 3–year bond must be sufficient so that the returns from the two maturity strategies give the same final wealth for equal investments. It must be that:

$$1.095^5 = 1.088^2 \, (1 + x)^3$$

where x equals the expected yield on the 3–year bond to cover the period from time = 2 to time = 5. What then is the value of x? Solving this equation for x gives:

$$1.5742 = 1.1837(1 + x)^3$$

$$(1 + x)^3 = 1.5742/1.1837$$

$$(1 + x) = \sqrt[3]{\frac{1.5742}{1.1837}}$$

$$x = 9.97\%$$

Notice that this expected interest rate for the 3–year bond exactly equals the forward rate for the same bond previously calculated. This is the crux of the argument for the pure expectations theory. If expected returns from all maturity strategies are equal, forward rates must necessarily equal expected future spot rates. The equality of forward rates and expected future spot rates follows logically from the view that all maturity strategies have the same expected return over any given holding period. If there are enough investors who do not care about the maturity of the instruments they hold and merely seek the highest expected return, they will ensure that all different maturity strategies have the same expected return, and they will force the major conclusion of the pure expectations theory to be true, namely, that forward rates equal expected future spot rates. Ultimately, the truth of the pure expectations theory depends upon the presence of bond investors who are indifferent to the maturities of the bonds they hold and who seek the greatest expected returns.

The Liquidity Premium Theory

In many ways, the liquidity premium theory resembles the pure expectations theory. At least both theories see the problem in very similar terms. The **liquidity premium theory** can also be stated by reference to forward rates:

Forward rates are upwardly biased estimators of expected future spot rates; that is, the estimates are too high.

or

Forward Rates > Expected Future Spot Rates

The liquidity premium theorists acknowledge the pure expectations theory claim that if enough bond investors care only about returns, they will trade to ensure that all maturity strategies over a given time span have the same expected return. However, they reject the claim that there are numerous investors who are indifferent about the maturities of the bonds they hold.

The defenders of the liquidity premium theory assert that bondholders greatly prefer to hold short–term bonds rather than long–term bonds. The short–term bonds have less interest rate risk. As explained in Chapter 7, the shorter the maturity, the less interest rate risk there will be. The fact that prices of short–term bonds will not change dramatically when interest rates change makes them more attractive than long–term bonds to many investors. According to the liquidity premium theory, short–term bonds are so much more attractive than long–term bonds that investors are willing to pay more for short–term bonds than for long–term bonds. This extra amount they are willing to pay is the **liquidity premium**.

The willingness of investors to pay a liquidity premium for the short–term bonds also implies that yields on short–term bonds will be lower than the yields on long–term bonds, other things being equal. Another way of saying the same thing is to notice that long–term bonds must pay a greater return than short–term bonds to induce investors to commit their funds to the long–term instruments.

If yields on short–term instruments are normally lower than those on long–term bonds, total returns from investing in short maturities will be less than the total return from investing in long maturities, even when the two strategies cover the identical time interval. For example, assume that a 5–year bond must pay 1/10 of 1 percent greater yield than a 1–year bond because of investor preferences for short–term securities. Using the values of our continuing example, the 5–year bond returns 9.5 percent over its life. With a 1/10 of 1 percent higher yield per annum for the 5–year over the 1–year instrument, the strategy of holding five 1–year bonds in succession must return only 9.4 percent over the 5–year period. The 1–year spot instrument has a yield of 8 percent. So the yield on the four following 1–year bonds must be such that the average annual yield on the strategy of holding the 1–year bonds turns out to be 9.4 percent:

$$(1.094)^5 = (1.08) (1 + x)^4$$

$$x = 9.753\%$$

If the total realized return over the 5–year period is to be 9.4 percent per year from the strategy of holding 1–year bonds, the expected average return per year for years 2 through year 5 must be 9.753 percent.[1] The forward rate $r_{1,5}$ can be calculated as well:

----

[1]Here it is not possible to say what the expected rate for each of the 1–year bonds would be. But the geometric average of these returns must be 9.753 percent. Fortunately, that is enough for the present purpose.

$$(1 + r_{0,5})^5 = (1 + r_{0,1})(1 + r_{1,5})^4$$

$$(1.095)^5 = (1.08)(1 + r_{1,5})^4$$

$$(1 + r_{1,5}) = \sqrt[4]{\frac{1.5742}{1.08}}$$

$$r_{1,5} = 9.88\%$$

According to the key claim of the liquidity premium theory, the expected rate of return on a succession of 1–year bonds must be less than the expected rate of return on a long–term bond when the two maturity strategies are pursued over the same time. The returns would differ by the amount of the liquidity premium, other things being equal. In this example, the assumed yield differential between the 5–year and the 1–year bonds, caused by the liquidity premium, was 1/10 of 1 percent. This implied that the expected rate of return on the 1–year bonds covering the last four of the five years was 9.753 percent. However, the forward rate for the same 4–year period was 9.88 percent.

Notice that this result is exactly consistent with the claims of the liquidity premium theory. The forward rate (9.88 percent) is greater than the expected rate (9.753 percent) over this 4–year period. If the liquidity premium theory is correct, using forward rates to estimate future spot rates of interest gives estimates that are too high due to the presence of the liquidity premium.

Both the pure expectations and liquidity premium theories are rigorous and follow logically from their respective beliefs about the preferences and behavior of bond market participants. The basic disagreement between the two theories turns on whether bondholders prefer short–term instruments to long–term instruments.

The Market Segmentation Theory

Unlike the pure expectations theory and the liquidity premium theory, the market segmentation theory is not expressly stated in terms of forward rates. Rather, the **market segmentation theory** takes a more institutional approach. According to this theory, the yield curve reflects the actions and preferences of certain major participants in the bond market. To a large extent, the bond market is dominated by large financial institutions, with each kind of institution having strong maturity preferences stemming from the kind of business it pursues. Commercial banks, for example, have relatively short–term liabilities in the form of demand deposits and certificates of deposit (CDs). As a consequence, they prefer to invest in relatively short–term bonds.[2] Life insurance companies, by contrast, have their liabilities falling due far in the future upon the death of policyholders. Correspondingly, life

---

[2] The reasons for these kinds of preferences are explained later in the section on Portfolio Immunization Techniques.

insurance companies prefer long–term bonds. Casualty insurers, such as those writing auto and home insurance, have liabilities that fall due in the medium term and, therefore, favor medium–maturity bonds for their investments.

These preferences of different types of financial institutions stem from the nature of their businesses and a desire to match the maturity of their assets and liabilities in order to control risk. Because of these preferences, the institutions tend to trade bonds only in their respective maturity ranges. For example, to induce a bank to invest in long–term bonds, the bonds must pay an attractively higher yield in comparison to the short–term bonds that banks prefer for business reasons. The desire of these different institutions to participate only in certain maturity segments of the bond market leads directly to the segmented markets hypothesis:

> *The yield curve is determined by the interplay of supply and demand factors in different segments of the maturity spectrum of the bond market. Financial institutions with strong maturity preferences occupy those different segments and effectively cause the bond market to splinter into different market segments based on maturity.*

These preferences for certain maturity ranges, it must be stressed, are not absolute. If the institutions dominated the bond market and never left their preferred maturity habitats, it might even be possible to observe a discontinuous yield curve, such as that shown in Figure 8.3. However, according to the market segmentation

Figure 8.3

An Extreme Case of a Segmented Bond Market

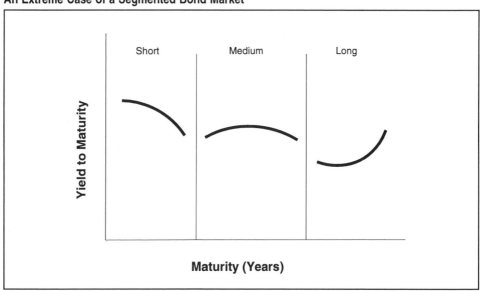

theory (also known as the preferred habitat theory), the institutions have preferred maturity ranges, but the preference is not absolute. In a situation such as that in Figure 8.3, the casualty insurers could make themselves much better off by taking a slightly shorter maturity than their currently shortest maturity and taking a slightly longer maturity than their currently longest maturity. In both cases, the yields on those bonds would increase. In fact, this is clearly what bond market participants would do in such a case. As a consequence, a discontinuous yield curve is not found in the actual market.

How the Three Theories Explain Different Observed Yield Curves

To understand these three theories of the term structure, it is important to realize that each theory is capable of explaining any observed market yield curve. For example, if the yield curve slopes upward, the forward rates increase as they go further into the future. According to the pure expectations theory, this means that short–term interest rates are expected to rise. With a flat yield curve, all forward rates equal the current short–term spot rate, so the pure expectations theory interprets this as the market's belief that interest rates will remain constant. For a downward–sloping yield curve, the pure expectations theory stresses the fact that forward rates will be smaller the farther they are in the future and interprets this as the market's belief that short–term interest rates are expected to fall.

The liquidity premium theory can explain any observed yield curve with equal facility, but the liquidity premium makes the explanation more complicated. To see the effect of the liquidity premium, assume the market expects short–term interest rates to be constant forever. The liquidity premium would then force a long–term bond to pay a higher yield. According to the liquidity premium theory, this means that the yield curve will be sloping slightly upward even when short–term rates are expected to remain constant. The tendency for the yield curve to slope upward would be due strictly to the impact of the liquidity premium. This situation is shown in Figure 8.4. The dotted line in the figure is at the level of the constant expected short–term interest rates. Nonetheless, the yield curve slopes upward because of the liquidity premium. For this reason, many people believe that an upward sloping yield curve, such as that shown in Figure 8.1, is the normal shape of the yield curve.

The liquidity premium theory cites two factors favoring a strongly upward–sloping yield curve: the impact of the liquidity premium and the market's expectation of higher interest rates, as in Figure 8.5. The dotted line indicates where the yield curve would be with just a liquidity premium and no expectation of higher rates in the future. The liquidity premium always makes the observed yield curve more strongly upward–sloping than it would be otherwise. The actual yield curve lies above the dotted line because interest rates are also expected to rise in this example.

For a downward–sloping yield curve, the liquidity premium theory argues that interest rates are expected to fall by an amount greater than the effect of the liquidity premium. The liquidity premium always has the effect of making the yield curve slope upward more than it otherwise would. An observed downward slope

Figure 8.4

**The Yield Curve with Equal Expected Future Short–Term Rates
According to the Liquidity Premium Theory**

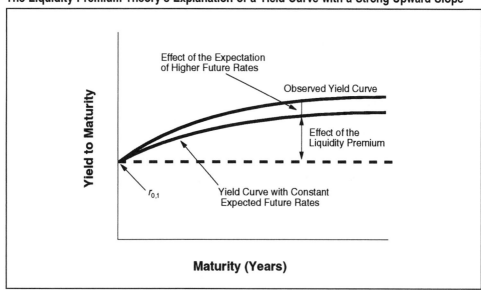

Figure 8.5

The Liquidity Premium Theory's Explanation of a Yield Curve with a Strong Upward Slope

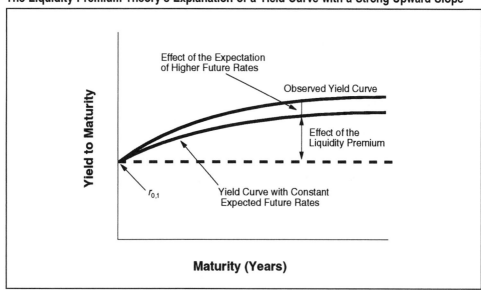

indicates that the market must be expecting a drop in interest rates sufficiently large to offset the effect of the liquidity premium.

The market segmentation hypothesis explains all observed yield curve shapes as resulting from the supply and demand factors in each segment of the bond market. According to this view, expectations are also important, but the emphasis is on the interest and maturity preferences of the different institutional participants.

Evidence on the Three Theories

The competing theories of the term structure have given rise to many attempts to determine which theory is correct. Not surprisingly, the issue is still not fully determined. In spite of some evidence in support of the market segmentation theory, there does seem to be a consensus that it alone cannot explain the yield curve.[3] As a consequence, the real struggle is between the pure expectations theory and the liquidity premium theory.

Meiselman and Santomero both find empirical evidence supporting the pure expectations hypothesis.[4] Opposed to these results is research by Nelson and McCulloch.[5] McCulloch finds a definite, but small, liquidity premium and also finds that virtually all of this premium is confined to very short maturities of about one year or less. Froot finds that the expectations hypothesis has little merit for short–term rates, but that it works well for long–term rates.[6] Cook and Hahn find limited support for the expectations hypothesis as well, although they regard the

---

[3] The market segmentation theory was first advanced by Franco Modigliani and Richard Sutch, "Innovations in Interest Rate Policy," *American Economic Review*, May 1966. Empirical support for the theory can be found in Edward J. Kane and Burton G. Malkiel, "The Term Structure of Interest Rates: An Analysis of a Survey of Interest Rate Expectations," *Review of Economics and Statistics*, August 1967; Wayne Lee, Terry Maness, and Donald Tuttle, "Nonspeculative Behavior and the Term Structure," *Journal of Financial and Quantitative Analysis*, March 1980; and J. W. Elliot and M. E. Echols, "Market Segmentation, Speculative Behavior, and the Term Structure of Interest Rates," *Review of Economics and Statistics*, February 1976.

[4] David Meiselman, *The Term Structure of Interest Rates*, Englewood Cliffs, NJ: Prentice Hall, 1962; Anthony M. Santomero, "The Error Learning Hypothesis and the Term Structure of Interest Rates in Eurodollars," *Journal of Finance*, June 1975.

[5] Charles Nelson, "Estimation of Term Premiums from Average Yield Differentials in the Term Structure of Interest Rates," *Econometrica*, March 1972; J. Huston McCulloch, "An Estimate of the Liquidity Premium," *Journal of Political Economy*, February 1975.

[6] K. A. Froot, "New Hope for the Expectations Hypothesis of the Term Structure of Interest Rates," *Journal of Finance*, 44:2, June 1989, pp. 283–305.

expectations contained in the term structure not to be very accurate forecasts of future interest rates.[7]

While the different theories of the term structure are sure to survive and to attract more research, it is important not to be misled by minor differences of opinion when there is major agreement. Most theorists would agree on the fundamental proposition that the shape of the yield curve expresses the market's opinion about future interest rates. In general, an upward–sloping yield curve implies that rates are expected to rise; a downward–sloping yield curve implies that rates are expected to fall. Further, if a liquidity premium does exist, it is not very large, so forward rates still provide a very good guide to the market's expectation of future interest rates. In fact, the forward rates of interest often provide better forecasts of future interest rates than professional forecasting services.

The Risk Structure of Interest Rates

Just as there is a term structure, there is also a risk structure of interest rates. The risk structure of interest rates analyzes the differences in risk among different classes of bonds. Since it focuses only on risk differences, the risk structure holds constant other factors affecting yield, such as maturity, callability, mortgage features, sinking funds, and the other important institutional features of bonds discussed in Chapter 2.

For two classes of bonds differing only in their risk level, the yield difference that results from a difference in risk is called a **yield differential**, **yield spread**, or **risk differential**. The yield spread can be observed between any two classes of bonds that differ in their risk level. Figure 8.6 presents a graph of the risk structure of interest rates over the recent past for different classes of long–term bonds. In Figure 8.6, it is possible to examine the risk structure of interest rates using U.S. government bonds and Moody's Aaa and Baa Corporate Bond indexes. These different classes of bonds are similar in tax status, maturity, and other features, but differ in their risk levels. Treasury bonds have the lowest risk and pay the lowest rate of return.

In comparing risk–free Treasury bonds and risky corporate bonds, the yield differential is also known as the **risk premium**. While the rate of return on Treasury bonds is always less than that for corporate bonds, the size of the yield differential varies dramatically over time. In the early 1930s, for example, the risk premium suddenly became very large. In other periods, such as the late 1950s, the risk premium for Aaa bonds was almost zero. For an investor, an understanding of these risk premiums and the way in which they fluctuate can be very important. For an aggressive investor, the greater risk premium that is sometimes available might be a good reason to hold riskier bonds.

---

[7]T. Cook and T. Hahn, "Interest Rate Expectations and the Slope of the Money Market Yield Curve," Federal Reserve Bank of Richmond *Economic Review*, 76:5, September/October 1990, pp. 3–26.

Figure 8.6

The Risk Structure of Interest Rates

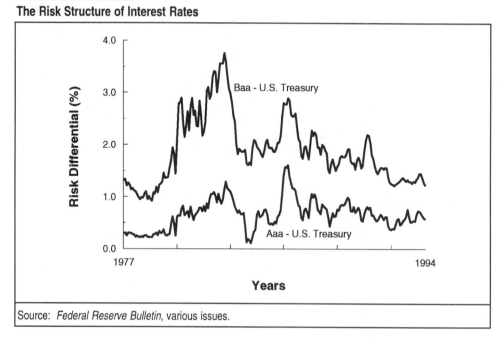

Source: *Federal Reserve Bulletin*, various issues.

Determinants of the Risk Premium

Certain relationships between the risk premium and other economic variables are important in understanding why the risk premium behaves as it does. One of the largest risk premiums in U.S. history occurred in the early 1930s when the Great Depression was at its worst. In times of economic prosperity, the risk premium tends to be much smaller. For example, in the boom year of 1967, the risk premium for Aaa corporate bonds almost vanished. Clearly, the risk premium varies inversely with the business cycle. Yield spreads are large in recessions and small in booms, other things being equal.[8] In times of economic hardship, weaker companies move much closer, relatively speaking, to the brink of disaster, than do

---

[8]This observation has been formally substantiated by a number of studies. See, for example: Calvin M. Boardman and Richard W. McEnally, "Factors Affecting Seasoned Corporate Bond Prices," *Journal of Financial and Quantitative Analysis*, 16:2, 1981, pp. 207–226; Dwight M. Jaffee, "Cyclical Variation in the Risk Structure of Interest Rates," *Journal of Monetary Economics*, 1, 1975, pp. 309–325; and David S. Kidwell and Timothy W. Koch, "The Behavior of the Interest Rate Differential Between Tax–Exempt Revenue and General Obligation Bonds: A Test of Risk Preferences and Market Segmentation," *Journal of Finance*, March 1982, pp. 73–85.

the firms issuing high–quality bonds. In times of prosperity, even the weaker companies can survive with relative ease. Accordingly, the risk premium should be larger the worse the general economic conditions.

Other factors seem to be of potential importance in explaining the risk structure of interest rates, but there is little conclusive evidence on the significance of the other factors. The level of interest rates appears to have some importance. In general, when interest rates are high, risk premiums tend to be large. The maturity of the instruments seems to have some bearing on the yield spread as well. The evidence on the importance of the maturity of particular bonds on the yield spread is somewhat mixed, but it tends to support the view that the longer the maturity of the bond, the greater the yield spread.[9] Also, there is evidence that the marketability of the particular bond issue affects the size of the risk premium.[10] While the risk premium seems to be sensitive to all of these factors—business conditions, maturity, marketability, and the level of interest rates—the size of the risk premium is itself a gauge of another more important factor. The risk premium essentially measures the risk of default.

The Risk Premium as a Measure of Default Risk

The greater the chance of default, the larger is the risk premium that a bond must pay to attract investors. The main reason that the risk premium seems to be so closely related to the business cycle is that the chance of default is much greater in periods of economic distress. If the marketability of a bond issue helps to keep a bond's risk premium smaller, it is because a risky (but highly marketable) bond can be sold more easily before default in comparison with a less marketable bond.

The bond rating services, such as Moody's and Standard & Poor's, attempt to summarize all factors that affect default risk and determine the risk premium in their bond ratings. As Figure 8.6 shows, low–rated bonds tend to have greater risk premiums than high–rated bonds. In fact, historical default experience matches the ratings very closely. Table 8.1 summarizes some results of a study by W. B.

---

[9] The impact of the maturity has been assessed by a number of authors who have reached different conclusions. See Lawrence Fisher, "Determinants of Risk Premiums on Corporate Bonds," *The Journal of Political Economy*, June 1959, pp. 217–237; Ramon E. Johnson, "Term Structure of Corporate Bond Yields as a Function of Risk of Default," *Journal of Finance*, May 1967, pp. 313–345; Thomas H. McInish, "Behavior of Municipal Bond Default–Risk Premiums by Maturity," *Journal of Business Research*, 8, 1980, pp. 413–418; Roland T. Robinson, *Postwar Market for State and Local Government Securities*, National Bureau of Economic Research, New York, 1960, pp. 184–188; and James C. Van Horne, "Behavior of Default–Risk Premiums for Corporate Bonds and Commercial Paper," *Journal of Business Research*, 7, December 1979, pp. 310–313.

[10] Lawrence Fisher, "Determinants of Risk Premiums on Corporate Bonds," *The Journal of Political Economy*, June 1959, pp. 217–237; and Calvin M. Boardman and Richard W. McEnally, "Factors Affecting Seasoned Corporate Bond Prices," *Journal of Financial and Quantitative Analysis*, 16:2, 1981, pp. 207–226.

Table 8.1
━━━━━━━━━━━

Default Experience for Corporate Bonds

Rating Category	Comparable S&P Rating	Percent Defaulting
I	AAA	6
II	AAA	6
III	AAA	13
IV	BBB	19
V—IX	below BBB	42

Source: W. B. Hickman, *Corporate Bond Quality and Investor Experience*, Princeton University Press, 1985, as cited in Robert C. Radcliffe, *Investment: Concepts, Analysis, and Strategy*, Glenview, IL: Scott, Foresman, 1987, p. 234.

Hickman, who examined the default experience of all corporate bonds issued between 1900 and 1943, grouping the bonds by their ratings.[11] Figure 8.7 provides

Figure 8.7
━━━━━━━━━━━

One–Year Speculative Grade Default Rates

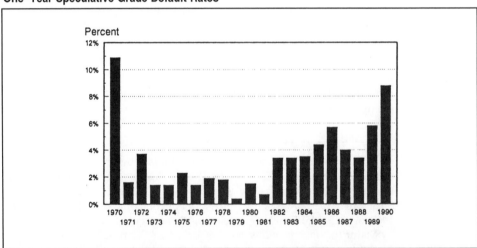

Source: J. S. Fons and A. E. Kimball, "Corporate Bond Defaults and Default Rates 1970–1990," *The Journal of Fixed Income*, 1:1, June 1991, pp. 36–47. This copyrighted material is reproduced with permission from Institutional Investor, Inc.

---

[11]See W. B. Hickman, *Corporate Bond Quality and Investor Experience*, Princeton, NJ: Princeton University Press, 1958.

Figure 8.8

One–Year Default Rates for Various Grades of Bonds

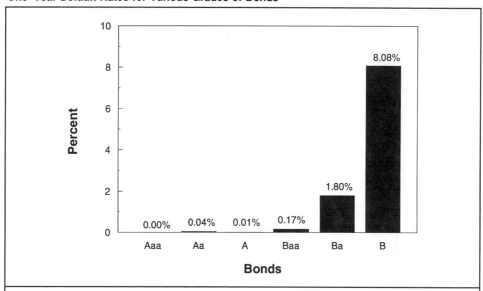

Source: J. S. Fons and A. E. Kimball, "Corporate Bond Defaults and Default Rates 1970–1990," *The Journal of Fixed Income*, 1:1, June 1991, pp. 36–47. This copyrighted material is reproduced with permission from Institutional Investor, Inc.

more recent evidence on default rates, covering the period 1970–1990. It shows the percentage of speculative grade bonds defaulting for each year. Specifically, for bonds with a speculative rating at the beginning of a year, it shows the proportion that defaulted within that year. (A speculative grade bond has a Moody's rating of Ba or lower.) As the graph shows, 1970 and 1990 were the worst years, with default rates around 9–11 percent.

When a bond is issued it receives an initial rating. Later, Moody's or Standard & Poor's might change their rating. Figure 8.8 shows the default experience for bonds within one year of their issuance, with the defaults being categorized by the original rating. Thus, as the figure shows, there were no defaults among Aaa rated bonds in the first year, while 8.08 percent of B rated bonds defaulted in the first year. Figure 8.9 shows the default experience for bonds within their first ten years of life. Of bonds that received an initial rate of Aaa, only 0.37 percent had defaulted within ten years. By contrast, 24.17 percent of bonds with an initial rating of B had defaulted within ten years.

Earlier we noted that yields tend to match the ratings very closely. This fact, along with Hickman's evidence, shows very clearly that the risk premium is a good indicator of default risk. This is only appropriate, because as an investor accepts riskier bonds to capture greater expected returns, he or she also must accept a

Figure 8.9

Ten–Year Default Rates for Various Grades of Bonds

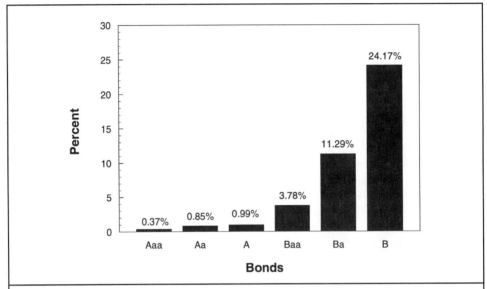

Source: J. S. Fons and A. E. Kimball, "Corporate Bond Defaults and Default Rates 1970–1990," *The Journal of Fixed Income*, 1:1, June 1991, pp. 36–47. This copyrighted material is reproduced with permission from Institutional Investor, Inc.

greater chance of default risk. Choosing the appropriate level of default risk is one of the chief decisions that a bond investor must make. The decision turns on the investor's tolerance of risk. While it is not possible to specify a general rule for how much default risk should be undertaken, it is clear that the promised return will increase with greater default risk.

Bond Portfolio Maturity Strategies

In discussing the term structure, we saw that the choice of maturities is a very important issue for any bondholder. When numerous bonds are held in a portfolio, there will be some average maturity of the portfolio. Even after the average maturity for the portfolio is chosen, there is still another important investment decision that concerns the maturity structure or the duration structure of the bond portfolio.[12] The maturity structure of the portfolio concerns the way in which

---

[12] The ideas of this section may be stated with respect to both maturity and duration. For convenience, the focus here is on maturity.

Figure 8.10

The Laddered Maturity Strategy for a Bond Portfolio

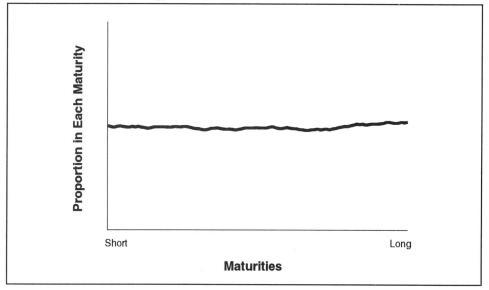

funds are allocated to bonds of differing maturities. Depending on the technique chosen, the bond portfolio manager can make the portfolio easy to administer, or the manager can choose maturities to allow dramatic changes in the interest rate sensitivity of the portfolio.

There are two basic approaches, one called the **laddered strategy** and the other the **dumbbell strategy** or **barbell strategy**. Each has its own advantages and disadvantages. In the laddered strategy, funds in the bond portfolio are distributed approximately evenly over the range of maturities. This approach is shown graphically in Figure 8.10. (The name of the laddered strategy comes from the fact that funds are evenly distributed across the maturity range, just as the rungs of a ladder are evenly spaced.) The main advantage of the laddered strategy is ease of management. Each year, the short–term bonds mature, and the funds provided from this source are committed to long–term bonds. Thus, it is very easy to maintain the same kind of maturity distribution with very low transaction costs.

The disadvantage of the laddered approach is the difficulty in changing the maturity composition of the portfolio. Aggressive bond portfolio managers sometimes wish to change the maturity structure of a bond portfolio to take advantage of anticipated shifts in yields. (Recall the bond pricing principles from Chapter 7 which noted that a drop in yields would cause an increase in bond prices and that the effect of a given drop in yields would be greater the longer the maturity of a particular bond, other factors being equal.) With that principle in mind, if a bond manager believes interest rates will soon drop by a large amount, he or she might wish to lengthen the average maturity of the portfolio to get a

Figure 8.11

The Dumbbell Maturity Strategy for a Bond Portfolio

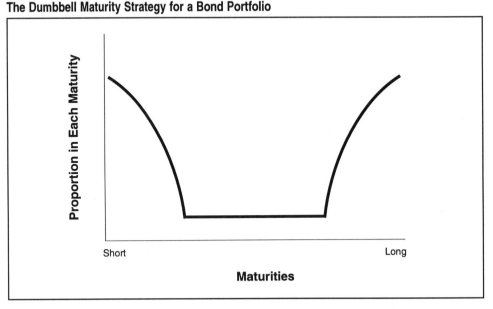

bigger effect when the drop in yields causes an increase in the price of bonds. With the laddered strategy, it is difficult to have a major effect on the portfolio's maturity without trading many bonds. To lengthen the average maturity of the portfolio, the manager would sell bonds with the shortest maturities and invest the funds in the bonds with the longest maturities. However, with all of the maturities receiving roughly equal investment, there will be too few short–term bonds to sell to have a major effect on the average maturity of the portfolio. After the short–maturity bonds are exhausted, the manager would sell medium–maturity bonds and use the proceeds to buy long–maturity bonds. But shifting funds from medium– to long–maturity bonds has relatively little effect on the average maturity of the portfolio. As a consequence, the laddered portfolio strategy makes it more difficult to shift the portfolio's maturity structure by large amounts.

With the dumbbell approach, the funds in the bond portfolio are divided between short–maturity and very long–maturity bonds. This distribution of maturities is shown graphically in Figure 8.11. As the graph shows, the shape of the maturities looks like a dumbbell, with the bells being the bulges of funds in the short and long maturities and the bar being formed by the virtually vacant middle–maturity range. The active bond manager using the dumbbell strategy can easily shorten or lengthen the maturity structure of the portfolio, because funds can be shifted between very short and very long maturities, respectively.

The dumbbell approach has its disadvantages, however. In many ways, the dumbbell strategy is like having two portfolios—one with very long maturities and one with very short maturities, each requiring separate management. For the short–maturity portion of the portfolio, the manager must keep reinvesting proceeds from maturing bonds. This need to roll over the maturing funds requires considerable management attention. For the long– maturity portion of the portfolio, the problems are even more acute. Over time, the long–maturity bonds become middle–maturity bonds. To maintain the dumbbell shape, middle–maturity bonds must be sold and the proceeds reinvested in long–maturity bonds. This requires active management as well. Selling these bonds and purchasing new long–term bonds produces higher transaction costs. In general, the dumbbell strategy has the disadvantages of requiring considerably greater management effort and higher transaction costs.

The choice of strategy depends on whether or not one wishes to engage in active management of the bond portfolio. Active management consists essentially of attempting to alter the maturity structure of the bond portfolio in order to take advantage of forecasted changes in interest rates. For the active manager, the dumbbell strategy is clearly preferred. The advisability of active bond management depends on the ability to forecast interest rates. Some portfolio managers believe that it is impossible to forecast interest rates with sufficient accuracy to make active bond portfolio management practical. These managers engage in a passive management strategy. For them, the key is to avoid unnecessary management expense and to control transaction costs, leading naturally to a preference for the laddered portfolio strategy. The decision to follow an active or passive management strategy depends on the manager's beliefs about his or her interest rate forecasts.

Interest Rate Forecasting

Knowledge of future interest rates would be sufficient to make virtually anyone a millionaire in a short period of time. Obviously, bond portfolio managers are extremely interested in being able to make good forecasts of interest rates. It is not a question of perfect foresight, but of just being able to anticipate interest rate movements better than the market.

For example, if the pure expectations theory is correct, the market's forecast equals the forward rate of interest. In this case, a successful forecast—one that beats the market forecast—is simply a forecast that performs better than the forward rate of interest. Because it is so widely available and constitutes an objective forecast that can be calculated from market data, the forward rate of interest is a useful bench mark for the adequacy of other forecasts. If other interest rate forecasts cannot outperform the forward rate of interest, they are not worthy of attention.

An easier criterion, and one that this section focuses on, is whether an interest rate forecast can beat the simplest forecast of all: no change. In other words, can a sophisticated forecast do better than a naive forecast that says that the future interest rate will be the same as the current interest rate? If the sophisticated forecast does not outperform the no–change forecast, then it merits no attention.

Two of the more popular kinds of interest rate forecasts come from various "experts" and from large sophisticated econometric models. Historically, neither has done very well against the no–change model. As a group, experts do not do very

Table 8.2

▬▬▬▬▬▬

The Range of Interest Rate Forecasts for Federal Funds One Year into the Future

	Forecast Made at Year–End for One Year Later	
	1981	**1989**
Forecast Based on Forward Rate	12.75%	8.5%
Forecaster 1	8.00	9.6
Forecaster 2	11.00	8.1
Forecaster 3	14.00	6.7
Forecaster 4	16.00	10.4
Forecaster 5	17.00	5.3
Range of Professional Forecasts	9.00%	9.72%
Mean of Professional Forecasts	13.20%	5.10%

Source: Adapted from W. David Woolford, "Forecasting Interest Rates," in F. J. Fabozzi, T. D. Fabozzi, and I. M. Pollack (eds.), *The Handbook of Fixed Income Securities*, 3e, Homewood, IL: Dow Jones–Irwin, 1991, p. 1337.

well in comparison with the no–change forecast, partly because the experts so seldom agree among themselves. Table 8.2 shows some forecasts made for the rate on Fed Funds in 1981 and 1989. The forecasters were trying to predict the Fed Funds rate one year into the future. Notice that the range of the professional forecasts was larger than some of the forecasts themselves. The experts really had very little basis for agreement. When there is so much disagreement, it is clear that most of the forecasts will be wrong. It is also an indication that one cannot rely on expert forecasts in general. At the very least, one must use forecasts with considerable care.

The ability of expert forecasters has also been tested formally to see whether the experts could outperform the no–change forecasts. As a group, they are unable to do so.[13] However, what may be true of the group is not necessarily true of each member of the group. It is possible that some particular expert forecaster may actually have an ability to outperform the no–change forecast. Unfortunately, it is very difficult to substantiate such an ability, because a good forecasting record might be due to chance alone. Even if a forecaster emerges who has a very long

---

[13] The following studies tested the value of expert forecasts and found them to be less accurate that the naive model of no change. D. R. Fraser, "On the Accuracy and Usefulness of Interest Rate Forecasts," *Business Economics*, September 1977; James E. Pesando, "Forecasting Interest Rates: An Efficient Markets Perspective," Mimeograph, University of Toronto, August 1979; M. J. Prell, "How Well Do the Experts Forecast Interest Rates?" Federal Reserve Bank of Kansas City, *Monthly Review*, September–October 1973.

track record of success, the forecaster may not have real ability and may just have been lucky. With a larger number of forecasters making predictions, some forecasters will have a very good record of accuracy just by chance.

One other major source of forecasts does not rely on individual talent, but utilizes recent innovations in economic theory and econometrics.[14] These attempts develop statistical models of the economy, some of the models containing hundreds of equations that must all be solved simultaneously. One might expect these models to perform better than the forecasts of individual experts. Unfortunately, tests of 19 forecasts find that econometric models are unable to beat the no–change forecast.[15]

In view of the enormous amount of energy directed toward forecasting interest rates and in view of the virtually total lack of success, we can conclude that interest rate forecasts deserve the same respect as the prediction inside a fortune cookie.

Portfolio Immunization Techniques

While it is difficult to believe that we cannot forecast interest rates, bond portfolio managers are beginning to accept that view. If one holds the position that it is impossible to forecast interest rates, active bond portfolio management has little appeal. If the bond manager does not know how to alter a portfolio to take advantage of an expected shift in interest rates because he or she has no good reason to expect one shift rather than another, active portfolio management has no useful role.

As bond managers have accepted this perspective, passive strategies have become more popular, particularly a set of techniques known as **portfolio immunization**. For an **immunized bond portfolio**, the investment result is not affected by a change in interest rates. In recognition of an inability to predict interest rates, many bond managers find it makes sense to immunize their portfolios against losses caused by changes in interest rates. These immunization techniques fall into two categories—the Bank Immunization Case and the Planning Period Case, both relying heavily on the concept of duration.

The Bank Immunization Case

This form of immunization gets its name from the fact that it first came into prominence in commercial banking. In its simplest possible form, a commercial

---

[14] *Econometrics* is the branch of statistics specializing in techniques appropriate to the statistical problems that one encounters in economics.

[15] Stephen K. McNees, "The Recent Record of Thirteen Forecasters," Federal Reserve Bank of Boston, *New England Economic Review*, September/October 1981; J. Walter Elliot and Jerome R. Baier, "Econometric Models and Current Interest Rates: How Well Do They Predict Future Rates?" *Journal of Finance*, September 1979, pp. 975–986.

Table 8.3

_____

The Balance Sheet of Simple National Bank

PANEL A

Assets		Liabilities	
Loan Portfolio	$1,000	Deposit Portfolio	$1,000
Portfolio Duration	5 years	Portfolio Duration	1 year
Interest Rate	10%	Interest Rate	10%
		Owner's Equity	$0

PANEL B

Assets		Liabilities	
Loan Portfolio	$909	Deposit Portfolio	$982
Interest Rate	12%	Interest Rate	12%
		Owner's Equity	−$73

bank borrows money by accepting deposits and makes loans with those funds. The portfolio of deposits and the portfolio of loans may be viewed as two bond portfolios, with the deposit portfolio constituting the liability portfolio and the loan portfolio constituting the asset portfolio. One of the problems in commercial banking is the short duration of the deposit portfolio, because most deposits can be withdrawn on very short notice. By contrast, the loan portfolio consists of obligations to provide funds for longer periods, since banks make commercial and consumer loans and also provide mortgage financing.

In Table 8.3, Panel A shows the position of Simple National Bank, which holds a deposit portfolio and liability portfolio with book and market values of $1,000 each. (We assume that the bank has zero equity for convenience, but in today's market this is barely an assumption at all!) The duration of the liability portfolio is one year, and the duration of the asset portfolio is five years. Assume, for the sake of simplicity, that the interest rate being earned on both portfolios is 10 percent. With different durations on the two portfolios, the bank has considerable interest rate risk. As we saw in Chapter 7, if interest rates fall, bond values will rise, so the value of both portfolios rises as well. But the asset portfolio is about five times as sensitive to a change in interest rates as the liability portfolio because its duration is five times as large. If interest rates rise, however, all bond values fall, and the asset portfolio will fall in value much more than the liability portfolio.

To see the effect of this on the bank, assume that interest rates rise from 10 percent to 12 percent on both the deposit and loan portfolios. The duration price change formula states:

$$\Delta P \approx -D_m \frac{\Delta (1 + r)}{(1 + r)} P$$

where:

P = the original bond price
D_m = the Macaulay duration of the bond
r = the initial rate of interest

For Simple National Bank, the change in the value of the deposit portfolio will be:

$$\Delta P \approx -1 \left(\frac{+.02}{1.10} \right) \$1,000 = -\$18.18$$

For the loan portfolio, the same change in rates creates a much larger drop in the portfolio's value:

$$\Delta P \approx -5 \left(\frac{+.02}{1.10} \right) \$1,000 = -\$90.91$$

The effects on the bank are shown in Panel B of Table 8.3. Because the duration of the asset portfolio is so much greater, the effect of the rise in rates caused its value to drop much more. Starting from a position of no owners' equity, the bank moved to a position of negative equity, or technical insolvency.

By careful management of the liabilities and the assets, the bank might have achieved the immunized position shown in Panel A of Table 8.4, where both the asset and liability portfolios have a duration of 3.0. Then, with the same shift in rates from 10 percent to 12 percent, each portfolio has the same change in value, since the durations are equal.[16]

$$\Delta P \approx -3 \left(\frac{+.02}{1.10} \right) \$1,000 = -\$54.55$$

With the value of both portfolios falling by the same amount, the owners' equity would be unchanged, as shown in Panel B of Table 8.4. The bank is immunized

---

[16]Notice that we are ignoring the second order effects due to convexity as discussed in Chapter 7.

Table 8.4

![divider]

The Immunized Balance Sheet of Simple National Bank

PANEL A

Assets		Liabilities	
Loan Portfolio	$1,000	Deposit Portfolio	$1,000
Portfolio Duration	3 years	Portfolio Duration	3 years
Interest Rate	10%	Interest Rate	10%
		Owner's Equity	$0

PANEL B

Assets		Liabilities	
Loan Portfolio	$945	Deposit Portfolio	$945
Interest Rate	12%	Interest Rate	12%
		Owner's Equity	$0

against a change in interest rates, because the change in rates leaves the equity position of the bank unchanged.

It must be noted that perfect immunization is very difficult for many financial institutions to achieve. Due to the nature of commercial banking, which involves accepting short–term deposits and making long–term loans, making the durations of the two portfolios equal is a real problem. However, managing the difference in the durations of the two portfolios helps offset the effects of changes in interest rates, even if perfect immunization cannot be achieved. In fact, virtually every bank in the country has an asset/liability management committee. The committee plays a crucial role in the management of the bank, and the maturity and duration structure of the two sides of the bank's balance sheet is among the most important issues the committee addresses.[17]

The Planning Period Case

The second basic type of immunization for bond portfolios concerns managing a portfolio toward a horizon date. For many bond portfolios, there is a definite planning period, with the goal being to achieve a target value for the portfolio at the end of the planning period. For example, a wealthy family might establish a trust fund for a child, with instructions that the child have access to the funds on his or her twenty–first birthday. In such a situation, the portfolio should be

---

[17]For a more thorough discussion of the asset/liability management problem in commercial banks, see Joseph F. Sinkey, Jr., *Commercial Bank Financial Management*, New York: Macmillan Co., 1986.

managed with that horizon or planning period in view. A similar problem occurs in pension fund management, with the bond manager managing the bonds in the pension fund with a horizon date set in the future when pensions become payable.

The problem confronting the bond manager in this case concerns the effect of changing interest rates on the immediate value of the bond portfolio and on the **reinvestment rate**—the rate at which cash thrown off by the bond portfolio can be reinvested. As we saw in Chapter 7, a change in interest rates can dramatically affect the realized compound yield to maturity (RCYTM). For example, assume that a bond portfolio consists of one 10 percent annual coupon bond with a face value of $1,000, which matures in five years. If interest rates are currently at 10 percent and remain steady for the 5–year period, all of the coupon payments may be invested at 10 percent. In this case, the RCYTM will be 10 percent over that 5–year period. On the maturity date, the total value of the bond and all reinvested proceeds will be:

The value of all of the reinvested coupons:
$100 \, (1.10)^4 + \$100 \, (1.10)^3 + \$100 \, (1.10)^2 + \$100 \, (1.10) = \$510.51$

plus the final coupon payment and the return of principal:
= $1,100

This gives a total future value of $1,610.51. With interest rates at 10 percent, the initial value of the bond must have been $1,000, so the RCYTM is:

$$\text{RCYTM} = \sqrt[5]{\frac{\text{Future Value}}{\text{Present Value}}} - 1$$

$$= \sqrt[5]{\frac{\$1,610.51}{\$1,000.00}} - 1$$

$$= 10\%$$

If interest rates had suddenly dropped at the beginning of the investment period from 10 percent to 8 percent, the RCYTM would have been different. The coupons could have been reinvested only at the new rate of 8 percent, so the future value of the coupon payments would be only $486.66.

The value of all of the reinvested coupons:
$100 \, (1.08)^4 + \$100 \, (1.08)^3 + \$100 \, (1.08)^2 + \$100 \, (1.08) = \$486.66$

plus the final coupon payment and the return of principal:
= $1,100

This gives a total future value of $1,586.66, so the RCYTM on this investment would be:

$$\text{RCYTM} = \sqrt[5]{\frac{\$1,586.66}{\$1,000.00}} - 1$$

$$= 9.67\%$$

By using the technique of planning period immunization, we can avoid this result. If the duration of the portfolio equals the number of years in the planning period, the portfolio will be immunized. This means that a shift in interest rates will not affect the RCYTM over a given planning period.

In this example, the problem arises from the fact that the duration of the bond was less than the planning period. For this particular bond, the duration was 4.17, but the planning period was five years. Assume now that a longer duration bond was also available, one having eight years to maturity, a 10 percent coupon rate, and a yield to maturity of 10 percent. With initial yields at 10 percent, this bond would have a price of $1,000 and a duration of 5.87.

For the planning period of five years, and with the availability of these two bonds, we can create a portfolio with a duration of 5 that would be immunized for the holding period. To create the new portfolio, we allocate funds to the two bonds so the average duration of the portfolio is 5. If 51.18 percent of the portfolio's value is committed to the 5–year bond, and 48.82 percent is committed to the 8–year bond, the resulting portfolio will have an average duration of 5.

$$.5118(4.17) + .4882(5.87) = 5$$

To apply this to the original example, assume that the bonds are divisible so that $511.80 is committed to the 5–year bond and $488.20 is committed to the 8–year bond. In other words, the portfolio is made up of fractions of the two bonds. With these fractions, the cash flows from the portfolio will still be $100 in coupon per year for the first four years. At year 5, the 5–year bond will mature. Since the portfolio owns 51.18 percent of that bond, it will receive .5118 x $1,100 = $562.98. Also, since the planning horizon is five years, the longer maturity bond will pay its fifth coupon and then be sold at that time, for a price that depends on market conditions.

To see how the immunization works in this case, assume once again that interest rates change from 10 percent to 8 percent as soon as the portfolio is established. In this case, the future value of the coupons (measured as of year 5) will be the same as before—$486.66. With interest rates at 8 percent at year 5, the longer maturity bond still has three years to maturity, and its market price will be $1,051.54.

$$P = \frac{100}{(1.08)} + \frac{100}{(1.08)^2} + \frac{1,100}{(1.08)^3} = \$1,051.54$$

Since the portfolio owns 48.82 percent of this bond, its value in the portfolio will be $513.36 (.4882) ($1,051.54) at year 5. The total future value of the portfolio at year 5 comes from four sources:

Future value of reinvested coupons received during years 1–4:	$486.66
Future value of payoff on 5–year bond (51.18% of $1,100 final payment):	562.98
The coupon payment at year 5 on the long–term bond (for the portfolio .4882 × $100):	48.82
Sale at year 5 of the long–maturity bond (48.82% of $1,051.54 market value):	513.36
Total Future Value	$1,611.82

In this case the RCYTM will be:

$$RCYTM = \sqrt[5]{\frac{\$1,611.82}{\$1,000.00}} - 1$$

$$= 10.02\%$$

This is almost exactly identical to the RCYTM had there been no change in rates whatsoever. A change in interest rates has two different effects. In this example, the drop in interest rates caused coupons to be reinvested at a lower rate than they would have been had there been no change. Another effect of the drop in interest rates was the capital gain on the two bonds. For the bond maturing in five years, this gain was never realized, but for the 8–year bond, the capital gain was an important part of the immunization. In fact, when duration equals the planning period, a change in interest rates will have a reinvestment rate effect that almost exactly offsets the capital gain or loss, which is also caused by the change in interest rates.[18]

This becomes clear by looking at the same example in a slightly different way. At the outset, the portfolio was constituted as follows:

---

[18]Again, we are not considering convexity, which accounts in part for the fact that the RCYTM was 10.06 in this example, rather than 10.00.

$$5\text{–year bond:} \quad D = 4.17 \qquad \text{Investment} = \quad \$511.80$$
$$8\text{–year bond:} \quad D = 5.87 \qquad \text{Investment} = \quad \$488.20$$
$$\text{Total Investment} \qquad\qquad\qquad = \$1,000.00$$

A drop in interest rates from 10 percent to 8 percent would change the value of the two bonds in the following way:

$$5\text{-year bond:} \quad \Delta P \approx -4.17 \left(\frac{-.02}{1.10} \right) \$511.80 = \$38.80$$

$$8\text{-year bond:} \quad \Delta P \approx -5.87 \left(\frac{-.02}{1.10} \right) \$488.20 = \$52.10$$

$$\text{Total New Value} \approx \$1,000 + \$38.80 + \$52.10 = \$1,090.90$$

This amount can only be invested at 8 percent because interest rates have already changed. Over a 5–year horizon, this initial amount will grow to $1,602.89 [$1,090.90(1.08)^5$], and this gives a RCYTM of almost exactly 10 percent as well:

$$\text{RCYTM} = \sqrt[5]{\frac{\$1,602.80}{\$1,000.00}} - 1$$
$$= 9.90\%$$

Here it is clear that the price increase caused by the drop in rates almost exactly offsets the drop in the available reinvestment rate over the 5–year planning period.

Contingent Immunization

Contingent immunization offers a mixed policy of active bond management with immunization under certain circumstances. At the time a bond portfolio is established and a horizon is chosen, specified RCYTM over the planning period can be achieved. However, the maximum possible immunized return can be guaranteed only if the portfolio is immunized immediately. This commits the bond manager to a passive strategy over the entire planning period. In **contingent immunization**, the bond manager guarantees a certain RCYTM over the planning period, but this guaranteed yield is less than the maximum that can be achieved. As long as the bond manager can guarantee the specified return, he or she is free to pursue a policy of active management in pursuit of higher returns.

Figure 8.12

Portfolio Values and Contingent Immunization

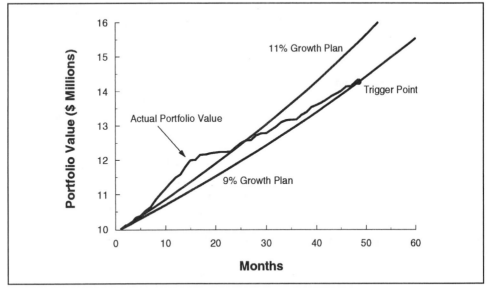

We can illustrate the policy of contingent immunization with the following example. Assume that the planning period is seven years and the initial value to be committed to bonds is $10 million. By following a strategy of immediate immunization, the manager is confident of achieving an RCYTM of 11 percent compounded monthly over the seven–year planning period. This would generate a total portfolio value of $21,522,036 at the horizon date. The portfolio value for an 11 percent growth rate is shown in Figure 8.12 as the top slightly curved line.

However, the manager also believes that it is possible to generate a higher return through active management. Yet active management entails risk—the duration will not be kept equal to the time remaining in the planning period. Therefore, the manager promises a lower return of 9 percent and asks for the right to manage the portfolio actively, subject to the guarantee of 9 percent.

The bond manager can actively manage the portfolio and guarantee the lower rate of return because of the policy of contingent immunization. The manager will manage the portfolio actively unless the value of the portfolio falls to the trigger point. The trigger point is a portfolio value requiring immediate immunization to lock in the guaranteed 9 percent return. If the portfolio value falls to a trigger point, the manager abandons active management and moves immediately to a fully immunized position.

What determines the trigger point? The **trigger point** is the minimum portfolio value at any time that is necessary to secure an immunized RCYTM equal to the guaranteed return. In Figure 8.12, the trigger point is any point on the 9 percent growth path. Figure 8.12 shows actual portfolio values in addition to the

9 percent and 11 percent growth paths. In the figure, active management secures portfolio values in excess of the 11 percent growth path early in the planning period. Later, at about month 25, the actual portfolio value crosses the 11 percent growth path, and then falls to the 9 percent growth path at about month 48.

If the portfolio value were allowed to fall below the 9 percent growth path, it would not be possible to guarantee even a 9 percent return. With contingent immunization and a guaranteed 9 percent return, the manager must immunize the portfolio at this point (month 48) to achieve the 9 percent return and the terminal portfolio value of $18,732,019.

Based on the result shown in Figure 8.12, the portfolio owner has gambled and lost. At the outset, it was possible to achieve a terminal value of $21,522,036 with full immunization. (This is the terminal value if the manager holds an immunized portfolio earning 11 percent over the entire seven–year period.) Hoping to earn more, the investor risked achieving a final terminal value of only $18,732,019, which occurred in this example. (This happens because the manager immunizes at the trigger point to ensure a 9 percent return over the horizon.)

Some Complications with Immunization

The preceding discussion did not consider several important points about immunization that are worth noting. In the examples, we assumed that interest rates change by the same amount for all different maturities. In the equation for Macaulay's duration, this is reflected by the fact that all cash flows are discounted at the same rate no matter when they occur. This is equivalent to assuming that the yield curve is flat and that it makes only parallel shifts. Such is patently not the case, as the evidence in Figure 8.1 proves. Faced with twisting yield curves, immunization based on Macaulay's duration will not hold exactly.

Duration for Yield Curves with Shape

Thus far, we have considered only the measure known as Macaulay's duration, but other more complicated duration measures can immunize a portfolio when yield curves change in a nonparallel fashion. However, for any particular duration measure, there is some possible yield curve change that will interfere with the immunization.[19]

As an example of an alternative duration measure, let us consider D_2, which reflects the slope of the yield curve but still assumes that yield curves shift in a parallel or additive fashion. The equation for D_2 is given by:

---

[19] For more on duration, see G. O. Bierwag and G. G. Kaufman, "Coping with the Risk of Interest Rate Fluctuations: A Note," *Journal of Business*, July 1977, pp. 364–370; G. O. Bierwag, "Measures of Duration," *Economic Inquiry*, October 1978, pp. 497–507. For an application of duration and immunization to interest rate futures, see R. W. Kolb, *Understanding Futures Markets*, 4e, Miami: Kolb Publishing, 1994.

$$D_2 = \sum_{t=1}^{M} \frac{t \left(\dfrac{C_t}{\prod\limits_{t=1}^{M} (1 + r_{t,t+1})} \right)}{P} \qquad \text{8.1}$$

D_m assumes that the yield curve is flat, because it discounts all cash flows at the same rate. Therefore, when yields change, D_m also assumes that they all change by the same amount. As a result, the yield curve is flat before and after the shift, differing only by some value being added to all of the rates.

D_2 reflects shape in the yield curve by allowing each cash flow to be discounted at the rate uniquely appropriate to its timing. That is the function of the numerator in D_2:

$$t \left(\frac{C_t}{\prod\limits_{i=1}^{M} (1 + r_{t,t+1})} \right)$$

This term is essentially similar to the numerator of D_m, except that it allows for each payment from the bond to be discounted at a different rate. For example, let us consider the numerator's value for C_3. In this case, the numerator becomes:

$$t \left(\frac{C_t}{(1 + r_{0,1}) (1 + r_{1,2}) (1 + r_{2,3})} \right)$$

instead of the equivalent term in D_m:

$$t \left(\frac{C_t}{(1 + r_{0,3})^3} \right)$$

If the yield curve slopes upward, the rate of discount applied to distant payments should be greater than that applied to nearby payments. For example, consider the following term structure:

Maturity	Yield to Maturity	One–Period Rates	
$r_{0,1}$	.12	$r_{0,1}$	.1200
$r_{0,2}$	.125	$r_{1,2}$	.1300
$r_{0,3}$	.13	$r_{2,3}$	.1401
$r_{0,4}$	.135	$r_{3,4}$	.1501
$r_{0,5}$	.14	$r_{4,5}$	.1602

Clearly, the yield curve is rising sharply. For a 5–year maturity bond, the computation of D_m would use a rate of .14 to discount all of the cash flows. However, in the computation of D_2, a different rate for each cash flow would be applied. For example, consider a $1,000 par value bond with a coupon rate of 10 percent that yields 14 percent. For the payment occurring in year 3, the present value would be computed in D_m as $100/(1.14)^3 = \$67.50$. In the computation of D_2, we would have:

$$PV = \frac{C_t}{(1 + r_{0,1})(1 + r_{1,2})(1 + r_{2,3})} = \frac{\$100}{(1.12)(1.13)(1.1401)} = \$69.30$$

The more severe the shape of the yield curve, the greater the difference between D_m and D_2. Table 8.5 shows the differences for sample bonds in a rising yield curve environment. In general, the differences do not exceed 10 percent. However, we must remember that D_2 still assumes that yield curves shift in parallel fashion, although it does consider the shape of the yield curve.

Multiple Shifts in Interest Rates

A second complication with duration arises from the fact that the immunization result holds only for a single change in interest rates, even when rates change by the same amount for all maturities. Duration depends on the interest rate. So, if a portfolio is immunized and interest rates change, the portfolio loses its immunization because the duration of the various bonds can change in different ways. This is not critically important, but it shows that an immunization strategy requires periodic rebalancing to keep the durations of the various bonds aligned.

Dedicated Portfolios

Faced with these duration complications in immunizing a portfolio, some bond managers have adopted a strategy of creating dedicated portfolios to service a liability stream. A **dedicated portfolio** is a bond portfolio created such that its cash inflows from coupons and maturing bonds cover cash outflows that result from a given liability stream. For example, assume that a pension plan manager can

Table 8.5

Differences in D_M and D_2 for an Upward–Sloping Yield Curve

Years to Maturity	Zero Coupon Return (%)	5% Coupon		10% Coupon	
		D_M	D_2	D_M	D_2
1	6.10	0.99	0.99	0.98	0.98
2	6.20	1.93	1.93	1.87	1.87
3	6.30	2.82	2.82	2.68	2.68
4	6.40	3.67	3.66	3.43	3.43
5	6.50	4.47	4.46	4.13	4.12
6	6.60	5.22	5.22	4.77	4.76
7	6.70	5.94	5.92	5.37	5.35
8	6.80	6.61	6.59	5.93	5.90
9	6.90	7.24	7.20	6.45	6.40
10	7.00	7.83	7.78	6.93	6.86
11	7.10	8.38	8.31	7.39	7.29
12	7.20	8.90	8.79	7.81	7.69
13	7.30	9.37	9.24	8.21	8.05
14	7.40	9.82	9.64	8.58	8.38
15	7.50	10.23	10.00	8.92	8.68
16	7.60	10.60	10.32	9.25	8.95
17	7.70	10.95	10.60	9.56	9.20
18	7.80	11.26	10.85	9.84	9.42
19	7.90	11.56	11.06	10.11	9.62
20	8.00	11.82	11.24	10.36	9.80
21	8.10	12.06	11.39	10.60	9.95
22	8.20	12.28	11.52	10.82	10.10
23	8.30	12.47	11.61	11.03	10.22
24	8.40	12.65	11.68	11.23	10.33
25	8.50	12.81	11.74	11.41	10.42

Source: G. O. Bierwag and G. G. Kaufman, "Coping with the Risk of Interest Rate Fluctuations: A Note," *Journal of Business*, July 1977.

forecast future pension fund payments with considerable accuracy. The bond manager may know that $15 million in payments will be required in 12 years. The dedicated portfolio will be constructed to give the necessary payment shortly before the $15 million must be paid.

In actual practice, the cash flows can be much more complex, and the client may have concerns about the kinds of bonds included in the portfolio. For example, assume the fund wants to follow a **cash–flow matching** strategy—to create a bond portfolio that will generate cash flows that will allow it to pay each of the liability cash flows as they come due.

The bond portfolio manager's job is to find the portfolio of bonds that generates the matching set of cash flows. Usually, this portfolio must meet several other conditions besides merely matching the cash flows. Subject to the various constraints imposed by the client, the bond portfolio manager will attempt to create a portfolio that has the lowest cost. The client's constraints focus on the quality of bonds in the portfolio, whether the included bonds are callable, the industry concentration of the portfolio, and the concentration in a single issue. We consider each of these issues briefly.

First, the client may constrain the quality. For example, the client may have an obligation to create a portfolio that is composed of at least 20 percent Treasury securities and to contain no speculative grade securities. Second, the client may require that not too much of the portfolio be invested in a single industry. For example, the client may not allow more than 20 percent of the portfolio to be invested in bonds issued by electric utilities. Third, the client may restrict the overall portfolio duration. Even though it is following a cash–flow matching strategy, the fund might want to minimize the duration of the portfolio to avoid unnecessary interest rate sensitivity. Fourth, the client may want to avoid concentrating too much investment in a single issue. For example, the client may require that not more than 5 percent of the portfolio's value be invested in a single issue and may require that the maximum investment in any one issue not exceed 10 percent of the existing bonds. Finally, the client may want to avoid callable bonds, because a call could upset the cash–flow matching strategy altogether. The bond portfolio manager must work under these constraints to build a portfolio that meets the cash–flow matching goal with the lowest cost.

As a more realistic, but still simplified example, assume that a pension fund faces the liability stream shown below for the next 20 semiannual periods. The fund wants to meet this liability stream by creating a dedicated bond portfolio that follows a cash–flow matching strategy.

Period	Liability ($000)	Period	Liability ($000)
1	350	11	320
2	350	12	320
3	350	13	320
4	350	14	320
5	350	15	1820
6	350	16	260
7	350	17	260
8	350	18	260
9	350	19	260
10	950	20	4260

For this liability stream, consider how a bond manager might use the following four bonds to create a cash–flow matching portfolio:

Table 8.6

■■■■■■■■

Cash–Flow Matching Example

Period	Liability	Bond A	Bond A Total	Bond B	Bond B Total	Bond C	Bond C Total	Bond D	Bond D Total
1	350	5	30	6	240	4	60	2	20
2	350	5	30	6	240	4	60	2	20
3	350	5	30	6	240	4	60	2	20
4	350	5	30	6	240	4	60	2	20
5	350	5	30	6	240	4	60	2	20
6	350	5	30	6	240	4	60	2	20
7	350	5	30	6	240	4	60	2	20
8	350	5	30	6	240	4	60	2	20
9	350	5	30	6	240	4	60	2	20
10	950	105	630	6	240	4	60	2	20
11	320			6	240	4	60	2	20
12	320			6	240	4	60	2	20
13	320			6	240	4	60	2	20
14	320			6	240	4	60	2	20
15	1820			6	240	104	1560	2	20
16	260			6	240			2	20
17	260			6	240			2	20
18	260			6	240			2	20
19	260			6	240			2	20
20	4260			106	4240			2	20

Bond A: 5–year, 10% coupon
Bond B: 10–year, 12% coupon
Bond C: 7.5–year, 8% coupon
Bond D: 10–year, 4% coupon

We assume that each of Bonds A–D has a face value of $100,000 and that each has just paid a coupon. Table 8.6 shows the overall liability stream and the cash flows from each of these bonds. The bond portfolio manager creates the following portfolio:

6 Bond A
40 Bond B
15 Bond C
10 Bond D

The combined cash flows from these 71 bonds will match the cash flows for the pension fund's total liability stream. The bond manager formed this portfolio so that it meets the pension fund's constraints and, subject to those constraints, has the lowest possible cost.

For very long horizons with large outflows, it is difficult to choose the right collection of bonds that will fulfill all of the liabilities. What makes the task more difficult is that the bond manager must choose from thousands of available bonds, keeping in mind risk level, callability of the bonds, and many other factors. In order to select the best collection of bonds to constitute the dedicated portfolio, managers often use linear programming techniques to find the optimal set of bonds.

These complications indicate that bond portfolio managers must be very skilled to be successful. The bond portfolio manager need not expect to make a living by forecasting interest rates and by making dramatic investment decisions. Instead, the task requires a firm understanding of bond pricing principles and their application to the management of complex portfolios. In addition, more advanced mathematical techniques, such as linear programming, can also be important skills.

Summary

This chapter advanced the basic bond pricing principles introduced in Chapter 7 and focused primarily on those issues of greatest concern to bond portfolio managers. The yield curve, or the term structure of interest rates, expresses the relationship between yield to maturity and term to maturity for bonds of the same risk level. Because bond yields differ by maturity, an understanding of these relationships is important to the bond manager. The bond manager needs to understand the opportunities and risks inherent in pursuing higher yields, which led to an exploration of theories of the term structure. These theories generally concur in assigning a very important role to expectations of future interest rates in the explanation of the term structure.

Bond yields differ not only by maturity but also by the level of default risk, as expressed by the risk structure of interest rates. The bond portfolio manager must seek higher yields for the portfolio, while striving to avoid risk. Consequently, it is important to understand the factors contributing to the riskiness of bonds.

Even after the bond manager chooses the appropriate average maturity and the correct risk level, the choice of a bond maturity strategy is still an open question. The dumbbell strategy places the bonds in the very short and very long maturities, which makes it easy to shift the average maturity of the portfolio by trading relatively few bonds. Alternatively, the laddered portfolio strategy spreads the bonds out across the entire maturity range, which makes it quite easy to maintain the chosen maturity distribution of bonds.

All of these managerial issues would be of secondary importance, however, if the bond manager could forecast interest rates. However, in spite of tremendous efforts, the best evidence suggests that interest rates cannot be forecast accurately on a consistent basis.

Faced with an inability to forecast interest rates, many bond managers have adopted a passive strategy of portfolio immunization. An immunized portfolio is established to meet a certain target rate of return or to make the market value of a position insensitive to interest rate changes.

Questions and Problems

1. What are the three major theories of the term structure?
2. In examining the yield curve, why should you use bonds of the same risk level?
3. How could differences in tax status among bonds used in yield curve analysis affect the analysis?
4. Liquidity premium theorists would maintain that it is normal for the yield curve to slope upward. Are there instances in history of flat or downward-sloping yield curves?
5. How would the pure expectations theory and the liquidity premium theory explain a downward–sloping yield curve?
6. Consider holding five successive 1–year T–bills vs. holding one 5–year Treasury bond for five years. According to the liquidity premium theory of the term structure, which should have the greater expected return? Why? How would the pure expectations theory differ?
7. In order for the liquidity premium theory to be true, investors must have preferences for short–term bonds. How does the market segmentation theory make use of the idea that investors have different maturity preferences? Are these theories really the same?
8. In our discussion of bond pricing, we have seen that long maturity bonds have considerable "price risk" because their prices can move a great deal in response to a change in interest rates. How does this price risk differ from "default risk"? Which is analyzed by the risk structure of interest rates?
9. What is the "risk premium" and what factors are important in determining the size of the risk premium?
10. What are the advantages and disadvantages of the two major portfolio maturity strategies we have considered?
11. What is the practical use of being able to forecast interest rates? What success can you expect from professional forecasting firms?
12. Compare the value of professional interest rate forecasts with the simple forecast that says that the future spot rate of interest equals the current forward rate.
13. What is portfolio immunization and what role does duration play in an immunization attempt?
14. What is a "passive" portfolio management strategy?
15. What is the difference between the "bank immunization" and the "planning period" immunization cases? Which would be more appropriate for a bond manager managing a portfolio with a horizon date 8 years from now?
16. A 2–year bond is yielding 15 percent and a 1–year bond is yielding 11 percent. What is the forward rate for a bond to cover the second year? Does the yield curve slope upward in this case?
17. Consider the following rates for bonds of differing maturities:

Maturity (years)	Yield (%)
5	14
4	13
3	12
2	11
1	10

Compute all possible forward rates. (NOTE: There are a total of ten forward rates to calculate, four 1–year rates, three 2–year rates, two 3–year rates, and one 4–year rate.)

18. Using the data of the preceding problem, what would be the interest rate forecast of a pure expectations theorist for the 1–year rate three years from now? How would the forecast of the liquidity premium theorist differ?

19. Given two bonds with durations of 7.3 years and 2.2 years, you are asked to split investment funds between them so that the resulting portfolio will have a duration of 5 years. Assume that you have $1,000,000 to invest. How much would you commit to each bond?

20. A bank has hired you as a consultant to advise it on its interest rate exposure. The bank has an asset portfolio of $1,000,000 with a duration of 5 years, and the portfolio is currently yielding 12 percent. This asset portfolio is funded by a liability portfolio, also worth $1,000,000 with a duration of 1.5 years and which is yielding 10.5 percent. Your problem is to advise the bank on its risk exposure in case interest rates change by 1 percent in either direction. Analyze the resulting position of the bank for both of these cases.

21. Assume that you are asked to manage a $1,000,000 immunized portfolio with a horizon date of 3 years. Two bonds are available to you: a 5–year pure discount bond yielding 10 percent and a 2–year 12 percent annual coupon bond yielding 12 percent. How would you make up the immunized portfolio from these two bonds?

22. For the preceding problem, what will be the terminal wealth of the portfolio assuming that interest rates do not change for 3 years? What is the RCYTM over this period? Now assume that interest rates drop by 1 percent on both bonds. Calculate the terminal wealth at the end of 3 years. Do the same assuming a 2 percent rise in rates.

CFA Questions

A. The concepts of spot and forward rates are most closely associated with which *one* of the following explanations of the term structure of interest rates?
   a. Expectations hypothesis
   b. Liquidity premium theory
   c. Preferred habitat hypothesis
   d. Segmented market theory
B. Which *one* of the following statements about the term structure of interest rates is *true*?
   a. The expectations hypothesis indicates a flat yield curve if anticipated future short–term rates exceed current short–term rates.
   b. The expectations hypothesis contends that the long–term rate is equal to the anticipated short–term rate.
   c. The liquidity premium theory indicates that, all else being equal, longer maturities will have lower yields.
   d. The market segmentation theory contends that borrowers and lenders prefer particular segments of the yield curve.
C. A portfolio manager at Superior Trust Company is structuring a fixed–income portfolio to meet the objectives of a client. This client plans on retiring in 15 years and wants a substantial lump sum at that time. The client has specified the use of AAA–rated securities.

The portfolio manager compares coupon U.S. Treasuries with zero coupon stripped U.S. Treasuries and observes a significant yield advantage for the stripped bonds.

Maturity	Coupon U.S. Treasuries	Zero Coupon Stripped U.S. Treasuries
3 year	5.50%	5.80%
5 year	6.00%	6.60%
7 year	6.75%	7.25%
10 year	7.25%	7.60%
15 year	7.40%	8.80%
30 year	7.75%	7.75%

Briefly discuss *two* reasons why zero coupon stripped U.S. Treasuries could yield more than coupon U.S. Treasuries with the same final maturity.
D. Bill Peters is the investment officer of a $60 million pension fund. He has become concerned about the big price swings that have occurred lately in the fund's fixed–income securities. Peters has been told that such price behavior is only natural given the recent behavior of market yields. To deal with the problem, the pension fund's fixed–income money manager keeps track of exposure to price volatility by closely monitoring bond duration. The money

manager believes that price volatility can be kept to a reasonable level as long as portfolio duration is maintained at approximately seven to eight years.

a. **Discuss** the concepts of duration and convexity and **explain** how *each* fits into the price/yield relationship. In situation described above, **explain** why the money manager should have used both duration and convexity to monitor the bond portfolio's exposure to price volatility.

b. One of the bonds held in the portfolio is a 15–year, 8% U.S. Treasury bond with a modified duration of 8.0 years and a convexity of 94.36. It has been suggested that the fund swap out of the 15–year bond and into a barbell position made up of the following two U.S. Treasury issues:

Bond	Coupon	Maturity	Modified Duration	Convexity
1	8%	5 years	3.97 years	19.58
2	8%	30 years	9.73 years	167.56

Construct a barbell position from these two bonds that results in a modified duration of 8.0 years. **Compare** the price volatility of the barbell position to the bond currently held under *each* of the following interest rate environments:

    i.   market rates drop by 50 basis points (e.g., from 9% to 8.50%), and

    ii.   market rates drop by 250 basis points (e.g., from 9% to 6.50%).

E. Barney Gray, CFA, is Director of Fixed–Income Securities at Piedmont Security Advisors. In a recent meeting, one of his major endowment clients suggested investing in corporate bonds yielding 9%, rather than U.S. government bonds yielding 8%. Two bond issues—one U.S. Treasury and one corporate—were compared to illustrate the point.

    U.S. Treasury bond   8% due 6/15/2010   Priced at 100

    AJAX Manufacturing   9.5% due 6/15/2015   Priced at 105
    Rated AAA
    Callable @ 107.5
    on 6/15/1995

Gray wants to prepare a response based upon his expectation that long–term U.S. Treasury interest rates will fall sharply (at least 100 basis points) over the next three months.

a. **Evaluate** the return expectations for *each* bond under this scenario, and **support** an evaluation of which bond would be the superior performer. **Discuss** the price–yield measures that affect your conclusion.

Following Gray's response in Part a., his client wanted to know why a collateralized mortgage obligation, which is AAA rated and composed of only government–guaranteed bonds, should yield 9.5% when U.S. Treasury bonds yield only 8%. Both bonds have modified durations of seven years.

b. **Justify** the yield spread between these two securities that appear to have similar quality characteristics. **Discuss** the differences in return behavior in these two types of bonds.

Suggested REALDATA Exercises

The following *REALDATA* exercises explore the concepts developed in this chapter: Exercises 57, 59, 61, 62, 64, 65.

Suggested Readings

Abken, P. A., "Innovations in Modeling the Term Structure of Interest Rates," Federal Reserve Bank of Atlanta *Economic Review*, 75:4, July/August 1990, pp. 2–27.

Altman, E. I., "The Anatomy of the High–Yield Bond Market," *Financial Analysts Journal*, 43:4, July/August 1987, pp. 12–25.

Altman, E. I. and M. L. Heine, "How 1989 Changed the Hierarchy of Fixed Income Security Performance," *Financial Analysts Journal*, 46:3, May/June 1990, pp. 9–12.

Becketti, S., "The Truth about Junk Bonds," Federal Reserve Bank of Kansas City *Economic Review*, July/August 1990, pp. 45–54.

Bernanke, B. S., "On the Predictive Power of Interest Rates and Interest Rate Spreads," Federal Reserve Bank of Boston *New England Economic Review*, November/December 1990, pp. 51–68.

Bierwag, G. O., *Duration Analysis: Managing Interest Rate Risk*, Cambridge, MA: Ballinger Publishing, 1987.

Blume, M. E. and D. B. Keim, "Lower–Grade Bonds: Their Risks and Returns," *Financial Analysts Journal*, 43:4, July/August 1987, pp. 26–33.

Blume, M. E., D. B. Keim, and S. A. Patel, "Returns and Volatility of Low– Grade Bonds, 1977–1989," *Journal of Finance*, 46:1, March 1991, pp. 49–74.

Brooks, R. and M. Livingston, "A Closed–Form Equation for Bond Convexity," *Financial Analysts Journal*, 45:6, November/December 1989, pp. 78–79.

Christensen, P. E., F. J. Fabozzi, and A. LoFaso, "Bond Immunization: An Asset Liability Optimization Strategy," *The Handbook of Fixed Income Securities*, 3e, Homewood, IL: Business Irwin One, 1991.

Christensen, P. E., F. J. Fabozzi, and A. LoFaso, "Dedicated Bond Portfolios," *The Handbook of Fixed Income Securities*, 3e, Homewood, IL: Business Irwin One, 1991.

Cook, T. and T. Hahn, "Interest Rate Expectations and the Slope of the Money Market Yield Curve," Federal Reserve Bank of Richmond *Economic Review*, 76:5, September/October 1990, pp. 3–26.

Cornell, B. and K. Green, "The Investment Performance of Low–Grade Bond Funds," *Journal of Finance*, 46:1, March 1991, pp. 29–48.

Fabozzi, T. D., T. Tong, and Y. Zhu, "Symmetric Cash Matching," *Financial Analysts Journal*, 46:5, September/October 1990, pp. 46–52.

Fons, J. S., "The Default Premium and Corporate Bond Experience," *Journal of Finance*, 42:1, March 1987, pp. 81–97.

Greshin, A. M. and M. D. Hadzima, "International Bond Investing and Portfolio Management," *The Handbook of Fixed Income Securities*, 3e, Homewood, IL: Business Irwin One, 1991.

Ho, T. S. Y., *Strategic Fixed–Income Investment*, Homewood, IL: Dow Jones–Irwin, 1990.

Hradsky, G. T. and R. D. Long, "High–Yield Default Losses and the Return Performance of Bankrupt Debt," *Financial Analysts Journal*, 45:4, July/August 1989, pp. 38–49.

Jones, F. J. and B. Wolkowitz, "The Determinants of Interest Rates on Fixed Income Securities," *The Handbook of Fixed Income Securities*, 3e, Homewood, IL: Business Irwin One, 1991.

Litterman, R. and J. Scheinkman, "Common Factors Affecting Bond Returns," *The Journal of Fixed Income*, 1:1, June 1991, pp. 54–61.

Litterman, R., J. Scheinkman, and L. Weiss, "Volatility and the Yield Curve," *The Journal of Fixed Income*, 1:1, June 1991, pp. 49–53.

McEnally, R. W. and J. V. Jordan, "The Term Structure of Interest Rates," *The Handbook of Fixed Income Securities*, 3e, Homewood, IL: Business Irwin One, 1991.

Rosenberg, M. R., "International Fixed Income Investing: Theory and Practice," *The Handbook of Fixed Income Securities*, 3e, Homewood, IL: Business Irwin One, 1991.

Sarig, O. and A. Warga, "Some Empirical Estimates of the Risk Structure of Interest Rates," *Journal of Finance*, 44:5, December 1989, pp. 1351–1360.

Woolford, W. D., "Forecasting Interest Rates," *The Handbook of Fixed Income Securities*, 3e, Homewood, IL: Business Irwin One, 1991.

Investing in Equities

Unlike bonds, equities offer no fixed promised payments. Instead, the owner of a share of stock is a part owner of the enterprise. This means that the stock owner has a residual claim on the firm—the stock owner receives payment only after the other claimants to the firm are satisfied. Bondholders must be paid before stock owners can receive their compensation.

Compared to bondholders, the residual position of the stockholder implies that stock investing is generally more risky. This greater risk emphasizes the need for careful analysis of stocks before investing. Chapter 9 introduces the basic principles of stock valuation. Essentially, the value of a share of stock equals the present value of all cash flows to come from the share of stock. In other words, Chapter 9 shows that the price of a share of stock should equal the present value of all future dividends to be paid by the stock.

Even if we know that the stock should be worth the present value of all future dividends, there is still the significant problem of trying to estimate and value those future dividends. This is the task of stock analysis, which is divided into three phases: analysis of the overall economy, analysis of the industry, and analysis of the individual firm.

Chapter 10 examines the principles underlying the analysis of the economy as a whole. As such it examines the factors that tend to affect all stocks, no matter from which industry or firm. Chapter 11 explores the analysis of particular industries, which are affected by changing consumption patterns and demographic trends. If the investor can understand present circumstances and anticipate future trends, there can be substantial opportunity to improve investment performance. Ultimately, stock investing requires a commitment to the stock of a particular company. This means that the analysis of the individual firm, which is the topic of Chapter 12, is also very important. Even if economy-wide and industry factors are favorable, there is still the question of selecting the best firm. Consequently, Chapter 12 considers questions of good management and similar issues that can affect the success of an individual firm.

CHAPTER NINE

Preferred and Common Stock Valuation

Overview

This chapter examines valuation principles for the second major segment of the capital market—preferred and common stock. As we will see, preferred stock is a hybrid security, sharing features of both bonds and common stock. As discussed earlier, common stock represents an ownership position in the firm.

When a firm issues either preferred or common stock, it undertakes an obligation to pay a return on the investor's commitment of funds to the corporation. Because of this commitment, which is necessary for the firm to secure the funds it needs to operate, it is essential to understand the principles that determine the value of stock. This chapter begins with a discussion of preferred stock, followed by a more detailed consideration of common stock.

Much work in finance studies the trade–off between risk and expected return. Common stock provides a laboratory for such study. Therefore, this chapter also focuses on the features of common stock that create value and risk. The chapter concludes with a brief discussion of the relationship between the risk an investor bears with different kinds of securities and the return the firm must expect to pay for different kinds of long–term financing.

Preferred Stock

Preferred stock is usually issued with a stated par value, such as $100. Payments made on preferred stock are called dividends and are usually expressed as a percentage of the par value. With a $100 par value and a 6 percent dividend, the annual dividend on a share of preferred stock would be $6.

In many respects, the dividend on a preferred stock is similar to the coupon payments made on a corporate bond. There are, however, important differences between preferred stock and corporate bonds. First, preferred stock never matures. In the normal course of events, the firm will make payments of preferred dividends forever. Second, as a consequence of the fact that preferred stock never matures, the purchaser never receives a return of the par value. Third, unlike the case of corporate bonds, the firm does not default if it misses a scheduled payment on preferred stock, and the preferred stockholder has no immediate legal remedy against the corporation.

Most preferred stock is cumulative. With **cumulative preferred stock**, any dividend payments that the firm misses must be paid later, as soon as the firm is able. In fact, the agreement between the firm and the cumulative preferred stockholders typically requires that dividends not be paid to the common stockholders until all late payments to the preferred stockholders have been made.

This cumulative feature offers partial protection for missed payments to the preferred stockholders. If a firm must temporarily suspend dividend payments to the holder of cumulative preferred stock, there is still a chance that the payments will be made up later. Even in such a case, however, the preferred stockholder loses the use of the money from the time the payment was scheduled to the time the payment is finally made. These features of no maturity, no return of principal, and no default when a payment is missed combine to make preferred stock riskier than a corporate bond issued by the same corporation.

Like many bonds, some preferred stock is callable. The issuing firm can require the preferred stockholders to surrender their shares in exchange for a cash payment. The amount of this cash payment, known as the call price, is specified in the agreement between the preferred stockholders and the firm.

Usually, preferred stockholders (like bondholders) are not allowed to vote on matters of concern to the firm. This contrasts with common stockholders who have the right to vote to choose management and to vote on a number of decisions that management refers to the shareholders. On occasion, the contract between the preferred stockholders and the firm allows the preferred stockholders to vote. Usually, the preferred stockholders are allowed to vote only when the firm is in serious financial difficulty.

Financing with Preferred Stock

Like virtually any financing method, preferred stock financing has its own special advantages and disadvantages as a financing vehicle for a corporation. Probably the greatest advantage of financing with preferred stock is its flexibility. If a payment on a bond is missed or delayed, the firm is technically bankrupt. As we have seen, this is not the case with preferred stock. At the worst, the firm may have to make up missed preferred stock dividend payments before it can pay its common stockholders.

The second major advantage of preferred stock also stems from its flexibility. By issuing preferred stock, the corporation secures financing without surrendering voting control in the firm. This combination of freedom from worry over bankruptcy when a dividend is missed, coupled with the fact that no control of the firm is surrendered, explains the attractiveness of preferred stock.

Preferred stock also has certain disadvantages, however. When a firm makes interest payments on a bond, the payment is made from the firm's before–tax income. Dividend payments to preferred stockholders are made from the firm's after–tax earnings. This distinction is very important because it has great bearing on the actual after–tax cost of the two financing methods for the firm.

To see the importance of before–tax payments versus after–tax payments, consider a firm in the 34 percent tax bracket that must pay $1,000 interest to its bondholders and $1,000 in dividends to its preferred stockholders. The amount of before–tax earnings necessary to cover these two payments is very different. To make a $1,000 interest payment takes only $1,000 of before–tax earnings, because the interest expense is deductible for tax purposes. For the preferred stock, the firm must pay taxes on all earnings before paying them as dividends. To generate the same $1,000 on an after–tax basis, the firm must have $1,515 in before–tax earnings. After the government takes its 34 percent tax, the firm will be left with the $1,000 to pay the preferred stockholders. Therefore, the firm must weigh the advantages of the greater flexibility of preferred stock financing against its potentially higher cost.

For the securities investor, preferred stock is similar to a **perpetuity**—a bond that makes interest payments of a fixed amount forever and never returns its principal. However, the holder of preferred stock has a weaker position among the firm's capital contributors than the bondholder does. The claims of bondholders must be satisfied before those of preferred stock investors. Also, payments from preferred stock are dividends, not interest payments, for purposes of federal taxation. Because 80 percent of dividends received by corporations are exempt from federal taxation, preferred stock may be more attractive to corporations than to private investors.

The Valuation of Preferred Stock

As is the case for all investments, the value or price of a share of preferred stock equals the present value of all cash flows that will come from the stock. Because the preferred stock is scheduled to make payments forever, it may be treated as a perpetuity for valuation purposes:

$$P = \frac{D_p}{k_p}$$ 9.1

where:

P = the price of the preferred share
D_p = the dividend payment from the preferred share
k_p = the discount rate appropriate to the preferred share

In this valuation formula, the obligated payments are known, because the dividend is given by the par value and the dividend rate on the shares. The rate of discount, k_p, is the rate of return required by the preferred stockholders and depends on the risk that the firm will go bankrupt or that it will delay some payments on the preferred stock.

As an example, consider a share of preferred stock with a par value of $100 that pays an 8 percent annual dividend. If the discount rate for this share should be 12 percent, the preferred stock would be worth:

$$P = \frac{\$8}{.12} = \$66.67$$

Common Stock Valuation

Holders of common stock commit their funds and assume the last–place claim on the value of the firm in hopes of securing substantial profits. While the stock is owned, the only cash flow from the shares is the cash dividend. Many firms, particularly new ones and those in financial distress, do not pay dividends. Dividends are so crucial for common stock that they play a key role in determining the value of a share of stock.

Stock prices emerge from the action of the marketplace, in which traders are always revising their opinions about what stocks are worth. For any investment, we know that the value of the investment depends on the cash flows that will be generated by the investment, the timing of those cash flows, and the rate of discount applied to those cash flows.

In the case of most bonds, the timing of the cash flows is quite clear, since the cash flows are promised to be paid on certain dates. The only cash flows that come from a share of stock are the dividends that are paid by the firm. The timing of the dividend payments is not always so clear. Some firms pay no dividends but hope to pay dividends at an unspecified time in the future. Each year, some firms that have paid dividends for a long period of time fall on hard times and either reduce or eliminate their dividends. Since dividends are not contractually obligated payments, their timing becomes much more a matter of prediction and speculation than is the case with bond coupon payments.

This speculative element in the amount and timing of dividend payments arouses great concern over risk assessment for equity securities. The perceived riskiness of shares is reflected in the rate of return required by stockholders, which is the discount rate applied to the firm's dividend stream.

The Dividend Valuation Model

For stocks, the value of a share can be expressed by the following equation, which we will call the **dividend valuation model**:

$$P_0 = \sum_{t=1}^{\infty} \frac{D_t}{(1 + k)^t} \qquad \text{9.2}$$

Equation 9.2 essentially states that the price of a share of stock equals the present value of all future dividends to be paid by the share. Equation 9.3 gives an alternative expression of Equation 9.2.

$$P_0 = \frac{D_1}{(1 + k)} + \frac{D_2}{(1 + k)^2} + \frac{D_3}{(1 + k)^3} + \frac{D_4}{(1 + k)^4} + \dots \qquad 9.3$$

where:
> P_t = the price of the share at time t
> D_t = the expected dividend to be paid at time t
> k = the discount rate appropriate to the riskiness of the expected dividends

Equation 9.2 states that the current stock price (P_0) equals the sum of the present values of all future expected dividends (D_t) when those dividends are discounted at the stockholder's required rate of return (k). This implies that the value of a share is determined solely by the present value of the cash flows to come from owning the stock.

Equation 9.2 appears to neglect **capital gains**, which are profits generated by an increase in the price of an asset. Many investors are primarily interested in capital gains when they buy stocks. These problems with Equation 9.2 are only apparent, not real, as the following discussion shows.

The Dividend Valuation Model and Capital Gains

According to the dividend valuation model, the only cash flows that matter to an investor in common stock are the dividends that are expected to be paid to the shareholder. Yet, many investors buy stocks for the expected capital gains. In fact, many investors buy stocks that pay no dividends, planning to sell them later for a profit. This behavior is quite rational. In the last 20 years, dividends have contributed an average return of about 4 percent of invested capital each year, ranging from about 3–5 percent. By contrast, capital gains have ranged from about –30 percent to +30 percent. Thus, while dividends are an important component of investment return, the total return is largely determined by the capital gain or loss the investor receives.

If the dividend valuation model were really saying that these capital gains did not matter to an intelligent investor, then so much the worse for the dividend valuation model. The investor would be wise to pocket the capital gains and ignore the model. The dividend valuation model does not ignore capital gains, but it treats them indirectly, through their relationship to dividends.

To see how the dividend valuation model takes account of capital gains, consider a stock that pays a dividend annually. An investor might buy such a stock, with a plan to hold it for three years. In this situation, the cash flows that would come to the investor would consist of the three annual dividends that are to be paid during the time the stock is held plus the value of the share when it is sold. In terms of the dividend valuation model, the value of such a share would be:

$$P_0 = \frac{D_1}{(1+k)} + \frac{D_2}{(1+k)^2} + \frac{D_3}{(1+k)^3} + \frac{P_3}{(1+k)^3} \qquad \text{9.4}$$

In this case, P_3 is the value of the share when it is sold three years after purchase, right after the third dividend is paid. An investor with the planned three–year holding period would be looking forward to receiving three dividends and would be hoping for a capital gain equal to the increase in the price of the stock over the three–year period, which would be equal to $P_3 - P_0$.

At first glance, Equation 9.4 appears to contradict the dividend valuation model of Equation 9.2, because it contains the term for the price at the end of the third year, P_3. This is only an apparent discrepancy, however. The value of the share in three years depends on the future dividends expected to be paid to shareholders from that time forward. In other words, the value of the share in the third year (P_3) depends on the dividends to be paid in subsequent years, D_4, D_5, and so on:

$$P_3 = \frac{D_4}{(1+k)} + \frac{D_5}{(1+k)^2} + \frac{D_6}{(1+k)^3} + \frac{D_7}{(1+k)^4} + \ldots \qquad \text{9.5}$$

Equation 9.5 is just like Equation 9.2 or 9.3 except that the subscripts denoting the timing of the dividends are changed to reflect the fact that the value of the share is being measured at the end of the third year instead of at time 0. If Equation 9.5 is substituted into Equation 9.4, the result is exactly the same as the original version of the dividend valuation model, namely Equation 9.3.

This discussion shows that the anticipated capital gain over the three years that the stock is to be held is due to the changing valuation of the future dividends. So even if capital gains are not *explicitly* shown in the dividend valuation model of Equation 9.2, they are reflected *implicitly*. One other way of seeing that the value of a share depends on the expected future dividends is to reflect upon the following question: How much is a share of stock worth, assuming that everyone knows it will absolutely never pay a dividend? In this case, investing in such shares would be investing in something that will never generate any cash flows. If the investment will generate no cash flows, it has no value and the price of such a share should be zero. To this, one might object that the share is not being purchased for dividends (since there are none) but is being purchased for prospective capital gains. The hope is to buy the stock now and sell it for a higher price to someone else. Under the circumstances, however, in which everyone knows that the stock will never pay a dividend, no one should be willing to pay anything for the share. If no one will pay anything for the share later on, its price will remain zero, and there will be no capital gains.

The hope of selling such a share for a capital gain is based on what is known as the *greater fool theory*.[1] To pay something for a stock that promises never to pay a cent in dividends is very foolish. To try and make money by buying the stock and selling it for a profit to someone else depends upon finding someone who is a "greater fool" than the original purchaser.

The Indefinite Future of Dividends

Another apparent problem with the dividend valuation model of Equation 9.2 is the possibly infinite number of dividends populating the right side of the equation. If one wishes to apply the model in actual practice, how is it possible to sum the present value of all of those dividends?

We have already seen in the case of preferred stock that the solution is very straightforward if the dividends are constant. As shown in Equation 9.1, the price is merely equal to a payment divided by the discount rate. However, if the dividends change over time, as is likely with common stock, no such easy solution is possible.

The Constant Growth Model

Even if dividends are not constant, there is still a way to apply the model and to avoid the pitfall of trying to add a potentially infinite number of dividends. Most successful firms hope to be able to pay increasingly larger dividends as time progresses, so that there may be some growth in dividends. If the dividends grow at a regular rate, g, then the dividend valuation model can be greatly simplified. In such a case, the dividend in the second year equals the dividend in the first year plus the growth in dividends, or:

$$D_2 = D_1(1 + g)$$

Likewise, the dividend in the third year is given by:

$$D_3 = D_2(1 + g) = D_1(1 + g)(1 + g) = D_1(1 + g)^2$$

In this case, knowing the value of D_1 provides enough information to calculate the value of all subsequent dividends. For this special case of a constant growth rate in dividends, the dividend valuation model is mathematically equal to:

$$P_0 = \frac{D_1}{k - g} \qquad \text{9.6}$$

---

[1]See Burton Malkiel's excellent book, *A Random Walk Down Wall Street*, for a very interesting and amusing discussion of the greater fool theory.

Table 9.1
▄▄▄▄▄▄▄▄▄▄▄

**Share Values for Stocks Paying $1 in Initial Dividends with
Different Growth Rates and Different Discount Rates**

Growth Rate	Cost of Capital (k)						
	.08	**.10**	**.12**	**.14**	**.16**	**.18**	**.20**
.00	12.50	10.00	8.33	7.14	6.25	5.56	5.00
.01	14.29	11.11	9.09	7.69	6.67	5.88	5.26
.02	16.67	12.50	10.00	8.33	7.14	6.25	5.56
.04	25.00	16.67	12.50	10.00	8.33	7.14	6.25
.06	50.00	25.00	16.67	12.50	10.00	8.33	7.14
.08	—	50.00	25.00	16.67	12.50	10.00	8.33
.10	—	—	50.00	25.00	16.67	12.50	10.00

This model is known as the **constant growth model**. The mathematics required to prove this result lie beyond the scope of this text. However, the essential technique employed to reach this result is to calculate the value of an infinite sum. There are several assumptions behind this simplification of the model:

1. The dividends grow each year at the constant growth rate g.
2. The dividends grow at the rate g forever.
3. The growth rate g is less than the discount rate k. (Otherwise, the denominator of Equation 9.4 would be zero or negative, and the resulting price would be meaningless.)

No firm is able to pay dividends at a constant rate of growth forever, so Equation 9.6 is a simplification of reality. Nevertheless, it is useful because it provides a way of dealing with the intractable problem of a potentially infinite series of dividends. To see how this simplified version of the dividend valuation model can be applied, consider a stock that you expect will pay $1.20 in dividends at the end of the year. Based on your assessment of the riskiness of the security, you believe that such an investment should pay a return of 17 percent, and you expect that the long–term growth rate for the dividends of the company should be 3 percent. According to Equation 9.6, the share should be worth $8.57, as shown below.

$$P_0 = \frac{D_1}{k - g} = \frac{\$1.20}{.17 - .03} = \$8.57$$

The value of a share of stock is highly sensitive to the discount rate or cost of capital, k, and the expected long–term growth rate in dividends, g. This sensitivity is reflected in Table 9.1, which shows the value of a share as given by Equation 9.6, assuming an initial level of dividends of $1 per share. For example, Table 9.1 shows that the share might be worth as much as $50.00, with a cost of capital of 12 percent and a growth rate in dividends of 10 percent. Alternatively, it could be worth as little as $5.00, if the cost of capital is 20 percent and dividends are not expected to grow.

The Dividend Valuation Model and Irregular Dividend Patterns

Thus far, it might appear that the dividend valuation model still has an insurmountable difficulty. On the one hand, Equation 9.2 has an infinite number of dividend payments to consider. On the other hand, the workable version of the model, presented in Equation 9.6, seems to hold only for the extremely improbable case of a dividend that grows at a constant rate forever. The model is really much more flexible than that, as this section will demonstrate.

Historically, many of the best buys in the stock market have been for shares that paid no dividends. In fact, many of the super growth firms are likely to pay no dividends early in their lives. This has been true of Coca– Cola, IBM, Xerox, and many other companies. One challenge for the dividend valuation model is its applicability to such stocks. Actually, the dividend valuation model can be applied quite directly to such shares. For a stock paying no current dividends, the dividend valuation model simply says that the future dividends are the cash flows that are worth worrying about, and the model can handle that quite well.

This can be illustrated by an example. Imagine a small new firm that is launching successful new products in the computer industry. All of its profits are being put back into new investment, so there is no money available to pay the shareholders a dividend. Currently, there are many such firms operating in the microcomputer industry, and without doubt, some of them will emerge as successful well–established firms. In 1994, an imaginary firm, Prune Computer, traded in the range of $23 to $30, and paid no current dividend. According to the dividend valuation model, that price of $23 to $30 must be based on the expected dividends that will come later from Prune. After serious investigation, you expect that Prune will not pay any dividends for the next three years, due to the need to reinvest all profits in new product development and the marketing of existing products. In the fourth year, however, you expect that Prune will be able to pay a dividend of $1.50 per share, and that they will be able to pay a dividend that grows at a long–term rate of 10 percent. On an investment as risky as Prune, you feel that you must demand a rate of return of 18 percent. The question is, how much is Prune worth, given these assumptions?

Consistent with these assumptions, here is the expected dividend stream for Prune for the next 10 years:

D_1	$0
D_2	0
D_3	0
D_4	1.50
D_5	1.65
D_6	1.82
D_7	2.00
D_8	2.20
D_9	2.42
D_{10}	2.66

Remember that the dividends are presumed to go on growing at a rate of 10 percent forever. The main point to observe is the way in which the dividend valuation model can be applied to a case similar to the Prune example, even where the dividend flows have not yet started.

To apply the dividend valuation model, a two–step procedure is necessary. First, there is a period, beginning with the fourth year, in which the imagined dividend pattern of Prune Computer matches the requirements of the dividend valuation model. From the vantage point of the end of the third year, the next year's dividend for Prune Computer is estimated to be $1.50, to grow at a growth rate, g, of 10 percent, and to warrant a cost of capital, k, or required rate of return, of 18 percent. According to the dividend valuation model, the value of the shares at year 3 must be given by the following expression:

$$P_3 = \frac{D_4}{k - g} = \frac{\$1.50}{.18 - .10} = \$18.75$$

If the time were three years from now, and the dividend stream from Prune were expected to start next year, then the price of a share of Prune computer should be $18.75.

However, what is really of interest is what the price of Prune should be now, at time $t = 0$, according to the dividend valuation model, not what the price should be three years from now. To convert the price at year 3 into the current price according to the model, the value of Prune Computer at year 3 must be discounted back to the present at Prune's appropriate discount rate:

$$P_0 = \frac{D_1}{(1 + k)} + \frac{D_2}{(1 + k)^2} + \frac{D_3}{(1 + k)^3} + \frac{P_3}{(1 + k)^3}$$

$$P_0 = \frac{\$0}{(1.18)} + \frac{\$0}{(1.18)^2} + \frac{\$0}{(1.18)^3} + \frac{\$18.75}{(1.18)^3}$$

$$= \$11.41$$

Figure 9.1

The Dividend Stream for Cellular Technodynamics

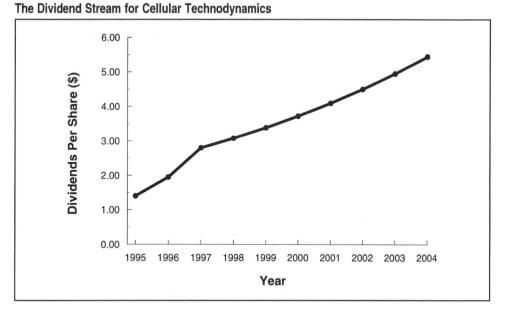

Notice that this example is really just like Equation 9.4, except that there are no dividends to consider in the first three years for Prune.

Another kind of situation is one in which there are irregular dividend payments in the near term. Industries, and the firms in them, often go through a cycle of growth. Normally, the growth is more rapid at the beginning and then settles down to a lower long–term growth rate.

As an example of such a firm, consider the imaginary mobile–phone company, Cellular Technodynamics. At the end of 1994, you forecast the following dividend stream. For 1995, you expect a dividend of $1.40, for 1996, $1.95, for 1997, $2.80, and then a long period of growth at 10 percent. These dividends are listed in the following table and are depicted graphically in Figure 9.1.

1995	$1.40
1996	1.95
1997	2.80

Then 10% growth thereafter:

1998	3.08
1999	3.39, etc.

Even for such an irregular flow of dividends, the dividend valuation model applies. The dividend stream from Cellular Technodynamics can be broken into two parts, the part with the regular growth rate of 10 percent and the earlier period of rapid growth. Clearly, the dividend discount model can handle the period of regular growth. At year–end 1997, the dividend expected for the next year is $3.08, followed by dividends that grow at a rate of 10 percent. Assuming a stockholder's required return of 16 percent, the price of a share of Cellular Technodynamics at the end of 1997 is given by:

$$P_{1997} = \frac{D_{1998}}{k - g} = \frac{\$3.08}{.16 - .10} = \$51.33$$

According to the dividend valuation model, the share price at year–end of 1997 is expected to be $51.33. It remains only to take account of the value of the earlier dividend payments and the fact that a price must be calculated for the present, which is the end of 1994. The value of Cellular Technodynamics depends on the dividends received in the years before the dividend becomes smooth, plus the value of the shares at the time the dividend growth rate becomes constant, 1997.

$$
\begin{aligned}
P_{1994} &= \frac{D_{1995}}{(1 + k)} + \frac{D_{1996}}{(1 + k)^2} + \frac{D_{1997}}{(1 + k)^3} + \frac{P_{1997}}{(1 + k)^3} \\
&= \frac{\$1.40}{(1.16)} + \frac{1.95}{(1.16)^2} + \frac{2.80}{(1.16)^3} + \frac{51.33}{(1.16)^3} \\
&= 1.21 + 1.45 + 1.79 + 32.88 = \$37.33
\end{aligned}
$$

Notice that the price expected for the end of 1997 must also be discounted back to the present. Also, it should be noted that the dividend to be paid at year–end of 1997 and the value of the shares in 1997 are both discounted back for three years. The assumption here is that the $51.33 expected value of the shares at the end of 1997 is the value immediately after the 1997 dividend has been paid.

These examples illustrate the flexibility of the dividend valuation model. With minor adjustments, it can handle more realistic situations, such as those for firms with initially irregular dividend streams, or even for those firms paying no current dividends. The model is not applicable, however, to firms that will never have any regular growth in dividends, but in practice this is a minor problem.

The Dividend Valuation Model and Earnings

Thus far in the discussion, the entire emphasis has been directed toward dividends. Yet, the reader of the financial press knows that market professionals pay great attention to earnings reports and the earnings prospects of different firms. Not surprisingly, there is an intimate link between earnings and dividends, which is reflected in the dividend valuation model.

The earnings that a firm generates have three, and only three, outlets according to accounting convention. They must be:

Figure 9.2

The Allocation of Corporate Profits

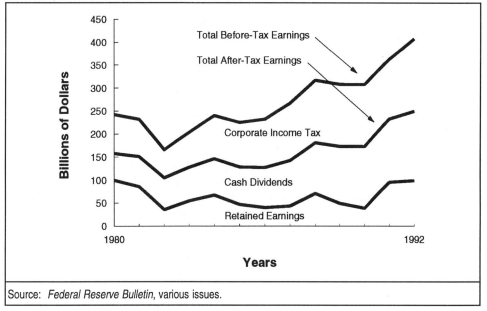

Source: *Federal Reserve Bulletin*, various issues.

1. paid in taxes,
2. paid as dividends, or
3. retained for further investment in the firm.

Figure 9.2 shows how U.S. corporate profits have been divided among these three uses. As Figure 9.2 shows, profits have been quite variable and now stand at over $300 billion annually. There has been a strong tendency toward a greater level of total dividends in the economy, even though the amount of dividends paid has varied considerably over time.

Growing firms typically pay small dividends because it is often important to generate as much cash as possible for reinvestment in the firm. Well–established firms that are paying dividends typically try to make those dividends increase, while taking precautions to avoid ever reducing their dividends.

The dividend valuation model recognizes the very close relationship between earnings and dividends by applying this accounting convention. Focusing now just on after–tax earnings, every dollar of earnings a firm achieves goes either to retained earnings or is paid as a cash dividend. The portion of earnings retained can be represented as a percentage, b. The remainder of the dollar of earnings, $(1 - b)$, the firm pays in cash dividends. Firms always paying a fixed percentage of their earnings follow a dividend policy that is called a **constant payout policy**. For such firms, there is a lawlike relationship between earnings and dividends; that is, dividends are always a fixed fraction of earnings.

For a firm with a constant payout policy, knowing the level of earnings is enough to determine the level of dividends. In a given year t, the dividend is given by the following expression, where $(1 - b)$ is the percentage of earnings paid as a dividend:

$$D_t = (1 - b) \, E_t$$

For a firm following a constant payout dividend policy, estimating the dividend payments to be made is the same problem as estimating the future earnings stream. For example, consider a well–established firm growing at its long–term growth rate, $g = 4$ percent. Next year's earnings are expected to be \$3.60 per share, and the firm follows the practice of paying 60 percent and retaining 40 percent of its earnings. Further, assume that the required rate of return, or the cost of capital, for such a firm's shares is 14 percent. How much is the firm worth? The dividend valuation model provides an easily calculated answer.

$$P_0 = \frac{D_1}{k - g} = \frac{(1 - b)E_1}{k - g}$$

$$= \frac{(1 - .4)\$3.60}{.14 - .04} = \$21.60$$

According to the dividend valuation model, the price of a share should be \$21.60.

The Dividend Valuation Model and the P–E Ratio

Having observed the intimate link among dividends, earnings, and share price, we are in a position to see how important earnings growth can be to a firm. The financial manager knows that, other things being equal, causing earnings to grow will help the stock price. While some managers may become obsessed with earnings, the clever manager knows that increased earnings are important only because of their effect on the share price. The investor is also interested in earnings, because firms with rapidly increasing earnings often have increasing stock prices.

The stocks of firms expected to enjoy a rapid increase in earning are known as **growth stocks**. For example, in the mid–1980s, Genentech led the field of genetic engineering and was a typical growth stock. From its founding, Genentech had high hopes, an ambitious research program, literally no dividends, and virtually no earnings. Nonetheless, the stock price of Genentech was relatively high through the 1980s.

One measure of the height of the stock price is known as the **price–earnings ratio** or **P–E ratio**, which is defined as the ratio of the stock price to the firm's annual earnings.

P–E Ratio = Stock Price/Current Annual Earnings per Share

A high P–E ratio usually indicates the prospect of rapid future growth in earnings. Typically, growth stocks also have high P–E ratios.

The Dividend Valuation Model and Constant Payout Policies

For firms with constant payout policies, there are a number of useful relationships to consider. The basic constant growth version of the dividend valuation model states that:

$$P_0 = \frac{D_1}{k - g}$$

By a simple rearrangement of the terms, it follows that:

$$k = \frac{D_1}{P_0} + g \qquad\qquad 9.7$$

The term D_1/P_0 is known as the **dividend yield**. So, Equation 9.7 says that the cost of equity capital for a firm equals the dividend yield plus the long–term growth rate in dividends. For a firm with zero growth, the cost of equity capital equals the dividend yield.

To illustrate this idea, consider a firm with a share price of $100 and a dividend yield of 5 percent. This implies a dividend of $5 per year. Assuming that the growth rate of dividends is zero, Equation 9.7 implies that the appropriate rate of discount for the dividends is also 5 percent—equal to the dividend yield. In other words, Equation 9.3 implies that the price of the share should be given by the following:

$$P = \frac{\$5}{(1.05)} = \frac{\$5}{(1.05)^2} + \frac{\$5}{(1.05)^3} + \frac{\$5}{(1.05)^4} + \dots$$

This reflects the constant dividend of $5 continuing forever.

The value of a perpetuity of N per period is given by the following expression:

$$P = \frac{N}{k} \qquad\qquad 9.8$$

where:
N = the amount of the payment
k = the discount rate

In our example, the constant dividend is $5 and the discount rate is 5 percent, so the value of the share of stock is given by:

$$P = \frac{N}{k} = \frac{\$5}{.05} = \$100$$

It also follows from Equation 9.7 that:

$$k = \frac{(1 - b)E_1}{P_0} + g \qquad\qquad \textbf{9.9}$$

For a firm with a zero growth rate and a policy of paying all earnings as dividends so that the retention ratio is zero (that is, $b = 0$), it must also be the case that:

$$k = \frac{E_1}{P_0} \qquad\qquad \textbf{9.10}$$

In this special case, $D_t = E_t$. As a consequence, the discount rate must equal the dividend payout ratio and the P–E ratio. In our example, if the firm that pays a $5 dividend is paying out all of its earnings, the earnings must also be $5 per year, and we can calculate the cost of equity capital using Equation 9.10.

$$k = \frac{E_1}{P_0} = \frac{\$5}{\$100} = .05$$

What happens to the growth rate in this situation? If all of the earnings are paid as dividends, retained earnings (b) must be zero. This means that there are no new funds to reinvest in the firm to generate increases in future earnings. As a consequence, the firm that pays all of its earnings in dividends is merely maintaining the present level of its capital stock but never increasing it. Accordingly, earnings can remain at their current level because the present capital stock is being maintained, but the earnings cannot increase because the capital stock is not being increased.

These relationships are useful because they provide the stock analyst with a technique for making estimates of the cost of capital to be applied to dividend streams. Being able to see these other relationships implied by the dividend valuation model is also important for the additional insight they provide. For example, Equations 9.7 and 9.9 clearly show that growth firms will have higher costs for equity capital than will nongrowth firms.

One of the most often–cited statistics about common stock is the inverse of the earnings–price ratio of Equation 9.10. It is the price–earnings ratio, or simply the P–E ratio. As will become clearer in the following chapters, a high P–E ratio is often the mark of a growth firm.

These measures are all useful ways of summarizing characteristics of different stocks. For example, an investor interested in income from a common stock portfolio would be particularly interested in the dividend yield, since that is the percentage cash return on the portfolio. Such an investor might reasonably prefer stocks with high dividend–price ratios or might try to invest at a time when the dividend yield is particularly high. Similarly, the earnings–price ratio is also important for many investors. Some evidence exists (and will be reviewed in Chapter 12) to suggest that stocks with high earnings–price ratios tend to outperform those with low earnings–price ratios.

Dividends and Share Prices in the Economy

In this section, we apply the principles of the dividend valuation model to the economy as a whole. The purpose here is to use real–world data to provide a broad understanding of the relationship among dividends, earnings, the retention ratio, the growth rate, and their effect on stock prices.

Figure 9.3 shows the history of the dividend–price ratio for the post–World War II period. Over this period, the average dividend–price ratio was 4.2 percent. If we focus for a moment on a typical dividend–price ratio of 4 percent, we can see that the dividend valuation model can relate this typical dividend–price ratio to the discount rate and the growth rate. For example, consider a firm with a dividend growth rate of 3 percent. It follows that the difference between the discount rate and the growth rate must equal the dividend–price ratio:

Figure 9.3

The Dividend–Price Ratio

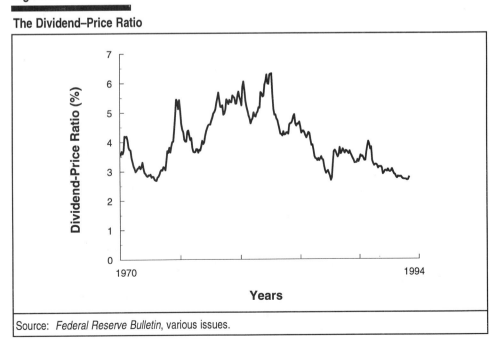

Source: *Federal Reserve Bulletin*, various issues.

Figure 9.4

Dividend–Price Ratios, Growth Rates, and Discount Rates

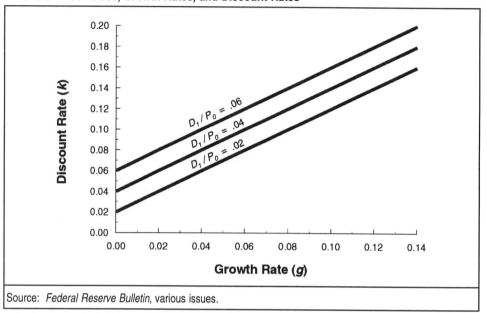

Source: *Federal Reserve Bulletin*, various issues.

$$\frac{D_1}{P_0} = k - g$$

Thus, a dividend–price ratio of 4 percent and a growth rate of 3 percent imply that the discount rate for dividends is 7 percent. Figure 9.4 shows this relationship for dividend–price ratios of 2, 4, and 6 percent. Each dividend–price ratio is consistent with different combinations of k and g. In the figure, different growth rates are shown on the horizontal axis, with the resulting discount rate on the vertical axis. The line for each dividend–price ratio in the figure begins with a discount rate equal to that ratio. This reflects the fact that a firm with zero growth will have a discount rate equal to the dividend–price ratio. As the growth rate increases, the discount rate increases as well.

In the long run, extremely high growth rates are impossible to sustain. For example, a firm paying a dividend of $1 million and growing at a rate of 12 percent for 100 years would be paying a dividend of over $83 trillion at the end of the period. A more realistic long–term growth rate for most firms is 3–4 percent, roughly consistent with the overall growth rate of the economy. As Figure 9.4 shows, a growth rate of 3–4 percent and a normal dividend–price ratio of 4 percent implies a discount rate of 7–8 percent.

Figure 9.5

The Price–Earnings Ratio

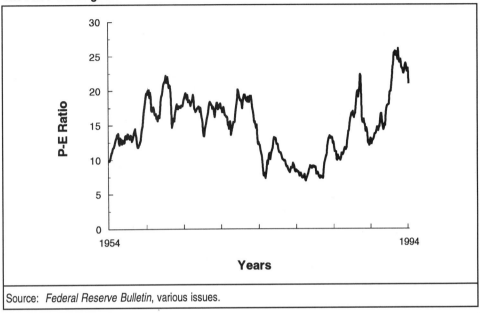

Source: *Federal Reserve Bulletin*, various issues.

Figure 9.5 shows the history of the P–E ratio in recent years. While the graph shows a high variability in the ratio, the average P–E ratio is about 14, consistent with an average earnings–price ratio of about 7 percent. With economy–wide average earnings–price ratios of 7 percent and dividend–price ratios of about 4 percent, the average percentage of earnings paid as dividends must be about 60 percent. (Dividing 4 by 7 gives approximately 0.60.) This implies a retention ratio of about 40 percent. Figure 9.6 shows how different P–E ratios and different payout ratios are consistent with different combinations of growth (g) and discount (k) rates. For example, for a fairly typical firm with a P–E ratio of 14, a payout ratio of 60 percent, and a growth rate of 3 percent, the discount rate would be 0.0741. We can see this by rearranging the terms in the dividend valuation model:

$$k = \frac{E_0}{P_0} \, (1 - b) \, (1 + g) + g$$

$$= .0714 \, (.6) \, (1.03) + .03$$

$$= .0741$$

Representative values appear in Figure 9.6 for combinations of P–E ratios and payout ratios.

Figure 9.6

P–E and Payout Ratios, Growth and Discount Rates

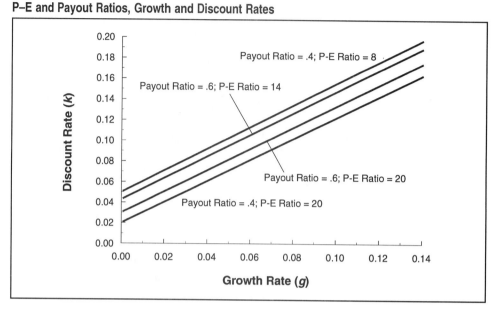

The Dividend Valuation Model and Equity Investing

So far, this chapter has explored the fundamental features of the dividend valuation model and the relationship between dividends and earnings. The ultimate purpose of this model is to provide a rational and coherent way of thinking about the value of common stocks. The value of any share of stock depends on the dividends paid to its owner. Earnings are important also because it is out of earnings that firms generate both the current dividends paid to investors now and the retained earnings, which will be reinvested to produce future dividends for stock owners.

By estimating the future flow of dividends and earnings, and the appropriate rate of discount to be applied to those dividends and earnings, it is possible to calculate a value for the stock using the dividend valuation model. This calculated value is known as the **intrinsic value** of the share, which may differ from the **market value** of the stock. The price calculated according to the dividend valuation model is an intrinsic value because it is an estimate of what the share is truly worth. By contrast, the market value of the share is simply the current price of the share in the stock market.

If the calculated intrinsic value differs from the market value of the share, there is an opportunity for investment, according to the following investment rule:

If the intrinsic value exceeds the market value:
Buy the stock.

If the market value exceeds the intrinsic value:
Sell the stock.

The investment rule is quite simple, but it depends critically on the accuracy of the intrinsic value calculation. If estimates of dividends, earnings, and discount rates are inaccurate, the calculated intrinsic value for the shares will be inaccurate as well and will lead to a poor investment decision. Also, the application of this rule depends on the belief that the market will eventually come to realize the intrinsic value of the stock. When that happens, the intrinsic value and the market value will be the same. It is that convergence of intrinsic value and market value that generates a profit. If other investors never recognize the intrinsic value of a stock, there will be no economic force to move the market price toward the intrinsic value, and there will be no profit for the investor who has correctly discerned the intrinsic value.

The successful application of the dividend valuation model is quite difficult, largely due to the tremendous number and complexity of factors that can affect the dividend and earnings streams and the discount rates applied to those streams.

The next three chapters examine the various factors that affect the inputs to the dividend valuation model. Chapter 10 considers the overall economic variables, such as the business cycle and the level of interest rates, that affect virtually all firms in the economy. Chapter 11 is more specific, focusing on trends that affect particular industries. The health of an industry is crucial to the success of the individual firms within that industry. For example, a widespread antipathy to nuclear power could have a major effect on all firms in that industry. Finally, Chapter 12 studies the factors that are specific to individual firms, such as quality of management and labor relations. The analysis moves from a concern with the broad factors affecting the economy as a whole, through the more specific industry factors, to an analysis of the company–specific factors. The application of the dividend valuation model to determine an accurate intrinsic value for the shares requires care and insight at each level of the analysis.

The Dividend Valuation Model and Stock Analysis

Imagine a situation in which many scientists with excellent training compete to solve a research problem. They work independently, with the prospect of huge financial rewards for the victors. The reward is largest if only one scientist reaches the correct solution and the others fail totally. If two or more solve the problem at the same time, the rewards will be divided among them. If all of the scientists reach the correct conclusion at the same time, no reward will be given.

Stock analysis is very similar to this situation. If all stock analysts correctly analyze the value of a given stock, they will all be willing to pay the same amount for it. In such a situation, the intrinsic value will equal the market value of the stock. When that happens, there is no chance for profit. It is not enough for a successful analyst to be correct about the true worth of a stock; one must also be correct when others are wrong. Just as with the scientific research competition, the rewards in analyzing stocks are greatest for the one analyst who correctly estimates the intrinsic value of a stock at a time when other analysts err.

The greater the discrepancy between the intrinsic value and the market value of a share, the greater the opportunity for profit. This fact highlights the importance and difficulty of being a "superior analyst"—one who discovers information overlooked by other analysts or one who analyzes the commonly available information in a superior way. In fact, as we shall see in Chapters 13–15, there is even reason to believe that the process of analysis is impossibly difficult. Nonetheless, the enormous potential reward of correct analysis continues to call forth the efforts of very intelligent people anxious to learn the techniques of analysis in the hope of applying them to generate spectacular wealth.

Risk and the Required Rate of Return

We have now surveyed the principal instruments of the capital market and have discussed the valuation principles that apply to different kinds of bonds, to preferred stock, and to common stock. Each represents a different source of financing for the firm and each has its own particular characteristics. One of the major differences among these different financing vehicles is the risk that the owner takes in giving money to the firm in exchange for promises of future cash flows from the company.

Figure 9.7

The Risk–Expected Return Relationship

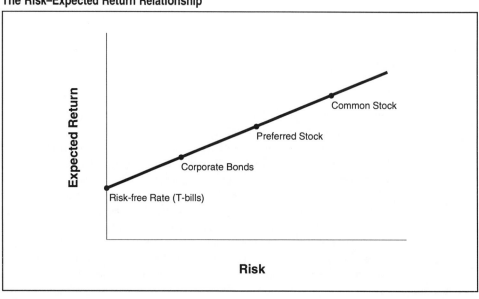

Not surprisingly, investors demand greater compensation for bearing risk. For instance, we have already noted that the owner of a first mortgage bond has a more secure position than the holder of the same firm's debenture. In general, all bondholders have a safer position than holders of stock, and preferred stockholders bear less risk than common stockholders. The differences in risk levels are reflected in the different rates of return that these various securities earn. Figure 9.7 presents this general relationship in a schematic form. The basic principle is clear: The greater the risk, the greater must be the expected return to encourage investors to commit their funds.

Summary

This chapter examined two major elements of the capital market—preferred stock and common stock. Preferred stock is a hybrid security, having features of both corporate bonds and common stock. Preferred stock normally pays a fixed dividend rate, similar to the coupon rate on a corporate bond. However, unlike most corporate bonds, preferred stock has no maturity date, so the preferred stock dividends are intended to be paid forever. The fact that preferred stock does not mature means that the firm need never repay the par value of the stock.

Preferred stock provides the firm with a flexible financing alternative, because the dividend payments on preferred stock are not contractual obligations (as they are with most bonds) and preferred stockholders do not normally have voting rights (as do common stockholders). This advantage of flexibility is partially offset by the fact that preferred stock dividends must be paid from the firm's after–tax earnings. Interest payments on bonds, by contrast, are paid from before–tax earnings.

Common stock is the one kind of financing common to all corporations, because ownership of common stock represents ownership in the corporation. The corporation need not sell preferred stock or bonds, but there must be common stock. Common stockholders are entitled to receive dividends from the firm as a return on their investment. However, because the stockholders receive dividends only after the other claimants of the firm are satisfied, there is no assurance that they will actually receive dividends. Of all of the financing instruments issued by a corporation, common stock is the riskiest, with much of that risk originating from broad economic movements.

The value of both preferred and common stock follows the basic rule that the value of any investment equals the present value of all of the cash flows expected from the investment. In the case of preferred stock, the flows are stated as a percentage of the face value. This practice implies a fixed dollar dividend, so preferred stock may be valued as a perpetuity. In the case of common stock, the matter is more complicated. The dividends may not exist at the present, or, if they do exist, they may grow yet larger. For those periods when dividends are growing at a constant rate, they may be valued with the constant growth model. This valuation technique is also useful under even more restrictive circumstances.

Questions and Problems

1. A new firm makes a 100 percent believable commitment never to pay dividends. What should the price of the shares in that firm be worth? Why?

2. Respond to the following claim: "The dividend valuation model is worthless as a guide to stock prices because it completely neglects capital gains."

3. Why do many new firms pay no dividends? Does this imply that their share prices should be zero? Why or why not?

4. React to the following criticism: "The dividend valuation model is not very useful, because it can only be applied to firms having smoothly growing dividends. For example, it cannot be applied to firms that might experience a period of rapidly and erratically growing dividends."

5. How would you respond to the following attack on the dividend valuation model? "The dividend valuation model assumes that dividends grow at a rate g forever. This is obviously unrealistic, so the model cannot be applied in practice."

6. In terms of the dividend valuation model, why does a firm with a higher growth rate of dividends have a higher discount rate?

7. What are the three possible outlets for a firm's earnings?

8. What is the cost of equity capital for a firm that pays 100 percent of its earnings as a dividend? What will be the growth rate in dividends for such a firm?

9. What is the intrinsic value of a share of stock?

10. State the basic investment rule using the concept of intrinsic value.

11. What relationship do you think normally exists between the intrinsic value of a share of stock and the market price of the share? Why?

12. If a firm cuts its dividend, should its price fall according to the dividend valuation model?

13. Consider a firm that announces a very attractive new investment opportunity and also announces that it is eliminating its dividend in order to finance the new investment. What should happen to the stock price according to the dividend valuation model?

14. Consider a firm that pays a dividend in the next period of $.70 and that has a growth rate of 11 percent for the next four years. What are the dividends for these periods? Assume that the firm will never pay any dividends beyond the fifth year. According to the dividend valuation model, what should be the price of this share, if the discount rate is 12 percent?

15. For a share paying a dividend in the coming period of $1.20, with a long-term growth rate of 4 percent and a cost of equity capital of 10 percent, what is the share price according to the dividend valuation model?

16. What happens, for the previous share, as the growth rate accelerates and other factors are held constant? Graph the share price as a function of the difference between the cost of equity capital 10 percent and the growth rate, as the growth rate increases.

17. You estimate that a firm will have the following dividends for the next three periods: $1.17, $1.44, $1.88. After these dividends you expect dividends to grow at their long–term growth rate of 3 percent. What is the share price according to the dividend valuation model? What would it be if the long–term growth rate were 5 percent rather than 3 percent? Assume $k = 10$ percent.

18. A fully mature firm follows the policy of paying 60 percent of its earnings in dividends, and these earnings have been growing at the long–term growth rate of 4 percent. Further increases in earnings are expected to remain at the 4 percent level as well. If the earnings in the current period are $1.20 per share, what is the value of this share according to the dividend discount model, assuming a 12 percent cost–of–equity capital?

19. For the firm in the preceding example, assume that the payout ratio is 100 percent rather than 60 percent. What does this imply about the growth rate and what should be the value of the share?

CFA Questions

All CFA examination questions are reprinted, with permission, from the Level I *1992–1994, CFA Candidate Study and Examination Program Review.* Copyright 1992–1994, Association for Investment Management and Research, Charlottesville, Va. All rights reserved.

A. Assume that at the end of the next year, Company A will pay a $2.00 dividend per share, an increase from the current dividend of $1.50 per share. After that, the dividend is expected to increase at a constant rate of 5%. If you require a 12% return on the stock, what is the value of the stock?
   a. $28.57
   b. $28.79
   c. $30.00
   d. $31.78

B. You are considering acquiring a common stock that you would like to hold for one year. You expect to receive both $1.50 in dividends and $26 from the sale of stock at the end of the year. What is the maximum price you would pay for the stock today if you wanted to earn a 15% return?
   a. $23.91
   b. $24.11
   c. $27.30
   d. $27.50

C. Company B paid a $1.00 dividend per share last year and is expected to continue to pay out 40% of its earnings as dividends for the foreseeable future. If the firm is expected to generate a 10% return on equity in the future, and if you require a 12% return on the stock, what is the value of the stock?
   a. $12.50
   b. $13.00
   c. $16.67
   d. $17.67

D. As a firm operating in mature industry, Arbot Industries is expected to maintain a constant dividend payout ratio and constant growth rate of earnings for the foreseeable future. Earnings were $4.50 per share in the recently completed fiscal year. The dividend payout ratio has been a constant 55% in recent years and is expected to remain so. Arbot's return on equity (ROE) is expected to remain at 10% in the future, and you require an 11% return on the stock.
   a. Using the constant growth dividend discount model, **calculate** the current value of Arbot common stock. *Show* your calculations.

   After an aggressive acquisition and marketing program, it now appears that Arbot's earnings per share and ROE will grow rapidly over the next two years. You are aware that the dividend discount model can be useful in estimating the value of common stock even when the assumption of constant growth does not apply.

   b. *Calculate* the current value of Arbot's common stock using the dividend discount model assuming Arbot's dividend will grow at a 15% rate for the next two years, returning in the third year to the historical growth rate and continuing to grow at the historical rate for the foreseeable future. **Show** your calculations.

Suggested REALDATA Exercises

The following *REALDATA* exercises explore the concepts developed in this chapter: Exercises 31, 32.

Suggested Readings

Ang, J. S., "Do Dividends Matter? A Review of Corporate Dividend Theories and Evidence," *Monograph Series in Finance and Economics*, Vol. 2, 1987.

Angell, R. J. and A. Redmon, "How to Judge a P/E? Examine the Expected Growth Rate," *American Association of Individual Investors*, 12:3, March 1990, pp. 16–17.

Bagwell, L. and J. B. Shoven, "Cash Distributions to Shareholders," *Journal of Economic Perspectives*, 3:3, Summer 1989, pp. 129–140.

Bailey, W., "Canada's Dual Class Shares: Further Evidence on the Market Value of Cash Dividends," *Journal of Finance*, 43:5, December 1988, pp. 1143–1160.

Campbell, J. Y. and R. J. Shiller, "Stock Prices, Earnings, and Expected Dividends," *Journal of Finance*, 43:3, July 1988, pp. 661–676.

DeAngelo, H. and L. DeAngelo, "Dividend Policy and Financial Distress: An Empirical Investigation of Troubled NYSE Firms," *Journal of Finance*, 45:5, December 1990, pp. 1415–1431.

Pearce, D. K. and V. V. Roley, "Firm Characteristics, Unanticipated Inflation, and Stock Returns," *Journal of Finance*, 43:4, September 1988, pp. 965–981.

Wilson, R. S., "Nonconvertible Preferred Stock," *The Handbook of Fixed Income Securities*, 3e, Homewood, IL: Business Irwin One, 1991.

CHAPTER TEN

Economic Analysis and the Stock Market

Overview

October 1987 was the most incredible month in the history of Wall Street. On Monday, October 19, the Dow Jones average fell 508 points, the largest one–day loss in the history of the index. On that one day, the Dow Jones Industrial Average lost more than 22 percent of its value. For the first time, the New York Stock Exchange traded over 600 million shares in a single day, doubling the previous volume record set earlier in the same year. Such wide swings in stock values occur only when stocks tend to move together—experiencing gains or losses on the same day. Clearly, stocks tend to move together.

In fact, stocks tend to act as a herd, moving up or down together. This is true whether one considers short time periods, like a single day, or whether the emphasis is on longer time spans. This chapter examines long–term economic factors and their effect on the stock market as a whole. The general effect of broad economic movements on the stock market has been compared to the effect of a tide. When the tide comes in, virtually all stocks tend to rise. Without question, some may rise faster than others, and others may be beached at the high–water mark. For the most part, however, the economic factors that form the subject matter of this chapter carry individual stocks with them, whether the tide floods or ebbs.

As defined in the last chapter, the value of a share of stock equals the present value of future dividends to be paid from the share. How can we reconcile this view with the fact that stocks tend to move together, as though they are carried on a tide? There is good reason for stock prices to move in unison, and the alert investor needs to know the basic relationships between broad economic movements in production, interest rates, and fiscal and monetary policy, on the one hand, and stock prices on the other. These factors tend to affect most stocks in similar ways, even if the degree of the effect varies, depending upon the particular industry and firm. Also, as we will see, the same basic relationships appear to be true of foreign stock markets as well.

In terms of the dividend valuation model introduced in the preceding chapter, changes in these basic economic variables have a general effect on the market's assessment of future dividend streams from all stocks. Similarly, these same basic economic factors can have an impact on discount rates in general. Together, they can have a profound effect on stock prices in general.

Once we acknowledge the importance of these broad economic factors, the next issue becomes one of attempting to predict the economic movements. If one could predict changes in broad economic measures correctly, then it might be possible to use those predictions to guide a successful trading strategy in the stock market. This chapter concludes with a brief survey of some of the more popular forecasting techniques and an appraisal of their usefulness.

Tidal Movements

It is a fact of economic life that there are cycles of boom and bust. These range from the Great Depression of the 1930s, which affected virtually all phases of economic life, to the "go–go" stock market years of the 1960s. The boom–and–bust cycle in the stock market is just part of the same cycle for the economy as a whole. Since there is a clear relationship between price movements in the stock market and the health of the economy as a whole, the hope is that studying economic developments will help the stock investor to invest more wisely.

Figure 10.1

Long–Term Stock Price Movements, S&P 500 and Consumer Stocks

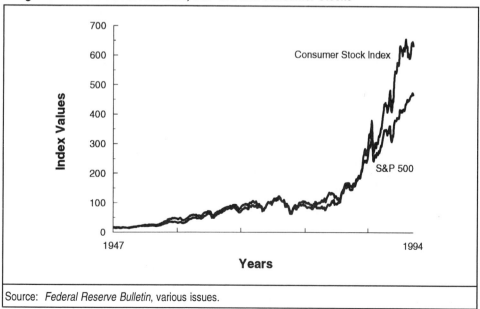

Source: *Federal Reserve Bulletin*, various issues.

The Herd Instinct

The tendency of stocks to rise and fall together is an important and pervasive factor in understanding the price movement of any stock. In Chapter 14, we will explore a theory that explains the movement of each individual stock's price by its relationship to the market as a whole. For the present, we note the very close tendency of widely differing stocks to move together, and we defer the detailed analysis of this topic until Chapter 14.

As an example of the herd instinct, consider Figure 10.1, which shows the long–term tendency of stocks in the consumer goods industry to mirror the movement of the market as a whole. The graph shows two stock indexes, the S&P 500 and the S&P consumer goods stock index. Clearly, the two portfolios of stocks move very similarly. (The correlation in returns between the two portfolios is 92 percent.) This suggests that understanding the economy–wide factors that affect stock prices will help to unravel the secrets of price movements for individual stocks.

The Business Cycle

One of the most pervasive effects on the stock market is the **business cycle**, the periodic expansion and contraction of the economy. In an economic downturn, retail sales fall, orders for capital equipment stagnate, unemployment rates rise, and business inventories expand as firms are unable to sell their goods promptly. A **recession** is a sharp and significant reduction in overall business activity. In an economic expansion, sales quicken, firms order new capital equipment, jobs become easier to find, inventories contract, and firms employ most or all of their productive capacity.

Stock prices respond to the business cycle. Recessions are often accompanied by extended bear markets, and expansionary periods are often heralded by a bull market. Figure 10.2 presents the S&P 500 stock index and an index of industrial production, the chief component of the Gross National Product. While there does appear to be a positive relationship between the two, the link is by no means exact. Upon careful view, the figure indicates that the stock market often rises before industrial production. We will return to this idea later. Table 10.1 shows the periods of six recent recessions.

Stocks that are particularly sensitive to the business cycle are called **cyclical stocks**. These include firms that make heavy industrial equipment and capital goods used by other firms. For example, steel firms are a prime example of cyclical stocks. These cyclical stocks often lead the recovery as well. By contrast, some firms are relatively immune to the business cycle. Supermarkets attract shoppers throughout recessions, so their stock prices tend to be affected relatively little by the business cycle. Liquor distillers and tobacco firms often do fairly well in recessions, too. Table 10.2 shows the three best and three worst performing industry groups during the 1981–1982 recession. The better performers tend to be in businesses that people need all the time, while the worst performers are concentrated in heavy industry.

Figure 10.2

Stock Prices and Industrial Production

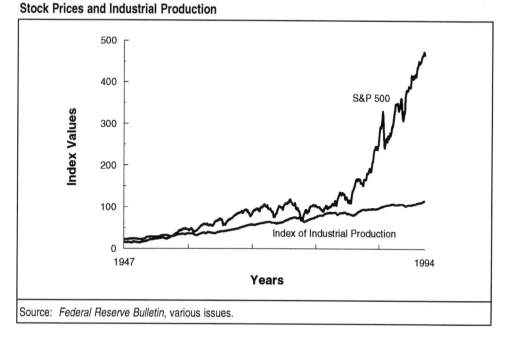

Source: *Federal Reserve Bulletin*, various issues.

This is a typical result, since capital goods industries tend to suffer more in recessions than most other industries.

Table 10.1

Recent Recessions

Starting Date	Ending Date	Duration in Months
April, 1960	February, 1961	10
December, 1969	November, 1970	11
November, 1973	March, 1975	16
January, 1980	July, 1980	6
July, 1981	November, 1982	16
July, 1990	March, 1991	8

Source: National Bureau of Economic Research (NBER).

Table 10.2

■■■■■■■■■■

Best and Worst Performing Industry Groups, 1981–1982 Recession

Industry Group	Returns (July, 1981—November, 1982)
Best Performers	
Beverages	29.7%
Home finance	28.9
Supermarkets	22.7
S&P 500 Benchmark	9.9
Worst Performers	
Shipping	-46.1
Oil services	-47.0
Steel	-49.6

Interest Rates and Inflation

In Chapter 7 we saw that the nominal rate of interest on a default–free bond, r, depended on the real rate of interest, r^*, and the expected rate of inflation, $E(I)$. The exact relationship, originally introduced as Equation 7.9, stated that:

$$(1 + r) = (1 + r^*)[1 + E(I)]$$

where:

r = the nominal rate of interest

r^* = the real rate of interest

$E(I)$ = the expected rate of inflation over the period

This equation stresses the very close relationship between expected inflation and interest rates. Consequently, this discussion of the impact of interest rates and inflation on stock prices will focus mainly on the relationship between inflation and stock returns.

As we have seen in Chapters 7 and 8, real returns are the relevant returns for measuring investment success, because real returns are the measure of changes in purchasing power. The change in purchasing power indicates the change in consumption opportunities, and every investor is ultimately interested in improving his or her consumption opportunities.

The inflation issue is particularly important for common stock investing because it appears that investing in common stock should protect an investor against the ravages of inflation. A share of common stock represents fractional ownership of the earning power and the physical assets of a corporation. In periods of inflation, these assets should also increase in nominal value, just as prices of

Table 10.3

Nominal and Real Common Stock Returns in High– and Low–Inflation Years

High–Inflation Years			
Year	Nominal Stock Returns	Inflation	Real Stock Returns
1946	– 8.07	18.17	–26.24
1979	18.44	13.31	5.13
1980	32.42	12.40	20.02
1974	–26.47	12.20	–38.67
1975	–11.59	9.72	<u>–21.31</u>
			Average –12.23

Low–Inflation Years			
Year	Nominal Stock Returns	Inflation	Real Stock Returns
1932	– 8.19	–10.30	2.11
1931	–43.34	– 9.52	–33.82
1930	–24.90	– 6.03	–18.87
1938	31.12	– 2.78	33.90
1927	37.49	– 2.08	<u>39.57</u>
			Average 4.58

Average for All Years, 1926–1993		
Nominal Stock Returns:	Inflation: 3.1%	Real Stock Returns:
Large firms: 10.3%		Large firms: 6.98%
Small firms: 12.4%		Small firms: 8.95%

Source: Ibbotson Associates, *Stocks, Bonds, Bills and Inflation: 1994 Yearbook*, Chicago: Ibbotson Associates, 1994.

goods and services of all types rise. If that is so, then the value of the common stock should also rise in tandem with the general price level. While this theory seems reasonable, it does not always work out that way. Table 10.3 presents the results for the five years of highest and lowest inflation rates for the years 1926 through 1993.

During the five years with the highest inflation, the average real return on common stocks was –12.23 percent. By contrast, in the low–inflation years, the real return on common stocks was 4.58 percent. Notice that during years of low inflation, *deflation* occurred and the price level actually fell. In addition, this period includes the years 1930–1932, from the heart of the Great Depression. While this evidence does not constitute a formal test, it does show that recent experience gives reason to favor low–inflation environments rather than high–inflation environments. Thus, it seems that common stock investment does not provide a perfect protection against inflation.

Figure 10.3

Stock Prices and the General Consumer Price Level

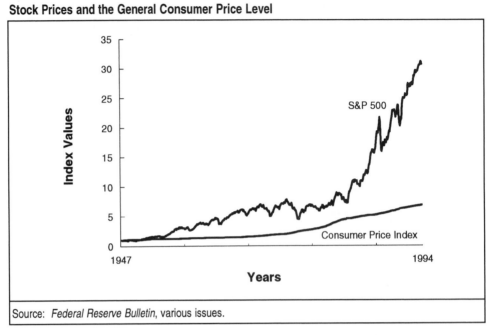

Source: *Federal Reserve Bulletin*, various issues.

In fact, both the periods of extremely high and low inflation were poor periods for common stock investment, relative to the 1926–1993 period as a whole. The arithmetic average annual real return for the common stocks of large firms over the entire period was 6.98 percent, and the average return for the stocks of small firms was 8.95 percent. These results beat the periods of both extremely high and low inflation.[1]

Figure 10.3 presents the changes in stock prices and the Consumer Price Index for the period following World War II. Both stock prices and the price level have tended to rise, but the recent past shows stock prices rising much more rapidly. This effect of inflation implies that the real value of stocks will fluctuate over time. Figure 10.4 shows the changes in the real value of stocks. The graph is drawn by assigning a value of 1.0 to January 1947. After reaching a peak in the mid–1960s, the real level of stock prices fell dramatically. During the 15–year period from 1965 to 1980, real stock prices fell by about 50 percent. During the 1980s and early 1990s, real stock prices rebounded and achieved parity with their 1960s highs.

Not surprisingly, there have been formal studies of the effects of inflation on stock returns. Most of these studies tend to support the more casual evidence

[1]See Ibbotson Associates, *Stocks, Bonds, Bills and Inflation: 1994 Yearbook*, Chicago: Ibbotson Associates, 1994.

Figure 10.4

Real Stock Prices

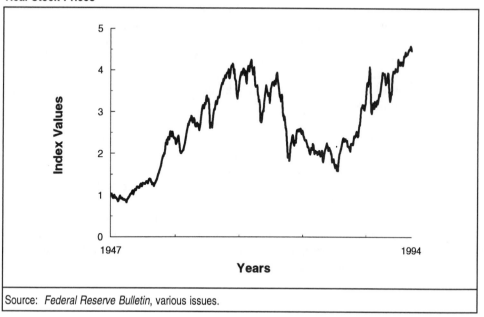

Source: *Federal Reserve Bulletin*, various issues.

offered by Table 10.3 and Figures 10.3 and 10.4.[2] Whether the inflation is anticipated or unanticipated, there seems to be a strong negative impact on stock returns, both nominal and real. It also appears that firms in other countries exhibit poorer stock performance during high–inflation periods.

In general, inflation is one of the stock investor's worst enemies. Even when high inflation is anticipated, real stock returns tend to be lower. The situation is worse, however, when the inflation is not anticipated, because real stock returns are typically negative during such periods.

The Federal Debt

One of the great social and political issues for the present and the near future is the growing federal debt. Fears have arisen that the debt is so huge that it will create an insuperable burden for subsequent generations. Politicians have been accused of "mortgaging the future" to avoid implementing unpleasant policies such as increasing taxes or reducing federal spending.

---

[2]See for example, Robert H. DeFina, "Does Inflation Depress the Stock Market," *Business Review*, Federal Reserve Bank of Philadelphia, November/December 1991, pp. 3–12.

For financial markets in general, and for the stock market in particular, it is feared that the burgeoning debt can have very severe consequences. With a permanently large debt, the financing needs of the U.S. Treasury may be so huge that a shortage of capital for private investment will result. Such a shortage would have immediate drastic effects for the bond market, but there would also be adverse effects for the stock market. In particular, an excessively high debt level keeps interest rates high, running the risk of high inflation. High interest rates could result from the excessive demand for funds on the part of the government, for which the government would need to pay a high rate of interest to attract the required volume of funds.

One other possible result of a high level of federal debt would be the decision to finance the debt by creating additional money. Basically, if the government wishes to spend more than its income, it can (1) borrow in the financial markets, or (2) increase the money supply. The likely result of increasing the money supply is to stimulate inflation, with the adverse effect on stock returns that was discussed in the preceding section. In simplest terms, creating too much additional money relative to the amount of goods available would probably generate inflation. As a result, the fixed amount of goods would be able to command larger sums of money, and when this happens the price level rises. It is simply a matter of "too much money chasing too few goods."

Figure 10.5

Debt of the Federal Government

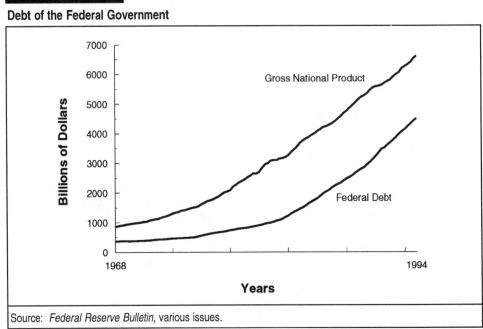

Source: *Federal Reserve Bulletin*, various issues.

Figure 10.6

Federal Debt as a Percentage of Gross National Product

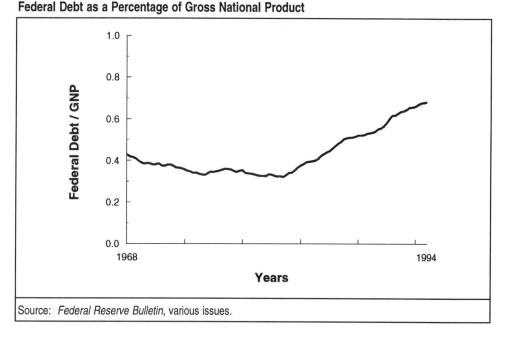

Source: *Federal Reserve Bulletin*, various issues.

Without question, an excessive level of federal debt bodes ill for the financial markets. The problem lies in identifying a situation in which there is too much debt. Figure 10.5 shows that the federal debt has tended to track the Gross National Product since 1968 with some accuracy, at least until recent years.

In the years immediately following World War II, federal debt stood at about 85 percent of GNP. In the ensuing years, that ratio fell as the economy expanded and the government repaid some of the debt undertaken to prosecute the war. By 1968, the ratio had been reduced to about 43 percent. Figure 10.6 shows the relationship between the level of federal debt and GNP by graphing the ratio of federal debt to GNP, starting in 1968. From 1968 onward, the ratio of federal debt to GNP continued to decline, hitting a low of about 33 percent in 1981. During the 1980s, federal debt grew much faster than the economy as a whole. By 1994, the federal debt had reached about 70 percent of GNP.

Whether this is dangerous or not is difficult to say. If the increase is merely temporary and a response to special factors, it may not be too ominous. On the other hand, if the present surge in the federal debt is only the first step in an uncontrollable increase, it may cause grave difficulties. One of the factors that makes the level of debt so difficult to control is the obligation of the federal government to make gigantic payments under various entitlement programs, such as Social Security. As the average age of Americans rises, the entitlement programs are likely to become increasingly burdensome. The course of the federal debt, and its effect on stock returns, depends on the way in which the competing claims of the beneficiaries of entitlement programs and the need for controlled federal spending are resolved.

In summary, how the deficit is handled will have a profound effect on the stock market. Uncontrolled increases in deficits, or the general expectation of such deficits, is bound to adversely affect the stock market. By contrast, implementing effective policies to reduce the deficit should have a beneficial effect on the market. For the stock investor, anticipating these decisions correctly could be very important.

Monetary Policy

In setting monetary policy, the Federal Reserve Board determines the rate at which the money supply will grow. If the money supply grows too quickly, there will be too much money relative to the amount of goods available and inflation will likely result. On the other hand, if the money supply grows too slowly, there will not be sufficient funds to support a robust economy. The goal of the Federal Reserve Board is to ensure that the money supply grows at the "right" speed. However, it is difficult to know what the right rate of growth is in every circumstance, and the policy instruments available to the Federal Reserve Board allow only partial control over the money supply anyway.

Without question, the growth of the money supply is related to general economic activity, including the stock market. To understand why there should be a relationship between monetary policy and the financial markets, we examine the transmission mechanism by which monetary policy is implemented. The most useful tool at the disposal of the Federal Reserve Board for the conduct of monetary policy is the open market operation. In an **open market operation**, the Federal Reserve Board increases the money supply by buying government securities or decreases the money supply by selling government securities.

When the Federal Reserve Board buys securities in the open market, new money enters the financial marketplace. This increase in the total pool of money eventually filters into every corner of the financial markets and the rest of the economy. The essential result of the increase in the supply of money is to drive up the prices of securities and other goods. Consequently, an increase in the supply of money generally should be expected to cause an increase in asset prices, including stock prices. By the same token, the Federal Reserve Board can decrease the money supply by selling federal securities. This withdraws money from the general economy, thereby reducing the price level of assets, including stocks.

There are, however, at least two important complications in this account. First, if an increase in the money supply is to have a beneficial effect on stock prices, the market must not regard the increase in the money supply as excessive or inappropriately large. Large increases in the money supply tend to be associated with higher inflation rates. If the market believes that the increase in the money supply will lead to higher inflation rates, stock prices may fall in response to inflationary fears.

Second, it is not even certain that monetary policy affects stock prices. If the stock market correctly anticipates a future change in monetary policy, the market may react in advance of the actual change in policy. This makes it necessary to distinguish between anticipated and unanticipated changes in the money supply. If the change in policy is correctly anticipated, implementing the policy is unlikely to have any effect. By contrast, if a policy change is unanticipated, a definite effect is likely.

According to **rational expectations theory**, market participants form expectations of future Federal Reserve Board actions that are rational in the sense that they reflect all available information. While the expectations regarding Fed actions may be wrong from time to time, they are unbiased. (An estimate is *unbiased* if it has an equal chance of being over or under the actual figure.) In this environment, Federal Reserve Board actions may have little or no effect because they are too well anticipated. If the market anticipates a certain Fed action, prices in the market will already adjust to reflect that forthcoming action. Under this theory, the Fed can only have an effect by "fooling" the market—the Fed action must be unanticipated to affect the economy.

There have been many research studies exploring the linkages between monetary policy and the prices of financial assets, including stocks. Early studies found that stock prices rose when the money supply expanded and that sudden contractions in the money supply were followed by stock price declines. However, more recent studies have emphasized the importance of the distinction between anticipated and unanticipated changes in the money supply. They generally find that stock prices move before changes in the money supply when the changes are anticipated.

The implications of these recent studies are very important. While admitting that unanticipated changes in the money supply affect stock prices, economists claim that stock prices already reflect anticipated changes in the money supply before the changes actually come about. For the investor, this implies that it is difficult to use changes in the money supply as signals for a successful trading strategy. An anticipated change in the money supply will have no effect on stock prices. While an unanticipated change in the money supply can affect stock prices, the investor's problem is being able to identify unanticipated changes in the money supply before the rest of the market. While there is a link between money supply changes and stock price movements, the investor must have a superior insight into the changes in monetary policy if following the money supply is to help generate stock market profits.

Fiscal Policy

The federal government establishes fiscal policy by setting tax and spending levels. Both policy actions have potentially profound effects on financial markets in general and on the stock market in particular. Through taxation, the federal government withdraws money from the economy as a whole. Large tax increases can have a depressing influence on stock prices, because money must go to pay taxes rather than to investment in the stock market. Also, high tax rates reduce the rewards for working. So the higher the tax rate, the less incentive people have to produce as much as they can. For this reason, tax cuts are generally believed to stimulate the economy.

In addition to collecting taxes, the federal government also spends. The goods and services acquired by federal expenditures increase the overall demand for these items and stimulate the economy. The public works projects sponsored by the federal government during the Great Depression are thought by many to have been an important stimulus to economic growth. Similarly, in 1991, the closing of many military bases reduced government spending in specific locations with profound effects on local economies.

Fiscal policy works in tandem with monetary policy in the overall management of the economy. Together, both policies can have great effects on interest rates, inflation, the federal deficit, and the stock market.[3] The actions of the federal government in the arenas of fiscal and monetary policy are among the major determinants of stock market movements. This fact justifies the investor's interest in the actions of the federal government. To turn a study of monetary and fiscal policy into usable strategic information for investing in the stock market, a successful investor needs earlier or better information than that possessed by other investors. If one has only the same information as other investors, prices will already reflect that common pool of information. By contrast, the investor with consistently good forecasts of future events that are made before other investors make similar forecasts could use that information to earn fantastic stock market profits. This explains the enormous amount of energy that has been applied to forecasting. With that in mind, we now turn to an examination of some basic economic forecasting techniques and an appraisal of their success.

Leading Indicators and the Business Cycle

Much attention in the economic community is directed toward trying to predict major economic swings. For example, most major banks have an economics department, which has as one of its main purposes the preparation of predictions regarding interest rates and other key economic variables. At the highest level of generality in the economy are business cycles. These cycles of economic growth and recession affect virtually all phases of the economy—employment, industrial production, corporate profitability, consumption, and GNP.

The business cycle is somewhat regular in its performance, which raises the possibility that the cycles can be predicted. Based on studies of many business cycles, the U.S. Department of Commerce has constructed several indexes of the business cycle. While there are hundreds of economic variables related to the

---

[3]There is still a surprising amount of disagreement on whether deficits really affect interest rates and other macroeconomic variables. See Charles E. Webster, Jr., "The Effects of Deficits on Interest Rates," *Economic Review*, Federal Reserve Bank of Kansas City, May 1983, pp. 19–28.

business cycle, some have proven more useful for forecasting than others, and these have been used to form composite indexes of economic performance. Three composite indexes are followed most closely: (1) the index of leading economic indicators, (2) the index of roughly coincident indicators, and (3) the index of lagging indicators.

As their names imply, one index leads movements in the economy as a whole, as measured by GNP. This means that the index of leading indicators tends to rise before increases in GNP and to fall before decreases in GNP. The roughly coincident indicators tend to reach their peaks and troughs at about the same time as GNP itself, and the lagging indicators reach their peaks and troughs after GNP does. Table 10.4 presents the components of the three indicator groups. Each month, *Business Conditions Digest*, published by the U.S. Commerce Department, reports the movement of the composite indexes and their various components.

Figure 10.7 presents the three composite indexes in graphical form for 1988–1994. The vertical lines in the graph indicate the recession that lasted from

Table 10.4

Closely Followed Economic Indicators

Components of the Index of 12 Leading Indicators

1. Average work week of production workers in manufacturing
2. Average weekly initial claims for state unemployment insurance
3. Index of new orders for consumer goods
4. Vendor performance, percentage of companies receiving slower deliveries
5. Index of new business formations
6. Index of contracts and orders for plant and equipment
7. Index of new building permits
8. Net change in inventory
9. Change in sensitive materials prices
10. Stock price index of 500 stocks
11. Money supply
12. Change in credit outstanding—business and consumer borrowing

Components of the Index of 4 Roughly Coincident Indicators

1. Number of nonagricultural employees
2. Index of industrial production
3. Index of personal income
4. Index of manufacturing and trade sales

Components of the Index of 6 Lagging Indicators

1. Average duration of employment
2. Manufacturing and trade inventories
3. Labor cost per unit of output in manufacturing
4. Commercial and industrial loans outstanding
5. Ratio of consumer installment debt to personal income
6. Average prime rate charged by banks

Figure 10.7

Composite Indexes of the Business Cycle

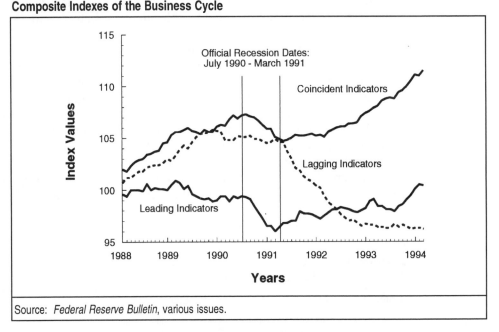

Source: *Federal Reserve Bulletin*, various issues.

July 1990 through March 1991. The index of leading indicators is the lowest line in the graph. Notice that this index had fallen in the year before the official start of the recession in July 1990, and it was stable by the time the recession began, although it fell during the recession. By contrast, the index of lagging indicators fell steeply after the recession was officially over. The index of coincident indicators fell during the recession and turned upward promptly upon the end of the recession in March 1991.

Historically, over many recessions and economic peaks, the composite index of leading indicators has shown a lead time in the range of three to 23 months for economic peaks and a lead time of one to eight months for economic troughs. By contrast, the composite index of lagging indicators generally reaches its peak after GNP reaches its high, with the lag time ranging between two and 13 months. For troughs in GNP, the composite index of lagging indicators reached its trough later, following GNP by four to 15 months.

For the stock market investor, the main interest of the indicator series is in finding some indicator that leads the stock market itself. For example, if we could find a reliable leading indicator of the stock market, it could be used to signal investment prior to market peaks. Not surprisingly, however, the stock market itself acts as a leading indicator. Also, changes in the money supply are leading indicators of GNP. This relationship between the level of stock prices and industrial production was presented in Figure 10.2, which showed their close relationship and the fact that the stock market led industrial production. In Figure 10.2, for example, the stock market bottomed out in October 1990, but industrial production increased through September 1990 and then began to fall.

But if other leading indicators led the stock market, it might still provide the stock market investor with valuable information. Table 10.5 presents a summary of the performance of the leading indicators. At first glance, it appears that there is real hope in being able to predict stock market peaks and troughs. The stock market led GNP by approximately nine months for peaks, but other leading indicators led GNP by even greater periods. For example, the net change in the index of prices for crude materials led peak GNP by 15 months and the money supply led peak GNP by 10 months. These indicators, and several others, led the stock market as well. In a sense, these leading indicators might be useful as leading indicators of the stock market, giving rise to an investment rule. One potential rule might be: Invest at the peak of the net change in sensitive prices. Sell six months later. If the sensitive prices were leading the peak stock market period by six months, this would capture the run up in stock prices and would have the investor selling out of the stock market at the peak.

A closer examination of Table 10.5 erodes most of this optimism, however. There are four reasons for caution in using this approach. First, the lead times before peaks are median lead times, so one would not know how much one variable leads another in a particular economic cycle. For one cycle, the net changes in sensitive prices might lead the stock market by six months, the next time by three or nine months. Because of this variability, the indicator approach cannot be expected to be a very accurate timing guide. Second, it is very difficult or impossible to know when an economic variable reaches its peak at the time of its peak. One can identify peaks only in retrospect, after the variable has turned down. For example, in Figure 10.7, has the index of leading economic indicators reached its peak for the last period shown? It is not clear, and one can be sure only later. Because of this, it will be very difficult to derive timely buy or sell signals from the indicators. Third, the leading indicators occasionally give false signals or fail to signal.[4] With false signals, the investor could be buying and selling at just the wrong times. Table 10.6 presents the results of a study of the frequency of true and false turns made by the index of leading economic indicators. Overall, there were more false turns than true turns. The results of Table 10.6 highlight the difficulty of identifying turns in the leading indicators, since the number of false signals was much higher when the leading indicators had gone up or down for just one month. Finally, as Table 10.5 shows, the stock market itself has the greatest overall score as a leading indicator. Attempts to use other leading indicators to guide stock market investment would be using a less reliable indicator to predict a more reliable indicator. For these reasons, it is unlikely that the indicator approach can yield predictions that will be successful in stock market investing. The leading

---

[4]See Clyde Farnsworth, *Monthly Review*, Federal Reserve Bank of Richmond, August 1971.

Table 10.5

Performance of the Leading Indicators

| Number and Title of Series | Median Leads (–) or Lags (+) (in months) | | | Scores | | | | | | |
	Peaks	Troughs	All Turns	Economic Significance	Statistical Adequacy	Timing	Conformity	Smoothness	Currency	Total
12 Components of New Index										
Average Workweek, Manufacturing	–12	–2	–5	70	80	81	60	60	80	73
Layoff Rate, Mfg. (Inverted)	–11	–1	–6.5	70	80	79	80	60	80	76
New Orders, Consumer Goods and Materials 1967 dollars	–6	–1	–4.5	80	75	76	70	60	80	74
Vendor Performance	–6	–5	–6	70	75	79	46	60	80	69
Net Bus. Formation	–11	–2	–3	80	61	78	59	80	80	73
Contracts and Orders, Plant and Equipment, 1967 dollars	–9	–2	–5.5	90	50	87	72	40	80	72
New Building Permits, Private Housing Units	–13	–8	–9.5	90	70	80	55	80	80	76
Change in Stocks on Hand and on Order, 1967 dollars	–5	–4	–4.5	90	53	83	60	80	40	71
Stock Price Index, 500 Common Stocks	–9	–4	–5.5	80	85	89	51	80	100	80
Pct. Change, Price Index for Crude Materials	–15	–5	–5.5	70	80	82	60	60	66	72
Money Supply, 1967 dol. (M1/CPI)	–10	–8	–9	90	85	80	41	100	80	79
Pct. Change, Liquid Assets	–6.5	–6	–6	90	81	84	41	80	66	75

Source: Victor Zarnowitz and Charlotte Boschan, "Cyclical Indicators: An Evaluation and New Leading Index," *Business Conditions Digest*, May 1975, pp. V–XXII.

Table 10.6

False Turns by the Leading Indicators

Criterion	Peaks			Troughs		
Number of Months Up or Down	Average Lead	Number of True Turns	Number of False Turns	Average Lead	Number of True Turns	Number of False Turns
1	1.6	5	24	4.0	5	9
2	0.6	5	15	3.0	5	3
3	−0.4	5	9	2.0	5	2
4	−1.4	5	5	1.0	5	1
5 or more	−2.4	5	3	0.0	5	0

A negative number for "average lead" means that the index is "predicting" turning points which have already happened.

Source: Gary Gorton, "Forecasting with the Index of Leading Indicators," *Business Review*, Federal Reserve Bank of Philadelphia, November–December 1982, p. 20. The table was adapted by Gorton from a study by H. O. Stekler and Martin Schepsman, "Forecasting with an Index of Leading Series," *Journal of the American Statistical Association*, June 1973, pp. 291–296.

indicators do, nonetheless, give useful information about future GNP.[5] However, there is little reason to hope that this information could be used to guide an investment strategy.

Professional Forecasting Techniques

Because of its importance, economic forecasting of all types of variables excites tremendous interest. This section discusses the various types of forecasts that are made and examines some recent results for predictions of important economy–wide variables, such as GNP, interest rates, inflation, and broad stock market movements. It is possible to classify the forecasts of economic variables into four basic groups that hold whether the variables being forecasted are broad economy–wide variables or the prices of individual stocks. The groups include:

[5] Some scholars believe that the index of leading indicators is not at all useful in predicting recessions and expansions. See, for example, Evan F. Koenig and Kenneth M. Emery, "Misleading Indicators? Using the Composite Leading Indicators to Predict Cyclical Turning Points," Federal Reserve Bank of Dallas *Economic Review*, July 1991, pp. 1–14.

1. time series models
2. econometric models
3. judgmental forecasts
4. technical forecasts

In discussing these, keep in mind that an individual forecast might be based on a combination of these methods.

Time Series Models

The last decade witnessed the growing popularity of **time series models** as a forecasting tool in economics, stemming from the work of Box and Jenkins.[6] A time series model is a statistical model that relates the current value of a variable to some function of the history of that same variable. For example, a time series of GNP might express the current value of GNP as depending upon the average values of GNP over some past period relative to the current value. One such model might state that the current value of GNP equals the average of GNP over the immediately preceding four periods, plus some other components. These models can become quite complex in their statistical structure, but they are all similar in that they use only the past history of the variable itself to make a prediction, and they use statistical rules to formulate the exact prediction. Since they use no other information except the history of the variable in question, they are often regarded as quite simple models. Nonetheless, there are numerous instances of surprising success with time series models.

Recently there have been a number of important innovations in time series models that promise better forecasting results. A new battery of techniques known as **ARCH models** (for autoregressive conditional heteroscedasticity) may allow for better forecasts of an economic variable based on past values of the same variable. For example, in forecasting GNP, an ARCH model would consider how one observation in the series is linked to past observations (the autoregressive part), and it would also take into account changes in the volatility of the series (the conditional heteroscedastic part).

Another increasingly popular concept is the idea of **cointegration**, a statistical relationship that arises when changes in two variables can be combined to create a statistically stable third variable. If we consider two economic variables observed over the same time periods, we may find that their behavior is linked. If changes in the values of one variable are statistically linked with changes in the value of the other variable, we can define a relationship between changes in the two variables that results in a composite variable that is stable; then the two original variables are said to be cointegrated. The practical point of this statistical concept is that two variables that are cointegrated cannot wander too far apart. While the mathematics

---

[6]G. E. P. Box and G. M. Jenkins, *Time Series Analysis*, San Francisco: Holden–Day, 1976.

of ARCH models and cointegration are complex, they do hold substantial promise for improving forecasting results in time series models.[7]

Econometric Models

Econometric models are also statistically based models, but they are much more complicated in theory and design than a time series model. A time series model usually emerges from experimentation with the data. In some sense, a time series model "allows the data to speak." By contrast, the designer of an econometric model builds into the model the economic relationships that he or she believes to hold. This is done by expressing these relationships in mathematical equations. The simplest kind of econometric model would be a single equation, expressing some dependent variable as a function of some other set of variables. For example, GNP might be expressed as a function of past GNP, the level of interest rates, changes in the unemployment rate, and home–building activity. There are econometric models that attempt to capture the complexity of the entire economy, and these models may contain hundreds of equations that must all be estimated simultaneously.

Judgmental Forecasts

Traditionally, judgmental forecasts have played a dominant role in economic forecasting. A judgmental forecast emerges from the reflection of a group of people or a single individual. The fact that it is judgmental means that it is essentially nonmathematical. The forecaster studies the current features of the economy that seem most important and might use mathematical techniques in the analysis. The ultimate judgmental forecast relies on the judgment of the forecaster, who takes all of the information into account and expresses a judgment about its meaning for the variable being predicted. For example, an economist might keep informed about recent trends in the stock market, the money supply, and other economic indicators and, weighing all of these factors, conclude that GNP will rise over the next year by 5.5 percent.

Often the judgmental forecast is superimposed upon some mechanical, or entirely non–judgmental, forecast. For example, a firm might begin with the forecasts from an econometric model and obtain forecasts of key variables from the statistical analysis. Forecasters may then use judgment to alter the statistical forecast in the hopes of improved accuracy. Some recent research finds that adjusting mechanical forecasts improves forecast results, but that the forecasters often

---

[7]For an introduction to cointegration, see D. A. Dickey, D. W. Janse, and D. L. Thornton, "A Primer on Cointegration with an Application to Money and Income," Federal Reserve Bank of St. Louis *Review*, 73:2, March/April 1991, pp. 58–78.

over–adjust the mechanical forecast. The result is still an improved forecast, but one that would have been even better if it had not been adjusted too much.[8]

Technical Forecasts

Technical analysis uses previous values of economic variables to forecast future values. In some respects, this type of analysis is similar to the time series models described earlier, although technical analysis has not used statistical techniques traditionally. The technical analyst attempting to predict future stock market movements, for example, would look at the historical performance of key variables in an attempt to identify recurring patterns. These patterns have been interpreted quite literally by some analysts, who believe in charting price movements on graph paper or with special charting software on computers. Recognizable patterns on the charts are believed to signal certain future movements in the variable being predicted. For example, when the chart of stock prices forms a pattern that looks like a head and shoulders, some technical analysts would interpret this as a signal of a major price reversal. In many respects, technical analysis is similar to time series analysis. In fact, technical analysis has begun to adopt the methods of time series analysis.

As a more concrete example of the kinds of information that technical analysts watch, consider a moving average. A **moving average** is the average of some variable over a certain period. Each period, the average is updated by dropping the oldest value from consideration and including the newest observation. For example, in a 30–month moving average, the last 30 months of data are used to form the average. Next month, the oldest month of data is dropped, and the new month replaces it to keep 30 months of data included in the average. Technical analysts might compare the moving average of the S&P 500 to the current level of the S&P 500 itself.

Figure 10.8 shows the current month's value and the 30–month moving average of the S&P 500 from 1981 to early 1994. As the graph shows, the moving average tends to be much more stable than the month–to–month value of the index itself. According to some technical analysts, a buy signal arises based on the relationship between the index and its moving average. For example, in September 1982, the S&P 500 index exceeded its moving average at about the 120.00 level. If an investor bought upon this signal, she could have enjoyed the long bull market that ended in 1987. The S&P 500 index remained above its moving average until October 1987, reflecting the Crash. Note, however, that the investor who sold in October 1987 would have missed some of the gains that followed in the 1987–1994 period.

As another example of technical analysis, some market observers believe that the P–E ratio and the dividend yield also provide useful buy and sell indicators. A P–E ratio that is too high indicates that the investor should sell, while a low P–E

---

[8]See S. K. McNees, "Man vs. Model? The Role of Judgment in Forecasting," Federal Reserve Bank of Boston *New England Economic Review*, July/August 1990, pp. 41–52.

Figure 10.8

The S&P 500 Index and Its 30–Month Moving Average

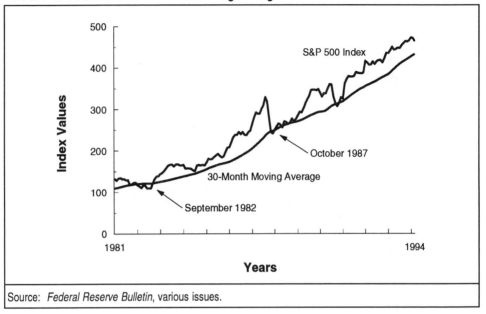

Source: *Federal Reserve Bulletin*, various issues.

indicates a buying opportunity. A high P–E ratio is a sell signal because it indicates that prices are unsustainably high relative to the earnings that the firms are generating. Similarly, if the dividend–price ratio is too high, then stock prices are too low. The problem with both methods, of course, is finding some useful definition of "too high" and "too low." Figure 10.9 shows the P–E and dividend–price ratios for the market as a whole from 1954–1994. Over this period, it does appear that a P–E ratio above 20 has not been sustainable. Notice also that the dividend–price ratio and the P–E ratio tend to reflect each other; high P–E ratios occur at the same time as low dividend–price ratios. This relationship essentially follows from the definitions of the two ratios.

As a final example of a technical indicator, we consider the activity of corporate insiders. Since the insiders presumably know more than the rest of us about their stocks, technical analysts believe it is a good idea to buy when the insiders buy. Some technical analysts believe that when more than 35 percent of insider transactions are purchases, it indicates a bull market. In Chapter 16, we consider the performance of technical analysis and cast a critical eye on the validity of these technical methods.

Figure 10.9

The Market's P–E and Dividend–Price Ratios

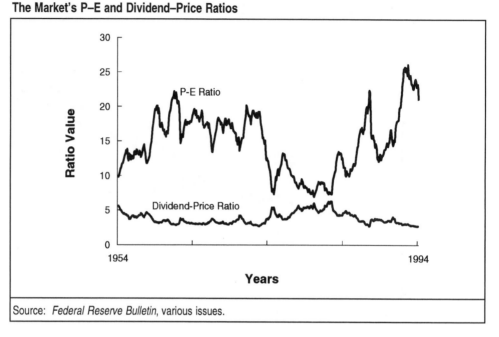

Source: *Federal Reserve Bulletin*, various issues.

Some Recent Forecasting Results

To the new student of financial markets and economic forecasting, it may seem scandalous that predictions of economic variables are often so poor. (Actually, there is good reason why predictions should be very difficult, as we will see in Chapter 16.) The purpose of this section is to introduce the reader to some recent forecasting results. Although particular forecasts are mentioned which are not very successful, they have no special claim on inaccuracy. Instead, inaccuracy is extremely typical, just as the results discussed in this section may be regarded as fairly typical of past forecasts and provide a reasonable guide as to the accuracy one may expect in future forecasts.

Time Series Models vs. Econometric Models

Since time series models use such a limited information set, forecasts of economic variables arrived at using time series techniques can be used as a minimal standard. Other more complex and expensive models should be able to beat that standard if they are worth the effort. A single individual, for example, could create a time series model forecast of GNP in one or two days. By contrast, a full–scale

Table 10.7

━━━━━━━━━━━━━━━━━

Forecast Errors for GNP Growth

	Forecast Errors					
Horizon	Benchmark	Chase	Conference Board	DRI	Kent	Michigan
One Quarter	4.3	3.9	3.1	3.6	4.3	3.5
Two Quarters	4.2	5.0	4.6	4.0	4.5	4.5
Three Quarters	4.3	5.7	4.9	4.7	4.9	4.8
Four Quarters	4.6	5.7	6.0	5.3	4.9	4.9
Average	4.35	5.08	4.65	4.4	4.65	4.43

Errors reported are mean absolute errors for the GNP growth rate, in percent, at an annual rate. Forecasts covered the second quarter 1976 through fourth quarter 1982.

Source: Charles R. Nelson, "A Benchmark for the Accuracy of Econometric Forecasts of GNP," *Business Economics*, April 1984, pp. 52–58.

econometric model might take many personyears of effort to construct. To justify that additional effort and expense, the large econometric model should be able to out–perform the time series model.

With this idea in mind, Charles R. Nelson set out to construct a time series forecast of GNP growth and to test a variety of very large econometric model forecasts against the benchmark forecast provided by the time series model. The benchmark forecast was tested against the forecasts of five econometric models: those of Data Resources, Inc., Chase Econometric Associates, Inc., The Conference Board, Michigan Research Seminar in Quantitative Economics, and Kent Economic Institute.[9]

Table 10.7 presents a portion of Nelson's results. Forecasts of GNP were made for one, two, three, and four quarters ahead. Compared with all of the econometric models, the benchmark forecast had smaller errors overall than did any other model. When the forecast horizon was only one quarter ahead, the econometric models outperformed the time series benchmark forecast. For all other forecast horizons, the benchmark forecast was superior, on average. In fact, not a single econometric model beat the benchmark for forecasts three or four quarters into the future, and only one of the five econometric forecasts outperformed the benchmark for forecasts two quarters into the future.

As Nelson concludes, because time series models are "cheap and uncompli-cated, these results would suggest that the value of econometric modeling for

―――――――――――

[9]For full details of the test, see Charles R. Nelson, "A Benchmark for the Accuracy of Econometric Forecasts of GNP," *Business Economics*, April 1984, pp. 52–58.

forecasting needs to be re–evaluated."[10] In fact, difficulties with these econometric models are well known and have been the subject of considerable debate in economics.[11]

Judgmental Forecasts vs. Econometric Models

Each year, *Business Week* surveys a group of economists for forecasts of key economic variables such as GNP growth, interest rates, and the unemployment rate. Thomas Fomby collected these forecasts for the years 1972–1981 and compared them to forecasts for econometric models.[12]

Table 10.8 presents the critical results from Fomby's study for forecasts of inflation, real GNP growth, and the unemployment rate. In the table, the forecasts are ordered in terms of increasing complexity. The first is the most naive and cheapest to produce, the **no–change forecast**. In other words, this forecast says that the unemployment rate, for example, will be the same next year as it is now. As a forecast, it is not very sophisticated, but for cheapness it cannot be beat. More complex forecasting techniques must be able to beat the no–change forecast to earn their keep. The next forecast is the **time series forecast**, which performs a little

Table 10.8

Relative Accuracy of Judgmental and Econometric Forecasts

	Inflation	Real GNP Growth	Unemployment
No–Change Forecast	2.325	3.138	.925
Time Series Model	2.378	2.522	.833
Business Week			
Economists	2.025	1.850	.400
Econometric Models	2.088	1.850	.488

Errors reported are mean absolute forecast errors in percent.

Source: Thomas B. Fomby, "A Comparison of Judgmental and Econometric Forecasts of the Economy: The Business Week Survey," *Economic Review*, Federal Reserve Bank of Dallas, September 1982, p. 7.

---

[10]Charles R. Nelson, "A Benchmark for the Accuracy of Econometric Forecasts of GNP," *Business Economics*, April 1984, p. 58.

[11]See "Where the Big Econometric Models Go Wrong," *Business Week*, March 30, 1981. For a readable review of academic thinking on the issue, see Richard W. Lang, "Using Econometric Models to Make Economic Policy: A Continuing Controversy," *Business Review*, Federal Reserve Bank of Philadelphia, January/February 1983, pp. 3–13.

[12]Thomas B. Fomby, "A Comparison of Judgmental and Econometric Forecasts of the Economy: The Business Week Survey," *Economic Review*, Federal Reserve Bank of Dallas, September 1982, pp. 1–10.

better than the no–change forecast. Next is the **consensus forecast** of the economists polled by *Business Week*. The consensus forecasts were obtained by averaging the forecasts of the individuals taking part in the study. Their performance, when taken as a whole, shows a marked improvement over the time series model. Finally, the errors of the econometric models, taken as a whole, are presented as well. They perform worse for all predictions than those drawn from the panel of economists. Even when the individual econometric models are compared with the consensus of the economists, the models typically performed worse.

Comparing these average, or consensus, forecasts obscures the tremendous variation in the size of errors from one forecaster to another. *Institutional Investor* surveyed a number of economists for their interest rate predictions. The magazine reported the results of interest rate predictions by 50 economists. These economists predicted commercial paper, prime, Treasury note, and Treasury bond interest rates for six months into the future. Among the 200 individual forecasts, the errors ranged from 0 to 2.97 percent, and the average error across predictions for the four rates ranged from .3125 percent to 2.8375 percent.[13] These results show the tremendous range of results that one can expect from a group of forecasters. Unfortunately, there seems to be little consistency from one period to the next. The best forecaster in one period is quite likely to be among the worst in the next period. Not surprisingly, there are some exceptions to this general rule, and some individual forecasters have records worthy of envy.

Summary

This chapter examined one major class of influences on stock prices—general economic factors. Movements in economic variables affect the market's beliefs about future dividend flows and the discount rate that should be applied to those flows in the dividend valuation model. These major factors include interest rates, inflation, the level of the federal debt, monetary policy, and fiscal policy. Unfavorable movements in any of these variables will cause a reassessment of a firm's abilities to pay dividends in the future or will raise the discount rate applied to those dividends.

Because economic variables influence stock prices, much effort is given to predicting movements in these variables. The techniques that are commonly employed are the time series models, econometric models, judgmental forecasts, and technical forecasts. On the whole, however, it is difficult to be optimistic about the usefulness of forecasting techniques. Some economists even believe that the enterprise is doomed to fail. The difficulties in predicting macroeconomic variables illustrated in this chapter also plague attempts to predict microeconomic variables, such as the movement of individual stock prices. In spite of the difficulties, however, the huge potential rewards continue to attract the efforts of almost all

---

[13] Tina Aridas, "The Economists' Batting Averages," *Institutional Investor*, March 1984, pp. 243–247.

major investment houses to predict the future of economic variables that are related to stock prices.

In addition to the macroeconomic variables that have been discussed in this chapter, there are two other classes of variables that have a large impact on stock prices. These are industry factors and firm–specific factors, which are the subject of the next two chapters. Industry–wide influences affect the market's expectation about future dividend streams and discount rates for firms in a specific industry. As we will see in the next chapter, these industry–wide influences include demographic changes and changing tastes and life–styles, and these changes can have dramatic effects on all of the firms operating in a given industry.

Questions and Problems

1. Why should stock prices, in general, tend to move together?
2. Evaluate the following claim: "As anyone knows, a rise in interest rates causes bond prices to fall. This has the effect of driving money out of bond investment, and some of that money naturally goes into the stock market. This causes stock prices to rise. As a consequence, increasing interest rates are good for stock investing."
3. Why is a higher level of anticipated inflation generally bad for stock prices? Why should this be, considering that share ownership constitutes ownership in the real productive assets of corporations?
4. If returns on all real investment were certain, what should be the relationship between the real and nominal rates of interest?
5. Explain the difference between anticipated and unanticipated inflation.
6. How could an increase in the money supply cause a higher rate of inflation?
7. Explain how a cut in taxes might help the stock market.
8. Can leading indicators predict changes in GNP? Can leading indicators be used to predict stock prices?
9. What are the four major classes of forecasting techniques?
10. Compared to most forecasting services, the Super Bowl predictor seems to work quite well. Would it be reasonable to base investment on this forecasting tool? Why or why not?
11. One of the leading indicators is the "index of new business formations." Explain why this index should be a leading indicator.
12. According to most studies, stock returns in foreign countries are positively correlated with U.S. stock returns. Why should this be expected?

CFA Questions

All CFA examination questions are reprinted, with permission, from the Level I *1992–1994, CFA Candidate Study and Examination Program Review*. Copyright 1992–1994, Association for Investment Management and Research, Charlottesville, Va. All rights reserved.

A. Assume that between 1974 and 1991, the nominal GNP of an economy increased from $1 trillion to $5 trillion and that the appropriate index of prices increased from 100 to 250. Which *one* of the following expresses GNP for 1991 in terms of 1974 process?
  a. $1.5 trillion
  b. $2.0 trillion
  c. $2.5 trillion
  d. $5.0 trillion

B. What impact do budget deficits have on the inflation rate?
  a. Budget deficits will stimulate aggregate demand and lead to an acceleration in the inflation rate.
  b. Empirical evidence indicates the inflation rate is directly related to the size of the budget deficit as a share of GNP.
  c. Empirical evidence indicates the inflation rate is inversely related to the size of the budget deficit as a share of GNP.
  d. Empirical evidence does not show any significant relationship between budget deficits and the inflation rate.

Suggested REALDATA Exercises

The following *REALDATA* exercises explore the concepts developed in this chapter: Exercises 1, 2, 3, 7, 8, 9, 14, 15, 16, 17, 18, 19, 73, 74.

Suggested Readings

Aiyagari, S., "Deflating the Case for Zero Inflation," Federal Reserve Bank of Minneapolis *Quarterly Review*, 14:3, Summer 1990, pp. 2–11.

Belongia, M. T. and J. A. Chalfant, "Alternative Measures of Money as Indicators of Inflation: A Survey and Some New Evidence," Federal Reserve Bank of St. Louis *Review*, 72:6, November/December 1990, pp. 20–33.

Bennett, P., "The Influence of Financial Changes on Interest Rates and Monetary Policy: A Review of Recent Evidence," Federal Reserve Bank of New York *Quarterly Review*, 15:2, Summer 1990, pp. 8–30.

Bernanke, B., "Is There Too Much Corporate Debt?" Federal Reserve Bank of Philadelphia *Business Review*, September/October 1989, pp. 3–13.

Carlson, K. M., "Do Price Indexes Tell Us About Inflation? A Review of the Issues," Federal Reserve Bank of St. Louis *Review*, 71:6, November/December 1989, pp. 12–30.

Dwyer, Jr., G. P. and R. W. Hafer, "Interest Rates and Economic Announcements," Federal Reserve Bank of St. Louis *Review*, 71:2, March/April 1989, pp. 34–46.

Ely, D. P. and K. J. Robinson, "The Stock Market and Inflation: A Synthesis of the Theory and Evidence," Federal Reserve Bank of Dallas *Economic Review*, March 1989, pp. 17–29.

Englander, A. and G. Stone, "Inflation Expectations Surveys as Predictors of Inflation and Behavior in Financial and Labor Markets," Federal Reserve Bank of New York *Quarterly Review*, 14:3, Autumn 1989, pp. 20–32.

Faust, J., "Will Higher Corporate Debt Worsen Future Recessions?" Federal Reserve Bank of Kansas City *Economic Review*, March/April 1990, pp. 19–33.

Garfinkel, M. R., "What Is an "Acceptable" Rate of Inflation?–A Review of the Issues," Federal Reserve Bank of St. Louis *Review*, 71:4, July/August 1989, pp. 3–15.

Garner, C. and R. E. Wurtz, "Is the Business Cycle Disappearing?" Federal Reserve Bank of Kansas City *Economic Review*, May/June 1990, pp. 25–39.

Gittings, T. A., "Capacity Utilization and Inflation," Federal Reserve Bank of Chicago *Economic Perspectives*, 13:3, May/June 1989, pp. 2–9.

Hafer, R. W., "Does Dollar Depreciation Cause Inflation?" Federal Reserve Bank of St. Louis *Review*, 71:4, July/August 1989, pp. 16–28.

Harris, L., "S&P 500 Cash Stock Price Volatilities," *Journal of Finance*, 44:5, December 1989, pp. 1155–1175.

Haslag, J. H., "Monetary Aggregates and the Rate of Inflation," Federal Reserve Bank of Dallas *Economic Review*, March 1990, pp. 1–12.

Keane, M. P. and D. E. Runkle, "Are Economic Forecasts Rational?" Federal Reserve Bank of Minneapolis *Quarterly Review*, 13:2, Spring 1989, pp. 26–33.

Koenig, E. F. and K. M. Emery, "Misleading Indicators? Using the Composite Leading Indicators to Predict Cyclical Turning Points," Federal Reserve Bank of Dallas *Economic Review*, July 1991, pp. 1–14.

Kuttner, K. N., "Inflation and the Growth Rate of Money," Federal Reserve Bank of Chicago *Economic Perspectives*, 14:1, January/February 1990, pp. 2–11.

Loungani, P., M. Rush, and W. Tave, "Stock Market Dispersion and Business Cycles," Federal Reserve Bank of Chicago *Economic Perspectives*, 15:1, January/February 1991, pp. 2–8.

McNees, S. K., "Man vs. Model? The Role of Judgment in Forecasting," Federal Reserve Bank of Boston *New England Economic Review*, July/August 1990, pp. 41–52.

Meyer, S. A., "The U.S. as a Debtor Country: Causes, Prospects, and Policy Implications," Federal Reserve Bank of Philadelphia *Business Review*, November/December 1989, pp. 19–31.

Mills, L., "Can Stock Prices Reliably Predict Recessions?" Federal Reserve Bank of Philadelphia *Business Review*, September/October 1988, pp. 3–14.

Mote, L. R., "Looking Back: The Use of Interest Rates in Monetary Policy," Federal Reserve Bank of Chicago *Economic Perspectives*, 12:1, January/ February 1988, pp. 15–29.

Peek, J. and E. S. Rosengren, "The Stock Market and Economic Activity," Federal Reserve Bank of Boston *New England Economic Review*, May/June 1988, pp. 39–50.

Renshaw, E. and D. Molnar, "Recessions and Recovery: How the Stock Market Behaves," *American Association of Individual Investors*, 13:2, February 1991, pp. 7–9.

Schwert, G. W., "Why Does Stock Market Volatility Change Over Time?" *Journal of Finance*, 44:5, December 1989, pp. 1115–1153.

Smith, B. D., "The Relationship Between Money and Prices: Some Historical Evidence Reconsidered," Federal Reserve Bank of Minneapolis *Quarterly Review*, 12:3, Summer 1988, pp. 18–32.

Strongin, S. and P. S. Binkley, "A Policymakers' Guide to Economic Forecasts," Federal Reserve Bank of Chicago *Economic Perspectives*, 12:3, May/June 1988, pp. 3–10.

Thornton, D. L., "Do Government Deficits Matter?" Federal Reserve Bank of St. Louis *Review*, 72:5, September/October 1990, pp. 25–39.

Walter, J. R., "Monetary Aggregates: A User's Guide," Federal Reserve Bank of Richmond *Economic Review*, 75:1, January/February 1989, pp. 20–28.

Webb, R. H. and R. Willemse, "Macroeconomic Price Indexes," Federal Reserve Bank of Richmond *Economic Review*, 75:4, July/August 1989, pp. 22–32.

CHAPTER ELEVEN

Industry Analysis

Overview

As the analysis of the stock market moves from the most general to the more specific factors affecting security returns, this chapter focuses on industry analysis. In industry analysis, the analyst examines those features of the economic landscape that are particular to a given industry. The same factors that will affect one company in a given industry are likely to have similar effects on other firms in the same industry. One might say that industry analysis focuses on the "family resemblances" among the various firms in a given industry. Doing so provides important economies of analysis, since the entire analysis need not be repeated for each company. Company analysis does the job of interpreting the effect of the industry–wide factors on a particular firm.

These factors are important determinants of the future dividend stream that can be expected from the firms in the industry. Also, since firms in the same industry confront the same risks, common influences on the discount rate tend to affect the dividend stream. From the point of view of the dividend valuation model, these industry–wide factors are similar in importance and scope to the economy–wide factors examined in Chapter 10 and the company–specific factors to be analyzed in Chapter 12.

The study of industry analysis begins with a brief examination of the different performance experienced by various industries. Whether one looks at broad economic measures, such as productivity or output, or at the stock market returns, there are strong differences across industries. If one could merely select the industries that will experience higher than normal stock returns, this ability would be enough to ensure fantastic wealth.

Broad demographic factors and a changing society probably have the greatest impact in determining which industries will succeed. This chapter identifies five different factors that will probably determine which industries grow and which decline in the decades ahead. These factors include the changing age and income distribution of the population, migratory patterns within the United States, and the movement from a production–based to a service–oriented economy.

In addition to these broad social trends, there are certain patterns that characterize the developmental pattern of many industries. The industry life cycle describes that pattern of growth, maturity, and decay followed by many industries. Also, even in an age of deregulation, government regulation is an important factor for many industries, and it has a different effect from industry to industry.

The chapter concludes with a comparison of four very different kinds of industries to illustrate the growth and investment prospects available in the marketplace. These industries are paper, steel (general), toys, and the semiconductor industry. Following these cross–industry comparisons, the chapter analyzes the paper industry in greater detail.

For the investor, understanding these industry–wide factors can be an important input for the estimates of the future dividend streams for individual companies and for the correct discount rate to be applied to those estimated dividends in the dividend valuation model.

Table 11.1

Growth Rates for Selected Industries, 1987–1994

Fastest Growing Industries	Compound Annual Growth Rate
Machine Tools	12.8
Electronic Components and Accessories	11.1
Surgical Appliances	10.0
Mobile Homes	9.4
Automotive Parts and Accessories	7.7
Surgical and Medical Instruments	7.0
Lighting Fixtures	6.6
Mattresses and Bedsprings	6.4
Leather Tanning and Finishing	6.0
Analytical Instruments	6.0
Slowest Growing Industries	**Compound Annual Growth Rate**
Space Vehicle Equipment	–3.9
Phosphate Fertilizers	–4.8
Manifold Business Forms	–5.0
Personal Leather Goods	–5.2
Space Propulsion Units and Parts	–5.3
Ship Building and Repairing	–6.6
Search and Navigation Equipment	–6.6
Aircraft	–11.3
Aircraft Engines and Engine Parts	–20.0
Aircraft Parts and Engines	–24.3

Source: U.S. Department of Commerce, *1994 U.S. Industrial Outlook*, 1994.

Differences in Growth and Investment Performance Across Industries

The U.S. Department of Commerce studied the output and productivity growth rates of different industries for the recent past and presented the results of that study in the *1994 U.S. Industrial Outlook*. Table 11.1 presents a summary of a portion of that study, showing growth rates for the best– and worst–performing manufacturing industries. The ten fastest growing industries are concentrated in areas that reflect domestic demand rather than exports. The rapid growth in mobile homes, for example, was due to replacement housing in the aftermath of Hurricane Andrew. The slowest growing industries were those dealing with defense. For example, the three worst–performing industries were concentrated in the aircraft industry.

Table 11.2

Stock Market Performance by Industry, First Quarter 1994

Best Performing Industries	Stock Returns
Engineering and Construction	20.2
Hospital Management	18.6
Electronic Semiconductors	12.8
Retail Specialty—Apparel	12.5
Computer Systems	10.4
Shoes	10.4
Truckers	9.5
Beverages—Alcoholic	6.4
Retail Food Chains	6.3
Machinery, Diversified	5.7

Worst Performing Industries	Stock Returns
Pharmaceutical Composite	−13.4
Broadcast Media	−13.4
Housewares	−13.7
Electric Companies	−13.8
Building Materials	−14.8
Oil and Gas Drilling	−14.8
Health Care Miscellaneous	−15.5
Health Care Drugs	−15.8
Airlines	−16.1
Homebuilding	−22.0

Source: Standard & Poor's Corporation, *Stock Market Encyclopedia*, Summer 1994.

Just as these economic indicators differ widely, the investment performance can also be highly divergent. Table 11.2 shows industry–wide stock returns for the best and worst industry groups over a recent quarter. Notice the extremely divergent returns from the large percentage increase for the leading industry to the dismal performance of the worst industry. These differences in growth rates and investment returns across industries emphasize the importance of understanding industry–specific factors for the stock market investor. In terms of the dividend valuation model, lack of attention to industry–wide factors can mean lost opportunity in identifying industries whose firms will enjoy larger dividend increases than firms as a whole.

Demographic Factors and Social Change

Large–scale demographic and social changes, in addition to governmental policies, can have sweeping effects on the stock market. The recent dramatic increase of women in the paid work force, the increasing proportion of part–time workers, the fitness movement, the growing number of one person families, the scare over AIDS health care costs, the growing economy of foreign countries such as Japan, and the population shift toward the Sun Belt are all major trends that can affect the economy. This section focuses on four such movements—the aging of the American population, trends toward income extremes, the emergence of a service–oriented economy, and recent migratory patterns.

Aging America

Americans are getting older. This statement may sound too obvious for words, but it is extremely important for the future of the stock market. For some time now, the average age of Americans has been increasing, and it certainly will continue to do so for some time to come. People of different ages have different interests and needs in life, which are reflected in their spending habits. Firms meeting the needs of age groups that are increasing in size can look forward to correspondingly larger sales.

Figure 11.1 shows how the age distribution of the United States will change between 1950 and 2000. In 1950, 19 percent of the population was under the age of nine and only 5 percent was above age 70. In the year 2000, less than 14 percent of the population will be below age 9 and almost 10 percent will be 70 or older. Currently, the median age in America is about 30, but by the year 2000, there will be 1.45 Americans above age 30 for every one 30 or below. Similarly, the proportion of people age 50 or above has been increasing steadily and will continue to do so. Figure 11.2 shows the rising percentage of Americans over age 50. In 1900, there were 13.2 percent, but by the year 2000, 27.6 percent of the population will be 50 years or older.

These changes in the age distribution of the population result from changes in fertility rates and advances in health care, meaning Americans are living longer.

Figure 11.1

Age Distribution of Americans, 1950–2000

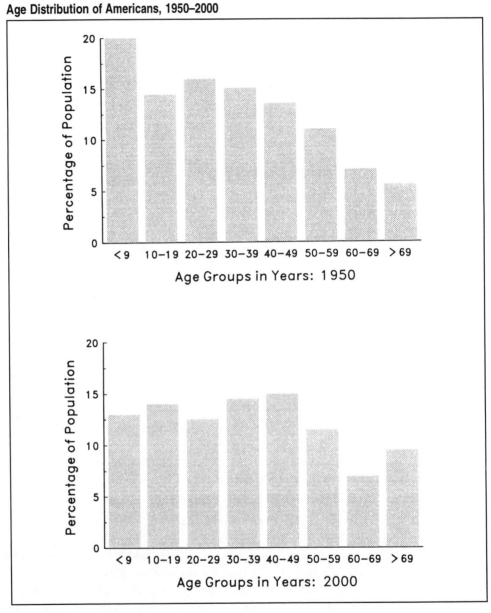

The dramatic change in the age distribution will have profound effects on the economy. In broadest terms, more Americans are in the age of home ownership, so there is a surge in the home–building industry. Likewise, there should be a boom for those industries catering to the older segment of the population, a segment that

Figure 11.2

Percentage of U.S. Population Age 50 or Older

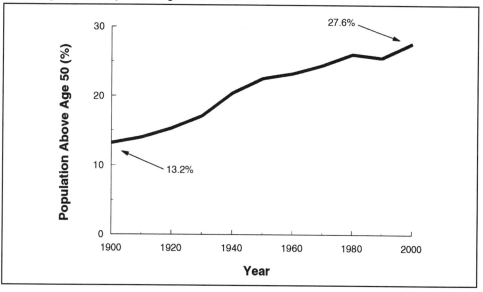

tends to have more disposable income than their younger counterparts. Clearly, the health care industry can expect to grow, while at the same time, youth–oriented industries can expect to suffer. The investor in the stock market needs to be aware of this kind of trend. For example, one might wonder whether now is the best time for long–term investment in the toy or the video game industries.

Changing Income Distribution

At the same time the age distribution is changing, the income distribution of Americans will be changing. The two movements are related. Figure 11.3 shows some of the changes that occurred during the 1980s. Considering all U.S. families and measuring income in constant 1988 dollars, average income rose by 8.3 percent over the decade. However, the distribution varied greatly by income group. Figure 11.3 classifies families into five groups based on income. As the figure shows, the poorest quintile actually had a reduction in family income, with family income falling 5.4 percent over the decade. By contrast, the richest quintile had the largest increase, 14.7 percent over the decade. Thus, the rich got richer and the poor got poorer.

These statistics do not reflect the fortunes of particular families. The analysis considers quintiles formed at the beginning and end of the 1980s and compares their incomes. This does not mean that the same families are in the same quintiles at the two measuring points. For instance, a family in the poorest quintile at the beginning of the period could be in a higher quintile at the end of the period. The

Figure 11.3

Changing Household Income Distribution, All Families

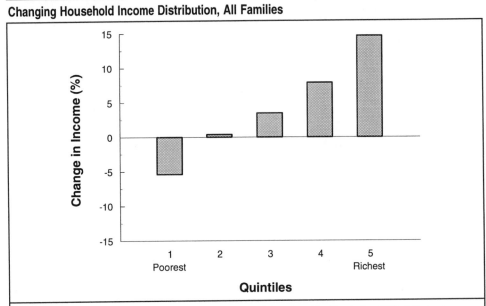

Source: Katharine L. Bradbury, "The Changing Fortunes of American Families in the 1980s," Federal Reserve Bank of Boston *New England Economic Review*, July/August 1990, pp. 24–40.

Table 11.3

Incomes of Elderly Families

Quintile	Percentage of Elderly Families in Each Family Income Quintile	
	1979	1988
First (poorest)	41.6	30.1
Second	28.4	30.3
Third	14.0	18.2
Fourth	8.7	11.4
Fifth (richest)	7.4	10.0
Average Income	$23,400	$28,550

Note: Income figures are in constant 1988 dollars.

Source: Katharine L. Bradbury, "The Changing Fortunes of American Families in the 1980s," Federal Reserve Bank of Boston *New England Economic Review*, July/August 1990, pp. 24–40.

statistics do show that poorest families at the end of the 1980s were worse off than the poorest families at the beginning of the 1980s.

During the 1980s, one group that advanced the most in income was the elderly. Table 11.3 shows the portion of elderly families in each family income quintile in 1979 and 1988. An elderly family is one headed by a person 65 or older. While 41.6 percent of elderly families were in the bottom quintile at the beginning of the period, only 30.1 percent of elderly families were in the bottom quintile in 1988, and average elderly family income rose from $23,400 to $28,550, for a 22 percent gain over the decade. In spite of their gains, however, elderly families still have a substantially lower average income than non–elderly families.

Figure 11.4 has the same structure as Figure 11.3 and shows the percentage change in incomes for non–elderly families in each income quintile. Because family incomes of the elderly rose so much in percentage terms during the 1980s, Figure 11.4 shows the poorer performance of younger families. During the decade, non–elderly family income rose only 7.1 percent. Further, the lowest quintile had a substantial drop in family income of 12.5 percent.

There are other interesting statistics not shown in the figures. First, almost half of young families (those headed by a person 25 or younger) were in the lowest quintile at the end of the 1980s. Families with a husband and wife did well over the decade, with a 10 percent increase in real income. Also, families without husbands

Figure 11.4

Changing Household Income Distribution, Non–Elderly Families

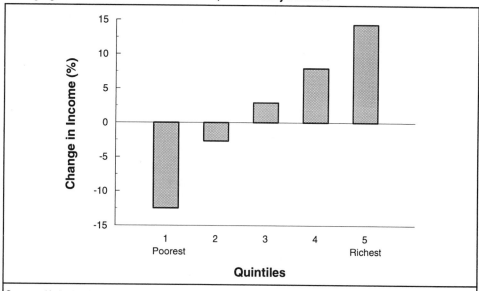

Source: Katharine L. Bradbury, "The Changing Fortunes of American Families in the 1980s," Federal Reserve Bank of Boston *New England Economic Review*, July/August 1990, pp. 24–40.

had increased real income of 35 percent. Families headed by a male, but with no wife present, did not fare well, recording a drop of 1.7 percent. In spite of the relative success of female headed families compared to male headed families, male headed families still had substantially higher incomes at the end of the 1980s.[1]

These figures are important because they show a growing affluence in the population as a whole, and, even more dramatically, they show an increasing variability in income. The gulf between the lowest and highest income groups definitely got larger during the 1980s. These demographic changes in family income point to the development of niche markets, with an increasing difference between the types of goods that might appeal to the poorest and richest families.

For the fortunate upper–income group, there is more disposable income, allowing concentration on luxury and leisure goods. Also, upper–income consumers exhibit a wider diversity of tastes. In the economy, this trend means good news for those firms and industries catering to specialized and expensive tastes. By the same token, there may be more interest in inexpensive, staple goods among those families in the lower income strata. Being able to anticipate these changes could lead to better anticipation of dividend streams and to wiser stock selection.

From an investment point of view, these statistics on family income point to a fragmentation of consumer markets. The greater gulf in income between rich and poor suggests an investment strategy that looks for companies that appeal to these developing and distinct niches. As a merely suggestive example, consider what has already happened in retailing. For more than a century, Sears has attempted to appeal to all tastes. By contrast, Wal–Mart aims at the no–frills, cost conscious shopper. Yet the 1980s saw the development of many upper–end specialized retailers, such as Ralph Lauren and Benetton. The success and failure of these companies may have been due largely to non–demographic factors, such as management performance. Nonetheless, it may be that a strategy of specializing in either the high or low end of the market may be more successful than the traditional middle–of–the–road approach represented by Sears.

The Changing Industrial Mix in the United States

Another important nationwide trend is a dramatic change in the industrial mix in the United States. There is a strong movement away from smokestack industries and toward high–technology industries, away from manufacturing and toward service industries. The joint operation of these two movements promises to transform the U.S. economy in the next decade. In fact, much of the change is already observable. Smokestack industries, such as automobile manufacturing, steel, and mining, have taken a severe beating in the last decade, with a major decrease in employment. During the same period, high–technology industries, such as computing, pharmaceuticals, and medical equipment, have exhibited significant

---

[1]These statistics on family income are drawn from Katharine L. Bradbury, "The Changing Fortunes of American Families in the 1980s," Federal Reserve Bank of Boston *New England Economic Review*, July/August 1990, pp. 24–40.

growth. During the 1980s, a tremendous transformation occurred in U.S. industry, with high–technology industries gaining about 20 percent in the level of employment and smokestack industries losing almost 20 percent.

Not only is there a broad movement from smokestack to high–technology industries, but there is an equally strong movement from manufacturing to the service sector of the economy. Most of the loss for the goods–producing sector came at the expense of manufacturing. Not all service industries are prospering, however. There is a very strong tendency for the movement to high–technology industries to carry over into the service sector, with some service industries even declining. Generally, service industries requiring more skilled employees (computing, accounting and finance, medical services) seem to be prospering relative to those service industries relying on low–skilled employees (taxis, movie theaters, fast food franchises). By anticipating future trends, investors can anticipate those sectors of the economy in which firms are likely to experience higher than anticipated growth in dividends. As the dividend valuation model shows, this can lead to stock price increases.

Regional Employment Patterns

Accompanying these changes in employment by sector and type of industry is yet another major social movement in the United States—the shifting of population and employment toward the Sun Belt and the West, and away from the industrial Northeast. Table 11.4 presents the comparative growth rates for different sectors of the country. Overall, higher growth rates are recorded in the West and the South.

Table 11.4

Population Growth by Regions, 1980–1990

Region	Population Change
Mountain	22.0%
West	20.5
Pacific	19.9
South Atlantic	17.9
West South Central	17.4
South	15.4
New England	6.4
East South Central	6.1
West North Central	3.7
Northeast	3.6
Middle Atlantic	2.7
Midwest	1.8
East North Central	1.0

Source: *The Wall Street Journal*, March 9, 1990.

Table 11.5

Population Growth for Selected States, 1980–1990

Fastest Growing States	Percentage Change in Population
Nevada	38.9%
Alaska	31.1
Arizona	30.8
Florida	30.0
California	22.8

Slowest Growing States	Percentage Change in Population
Pennsylvania	1.5%
Wyoming	1.1
North Dakota	1.1
Michigan	−1.0
Iowa	−2.5

Source: *The Wall Street Journal*, March 9, 1990.

However, the growth rates for high–technology employment are much more rapid for the western half of the country. Table 11.5 shows population growth rates for the states that grew the fastest and slowest over the 1980s. The location of these states confirms the regional population shifts noted in Table 11.4. In addition to the purely economic factors that are contributing to this difference in regional growth rates, there may be changing life–style preferences, particularly for the more casual life styles and better weather typical of the Sun Belt and the West. This change in preferences is probably both a cause and a result of some of the changes in the economic environment, such as the shift in jobs to the Sun Belt and the West.

It is quite likely that the social and demographic trends discussed in this chapter will have a large impact on the economy and the stock market. Being aware of these trends is important to any investor. From this, however, it does not follow that one can now expect shares of firms directed toward older consumers, for example, to outperform the shares of youth–oriented firms. To exploit a knowledge of these major trends in society, one must have a superior knowledge of them, relative to other investors. Surely, there are many investors who know what the age distribution in the United States will likely be over the next 20 years. Presumably, these investors already have used this knowledge in forming their investment plans. To the extent they have done so, they have already affected the price of shares. A newcomer to the game is unlikely to achieve any benefit from investing on the basis of generally accepted information.

Often, however, the mere facts are not the important part of the story. Most investors have access to the same general set of facts; it is the interpretation of those facts that can make the difference. To exploit the kinds of social and demographic analyses discussed here, investors must either get the information earlier than other market participants, or they must interpret it more wisely.

The Industry Life Cycle

One of the most important factors in determining stock prices is the growth rate of dividends and earnings. In general, dividend growth and the rate of discount applied to those dividends, as in the dividend valuation model, determine the value of those shares.

The success of firms in establishing good growth records depends to a great extent on the growth opportunities in their industry. These industry growth opportunities depend, in turn, on the point the industry as a whole occupies in the industry life cycle.

The **industry life cycle** refers to a regular pattern of growth, maturity, and decay experienced by many industries, and it is illustrated in Figure 11.5.[2] As the figure shows, industry–wide sales begin at a zero level as the new industry is created, pass through a growth stage, into a phase of maturity, followed by an inevitable decline.

Figure 11.5

The Industry Life Cycle

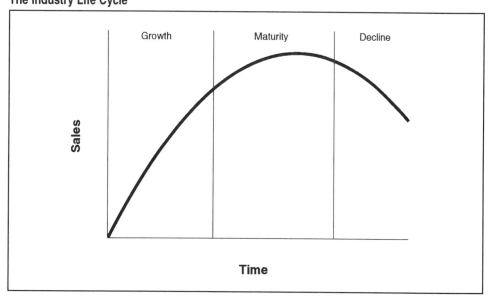

---

[2]This concept of an industry life cycle is closely related to the idea of a "product life cycle" that may be familiar from marketing.

The creation of a new industry is generally brought about by the introduction of some product, and this new product is generally the fruit of some technological leap. Examples of new products that created new industries are the automobile, the dry toner copier, and the personal computer. In each of these cases, there was some advance that made the new industry possible. Henry Ford successfully applied mass production techniques to the automobile, bringing the car within the economic reach of a wider public. Xerox Corporation created and patented a new copying process which could be carried out in the office setting and without expertise. Apple Computer introduced the personal computer and defined a market where there was not one previously. Often, in the creation stage, there is only one firm in the industry, or at least there is one firm that is totally dominant. That was the case with Ford, Xerox, and Apple.

After the creation stage and initial acceptance of the new industry, new competitors enter. As a result, the competitive structure in the industry changes from a monopoly to an oligopoly. The newcomers to the industry must be very aggressive in defining their own market niche and in differentiating their products from those of the industry founder and leader. General Motors was able to do this by doing a better job of meeting consumer demands for styling. IBM forced entry into the copier field largely through the flexing of its marketing muscle. In the personal computer industry, Apple's initial dominance was challenged by a number of small upstart companies, but these challenges were beaten back. Again, IBM, with its marketing skill, entered the personal computer market, forcing Apple into the second position. Now IBM is under a strong attack from smaller, more innovative personal computer companies that threaten its premier position in the industry.

After an initial growth phase, the industry matures. The period of maturation is characterized by slowly growing sales and a movement within the industry to a highly competitive environment. Normally, there will be a number of firms competing, and price tends to become a major competitive weapon. Clearly, the copying industry has reached maturity, with a wide variety of copiers from many vendors in the marketplace. This is true even though technological advances continue to be made.

As industries begin to decline, profit margins are reduced and the emphasis turns to production efficiencies, with price competition continuing to be a major threat to profits. The automobile industry appears to be in its declining phase, although one characterization of dying industries is the potential emergence of a replacement product. There does not seem to be such a replacement for the automobile on the horizon. A better example of a declining industry in the United States is given by the integrated steel producers, those makers of bulk steel items, as opposed to specialty steel manufacturers. Beset by aged plants, the failure to invest in technological upgrades, and stiff competition from technologically superior foreign producers, the steel industry has most of the hallmarks of a declining industry. The technological advances in plastics and ceramics in the last 20 years have resulted in substitutes for steel in many uses. For declining industries, it does not necessarily follow that they pass out of existence. Currently, there is little reason to think that the automobile and steel industries will cease to exist. However, one can be fairly certain that these industries will not be future growth industries.

As reflected in the dividend valuation model, investors should prefer growth industries, other factors being equal, because these industries will be the ones to generate growing dividends. However, growing industries are often the most risky as well, so the rate of discount applied by the market to those growing dividends will tend to be larger. The investor's job is to interpret the growth prospects of industries relative to the risks—and to find the best trade-offs.

The Federal Government and Industry Analysis

One of the major differences among industries concerns their different interactions with the federal government. This interaction can be either beneficial or detrimental to the earnings prospects of firms in the industry. The federal government can affect industries through regulation, taxation, and subsidies.

Regulation

The most obvious example of the way in which federal action can affect industries comes through regulation imposed by the government, and this regulation has different effects on different industries. The decades of the 1960s and 1970s witnessed ever broader penetration of economic life in the U.S. by the federal government. Regulation during this period had a major impact on the financial services industry, automobiles, airlines and other forms of inter–state commerce, the pharmaceutical industry, and many others. The 1980s brought with it a very strong trend toward deregulation, which has had a different impact on these same industries. In the early 1990s, federal regulation appears to be gaining strength. For example, in 1991, the Food and Drug Administration launched a strong attack on food labeling practices. The result of these studies were new and more easily understood labels, which started appearing in 1994. An attempt is currently being made to reorganize health care as a result of federal action.

As an example of the effects of federal regulation, consider the airline industry. When rates on interstate flights were freed from regulation by the federal government, prices for air travel generally fell as the industry became more competitive. Air Florida, Braniff, and Eastern went into bankruptcy and ceased operations. These firms were closely followed into bankruptcy by Continental and the once powerful Pan Am. It seems increasingly clear that the industry will be dominated by just a few mega–airlines, and that these will be challenged aggressively by regional carriers such as Southwest Airlines. In retrospect, it now appears that federal regulation had been providing a shelter from competition in the airline industry.

While many economists believe that governmental regulation often acts to shelter industries from competition, governmental regulation is often not helpful to industry earnings. In the early 1970s, cyclamates were very popular as a dietetic sweetener for many products. After testing determined cyclamates might cause cancer, they were banned from the U.S. market. This segment of the pharmaceutical industry was totally destroyed by governmental action.

These examples show that governmental regulation can have a major impact on industry earnings, causing them to be either higher or lower than they otherwise would be. Further, the impact of federal intervention falls with different weight on different industries. For example, there is little regulation of the leisure products, entertainment, publishing, or the tire and rubber industry. By contrast, there is a great deal of regulation in chemicals, hospital management, transportation, and pharmaceuticals. In conducting an industry analysis, it is important to take these factors into account.

In addition, the impact of government on the future of a particular industry cannot be measured by looking only at the current situation. As the level of regulation changes, one must also look at the likely future impact of regulation. For transportation and financial services, the impact of regulation will probably continue to diminish. A likely exception to this is an increase in regulation of federally insured deposit institutions. On the other hand, in industries focusing on human services or where carcinogens or likely carcinogens are involved, there will probably be an increasing amount of regulation.

Taxation and Subsidies

Federal taxation falls unevenly on different industries. Rules for depreciation, tax–loss carries, and reinvestment incentives are written in a way that benefit some industries and deny those benefits to others. The Tax Reform Act of 1986, for instance, affected various industries differently. Congress has repeatedly changed the rules for depreciation, allowing tax write–offs at a sometimes slower and sometimes faster rate. Since industries differ in their levels of capital intensity, changing rules about depreciation have different effects. Clearly, firms that are highly capital intensive (such as electrical utilities) are helped more than industries that are less capital intensive (such as a service industry) when the depreciation rules are liberalized.

As an example of the effect of tax changes on businesses, consider the investment tax credit. Before the 1986 tax act, a firm buying a good for investment could subtract 10 percent of the value of the good from its tax bill. For example, if a firm bought a computer for $100,000 in 1985, it could take the investment tax credit and subtract $10,000 from its tax bill that same year. If the firm bought the same computer in 1987, it could not take any tax credit. This feature of the Tax Reform Act clearly penalizes capital intense businesses relative to those using relatively little capital.

Currently, all interest paid by businesses, for whatever purpose, is tax deductible. Under the 1986 act, individuals may no longer deduct credit card interest, but they still may deduct interest paid on the mortgage for their first and second homes. Making the interest paid on home mortgages nondeductible, for example, could have a drastic effect on the housing industry. A homeowner paying $1,000 interest per month with a 30 percent marginal tax rate pays only $700 of that

$1,000 on an after–tax basis under the present rules. If the interest were not deductible, his or her after–tax cost would be the full $1,000. While this change is not likely to be made, there could be little doubt that such a change would dramatically affect the home–building industry.

It is difficult to distinguish fully between subsidies and the tax system, since many so–called subsidies are implemented through favorable tax treatment. The deductibility of mortgage interest is regarded as a subsidy by many observers. But perhaps the clearest instance of a subsidy by the federal government is the program of federal price supports for the agricultural industry. In many instances, the federal government puts a floor under prices of certain commodities, guaranteeing to buy produce at a given price. If market prices fall too low, the farmer can still be sure of receiving at least the support price. While much of this subsidy goes to family farmers, it is also paid to large agricultural firms. The sudden withdrawal of this subsidy could have a very severe impact on such firms.

In the past, the Medicare program has given a large boost to hospitals, to hospital management and supply firms, and to pharmaceutical companies. That subsidization is now waning, as new rules are implemented to control payments. Under the new rules, various medical procedures will only receive a fixed Medicare compensation. The control of this subsidy might be expected to have a negative impact on firms in the health care industry.

Another way in which the federal government subsidizes certain industries at the expense of others is through tariffs and quotas on imported goods. In the early 1980s, the government–invoked quotas on Japanese automobiles provided a large benefit to American automobile manufacturers. Without these quotas, earnings at U.S. automobile firms would certainly have been lower. Now those quotas have been removed and U.S. firms face stiffer foreign competition. Similarly, the steel industry has been seeking import quotas or higher tariffs on foreign steel. While these subsidies have not been granted, the fortunes of the steel industry would be greatly improved if the quotas were to be put into effect. Of course, subsidies granted to the steel industry must be paid by someone else.

The federal government has such a large potential impact on firms in certain industries that these firms employ staffs to follow and influence governmental policy. This emphasizes the importance of governmental action on the dividend stream and the risk level of firms in such industries. Anticipating governmental impact on a given industry can be an important factor when deciding whether to invest in a given industry. The investor who can anticipate the effect of future governmental action has a chance to select the best industries for investment and the best chance to avoid investment in industries likely to suffer from governmental intervention.

A Typical Industry Analysis

As an example of how to apply these principles of industry analysis, the remainder of this chapter focuses on a comparison of four industries: paper, general steel, toys, and semiconductor industries. These diverse industries are first compared with respect to many of their key financial ratios, and then closer attention is focused on one of these industries, the paper industry.

Industry Comparisons

Examining financial statistics for different industries can reveal the extent of their success and can also give some insight into their future sales and earnings growth. The key measures to be discussed here focus on accounting measures of profitability, the disposition of earnings, the P–E ratio, and the cash yield to the shareholder. The **return on assets** (ROA) and the **return on equity** (ROE) measures are both gauges of accounting profitability and appear in Tables 11.6 and 11.7, respectively. The two tables reveal large differences in these ratios across industries, and, in general, these kinds of measures of profitability are not comparable across industries.

The ROA is defined as:

$$\text{Return on Assets} = \frac{\text{Net Income}}{\text{Total Assets}}$$

Other things being equal, firms and industries with relatively large amounts of assets on their books will turn in low ROA figures. For capital–intensive industries, such as the steel industry, one can normally expect lower ROA figures. With large investment in capital equipment, the denominator in the ROA formula is very large. By contrast, service or marketing firms having relatively small amounts of physical capital on their books should have higher ROA figures. In Table 11.6, we find that steel actually performs quite well, particularly considering the recession that began in 1990. The most striking feature of Table 11.6 is the variability in the ROA across time. For instance, paper and semiconductors reported quite volatile ROA figures. Because of the different levels of capital intensity, ROA figures are difficult to

Table 11.6

Comparative Industry Percentage Return on Assets (ROA)

Industry	1990	1991	1992	1993	1994
Paper	7.3	4.0	3.5	3.0	4.5
Steel (General)	11.7	8.9	8.1	10.0	12.0
Toys	12.2	13.4	14.1	14.2	14.5
Semiconductors	7.7	7.1	11.8	17.0	15.0

NMF = Not meaningful; NA = Not Available; Figures for 1994 are Value Line estimates.

Source: Value Line Publishing, Inc., *The Value Line Investment Survey*, various issues.

Table 11.7

<hr>

Comparative Industry Percentage Return on Equity (ROE)

Industry	1990	1991	1992	1993	1994
Paper	9.4	3.3	2.8	2.0	4.5
Steel (General)	13.6	9.9	9.3	11.0	14.0
Toys	13.9	16.6	17.4	16.6	18.0
Semiconductors	8.4	7.6	13.1	20.0	16.5

NMF = Not meaningful; NA = Not Available; Figures for 1994 are Value Line estimates.

Source: Value Line Publishing, Inc., *The Value Line Investment Survey*, various issues.

compare across industries. This means that time series analysis of the figure within a given industry is likely to be more meaningful.

Similar care must be taken in the interpretation of the ROE figures shown in Table 11.7. ROE is defined as:

$$\text{Return on Equity} = \frac{\text{Net Income}}{\text{Total Equity}}$$

The interpretation of the ROE figure across industries is hazardous because of the different capital structure employed in different industries. **Capital structure** is the division of the firm's financing between debt and equity. Other things being equal, the higher the proportion of debt, the greater will be the ROE, assuming that there is at least some net income. In comparing the two tables for ROA and ROE, the differences stem from the varying proportions of debt used by the firms. For an entirely equity–financed firm, the ROA and ROE would be equal. Comparing Tables 11.6 and 11.7, we note the largest difference in ROA and ROE occurs for the paper industry.

Table 11.8 shows the industry figures for the debt levels where it is measured as:

$$\text{Debt to Equity} = \frac{\text{Long-Term Debt}}{\text{Total Equity}}$$

The paper industry has a very high debt proportion, which greatly enhances profitability in good years. By contrast, the semiconductor industry has used a small proportion of debt. Differences in debt levels characterize different industries, but

Table 11.8

Comparative Industry Debt–to–Equity Ratios

Industry	1990	1991	1992	1993	1994
Paper	79.7	83.9	88.6	90.2	88.1
Steel (General)	16.3	20.2	26.1	29.2	25.0
Toys	28.2	40.9	34.5	29.2	26.9
Semiconductors	19.0	19.6	18.7	15.8	17.3

NMF = Not meaningful; NA = Not Available; Figures for 1994 are Value Line estimates.

Source: Value Line Publishing, Inc., *The Value Line Investment Survey*, various issues.

within industries firms tend to have very similar capital structures.[3] The industry analyst must be sensitive to the differences in debt proportions that characterize different industries. All of these ratios discussed so far are not comparable across industries because of the long–standing traditional differences in their normal values.

Table 11.9 presents the average P–E ratios for the four industries, and we can once again note systematic differences. Until recently, steel had a very low P–E ratio. In 1980 it was 5.9, and in 1981 it was 3.6. Notice, however, that the P–E ratios for steel in Table 11.9 are sizeable, reflecting the comeback of steel in recent years.

In many respects, the P–E ratio may be interpreted as a measure of prospective growth rates in earnings and dividends that are anticipated by the market. In the case of the semiconductor industry, competition has been growing very rapidly and the industry has matured considerably after the introduction of the personal computer.

In Chapter 10, we noted that P–E ratios are quite cyclical. In the 1990–91 period, P–E ratios were at a cyclical low, reflecting the recessionary environment. Thus, in comparing P–E ratios across time for a particular firm or industry, we should be aware of the overall P–E ratios in the marketplace. Also, as we will see in Chapter 12, it is useful to compare P–E ratios for individual firms with the industry average P–E ratio and the P–E ratios of other firms in the same industry.

Closely related to the P–E ratio is the **payout ratio**, which is the percentage of earnings paid by a firm in dividends.

---

[3]Capital structure is one of the poorly understood, but much studied, central problems of finance. See Stewart C. Myers, "The Capital Structure Puzzle," *Journal of Finance*, July 1984, pp. 575–592, where he says: "I will start by asking, 'How do firms choose their capital structures?' Again, the answer is, we don't know." p. 575.

Table 11.9

Comparative Industry P–E Ratios

Industry	1990	1991	1992	1993	1994
Paper	11.2	NMF	NMF	NMF	NA
Steel (General)	14.9	21.7	27.1	NA	NA
Toys	11.5	11.8	15.5	18.3	NA
Semiconductors	21.0	23.8	15.8	NA	NA

NMF = Not meaningful; NA = Not Available; Figures for 1994 are Value Line estimates.

Source: Value Line Publishing, Inc., *The Value Line Investment Survey*, various issues.

$$\text{Payout Ratio} = \frac{\text{Cash Dividends}}{\text{Net Income}}$$

If a firm is to sustain a high rate of growth in earnings and dividends, it will need considerable financing for new investment. If the firm pays a large cash dividend, then it gives up one source of financing. As a consequence, high–growth industries are normally characterized by low payout ratios. This is reflected in Table 11.10, which shows very high–payout ratios for the mature industries of steel and paper. The paper industry paid more in dividends than it earned in 1991 and 1992. Not surprisingly, high–P–E ratios tend to go with low payout ratios, both being associated with higher growth rates. The extremely high dividend payout ratios for the paper industry result largely from falling earnings coupled with a stable dividend. In general, the variability in payout ratios shown in Table 11.10 comes more from fluctuations in earnings, rather than from changing dividend levels. In

Table 11.10

Comparative Industry Percentage Dividend Payout Ratios

Industry	1990	1991	1992	1993	1994
Paper	44.0	122.0	141.0	NMF	85.0
Steel (General)	26.0	34.0	38.0	34.0	30.0
Toys	8.0	8.0	10.0	13.0	13.0
Semiconductors	18.0	19.0	11.0	10.0	11.0

NMF = Not meaningful; NA = Not Available; Figures for 1994 are Value Line estimates.

Source: Value Line Publishing, Inc., *The Value Line Investment Survey*, various issues.

Table 11.11

■■■■■■■■■■■■■■■

Comparative Industry Dividend Yields

Industry	1990	1991	1992	1993	1994
Paper	3.8	3.0	2.6	2.5	NA
Steel (General)	1.6	1.6	1.3	NA	NA
Toys	0.7	0.7	0.6	0.7	NA
Semiconductors	0.7	0.6	0.5	NA	NA

NMF = Not meaningful; NA = Not Available; Figures for 1994 are Value Line estimates.

Source: Value Line Publishing, Inc., *The Value Line Investment Survey*, various issues.

general, the higher the payout ratio in a given industry, the more important dividends are to shareholders. For a firm in a high–growth industry, a dividend cut might be regarded as bad news, but it is unlikely that it would have such a drastic effect.

Table 11.11 shows another measure of dividends.

$$\text{Dividend Yield} = \frac{\text{Dividends for the Year}}{\text{Stock Price at the Beginning of the Year}}$$

The dividend yield is an important measure since it makes up one of the two components of the stock investor's return. The other is the capital gain. From Table 11.11, it is clear that the dividend yield varies significantly across industries. By contrast, the investor in the semiconductor industry must be anticipating significant capital gains as the dividend yield in that industry has been less than 1 percent. In general, the lower the dividend yield, the greater must be the anticipated price appreciation.

All of these key ratios discussed in this section are important to the prospective investor, but all must be interpreted cautiously. The aspiring industry analyst must remember the following:

1. Most of the ratios vary across industries.
2. Most of the ratios vary across time within a given industry.
3. Most of the ratios are sensitive to the particular practices within a given industry, such as the use of debt.

To a large extent, these ratios are determined by the marketplace. In order to make superior investment returns, investors must do a better job of determining what the values of these ratios should be. They must anticipate what the market will come to perceive as the correct prices for the various stocks, and this will be a function of the correct valuation of measures such as the P–E ratio and the dividend yield.

To develop these ideas further, this chapter concludes with a closer examination of the paper industry.

The Paper Industry

This section focuses on the paper industry to illustrate some of the major considerations in an industry analysis. Industry analysts are employed by major brokerage houses and investment banking firms. Their analysts prepare professional analyses that may be very long and exhaustively researched. Their efforts include reading everything available about the paper industry and meeting with top executives of the major firms in the industry. This section provides an overview of industry analysis and shows the kinds of issues that must be addressed in a successful industry analysis.

Industrial Classifications

One of the first issues that must be addressed in any potential industry analysis is the proper definition of the industry. For our purposes, we will use the Standard Industrial Classification (SIC) code. The paper industry is defined as all firms having an SIC code of 2600. This is a two–digit code. By substituting digits for the last two zeroes of the code, a tighter industry specification can be created.

To make the number of firms manageable, we focus on the 12 paper firms with a market value in 1994 of $2 billion or more. Table 11.12 presents the firms

Table 11.12

Major Firms in the Paper Industry, June 1994

Firm	Ticker Symbol	Market Value ($ millions)
Champion International	CHA	2953.6
Georgia–Pacific	GP	5788.5
International Paper	IP	8672.2
Louisiana–Pacific	LPX	3718.6
Macmillan Bloedel, Ltd.	MB.TO	2304.5
Mead Corporation	MEA	2663.3
Scott Paper	SPP	3525.7
Temple–Inland	TIN	2781.0
Union Camp	UCC	3264.7
Westvaco Corp.	W	2173.8
Weyerhaeuser	WY	8613.7
Willamette Industries	WMTT	2511.6

Source: Value Line Publishing, Inc., *The Value Line Investment Survey*, various issues.

Table 11.13

■■■■■■■■■■■■■■

Distribution of Sales for Paper Firms, 1993

Firm	Paper, Pulp, and Packaging	Wood and Building Products	Other
Champion International	76%	24%	–
Georgia–Pacific	57%	42%	1%
International Paper	60%	10%	30%
Union Camp	73%	8%	19%
Weyerhauser	37%	37%	17%

Source: Standard & Poor's, *Industry Surveys*, various issues.

that we will consider, the ticker symbol, and the market value for each firm. This definition, though, leaves out many well–known paper firms, such as Federal Paper Board, Stone Container, and Potlatch Corp. The second problem in industry definition comes from the fact that large firms almost always operate in two or more different industry areas. In the case of the paper industry, most of these firms are also engaged in the forest products industry. As an example, Table 11.13 reports the sources of sales for several of the companies that constitute our industry. The sales from paper, pulp, and packaging range from 37 percent for Weyerhauser to 76 percent for Champion International. These differences can be important when it comes to selecting particular firms in the industry for investment.

Paper Industry Overview

In 1994, U.S. paper consumption exceeded 700 pounds per person per year. Table 11.14 shows the breakdown of paper and paperboard into the specialty products that comprise the total. Paper and paperboard are almost exactly equal in volume produced, with 1993 production of each reaching about 42 million tons.

Paper is clearly a commodity good. If we think of the industry life–cycle analysis, we must regard paper as a mature industry. While technological advances in papermaking will continue, we cannot expect any radical breakthroughs. Further, because paper is a commodity good, we might expect paper and related products to have price fluctuations similar to other commodities. During the recession of 1981–1982, paper prices typically fell, but rebounded sharply in late 1983 and 1984. Prices followed a similar pattern after the 1990–1991 recession.

In the late 1980s and early 1990s, the paper industry suffered, with excess capacity being a particular problem in 1990–1991. This excess capacity resulted in part from plant expansion, but also from more aggressive recycling efforts. For example, in 1993 slightly more than 40 percent of total paper use was from recycled paper. Paper is generally quite cyclical, so production will probably expand in line with general industrial production. Further, paper prices are very elastic and respond dramatically to small shifts in capacity utilization. The ability to raise

Table 11.14
■■■■■■■■■■■■■■■■■■■■■■■
Production of Paper and Paperboard

Paper	Percentage of Total Paper
Newsprint	17%
Printing and writing papers	58%
Tissue paper	14%
Packaging and other papers	11%

Paperboard	Percentage of Total Paperboard
Unbleached Kraft linerboard	50%
Bleached Kraft linerboard	14%
Semi–Chemical paperboard	11%
Recycled paperboard	25%

Source: Standard & Poor's, *Industry Surveys*, March 31, 1994.

prices depends on a high capacity utilization rate, but there are already signs that the economy may be slowing.

Environmental Concerns

Growing environmental awareness threatens the paper industry in two ways. First, we have already noted a growing willingness for consumers to recycle paper products. Recycling efforts will clearly reduce demand for new paper products. Second, the paper industry employs some highly toxic chemicals. In some respects, the industry has had an unenviable record in pollution.

Paper production creates significant amounts of sulphur dioxide. When emitted into the air, this chemical is a significant contributor to acid rain. New legislative initiatives aimed at curbing acid rain will have a significant impact on the paper industry. Paper making uses significant amounts of water, so paper plants are always located near lakes or rivers. Making white paper requires using chlorine to bleach naturally brown wood pulp. This process generates waste chlorine and dioxins. Some plants continue to discharge substantial amounts of polluted waste water. Finally, paper production generates solid sludge from waste pulp. To date, no economic means of recycling this sludge has been found.

Environmental concerns will have a major impact on the industry. For example, the industry is projected to spend about $11 billion on capital projects in coming years, with about 40 percent of that total being directed to comply with environmental restrictions. These include secondary treatment plants, efforts to control plant emissions and to reduce the use of chlorine, and initiatives to promote recycling. Environmental groups and state governments are becoming more aggressive in raising legal challenges to paper producers. In Mississippi, International Paper and Georgia–Pacific have been sued for discharging dioxins into rivers.

From an investment perspective, firms that have already incurred substantial pollution control expenses may be positioned to perform better in the years ahead, to the extent that this early expenditure is not already fully reflected in share prices. Similarly, firms with operations in more tolerant jurisdictions may be able to avoid the full cost of their pollution.

The U.S.–Canada Connection

Table 11.15 shows the flows of paper and paperboard between the United States and Canada for 1993. All numbers express tons of paper. In virtually every category, Canada is a net exporter of paper to the United States. This is not too surprising given the vast forests of Canada and the much greater demand for paper in the U.S. economy.

In spite of its large exports to the United States, Canada supplies a relatively small portion of U.S. needs. For example, total paper production in the United States in 1993 was almost 41 million tons. In 1993, U.S. newsprint production was about 7.1 million tons. As Table 11.15 shows, the U.S. imported almost 8 million tons of additional newsprint from Canada. Obviously, U.S.–Canada trade in paper is critical to U.S. supplies.

In light of the importance of Canada, it is not surprising that many of the paper firms that we are considering have significant Canadian operations. For example, Abitibi–Price is the largest newsprint manufacturer in the world, and it holds cutting rights on 19 million acres, largely in Canada. Similarly, Champion International owns about 85 percent of Weldwood of Canada, a pulp and wood products company. Champion also owns or controls 2.5 million acres in Canada. As a final example, Weyerhauser has cutting rights on 13.5 million Canadian acres.

Table 11.15

U.S.–Canada Paper Trade, 1993

Product	Tons Exported to Canada	Tons Imported from Canada	Net Imports from Canada
Newsprint	14,376	7,630,129	7,615,753
Printing and writing paper	480,105	2,280,553	1,800,448
Packaging papers	56,540	204,576	148,036
Special industrial papers	85,450	60,409	−25,041
Tissue paper	35,031	73,952	38,921
Total paper	671,502	10,249,618	9,578,116
Total paperboard	554,375	921,094	366,719

Source: American Paper Institute, *Paper, Paperboard & Wood Pulp*, February, 1994.

Internationalization

Beyond trade with Canada, the U.S. paper industry is moving toward even more complete internationalization. Currently, world production of paper and paperboard is about 250 million metric tons, and U.S. firms have about 30 percent of that market. U.S. firms are moving to capture more of that market and appear to be well situated to capitalize on some inherent advantages. First, U.S. paper plants are the most modern and technologically advanced in the world. This situation contrasts with the U.S. auto industry, which was impeded by its decaying capital base. Second, compared to many countries that might compete in paper production, the United States is endowed with a very rich resource base. In comparison, Europe has the technology and capital to produce paper, but it is poor in wood pulp. Third, the paper industry is capital intensive, not labor intensive. Therefore, the paper industry is not as subject to competition from low labor cost environments as some other industries would be.

Currently, U.S. paper firms are securing operating facilities and raw materials overseas. Champion International, for example, owns a Brazilian pulp and paper subsidiary, and garnered 17 percent of operating income from foreign sources in 1993. James River Corporation has 126 facilities scattered through the United States, Canada, Mexico, and Europe. Stone Container has operations in Mexico, Germany, the United Kingdom, and Holland, with foreign operations accounting for 27 percent of 1993 sales. Scott Paper derives about 36 percent of its sales abroad.

By contrast, some firms are highly concentrated in North America. Weyerhauser has huge timber holdings, but these are almost all concentrated in the United States and Canada. These lands provide virtually all of Weyerhauser's fiber needs, but leave it vulnerable to the development of cheaper foreign sources. Georgia–Pacific recently acquired Great Northern Nekoosa, another paper firm. This acquisition makes Georgia–Pacific the largest owner of timberland in North America.

From an investment point of view, the movement to internationalization is potentially of great importance. The U.S. market is quite mature, so firms may do well to seek higher growth markets in less industrialized countries. As we noted, U.S. annual paper consumption is 700 pounds per person, but in the Philippines, consumption is only 20 pounds. Faced with these statistics, it seems apparent that growth opportunities are likely to be better overseas, at least in the long run. Second, environmental concerns in the United States are higher than elsewhere, so foreign operations may help firms to avoid environmental pressures at home. Third, by obtaining rights to foreign pulp sources, firms may be able to diversify their resource base in a way that will protect them from fluctuating exchange rates.

New Federal Initiatives on Forest Resource Management

Commercial forest land covers about 20 percent of the United States, with about 70 percent of this land in private hands. Although tree growth exceeds harvest by about 30 percent each year, federal lands provide a critical supply of lumber, at least in the view of the paper and forest products industry. The most productive

Figure 11.6

Industry Analysis of the Paper Industry

April 22, 1994   **PAPER & FOREST PRODUCTS INDUSTRY**   **912**

The state of paper and pulp markets can best be described as a mixed bag. The first quarter of 1994 was marked by continued improvement in linerboard and pulp prices. But pricing for coated and uncoated free sheet, bleached board, and newsprint continued to slide. One explanation for this situation is the lack of a strong European export market. This has in turn forced more imported paper into the U.S., thereby weakening domestic paper markets. The strengthening of the dollar versus the currencies of Canada, Sweden, and Finland has exacerbated the problem. The stronger greenback has increased the relative cost competitiveness of Foreign producers when they sell their paper products in the U.S. Over the last year, imports have increased as much as 40% in some grades. As a result, domestic operating rates remain below the market equilibrium level and prices are at rock-bottom levels for printing papers.

Turning to the forest products segment, realizations from logs, lumber, and panelboard moved up in the first quarter from last year's fourth quarter levels. Spot prices, however, did begin to give way during the quarter probably due to the cramp harsh winter weather put on building activity in some parts of the country. A temporary overhang in new housing stock may also be responsible for the drop off in wood prices. In our opinion, though, any weakness in wood prices will be short lived. Long-term interest rates are still very low by historical standards and the U.S. economic recovery has a long way to go before it peters out. Thus, the general trend in housing starts should be upwards. Furthermore, environmentally inspired court injunctions have restricted the amount of logging on federal lands to virtually nil. This limit on supply is supportive of higher forest products prices.

Prices To Watch

Table 1 depicts the difficult market conditions pulp and paper producers face. Transaction prices (as opposed to list prices) for several grades are significantly lower on a year-over-year basis. Chart B reveals a generally strong long-term pricing trend for wood products as well as seasonal peaks and valleys.

INDUSTRY TIMELINESS: 76 (of 96)

TABLE 1: Pulp, Paper & Paperboard Prices
(per short ton except pulp and newsprint, metric tons)

	Current Price	Year Ago Price	% Change
Pulp (bleached softwood kraft)			
Canadian/U.S.	$460	$480	-4.2%
U.S. Southern	400	415	-3.6
Newsprint (30-lb)			
East ($685 list)	430	475	-9.5
West Coast ($630 list)	420	440	-4.6
Coated Publication			
No. 1, 70-lb sheets ($1,540 list)	1,500	1,500	0.0
No. 3, 60-lb rolls ($1,370 list)	970	1010	-4.0
No. 5, 40-lb offset rolls ($1,030 list)	770	770	0.0
Uncoated White			
Offset, 50-lb rolls ($860 list)	510	645	-20.9
No. 3 book offset ($1,020 list)	945	960	-1.6
Bond, No. 4 repro, 83 bright ($960 list)	705	690	2.2
Form bond, 15-lb rolls ($820 list)	645	680	-5.2
Tissue			
Sanitary paper products and stock (BLS index)	134.0	136.6	-1.9
Unbleached kraft paper			
Shipping sack, 50-lb ($580 list)	550	550	0.0
Grocery sack, 70-lb ($490 list)	360	370	-2.7
Grocery bag, 30-lb ($670 list)	585	630	-7.1
Linerboard (42-lb)			
East ($380 list)	350	330	6.1
West ($390 list)	370	350	5.7
Bleached kraft board,			
16-pt folding carton, C1S, 80 bright, rolls ($870 list)	730	790	-7.6

Source: Pulp & Paper Week, Value Line estimates

Paper Statistics And Prospects

The *American Paper Institute's* (API) annual survey of paper industry capacity expansion was released last December. The 1993 version forecasts capacity expan-

Composite Statistics: PAPER & FOREST PRODS. INDUSTRY						
1990	1991	1992	1993	1994	1995	97-99
91737	88500	91346	82000	95500	100000	Sales ($mill)
15.5%	12.2%	12.1%	12.0%	13.5%	15.0%	Operating Margin
5321.8	5714.8	6241.3	6500	6800	7150	Depreciation ($mill)
3967.7	1373.1	1157.6	910	1950	3150	Net Profit ($mill)
38.2%	44.1%	35.7%	38.0%	38.0%	38.0%	Income Tax Rate
4.4%	1.6%	1.3%	1.0%	2.0%	3.1%	Net Profit Margin
6371.2	5500.2	4817.5	4500	4500	4700	Working Cap'l ($mill)
33992	35345	36452	37000	37000	37000	Long-Term Debt ($mill)
42635	42128	41137	41000	42000	44000	Net Worth ($mill)
7.3%	4.0%	3.5%	3.0%	4.5%	6.0%	% Earned Total Cap'l
9.4%	3.3%	2.8%	2.0%	4.5%	7.0%	% Earned Net Worth
5.4%	NMF	NMF	NMF	.5%	3.5%	% Retained to Comm Eq
44%	122%	141%	NMF	85%	55%	% All Div'ds to Net Prof
11.2	NMF	NMF	NMF			Avg Ann'l P/E Ratio
.84	NMF	NMF	NMF			Relative P/E Ratio
3.8%	3.0%	2.6%	2.5%			Avg Ann'l Div'd Yield

120000	Sales ($mill)
18.0%	Operating Margin
8300	Depreciation ($mill)
7800	Net Profit ($mill)
37.5%	Income Tax Rate
6.5%	Net Profit Margin
6000	Working Cap'l ($mill)
27500	Long-Term Debt ($mill)
58000	Net Worth ($mill)
11.0%	% Earned Total Cap'l
13.5%	% Earned Net Worth
9.5%	% Retained to Comm Eq
32%	% All Div'ds to Net Prof
11.0	Avg Ann'l P/E Ratio
.85	Relative P/E Ratio
3.0%	Avg Ann'l Div'd Yield

Bold figures are Value Line estimates

Paper & Forest Products

RELATIVE STRENGTH (Ratio of Industry to Value Line Comp.)

Index: June, 1987 = 100

Factual material is obtained from sources believed to be reliable, but the publisher is not responsible for any errors or omissions contained herein. For the confidential use of subscribers. Reprinting, copying, and distribution by permission only. Copyright 1994 by Value Line Publishing, Inc. ® Reg. TM—Value Line, Inc. **To subscribe call 1-800-833-0046.**

Figure 11.6 Continued

sion over the three-year period 1994-96 based on plans announced prior to the survey's publication. The data indicates that paper and paperboard capacity are (1) slowing down; (2) below the long-term average; and, (3) below our forecast for real GDP growth. Specifically, the 1993 survey forecasts total paper and paperboard capacity growth slowing from a 2.2% average annual rate during the 1991-93 time frame to 1.9% over the 1994-96 stretch. These growth rates are below the 10-year figure of 2.3% and well below our projection for real GDP growth over the next three years, which ranges from 3.3% in 1994 to 3.4% in 1996.

The API data suggests a rise in industrywide operating rates from about 92.5% in 1993, to nearly 93.5% in 1994, 94.5% in 1995, and 95.5% in 1996. Because prices have historically started to move up when operating rates reached 93%, we continue to look for some modest pricing improvements to take place across the whole spectrum of paper and paperboard grades in 1994—particularly in the latter part of the year when worldwide economies should be doing better.

Ironically, Stricter EPA Regulations Could Actually Help The Industry

Although manufacturers are opposed to tighter regulations, which are usually very expensive to comply with, last November's proposal by the EPA for more stringent pollution regulations could eventually strengthen the Paper industry's prospects. Because paper producers would have to devote more of their resources to environmental equipment as opposed to plant expansions, the rate of capacity growth could be even less than what the API data would otherwise suggest. The restriction on supply would lead to higher operating rates—sparking increased prices.

The Outlook For Wood Products Markets

In the Pacific Northwest, environmentally inspired court injunctions have reduced the volume of federal and state timber sales to only about 10% and 35%, respectively, of their historical levels. These injunctions have led to a 10% to 15% reduction in the entire U.S. wood products level of supply experienced in the mid-1980s.

The Clinton Administration has come up with a compromise to deal with the issue of the court-ordered curtailments on logging from federal lands. The proposal calls for a timber program that will result in considerably more federal timber sales than what is currently being sold. However, the plan would still result in substantially smaller annual harvests from federal forests than the norm over the last decade. Under the Clinton proposal, annual board feet over the next 10 years are to average 1.2 billion as compared to the 5 billion board feet averaged throughout the Eighties and the 3 billion averaged just prior to the court injunctions. In our opinion, this plan will support higher wood product prices, especially as the recovery progresses because of a likely pickup in construction. This should be a boon to those forest product firms that own a significant amount of private timber acreage and/or have cutting rights on land outside of the U.S.

Higher Profits Ahead

Over the next year we look for industrywide earnings to more than double on a 3%-4% sales gain. Even assuming such a strong year-over-year gain in 1994, the profit figures would still be considerably below the 1988-89 peak levels. By 1997-99, however, industrywide earnings should achieve record heights. We continue to base our projection on a number of assumptions, including: (1) growing demand resulting from a synchronized worldwide economic expansion; (2) a pricing recovery in paper primarily due to higher paper plant utilization rates; (3) persistent price strength in lumber products as a result of stronger construction activity and restrictive environmental policies that significantly limit the harvest of trees from federal lands; and lastly, (4) further productivity gains and higher operating efficiencies as volume picks up.

Investment Advice

On the whole, the paper and forest products group is ranked to underperform most of the industries under our review in the coming six to 12 months. Investors with a longer view, however, may find the 3- to 5-year capital appreciation potential of some of these stocks appealing.

Anthony J. Glennon

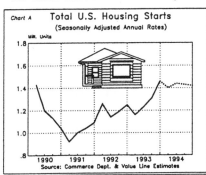

Chart A **Total U.S. Housing Starts**
(Seasonally Adjusted Annual Rates)
Source: Commerce Dept. & Value Line Estimates

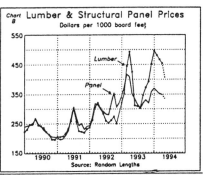

Chart B **Lumber & Structural Panel Prices**
Dollars per 1000 board feet
Source: Random Lengths

Source: Value Line Publishing, Inc., *The Value Line Investment Survey*, April 22, 1994, p. 912–913.

forest lands are old growth forests, located mainly in the Pacific Northwest. In this region, there are about 5.3 million acres of old growth forest, with about 1.5 million acres in national forest. Traditionally, the federal government has allowed logging on about half of national forest land. In February 1994, the Clinton Administration launched an effort to restrict logging in national forests. These restrictions, coupled with court injunctions, have led to a 10 to 15 percent reduction in the domestic supply of wood products.

These restrictions on logging constrict supply and help to keep prices for wood products high. This may actually benefit some firms in the industry, but it will be quite certain to have a differential effect on firms in the industry, depending on the firm's source of raw materials for the paper–making process.

Investment Prospects in the Paper Industry

The *Value Line Investment Survey* reviews 96 industries and groups firms according to its own classification. Figure 11.6 presents the first of two pages from Value Line's recent analysis of the Paper and Forest Products Industry. Notice that Value Line ranks the paper industry 76th in attractiveness among the 96 industries that it follows. The following quotation from Value Line summarizes their view of the paper industry: "On the whole, the paper and forest products group is ranked to underperform most of the industries under our reveiw in the coming six to 12 months."

Summary

This chapter emphasized the importance of industry selection for successful stock investing. At any time, the investment prospects of different industries can vary widely. If an investor could correctly select promising industries, this skill by itself would be enough to virtually guarantee success.

In a dynamic economy, such as that in the United States, the fortunes of different industries are determined to a large extent by the social and demographic changes affecting the entire society. This chapter identified and discussed some of the most prominent changes, including the changing age and income distributions, and the changing industrial mix and shifts in regional employment patterns. Each of these factors is likely to be important in the years ahead.

One tool used in industry analysis is the concept of the industry life cycle—the idea that industries go through a normal cycle of birth, development, and decay. Because the growth cycle of an industry is important for the dividends that firms in a given industry will be able to pay, the position of a firm in the life cycle is potentially important to the stock investor.

The federal government is also an important factor in the fortune of industries. Some industries are relatively free from governmental intervention, while others are closely supervised. Some industries are hurt by governmental actions, while others are helped. Anticipating future effects of governmental actions can be important in the process of industry analysis.

As a guide to practical application of industry analysis techniques, four industries were compared. Performance measures and financial measures differ widely across these industries, so the investor needs to know techniques for comparing industries with each other and for analyzing a single industry across time. Finally, the chapter concluded with a discussion of a particular industry—the paper industry. Having focused on the economy–wide factors in the preceding chapter and the industry–wide factors in this chapter, the next chapter examines the individual firm, concluding the cycle of analysis of stocks and the factors that affect their dividends.

Questions and Problems

1. Explain why stocks in one industry might differ in their general performance from those in another industry.
2. The increase in the average age of Americans is virtually certain to affect the economy in that industries serving the needs of older people will probably grow. Does this mean that stock of firms in those industries will perform well relative to the economy as a whole? Explain.
3. As argued in the chapter, there is a major movement in the industrial mix of the United States—away from manufacturing and toward service industries. Does this mean that it is now generally wiser to invest in service industries rather than manufacturing industries?
4. Apply the concept of the industry life cycle to the personal computer industry. What phase is the industry in now? Apply the same kind of analysis to the "genetic engineering" industry.
5. There are often marked differences in firms across different industries in terms of their balance sheet and income statement ratios. Explain why these differences might exist. Do the differences imply which industries are better suited for investment?

Suggested REALDATA Exercises

The following *REALDATA* exercises explore the concepts developed in this chapter: Exercises 52, 100, 101, 103.

Suggested Readings

Bradbury, K. L., "The Changing Fortunes of American Families in the 1980s," Federal Reserve Bank of Boston *New England Economic Review*, July/August 1990, pp. 25–40.

Crone, T. M., "The Aging of America: Impacts on the Marketplace and Workplace," Federal Reserve Bank of Philadelphia *Business Review*, May/June 1990, pp. 3–13.

Morris, F. E., "The Changing American Attitude toward Debt, and Its Consequences," Federal Reserve Bank of Boston *New England Economic Review*, May/June 1990, pp. 34–39.

CHAPTER TWELVE

Company Analysis

Overview

This chapter focuses on the analysis of the individual firm for the stock market investor. The two preceding chapters focused on the economy–wide and industry–wide factors affecting stock prices. These two chapters, together with this chapter analyzing individual firm effects, provide the basic inputs for the application of the dividend valuation model. In essence, the factors affecting the future dividend stream and the discount rate to be applied to those dividends fall into one of the three categories: economy–wide factors, industry–wide factors, and company–specific factors. This chapter begins by introducing a technique for estimating the value of stocks of individual firms called the fundamental analyst's model. This model is an outgrowth of the dividend valuation model in a form that is particularly easy to apply. The fundamental analyst's model relies most heavily on estimates of future earnings and on estimated P–E ratios, so both topics receive considerable attention in this chapter. After introducing the key ideas of company analysis, the discussion turns to an extended example. Just as the paper industry was used to highlight the principles and aims of industry analysis, this chapter contrasts the characteristics of several paper firms. Putting particular firms under the microscope to see how they differ, and how those differences might be important for investors, sets the stage for a detailed examination of the financial characteristics of a single firm. The chapter also includes a more detailed examination of the financial statements of International Paper.

The Fundamental Analyst's Model

The **fundamental analyst's model** is a straightforward technique for gauging the intrinsic value of a share of stock. It is deceptively simple, because it can be stated so easily:

$$\text{Stock Value = Expected Earnings} \times \text{Justified P–E Ratio} \qquad \textbf{12.1}$$

The model simply states that the intrinsic value of a share of stock equals the expected earnings for the firm in the next period, multiplied by the justified P–E ratio for the firm's shares. Each of the three terms in the equation requires elaboration, with the most important being the justified P–E ratio. As a shorthand definition, we can say that the **justified P–E ratio** is the correct ratio of share price to current earnings that reflects both the firm's future growth prospects in earnings and the level of risk associated with future earnings.

Price versus Value

Generally, in economics and finance, the value of a good is thought to equal its price. However, the fundamental analyst's model makes a distinction between price and value because it is a technique designed to find discrepancies between the two. The fundamental analyst attempts to find securities for which the market has incorrectly estimated the true value of the security. In such a situation, the market price will not equal the true value. Upon finding such a stock whose market price is less than its true value, the investor buys. When the rest of the market comes to realize what the security is truly worth, the stock price will rise until the stock's price equals its value again. In short, the analyst is estimating stock values to find situations where the market pricing mechanism has made a mistake, allowing the stock's price to diverge from its true value. This gives rise to the two following investment rules:

> If the estimated value > market price, **buy** the stock.
> If the estimated value < market price, **sell** the stock.

When the other participants in the market finally realize what the stock is truly worth, traders will force the market price to adjust until the stock's price equals the true value of the stock. For example, if the true value of a share is $15, and the market price is $12, the investor would buy the stock. When the other participants in the market realize that the share is really worth $15, they will start to buy it. As they buy the stock in increasing numbers, the excess demand for the shares at the price of $12 causes the share price to rise. The share price must rise as long as most of the traders are trying to buy the shares. The traders will keep trying to buy the shares as long as the market price lies below the now acknowledged true value of the shares. This process of adjustment will cease only when the market price reaches $15, the true value of the share in this example.

Three Requirements for Applying the Model

To profit by following this strategy requires three conditions:

1. The estimate of the true value of a share must be correct.

2. The true value must be estimated before the rest of the market discovers the true value.
3. The other participants in the market must come to recognize that the share is worth its estimated value.

Clearly, if the estimates of value are incorrect, the investor cannot hope to make any money. Rather, it is much more likely that he or she will lose money. Second, if the analyst is slow in reaching the correct conclusion, there will be little chance for profit. If other traders know the true value before you, the price will have already converged to its true value, and no profit opportunity will remain. Finally, the market must eventually come to recognize the true value of a security. Otherwise, there will be no price movement to generate a profit. To see how necessary this is, imagine an analyst saying that IBM is worth $300 while the market price is $120, and that IBM has been worth $300 for the last 15 years but the market is too stupid to recognize this true value. Such an analyst would appear ridiculous. Even worse, there would be no profit. The analyst might even be correct about IBM, but unless other traders in the market come to share the analyst's view, there will be no market forces to make the market price of IBM converge to its true value of $300.

Actually, it should not be long before intelligent and profit–hungry traders in the stock market recognize the true value of a security. It is probably impossible, however, to beat the market consistently in recognizing the true value of securities. That is a recurrent theme throughout this book and will be discussed at length in Chapters 14–16. For now, however, the first step is to learn to make the best possible estimate of a stock's true value. Since any estimate is only as good as its inputs, attention must focus on the two key inputs to the fundamental analyst's model—the expected earnings and the justified P–E ratio.

Earnings Growth

The growth rate and pattern of earnings and dividends are crucial for both the justified P–E ratio and the expected earnings estimate. If the investor knew the present level of earnings and the growth rate to be experienced over the next period, the earnings for the next period could be estimated with total accuracy. By the same token, the central determinant of the justified P–E ratio is the expected earnings growth for the future.

Table 12.1 presents earnings data for the 12 large paper firms that we will consider. The first column of data shows how the earnings–per–share have changed over the last year for these companies. On the whole, these firms have experienced a significant decline in earnings over the last five years, while the shorter–term experience has been more diverse. Some firms had negative earnings, so percentage changes were not computed. For most of these firms, the P–E ratio is also quite high. These high P–E ratios tend to reflect somewhat low earnings, rather than the expectation of rapidly growing profits.

Table 12.1

━━━━━━━━━━

Earnings

Company Name	12–Month EPS % Change	5–Year EPS Growth	Current P–E
Champion International	NMF	NMF	NMF
Georgia–Pacific	NMF	NMF	NMF
International Paper	–13.0	–5.0	24.4
Louisiana–Pacific	11.2	9.5	11.8
Macmillan Bloedel, Ltd.	NMF	NMF	25.2
Mead Corporation	8.3	–8.5	17.9
Scott Paper	–19.3	–11.0	23.7
Temple–Inland	–55.6	–2.5	24.2
Union Camp	–2.0	–15.0	42.5
Westvaco Corp.	–21.8	–3.0	23.2
Weyerhaeuser	8.8	–4.0	15.5
Willamette Industries	34.0	–8.5	18.4

Source: Value Line Publishing, Inc., *The Value Line Investment Survey*, various issues. Data are current through June 1994. NMF = Not Meaningful; NA = Not Available.

Forecasting Earnings

While it is important to be able to measure historical earnings growth, the main emphasis should be on future growth in earnings. Future growth determines future earnings figures, and this helps determine the justified P–E ratio. There are many ways to estimate future earnings, including accounting–based approaches, mathematical models, and judgmental forecasts. This section presents and briefly discusses each type.

The Percentage of Revenue Technique

The intuition behind this technique is to assume that a firm will continue to earn the same percentage on each dollar of sales as it has done in the past. Then, if one can forecast sales for the next period, it is possible to derive a forecast of earnings. Essentially, this technique avoids a direct estimation of future earnings by substituting the problem of estimating revenues. However, in many instances, it will be easier to forecast revenues than to forecast earnings directly. Table 12.2 presents the net income as a percent of revenues for our 12 firms from the paper industry. As the data in the table indicate, the typical profit margin on sales is in the range of 2 to 4 percent, although Louisiana–Pacific fared much better. In the case of International Paper, the value is 2.29 percent. Assuming International Paper

Table 12.2
━━━━━━━━━━━━━━━

Net Income as a Percentage of Revenues

Company Name	Net Profit	Sales	Profit/Sales (%)
Champion International	–106.7	5068.8	2.11
Georgia–Pacific	–18.0	12330.0	0.15
International Paper	314.0	13685.0	2.29
Louisiana–Pacific	258.8	2511.3	10.31
Macmillan Bloedel, Ltd.	14.2	3762.0	0.38
Mead Corporation	131.7	4790.3	2.75
Scott Paper	116.5	4748.9	2.45
Temple–Inland	67.4	2100.7	3.21
Union Camp	68.8	3120.4	2.20
Westvaco Corp.	96.4	2344.6	4.11
Weyerhaeuser	462.7	9544.8	4.85
Willamette Industries	116.5	2622.2	4.44

Source: Value Line Publishing, Inc., *The Value Line Investment Survey*, various issues. Data are current through June 1994. NMF = Not Meaningful; NA = Not Available.

can control its costs, we might reasonably expect it to earn two cents per dollar of revenue. As an example, if we estimate the increase in revenues per share to be $2.00, we would estimate the new earnings level to be $.04 greater than the previous year's. With earnings per share of $2.87 in 1993, this technique would lead us to forecast an earnings level of about $2.91 per share for 1994.

This technique has both advantages and disadvantages. First, it is easy to apply and calculate. However, one needs to have reliable estimates of profitability and revenue. Thus, the main weakness of this approach to forecasting earnings is that it substitutes the problem of forecasting revenues and profit margins for the original problem of forecasting earnings.

Trend Analysis

A common mathematical technique that might be used to forecast future earnings is **trend analysis**. Figure 12.1 presents the EPS figures for International Paper for the 19–year period from 1975–1993. The values shown there present a clearly discernible trend, which the straight line indicates. This straight line was found by regressing the EPS values on a time index. The regression analysis determines the line of best fit according to a standardized criterion. Based on this technique, the forecast earnings for 1994 is $4.25. However, the relationship is not very strong; the R^2 is only 3 percent, so the forecast certainly does not inspire confidence.

Another kind of mathematical technique that could be used to fit the data of Figure 12.1 is a collection of statistical tools known as **time series analysis**. Many statisticians believe that time series analysis offers better forecasts of some types of

Figure 12.1

Nineteen Years of Earnings for International Paper

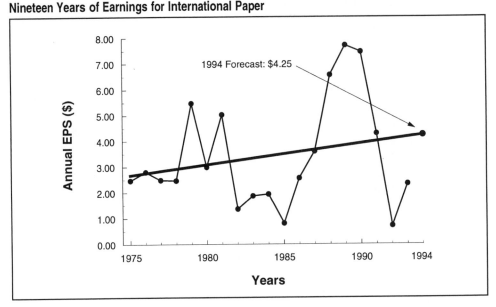

variables than does straightforward trend analysis. The trend line fit to the data in Figure 12.1 can also be used to prepare a forecast. If one follows the trend line to the next period, then the line indicates a forecasted value for the next period's earnings. (This point is also shown in Figure 12.1.) The trend line can be used to forecast as far into the future as the investor wishes. The difficulty with this kind of analysis, whether the trend line is fit by eyeball or by regression analysis, is that it assumes the future will be like the past. In fact, it assumes that whatever growth rate characterized the sample period will continue in the future. This assumption is very hazardous.

In Chapter 11 we noted that many firms follow a life cycle. If the data used to fit the trend line are drawn from the high–growth period, and the forecast is made for the mature period, serious errors can occur. Consequently, this forecasting technique, like all of the others, must be used with care. In general, the longer into the future the forecast is made, the greater will be the size of the probable errors.

Judgmental Forecasts

Another major type of forecast is the judgmental forecast. This type of forecast may employ the kinds of mathematical or accounting techniques discussed earlier in this section, but those techniques are used just for informational purposes. As the name implies, judgmental forecasts ultimately rely on the (one hopes) informed judgment of the forecaster. As such, a number of factors in addition to the past data on earnings and revenues are considered. While the judgmental forecaster will

Table 12.3

█████████████

Paper Firms' Growth Rates

Company Name	Current EPS	Projected EPS Growth
Champion International	−1.05	NMF
Georgia–Pacific	1.04	NA
International Paper	2.87	18.5
Louisiana–Pacific	2.86	20.5
Macmillan Bloedel, Ltd.	0.74	NA
Mead Corporation	2.52	21.5
Scott Paper	2.01	22.5
Temple–Inland	2.07	17.0
Union Camp	1.10	27.0
Westvaco Corp.	1.40	10.5
Weyerhaeuser	2.71	22.0
Willamette Industries	2.49	21.0

Source: Value Line Publishing, Inc., *The Value Line Investment Survey*, various issues. Data are current through June 1994. NMF = Not Meaningful; NA = Not Available.

certainly be interested in recent performance, he or she will also be sure to concentrate on the future prospects of the company. The analysis might focus on issues such as financial stability, market share, and quality of management. Many of these are reviewed in the following sections.

Table 12.3 presents Value Line's forecast for firms in the paper industry. The first column of figures gives the current EPS for each firm. The last column gives the projected change in EPS over the next fiscal year. Notice that Value Line believes EPS will surge dramatically over the next year for most firms, with most estimated increases being about 20 percent. Notice that Champion International has a negative current EPS, making a growth projection impossible.

The investor using the fundamental analyst's model should be able to apply one or more of these forecasting techniques to form a reasonable forecast of future earnings. This will provide one of the key inputs into the model—the expected earnings. The next step is to estimate the justified P–E ratio.

The Justified P–E Ratio

After obtaining the best estimate of the expected earnings, the investor must include the justified P–E ratio in the fundamental analyst's model. The analyst multiplies these two terms in the model to give the stock's value. A number of factors operate together to determine the justified P–E ratio for a particular firm. Many of these factors are also important for judgmental estimates of future earnings. This section discusses three broad categories of factors affecting the justified P–E ratio: firm financial characteristics, managerial style, and special firm characteristics.

Justified P–E Ratios and Firm Financial Characteristics

Financial characteristics both reflect and help to determine the justified P–E ratio of particular firms. The following accounting and financial issues are discussed in this section:

1. Accounting earnings
2. Dividend policy
3. Financial leverage
4. Notes to the financial statements

This discussion begins by focusing on earnings. However, the emphasis is on the interpretation and validity of the reported earnings figures. In addition to earnings, measures of profitability are also important gauges of a firm's performance and useful guides to the firm's likely prospects. The dividend policy that the firm follows helps to shape the firm's future prospects for earnings growth, and thereby influences the justified P–E ratio. The same is true of the yield that shares offer and the way in which the firm uses leverage.

Accounting Earnings. One of the most important aspects of company analysis is the normalization and interpretation of the accounting earnings figures that firms present in their annual reports and other public releases. Since the earnings values play such a central role in the fundamental analyst's model, it is clear that the predictions from the model can be only as good as the earnings figures that are used as inputs. The importance of interpreting the earnings figures stems from the fact that accounting earnings are not always what they seem. In fact, two companies that are identical in all of their physical operating characteristics could justifiably present radically different earnings figures in their annual reports. This possibility arises because accounting earnings are not the same as economic earnings. **Accounting earnings** may be thought of as the results of applying a set of accounting rules to the operations of the firm. However, there is considerable permissible variation in the application of the accounting rules. As a result, two equally honest and diligent accounting firms might arrive at different earnings figures for a given firm in the same time period.

The important implication of these facts is that accounting earnings must be interpreted with care, because they are imperfect measures of economic earnings. **Economic earnings** equal the change in purchasing power earned by the firm in a given period. Economic earnings reflect all profits earned, all exhaustion of capital, all effects of inflation, and the like. From this, it is clear that the conception of economic earnings is very difficult to specify with precision. In spite of the fact that the accounting earnings should ideally reflect the economic earnings, there is often discrepancy between the two. Since economic earnings truly measure the operating

Table 12.4

Income Statements for Bigern Corp. and Conserv, Inc.

	Income Statements	
	Bigern Corp.	Conserv, Inc.
1. Gross Sales	$1,000	$910
2. Cost of Goods Sold	(600)	(640)
Operating Income	$ 400	$270
Depreciation Expense	(140)	(140)
Earnings Before Interest and Taxes	$ 260	$130

1. *Gross Revenue*: Bigern recognizes sales when orders are placed. Conserv recognizes sales only when goods are shipped.

2. *Cost of Goods Sold*: Bigern uses FIFO accounting, assuming that the first items put into a given inventory category were the first to be used. (FIFO: first in/first out.) Conserv uses LIFO accounting, assuming that the last items put into a given inventory category were the first to be used. (LIFO: last in/first out.)

results of the firm, the fundamental analyst must be careful to reconcile any discrepancy between the accounting earnings and the estimated economic earnings.

To see the importance of these differences, consider two firms that are identical in all respects except for the decisions they make about how to treat certain events for accounting purposes. Bigern Corporation chooses the accounting treatment that results in larger reported earnings at every opportunity. By contrast, Conserv Incorporated always chooses the accounting standard that results in lower reported earnings. In spite of the fact that both firms have identical operations, except in the accounting department, the two firms report drastically different earnings for the same period. Table 12.4 presents a highly simplified pair of income statements to illustrate how the accounting choices can dramatically affect the reported earnings.

First, Bigern is very aggressive in recognizing sales. The moment an order is received, Bigern regards the sale as completed. By contrast, Conserv waits until it actually ships the goods. Because Bigern recognizes sales sooner than Conserv does, Bigern will always report larger sales, as long as business is growing. Second, Bigern uses the **FIFO method** of inventory accounting, which assumes that the first item of a given type that was purchased and put into inventory was the first used. By contrast, Conserv uses the **LIFO method**, which assumes that the most recently acquired item in an inventory was used. When prices for goods are rising, there can be dramatic differences in the purchase price of the first and last items of a given type that were acquired for inventory. In an inventory of screws, for example, the first might have been purchased in 1950 and the last in 1994. Assuming that the 1950 screw was used rather than the 1994 screw could mean a big difference in the cost of goods sold, particularly when this effect is added up across all of the components used to make a given product. In the example of Table 12.4, these differences together resulted in Bigern's having before–tax earnings that are twice as large as Conserv's. Occasionally, dramatic reports of conscious attempts to manipulate earnings figures come to light. Not all are based on simple choices among equally permissible accounting techniques.

The fact that firms can manage their earnings means that it is sometimes possible to fabricate an amazing growth record in earnings. This is possible even when there is no real improvement in cash flow. In some actual cases, the market has apparently been fooled by such accounting sleight–of–hand into rewarding firms with very large P–E ratios. When the real financial status of such firms comes to light, the market often reacts very swiftly to reflect the new information that calls for a new P–E ratio.[1]

For the analyst, these different accounting strategies mean that the reported earnings must be adjusted to reveal the true economic earnings more accurately. This has particular significance because past earnings will generally be important in determining the next period's expected earnings and in estimating the growth rate in earnings. As such, the earnings estimates affect both elements of the fundamental analyst's model: the expected earnings and the justified P–E ratio.

Dividend Policy.   As we have seen, dividends are the essential cash flows that determine the share price in the dividend valuation model. However, dividends are also important in the fundamental analyst's model. A firm's earnings that escape taxation may be retained for reinvestment or they may be paid as cash dividends. Funds paid as dividends are no longer available for reinvestment. A firm that pays a large dividend must either reduce its investment program or raise new funds in the capital market. If the firm reduces investment, future earnings are likely to be smaller than they otherwise would be.

In the fundamental analyst's model, the importance of a dividend policy lies in its implications for future earnings growth and the justified P–E ratio that depends so heavily on future earnings growth. Dividend policy is one of the features of corporate finance that is poorly understood.[2] It continues to be an important decision for corporate managers, and it can also be important to security investors, both for the information the dividend decision may convey and for the cash flows that constitute the dividend.

---

[1]Abraham J. Briloff has made a careful study of many of the more amazing reversals of a firm's earnings, due to the firm's accounting techniques. He explains the techniques used and the results of the gimmickry in a very entertaining and informative way in his books. See *Unaccountable Accounting*, (New York: Harper & Row, 1972), and *More Debits than Credits*, (New York: Harper & Row, 1976), for writing about accounting that can be simultaneously informative, interesting, and even entertaining.

[2]See Fischer Black, "The Dividend Puzzle," *Journal of Portfolio Management*, 2, Winter 1976.

Table 12.5

Dividend Data for Paper Industry Firms

Company Name	Current Dividend	Current Dividend Yield	5–Year Dividend Growth	Projected Dividend Growth
Champion International	0.20	0.6	−23.0	35.5
Georgia–Pacific	1.61	2.5	9.0	2.0
International Paper	1.68	2.4	6.5	3.0
Louisiana–Pacific	0.50	1.5	7.5	8.5
Macmillan Bloedel, Ltd.	0.60	3.2	−2.0	2.5
Mead Corporation	1.00	2.2	8.5	7.0
Scott Paper	0.80	1.7	3.0	7.5
Temple–Inland	1.02	2.0	22.0	6.5
Union Camp	1.60	3.4	6.5	2.5
Westvaco Corp.	1.11	3.4	9.0	4.5
Weyerhaeuser	1.20	2.9	4.5	9.0
Willamette Industries	1.00	2.2	9.0	8.0

Source: Value Line Publishing, Inc., *The Value Line Investment Survey*, various issues. Data are current through June 1994. NMF = Not Meaningful; NA = Not Available.

Table 12.5 presents dividend information for the 12 firms in the paper industry example. The first column of figures shows the actual dollar dividend per share, ranging from $.20 to $1.68. These figures are not very meaningful as a basis of comparison. To compare dividends, one should consider the dividend yield or current yield, shown as the second column of figures. This current yield is the ratio of the dollar dividend divided by the price, and it is expressed in percentage terms. The dividend yields range from 0.6 percent to 3.4 percent. These are relatively low dividends yields, lower than the average of the market as a whole.

Table 12.5 also presents the five–year growth rate in dividends for each firm. These range from a low for Champion International of a 23 percent cut in dividends to a high of 22.0 percent for Temple–Inland. In 1981, Champion paid dividends of $1.48, but by 1986 it had cut its dividend to $.52. After 1986, dividends have risen sharply to $1.10 in 1990. However, Champion slashed its dividend in mid–1991 to $.20 per share per year, where it has remained until 1994. Value Line dividend growth projections appear in the last column of Table 12.5.

The dividend payout ratio also indicates the percentage of the firm's earnings being paid in dividends. Table 12.6 presents the dollar dividends per share, the current annual earnings per share, and the dividend payout ratio. The dividend payout ratio equals the dollar dividends divided by the EPS. As the table shows, these range from 17.48 percent for Louisiana–Pacific to 154.81 percent for Georgia–Pacific. Champion is paying its dividend even though it lost money in 1993. As Georgia–Pacific, Union Camp, and Champion are all paying a dividend

Table 12.6

The Dividend Payout Ratio for the Paper Companies

Company Name	Current Dividend	Current EPS	Dividend Payout Ratio (%)
Champion International	0.20	−1.05	NMF
Georgia–Pacific	1.61	1.04	154.81
International Paper	1.68	2.87	58.54
Louisiana–Pacific	0.50	2.86	17.48
Macmillan Bloedel, Ltd.	0.60	0.74	81.08
Mead Corporation	1.00	2.52	39.68
Scott Paper	0.80	2.01	39.80
Temple–Inland	1.02	2.07	48.41
Union Camp	1.60	1.10	145.45
Westvaco Corp.	1.11	1.40	79.29
Weyerhaeuser	1.20	2.71	44.28
Willamette Industries	1.00	2.49	40.16

Source: Value Line Publishing, Inc., *The Value Line Investment Survey*, various issues. Data are current through June 1994. NMF = Not Meaningful; NA = Not Available.

that exceeds earnings, these firms will be forced to cut their dividends or to improve their earnings substantially.

Managers often signal the growth prospects of their firms by the way in which they manage their dividend policies. A policy of increasing the dividend payout ratio may well mean that managers foresee slower growth. By the same token, a policy of low or zero dividends might signal the expectation of continuing growth, because funds are being conserved for investment. Alternatively, it might signal management's fears about being able to sustain the dividend. For the paper industry, the dividend reductions clearly signal management concerns about sustaining cash flows to pay the dividends.

In the marketplace in general, firms with high dividend payout ratios tend to have relatively lower P–E ratios. This is probably due to the recognition by the market of the lower growth prospects signaled by the decision to pay large dividends. According to this line of reasoning, a dividend increase that is large relative to the increase in earnings might well signal diminishing growth prospects and could justify a lower P–E ratio.

Financial Leverage. When firms use debt as a source of financing, the fixed payments that must be made on the bonds give rise to **financial leverage**. The use of debt has two important effects on the justified P–E ratio. The first effect arises from the tax deductibility of interest payments, which may convey a real advantage to a firm with some debt in its capital structure. The second effect arises from the fact that a firm may use debt to increase its EPS, assuming that it has positive earnings. To

Table 12.7

Results of Different Capital Structures

	Alleq, Inc.	Bigdebt Corp.
Common Stock	(200 Shares at $10) $2,000	(100 Shares at $10) $1,000
Debt at 10%	0	1,000
Total Capitalization	$2,000	$2,000
	Income Statements	
Sales	$1,000	$1,000
Cost of Goods Sold	(600)	(600)
Operating Income	$ 400	$ 400
Depreciation	(150)	(150)
Earnings Before Interest and Taxes	$ 250	$ 250
Interest Expense	0	(100)
Earnings Before Taxes	$ 250	$ 150
Taxes at 34%	(85)	(51)
Net Income	$ 165	$ 99
Earnings per Share	$ .83	$ .99

see the effect of debt on EPS, and through EPS on the justified P–E ratio, consider two firms that are identical in all of their operating characteristics. The only difference between the two firms is a difference in their capital structure, which is shown in Table 12.7. Alleq is financed totally with equity, while Bigdebt raised half its funds from debt. The use of debt gives Bigdebt a tax break, and because the firm had positive earnings, it enjoys a higher level of EPS than the identical firm that is financed totally with equity. This indicates that it may be possible for a firm to manufacture the appearance of rapid earnings growth by the use of more and more debt. Since the justified P–E ratio and earnings growth are intimately related, the appropriate P–E ratio will depend to some extent on the degree of financial leverage.

To the extent that the earnings growth is merely a product of changing financial leverage, it should not justify a larger P–E ratio for Bigdebt. This is the case because Alleq and Bigdebt maintain identical operating characteristics. However, financial leverage may confer real benefits on Bigdebt if the tax savings outweigh the increase in risk due to using debt. The use of debt generates tax savings because interest payments are made from before–tax earnings. Therefore, the debtholders can be paid with before tax–dollars. The equity holders, by contrast, must be paid with dividends, which are paid from after–tax earnings. The use of debt, however, may increase the risk level of the firm, because the debt payments must be made no matter what the earnings of the firm are.

Another way to see this same point is to consider two firms with similar growth rates in earnings, with one firm being totally financed by equity, while the other uses debt. The all–equity firm has a greater unused debt capacity than the leveraged firm. **Debt capacity** refers to the amount of debt a firm may safely or appropriately use. Because the two firms are alike in their operating characteristics, they must have the same total debt capacity. If one firm has sustained the identical growth record as the other but has used no debt, it should have the greater P–E ratio, because it still has the resource of a greater untapped debt capacity.

These considerations mean that the justified P–E ratio depends to some extent on the amount of leverage that is being used. If leverage is used in such a way that real tax benefits are captured, the firm with debt may well have a higher justified P–E ratio. Otherwise, the low–debt or zero–debt firm should have the higher P–E ratio, other factors being equal. For the financial analyst, the degree of financial leverage is important in determining the P–E ratio for both its effects on the risk level of the firm and the effect of the use of leverage in generating earnings growth.

Table 12.8 presents leverage figures for our 12 paper companies. The leverage measures are the ratio of debt to total assets and the ratio of debt to equity. The higher the debt ratios, the riskier the financial position of the firm, other factors being equal. For these firms, the debt–to–assets ratio ranges from 11.70 percent for Louisiana–Pacific to 39.42 percent for Georgia–Pacific. The debt–to–assets and debt–to–equity measures are highly correlated, as they must be, given their definitions.

Table 12.8

Debt Ratios for the Paper Companies

Company Name	Debt/Total Assets (%)	Debt/Net Worth (%)
Champion International	36.27	102.03
Georgia–Pacific	39.42	173.06
International Paper	21.65	57.85
Louisiana–Pacific	11.70	18.37
Macmillan Bloedel, Ltd.	39.01	100.63
Mead Corporation	32.87	86.74
Scott Paper	35.72	150.17
Temple–Inland	30.70	61.45
Union Camp	26.57	68.56
Westvaco Corp.	32.04	68.99
Weyerhaeuser	31.26	75.59
Willamette Industries	33.58	74.86

Source: Value Line Publishing, Inc., *The Value Line Investment Survey*, various issues. Data are current through June 1994. NMF = Not Meaningful; NA = Not Available.

Notes to the Financial Statements.   In addition to the issues of accounting earnings, dividend policy, and financial leverage, the obscure parts of the financial statements can also be important for applying the fundamental analyst's model. In examining the financial statements of a firm, the financial analyst must also attend to the dreary footnotes in the annual report. On occasion, these footnotes have proven to be of extreme importance in determining the justified P–E ratio. An example from the use of convertible debt illustrates the point. As noted, earnings growth records have a great influence on P–E ratios. The P–E ratio should be higher the greater the expected rate of earnings growth in the future. One guide to future earnings growth, however, is the recent record of earnings growth.

As just noted, earnings growth can be temporarily fabricated by the clever use of ever–increasing amounts of debt. If EPS is measured simply as net income divided by the number of shares outstanding, the EPS can always be increased by finding financing sources that will finance increases in net income without affecting the number of shares outstanding. Debt, however, sticks out like a sore thumb on the balance sheet.

In the 1960s, another, less obvious technique of financing was used that did not affect the number of shares outstanding, yet allowed for reporting increased EPS. This technique involved issuing convertible debt. A convertible bond is a hybrid security with characteristics of both debt and equity. At the wish of the bondholder, a convertible bond can be exchanged for shares of stock. As such, it is more complicated than either a straight debt issue or a simple share of stock. If convertible debt were used as a financing source, then EPS could be increased without any real improvement in the operating results of a firm.

Abuses of this technique were so common in the 1960s that accounting rules were changed to eliminate the confusion. Now firms must report their EPS figures on a fully diluted basis. The **fully diluted basis** is calculated by assuming that all securities that could be converted into common stock are already converted. With this change in rules, the EPS–building advantage of convertible debt was taken away.

There are other important factors that are sometimes buried in the notes to financial statements. For example, pending litigation is reported in the notes. In some instances, overhanging suits may have a deleterious impact on future earnings and could require an adjustment to the justified P–E ratio.

Many firms also have liabilities to their pension plans that have not yet been funded. **Unfunded pension liabilities** are often discussed in the notes, and these liabilities are quite large for some firms, large enough to have an impact on their earnings growth and on their justified P–E ratios. For example, in mid–year 1994, Union Camp had a substantial unfunded pension liability. By contrast, International Paper's pension liability was fully funded.

Summary.   As we have seen, a firm's financial characteristics—accounting earnings, dividend policy, financial leverage, and even the notes to the accounting statements—are important for the fundamental analyst's model because they affect the basic inputs to the model, either the expected earnings for the next period or the justified P–E ratio. If the firm's financial picture gives a misleading indication of the growth prospects in earnings, the analyst must be prepared to adjust for this possibility and to make accurate estimates of the firm's growth prospects. Only then can accurate estimates of the expected earnings and the justified P–E be possible.

Justified P–E Ratios and Managerial Style

This section discusses some of the more important managerial characteristics that are likely to affect the justified P–E ratio and stock values. These are:

1. Public perception and investment value
2. Management quality
3. Reputation for quality of products or services
4. Innovation—research and development
5. Social responsibility

For most of these factors, the key issue is often one of public perception. But the perception of the firm by the investing public can affect the value of the shares, because managerial style can affect the justified P–E ratio. Remember that this is not necessarily the same as the present P–E ratio, but it is the P–E ratio that should prevail for a given stock if the market were valuing it correctly. The analyst's job is to evaluate the key managerial factors that should influence the P–E ratio in order to estimate the justified P–E ratio. As will become clear, managerial style is important because it helps to determine the future prospects for growth in earnings and dividends.

Table 12.9

Most and Least Admired Large Corporations, 1994

Most Admired	Industry
1. Rubbermaid	Rubber and plastic products
2. Home Depot	Specialist retailers
3. Coca–Cola	Beverages
4. Microsoft	Computer and data services
5. 3M	Scientific, photograhic, and control equipment

Least Admired	
400. Northwest Airlines	Airlines
401. Gitano Group	Apparel
402. Leslie Fay	Apparel
403. Trans World Airlines	Airlines
404. Brooke Group	Tobacco

Source: Tricia Welsh, "America's Most Admired Corporations," *Fortune*, February 7, 1994.

Public Perception and Investment Value. The prime focus of an investor's interest is on investment opportunity. Generally, the investor is not too interested in other aspects of the firm, such as its corporate reputation. However, these two features are often related. Each year *Fortune* magazine surveys leading executives to determine the most and least admired "Fortune 500" firms from selected industries. Table 12.9 shows the most and least admired firms among the firms included in the 1994 rankings. Among the 404 firms in the *Fortune* survey, Rubbermaid, Home Depot, Coca–Cola, Microsoft, and 3M were ranked as most admired. Three airlines were among the ten least admired firms, along with Glendale Federal, a savings and loan institution. In large part, these rankings seem to parallel recent investment performance. These rankings, by themselves, say little about the investment opportunities available with these different firms. However, the general perception of these firms is tied to more specific factors. Further, overall investor perceptions about the admirability of firms will clearly have an impact on their investment decisions. Management quality is one of the most important factors in deciding which companies are admirable and is critically important for the investment prospects of a firm.

Management Quality. Managers of corporations make all of the key decisions about the way in which the assets of a corporation are to be deployed, about the lines of business that will be pursued and abandoned, about the financial structure of the firm, and about the utilization and development of personnel.

Closely related to overall management quality is the issue of managing people. Table 12.10 shows the results of the *Fortune* ranking for management quality and the ability to attract, develop, and keep talented people. Not surprisingly, there

Table 12.10

Rankings for Management Quality

Overall Management Quality	
Most Admired	**Least Admired**
1. Home Depot	402. California Federal Bank
2. Rubbermaid	403. Brooke Group
3. J. P. Morgan	404. Leslie Fay

Ability to Attract, Develop, and Keep Talented People	
Most Admired	**Least Admired**
1. Microsoft	402. Northwest Airlines
2. J. P. Morgan	403. Brooke Group
3. Home Depot	404. Trans World Airlines

Source: Tricia Welsh, "America's Most Admired Corporations," *Fortune*, February 7, 1994.

is considerable overlap between the best overall management and the best management of the firm's personnel resources. Management quality is very difficult to assess, particularly for the outside investor. In the case of the very largest corporations, such as those in the *Fortune* survey, assessment is somewhat easier. Top management personnel for these firms are often featured in stories in the financial press, such as *Business Week*, *Fortune*, and *Forbes*. Readers of these publications can at least become acquainted with the personalities and major plans of these corporate leaders. The situation is much more difficult for smaller firms. For example, what is known by the generally informed public about the management of National Starch, Incorporated?

For professional analysts, one of the key means of assessing management quality is attending company presentations and visiting the facilities of the corporation. Most companies make presentations before the societies of financial analysts in major cities on a fairly regular basis, with the largest of these societies being located in New York. Managers typically view these presentations as an opportunity to present themselves and their corporations in a favorable light. The financial analyst can begin to appraise top management's quality by evaluating these performances. In addition, at the larger brokerage houses, analysts are assigned to cover a number of firms, often in a single industry. As part of their research, they occasionally visit the headquarters of the companies and have the opportunity to meet with key management. This allows a further means to acquire information about the quality of management.

Top corporate management has a great deal of discretion about how it runs the corporation, and this discretion extends to compensation for management itself. In standard corporate finance theory, the firm's managers are employed to act as the agent of the shareholders, who are the principals in the firm. The shareholders are regarded as principals because they actually own the firm. This separation between ownership and management can lead to **agency problems**—a situation that arises when the agent does not act in the interest of the principal.

Given the discretion that corporate management enjoys, it is easy to see how agency problems can become acute. The CEO of a corporation may pack the board of directors with cronies and arrange outlandish compensation. In many instances, the compensation that top management receives bears little or no relationship to the firm's success. On occasion, top executives arrange tremendous perquisites for themselves to the detriment of the shareholders. One recent and famous example is David Paul, leader of the now defunct savings bank, Centrust. Media attention spotlighted the gold bathroom fixtures in Centrust's corporate headquarters, a feature hardly beneficial to Centrust's beleaguered shareholders. Also, Paul purchased a number of pieces of valuable art with corporate funds and displayed this art at his home. When management fails to attend to corporate business, shareholders can suffer dramatically.

Reputation for Quality of Products or Services.   Corporate reputations for the quality of their products and services can also be an important influence on the investment prospects of a particular firm. As shown in Table 12.11, Rubbermaid, Procter & Gamble, and Walt Disney lead for the estimates of the quality of their products and

Table 12.11

━━━━━━━━━━━━━━

Rankings for Quality of Products or Services

Most Admired	Least Admired
1. Rubbermaid	402. Trans World Airlines
2. Procter & Gamble	403. Brooke Group
3. Walt Disney	404. Southern Pacific Transportation

Source: Tricia Welsh, "America's Most Admired Corporations," *Fortune*, February 7, 1994.

services. To see the importance of this factor, consider pharmaceutical production and the cost to Merck if it lost its reputation for producing quality products. In pharmaceuticals, public perception of quality is extremely important and fragile. Fear over the safety of a particular drug could have disastrous effects on company sales.

Innovation—Research and Development. In some industries, the speed of innovation is great. Firms may view a changing environment as providing an opportunity or as posing a threat. In other industries, there may be little opportunity for innovation. For instance, the pace of innovation in the paper industry seems rather slow. An investor would likely find the greater returns (along with greater risk) in the developing industries, those with rapid change and greater growth prospects. In terms of the industry life–cycle hypothesis elaborated on in Chapter 11, the best opportunities are likely to be found in emerging industries. One fast–changing industry is the financial services industry. With the relaxation of banking and other types of financial regulation, there is considerable opportunity for financial service firms to expand into other lines of business. Citicorp, for example, has been very aggressive in marketing its VISA card nationwide and in expanding into many states in what appears to be a major step toward nationwide branch banking. Merrill Lynch, for its part, introduced its "Asset Management Account." For larger customers, this is a unified account that incorporates most of the features of a credit account, brokerage account, savings account, and checking account. The three companies least admired for innovation are Borden, Southern Pacific Transportation, and Brooke Group. Poor financial performance seems to be the key featuring linking these disparate firms.

Social Responsibility. In recent years, the social responsibility of corporations has also become increasingly important for investors. Companies that disregard the health of their customers or the well–being of the environment may incur large losses from lawsuits or governmental intervention. Also, corporate reputation in the area of social responsibility is very important. In the *Fortune* survey, Rubbermaid, Corning, and Johnson & Johnson were ranked highest for community and environmental responsibility, while Food Lion, Gitano Group, and Brook Group were ranked lowest.

Focusing on the best and worst in this category shows the importance of social responsibility. Johnson & Johnson is the maker of Tylenol. The deaths caused by Tylenol capsules that had been intentionally poisoned after leaving Johnson & Johnson's warehouses threatened to destroy that leading product and the reputation of Johnson & Johnson. One possible line of response to the crisis might have been to try to "tough it out"—keep the product on the shelves and deny any wrongdoing or responsibility. Johnson & Johnson took a more aggressive approach, one that saved the product and the firm's reputation. Johnson & Johnson immediately removed all Tylenol from store shelves, held the product off the market while the poisoning case was being investigated and then reintroduced Tylenol with a new tamper–resistant packaging. Clearly, Johnson & Johnson was not responsible for the deaths in any way. In spite of this, their move to aggressively protect the public from any further danger, and to assume responsibility where it could have been avoided, earned high marks in the public eye. Further, when the product was reintroduced, it quickly became the market leader again and regained almost its entire market share. Even though the Tylenol scare occurred several years ago, the treatment of that situation has helped Johnson & Johnson's reputation over the years. At the lower end of the spectrum, Brooke Group and Gitano Group lost about one–third of their value in 1993. Brooke Group continues struggling with a net worth of –$500 million, while Gitano Group continues to lose money.

We have already discussed the paper industry's problems with pollution. Paper firms have a large impact on the environment, and the failure to exercise corporate responsibility could lead to serious lawsuits, consumer backlash, and costly restrictions on future operations. In this period of heightened ecological concern, investment results for a paper firm could be particularly sensitive to the firm's ecological responsibility.

Justified P–E Ratios and Special Firm Characteristics

Having examined the connection between the justified P–E ratio, firm financial characteristics, and managerial style, we now turn to a third major group of influences—special firm characteristics. In addition to the managerially determined factors discussed in the preceding section, there are a number of essentially financial factors that also have a large impact on the justified P–E ratios of firms. Many of these factors are not within the direct control of management, or at least they cannot be altered within a short period of time. Instead, they are often associated with the point occupied by the firm and industry in the life cycle and also depend on the nature of the business in which the firm is engaged.

Small Capitalization Firms.   For most of this century, small firms have tended to outperform larger firms. This appears true even when sophisticated allowances are made for differences in risk level. This suggests to the investor that investing in smaller firms is likely to prove more rewarding in the long run. However, there is no guarantee that the future will be like the past. Smaller firms tend to have greater rates of earnings growth than do larger firms because small firms tend to be in new industries where the growth opportunities are naturally greater. Also, as firms get larger, they tend to diversify into other product lines in addition to those that made them successful. One result of diversification is to limit growth, since the growth of the whole firm will depend on the growth of the parts and the relationship among the success rates for the different sectors.

Merger Potential.   Another important financial consideration for investors is the merger potential of a firm. Firms that are acquired tend to experience statistically significant price increases. These price increases become very large if two or more buyers begin to compete to acquire a given firm. Merger potential is greater for small firms, largely because they are easier for a bigger firm to acquire. It is difficult in many cases to say why a given merger occurs. One of the attributes that makes a company attractive as a takeover target, however, is the existence of a large pool of liquid assets or a large pool of temporarily undervalued assets. A company with a large amount of cash is a clear takeover target, for example. In certain industries, the characteristics of takeover targets are less clear. In the oil industry, for example, oil reserves are often the motivator for a takeover attempt.

These kinds of special firm characteristics—such as firm size and merger potential—are important in valuing the firm. While they are subject to management control in the long run, there is little that a manager can do to change these kind of characteristics in the short run. Nonetheless, they are potentially important to the investor, because they can affect the justified P–E ratio.

Summary

This chapter extends the cycle of analysis begun in Chapter 10. Chapter 10 introduced the dividend valuation model, while Chapters 11–12 considered the economy, industry, and firm specific factors that affect the inputs to the dividend valuation model—the expected dividends for the firm and the appropriate rate of discount. This chapter also introduced the fundamental analyst's model, which allows an easier application of the ideas behind the dividend valuation model. The fundamental analyst's model says that the value of a share of stock equals the expected earnings for the coming period multiplied by the justified P–E ratio for the firm.

In applying the fundamental analyst's model, this chapter examined the factors that affect the value of a share of stock—the expected earnings and the justified P–E ratio. Three basic types of models are employed to forecast earnings: the percentage of revenue technique, trend analysis, and judgmental forecasts. Earnings, however, are difficult to forecast accurately, no matter which technique is used. The justified P–E ratio is also critically important to the successful application of the fundamental analyst's model. Three basic classes of influences on the justified P–E ratio were discussed: firm financial characteristics, managerial style, and special firm characteristics. The analyst must consider each class of factors in order to successfully apply the fundamental analyst's model.

Questions and Problems

1. According to analysts that use the fundamental analyst's model, does price always equal value for stocks? What would it imply for stock investing if price and value were always the same?

2. Assume that you are a skilled analyst and that you reach your correct conclusions about the value of shares at the same time the market does. How can you profit from your analysis?

3. Assume that you are a skilled analyst and that you reach your correct conclusions about the value of shares, but the market never comes to share your perceptions. How can you profit from your analysis?

4. Explain one way in which accounting statements affect earnings growth estimates and how this might affect the estimated justified P/E ratio.

5. In forecasting earnings, explain some of the advantages and disadvantages of the percentage of revenue technique.

6. What is the basic difficulty with trend analysis as a technique for predicting future earnings?

7. How might financial leverage affect the justified P/E ratio?

8. At some times, P/E ratios for stocks as a whole tend to be high. At other times they tend to be low. Should this be true? Why or why not?

9. Our discussion of stock investing employs the dividend valuation and fundamental analyst's model. Are these two models consistent?

10. Respond to the following claim: "The fundamental analyst's model takes no account of capital gains. Its entire focus is on earnings and the way in which the market values those earnings. But this leaves out capital gains, so the model cannot be correct."

11. Respond to the following claim: "The market price of a share is the best estimate we have of the share's true value, because the price reflects the combined wisdom of all market participants. Further, investors are like voters, who vote with their investment decisions to determine the correct value of shares. Naturally, this collective intelligence is better than the efforts of any particular analyst."

12. How would the speaker in the preceding question explain the existence of analysts with spectacular records of correct stock predictions?

13. If a firm earned $1.44 per share in 1990 and $2.56 in 1994, what was the growth rate in earnings over this period?

14. For a firm with current EPS of $1.09, you have estimated next period's earnings will grow by 10 percent, and you have estimated the justified P/E ratio to be 14. What should the value of this share be next period? If the share is selling for $15 now, what would you do? Assume now that the risk–free rate of interest is 12 percent. Does this change your answer?

Suggested REALDATA Exercises

The following *REALDATA* exercises explore the concepts developed in this chapter: Exercises 66, 67, 68.

Suggested Readings

Bauman, W. S. and R. Dowen, "Growth Projections and Common Stock Returns," *Financial Analysts Journal*, 44:4, July/August 1988, pp. 79–80.

Black, F., "The Dividend Puzzle," *Journal of Portfolio Management*, 2:2, Winter 1976.

Briloff, A. J., *More Debits than Credits*, New York: Harper & Row, 1976.

Briloff, A. J., *Unaccountable Accounting*, New York: Harper & Row, 1972.

Carter, R. B. and H. E. Van Auken, "Security Analysis and Portfolio Management: A Survey and Analysis," *The Journal of Portfolio Management*, 16:3, Spring 1990, pp. 81–85.

Reinganum, M. R., "The Anatomy of a Stock Market Winner," *Financial Analysts Journal*, 44:2, March/April 1988, pp. 16–28.

Worthy, F. S., "Manipulating Profits: How It's Done," *Fortune*, June 25, 1984, pp. 50–54.

Portfolio Management

As was the case with bond investing, stocks are most often held in portfolios. The reasons for holding securities in portfolios are very well understood, particularly with respect to stock portfolios. This part of the book presents the basic ideas underlying portfolio management—the combining of securities to achieve the best return for a given level of risk.

Chapter 13 presents the rationale for diversification, the holding of securities with differing characteristics in a single portfolio. As we will see, by diversifying, the investor can greatly reduce risk without adversely affecting return. Chapter 14 presents one of the basic ideas of finance: investors may expect rewards in financial markets as compensation for the risk-bearing services that they provide to society. In fact, there is even a market-determined level of compensation that is paid for that risk-bearing service. Chapters 13 and 14 are the most theoretical of the book, but they may also be the most important. Essentially, they provide the basic rationale to help us understand a great deal about how investors actually behave and how they ought to behave.

Chapter 15 examines the actual behavior of markets to determine whether prices behave in the manner specified by theory. As we will see, markets in general behave very much as theory predicts. However, there are some important exceptions to this general conclusion. Seeing the connection between theory and the actual behavior of security prices has important implications for investor strategy. In essence, the theory suggests that investors should hold well-diversified portfolios with a risk level they can tolerate.

Given the wisdom of holding well-diversified portfolios, it is no accident that an entire industry exists to meet the need of providing ready-made diversified portfolios. Chapter 16 discusses investment companies. An investment company is a firm that collects funds from a variety of investors and uses those funds to construct a portfolio. Each investor owns a fraction of the created portfolio that is proportional to each individual's investment. In addition to explaining how the different kinds of investment companies function, Chapter 16 also analyzes their investment performance to see whether it matches theory. This examination provides a summary of the theory and additional evidence about the kinds of investment performance investors should expect.

CHAPTER THIRTEEN

Diversification and Portfolio Formation

Overview

Having discussed the details of the money, bond, and equity markets, we can now analyze the ways in which different securities can be combined to form a portfolio. A **portfolio** is a collection of securities held by a single investor, whether an individual or institution. As this chapter explains in detail, one of the main incentives for forming portfolios is **diversification**, which is the allocation of investable funds to a variety of securities. By diversifying, investors reduce the risk that they would otherwise bear. Also, the risk reduction benefits of diversification can be achieved without reducing the returns on investments.

This chapter begins by examining the features of portfolios under certain simplifying assumptions. Initially, we consider the simple case of two–asset portfolios. Gradually, we include more complicated factors, such as the presence of riskier securities and differences in investor preferences. Compared with preceding chapters, this chapter requires more statistical reasoning, which is necessary to achieve the benefits of diversification. To make the application of these principles more concrete, specific examples of certain assets are considered, such as the properties of gold as a useful asset for achieving diversification.

Assumptions of the Analysis

To make the following discussion more manageable, we make certain simplifying assumptions about market operation and the psychology of investors. Together these assumptions imply that the financial market is perfect. A **perfect market** is a market without any impediments to trading, such as transaction costs or costly information. While these assumptions are not necessarily true, examining them helps us gain insights into very complicated processes. Also, while the assumptions themselves are not necessarily realistic, markets behave very much as if the assumptions were true. This will be shown in Chapters 14–17.

The Assumptions

We make five assumptions, which we list here and then discuss in turn:

1. There are no transaction costs in securities markets.
2. Information is free.
3. Investors appraise information in the same way.
4. Investors care only about expected return and risk in their investments.
5. Investors have a time horizon of one period.

No Transaction Costs.   In assuming that securities markets operate with no transaction costs, we assume away the existence of commission costs and taxes. This assumption is quite strong. For example, if there are no transaction costs, investors can also trade fractional shares because each security is assumed to be infinitely divisible.

Free Information.   We assume that all investors have free access to the complete body of information about securities and everything relevant to the pricing of securities. This assumption rules out a privileged access that some investors may enjoy from time to time in actual markets. In effect, it levels the playing field as investors compete to create portfolios that have the best combination of risk and expected return.

Common Appraisal of Information.   As a parallel assumption to the assumption of free information, assume that investors appraise the available information in a similar way. In assuming the same appraisal of information, we ensure that two investors with the same information about securities would reach the same assessment of risk and expected return. Because investors have the same information and the same mode of analysis, they will have identical expectations about the risk and expected return of the securities in the markets. Another way of stating this assumption is to say that investors have **homogeneous expectations**—they expect the same risk and return for securities.

The assumption of free information and a common mode of appraising that information essentially mean that we can gain insight into the entire market by considering the market from the point of view of any one investor. After all, if all investors have the same information and appraise it the same way, they will have a common set of expectations about risk and expected return. In effect, these two assumptions ensure that each investor is a clone of every other investor in terms of the expectations that they form about risk and expected return. However, this does not mean that every investor has the same tastes about risk and expected return. As we see later in this chapter, different tastes regarding risk and return give investors with identical expectations reasons to choose different portfolios.

Investors Care Only About Risk and Expected Return.   We assume that investors care only about the risk and expected return characteristics of securities. More specifically, we assume that all investors seek securities with higher expected returns, and all investors try to avoid risk. This assumption, coupled with the assumption that investors have homogeneous expectations about return and risk, means that all investors evaluate the risk and expected return characteristics of securities in the same way.

In assuming that investors care only about risk and expected return, we rule out other investor interests in owning securities. For example, if an investor gets enjoyment from owning the same securities as her friends, we do not consider that benefit. Focusing on risk and expected return means focusing only on the monetary characteristics of investing. Also, we do not consider other statistical characteristics of the probability distribution of returns, such as skewness. A probability distribution is skewed if it is not symmetrical. Thus, assuming a concern with only risk and expected return is virtually equivalent to assuming that the distribution of security returns is symmetrical.

Investors Have a One–Period Horizon.   We assume that all of the investors in the marketplace have the same one–period time horizon. If we did not make this assumption, we would have to consider the much more complex problem of evaluating many periods at once. This would greatly increase the mathematical complexity of the problem without necessarily providing more insight.

By assuming that investors have a one–period horizon, we can still accommodate many situations. For example, we can define the period of interest to be a day, week, or year as convenient. This assumption of a single period is equivalent to assuming that we are interested in only two dates, the present and some future date that is the end of the single period in question.

The Role of the Assumptions

These assumptions are useful for simplifying the analysis of diversification, and the assumptions can be judged by the extent to which they enable us to understand the formation of portfolios and the effect of diversification. While the assumptions are not realistic (for example, transactions costs are not zero), their lack of realism is more apparent than real. These strict assumptions are needed to allow mathematical precision in the derivation of the results we examine. Relaxing the assumptions makes the mathematics much more complicated, but the basic ideas do not change. As an example, consider the assumption of zero transaction costs. While this assumption is necessary for the mathematical derivations, the important issue is whether there are enough investors with low transaction costs so that markets behave as though the costs were zero. In fact, there are many traders (such as members of stock exchanges) that have extremely low transaction costs. So while this assumption is not literally true, it is a close approximation of the truth, and it greatly simplifies the analysis. The same is true of most of the other assumptions.

Table 13.1
▬▬▬▬▬▬▬▬
Historical Returns for Assets A and B

Year	Asset A	Asset B
1990	.18	.14
1991	.15	.09
1992	−.13	.02
1993	.05	−.03
1994	.14	.07
Mean	.078	.058
σ^2	.0127	.0034
σ	.1127	.0582

Risk/Expected Return Space

To illustrate the idea of a risk/expected return space and subsequent calculations for the two–asset risky portfolio, consider the data presented in Table 13.1 for two risky assets. These five years are percentage returns including dividends. The table also presents the arithmetic mean returns, standard deviations, and variances of returns for each security. Since the calculated mean and variance are based on the past data, they are the historical mean and variance. According to our assumptions, however, investors are interested in the expected return and variance.

For the sake of simplicity, assume that variance is constant. However, the estimated future expected return is equal to the past mean return. For the two securities in Table 13.1, this means that the expected return of Security A is estimated to be 7.8 percent and the expected return of Security B is 5.8 percent. Figure 13.1 presents the probability distribution of expected returns for Securities A and B. Security B has a lower expected return, but it also has a smaller level of risk, as measured by the variance or the standard deviation. In graphical terms, this is reflected by the greater spread in the probability distribution graph of Asset A.[1]

Risk/Expected Return Axes. Since investors are interested in only the expected return and the risk of securities, another very useful way of depicting their characteristics is in risk/expected return space, as Figure 13.2 shows. This graph depicts the lower expected return of Security B in comparison with A and the correspondingly lower risk level of B. As Figure 13.2 makes clear, an investor considering Securities A and

---

[1]At this point, the reader should be sure that he or she can calculate the expected returns and risk measures shown in Table 13.1. The details of this kind of calculation were presented in Chapter 1.

Figure 13.1

Probability Distributions of Returns for Securities A and B

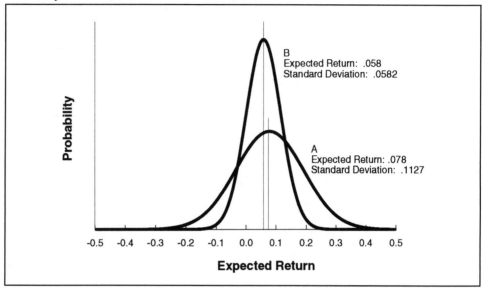

Figure 13.2

Securities A and B in Risk/Expected Return Space

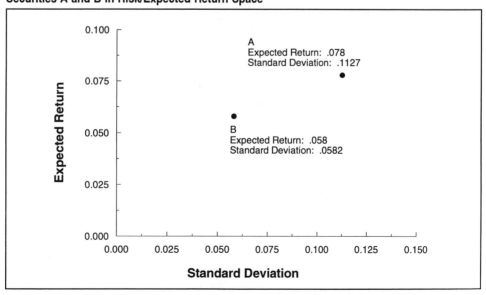

Figure 13.3

Dominance Relationships Among Securities in Risk/Expected Return Space

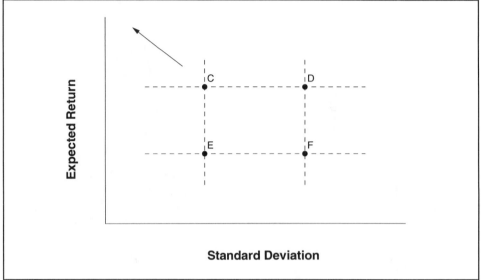

B faces a risk/return trade–off, or more exactly, a risk/expected return trade–off. However, it is customary to speak simply of the risk/return trade–off. The trade–off stems from the fact that the expected return of A is greater than that of B, but to get the higher expected return for investing in A, the investor must also accept the greater risk of Security A. Therefore, one must sacrifice higher expected return to obtain lower risk, or vice versa. Not surprisingly, this trade–off is the normal circumstance faced by investors.

The Concept of Dominance.   When an investor has investment opportunities in which this risk/return trade–off is not confronted, one investment opportunity *dominates* the other. Figure 13.3 illustrates the concept of dominance. Figure 13.3 shows four other securities in risk/return space. The arrow in the figure points toward the northwest. This is the preferred direction for all investors, because we assume they seek greater expected returns and avoid risk.

　　　Given the assumption that investors prefer greater expected returns and wish to avoid risk, it is also apparent that any investor would prefer Security C to Security E. Security C offers greater expected returns than Security E, but the two securities have the same level of risk. Therefore, any investor would prefer Security C to Security E. If we compare Security C to Security D, it is also clear that every investor would prefer Security C to Security D. Although C and D offer the same level of expected returns, C has less risk than D, so all investors would prefer C to D. Also, every investor would prefer Security C to Security F, because C offers both greater expected returns and less risk than F. By the same reasoning, it is also clear that all investors would prefer Security E to Security F, and that all investors would prefer Security D to Security F.

These relationships help to formulate a definition of **dominance**. One security dominates another if it meets at least one of the following three conditions:

1. If a given security offers greater expected return and the same risk level than a second security, then the first security dominates the second.
2. If a given security has the same expected return and a lower risk level than a second security, then the first security dominates the second.
3. If a given security has both a greater expected return and a lower risk level than a second security, then the first security dominates the second.

In terms of Figure 13.3, Security C dominates E and Security D dominates F by the first of these rules. Security C dominates D and Security E dominates F by the second of the rules. Finally, Security C dominates F by the third of the rules. Note also that the dominance relationship is transitive. Because C dominates E and E dominates F, it is necessarily the case that C dominates F.

Sometimes, however, it is not possible to say in advance that all investors would prefer one security to another. When comparing Securities D and E in Figure 13.3, some investors might prefer Security E, while others could reasonably prefer Security D. Their preferences would depend on their willingness to accept additional risk in order to capture additional expected returns. In other words, the choice between E and D depends on the individual investor's risk/return trade–off. In this case, D does not dominate E and E does not dominate D. This idea of dominance will be employed throughout our discussion of portfolios.

Two–Asset Risky Portfolios

A two–asset risky portfolio is just that—a portfolio made up of two risky assets. It is the simplest kind of portfolio we can use to illustrate the concept of diversification and the building of portfolios. The expected return on a two–asset portfolio depends on the expected returns of the individual assets and the relative weight or percentage of funds invested in each.

Expected Return of a Two–Asset Risky Portfolio

The expected return of a two–asset portfolio is given by:

$$E(R_p) = W_i E(R_i) + W_j E(R_j)$$

13.1

where:

W_i, W_j = percentage of funds, or weight committed to Assets i and j, respectively

$$E(R_p),\ E(R_i),\ E(R_j)\ =\ \text{the expected return on the portfolio, and individual Assets}\ i\ \text{and}\ j,\ \text{respectively}$$

Notice also that:

$$W_i + W_j = 1$$

The weights sum to 1.0 because all the funds under consideration are committed to one asset or another to form the portfolio. This also implies that:

$$W_j = 1 - W_i$$

So it is possible to express both weights in terms of just one.

To illustrate the central ideas behind two–asset risky portfolios, we will continue to use Securities A and B (introduced in Table 13.1) for many subsequent computations. Applying Equation 13.1 to Assets A and B, it is possible to answer questions such as: What is the expected return on a portfolio in which 70 percent of the funds are committed to Security A and 30 percent are committed to Security B? Adapting Equation 13.1 to fit our choice of securities gives:

$$E(R_p) = W_a E(R_a) + W_b E(R_b)$$

For this example, we know that:

$$W_a = .7 \qquad E(R_a) = .078$$
$$W_b = .3 \qquad E(R_b) = .058$$

Substituting these values into Equation 13.1 gives:

$$E(R_p) = (.7)\ (.078) + (.3)\ (.058)$$
$$= .072$$
$$= 7.2\%$$

As this calculation illustrates, the expected return of a two–asset portfolio is a simple weighted average of the expected returns of the individual assets. Since Asset A has a greater expected return, the portfolio's expected return will always be larger the greater the proportion of funds invested in Asset A. The maximum expected return of .078 occurs when all funds are invested in A.

The Risk of a Two–Asset Portfolio

The next calculation necessary for a two–asset portfolio is the computation of risk as measured by the variance or standard deviation of returns. As we will see, the riskiness of a portfolio depends on the tendency of the returns of the assets in the portfolio to move together. Returns move together when they tend to be high in the same time period and low in the same period. Mathematically, this tendency for returns to move together can be measured by the covariance of returns.

Definition of Variance.   Equation 13.2 presents the variance of a two–asset portfolio, which we denote by σ^2.

$$\sigma_p^2 = W_i^2 \sigma_i^2 + W_j^2 \sigma_j^2 + 2W_i W_j \sigma_{i,j}$$ **13.2**

where:
  $\sigma_{i,j}$ = the covariance of returns between Assets i and j (the other terms are as defined previously).

To calculate the variance of a two–asset portfolio, we need to know the proportion of funds committed to each asset, the variance or standard deviation of each asset, and the covariance between the returns of the two assets.

Definition of Covariance.   The **covariance** is simply a measure of the tendency of the returns to move in the same direction, and it is given by Equation 13.3.

$$\sigma_{i,j} = \frac{\sum_{t=1}^{T} [R_{i,t} - E(R_i)][R_{j,t} - E(R_j)]}{T}$$ **13.3**

where T = the number of periods used to calculate the covariance.

Calculating the Covariance.   To calculate the covariance of returns for two assets, the investor needs to know the returns for each asset for each period. The calculation of the covariance can be illustrated using the returns for Securities A and B, which were presented in Table 13.1, and by following these steps.

Step 1: Calculate the deviations for each security by subtracting the mean return from the return in each period.

	Asset A					**Asset B**				
	Return	–	Mean	=	Deviation	Return	–	Mean	=	Deviation
1990	.18	–	.078	=	.102	.14	–	.058	=	.082
1991	.15	–	.078	=	.072	.09	–	.058	=	.032
1992	−.13	–	.078	=	−.208	.02	–	.058	=	−.038
1993	.05	–	.078	=	−.028	−.03	–	.058	=	−.088
1994	.14	–	.078	=	.062	.07	–	.058	=	.012

If this calculation has been made correctly, the sum of all of the deviations for each security will equal zero.

Step 2: For each period, multiply the respective deviation for one asset by the deviation for the other asset and compute the sum of all of the products.

	Asset A Deviation	×	Asset B Deviation	=	Products
1990	.102	×	.082	=	.0084
1991	.072	×	.032	=	.0023
1992	−.208	×	−.038	=	.0079
1993	−.028	×	−.088	=	.0025
1994	.062	×	.012	=	.0007
					.0218

Step 3: Divide the sum of the products computed above by T, the number of periods used to compute the products. The answer is the covariance.

$$\sigma_{a,b} = \frac{.0218}{5} = .0044$$

As shown in the example for Securities A and B, the covariance of returns for the period under analysis is .0044. This covariance, in addition to our other information, is enough to compute the variance and standard deviation of a two–asset portfolio composed of Securities A and B.

Calculating the Variance.   To compute the variance of a two–asset portfolio, we need several pieces of information. We need to know the proportion of funds committed to each asset (the weights), the standard deviation or variance of returns for each asset, and the covariance between the returns for the two assets. Stating the equation for the variance of a two–asset portfolio as it applies to Assets A and B and using our sample data gives the following results:

$$\sigma_p^2 = W_a^2 \sigma_a^2 + W_b^2 \sigma_b^2 + 2W_a W_b \sigma_{a,b}$$
$$= (.7)^2 (.0127) + (.3)^2 (.0034) + (2)(.7)(.3)(.0044)$$
$$= .0084$$

The standard deviation of a variable is simply the square root of the variance of that variable. Accordingly, the standard deviation of returns for a portfolio is given by:

$$\sigma_p = \sqrt{\sigma_p^2}$$

$$= \sqrt{.0084}$$

$$= .09165$$

Because the standard deviation is in the same units as the original variable, it is often more intuitively meaningful than the variance. In this case, the computed standard deviation of our portfolio is 9.165 percent per year.

The Correlation Coefficient.   The risk measures for portfolios can also be expressed using the correlation coefficient instead of the covariance. The correlation and covariance are very closely related, as shown by the following formula:

$$\rho_{a,b} = \frac{\sigma_{a,b}}{\sigma_a \sigma_b} \qquad\qquad 13.4$$

In terms of our example, this means that the correlation between the returns of Securities A and B is:

$$\rho_{a,b} = \frac{.0044}{(.1127)\,(.0582)} = .6708$$

The equation for the variance of a two–asset portfolio may also be expressed using the correlation instead of the covariance:

$$\sigma_p^2 = W_i^2\sigma_i^2 + W_j^2\sigma_j^2 + 2W_iW_j\rho_{i,j}\sigma_i\sigma_j \qquad\qquad 13.5$$

The correlation coefficient is essentially a **scaled** covariance. The scaling means that the correlation must fall between –1 and +1. A correlation greater than zero means that the two variables tend to move in the same direction when they change. A negative value for the correlation indicates that the two variables tend to move in opposite directions. If the correlation between two variables equals zero, there is no correlation between them, and they are regarded as independent.

Risk, Covariance, and Correlation

In portfolio building, one of the most important factors affecting the risk of any portfolio is the extent of covariance or correlation among the individual assets comprising the portfolio. This is true no matter how many assets are in the portfolio, and we can illustrate this principle using a portfolio made up of two risky assets. Consider the two imaginary Securities, ABC and XYZ, and assume that they have the following risk and expected return characteristics.

	ABC	XYZ
Expected Return	.10	.18
Standard Deviation of Returns	.08	.22
Weight in Portfolio	.4	.6

Although it is one of the prime determinants of a portfolio's risk, the correlation between two securities has no effect whatsoever on the overall return of the portfolio composed of those two securities. This is clear from the formula for the expected return of a portfolio. In the case of our portfolio made up of ABC and XYZ, the expected return on the portfolio is given by:

$$E(R_p) = (.4)(.10) + (.6)(.18)$$
$$= .148$$
$$= 14.8\%$$

However, the importance of the correlation between securities in determining the risk level of a portfolio is difficult to exaggerate. To see the importance of the correlation of returns in determining the total risk of a portfolio, let us consider two special cases and examine the effect on the total risk of our portfolio made up of ABC and XYZ. The first special case arises when the correlation between the assets equals +1.0, with the second special case arising when the correlation equals –1.0.

Correlation = +1.0

The formula for the variance of a two-asset portfolio using the correlation coefficient is:

$$\sigma_p^2 = W_i^2 \sigma_i^2 + W_j^2 \sigma_j^2 + 2 W_i W_j \rho_{i,j} \sigma_i \sigma_j$$

If the correlation coefficient equals 1, the last term can be simplified to:

$$2 W_i W_j \sigma_i \sigma_j$$

because the correlation coefficient will drop out. In this special case, the expression for the variance becomes a perfect square:

$$\sigma_p^2 = W_i^2 \sigma_i^2 + W_j^2 \sigma_j^2 + 2 W_i W_j \sigma_i \sigma_j$$

Because this is a perfect square, we can easily take the square root of the variance formula, obtaining:

$$\sigma_p = W_i \sigma_i + W_j \sigma_j$$

In the special case of the correlation equaling 1, the risk of the portfolio depends only on the risk of the individual assets and on the weight that they represent in the portfolio. In the case of the portfolio of ABC and XYZ, the standard deviation of the portfolio is:

$$\sigma_p = (.4)(.08) + (.6)(.22)$$
$$= .164$$
$$= 16.4\%$$

Other portfolio weights would give portfolios of different risk levels. In fact, if we imagine that different portfolios were constructed of ABC and XYZ by just

Figure 13.4

Possible Risk/Return Combinations of ABC and XYZ When the Correlation of Returns = 1

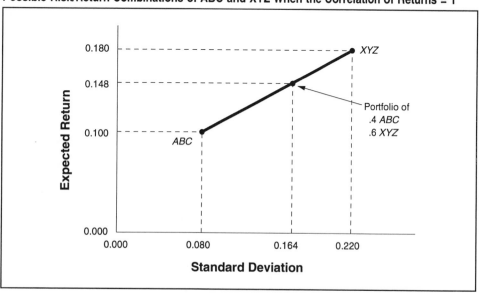

choosing different weights, it is possible to calculate where all of the possible portfolios made up of ABC and XYZ would lie in risk/return space.

Figure 13.4 shows the position of ABC and XYZ in risk/return space. The portfolio made up of 40 percent ABC and 60 percent XYZ is also shown. When the correlation between ABC and XYZ is 1.0, all of the risk/return possibilities that can be achieved lie on the straight line between ABC and XYZ as shown in Figure 13.4. This must be so because of the mathematics of the case. As we've already seen, when the correlation coefficient equals 1.0, the standard deviation of the portfolio is just a simple weighted average of the standard deviations of the individual assets.

Correlation = −1.0

The second special case arises when the correlation between the two assets equals −1.0. Returning again to the formula for the variance, we have:

$$\sigma_p^2 = W_i^2\sigma_i^2 + W_j^2\sigma_j^2 + 2W_iW_i\rho_{i,j}\sigma_i\sigma_j$$

If the correlation coefficient equals −1, the last term can be simplified to:

$$-2W_iW_j\sigma_i\sigma_j$$

Once again, the expression for the variance becomes a perfect square:

$$\sigma_p^2 = W_i^2\sigma_i^2 + W_j^2\sigma_j^2 - 2W_iW_j\sigma_i\sigma_j$$

This allows us to take the square root of the variance formula, obtaining:

$$\sigma_p = W_i\sigma_i - W_j\sigma_j$$

This is almost the same as the standard deviation for the special case of the correlation equaling 1.0, except now the second term has a negative sign.[2] For our same portfolio of ABC and XYZ, the standard deviation would be:

$$\sigma_p = (.6)(.22) - (.4)(.08) = .10$$

---

[2] There is a second root to this equation, namely $\sigma_p = W_a\sigma_a - W_b\sigma_b$. However, the calculated value using this root is −.1. Because the standard deviation can never be negative, by definition, we know that the other root is the one we seek.

Note that this is considerably less than the risk of the portfolio had the assets been perfectly correlated. Examination of the formula for the standard deviation when the correlation equals −1.0 shows that it might be possible to form a riskless portfolio. By setting the standard deviation equal to zero for this case and solving for the appropriate weights, we get:

$$\sigma_p = W_i \sigma_i - W_j \sigma_j = 0$$

Recalling that $W_b = 1 - W_a$, and substituting this value into the preceding equation, gives:

$$\sigma_p = W_a \sigma_a - (1 - W_a) \sigma_b = 0$$

Rearranging terms, and solving for W_a gives:

$$W_a \sigma_a - \sigma_b + W_a \sigma_b = 0$$
$$W_a \sigma_a + W_a \sigma_b = \sigma_b$$
$$W_a = \frac{\sigma_b}{\sigma_a + \sigma_b}$$

To create a riskless portfolio, we invest proportion W_a in Asset ABC. The remainder of the funds we invest in Asset XYZ.

$$W_a = \frac{\sigma_b}{\sigma_a + \sigma_b} = \frac{.22}{.08 + .22} = .7333$$

This can be confirmed by making the appropriate substitutions into the formula for the standard deviation.

$$\sigma_p = (.2667)(.22) - (.7333)(.08) = 0$$

This example illustrates a very important principle. Whenever two assets have a perfectly negative correlation, it is possible to form a risk–free portfolio. Figure 13.5 shows the possible portfolio combinations that can be constructed from ABC and XYZ when the correlation between them equals −1. The two lines from XYZ to the vertical axis and from ABC to the vertical axis define the opportunities, which include a risk–free portfolio, DEF.

Figure 13.5 also illustrates the idea of dominance that was introduced earlier. By combining ABC and XYZ in the correct amounts, it is possible to form a portfolio that will lie at point GHI on the line between XYZ and the vertical axis.

Figure 13.5

Possible Risk/Return Combinations of ABC and XYZ When the Correlation of Returns = –1

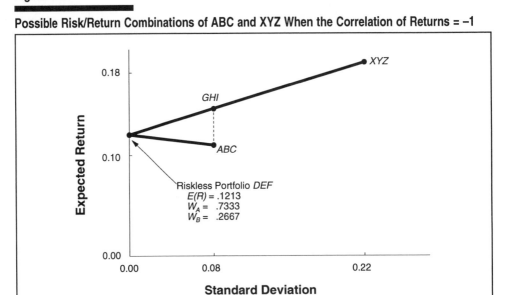

GHI dominates Asset ABC because GHI has the same level of risk as ABC but offers greater expected return. In fact, all of the portfolios on the line from ABC to DEF are dominated by some asset or portfolio on the line DEF to XYZ. The fact that ABC is dominated means that no investor should hold ABC alone. By mixing ABC with XYZ in varying amounts, portfolios can be created that are clearly superior to ABC alone.

Correlation Between –1 and +1

Thus far, we have considered two extreme cases, the situation when the correlation between two assets is either +1 or –1. Because the correlation must lie within this range, these two extremes define the entire realm of possibilities for risk/return combinations that can be formed for our two sample securities, ABC and XYZ. Figure 13.6, which combines the information from Figures 13.4 and 13.5, shows that the triangle (formed by the points ABC, DEF, XYZ) defines the total space that could be occupied by any two–asset portfolio made up of ABC and XYZ. This includes the points ABC and XYZ themselves, which are simply the portfolios that arise when all of the funds are placed in one asset and nothing in the other. The dashed line from ABC to XYZ in Figure 13.6 indicates all of the possible portfolio combinations when the correlation between ABC and XYZ equals 1. The two lines, from ABC to DEF and from XYZ to DEF, together define all of the possible portfolio combinations when the correlation between ABC and XYZ equals –1.

Figure 13.6

Possible Risk/Return Combinations of ABC and XYZ for All Possible Combinations

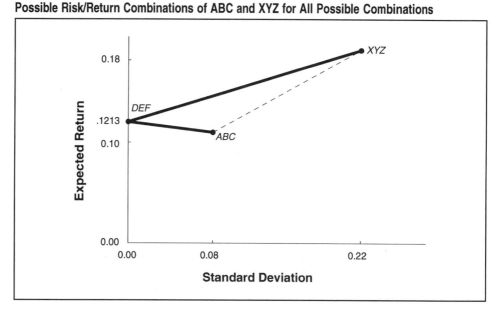

Typical Correlations Between Securities.   However, for the vast majority of security pairs, the correlation of returns between them lies at neither extreme of 1 or –1. Most securities, in fact, are positively correlated with each other. Earlier in this chapter, we used Securities A and B as examples and plotted the individual securities in risk/return space in Figure 13.2. We also calculated the correlation between the returns of Securities A and B and found it to be .6708. While A and B are only examples, the computed correlation between them is typical of the actual correlation values found in the market. Figure 13.7 shows the portfolios that could be created from Securities A and B given this correlation. As the figure shows, the possible portfolios lie along the curved line from A to B. In contrast with the extreme values that we have been examining, a correlation between +1 and –1 results in a curved line for the portfolio possibilities. The lower the correlation between the securities, the greater is the amount of curvature in the line indicating the portfolio possibilities.

Figure 13.8 shows how the portfolio possibilities between ABC and XYZ change for different correlations. The straight line between ABC and XYZ indicates the possible portfolios with perfect correlation and the two straight lines from XYZ to DEF to ABC indicate the possibilities with perfect negative correlation. The curved lines in the interior indicate the increasingly better opportunities as the correlation is assumed to fall from +1 toward –1. On the curved line labeled number 1, there is still a quite high correlation between the assets. Notice, however, that an investor would still be better off with curve 1 than with the perfect correlation line. In other words, any decrease in correlation benefits the investor.

Figure 13.7

Possible Risk/Return Combinations of Securities A and B

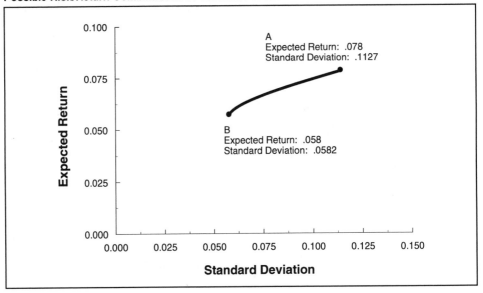

Figure 13.8

Possible Risk/Return Combinations of Securities ABC and XYZ with Diverse Correlations

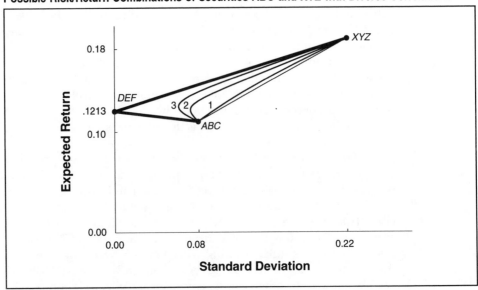

This is clear from the fact that points on curved line 1 dominate points on the straight line from ABC to XYZ. Curved lines 2 and 3, however, have points that dominate points on line 1. The best situation for the investor arises with perfect negative correlation. Then it is possible to achieve points on the line DEF to XYZ, and some point on this line will dominate all of the possibilities on all of the curved lines. One exception to this is point XYZ, which is common to all of the portfolio possibilities. No portfolio dominates Security XYZ. In general, the one asset with the greatest expected return can never be dominated.

An Intuitive Approach to Multiple Risky Assets

Before turning to the calculation of the expected return and risk of a multiple–asset portfolio, we can illustrate graphically the essential features of the multiple–asset case, as shown in Figure 13.9. The three individual assets in this figure are labeled 1, 2, and 3. We can combine any two assets to form a two–asset portfolio, and the figure shows the possibilities for combining Assets 1 and 2 into one portfolio and for combining Assets 2 and 3 into another portfolio. One of the combinations possible from combining Assets 1 and 2 is Portfolio 4, while similarly, Assets 2 and 3 could be combined to form Portfolio 5. Portfolios 4 and 5 have no special significance; many other portfolios could have been formed by giving different weights to the individual Assets 1, 2, and 3.

Figure 13.9

Portfolio Possibilities with Multiple Risky Assets

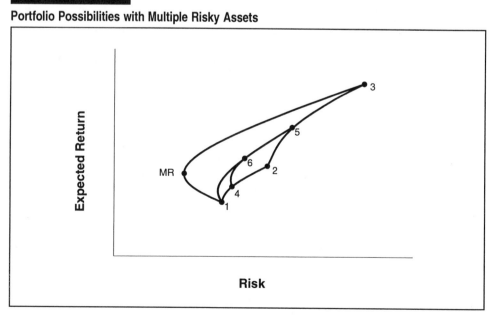

Treating Portfolios as Single Assets

For purposes of analyzing risk and expected return characteristics, however, we can treat a portfolio as a single asset. In the example of Figure 13.9, Portfolios 4 and 5 could be combined (as if they were single assets), to form other portfolios, such as those lying on the curved line from Portfolio 4 to Portfolio 5. By taking the right combinations of Portfolios 4 and 5, a possible new portfolio is shown as Portfolio 6. Portfolio 6, for its part, might be combined with Asset 1 to form another new set of possibilities shown on the curved line from Asset 1 to Portfolio 6.

How Portfolios Dominate Single Assets

This process of combining new portfolios out of the individual assets and other previously created portfolios has two interesting results. First, some of the new portfolios dominate the individual assets and some other portfolios. For example, in Figure 13.9, Portfolio 4 is dominated by some of the portfolios that could be constructed from Portfolio 6 and Asset 1. The second point to notice is that this process does not go on forever but stops when the curved line from Asset 1 to Asset 3 is reached. While this line goes from Asset 1 to Asset 3, many of the portfolios on this line include Asset 2. Among the many possible portfolios are some that are not dominated by any other. In Figure 13.9, the set of portfolios that is not dominated by any others lies on the curved line connecting Asset 1 and Asset 3, but only on that segment between Asset 3 and the portfolio indicated as MR.

The Minimum Risk Portfolio

In other words, given the initial set of only three assets, there are limits to what can be achieved through diversification, and these are shown on the curved line from Asset 1 to Asset 3 in Figure 13.9. However, not every possible portfolio on the line from Asset 1 to Asset 3 escapes domination. Portfolio MR is the minimum–risk portfolio that could be achieved from Assets 1, 2, and 3. All of those portfolios that lie on the curve from 1 to MR are dominated. This can be verified immediately by noting that for each of these portfolios there is one other directly above it on the segment of the curve running from Portfolio MR to Asset 3. Since any portfolio on the segment of the curve from MR to 3 offers the same risk level but greater expected return than any asset or portfolio directly below it, any portfolio on the curve from Asset 1 to MR will be dominated. In Figure 13.9, it is also clear that Asset 3 is not itself dominated. While Assets 1 and 2 are dominated, Asset 3 is not because no other asset or portfolio meets the criteria for dominating Asset 3 that were discussed earlier.

Risk and Expected Return
of Multiple–Asset Portfolios

All of the basic ideas introduced in the context of two–asset portfolios hold when investors are allowed to construct portfolios of many assets, as shown in Figure 13.9. However, the mathematical analyses of the expected return and risk of a portfolio with many assets are essentially the same as they were for the two–asset case, only somewhat more complicated.

Computing Risk and Expected Return for Multi–Asset Portfolios

In general, the expected return for a multiple asset risky portfolio is:

$$E(R_p) = \sum_{i=1}^{n} W_i E(R_i)$$ 13.6

and the variance of a multi–asset portfolio is given by:

$$\sigma_p^2 = \sum_{i=1}^{n} \sum_{j=1}^{n} W_i W_j \sigma_{i,j}$$ 13.7

These equations are really only extensions of the two–asset case that we have already examined in detail.

A Sample Calculation

These equations can be applied to a portfolio of any size using just three assets. The following table gives some values for three assets I, J, and K, and they can be used to illustrate the principles involved. The table assumes that the reader now knows how to calculate the expected return, standard deviation, and variance for individual assets, and the correlation of returns between any pair of assets.

Asset	Expected Return	Portfolio Weight	Standard Deviation
I	.10	.25	.17
J	.15	.40	.23
K	.20	.35	.29

The correlations among the three assets are shown in the following correlation matrix:

	Asset		
	I	**J**	**K**
I	1.00		
Asset **J**	.80	1.00	
K	.72	.65	1.00

Because the formula of Equation 13.7 uses the covariance term, the following matrix is the variance–covariance matrix that is consistent with the preceding correlation matrix.

	Asset		
	I	**J**	**K**
I	.0289		
Asset **J**	.0313	.0529	
K	.0355	.0434	.0841

The correlation and variance–covariance matrices show the correlation between all possible pairs of assets in our set. Notice that the correlation of each asset with itself is 1.00. Naturally, the returns of an asset are perfectly correlated with themselves. In the variance–covariance matrix, the variance terms lie on the **main diagonal**—the diagonal running from the northwest to the southeast. The covariance of an asset with itself is just the variance of the asset. For example:

$$\sigma_{i,i} = \sigma_i^2 = .0289$$

All of the off–diagonal terms are the covariances. With all of this information, it is possible to unpack our general Equations 13.4 and 13.5.

Computing the Expected Return. The expected return of our three–asset portfolio is:

$$E(R_p) = W_i E(R_i) + W_j E(R_j) + W_k E(R_k)$$
$$= (.25)(.10) + (.40)(.15) + (.35)(.20)$$
$$= .155$$
$$= 15.5\%$$

Computing the Variance. For the variance calculation, we must know how to interpret the double summation sign. Double summation means that we should let $i = 1$ first, and then sum all of the different values for j, as j equals 1, 2, . . . , n. Then we should let $i = 2$, and repeat the entire process for j. We should continue repeating this process until we have performed the entire calculation n times. This means that we will have made n^2 such calculations. As the number of securities becomes larger, the number of calculations to perform becomes gigantic.

With three assets we will first let the outer summation sign take on the value I, while the inner takes the three different values I, J, and K. Then the outer summation sign will take the value J, while the inner takes the values I, J, and K. Finally, the outer summation sign will take the value K, and the process will be repeated a final time. When the process is completed for the case of three securities, there will be $3^2 = 9$ terms to consider, as shown in the following table.

Outer/Inner Summation	Term	Numerical Value	Numerical Result
I / I	$W_i W_i \sigma_{i,i}$	(.25)(.25)(.0289)	.0018
I / J	$W_i W_j \sigma_{i,j}$	(.25)(.40)(.0313)	.0031
I / K	$W_i W_k \sigma_{i,k}$	(.25)(.35)(.0355)	.0031
J / I	$W_j W_i \sigma_{j,i}$	(.40)(.25)(.0313)	.0031
J / J	$W_j W_j \sigma_{j,j}$	(.40)(.40)(.0529)	.0085
J / K	$W_j W_k \sigma_{j,k}$	(.40)(.35)(.0434)	.0061
K / I	$W_k W_i \sigma_{k,i}$	(.35)(.25)(.0355)	.0031
K / J	$W_k W_j \sigma_{k,j}$	(.35)(.40)(.0434)	.0061
K / K	$W_k W_k \sigma_{k,k}$	(.35)(.35)(.0841)	.0103
			$\sigma_p^2 = .0452$

To compute the variance of this portfolio, we need to compute each of the nine terms shown and sum them. All of the numerical values are shown in the last column. The sum of these nine values, .0452, is the variance. The standard deviation of returns for this portfolio is just the square root of the variance, or .2126. In comparison with the individual assets, the portfolio has a standard deviation that is less than that of Asset J or K, but greater than that of Asset I.

The location of the three assets and the portfolio are shown in risk/return space in Figure 13.10. The expected return of 15.5 percent and the standard deviation of returns of 21.26 percent for the portfolio means that the portfolio dominates Asset J. This is the case because the portfolio offers both greater expected return and lower risk than Asset J. It may well be possible to create other portfolios of these three securities that would dominate the portfolio we have created.

The Efficient Set and the Efficient Frontier

In a market with many securities, the final result of portfolio building is likely to look like Figure 13.11. The points on the interior of the curve represent individual

Figure 13.10

Three Assets and a Portfolio in Risk/Return Space

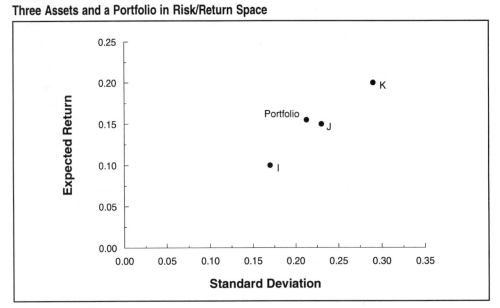

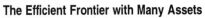

Figure 13.11

The Efficient Frontier with Many Assets

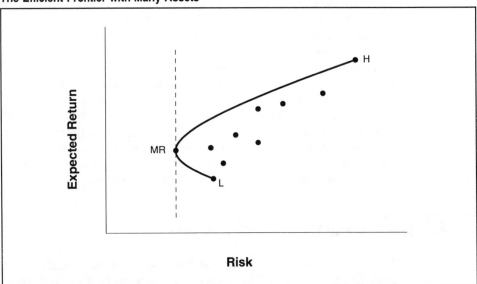

assets, while the curve running from L to H represents the ultimate portfolios that can be created from the many individual assets available in the marketplace. Once again, certain portfolios on the curve from L to H are dominated. All of those portfolios on the curve from L to MR are dominated. The minimum–risk portfolio, MR, is not dominated, nor are any of the portfolios from H to MR.

All of the portfolios, and the single Asset H, which lie on the line from H to MR are not dominated and accordingly form the efficient set. The **efficient set** is the set of all assets and portfolios that are not dominated. The **efficient frontier** is the graphical representation of the elements of the efficient set. In Figure 13.11, the efficient frontier is the line from H to MR.

The efficient set and the efficient frontier have a special significance for investors. All investors who desire higher expected returns and who wish to avoid risk will want to invest in portfolios that are members of the efficient set. In other words, they want portfolios that lie on the efficient frontier running from H to MR. This desire is completely reasonable, because any other portfolio that an investor might consider will be dominated by one that does lie on the efficient frontier.

The Dramatic Effects of Diversification

While it may seem that diversification is a nice idea in theory, an investor might still wonder whether it matters in practice. This important question was studied with very dramatic results by Wagner and Lau.[3] Their strategy was to form many portfolios with varying numbers of stocks in each portfolio. To do this, they selected stocks at random from the New York Stock Exchange and formed many one–stock portfolios, two–stock portfolios, and so on, up to 20–stock portfolios. They then computed the average standard deviation of each of the different sizes of portfolios. These average standard deviations for each of the portfolios of a different size are summarized in Figure 13.12.

The portfolios with the highest average risk level were the one–stock portfolios. The two–stock portfolios had lower risk, and so on to the 20–stock portfolios, which had the lowest average risk. The average standard deviation of the one–stock portfolio is just the average standard deviation of a single stock in the New York Stock Exchange. Compared with the level of risk for a single stock, a 20–stock portfolio has about 40 percent less risk. In other words, by choosing a 20–stock portfolio at random, an investor can avoid about 40 percent of the risk of an average share of stock.

This process of choosing stocks at random to construct a portfolio is called **naive diversification**. It is also possible, by using certain mathematical program-ming techniques, to find the portfolios that lie on the efficient frontier. This more sophisticated technique of diversification is known as **Markowitz diversification**,

---

[3]W. Wagner and S. Lau, "The Effect of Diversification on Risk," *Financial Analysts Journal*, 26, November–December 1971, p. 50.

Figure 13.12

The Effect of Diversification

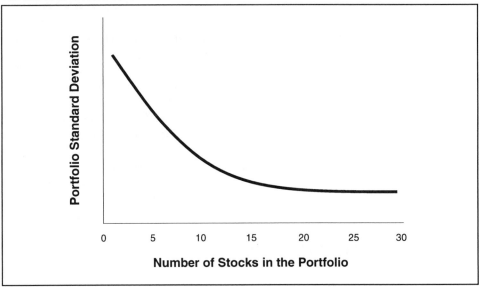

named after its creator, Harry Markowitz.[4] Markowitz won the Nobel Prize for Economics in 1990, largely for his work on diversification theory.

International Diversification

If diversification is a good idea, and if it depends on getting stocks that have returns that are not highly correlated, perhaps even greater diversification benefits could be achieved by diversifying a stock portfolio across national boundaries. In fact, this appears to be exactly the situation.

This problem was studied by Bruno Solnik, who examined the benefits of diversification for a number of major stock markets. He followed a technique of forming portfolios of varying sizes and computed the amount of diversification benefit that was achieved in the stock market for each country. He measured this by finding the standard deviation for a typical stock in each of the national stock markets. This he defined as 100 percent. As we have seen, as the investor increases the number of stocks in the portfolio, risk falls. This is true for every national market. Figure 13.13 is reproduced from Solnik's study. It shows the percentage reduction in risk for purely domestic diversification in each of six national markets. For example, the U.S. investor can diversify away about 60 percent of the risk in a

---

[4]See Harry Markowitz, "Portfolio Selection," *Journal of Finance*, March 1952.

Figure 13.13

Diversification in National Markets

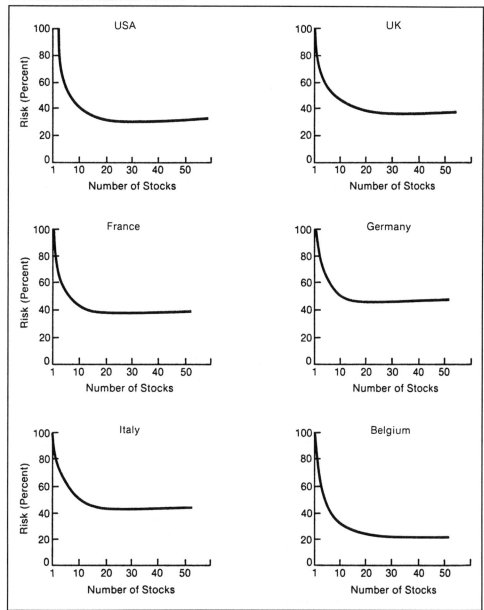

Figure 13.14

A Comparison of Domestic and International Diversification

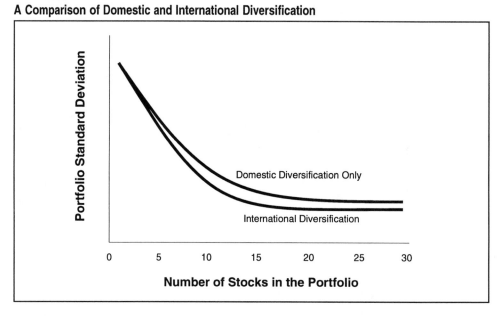

typical single stock by holding a portfolio of about 30 stocks. By contrast, the Belgian investor can diversify away about 73 percent of risk.

Solnik then considered the additional diversification benefit that is available to an investor by diversifying beyond the investor's national market. Figure 13.14 illustrates the key idea by showing how risk falls for purely domestic diversification versus investing internationally. The upper line shows the diversification benefits that can be achieved by domestic diversification. The lower line shows the portfolio risk when an investor selects stocks from an international smorgasbord. The vertical difference between the two lines is the reduction in risk achieved by diversifying internationally rather than just domestically.

This analysis can be performed from the point of view of any country. The benefits of going international differ from one country to another. For example, the U.S. market is already internationally diversified in many ways, because so many large U.S. corporations have extensive foreign operations. However, an investor in a small country with a stock market that is not very well diversified can achieve even greater benefits by diversifying internationally. This fact has not escaped portfolio managers; there is a strong and continuing movement toward international diversification under way.

Investors' Preferences

Even though we have assumed that investors prefer higher expected returns and seek lower risk, we still do not know which portfolio a given investor will prefer. Certainly he or she will prefer one of the portfolios on the efficient frontier, such as that depicted in Figure 13.11. However, there are still many portfolios to choose from.

It is impossible to say which of these many risky portfolios an investor will prefer because each investor may have his or her own special preferences regarding risk and return. For example, it is possible to imagine a very aggressive investor who is willing to bear considerable risk to gain additional expected return. Another investor may be determined to avoid risk to a greater extent, foregoing additional expected return to escape risk. To see the effect of different preferences and life situations, contrast a 70–year–old retiree and a 35–year–old yuppie. For the retiree, investment income is probably a very important component in his consumption income. Accordingly, the investment strategy cannot be too risky. For the yuppie, who presumably has a high income, a riskier strategy might be preferred. The yuppie can afford the temporary setbacks that might come from a high–risk investment strategy, because she has employment income that is large enough to meet basic needs.

Indifference Curves

These differences in investor preferences can be illustrated graphically in the return/risk space of Figure 13.15 for two hypothetical investors. Consider first the set of curves for the conservative investor. The curves are constructed so that each individual line represents different combinations of expected return and risk that are equally attractive for an investor. In Curve 1, for example, the conservative investor would be indifferent between positions A and B. A offers less expected return than B, but A also involves less risk. The conservative investor is indifferent between opportunities A and B, so this kind of curve is called an **indifference curve** because the investor is indifferent among all of the different opportunities that lie on a particular curve. The aggressive investor, for example, would be indifferent between positions C and D.

For each of the investors, there is a set of curves constructed in a way that expresses different levels of satisfaction or utility. The conservative investor would find all the points on Curve 2 equally attractive but would prefer to be at any point on Curve 2 rather than to be at any point on Curve 1. In terms of the graph, the conservative investor would prefer to be on the highest obtainable curve, and the same is true for the aggressive investor.

It may not be possible, however, for these investors to reach the higher curves. Attaining any position on any of the indifference curves depends upon the investment opportunities available in the marketplace. Given a set of preferences that are implied by the utility curves, and given information about the investment

Figure 13.15

Utility Curves for Different Investors

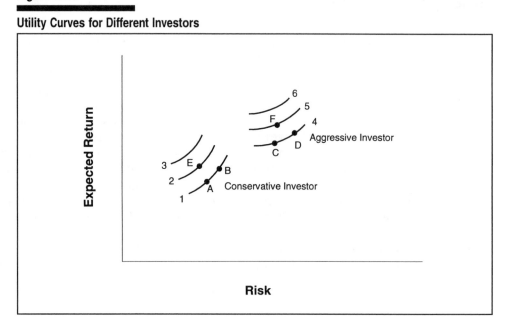

opportunities that the investors have available to them, it is possible to determine which investment opportunities will actually be chosen by the different investors.

Combining Investors' Preferences with the Opportunity Set

Figure 13.16 puts together the preferences of the conservative and aggressive investors from Figure 13.15 and the investment opportunities from Figure 13.11. The efficient set, shown on the curve from H to MR in Figure 13.11, indicates the best opportunities available to investors. The conservative investor can easily obtain a position on indifference Curve 1. However, it is possible for the conservative investor to achieve a point on indifference Curve 2 by holding Portfolio E. Likewise, the aggressive investor will hold Portfolio F to obtain a position on indifference Curve 5. In general, an investor will do best by holding a portfolio that is just tangent to an indifference curve. At that point, the investor will attain the highest possible indifference curve and will be better off by holding the tangent portfolio than by holding any other portfolio.

Both the conservative investor and the aggressive investor choose portfolios that lie on the efficient frontier, but they choose portfolios with different risk and return characteristics. These choices are consistent with the investors' attitudes toward risk and return. The fact that the slope on the conservative investor's indifference curves is steeper reflects a greater degree of risk aversion. The more nearly horizontal slope of the aggressive investor's indifference curves indicates a

Figure 13.16

Investment Preferences and Attitudes Toward Risk

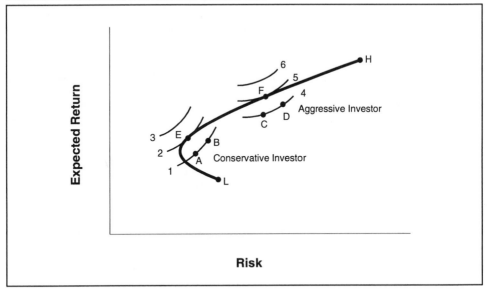

greater willingness to accept risk. These different attitudes toward risk are shown in Figure 13.17.

For the conservative and aggressive investors, consider the additional risk that is represented by X and X', respectively, where X = X'. To induce the conservative investor to accept X = X' more risk, the investor must receive an additional expected return equal to or exceeding Y in Figure 13.17. If this much additional expected return is not available, the conservative investor would not accept the additional X units of risk, because such an exchange would reduce utility. This is clear because both of the points touched by the X and Y line segments are on the same indifference curve. The aggressive investor, however, is willing to accept an additional amount of risk equal to X = X' for an increase in expected return equal to Y'. Because Y' < Y, and X = X', the aggressive investor must be relatively more *risk tolerant*, while the conservative investor is relatively more *risk averse*. For the aggressive investor, accepting X = X' more risk requires a compensating increase in expected return of only Y'. To get the conservative investor to accept the same amount of additional risk requires a greater increase in expected return. This makes sense, because we expect aggressive investors to be more risk tolerant and conservative investors to be more risk averse. That is, the increase in expected return demanded by the aggressive investor (Y') is less than the increase in expected return demanded by the conservative investor (Y) for the same increase in risk (X = X').

Figure 13.17

Indifference Curves and the Variety of Attitudes Toward Risk

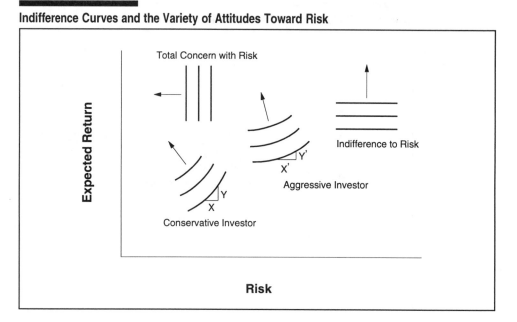

The Range of Investors' Preferences

Figure 13.17 also shows two extreme positions. The horizontal indifference curves reflect a total indifference to risk. An investor with such indifference curves is said to be *risk neutral*, because a given level of expected return is the only factor that determines the utility that such an investor receives. Because the indifference curves are horizontal, any point on the curve gives the same level of satisfaction. However, different points on a given curve have radically different risk levels.

The vertical indifference curves reflect a total concern with risk. In this case, the level of expected return does not affect the utility received by the investor. Rather, the total concern is with risk. The horizontal and vertical indifference curves are clearly extremes. Both sets of indifference curves show that there is no concern whatsoever with a risk/return trade–off. Instead, the total concern expressed by the indifference curves is with return for the risk–neutral investor and is with risk for the risk abhorrent investor. More normal indifference curves are those shown for the conservative and aggressive investors. As long as the lines are curved, as they are for these two types of investors, there is some trade–off between risk and return.

Summary

Using simplifying assumptions, such as zero transaction costs, free access to information, and no taxes, this chapter analyzed the effects of holding different securities in portfolios. By defining the risk/expected return space, we were able to see graphically how individual securities and portfolios plot. Assuming that investors desire portfolios with high expected return and low risk showed the important benefits of diversification that arise from combining individual securities into portfolios.

When assets are combined to form portfolios, the expected return of the portfolio is a simple weighted average of the expected return of the individual securities. The risk of a portfolio depends on the risk of the individual securities, the weight given to each security, and the covariance of returns among all of the possible pairs of securities in the portfolio.

The covariance or correlation of returns—both of which measure the tendency of returns on two investments to move together—is crucial in determining the risk of the portfolio. In fact, the tendency of returns to move together is the most important determinant of portfolio risk.

As shown in the case of the two–asset portfolio, when returns are perfectly correlated, the standard deviation of a portfolio is a weighted average of the standard deviations of the individual securities. In any other case, the correlation will be less than one, and the risk of the portfolio will be reduced. At the other extreme, when the correlation is –1, it will be possible to construct a riskless portfolio from the two risky assets. In the more normal case, the correlation is less than +1 and greater than –1. In this situation, forming portfolios will reduce risk, but it will not be able to eliminate risk altogether. In a market with many risky assets, there will be many investment opportunities that are not dominated.

The non–dominated investment opportunities constitute the efficient set and may be graphed in risk/return space as the efficient frontier. Investors will choose a non–dominated investment alternative, but with different attitudes toward risk, investors may choose different risky portfolios. Risk–tolerant investors will choose portfolios that offer high expected returns and high risk, while conservative investors will choose portfolios with lower expected returns and lower risk. In a market with only risky assets, investors will hold diversified portfolios that lie on the efficient frontier and will choose particular portfolios that are consistent with their attitudes toward risk and return. In the next chapter, we take a step toward a more realistic environment and consider the investor's choices when a risk–free asset exists as well as the set of risky assets. Then the investor must choose one risky portfolio and must decide how much to invest in the risk–free asset.

Questions and Problems

1. Which is important to the investor's decision as we have defined it, return or expected return?

2. Security A has an expected return of 14 percent, while Security B has an expected return of 12 percent. Is this enough information to determine whether A dominates B?

3. Security A has an expected return of 14 percent and a standard deviation of returns of .20, while Security B has an expected return of 12 percent, and a standard deviation of returns of .19. Does A dominate B? Why or why not?

4. Your broker tells you that it is important to diversify because doing so will increase your expected returns, even if you diversify by randomly selecting stocks. What should you do?

5. Why do the weights committed to different securities in a portfolio have to sum to 1? Can a weight be negative? If so, what would this mean?

6. Your broker tells you that the standard deviation of returns for a portfolio depends only on the standard deviations of the individual securities and the amount of funds invested in each. What should be your response? Why?

7. What is the relationship between the covariance of returns and the correlation of returns?

8. You already have a one–stock portfolio and, after reading this chapter, you are considering adding a second. Your broker recommends against the one you were considering because it has a high covariance with the stock you already own. However, he does not know the standard deviation of either stock's returns. What should you do? Why?

9. Securities C and D have returns with a correlation of –.9. Can you combine them to form a risk–free portfolio?

10. Your new broker is helping you form a new portfolio and recommends that you select from 30 stocks that the research department says lie on the efficient frontier. What should you do? Why?

11. Your second new broker says that no individual stock could ever lie on the efficient frontier. Is this correct? Why or why not?

12. Stock F has an expected return of .22 and a standard deviation of .18 and Stock G has an expected return of .20 and a standard deviation of .16. However, Stock G lies on a higher indifference curve than Stock F. Does Stock G dominate Stock F? Why or why not?

13. In the case of many risky assets, why does the efficient frontier stop at the minimum risk investment opportunity?

14. Security X has an expected return of .25 and a standard deviation of returns of .20. Security Y has an expected return of .18 and a standard deviation of returns of .18. Plot the two securities in risk/return space. Does one dominate the other?

15. What is the expected return of a portfolio with 30 percent invested in Security X of the preceding problem and with 70 percent invested in Security Y?

16. Over three years, Security Q had returns of 10 percent, 14 percent, and –3 percent. For the same three years, Security R had returns of 12 percent, 10 percent, and 5 percent. What is the variance and standard deviation of returns for these two securities? What is the covariance of returns between these securities? What is the correlation of returns?

17. Consider a portfolio with 40 percent of the funds invested in Security Q from the preceding question and with 60 percent invested in Security R. What is the variance of returns for this two–asset portfolio?

18. Security V has an expected return of 13 percent and a standard deviation of .20 and Security W has an expected return of 5 percent and a standard deviation of .13. If the two securities are perfectly negatively correlated, how much money would you put in each to have a zero risk portfolio? What would be the expected return of the portfolio?

CFA Questions

All CFA examination questions are reprinted, with permission, from the Level I *1992–1994, CFA Candidate Study and Examination Program Review*. Copyright 1992–1994, Association for Investment Management and Research, Charlottesville, Va. All rights reserved.

A. Portfolio theory as described by Markowitz is most concerned with:
   a. the elimination of systematic risk.
   b. the effect of diversification on portfolio risk.
   c. the identification of unsystematic risk.
   d. active portfolio management to enhance return.

B. The measure of risk in a Markowitz efficient frontier is:
   a. specific risk.
   b. standard deviation of returns.
   c. reinvestment risk.
   d. beta.

C. Which *one* of the following portfolios cannot lie on the efficient frontier as described by Markowitz?

	Portfolio	Expected Return	Standard Deviation
a.	W	9%	21%
b.	X	5%	7%
c.	Y	15%	36%
d.	Z	12%	15%

D. The standard deviation of variable X is .20. The standard deviation of variable Y is .12. The covariance between X and Y is .0096. The correlation between X and Y is then:
  a. 0.20
  b. 0.24
  c. 0.36
  d. 0.40

E. Which *one* of the following portfolios *cannot* lie on the efficient frontier as described by Markowitz?

	Portfolio	Expected Return	Standard Deviation
a.	W	15%	36%
b.	X	12%	15%
c.	Y	5%	7%
d.	Z	9%	21%

F. Which statement about portfolio diversification is *correct*?
  a. Proper diversification can reduce or eliminate systematic risk.
  b. Diversification reduces the portfolio's expected return because diversification reduces a portfolio's total risk.
  c. As more securities are added to a portfolio, total risk typically would be expected to fall at a decreasing rate.
  d. The risk–reducing benefits of diversification do not occur meaningfully until at least 30 individual securities are included in the portfolio.

G. For a two–stock portfolio, what would be the preferred correlation coefficient between the two stocks?
  a. +1.00
  b. +0.50
  c. 0
  d. –1.00

H. Given the following:
    Stock A standard deviation = 0.45
    Stock B standard deviation = 0.32
  If Stock A and B have a perfect positive correlation, which portfolio combination represents the minimum variance portfolio?
  a. 100% Stock A
  b. 50% Stock A/50% Stock B
  c. 100% Stock B
  d. 30% Stock A/70% Stock B

I. A measure of how much the returns of two risky assets move together is:
  a. variance.
  b. standard deviation.
  c. covariance.
  d. semi–variance.

J. Stocks A, B, and C each have the same expected return and standard deviation. Given the following correlations, which portfolio constructed from these stocks has the lowest risk?

Correlation Matrix

Stock	A	B	C
A	+1.0		
B	+0.9	+1.0	
C	+0.1	−0.4	+1.0

  a. A portfolio equally invested in Stocks A and B
  b. A portfolio equally invested in Stocks A and C
  c. A portfolio equally invested in Stocks B and C
  d. A portfolio totally invested in Stock C

K. Portfolio diversification is one reason for investing in international bonds. The benefits of international diversification are derived from the fact that:
  a. the variability of returns on foreign (non–U.S.) bonds are generally lower than domestic (U.S.) bonds.
  b. the returns on foreign bonds are generally lower than domestic bonds, but there are greater opportunities for profits because of the wider price swings in foreign markets.
  c. foreign bonds not only offer the potential for higher returns, but also offer a relatively low correlation with the returns on domestic bonds.
  d. the return behavior of foreign bond markets is very closely linked with the return performance of domestic bonds, so it provides investors with an even wider array of investment opportunities.

Suggested REALDATA Exercises

The following *REALDATA* exercises explore the concepts developed in this chapter:
    Exercises 40, 41, 42, 43, 46, 53.

Suggested Readings

Alexander, G. J. and J. C. Francis, *Portfolio Analysis*, 3e, Englewood Cliffs, NJ: Prentice Hall, 1986.

Brinson, G. P. and N. Fachler, "Measuring Non–U.S. Equity Portfolio Performance," *The Institutional Investor Focus on Investment Management*, Cambridge, MA: Ballinger Publishing, 1989, pp. 251–258.

French, K. R. and J. M. Poterba, "Investor Diversification and International Equity Markets," *The American Economic Review*, 81:2, May 1991, pp. 222–226.

Grauer, R. R. and N. H. Hakansson, "Gains from International Diversification: 1968–85 Returns on Portfolios of Stocks and Bonds," *Journal of Finance*, 42:3, July 1989, pp. 721–741.

Hsieh, D. A. and M. H. Miller, "Margin Regulation and Stock Market Volatility," *Journal of Finance*, 45:1, March 1990, pp. 3–29.

Jaffe, J. F., "Gold and Gold Stocks as Investments for Institutional Portfolios," *Financial Analysts Journal*, 45:2, March/April 1989, pp. 53–59.

Markowitz, H., "Portfolio Selection," *Journal of Finance*, 7:1, March 1952.

Renshaw, A. and E. Renshaw, "Does Gold Have a Role in Investment Portfolios?" *Journal of Portfolio Management*, 8:3, Spring 1982, p. 29.

Sharpe, W. F., "A Simplified Model for Portfolio Analysis," *Management Science*, January 1963, pp. 277–293.

Solnik, B., "Why Not Diversify Internationally Rather than Domestically?" *Financial Analysts Journal*, 30:4, July–August 1974, pp. 48–54.

Wagner, W. and S. Lau, "The Effect of Diversification on Risk," *Financial Analysts Journal*, 27:5, November–December 1971, p. 50.

CHAPTER FOURTEEN

The Market Price of Risk

Overview

Chapter 13 demonstrated how investors who sought high expected returns and were anxious to avoid risk would react to a market in which only risky securities were traded under certain idealized assumptions, such as the existence of perfect markets. This chapter continues developing this model by introducing a risk–free asset. In the idealized world under investigation, this chapter shows how the presence of the risk–free asset greatly increases the investor's opportunities and how it makes virtually all investors better off than they would be in a market with only risky assets.

The chapter then shows how the introduction of the risk–free asset gives rise to a market standard against which other investment opportunities can be compared. We also examine the **Separation Theorem**, which states that all investors should hold the same portfolio of risky assets, no matter how risk tolerant or risk averse they may be. The chapter leads to an exposition of the **Capital Asset Pricing Model** (CAPM), a general model that expresses the equilibrium rate of expected return for an asset as a function of its inherent risk characteristics.

Most of this chapter focuses on building a model that relies on some unrealistic assumptions. The reader should not forget that the purpose of the model is to examine the factors that affect security pricing in the real world. While the assumptions employed to construct the model may not hold in reality, they help us improve our understanding of security pricing. Also, as the next chapter explains, security prices actually behave in a way that is highly consistent with the predictions of our simplified model.

Introduction of the Risk–Free Asset

This section extends our analysis of two–asset portfolios to the special case in which one of the two assets is risk free. In deciding how to combine a risk–free asset with a portfolio of risky assets, remember that we are considering a one–period model.

In this context, a risk–free asset is one that is free of default risk, so that it is certain to pay its expected return. By the same token, the restriction of the model to a consideration of only one period means that there can be no variance of returns for the risk–free asset either. Thus, the risk–free asset has three important features. First, it has no default risk. Second, its expected return is certain. Third, the variance of returns for the risk–free asset is zero.

Two–Asset Portfolios: A Brief Review

As explained in Chapter 13, the expected return of a two–asset portfolio is given by:

$$E(R_P) = W_i\, E(R_i) + W_j\, E(R_j) \qquad\qquad \textbf{14.1}$$

where:

$$W_i,\, W_j = \text{percentage of funds committed to Assets } i \text{ and } j, \text{ respectively}$$
$$E(R_P),\, E(R_i),\, E(R_j) = \text{the expected return on the portfolio, and individual Assets}$$
$$i \text{ and } j, \text{ respectively}$$

Likewise, the original equation for the variance of a two–asset portfolio still holds and is given by Equation 14.2:

$$\sigma_P^2 = W_i^2 \sigma_i^2 + W_j^2 \sigma_j^2 + 2 W_i W_j \sigma_{i,j} \qquad\qquad \textbf{14.2}$$

where:

$$\sigma_{i,j} = \text{the covariance of returns between Assets } i \text{ and } j$$

and the other terms are as defined previously.

Expected Return of a Two–Asset Portfolio with a Risk–Free Asset

To find the expected return of a two–asset portfolio when one asset is the risk–free asset, we use Equation 14.1 and replace one asset with the risk–free asset. In this case, we replace Asset i with the risk–free asset, which we denote as R_f. Nothing essential about Equation 14.1 changes; the formula holds just as before. The expected return of a portfolio composed of the risk–free asset, R_f, and the risky portfolio or Asset j is just the weighted average of the two expected returns, where the weights are the percentage of funds committed to the two assets:

$$E(R_P) = W_f\, E(R_f) + W_j\, E(R_j)$$

where:
$$W_f = \text{the weight given to the risk–free asset}$$

However, in the case of the risk–free asset, the expected return is certain, because there is no default risk. Therefore:

$$E(R_f) = R_f$$

Because the expected return on the risk–free asset is constant, the expected return for the portfolio involving the risk–free asset is:

$$E(R_P) = W_f \, \bar{R}_f + W_j \, E(R_j)$$

Variance of a Two–Asset Portfolio with a Risk–Free Asset

The fact that R_f is risk free dramatically affects the evaluation of variance in Equation 14.2. Because R_f is risk free:

$$\sigma_f^2 = 0$$

where:

σ_f^2 = the variance of returns for R_f, and:

$$\sigma_{f,j} = 0$$

The covariance between a constant (R_f) and a random variable, in this case the returns of Asset j, always equals 0. This must hold because a constant does not covary with any other asset. As the name implies, a constant is just constant.

In Equation 14.2 for the variance of a two–asset portfolio, any term involving multiplication by σ_f^2 or $\sigma_{f,j}$ will itself be zero. Making the relevant substitutions in Equation 14.2 to accommodate the risk–free asset, we have:

$$\sigma_P^2 = W_f^2 \sigma_f^2 + W_j^2 \sigma_j^2 + 2 W_f W_j \sigma_{f,j}$$

Because R_f is a constant, the first and third terms drop out, and the risk of a two–asset portfolio including R_f will be:

$$\sigma_P^2 = W_j^2 \sigma_j^2$$

and since this is a perfect square, the standard deviation of the portfolio is:

$$\sigma_P = W_j \sigma_j \qquad \text{14.3}$$

Equation 14.3 says that the standard deviation of a two–asset portfolio that includes one risk–free asset depends only on the risk level of the risky asset and the proportion of funds committed to it.

As noted in Chapter 13, the equation for the variance of a two–asset portfolio may also be expressed using the correlation instead of the covariance:

$$\sigma_p^2 = W_i^2\,\sigma_i^2 + W_j^2\,\sigma_j^2 + 2W_i W_j\,\rho_{i,j}\,\sigma_i\,\sigma_j \qquad\qquad \textbf{14.4}$$

If we apply this formula to a two–asset portfolio that includes one risk–free asset, the second and third terms on the right side of Equation 14.4 will equal zero. The second term will be zero because the variance of the risk–free asset is zero. The third term will equal zero because the correlation between the risk–free asset and any other asset will be zero. (Also, the standard deviation of the risk–free asset appears in the third term and will make the whole term zero.)

In Chapter 13, we noted that risk measures for portfolios can also be expressed using the correlation coefficient instead of the covariance. The correlation and covariance are very closely related, as shown by the following formula:

$$\rho_{i,j} = \frac{\sigma_{i,j}}{\sigma_i\,\sigma_j} \qquad\qquad \textbf{14.5}$$

This means that the correlation between any two assets will be zero whenever the covariance equals zero. This will always be the case when one of the assets is a constant, like R_f. As a consequence, we may drop all terms that are multiplied by σ_f^2 or $\rho_{f,j}$, in this special case.

Computing Expected Return and Risk for a Two–Asset Portfolio

To illustrate these principles, consider a portfolio that is to be made up of the risk–free Asset R_f and a risky Portfolio j, where the data for R_f and j are as follows:

	Risk–Free Asset	**Risky Asset j**
Expected Return	.10	.17
Standard Deviation	.00	.21
Portfolio Weight	.45	.55
$\sigma_{f,j}$	.00	

In this case, the expected return for the portfolio is given by:

$$E(R_P) = (.45)\,(.10) + (.55)\,(.17) = .1385$$

Figure 14.1

Combining the Risk–Free Asset with Risky Portfolio _j_

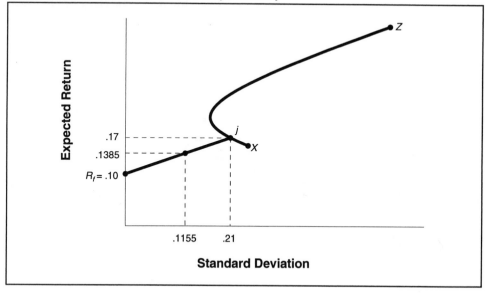

and the standard deviation of the portfolio is:

$$\sigma_p = (.55)\,(.21)$$
$$= .1155$$

Figure 14.1 shows the risk–free asset (R_f), the risky portfolio (j), and the combined portfolio (P) in risk–return space. By combining R_f and j, we achieve Portfolio P, which lies on a straight line in risk–return space between R_f and j. Any point on the line between R_f and j could be achieved by constructing a portfolio made up of just R_f and j.

Choosing the Best Risky Portfolio

In the example illustrated by Figure 14.1, risky Portfolio j was combined with the risk–free asset, R_f, to form a portfolio. However, investors may prefer to use other risky portfolios besides j to combine with R_f. In fact, as the argument of this section shows, all rational investors will choose the same particular risky portfolio to combine with the risk–free asset, and the preferred risky portfolio is certainly not j. No investor, regardless of his or her risk preferences, would want to invest in risky Portfolio j.

Figure 14.2

Combining the Risk–Free Asset with Risky Portfolio *j* versus Risky Portfolio *k*

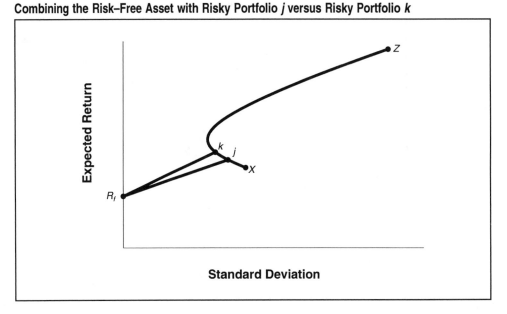

Avoiding Dominated Portfolios

To see why Portfolio *j* is not a desirable partner for the risk–free asset, consider Figure 14.2, which shows R_f, *j* and another risky portfolio, *k*. Just as we could combine R_f and *j* to achieve portfolios on the line $R_f j$, we can combine R_f and *k* to achieve portfolios on the line $R_f k$. Notice, however, that every portfolio on the line $R_f j$ is dominated by a portfolio on the line $R_f k$. This means that all investors would prefer to hold risky Portfolio *k* rather than risky Portfolio *j*, because they will always be better off. In Figure 14.2, it is clear that for any portfolio of R_f and *j*, we can construct a portfolio of R_f and *k* that dominates the portfolio of R_f and *j*.

The Optimal Portfolio

From this comparison between *j* and *k*, it is clear that one should move up the curve beyond *k* to find yet better risky portfolios. This process must cease, however, when the position cannot be improved. That will occur when the line from R_f to the risky portfolio is just tangent to the curve showing the efficient frontier for the risky assets, XZ. Figure 14.3 shows this portfolio of risky assets, M. When M is combined with R_f, any portfolio on the line R_fM can be reached with a new portfolio. The minimum–risk portfolio (MR) is also shown in Figure 14.3. MR is now dominated by portfolios along R_fM.

Figure 14.3

Combining the Risk–Free Asset with the Optimal Risky Portfolio M

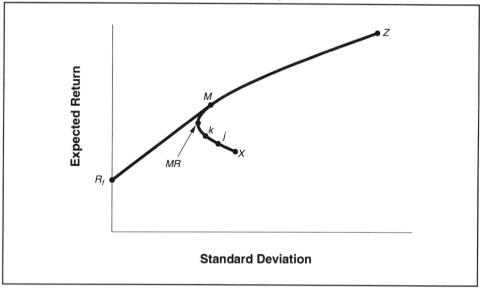

The Efficient Frontier with Investment in the Risk–Free Asset

The efficient frontier has been changed by the introduction of the risk–free asset. The new efficient frontier runs from R_f to M to Z. Any portfolio not lying on the line R_fMZ will be dominated. Thus, the introduction of the risk–free asset means that all of those risky portfolios lying on the curve from MR to M are no longer on the efficient frontier. This means that no investor will hold any risky portfolio on the curve between MR and M as a portfolio of risky assets because a better portfolio is available that can be made up of R_f and M.

Lending Portfolios

We have determined that investors will seek portfolios that lie on the line R_fMZ. How would one actually go about trading to obtain such portfolios? To construct portfolios that lie on the curve from M to Z, the investor need only select the correct risky portfolio and invest 100 percent of all funds in that portfolio. To build portfolios that lie on the line from R_f to M, the investor must hold the risky Portfolio M and also invest some money in the risk–free asset, such as Treasury bills. Investing in Treasury bills is simply lending to the government, so we may say that portfolios lying between R_f and M are **lending portfolios**, because they involve holding some stock and lending some funds to the government.

In Chapter 13, we considered investing in the universe of risky assets only, and we found that the efficient frontier extended along the curved line from X to Z in Figure 14.3. Now having introduced the possibility of lending by investing in the risk–free asset, we see that the efficient frontier extends from R_f to M to Z.

Borrowing Portfolios

The idea of a lending portfolio raises the possibility that there could also be a **borrowing portfolio**, one constructed by borrowing funds and investing the borrowed funds, in addition to the investor's original capital, in some risky portfolio. Because we are assuming perfect markets, it must be possible to both borrow and lend at the risk–free rate R_f. Of course, individual investors cannot borrow at the risk–free rate in actual markets, but large institutional investors can borrow at rates very close to the risk–free rate. Large banks and portfolio management firms have very low borrowing costs for loans using securities as collateral. Therefore, examining borrowing portfolios in the context of a perfect market is more realistic than it might appear.

Under our perfect market assumptions, it is possible to construct a borrowing portfolio by borrowing money at rate R_f and investing the loan proceeds in some risky portfolio. So far, we know that the investor would want to put funds into only those risky portfolios that lie on the curve from M to Z. Now, with the opportunity to borrow at rate R_f, the investor's opportunity set becomes much richer.

To illustrate how to create a borrowing portfolio, consider the following example, using the initial data:

Asset	R_f	M
Expected Return	.10	.23
Standard Deviation	.00	.18

Also assume an initial wealth of $1,000. If an investor puts half of all available funds in R_f and half in M, he or she has a lending portfolio in which $500 is being lent to the government. If all of the funds were put in Portfolio M, there would be neither borrowing nor lending. However, consider a situation in which the investor borrows $750 at rate R_f = 10 percent and invests the borrowed funds, plus the original capital of $1,000 in the risky Portfolio M. Table 14.1 shows the different portfolios, with their expected returns and standard deviations. These expected returns and standard deviations were calculated using the formulas developed earlier.

To illustrate the expected returns and risk of a borrowing portfolio, let us assume that the expected return for the portfolio happens to be the actual return in the period under analysis. In that case, the value of the portfolio at the end of the period will be the $1,750 that is invested times 1.23, or:

$$\$1,750 \times 1.23 = \$2,152.50$$

Table 14.1

Portfolios Constructed from the Risk–Free Asset and Risky Portfolio M

W_f	Funds in R_f	W_m	Funds in M	$E(R_p)$	σ_p
.5	$500	.5	$500	.165	.09
.0	0	1.0	$1,000	.23	.18
−.75	−$750	1.75	$1,750	.3275	.3150

The $750 loan must be repaid with 10 percent interest, which comes to $825. After the 23 percent return is earned on the risky portfolio and the debt of $825 is repaid, the investor still has $1,327.50. With an original capital of $1,000, this means that the return earned was 32.75 percent. This is only to be expected in this situation, because the risky portfolio earned exactly its expected return.

Not only does borrowing at R_f to invest in a risky portfolio increase the expected return, it also increases the risk. To see how risk increases, let us assume that the risky Portfolio M earns a return one standard deviation above or below its expected return and compute the returns on the borrowing portfolio.

If the risky portfolio earns one standard deviation less than its expected return, it will earn .23 − .18 = .05. In this situation, the borrowing portfolio will be worth 1.05 × $1,750 = $1,837.50. Out of this, the debt of $825 must be repaid, leaving $1,012.50, which gives a return of 1.25 percent on the original capital. If the return on the risky portfolio is one standard deviation above the expected return, the risky portfolio will earn .23 + .18 = .41. The portfolio will be worth 1.41 × $1,750 = $2,467.50 at the end of the period. Out of this, the $825 must be repaid, leaving $1,642.50. On the initial capital of $1,000, this is a return of 64.25 percent.

The Effect of Leverage on Risk and Expected Return

The use of borrowing, or **leverage**, increases both the expected returns and the variability of returns. Figure 14.4 shows the result of borrowing at R_f in order to invest in M. In the particular case already analyzed, we found that the expected return of the leveraged portfolio was 32.75 percent and the standard deviation of the portfolio was 31.50 percent. This leveraged portfolio (S) is shown in Figure 14.4. Notice that Portfolio S falls on the straight line R_fY. In fact, all leveraged portfolios fall on that line, with the possibility of creating portfolios with infinite expected returns.

The Efficient Frontier with Borrowing and Lending

In the previous section, before we introduced the possibility of borrowing to invest in a risky portfolio, we said that the efficient frontier ran from R_f to M to Z. With the possibility of borrowing, that is no longer the case. For example, consider

Figure 14.4

Portfolio Possibilities with Borrowing and Lending

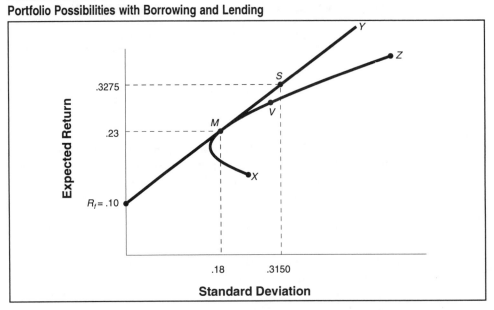

Portfolio V, which lies on the curve between M and Z. Formerly, it was in the efficient set, but now it is dominated by a leveraged portfolio that would lie between M and S. While a portfolio such as V might be combined with R_f, no investor would wish to do so. The resulting portfolios would lie on the straight line from R_f to V, and all portfolios on that line are dominated by portfolios lying on the line from R_f to M to Y.

In fact, there is only one risky portfolio that is not dominated, and that is Portfolio M. As a consequence, all investors will want to hold M as their risky portfolio, although they may put different proportions of their funds in M. Some will wish to invest a portion of their funds in M and some in R_f. Other, bolder, investors might choose to borrow funds at rate R_f and invest the proceeds in M along with their original capital. However, all investors who hold any of their funds in risky assets will put those funds in Portfolio M. Otherwise, they would be choosing a dominated portfolio. Since we have been assuming that investors seek larger expected returns and wish to avoid risk, investing any funds in a risky portfolio other than M would be irrational.

How well does this discussion of borrowing at the risk–free rate and investing at M fit with reality? While there are some borrowers that have very low borrowing costs that approximate the risk–free rate, they cannot borrow an unlimited amount of funds at that rate. Also, the Federal Reserve Board limits the amount of borrowing for securities investment with its margin requirements. Currently, only 50 percent of the funds invested in securities can be borrowed, so in practice investors cannot achieve unlimited leverage. In terms of Figure 14.4, there are practical limits to how far beyond M the investor can go on the line R_fMY.

Investor Utility and the Risk–Free Asset

As shown in Figure 14.4, the introduction of a risk–free asset creates a new range of investment options for investors. It also means that virtually every investor in the marketplace can improve his or her position. Now it is possible to select a portfolio that dominates the portfolio the investor would have selected from just the universe of risky assets alone. This means that investors will be able to reach a higher utility curve than would be possible without the existence of the risk–free asset.

Figure 14.5 repeats the investment opportunities shown in Figure 14.4 but includes two sets of utility curves to show how investors' utility differs under the new set of circumstances created by the introduction of the risk–free asset. For one investor, whose utility curves are numbered 1 through 3, there has been a dramatic increase in utility. In a universe of only risky assets, this investor would have chosen a portfolio at Point T, on the efficient frontier of risky assets. With only risky assets available, and risk–return preferences expressed by the family of utility curves numbered 1 through 3, Point T was the best portfolio available. With the risk–free asset, however, this same investor could obtain a portfolio on R_fMY at U, which will be preferred to Portfolio T. This is clear since Point U lies on a higher

Figure 14.5

Investor Utility Possibilities with the Introduction of the Risk–Free Asset

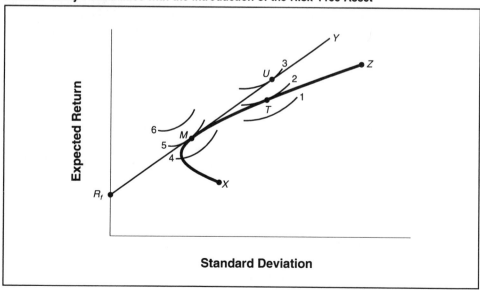

utility curve than Portfolio T. As drawn, U does not dominate T, however. Though U offers higher expected return than T, it also involves slightly more risk. While the investor may prefer U to T, that preference depends on the investor's risk/return trade–off. The investor has chosen U because it is the only possible portfolio that allows him or her to reach Utility Curve 3.

A second set of utility curves is numbered 4 through 6. For this investor, the preferred portfolio is M, which happens to be on both the line R_fMY and on the efficient frontier for risky assets considered alone. This particular investor will choose Portfolio M either in a world of only risky assets, or in a world including the risk–free asset. Because of this, the investor is not helped by the introduction of the risk–free asset. In this special case, the utility of this investor is not affected by the presence of the risk–free asset. However, for all other investors, the introduction of the risk–free asset means that a higher level of utility can be achieved. For all investors, the introduction of the risk–free asset increases the investment choices that are available. Almost all investors will be helped by the introduction of the risk–free asset because they will be able to find an investment combination that gives them a higher level of satisfaction by combining the risk–free asset with a risky portfolio.

The Market Portfolio

Thus far we have observed that all investors who commit any funds to risky securities will invest in Portfolio M in Figures 14.4 and 14.5. By doing so, they can achieve portfolios that yield greater utility than they would be able to achieve otherwise. A clear understanding of the characteristics of this special portfolio is essential.

In fact, Portfolio M must be the market portfolio. The **market portfolio** is the portfolio of risky assets that includes every risky security in the marketplace, with each security in the portfolio being weighted proportionally by its market value. For example, if the total market value of IBM's shares were $4 billion, and the market value of all securities were $100 billion, then the weight given to IBM in the market portfolio would be 4 percent. Accordingly, this portfolio is a **value weighted portfolio**.

Portfolio M must be the market portfolio because (1) investors hold M as their risky portfolio because they will be better off by doing so, and (2) all securities must be owned by someone. There are simply no securities floating around without owners. The only way that all securities can have an owner and all investors can have the same risky portfolio is for each investor to hold the market portfolio of risky securities.

The Separation Theorem

Because all investors who hold any risky assets will choose to hold Portfolio M, the choice of a risky portfolio is independent of the choice of a particular portfolio on the line R_fMY. This is known as the **separation theorem**, where the investment decision is separate from the financing decision. Every investor who chooses to hold any risky assets will hold Portfolio M. The financing decision, whether to borrow or lend and how much, is separate from the choice of the particular portfolio of risky assets. Another way of making the same point is to say that the choice of risky Portfolio M is separate from the decision about how much expected return to seek and how much risk to bear. This is clear, because any point along the line $R_f MY$ can be attained while holding only Portfolio M as the portfolio of risky assets.

The Capital Market Line

As noted earlier, and as shown in Figure 14.5, investors can obtain any point on the line $R_f MY$, and they will choose the exact combination of the risky Portfolio M and the risk–free Asset R_f that allows them to reach their highest utility curve. This will be at the point where $R_f MY$ is tangent to a utility curve. At this point on the utility curve, the slope of the utility curve will be identical to the slope of the line $R_f MY$. Otherwise, the utility curve and line $R_f MY$ could not be tangent to each other. The slope of the utility curve represents the trade–off that a particular investor is willing to make between risk and expected return. The choice of a portfolio in the marketplace is reached when the trade–off between risk and return available in the marketplace matches the trade–off that the investor is willing to make.

This means that line $R_f MY$ represents the trade–off between risk and return that is available in the marketplace. As such, it is called the **capital market line** (CML). The upward slope of the CML reveals graphically that the acquisition of greater expected return means that the investor must accept more risk. The slope of the CML is the rate of exchange between expected return and risk.

From algebra, we know that the equation of a straight line is given by:

$$y = mx + b$$

where:

y = the height on the vertical axis
m = the slope of the line
x = the value on the horizontal axis
b = the point at which the line cuts the y axis, the intercept

In Figure 14.6, line $R_f MY$ cuts the y axis at R_f. The slope of $R_f MY$ is given by:

$$\text{Slope} = \frac{\text{Change in Vertical Distance}}{\text{Change in Horizontal Distance}}$$

It is convenient to measure the slope using the origin as a reference point for risk and using point R_f as a reference point for the expected return. Because the line $R_f MY$ hits the vertical, or y axis, at R_f, expected return R_f can be achieved without

Figure 14.6

The Capital Market Line

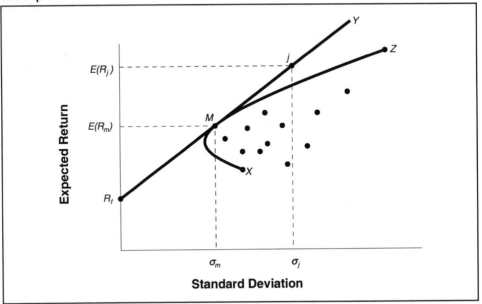

any risk being borne. However, if one is willing to accept a level of risk equal to σ_m, an increase in expected return can also be obtained. The expected return for bearing risk in the amount of σ_m is $E(R_m)$. Thus, if an investor is willing to accept a change in risk from 0 to σ_m, he or she can expect an increase in expected return from R_f to $E(R_m)$. This is exactly what we need to determine the slope of the capital market line:

$$\text{Slope of the Capital Market Line} = \frac{E(R_m) - R_f}{\sigma_m}$$

This is enough to give us all of the values we need to express the CML as an equation. Consider any portfolio, such as Portfolio j in Figure 14.6. From algebra, we know that the height of a value on the y axis, the expected return on portfolio j, $E(R_j)$, should equal the intercept, R_f, plus the slope of the line (given above) times the position on the x axis σ_j for Portfolio j. In equation form, this says:

$$E(R_j) = R_f + \sigma_j \left(\frac{E(R_m) - R_f}{\sigma_m} \right) \qquad \textbf{14.6}$$

and this is often written in the equivalent form:

$$E(R_j) = R_f + \frac{\sigma_j}{\sigma_m}\left[E(R_m) - R_f\right]$$　　**14.7**

Verbally, this equation says that the expected return on Portfolio j equals the risk–free rate plus the risk of Portfolio j relative to the risk of the market portfolio times the difference between the expected return on the market and the risk–free rate.

To apply this information, consider a situation in which the following values hold:

$$R_f = 10\%$$
$$E(R_m) = 17\%$$
$$\sigma_m = .24$$
$$\sigma_j = .34$$

These figures give us enough information to calculated the expected return of Portfolio j:

$$E(R_j) = R_f + \frac{\sigma_j}{\sigma_m}[E(R_m) - R_f]$$
$$= .10 + \frac{.34}{.24}[.17 - .10]$$
$$= .1992$$
$$= 19.92\%$$

The expected return for Portfolio j must be greater than the expected return on the market portfolio, because Portfolio j has higher risk than the market portfolio. Investors will hold the riskier Portfolio j, instead of the market portfolio, only if they are compensated for the additional risk by getting greater expected returns.

Risk and Expected Returns for Portfolios and Individual Securities

The most important feature of the CML is the relationship it expresses between the riskiness of a portfolio and its expected return. The slope of the CML reveals how much extra return can be expected for each extra unit of risk accepted. As such, the slope of the CML gives the market price of risk for fully diversified portfolios.

One limitation of the CML is that it pertains only to well–diversified portfolios. Since every portfolio on the CML is composed of a mix of the market portfolio and the risk–free asset, it is clear that it can hold only for portfolios that are very similar to the market portfolio, in the sense that they are well–diversified. As a consequence, it has very little to say about what returns should be expected for individual securities.

There is another relationship that gives the expected returns for an individual security, and it is called the **security market line** (SML). The security market line expresses a relationship between the expected returns of an individual security (or a portfolio) and its level of relevant risk. Much of the remainder of this chapter explains the SML.

What is this relevant risk for an individual security? This chapter argues that investors will hold only the market portfolio as their portfolio of risky assets. As far as individual securities are concerned, investors will be concerned with their risk level only to the extent that the individual security contributes to the risk of the market portfolio. From the preceding chapter, we know that much of the risk for most individual securities can be avoided by diversification.

Because investors will hold the market portfolio if they hold any risky assets at all, and because much of the risk of an individual security can be avoided, the relevant risk for an individual security is that part remaining after diversification. The part that cannot be diversified away will still be left in the market portfolio. It will be that unavoidable portion of the risk that will be compensated in the market. We need, therefore, some means of quantifying the unavoidable, relevant, nondiversifiable risk of an individual security or portfolio. This measure of risk is called the beta of a security or a portfolio. **Beta** is a measure of the nondiversifiable risk inherent in a security or portfolio.

Beta and the Risk of Individual Securities

The preceding chapter examined the behavior of two–asset risky portfolios in detail and observed that the riskiness of the portfolio depended largely on the extent of correlation between the two assets. Simply stated, the higher the correlation between two assets, the greater the risk of a portfolio consisting of those two assets. Now let us consider a two–asset portfolio consisting of the market portfolio as one asset and a single security as the second asset. If the individual security is added to the portfolio, its contribution to the risk of the market portfolio depends almost exclusively on the degree of correlation between the returns of the individual security and the market portfolio. Beta measures the riskiness of a security or portfolio by examining the correlation between the security or portfolio on the one hand, and the market portfolio on the other. For a security or Portfolio j, and the market Portfolio m, the beta of Security j, β_j, is given by the following expression:

$$\beta_j = \frac{\sigma_{j,m}}{\sigma_m^2} = \frac{\sigma_j}{\sigma_m} \rho_{j,m} \qquad \text{14.8}$$

In the two equivalent formulas, the crucial term is the one that measures the tendency of j's returns to move with those of the market portfolio. In the first, it is the covariance, and in the second, it is the correlation.

Beta and the Characteristic Line

The relationship between the returns of an individual security and the returns of the market, which is measured by beta (β), can also be shown graphically. Figure 14.7 shows the relationship between the returns of IBM and the market portfolio for 12 months. Each dot in the figure corresponds to the returns earned by IBM and the S&P 500 Index for a particular month. The data used in this figure are presented

Figure 14.7

The Characteristic Line for IBM

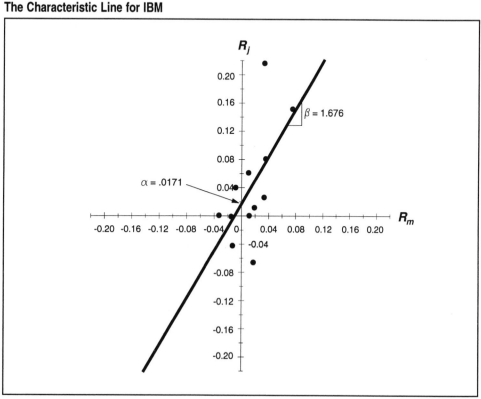

Table 14.2

Information for Security Betas

Month	S&P 500	AMI	Homestake	IBM
January	0.0331	−0.0329	0.1139	0.2162
February	0.0189	−0.1870	−0.2192	0.0117
March	0.0331	0.1498	−0.4450	0.0262
April	0.0749	−0.0207	0.0936	0.1515
May	−0.0124	0.0124	0.1318	−0.0415
June	0.0352	0.0521	0.0090	0.0809
July	−0.0331	−0.1423	0.0060	0.0008
August	0.0113	−0.0069	0.0820	0.0004
September	0.0101	−0.0172	−0.1851	0.0611
October	−0.0152	−0.1713	−0.1153	−0.0008
November	0.0174	−0.0085	0.1590	−0.0660
December	−0.0088	0.0212	−0.0199	0.0400
Avg. Return	0.0137	−0.0293	−0.0324	0.0400
σ^2	0.000769	0.008497	0.029386	0.005770
σ	0.027738	0.092178	0.171423	0.075958
β		1.300617	−0.056442	1.676015
Correlation with S&P 500		0.391378	−0.009132	.612038
R^2		.153177	.000083	.374591
α		−0.0471	−.0317	.0171

in Table 14.2, along with similar information for two other firms, American Medical International and Homestake Mining.

By plotting the return pairs for a security (like IBM) and the market portfolio (like the S&P 500), we can see the relationship between the returns on the security and the returns on the market. This relationship is summarized by the characteristic line shown in Figure 14.7. The **characteristic line** is a line chosen by regression analysis to fit the pattern of dots in the graph in the best way. Any straight line can be expressed mathematically by specifying its slope and the point at which it intercepts the vertical axis. For the characteristic line, regression analysis is used to find the line that best fits the data.

The Equation of the Characteristic Line. The regression equation, or the equation for the characteristic line, is given by the following equation for some Security i:

$$R_{i,t} = \alpha_i + \beta_i\, R_{m,t} + \varepsilon_{i,t}$$

where:

$R_{i,t}$ = the returns on Security i in Period t

$R_{m,t}$ = the returns on the market portfolio in Period t

α_i = the parameter for the intercept term (alpha)

β_i = the parameter for the slope coefficient (beta)

$\varepsilon_{i,t}$ = a random error term assumed to have a zero mean

Through regression analysis, the parameters in the regression equation, α_i and β_i, are estimated using historical data. If these parameters are stable across time, they may be used to predict the future relationship between the returns of one security and the market portfolio.

The Characteristic Line: An Example.   In Figure 14.7, the characteristic line for IBM has an intercept at .0171 and a slope of 1.676. The intercept is known as the alpha (α) and the slope of the characteristic line is called beta (β). This is exactly the beta that acts as a measure of a security's risk relative to the market. For IBM, the measured beta during this period was 1.676. This can be interpreted as follows: When the market goes up by 1 percent, IBM will tend to go up by 1.676 percent. When the market goes down by 1 percent, IBM will tend to go down by 1.676 percent. This means that IBM is riskier than the market as a whole, because the price of IBM moves a greater percentage amount than the market, on average. The Appendix to this chapter shows how to compute betas by illustrating the computation of IBM's beta.

Beta as a Measure of Relative Risk

The beta of a security or portfolio is a relative risk measure because it measures risk relative to the market portfolio. For example, treating the market portfolio as a security and plotting its returns against the market portfolio itself results in the characteristic line shown in Figure 14.8. The intercept (alpha) would be zero, and the slope of the characteristic line (beta) would be +1. This would have to be the case, because the plotted values of the market portfolio would always be equal, and that defines a line such as the one shown in Figure 14.8. Because the beta of the market portfolio must always be +1, by definition, it provides a standard against which to measure other securities or portfolios. A security or portfolio that has a beta greater than 1 is **aggressive** because it involves more risk than the market portfolio. A security or portfolio with a beta less than 1 is **defensive** because it has less risk than the market portfolio. By this standard, IBM with its estimated beta of 1.676 may be considered to be quite aggressive.

Not all securities are aggressive, by any means. In fact, the average beta of all portfolios in the market equals 1. This must be the case, because the market portfolio, which is composed of all securities, has a beta of 1. Figure 14.9 shows the characteristic line of IBM and American Medical International. American Medical International (AMI) has a beta of 1.301 and an alpha of −.0471. Like IBM, AMI may be considered an aggressive security, because its beta exceeds 1. Notice, however,

Figure 14.8

The Characteristic Line for the Market Portfolio

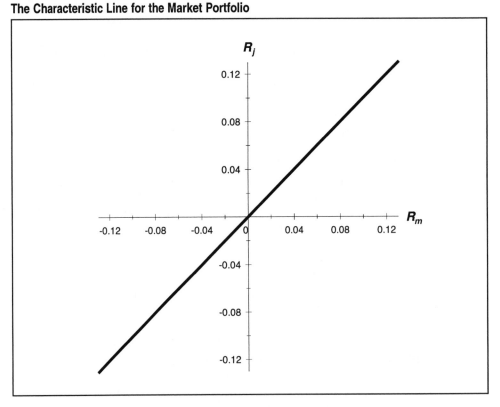

that its beta is still less than that of IBM, showing that its response to the market portfolio is more restrained than IBM's.

Homestake Mining is an interesting case. As calculated, its beta is actually negative by a very small amount, –.05644, and it has an alpha of –.03166. The negative beta means that Homestake Mining has a tendency for its returns to move opposite to the market as a whole. For example, when the market portfolio increases by 10 percent in value, an investor could expect Homestake to lose .005644, or a little more than one–half of one percent of its value. An investor would expect the opposite relationship if the market fell in value by 10 percent. This tendency of Homestake to move in a direction opposite to that of the market is a very valuable tool for diversification. For example, the radically different betas of IBM and Homestake suggest that they could be combined in a two–asset portfolio that would have very low risk. In summary, securities with differing betas can be combined to create a portfolio with the risk/return characteristics desired by the investor.

Figure 14.9

The Characteristic Lines of IBM and AMI

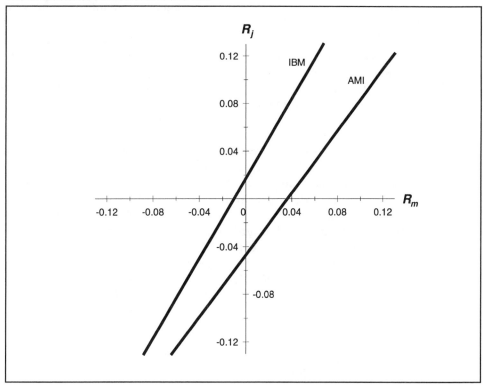

The Partition of Risk

As noted earlier, beta measures the risk of a given security or portfolio that depends on its relationship to the market portfolio. This raises the possibility that we can divide, or partition, the risk of a security into two parts. First, there is the portion of risk that depends on the market—known as **market risk, systematic risk,** or **nondiversifiable risk** of the security or portfolio. Second, the risk that does not depend on the market makes up the remainder. This portion of the risk is known as **nonmarket risk, unsystematic risk, nonsystematic risk,** or **diversifiable risk.**

The risk for a particular security or portfolio can be divided in the following equivalent ways:

Total Risk = Market Risk + Nonmarket Risk
Total Risk = Systematic Risk + Nonsystematic Risk
Total Risk = Nondiversifiable Risk + Diversifiable Risk

All three of these equations say exactly the same thing. The market risk is also systematic risk because the risk associated with the market is system–wide. By the same token, market risk is also nondiversifiable risk. This element of risk associated with fluctuations in the market portfolio makes it impossible to eliminate or reduce by diversification.

By contrast, nonmarket risk is associated with the unique or special features of a particular security or a portfolio that is not fully diversified. Consequently, its risk is nonsystematic—it is not tied to the performance of the market as a whole. For this reason, the nonmarket risk can be eliminated by further diversification, and it is properly regarded as diversifiable risk.

If the investor begins with a single security or a small portfolio, the investment has considerable diversifiable risk. By adding other securities to the portfolio, a greater degree of diversification can be achieved. This possibility is shown in Figure 14.10. For a single security, as noted in the previous chapter, there is a considerable degree of risk. However, by adding other securities to form a portfolio, it is possible to reduce the risk of an investor's position. Figure 14.10 shows this possibility by the curved line, which indicates how the riskiness of the portfolio tends to fall as additional securities are added to the portfolio.

However, after the first 10 to 20 securities are included in the portfolio, adding more securities offers little risk reduction. The graph reflects the waning benefit of continuing to add securities by the fact that the line becomes almost horizontal. Figure 14.10 shows market risk by the dashed line. As portfolios are

Figure 14.10

The Elimination of Nonsystematic Risk Through Diversification

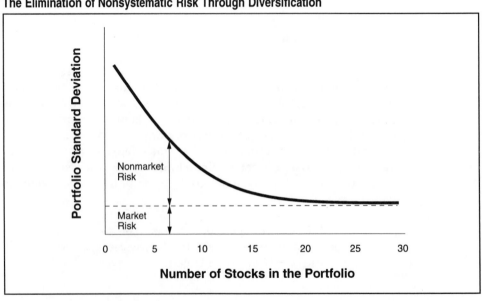

created by adding more securities, the risk level of the portfolio drops quickly to the level of risk inherent in the market. However, the portfolio's risk level can never go below the level of market risk. Consequently, the risk of a portfolio will approach the dashed line from above, as more and more securities are added to the portfolio. The risk level of a portfolio will only be as low as the market risk level when the portfolio is perfectly diversified, and this happens only when it is itself the market portfolio.

Portfolios that are not well diversified have nonmarket risk which can be eliminated through diversification. For a portfolio of any given size, the distance from the curved line of Figure 14.10 to the dashed line indicates the amount of risk that can still be eliminated by more complete diversification. As the graph makes clear, after about 20 securities are held in a portfolio, there is very little additional diversification benefit to be achieved by adding more securities to the portfolio.

The partition of risk between systematic and nonsystematic risk can also be explained in terms of the regression equation. The market risk of a security or portfolio is the risk associated with the $\beta_i R_{m,t}$ term in the equation for the characteristic line, while the nonmarket or unsystematic risk is the risk associated with the term $\varepsilon_{i,t}$. The Appendix to this chapter explains this idea in more detail.

The Expected Return of a Security

In the previous discussion of the capital market line, we noted that the expected return for a fully diversified portfolio depended largely on the risk level of the portfolio. Portfolios on the capital market line have no nonsystematic risk and are perfectly diversified because they are composed of the market portfolio as the only portfolio of risky assets. However, for individual securities and smaller portfolios, investors still need to know the factors that determine their expected returns.

As noted in the previous section, risk for an individual security is composed of two parts, the systematic and nonsystematic.[1] It is reasonable to suppose that the expected return of a security depends on its risk level. However, one difference between a single security and the fully diversified portfolios lying on the capital market line is the fact that the single security still has diversifiable risk, while the fully diversified portfolio on the CML is free of diversifiable risk. Consequently, the question is whether the nonsystematic diversifiable risk of a single security is compensated in the marketplace by a greater expected return.

In the market described by capital market theory, additional risk is compensated by additional expected return. However, only nondiversifiable risk is compensated. To see why this must be true, recall that markets are assumed to be perfect so that investors may trade securities without cost. For an investor with an initial position in a single security, there will be a considerable amount of

---

[1]The same holds true for portfolios that are not fully diversified. We will speak of single securities in this section, but the argument holds equally well for portfolios that are not fully diversified.

diversifiable risk. By selling a portion of the holdings in that security and investing the proceeds in other securities, the investor can reduce the diversifiable risk. This means that any investor may avoid all diversifiable risk without cost. As a consequence, the market will not reward investors for bearing diversifiable risk.

Another way to see the same point is to consider the function of bearing risk in society. Markets reward the bearing of risk with additional expected returns because the bearing of risk provides a service to society. In the economy overall, there are certain risks to be undertaken. Ownership of physical capital and the contribution of financial capital to risky ventures both involve risk. But only through undertaking risky projects does society achieve the benefits of a healthy economy. Therefore, those investors who bear risk for society deserve to be compensated for the service they render, and this compensation takes the form of additional expected returns on security investments.

The market should be organized to reward the bearers of risk for society, but there is no need to reward investors for bearing unnecessary risks. The investor who holds a single security bears both systematic risk and nonsystematic risk. The bearing of systematic risk is the bearing of a risk that is inherent in the economy and that must be undertaken by some investor. However, the investor who holds a single security also bears a considerable amount of nonsystematic risk. Since this risk can be eliminated by diversification, the bearing of this risk performs no useful function for society. Accordingly, there is no reason the investor should be rewarded for bearing the nonsystematic risk.

For an individual security, the expected return includes compensation for the passage of time, which is the risk–free rate, plus a reward for bearing systematic risk. The measure of the amount of systematic risk that is undertaken is beta. So the expected return of an individual security should equal the risk–free rate, plus an additional amount for the bearing of risk. This relationship is expressed by the security market line.

The Security Market Line

The security market line (SML) expresses the central idea of the capital asset pricing model (CAPM):

> The expected return of a security depends on the risk–free rate, plus additional compensation for the bearing of systematic risk, as measured by beta.

Figure 14.11 shows the linear relationship between beta and the expected returns of different securities. In equilibrium, the expected return of each security or portfolio lies on the SML. This includes every security or portfolio in the market, even the market portfolio. The SML begins at the risk–free rate, and the upward slope of the line indicates the greater expected return that accompanies higher levels of beta.

Figure 14.11

The Security Market Line

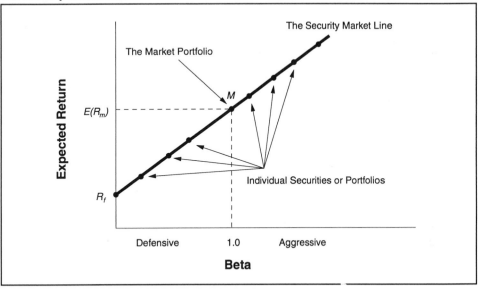

Each security lying on the SML receives compensation for its level of beta, as illustrated in Figure 14.11. Only systematic risk is rewarded, and any additional risk that holding a security might involve is not rewarded. The expected return of a Security i can also be expressed as the equation of the SML, which is the basic equation of the capital asset pricing model:

$$E(R_i) = R_f + \beta_i[E(R_m) - R_f] \qquad \textbf{14.9}$$

This equation gives the market risk premium by the term:

$$[E(R_m) - R_f]$$

and is shown graphically in Figure 14.12. The market risk premium is the additional return one can expect to earn by holding the market portfolio rather than the risk–free asset. If an investor holds a portfolio with a beta greater than that of the market portfolio (a beta greater than 1), he or she expects a return greater than the return on the market portfolio. In summary, the capital asset pricing model maintains that the expected return on any security or portfolio equals the risk–free rate plus the market risk premium multiplied by the beta of the security or portfolio. As we will see in the next chapter, this relationship breaks down in the real market for individual securities, but holds well for portfolios.

Figure 14.12

The Security Market Line and the Market Risk Premium

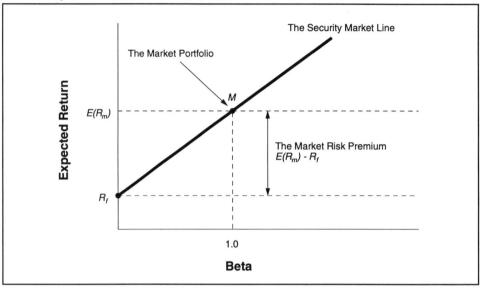

The Capital Market Line and the Security Market Line

To complete our discussion of the capital asset pricing model, it is useful to compare the capital market line in Figure 14.6 and the security market line in Figure 14.11 to see how they are mutually consistent. The major points of difference between the two can be summarized as follows:

1. The risk measure for the CML is the standard deviation, a measure of total risk, while the risk measure for the SML is beta, a measure of systematic risk.
2. In equilibrium, only fully diversified portfolios lie on the CML, while individual securities plot below the CML. For the SML, all securities and all portfolios fall exactly on the SML in equilibrium.

By using the standard deviation as its risk measure, the graph of the CML shows the total risk of the individual securities and portfolios in the risk–return space. However, the arguments given earlier have proven that not all of the risk of a security is relevant to determining the expected return. All of the individual securities shown in Figure 14.6 embody some nonsystematic risk. This portion of risk does not contribute to their expected returns, so there is no reason for their expected returns to lie on the CML. For the SML, Figure 14.11 uses beta as the risk measure. Since beta measures the systematic risk only, we can anticipate that the expected returns of securities reflect that kind of risk fully. If this is correct, each security should lie exactly on the SML when the market is in equilibrium.

The graph of the SML shows nothing about the total risk of the individual securities. Only the systematic risk, as measured by beta, is reflected because that is the only portion of the total risk relevant to determining the expected returns of a security. In the graph of the CML, many securities can plot below the CML. The graph of the CML shows the additional risk that is not relevant to pricing, due to the fact that the total risk of the securities is being presented. Only the systematic risk, as measured by beta, is priced.

International Capital Asset Pricing

One of the key features of the capital asset pricing model is the important role assigned to the market portfolio. The theory asserts that rational investors will seek to hold a portfolio of risky assets that is a miniature of the market portfolio. Because of this, it becomes very important to correctly identify the market portfolio.

Domestic versus World Market Portfolios

In practice, most analysts have used a portfolio of U.S. stocks to approximate the market portfolio. In theory, however, it appears that the real market portfolio is a world market portfolio. In this portfolio, all risky assets in the world would be included in proportion to their contribution to total world wealth.

It is already a simplification to pretend that only stocks are relevant and to use stock market portfolios as surrogates for all other assets. In particular, using only stocks tends to neglect the two greatest categories of world wealth—human capital and real estate. However, to restrict the market portfolio to only domestic stocks is even more restrictive. In this section, we show the advantages of regarding the world stock market index as the market portfolio in the capital asset pricing model.

Part of the reason for restricting attention to just the U.S. stock market has been the belief that capital markets across international boundaries are segmented. A **segmented market** is a market in which capital cannot move freely from one part of the market to another, and as we will see, this has important implications for investors' ability to diversify fully. If the equity markets of the world are segmented by various kinds of restrictions on the movement of capital or relevant information across national boundaries, it may be that a different capital asset pricing model would hold for each country. In other words, with segmented markets, the expected return of a security would depend only on the beta of that security when it is measured against the market portfolio from the same country. On the other hand, if international equity markets are not segmented, then the expected return of a security should depend on the beta of that security when it is measured against the world market portfolio.

This issue has great implications for the question of international diversification. In this chapter, we have seen that poorly diversified portfolios will have a risk level that is higher than necessary for the expected returns of the portfolio, and that this situation can be remedied by further diversification. In the preceding chapter, we explored the question of international diversification and found that investors have the chance to reduce their risk by diversifying beyond their national boundaries.

Markets can differ in the extent to which they are segmented. For example, if we consider geographical segmentation, the market for residential housing is a segmented market, because it is difficult to move the goods from one geographical market segment to another. The U.S. stock market is not geographically segmented at all, because capital can very easily be shifted from one location to another. If capital markets are strictly segmented, it will be impossible to diversify abroad. However, if capital markets are weakly segmented, there may be even greater potential gains to international diversification. A market might be weakly segmented if there are difficulties in moving capital or in acquiring information about activities in other market segments.

Table 14.3

Standard Deviations and Betas of National Stock Markets

Country	Standard Deviation of Returns	Beta
Australia	16.1	.51
Austria	13.0	.26
Belgium	11.4	.55
Canada	12.3	.95
Denmark	11.5	.10
France	17.1	.50
Germany	19.4	.86
Italy	21.6	.50
Japan	18.4	.49
Netherlands	14.8	.94
Norway	16.0	.21
Spain	12.7	.08
Sweden	13.6	.46
Switzerland	18.6	.96
U.K.	15.8	.61
U.S.A.	12.5	1.10
World	10.6	1.00

Note: Betas for each national stock market are measured against the world market portfolio.

Source: Donald R. Lessard, "World, Country, and Industry Relationships in Equity Returns: Implications for Risk Reduction Through International Diversification," *Financial Analysts Journal*, January/February 1976, pp. 32–38. Adapted, with permission, from *Financial Analysts Journal*, January/February 1976. Copyright 1976, Financial Analysts Federation, Charlottesville, VA. All rights reserved.

Risk Measures for Foreign Stock Markets

Table 14.3 shows the betas of domestic stock portfolios when the returns from domestic markets are regressed against the world market portfolio. In other words, each of the complete domestic equity markets from a foreign country was regressed against the world market portfolio to measure its beta. Notice the extreme diversity of betas, from the lows of .08 and .1 for Spain and Denmark, to the high of 1.1 for the United States. In fact, only the United States had a beta greater than one.

More important, however, is the relationship between beta and the expected returns on the portfolios. These are presented in Table 14.4. Using the betas for the domestic portfolios shown in Table 14.3, Lessard calculated the expected return for each of the domestic portfolios and then compared these to the risk equivalent world portfolio. The risk equivalent world portfolio is constructed of the world

Table 14.4

Differences in Expected Returns for Domestically versus Internationally Diversified Equity Portfolios

Country	Expected Return of Domestic Portfolio	Expected Return of Risk-Equivalent World Portfolio	Loss in Expected Return from Not Diversifying Internationally
Australia	8.02	12.08	4.06
Austria	7.04	10.92	3.88
Belgium	8.20	10.28	2.08
Canada	9.79	10.64	0.85
Denmark	6.40	10.36	3.96
France	8.01	12.48	4.47
Germany	9.45	13.32	3.87
Italy	8.02	14.16	6.14
Japan	7.95	12.96	5.01
Netherlands	9.77	11.60	1.83
Norway	6.85	12.04	5.19
Spain	6.30	10.80	4.50
Sweden	7.85	11.12	3.27
Switzerland	9.82	13.04	3.22
U.K.	8.46	11.46	3.00
U.S.A.	10.41	10.72	0.31

Note: The analysis assumes that the risk–free rate is 6 percent and the expected return on the world market portfolio is 10 percent.

Source: Donald R. Lessard, "World, Country, and Industry Relationships in Equity Returns: Implications for Risk Reduction Through International Diversification," *Financial Analysts Journal*, January/February 1976, pp. 32–38. Adapted, with permission, from *Financial Analysts Journal*, January/February 1976. Copyright 1976, Financial Analysts Federation, Charlottesville, VA. All rights reserved.

equity portfolio and the risk–free asset in proportions to match the risk of the domestic portfolio. For each of the countries, there would have been a gain in expected return by holding the world portfolio rather than just the domestic portfolio. The amount of this gain is shown in the last column of Table 14.4. This is the additional expected gain that could be realized by holding the world portfolio instead of the domestic portfolio, and it could be achieved without any additional risk beyond that which was already present in the purely domestic portfolio.

Figure 14.13 presents the same information graphically. Here the risk–free rate is taken as 6 percent, in accordance with Lessard's analysis, and the world market portfolio has an expected return of 10 percent. As an example, we find that Austria has a standard deviation of returns of 13 percent and an expected return of 7.04 percent. By comparison, an investment in the world portfolio, using leverage to bring the risk level to 13 percent to match Austria's, would have an expected return of 10.92 percent. For its risk level, an investment in Austria's market would be underperforming the market by 3.88 percent per annum. Similarly, an investment in any of the other countries would also be earning a lower return for its level of risk than the return that could be achieved by investing in the world market portfolio.

This indicates that there are substantial advantages to be gained from international diversification and the magnitude of these advantages depends upon the investor's home country. We have already seen that there are dramatic risk reduction possibilities. Now, we also see a way to quantify the shortfall in expected

Figure 14.13

The World Capital Market Line and Purely Domestic Portfolios

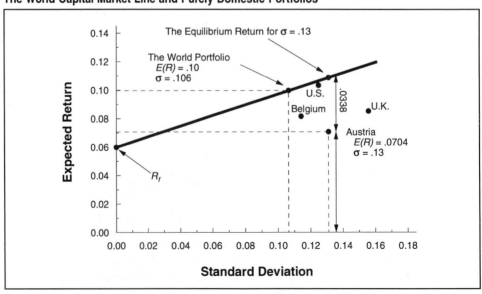

return that comes from holding poorly diversified portfolios. In this case, the poorly diversified portfolios are thoroughly diversified domestically but do not take advantage of international diversification. Also, as shown in Figure 14.13, the advantages of international diversification differ across countries. In the figure, the United States is almost on the world capital market line, so there is relatively little benefit for the U.S. investor to diversify internationally. The situation is very different for an Austrian investor, because the Austrian domestic portfolio lies well below the world CML. Though small, the relative benefits to the U.S. investor from international diversification are still significant. The importance of international diversification for U.S. investors has been emphasized by a recent strong trend in the United States toward international diversification. Further, as the United States stock market becomes smaller relative to the world market, as has been occurring in the last few years, international diversification will become increasingly important for U.S. investors.

The principle is clear. The investor, who holds a portfolio of only a few stocks, is not taking advantage of the available domestic diversification opportunities. Likewise, the investor that diversifies thoroughly, but who uses only the domestic market, is not taking advantage of the opportunities for international diversification. Both investors are earning a lower rate of return, for a given level of risk, than they could achieve by holding the world market portfolio.

Characteristics of Betas

The central importance of beta to the capital asset pricing model and all of capital market theory has made it the object of intense scrutiny. This section considers some important research about the behavior of betas and considers the distribution of betas found in the marketplace. First, betas tend to change in particular ways over time. Second, in spite of the fact that a given beta may be expected to change over time, the distribution of betas is remarkably stationary. Finally, the fact that individual betas can be expected to change but that the distribution of betas remains constant gives information about predicting the change in betas.

In two classic articles, Marshall Blume argued that betas exhibit a tendency to regress toward the mean of all betas, namely 1.0, a conclusion sustained by other researchers following in his footsteps.[2] For example, assume that the beta measured by regression analysis using current data is 1.6. According to Blume's analysis, we

---

[2] The central literature on the tendencies of betas to move toward 1.0 includes: Marshall E. Blume, "On the Assessment of Risk," *Journal of Finance*, March 1971, pp. 1–10 and "Betas and Their Regression Tendencies," *Journal of Finance*, June 1975, pp. 785–795; Frank J. Fabozzi and Jack Clark Francis, "Beta as a Random Coefficient," *Journal of Financial and Quantitative Analysis*, March 1978, pp. 101–116; Menachem Brenner and Seymour Smidt, "A Simple Model of Non–Stationarity of Systematic Risk," *Journal of Finance*, September 1977, pp. 1081–1092; Arthur E. Gooding and Terence P. O'Malley, "Market Phase and the Stationarity of Beta," *Journal of Financial and Quantitative Analysis*, December 1977, pp. 833–857.

should expect the beta for the same firm when it is measured in the next period to be closer to 1.0. Similarly, if the measured beta were 0.4 now, we would expect the beta to increase, becoming closer to 1.0. Part of this measured change is due to measurement error, but part is due to a real tendency for extreme betas to actually become closer to 1.0.

If this process continued over a long period of time, it would imply that betas in the marketplace would get closer and closer to 1.0, so that eventually all betas would be 1.0. However, that clearly does not seem to be happening. In fact, as Kolb and Rodriguez have shown, the distribution of betas is essentially stable over time.[3] The distribution is stable, because betas close to 1.0 have a high probability of moving away from 1.0, becoming either smaller or larger. This movement of betas near 1.0 away from the mean offsets the tendency of very small or very large betas to move closer to 1.0. The result is a fairly stable distribution of betas.

Figure 14.14

The Distribution of Betas 1926–1985

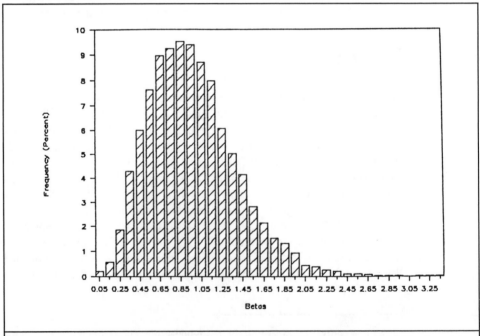

Source: R. Kolb, and R. Rodriguez, "The Regression Tendencies of Betas: A Reappraisal," *The Financial Review*, 24:2, May 1989, pp. 319-334. Reprinted with permission of *The Financial Review*.

---

[3]Robert W. Kolb and Ricardo Rodriguez, "The Regression Tendencies of Betas: A Reappraisal," *The Financial Review*, 24:2, May 1989.

Figure 14.14 shows the distribution of measured betas for the period 1926 to 1985. Each beta was computed using the equation for the characteristic line and 60 months of data. The figure reflects 10,625 measured betas. Notice that the distribution exhibits positive skewness. In particular, over half of the betas are lower than 1.0. There were essentially no betas measured with values below 0, and very few with values above 2.0. The overwhelming majority of betas fall in the interval of 0.6 to 1.4.

The stability of the distribution makes it possible to produce a table showing the likely change in betas from one measurement period to the next. Table 14.5 shows how betas can be expected to change from one five–year estimation period to the next. The left–hand column shows the value of a beta in the original estimation period, while the middle column shows the number of firms with betas in that range. For a beta different from 1.0, the beta in the next period can either move closer to or farther from the market average of 1.0. The last column of Table 14.5 gives the probability that a beta falling in one region in a given period will be found in another region in the next period. For example, if the beta was originally 0.2 or less in the original period, it is one of the 66 firms appearing in the first row of the table. For a beta so far from 1.0, there is a 93.94 percent chance that it will move closer to 1.0 in the next period. By contrast, if the beta was near 1.0 in the original period, it is likely to be farther from 1.0 in the next period. For example, in the original estimation period, there were 1547 betas in the range from 0.8 to 1.0. However, in the next period, only 23.01 percent of these betas moved closer to 1.0. Thus, if the beta is originally far from 1.0, it is likely to move closer to 1.0, but this is not true if the beta is already close to 1.0.

Table 14.5

Behavior of Interior Beta Sub–Samples

Sub–Sample*	Observations in Range in Period t	Percentage Closer to 1.0 in Period $t + 1$
$(-\infty, 0.2)$	66	93.94
$(0.2, 0.4)$	501	78.24
$(0.4, 0.6)$	1115	66.10
$(0.6, 0.8)$	1487	53.87
$(0.8, 1.0)$	1547	23.01
$(1.0, 1.2)$	1365	23.22
$(1.2, 1.4)$	907	52.37
$(1.4, 1.6)$	568	72.36
$(1.6, 1.8)$	300	75.33
$(1.8, 2.0)$	184	87.50
$(2.0, +\infty)$	155	92.26

*The sub–sample consists of all firms with betas in the indicated range in Period t.

Summary

This and the preceding chapter traced the main outlines of capital market theory as it developed over three decades. We have omitted a number of important developments in order to concentrate on the main argument. Also, it must be remembered that this theory has been developed under certain idealized conditions that do not hold in actual markets. Most importantly, we assumed that security markets are perfect, that investors have full information relevant to the pricing of securities, and that they all process the information in the same way.

Obviously, these assumptions are not true of the actual market and its participants. However, all theories simplify the full complexity of the subject matter they try to explain. If they can simplify that subject matter and still explain the essential features of the subject matter and its behavior, then doing so helps to validate the theory. There has been a great deal of study of the predictions of the capital asset pricing model and a great portion of the next chapter considers how well the CAPM fits markets as they actually exist.

Questions and Problems

1. For a two–asset portfolio made up of two risky assets with zero correlation between them, the possible portfolios lie on a curved line. For a two–asset portfolio made up of the risk–free asset and a risky portfolio, the resulting portfolios lie on a straight line. This is the case, even though the correlation between the risk–free asset and a risky portfolio is also zero. Explain.

2. Why should investors prefer the market portfolio as their portfolio of risky assets?

3. The relationships shown in the CML and SML hold strictly only in the idealized world defined by our assumptions. In a practical sense, what would an investor be likely to hold who wanted to construct a "real world" lending portfolio? A borrowing portfolio?

4. Graphically show the revised CML if the borrowing rate is 15 percent and the lending rate is 10 percent. Identify the efficient frontier under these circumstances.

5. What kind of investor does not benefit by the introduction of the risk–free asset, according to our analysis of the CML?

6. What is the "separation theorem"?

7. Consider the following two facts: (1) All investors will wish to hold the same risky portfolio in conjunction with the risk–free asset; (2) All securities are owned by someone. Explain how these two facts imply that the market portfolio is the risky portfolio preferred by all investors.

8. What is the interpretation of the slope of the CML? The slope of the SML?

9. What is the "market risk premium"?

10. Does the CML hold for individual securities? Why or why not?

11. Does the SML hold for individual securities? Why or why not?
12. What is the "characteristic line"? What is the interpretation of its slope?
13. Every security or portfolio has a total amount of risk. What are the measures of that risk? What kinds of risk go into that total risk?
14. If a portfolio has an estimated beta of 1.0 and an $R^2 = 1$, what is the portfolio? Why? Would it matter if the $R^2 = .8$?
15. You have computed a characteristic line equation and have found that the $R^2 = 1.2$. What does this mean? How can you interpret this R^2?
16. In equilibrium, will individual securities plot on the CML? On the SML? Why the difference?
17. In our discussion of international diversification, we noticed that U.S. investors receive smaller benefits relative to investors from other countries. Explain why this is true using the ideas of portfolio theory. (Hint: How does the U.S. market portfolio relate to the world market portfolio?)
18. A risky portfolio has an expected return of .33 and a standard deviation of .4. The risk–free rate is 12 percent. You construct a portfolio comprised of 40 percent investment in the risk–free asset and 60 percent in the risky portfolio. What is the expected return and standard deviation of this portfolio?
19. The market portfolio has an expected return of 22 percent and a standard deviation of 19 percent. The risk–free rate is 9 percent. How could you construct a portfolio with an expected return of 15 percent? What would the standard deviation of the portfolio be?
20. With a market portfolio having an expected return of 22 percent and a standard deviation of 19 percent, how would you construct a portfolio having an expected return of 30 percent? Assume that the risk–free rate is 9 percent. What would be the standard deviation of this portfolio?
21. A well–diversified portfolio has a standard deviation of .25. The risk–free rate is 11 percent and the market portfolio has an expected return of 20 percent and a standard deviation of .20. What is the expected return for the portfolio?
22. A security has a correlation with the market portfolio of .8 and a standard deviation of .15. The standard deviation of the market portfolio is .22. What is the beta of this security?
23. A security has a beta of 1.3 and a standard deviation of .22. The risk–free rate is 11 percent. The market portfolio has an expected return of .18 and a standard deviation of .20. What is the expected return of the security?
24. In five successive time periods, the market portfolio had a return of 10 percent, 12 percent, 6 percent, –4 percent, and 1 percent. A given security had the following returns in each period: 15 percent, 13 percent, 4 percent, –12 percent, and –2 percent. Calculate the following for this security: (1) the variance of returns, (2) the characteristic line, (3) the correlation of returns between the market portfolio and the security, (4) the R^2 of the characteristic line equation, (5) the systematic risk of the security, and (6) the non–systematic risk of the security.

CFA Questions

    A. Assume the correlation coefficient between Baker Fund and the S&P 500 Stock Index in 0.70. What percent of Baker Fund's total risk is specific (i.e., nonsystematic)?

      a. 35%
      b. 49%
      c. 51%
      d. 70%

    B. The correlation between the Charlottesville International Fund and the EAFE Index is 1.0. The expected return on the EAFE Index is 11%, the expected return on Charlottesville International Fund is 9%, and the risk–free return in EAFE countries is 3%. Based on this analysis, the implied beta of Charlottesville International is:

      a. negative.
      b. 0.75.
      c. 0.82.
      d. 1.00.

    C. You manage an equity fund with an expected risk premium of 10% and an expected standard deviation of 14%. The rate on Treasury bills is 6%. Your client chooses to invest $60,000 of her portfolio in your equity fund and $40,000 in a T–bill money market fund. What is the expected return and standard deviation of return on your client's portfolio?

	Expected Return	Standard Deviation of Return
a.	8.4%	8.4%
b.	8.4%	14.0%
c.	12.0%	8.4%
d.	12.0%	14.0%

    D. The concept of *beta* is most closely associated with:

      a. correlation coefficients.
      b. mean/variance analysis.
      c. nonsystematic risk.
      d. the Capital Asset Pricing Model.

E. Capital Asset Pricing Theory asserts that portfolio returns are best explained by:
   a. diversification.
   b. systematic risk.
   c. economic factors.
   d. specific risk.
F. The Security Market Line depicts:
   a. a security's expected return as a function of its systematic risk.
   b. the market portfolio as the optimal portfolio of risky securities.
   c. the relationship between a security's return and the return on an index.
   d. the complete portfolio as a combination of the market portfolio and the risk–free asset.
G. Within the context of the Capital Asset Pricing Model (CAPM), assume:
   - Expected return on the market = 15%
   - Risk free rate = 8%
   - Expected rate of return on XYZ security = 17%
   - Beta of XYZ security = 1.25
   Which *one* of the following is *correct*?
   a. XYZ is overpriced.
   b. XYZ is fairly priced.
   c. XYZ's alpha is –0.25%.
   d. XYZ's alpha is 0.25%.
H. Which *one* of the following is *not* a systematic risk factor?
   a. Interest rate risk
   b. Market risk
   c. Business risk
   d. Inflation risk
I. Fundamental analysis uses the following technique:
   a. earnings and dividends prospects.
   b. relative strength.
   c. price momentum.
   d. moving averages.
J. In terms of risk levels, the ultimate result that occurs in a portfolio when part of the equity portion of the portfolio is liquidated and subsequently reinvested in money market instruments is:
   a. a decline in portfolio liquidity.
   b. a dramatic reduction in the beta of the portfolio.
   c. a dramatic reduction in the beta of the equity portion of the portfolio.
   d. an increase in portfolio risk.
K. CAPM suggests that the return on a well–diversified portfolio should be most affected by:
   a. systematic risk.
   b. asset allocation.
   c. security selection.
   d. unsystematic risk.

L. Assuming a diversified portfolio of common stocks, which *one* of the following does *not* reduce portfolio risk?
   a. Selecting stocks with low systematic risk
   b. Investing in fixed–income securities
   c. Holding cash equivalents
   d. Selling stocks which appear overpriced

M. Standard Deviation and Beta both measure risk, but they are different in that:
   a. Beta measures both systematic and unsystematic risk while Standard Deviation measures only unsystematic risk.
   b. Beta measures only systematic risk while Standard Deviation is a measure of total risk.
   c. Beta measures only unsystematic risk while Standard Deviation is a measure of total risk.
   d. Beta measures both systematic and unsystematic risk while Standard Deviation measures only systematic risk.

N. What is the expected return of a zero–beta security?
   a. The market rate of return
   b. Zero rate of return
   c. A negative rate of return
   d. The risk–free rate of return

O. The unsystematic risk of a specific security:
   a. is likely to be higher in a rising market.
   b. results from its own unique factors.
   c. depends upon market volatility.
   d. cannot be diversified away.

Suggested REALDATA Exercises

The following *REALDATA* exercises explore the concepts developed in this chapter: Exercises 26, 27, 47, 48, 49, 50, 51.

Suggested Readings

Cheung, Y. and Y. Ho, "The Intertemporal Stability of the Relationships Between the Asian Emerging Equity Markets and the Developed Equity Markets," *Journal of Business Finance and Accounting*, 18:2, January 1991, pp. 235–254.

Friedman, M. and L. J. Savage, "The Utility Analysis of Choices Involving Risk," *The Journal of Political Economy*, August 1948, pp. 279–304.

Gandar, J., R. Zuber, T. O'Brien, and B. Russo, "Testing Rationality in the Point Spread Betting Market," *Journal of Finance*, 43:4, September 1988, pp. 995–1008.

Harrington, D. R., *Modern Portfolio Theory, The Capital Asset Pricing Model and Arbitrage Pricing Theory: A User's Guide*, 2e, Englewood Cliffs, NJ: Prentice Hall, 1987.

Harvey, C. R., "The World Price of Covariance Risk," *Journal of Finance*, 46:1, March 1991, pp. 111–157.

Ko, K. and S. Lee, "A Comparative Analysis of the Daily Behavior of Stock Returns: Japan, the U.S. and the Asian NICs," *Journal of Business Finance & Accounting*, 18:2, January 1991, pp. 219–234.

Krueger, T. M. and W. F. Kennedy, "An Examination of the Super Bowl Stock Market Predictor," *Journal of Finance*, 45:2, June 1990, pp. 691–697.

Mossin, J., "Security Pricing and Investment Criteria in Competitive Markets," *American Economic Review*, December 1969, pp. 749–756.

Sharpe, W. F., "Capital Asset Prices: A Theory of Market Equilibrium Under Conditions of Risk," *Journal of Finance*, September 1964, pp. 425–442.

Sharpe, W. F. and G. M. Cooper, "Risk–Return Classes of New York Stock Exchange Common Stocks, 1931–1967," *Financial Analysts Journal*, 28:2, March/April 1972, pp. 46–54, 81.

Appendix

Calculating the Simple Regression

This appendix shows how to calculate the parameters of the characteristic line regression equation and discusses the partition of risk into systematic and nonsystematic risk in more detail.

In Chapter 14, we saw that the equation of the characteristic line is given by:

$$R_{i,t} = \alpha_i + \beta_i R_{m,t} + \varepsilon_{i,t}$$

where:

$R_{i,t}$ = the returns on Security i in Period t
$R_{m,t}$ = the returns on the market portfolio in Period t
α_i = the parameter for the intercept term (alpha)
β_i = the parameter for the slope coefficient (beta)
$\varepsilon_{i,t}$ = a random error term assumed to have a zero mean

Consistent with this model, the value of beta is defined by:

$$\beta_i = \frac{\sigma_{i,m}}{\sigma_m^2} = \frac{\sigma_i}{\sigma_m} \rho_{i,m}$$

To illustrate the calculation of beta, we will use IBM as our stock and we will use the S&P 500 index as our market portfolio. For the sake of simplicity, we use only 12 months of data. In actual practice, portfolio managers use many more observations to obtain a better estimate. The returns for IBM and the S&P 500 are as follows:

Month	S&P 500	IBM
January	0.0331	0.2162
February	0.0189	0.0117
March	0.0331	0.0262
April	0.0749	0.1515
May	−0.0124	−0.0415
June	0.0352	0.0809
July	−0.0331	0.0008
August	0.0113	0.0004
September	0.0101	0.0611
October	−0.0152	−0.0008
November	0.0174	−0.0660
December	−0.0088	0.0400

Calculation of Beta and Alpha

Step 1: Calculate mean returns. The average return for the S&P 500 over this period was 1.37 percent per month, and for IBM it was 4 percent. These are arithmetic averages of the 12 monthly returns shown in the preceding table.

Step 2: Form deviation vectors. To calculate the various elements of our formula for beta, we need to know the deviations of IBM and the S&P 500 from their means. We find these deviations by subtracting the arithmetic mean return from the returns for each of the months.

Month	S&P 500 Deviation	IBM Deviation
January	0.0194	0.1762
February	0.0052	−0.0283
March	0.0194	−0.0138
April	0.0612	0.1115
May	−0.0261	−0.0815
June	0.0215	0.0409
July	−0.0468	−0.0392
August	−0.0024	−0.0396
September	−0.0036	0.0211
October	−0.0289	−0.0408
November	0.0037	−0.1060
December	−0.0225	0.0000

Step 3: Compute squared deviation and cross products of deviations. The deviation vectors are needed to calculate the standard deviation of returns for the S&P 500 and IBM and to calculate the covariance of returns between the two. For the standard deviations, we need to square each of the deviations, and for the covariance we need to compute the products of the month–by–month deviations across the S&P 500 and IBM. For example, in the first month we need to multiply the deviation for the S&P 500 (.0194) by the deviation for IBM in the same month (.1762).

Month	Squared S&P 500 Deviation	Squared IBM Deviation	S&P Deviation × IBM Deviation
January	0.000376	0.031046	−.003418
February	0.000027	0.000801	−.000147
March	0.000376	0.000190	−.000268
April	0.003745	0.012432	−.006824
May	0.000681	0.006642	−.002127
June	0.000462	0.001673	−.000879
July	0.002190	0.001537	−.001835
August	0.000006	0.001568	−.000095
September	0.000013	0.000445	−.000076
October	0.000835	0.001665	−.001179
November	0.000014	0.011236	−.000392
December	0.000506	0.000000	−.000000

Step 4: Compute variances and covariance.   Next we compute the variances and standard deviations of the S&P 500 and IBM and the covariance of returns between the index and IBM. For the variance, we sum the columns for the S&P 500 and IBM squared deviations and divide by the number of observations:

$$\sigma^2_{S\&P\ 500} = \frac{.009228}{12} = .000769$$

$$\sigma^2_{IBM} = \frac{.069240}{12} = .005770$$

The standard deviations are simply the square roots of the variances:

$$\sigma_{S\&P\ 500} = .027731$$
$$\sigma_{IBM} = .075961$$

The covariance of returns between the S&P 500 and IBM is the sum of the third column, divided by the number of observations:

$$\sigma_{S\&P\ 500,\ IBM} = \frac{.015474}{12} = .001290$$

Step 5: Make final beta calculation.   We now have all of the information necessary to calculate beta. As shown in the equation above, the beta equals the covariance of returns divided by the variance of the market portfolio:

$$\beta_{\text{IBM}} = \frac{.00129}{.000769} = 1.677503$$

Step 6: Calculate intercept term. The intercept term can now be calculated easily from the following formula.

$$\alpha_{\text{IBM}} = \text{Average IBM Return} - \beta_{\text{IBM(Average S\&P 500 Return)}}$$
$$= .0400 - (1.676853)(.0137)$$
$$= .017027$$

Together, the alpha and beta define the characteristic line for IBM.

In addition to knowing beta and alpha, it is also important to know the goodness–of–fit between IBM and the S&P 500. The better IBM tracks the market, the less of IBM's total risk is unsystematic risk. The best known measure of the goodness–of–fit for a regression line is the R–squared (R^2), or the "coefficient of determination." Essentially, it measures the correlation between the S&P 500 and IBM. In fact, R^2 simply equals the square of the correlation coefficient.

The correlation between IBM and the S&P 500 is given by the equation:

$$\rho_{\text{S\&P 500, IBM}} = \frac{\sigma_{\text{S\&P 500, IBM}}}{\sigma_{\text{S\&P 500}}\sigma_{\text{IBM}}}$$
$$= \frac{.001290}{(.027731)(.075958)}$$
$$= .612$$

and R^2 equals the square of the correlation coefficient:

$$R^2 = (.612422)^2$$
$$= .375$$

The Interpretation of the Coefficient of Determination and the Partition of Risk

The coefficient of determination, or the R^2, has a fairly straightforward interpretation. In the context of our sample problem, it means that 37.51 percent of the variability in the returns of IBM can be explained by the variability in the returns of the S&P 500. The remaining portion, 62.49 percent, is associated with other factors that are not specified in this equation.

In terms of the characteristic line equation, 37.51 percent of the variability of IBM is associated with movements in the S&P 500, and the remainder is associated with the random error term. For IBM, the following relationship holds true:

Total Risk = Systematic Risk + Nonsystematic Risk

Using the variance as a measure of the total risk, it must also be true that:

$$\sigma^2_{IBM} = (R^2)\sigma^2_{IBM} + (1 - R^2)\ \sigma^2_{IBM}$$

Using the values determined above for the variance and the R^2:

.005770 = (.3751) (.005770) + (1–.3751) (.005770)
.005770 = .002164 + .003606

In this way, we can very precisely state the total risk of IBM and partition that total risk into systematic and nonsystematic risk. The R^2 tells us what percentage of the total risk is associated with the market. It tells us nothing about how much total risk a security involves. The total risk is given by the variance or standard deviation.

CHAPTER FIFTEEN

Efficient Markets and the Capital Asset Pricing Model

Overview

Chapters 13 and 14 developed portfolio theory and the concept of the market price of risk. Having seen that there is a theoretical relationship between the expected returns of securities and their level of systematic risk, this chapter builds on this theoretical foundation. First, we introduce the concept of an **efficient market**—a market in which prices fully reflect a specified information set. We then examine how closely the actual performance of security returns matches the theoretical predictions developed in the last two chapters.

In briefest terms, an efficient market is one that responds well and quickly to new information. The response of a market to new information is very important for the issue of market equilibrium. While the capital asset pricing model (CAPM) may hypothesize an equilibrium relationship between expected return and risk, the entire theory would be devoid of practical application if markets never moved toward this equilibrium.

The rapid adjustment of market prices to new information is the mechanism by which the market moves toward equilibrium. If market prices do not respond to new information in a way that moves the market toward equilibrium, then there is no reason to think that actual markets behave as implied by the CAPM. Therefore, there is an intimate theoretical and practical connection between the CAPM and the **efficient markets hypothesis** (EMH).

In fact, the close conceptual relationship between the CAPM and the EMH means that the two ideas cannot really be tested independently of one another in many instances. Tests of the EMH try to determine whether markets process new information in a way that makes prices move quickly toward the new equilibrium. To evaluate that issue, however, there must be some definition of the equilibrium. Since the CAPM specifies the market equilibrium, the two theories are linked logically.

In spite of some difficulties in separating the CAPM and the EMH, a number of revealing empirical tests have been conducted. Taken together, these tests provide a very good indication of the adequacy of the CAPM and the efficiency of the financial markets. This chapter examines representative studies of the adequacy of the CAPM and the EMH.

In the last 10 to 15 years, a number of controversies surrounding the CAPM have arisen. Richard Roll raised general issues that question the entire CAPM framework. In addition, a number of market anomalies have been discovered that apparently violate either the CAPM or the EMH. These anomalies appear to be inconsistent with the ideas of market efficiency and equilibrium pricing.

Not surprisingly, the development of problems with the CAPM has given rise to an alternative theory—the **arbitrage pricing theory** (APT). While this theory is still in the process of definition and elaboration, it has attracted the interest of many serious researchers. This chapter presents a brief synopsis of the APT and its relationship to the CAPM.

While many of the issues addressed in this chapter lie at the very heart of finance, many of them are still unresolved and are currently the subject of controversy and spirited discussion. In spite of this, the investor needs to know as much as possible about the practical implications of these ideas for managing investments. Accordingly, the chapter concludes with some guidelines for investing in efficient markets.

The Efficient Markets Hypothesis

The efficient markets hypothesis is a key idea of modern finance. Unfortunately, the very name is misleading, because it seems to imply that a market is efficient in the same way that a street sweeper might be efficient. This potential confusion has prompted a need for clearer terminology. To this end, a market is **operationally efficient** if it works smoothly, with limited delays. For example, if orders can be transmitted from all parts of the world to a market very rapidly, with little chance of miscommunication, and if those orders can be executed and confirmed quickly, the market is operationally efficient.

A market may be operationally efficient, however, without being informationally efficient. Such a market would be one in which orders are handled very smoothly, but market prices adjust only slowly to new information. For our purposes, the key concept of efficiency is informational efficiency, and the discussion of efficiency pertains only to informational efficiency. With this restriction in mind, an **informationally efficient** market is defined as follows:

> A market is efficient with respect to some set of information, if prices in the market, at all times, fully reflect all information in the information set.

In this definition, the term "fully reflect" is very important. If market prices fully reflect a set of information, it means that prices have already completely adjusted to levels consistent with the new information. If a market is efficient with respect to some body of information, this also implies that information in that set cannot be used to guide a trading strategy to "beat the market." If prices already have completely adjusted to reflect the information in a given set, then there is no way to use that information to advantage in trading. Any bit of information in the set would already be reflected in the market prices.

Since this definition specifies that a market is efficient with respect to some body of information, it means that we can develop different versions of the market efficiency hypothesis by specifying different information sets. Following a classic article by Eugene Fama, it has become traditional to distinguish three versions of market efficiency: (1) weak, (2) semi–strong, and (3) strong.[1] These three versions of the EMH differ, because each claims that the market is efficient with respect to a different set of information.

Weak Form Efficiency

A market is **weak form efficient** if its prices fully reflect the information set that includes all historical market data. Historical market data include the complete history of market prices, volume figures, the amount of short positions outstanding, and similar data. If markets are weakly efficient, all such information is useless for directing a trading strategy. Analysis of this kind of information is known as technical analysis, so if the market is weakly efficient, technical analysis is without validity—at least from the point of view of trying to make money.

Semi–Strong Form Efficiency

A market is **semi–strong efficient** if prices in that market at all times fully reflect all public information. Public information includes all published reports, such as those found in newspapers, the financial press, and government publications and announcements. It includes television and radio news reports and investigative reports. Since the semi–strong efficiency hypothesis says that market prices reflect all public information, this includes all market data as well.

Strong Form Efficiency

A market is **strong form efficient** if its prices fully reflect all information, both public and private. Private information consists of information that is generated by government officials or corporate insiders that has not yet been made public. For example, members of the Federal Reserve Board often have access to private information. Imagine a meeting of the Federal Reserve Board in which new guidelines for the conduct of monetary policy are adopted. Such decisions are not revealed immediately to the public, so until the public announcement is made, Federal Reserve Board members have access to private information. As another example, imagine the case of a company that makes a major oil find, but that has

---

[1]See Eugene F. Fama, "Efficient Capital Markets: A Review of Theory and Empirical Work," reprinted in James Lorie and Richard Brealey, *Modern Developments in Investment Management*, New York: Praeger Publishers, 1972, pp. 109–161.

not yet announced the discovery. Before the discovery is announced, some employees of the corporation have access to that private information.

The strong form of the efficient market hypothesis implies that market prices already reflect this private information. The most important consequence of this claim, if true, is that such information could not be used to generate a trading profit that "beats the market." As the name implies, the strong form efficiency claim is very strong indeed.

Relationships Among the Three Forms of Market Efficiency

The three versions of the efficient markets hypothesis are ever more inclusive as we move from the weak form to the semi–strong form to the strong form. The weak form of the hypothesis says that financial markets are efficient with respect to a minimum core of information. The semi–strong form of market efficiency claims that markets reflect the minimum core of information plus all other types of public information. The strong form says that all information is reflected in market prices, including all public information, which in turn includes all market–related data. These relationships mean that any refutation of the weak–form hypothesis refutes both the semi–strong and the strong versions of the hypothesis. If the market is not efficient with respect to market–related information, it cannot be efficient with respect to all public information. Likewise, if the market is not efficient with respect to data related to the market, it cannot be efficient with respect to all information. So if the weak form hypothesis is shown to be false, both the semi–strong and the strong form are also false.

The truth of the weak form of the EMH is a necessary condition for the truth of the semi–strong and strong versions. It is not, however, a sufficient condition, because the weak form version could be true, and the semi–strong and strong versions could be false. Similarly, the truth of the semi–strong version is a necessary, but not sufficient, condition for the truth of the strong version. By contrast, if the strong form of the EMH is true, the semi–strong and weak form must be true. In this case, the truth of the strong form of the EMH is a sufficient condition for the truth of the semi–strong and weak form versions of the EMH.

The Practical Consequences of the Efficient Markets Hypothesis

Later in this chapter, we consider evidence for and against each of the forms of the efficient markets hypothesis. At this point, we emphasize the importance of the EMH, because it is not simply an academic theory. If the EMH in its different versions is true, it has extremely important implications for actual market conduct.

If the weak form is true, for example, it means that security prices already reflect all market–related data. As a consequence, analysis of such data cannot be useful for directing a trading strategy. The selling of charts of past price movements of securities is a multimillion dollar business in the United States, and customers buy such charts largely to help them formulate better investment strategies. If the weak form of the EMH is true, such charts are worthless and the money spent on them is totally wasted, to the extent that the charts are to be used for improving investment performance.[2] An immediate implication for investors that could be drawn from the truth of the weak form EMH is that investment in such services is wasted money.

If the semi–strong form of market efficiency is true, there are equally important practical consequences. Fundamental analysis, discussed in Chapters 12–14, examines publicly available information about the economy as a whole, about different industries, and about particular firms. If the semi–strong version is true, stock prices already reflect this information. As a consequence, analysis of this information would be purely wasted effort, and money spent on fundamental analysis would be money spent on services no better than the reading of tea leaves.

Currently, there are numerous laws on the books regarding the appropriate use of privileged information for directing securities–market trading. Transgressors of these laws are occasionally discovered and even imprisoned. If the strong form of the EMH is true, such laws are pointless. If markets are strongly efficient, attempts to use such information are pointless because security prices would already reflect all of this information. On the other hand, if the strong form of the EMH is false, then the laws have a much better claim to validity and may be worthy of more strict enforcement.

No matter whether these different versions of the EMH are true or not, and no matter how the issues are finally decided, the results have great importance for many practical applications—from how an individual investor should spend money to acquire securities information, to issues of public policy. Because of this, financial researchers have made the issue of efficient markets one of the prime targets of investigation for many years.

The CAPM and the Efficient Markets Hypothesis

As mentioned in the chapter overview, there is an intimate connection between the CAPM and the EMH. Essentially, the CAPM specifies the market standard for the relationship between risk and expected return, and tests of the EMH seek violations of that specified relationship. As an example, consider the fact that some stocks trade on both the New York and Pacific Stock Exchanges, and assume for the moment that there are no transaction costs. During parts of the day, both exchanges are open and engage in active trading of the same securities. Across the country, traders follow the trading activity on both exchanges. Now assume that a particular stock trades for $105 in New York and for $100 on the Pacific Exchange. Faced with these prices, a trader could simultaneously buy the stock on the Pacific Exchange and sell it on the New York Stock Exchange. Doing this would be riskless and would require no capital. The trade would be riskless because both trades were made simultaneously, and it would require no capital because both transactions

---

[2]The chart business is busy diversifying into home computer software that will allow owners of personal computers to download price histories from a central data management source and to construct charts via the client's own computer.

would be concluded at the same time. The result would be a profit of $5 per share on the transaction. Such a transaction, one which is riskless and requires no capital from the trader, is called an **arbitrage transaction**.

According to the CAPM, could such an opportunity exist? As shown by the SML, a riskless investment should earn the risk–free rate. However, the risk–free rate, say 10 percent, is for investment over some period of time. In the situation just described, there is no investment and no risk. For investment to occur, there must be the commitment of funds for some period of time. Also, there is no risk because both transactions are assumed to be executed simultaneously. Together, the two transactions lock in a sure profit. Therefore, according to the CAPM, the market should allow no arbitrage opportunities.

In this case, it is easy to see that a market that allows arbitrage opportunities is performing very poorly. The existence of arbitrage opportunities means that there are unexploited profit opportunities in the marketplace. In a very real sense, the presence of arbitrage opportunities means that there is money lying on the ground that no one is willing to pick up.

It is also apparent that the presence of arbitrage opportunities is inconsistent with equilibrium pricing. In our example, the price differential of $5 will be sure to attract trader interest. The traders will buy the stock on the Pacific Exchange for $100 and sell it in New York for $105. Doing so will generate excess demand for the stock at a price of $100 on the Pacific Exchange, because everyone will want to buy the stock at that price. Likewise, everyone will try to sell the stock for $105 in New York, creating an excess supply. With excess demand on the Pacific Exchange, the price must rise, and with excess supply on the New York Exchange, the price must fall. In fact, only when the two prices are the same can there be any equilibrium at all.[3]

How could arbitrage opportunities such as we have described exist? Remember the assumption that investors favor higher expected returns, all other factors being equal. If that is so, and if arbitrage opportunities persist, the implication is that the market prices are not reflecting all of the available information. In this case, the implication is proven by the fact that the same good sells for two different prices in two different markets. Also, the persistence of arbitrage opportunities would mean that the CAPM was violated. If we were faced with frequent arbitrage opportunities, we would have to admit that the market was not efficient, even in the weak sense, and that the CAPM was false.

In well–developed securities markets, one expects never to find arbitrage opportunities. As a consequence, most potential violations of the CAPM and the EMH are much more difficult to identify. Figure 15.1 shows a historical relationship

---

[3]Remember we assumed away transaction costs for purposes of this example. With transaction costs, a slight difference in the price of the stock on the two exchanges could persist if the transactions costs eroded the potential profits arising from the price discrepancy. For example, if the total transaction cost to exploit the arbitrage opportunity were $1 per share, there could be a persistent price differential of $1 or less. The moment the price differential exceeded $1, there would be an arbitrage opportunity again, and traders would have a strong profit incentive to trade in the way we have described here.

Figure 15.1

The SML with Securities Not in Equilibrium

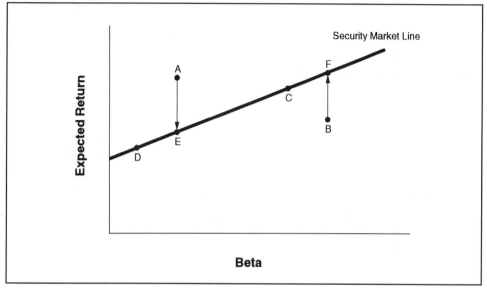

between risk and return, with the line being consistent with the SML. If we think of the line as expressing the predicted trade–off between risk and return, then Securities C and D are exactly consistent with the theory. Securities A and B, however, are not. Let us assume that the observed deviations from the predicted return line are not due to chance.

If we rule out chance as an explanation for the deviations of Securities A and B from the theoretically correct risk and return relationship, only two other explanations are possible. First, the market may not be responding to the relevant information about Securities A and B. In other words, the market may be inefficient. In a way, this is similar to the presence of continuing arbitrage opportunities discussed earlier. An investor could purchase Security A and receive a greater level of return than the market should allow. For the same level of systematic risk, the investor should receive a return like that of Security E. If A's returns always lie above the line representing the appropriate trade–off between risk and return, the market may be inefficient.

A second possible explanation for A being above and for B being below the prescribed level of return for their levels of risk could be that the CAPM incorrectly specifies the risk/return relationship. Perhaps expected return is not really a function of systematic risk. It may be that systematic risk is not really important at all and that the CAPM is completely false. A more probable explanation may be that returns depend on other factors besides systematic risk and that the CAPM does not give a complete explanation of the factors that generate returns.

The most important point, however, is that attempts to test the EMH or the CAPM turn out to be tests of both theories together. As just explained, given persistent occurrences of securities like A or B, the problem could lie either with the CAPM, the EMH, or both theories. From our tests, determining the source of discrepancy may be impossible.

Performance Measurement and "Beating the Market"

Implicit in the preceding discussion of the relationship between the EMH and the CAPM is the idea that the CAPM provides a measure of normal performance. In explaining the CAPM, we have stressed that it expresses the equilibrium level of expected returns for a given level of risk, and that the SML depicts this relationship graphically, as shown in Figure 15.1. We have already observed that this normal level of expected performance can be achieved by holding the market portfolio in conjunction with the risk–free asset.

As a consequence, any special efforts at investment analysis must focus on attempts to find securities like A or B in Figure 15.1. Security A offers too much return for its level of risk, while Security B offers too little. If we, as investors, could successfully identify such securities, we would want to buy securities like A and sell (or sell short) securities like B. When the other participants in the market realize that Securities A and B were mispriced, market forces would return A and B to their right level of return for their respective levels of risk. In the case of Security A, other participants in the market would buy the stock. This increase in buying interest would drive the price of A up and would drive the returns of A down, until A offered the correct level of returns for its level of risk. In Figure 15.1, Security A would be purchased until it came to occupy the same point as Security E, at which its returns are commensurate with its risk. Analogously, the price of Security B is too high for its level of risk. Consequently, when investors realize this, they would sell Security B out of their portfolios or would even sell it short. This selling pressure would drive down the price of B, thereby raising its returns. The process would continue until the price of B was low enough to give a level of returns like Security F, which has the same risk level.

The goal of investment analysis must be to find securities that lie off of the SML, and to trade to exploit those opportunities. The analyst who finds securities lying off the SML on a consistent basis is performing well. In other words, the successful analyst, one who beats the market, consistently finds investment opportunities that give a high return for their level of risk. In summary, within a CAPM framework, beating the market means that the investor finds securities that lie off of the SML.

Notice that high returns on a portfolio do not necessarily indicate successful performance. In Figure 15.1, Security B has a greater return than Security D. As a consequence, it might appear that B is the better investment. According to the CAPM, this is not true. Security B may offer high returns, but the returns it offers are not sufficient to justify its risk. Security D, on the other hand, offers a level of return than is warranted by its risk level. By contrast, B offers a level of returns that is too low to compensate for its risk. According to the CAPM, we should prefer Security D to Security B.

Because the CAPM expresses a relationship between *expected* return and risk, it can be difficult to validate a superior performance by an analyst. In any given year, some analysts are bound to do better than others just by chance. As a consequence, the mere report of a very good year for an investment portfolio should not earn too much respect from us. We would want to know both how much risk was involved in the particular portfolio and how consistently a particular analyst turned in a good performance.

If an analyst recommends a high beta portfolio in a year when the market happens to go up, it would be no surprise if the recommended portfolio performed well. However, we would rightly want to know how well this analyst's recommendations performed over a long period of time. In short, beating the market requires consistently finding securities lying off the SML. In order for us to believe that any such analyst is truly successful, his or her track record must be sufficiently good and sufficiently long to rule out the possibility that he or she produced such a record by chance.

Some scholars have even attempted to prove that it is impossible to beat the market. If security prices move randomly, in a sense to be defined in the next section, there would be no way to beat the market, and the efficiency hypothesis would be proven.

The Random Walk Hypothesis and Market Efficiency

The concept of market efficiency is often linked to the **random walk hypothesis**, a very strong statistical hypothesis that might be applied to any variable for which observations over time are possible. In spite of the odd implications of the name, the random walk hypothesis does not maintain that security prices are random in the sense of being uncaused. Instead, the random walk hypothesis consists of two sub–hypotheses. First, it asserts that successive returns are statistically independent, implying that the correlation between one period's return and the next is zero. Second, it asserts that the distribution of returns in all periods is identical. This second condition implies, for example, that the chance of a 50 percent loss is the same in every period.

While a full explication of the random walk hypothesis would be very mathematical, we can understand the implications of the hypothesis by considering an example. In a justly famous article, Harry Roberts used a table of random numbers to generate a series of artificial price changes with the assumption that these changes started from an initial price level of 450. In other words, changes from that initial value of 450 were created by selecting random numbers and applying those changes to the variable that started at 450, with this process continuing for 52 simulated weeks. Figure 15.2 shows those simulated changes. Not surprisingly, there seems to be no pattern in the changes. After all, they were generated at random. However, as Figure 15.3 shows, when those changes were applied to an initial assumed price level of 450, they appeared to generate some

Figure 15.2

Randomly Generated Artificial Price Changes

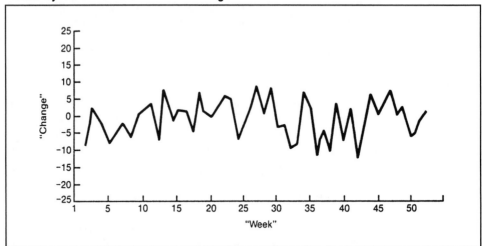

Source: H. V. Roberts, "Stock Market Patterns and Financial Analysis: Some Methodological Suggestions," *Journal of Finance*, March 1959, pp. 1–10. Reprinted with permission from the *Journal of Finance*.

Figure 15.3

Changes in an Artificial Price Level Generated by Random Price Changes

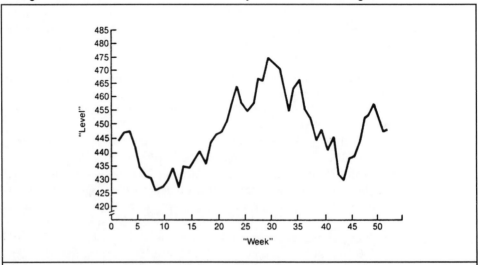

Source: H. V. Roberts, "Stock Market Patterns and Financial Analysis: Some Methodological Suggestions," *Journal of Finance*, March 1959, pp. 1–10. Reprinted with permission from the *Journal of Finance*.

Figure 15.4
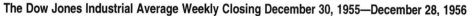

The Dow Jones Industrial Average Weekly Closing December 30, 1955—December 28, 1956

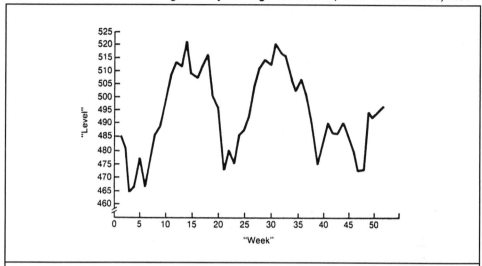

Source: H. V. Roberts, "Stock Market Patterns and Financial Analysis: Some Methodological Suggestions," *Journal of Finance*, March 1959, pp. 1–10. Reprinted with permission from the *Journal of Finance*.

strong patterns. For example, from about week 12 to week 28, there appears to be a very strong bull market. This experiment illustrates that purely random price changes can generate changes in price levels that appear to have important trends.

When we as investors look at the history of security prices, there appear to be strong trends. Figure 15.4 shows the weekly closing level of the Dow Jones Industrial Average for one year. Notice the strong patterns that correspond very closely to the patterns in Figure 15.3. However, if we examine the *changes* in the level for the same period, as illustrated in Figure 15.5, the changes appear to be quite random, just like the random price changes of Figure 15.2. For anyone who believes in examining price trends to forecast future prices, this should be very disturbing news.[4]

However, we must acknowledge that security prices do not follow a random walk, strictly speaking. Tests indicate that there are small, but statistically

---

[4]See Harry V. Roberts, "Stock Market 'Patterns' and Financial Analysis: Some Methodological Suggestions," *Journal of Finance*, March 1959, pp. 1–10.

Figure 15.5

Weekly Price Changes for the Dow Jones Industrial Average
January 6, 1956—December 28, 1956

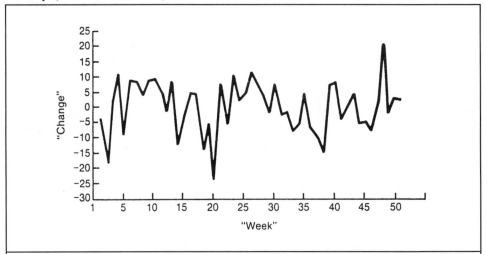

Source: H. V. Roberts, "Stock Market Patterns and Financial Analysis: Some Methodological Suggestions," *Journal of Finance*, March 1959, pp. 1–10. Reprinted with permission from the *Journal of Finance*.

significant, departures from randomness in most price change series.[5] As we shall see, this does not rule out market efficiency. Even if there are slight statistical regularities in the movements of security prices, these might not be significant enough to permit a profitable trading strategy. Therefore, a market may be efficient even if security prices do not, strictly speaking, follow a random walk.

Note that the random walk hypothesis is a statistical hypothesis, while the efficient markets hypothesis is an economic hypothesis. Essentially, to refute the efficient markets hypothesis there must be rules for trading to beat the market. Refuting the random walk hypothesis, albeit a very strong statistical hypothesis, does not show that markets are inefficient. This distinction between the *statistical* random walk hypothesis and the *economic* efficient markets hypothesis will be elaborated later when we examine some tests of the alternative versions of the efficient markets hypothesis.

---

[5]For a good summary of this evidence and its bearing on the random walk hypothesis and market efficiency, see Eugene F. Fama, "Efficient Capital Markets: A Review of Theory and Empirical Work," reprinted in James Lorie and Richard Brealey, *Modern Developments in Investment Management*, New York: Praeger Publishers, 1972, pp. 109–161.

Challenges to the Capital Asset Pricing Model

Given the apparently damaging evidence suggesting that markets cannot be semi–strong efficient if the CAPM expresses the correct relationship between risk and return, it is not surprising that important challenges have arisen to the CAPM. This section discusses two of the most important challenges. First, Richard Roll has challenged the CAPM regarding the validity of its measurements and the issue of whether the CAPM is truly testable as a scientific hypothesis. The second challenge has arisen in the form of an alternative theory of capital asset pricing, the arbitrage pricing theory.

Roll's Critique

In theory, the market portfolio used in the CAPM should include all assets in the world in proportion to their value. In practice, most tests use a stock index limited to U.S. firms. As mentioned earlier, this neglects any direct inclusion of the world's two largest asset categories, human capital and real estate. Further, it appears that there is no hope of being able to construct an adequate index of the true market portfolio, due to the practical difficulties of measuring and properly weighting the returns on all of the different asset categories for all of the different countries of the world.

Richard Roll has pointed out the consequences of this situation.[6] All important implications of the CAPM require that the market portfolio be efficient. The portfolio must be efficient in the sense of not being dominated by some other portfolio (as discussed in Chapter 13 on diversification). However, since we cannot observe the market portfolio, there is no way to test its efficiency. This means that all other tests of the CAPM must have uncertain results, since there will be constant uncertainty about the market portfolio. Further, even if the index used in practice is quite good, there can still be problems. As Roll has shown, even if two indexes have a .95 correlation, they could give different answers in issues of performance evaluation. To date, Roll's critique has not been answered, and it presents one of the major outstanding problems for the CAPM. Stated baldly, Roll concludes that the only legitimate empirical test of the CAPM would test whether the market portfolio is efficient.

Roll goes on to show the disastrous consequences his conclusions have for measuring performance within a CAPM framework. In any test, it will be necessary to use some market index, and that index can be efficient or inefficient. Whether the index is efficient or not does not matter too much because both efficiency and inefficiency of the index lead to disastrous results:

---

[6]See Richard Roll, "A Critique of the Asset Pricing Theory's Tests," *Journal of Financial Economics*, March 1977.

1. If the index is efficient, then the performance of every security examined will lie exactly on the security market line as a matter of mathematical necessity.
2. If the index is not efficient, then any ranking of performance is possible, and the particular ranking that a test gives will depend only on the way in which the index is inefficient.

Therefore, the CAPM provides a meaningless benchmark of performance. Either every security lies on the security market line or every security can diverge in unpredictable ways from the risk/expected return relationship expressed by the CAPM.

Arbitrage Pricing Theory

Given the present difficulties of the CAPM, it is not surprising that an alternative theory has emerged. It is called the **arbitrage pricing theory** (APT) and was created by Stephen Ross.[7] Ross maintains that there can be a number of risk factors that are priced in the market. If these factors do not affect the expected return of a security, there will be arbitrage opportunities. If we are willing to assume that there should be no unexploited arbitrage opportunities, Ross is able to show that we can express the expected return of a security as a function of the risk–free rate and a number of different factors, with each factor having a price.

The Arbitrage Pricing Model

The APT relies on four key assumptions:

1. Capital markets are perfect.
2. Investors have homogeneous expectations about the structure of security returns and the identity of factors affecting security returns.
3. There is some undetermined number (K) of factors common to all securities.
4. The number of securities (N) exceeds the number of common factors (K) determining security returns.

Under these assumptions, Ross is able to prove mathematically that the expected return on any Security j, $E(R_j)$, will depend on the risk–free rate of interest, R_f, and K factors, $\gamma_1 \ldots \gamma_K$, each multiplied by the market–determined price for each unit of that type of risk, $F_1 \ldots F_K$.

The Arbitrage Pricing Model

$$E(R_j) = R_f + \gamma_1 F_1 + \gamma_2 F_2 + \ldots + \gamma_K F_K$$

---

[7]See Stephen Ross, "The Arbitrage Theory of Capital Asset Pricing," *Journal of Economic Theory*, December 1976.

In the APT, the number of factors and their identification is an empirical issue. Early results indicate that there may be three to five significant factors and work is proceeding in an attempt to associate these factors with recognizable economic variables, such as unexpected inflation and unexpected changes in GNP.

It is also possible to view the CAPM as a special case of the APT. If there happens to be one significant factor and if it happens to be the systematic risk of the security (β_j), then the APT would be simplified to the CAPM. Early results indicate that this is unlikely to be the case. This is a rapidly developing area of research in finance, and we must await more concrete results before being sure how to assess this theory.

Tests of Efficient Markets and Pricing Models

This section reviews some of the more famous efforts to test the CAPM and the EMH. While these hypotheses have been tested for many different kinds of financial markets, the most famous tests have been conducted for the stock market. As a consequence, almost all of the tests discussed here pertain to the stock market.

The Joint Nature of Efficiency Tests

Scholars are often interested in determining whether a market is informationally efficient, and they would like to test that hypothesis directly. Unfortunately, such a direct test is essentially impossible. Testing for market efficiency involves testing whether prices in a market behave as they theoretically should. In other words, the tests amount to determining whether price behavior in a market meets a given standard. However, the standards provided by a theory of pricing such as the CAPM or the APT are not cast in stone. Instead, theories of pricing are themselves subject to debate.

To see the practical consequence of uncertainty over theoretically correct pricing, assume that we find a gross departure of price behavior from the CAPM. For example, we might find that low beta stocks consistently outperform high beta stocks, turning the central risk/expected return trade–off of the CAPM on its head. This evidence allows two interpretations. First, it could be solid evidence that the market is inefficient because prices do not reflect the systematic risk of stocks. Second, we could interpret this evidence as a repudiation of the CAPM. In other words, we could maintain that the market is still efficient, but that the CAPM does not describe how markets work. We can successfully interpret the empirical evidence in this case by rejecting either the efficient markets hypothesis or the CAPM. Consistency does not demand that we reject both.

Because we can achieve consistency by rejecting either the efficient markets hypothesis or the CAPM, we effectively have a joint test of market efficiency and the CAPM. In summary, when prices do not behave as theory suggests they should, that can mean either that the market is inefficient or the theory is no good. The joint nature of these tests has always plagued efforts to test for market efficiency.

The discussion of the traditional tests of the EMH and the CAPM is divided along the lines of the three versions of the EMH. First, we discuss tests of technical trading strategies. These strategies emerge from a study of historical market data and consist of trading rules based on observed events in the market such as the occurrence of particular price patterns. If technical trading strategies are useful for earning a profit above the risk–adjusted return predicted by the CAPM, then either the CAPM is false, or the weak form of the EMH is false. Second, we review tests of trading strategies based on fundamental analysis, which uses public information in the development of its trading strategies. Accordingly, if such strategies are useful in earning a profit above and beyond the predicted risk–adjusted return of the CAPM, either the semi–strong version of the EMH must be false, or the CAPM must be false. Third, we examine tests of strategies based on private information. If this information is useful in earning a supernormal return (that is, one above the prescribed risk–adjusted return), then either the strong form of the EMH is false, or the CAPM is false.

Tests of the Weak Form of Market Efficiency

In its purest form, technical analysis focuses on patterns of securities prices and measures of market mood or investor behavior. The strategies that focus on market mood consider matters such as the level of insider trading activity, the behavior of odd–lot traders, volume indicators, and other non–price indicators. Briefly, active net buying by corporate insiders provides a **buy signal**, because it means that the group with the best information is buying. The idea here is to follow the knowledgeable investors. The odd–lot trader is the small trader who trades shares in amounts less than a round lot, usually 100 shares. Odd–lot trading usually incurs higher transaction costs and is the province of the market participant with little capital. After all, such traders cannot even afford a round lot. According to technical analysis, the odd–lot traders are the least sophisticated traders in the market, so the odd–lot theory suggests that one should do exactly the opposite of the odd–lot traders. Heavy net buying by the odd–lot trader is a sell signal to the informed trader, according to this view.

The technical trading techniques that focus on price patterns have received more attention from researchers than strategies focusing on market mood, probably because they are more specific in their prescriptions for trading behavior. Following that trend in research, this section discusses three different techniques that test for the existence of price patterns in stock prices: (1) serial correlation tests, (2) runs tests, and (3) filter tests.

Serial Correlation Tests. If price changes behaved in regular ways from one day to the next, an investor could learn the regular rules for their behavior and use that information to earn fantastic returns. For example, if a large positive price change in one period is typically followed by a large positive price change in the next period, a smart trader could buy a stock after a big price increase and then capture the next big price increase. One way to test for this kind of possibility is to examine stock returns to determine whether such a rule persists.

Figure 15.6

Different Possible Patterns of Correlated and Uncorrelated Securities Returns

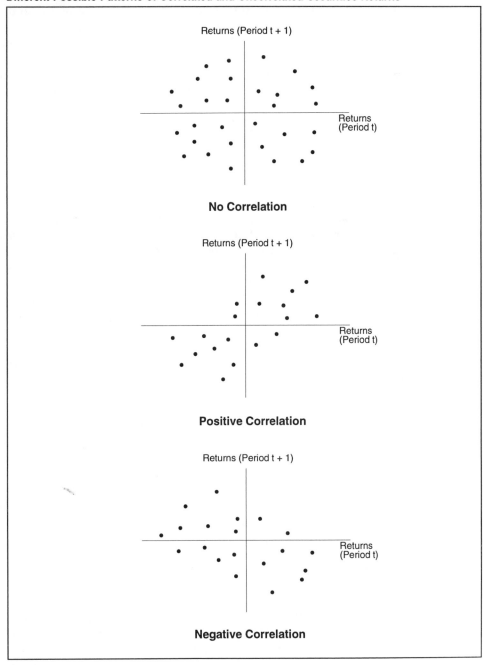

Graphically, we can plot the relationship between successive returns. The examination of successive returns for a single security over time focuses on the serial correlation, which differs from contemporaneous correlation. When we discussed diversification in Chapter 13, we were concerned with the tendency of two or more securities to have the same kinds of returns in the same period. Now the focus is on the relationship between the returns in different periods for the same security. For example, if a positive return in Period t happens to be followed by a positive return in Period $t + 1$, we could plot this pair of returns in the northeast quadrant on a pair of axes such as those shown in Figure 15.6. The top graph of Figure 15.6 shows how the returns would plot if there were no correlation between the returns in one period and the next. If there were positive correlation between returns, positive returns would tend to be followed by positive returns, leading to a point being plotted in the northeast quadrant. However, some positive returns would be followed by a negative return in the next period. Such a pair of returns would be plotted in the southeast quadrant. If there were no correlation between returns in successive periods, the graph would be a circular "cloud" of points centered around the origin, such as the top graph in Figure 15.6.

If there were positive correlation between successive returns, the graph would appear as shown in the middle graph of Figure 15.6, with positive returns being followed by more positive returns. In this case, most pairs of successive returns would tend to lie in the northeast and the southwest quadrants. Similarly, if returns were negatively correlated, most of the plotted pairs of returns would tend to lie in the southeast and the northwest quadrants, as is shown in the third graph.

Even if it were found that there were no correlation between returns in one period and the next, there could still be correlations between one period and a period that occurred earlier. For example, if there were a correlation of returns between one day and the trading day four days earlier, this could still be useful information. In such a case, there would be a correlation between one day and another day of "lag 4." Table 15.1 considers this possibility and reports calculated correlation values for stock returns when the lag is 1, 4, 9, and 16 days. All of the Dow Jones industrial stocks are shown in the table, revealing very low correlations. Theoretically, if these correlations were zero, there would be no way to devise a strategy of using high returns in one period to tell one what to do in another period. Actually, if the correlations are close to zero, there would not be much point in trying to use such information. For practical purposes, the correlations shown in Table 15.1 might as well be zero.

Having seen the principle of graphing the correlations of returns shown in Figure 15.6, and having seen the evidence of Table 15.1, it is not surprising that a graph of actual market values would look like Figure 15.7. Figure 15.7 graphs the monthly correlation of returns for the U.S. stock market for 1947–1994. As the graph clearly indicates, there is little tendency toward any correlation in the returns from one period to the next. In fact, this conclusion is highly consistent with formal tests to determine whether the correlation coefficients in such analyses are significantly different from zero. Most studies find small, but statistically significant, positive correlations. That is true of the data in Figure 15.7; there is a statistically significant

Table 15.1

Serial Correlation Coefficients for Dow Jones Industrial Stocks

Stock	Differencing Interval (Days)			
	1	4	9	16
Allied Chemical	0.017	0.029	−0.091	−0.118
Alcoa	0.118*	0.095	−0.112	−0.044
American Can	−0.087*	−0.124*	−0.600	0.031
A.T. & T.	−0.039	−0.010	−0.009	−0.003
American Tobacco	0.111*	−0.175*	0.033	0.007
Anaconda	0.067*	−0.068	−0.125	0.202
Bethlehem Steel	0.013	−0.122	−0.148	0.112
Chrysler	0.012	0.060	−0.026	0.040
DuPont	0.013	0.069	−0.043	−0.055
Eastman Kodak	0.025	−0.006	−0.053	−0.023
General Electric	0.011	0.020	−0.004	0.000
General Foods	0.061*	−0.005	−0.140	−0.098
General Motors	−0.004	−0.128*	0.009	−0.028
Goodyear	−0.123*	0.001	−0.037	0.033
International Harvester	−0.017	−0.068	−0.244*	0.116
International Nickel	0.096*	0.038	0.124	0.041
International Paper	0.046	0.060	−0.004	−0.010
Johns Manville	0.006	−0.068	−0.002	0.002
Owens Illinois	−0.021	−0.006	0.003	−0.022
Procter & Gamble	0.099*	−0.006	0.098	0.076
Sears	0.097*	−0.070	−0.113	0.041
Standard Oil (CA)	0.025	0.143*	−0.046	0.040
Standard Oil (NJ)	0.008	0.109	−0.082	−0.121
Swift & Co.	−0.004	−0.072	0.118	−0.197
Texaco	0.094*	−0.053	−0.047	−0.178
Union Carbide	0.107*	0.049	−0.101	0.124
United Aircraft	0.014	−0.190*	−0.192*	−0.040
U.S. Steel	0.040	−0.006	−0.056	0.236*
Westinghouse	−0.027	−0.097	−0.137	0.067
Woolworth	0.028	−0.033	−0.112	0.040

*Coefficient is twice its computed standard error.

Source: Eugene F. Fama, "Efficient Capital Markets: A Review of Theory and Empirical Work," reprinted in James Lorie and Richard Brealey, *Modern Developments in Investment Management*, New York: Praeger Publishers, 1972, p. 122.

positive correlation in returns from one month to the next. Even though these correlations are statistically significant, they are not large enough to allow a profitable trading strategy based on the correlation because the transaction costs

Figure 15.7

A Graph of Serial Correlation for the S&P 500 Index Using Monthly Returns, 1947–1994

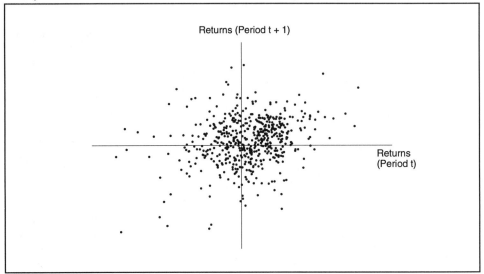

would be too large to leave any profit. As a consequence, these studies indicate that the random walk hypothesis is probably false, but the results do not provide evidence against the market efficiency hypothesis.[8] The reasons for this are clear from a consideration of the results of another kind of test called a **runs test**.

Runs Tests.   While tests for serial correlation reflect the size of returns, a **runs test** examines the tendencies for losses or gains to be followed by further losses or gains. These tests are often performed by examining a time series of returns for a security and testing whether the number of consecutive price gains (or the number of consecutive price drops) shows a pattern. If we let a price gain be represented by a plus sign (+) and a price drop be represented by a minus sign (–), we can represent the price movements of a security by a series of plus and minus signs. For example, one possible series might look like the following:

$$+ + + - + + + - + + + - + + + - + + + -$$

If price changes for a security exhibited this pattern of three gains followed by a loss, which was repeated over and over, it would lead to a very simple

---

[8]See Eugene F. Fama, "Efficient Capital Markets: A Review of Theory and Empirical Work," reprinted in James Lorie and Richard Brealey, *Modern Developments in Investment Management*, New York: Praeger Publishers, 1972, pp. 109–161.

strategy. We would buy the security at the close of a day with a loss, hold it for three days, and sell it at the close of the third day. Of course, this is an extreme kind of pattern; we would not really expect actual price movements to follow such a rigid rule. However, if price movements followed any rule, it would be useful to know the rule and to try to form a strategy to take advantage of the regularity.

To test for this possibility, researchers perform a runs test to determine whether the sequences of price gains and losses are similar to those which would be generated by chance. In a way, this is testing to determine the probability that the sequence of gains and losses could have been generated by tossing a coin. If we let heads represent a gain and tails represent a loss, what is the probability that the sequence could have been generated by coin flipping? If the sequence of gains and losses is random, then there is no information to be gleaned from trying to find patterns, just as there is no use trying to predict whether the next coin toss will be heads or tails by examining the past tosses.

Runs tests for the stock market were conducted by Niederhoffer and Osborne, and in another paper, by Fama. Niederhoffer and Osborne found statistically significant departures from randomness in runs of stock prices.[9] In particular, gains tended to follow gains and losses tended to follow losses. A trader might be able to use knowledge of this tendency to generate a simple, yet profitable, trading strategy. The rule would be to buy following a price rise and to sell following a loss. The first part of the rule would capture the subsequent gains that were more likely to occur, and the second part of the rule would avoid the subsequent losses that were more likely to occur.

Fama also tested for the presence of runs and found that the number of runs in the Dow Jones stocks was very close to the number we would expect if there were no tendency for runs to occur. In other words, even if there is no tendency for price increases to be followed by price increases, we will sometime observe these patterns simply by chance. Fama was testing to see whether the number of runs observed was consistent with the number we would expect to find even if there were no real patterns. Table 15.2 shows a portion of his results, where he calculated the expected number of runs of different lengths based on chance. These are shown as the expected runs. Also, he computed the actual number of runs of each different length of time. With the exception of the one–day runs, there is an exact correspondence between the actual and expected number of runs.[10]

In summation, stocks show a tendency to experience runs in a way not entirely consistent with chance. However, that is not enough to show that the

---

[9]See Victor Niederhoffer and M. F. M. Osborne, "Market Making and Reversal on the Stock Exchange," *Journal of the American Statistical Association*, December 1966, pp. 897–916. For a summary of this paper, and many others, see Eugene F. Fama, "Efficient Capital Markets: A Review of Theory and Empirical Work," reprinted in James Lorie and Richard Brealey, *Modern Developments in Investment Management*, New York: Praeger Publishers, 1972, pp. 109–161.

[10]See Eugene F. Fama, "The Behavior of Stock Market Prices," *Journal of Business*, January 1965, pp. 34–105.

Table 15.2

Actual and Expected Number of Runs of Different Lengths for Dow Jones Stocks

	1–Day Change		4–Day Change		9–Day Change		16–Day Change	
	Actual	Expected	Actual	Expected	Actual	Expected	Actual	Expected
Average Number of Runs	735	760	176	176	75	75	42	42

Source: Eugene F. Fama, "The Behavior of Stock Market Prices," *Journal of Business*, January 1965, pp. 34–105.

---

market is inefficient. It must also be possible to devise a trading strategy that will beat the market. While Niederhoffer and Osborne may have found departures from randomness that are *statistically* significant, that does not mean that they are *economically* significant, and it is economic significance that is important for the issue of market efficiency.

To take advantage of runs, one must be able to trade on the information. For a trader with absolutely no transactions costs, it would be possible to trade on the information provided by Niederhoffer and Osborne. However, every trader, even an exchange member, has some transaction costs. When even the lowest feasible transaction costs are taken into account, the prospective advantage from trading to take advantage of the runs disappears. We must conclude that the runs tests indicate only statistically significant, and not economically significant, departures from randomness. As a consequence, the evidence of Niederhoffer and Osborne, and of Fama, is perfectly consistent with the efficient markets hypothesis. Here the situation is similar to the results in the tests for serial correlation. While there may be statistically significant departures from randomness (which rule out the random walk hypothesis), the departures are not large enough to permit a supernormal return, so they do not refute market efficiency.

Filter Tests. The last kind of technical trading rule to be discussed is a **filter rule**. A filter rule has the following form:

> If the daily closing price of a security rises at least x%, buy the security and hold it until its price moves down at least x% from a subsequent high. At that point sell the security short and maintain the short position until the price rises at least x% above a subsequent low.[11]

---

[11]See R. A. Brealey, *An Introduction to Risk and Return from Common Stocks*, Cambridge, MA: The MIT Press, 1983, p. 13.

Table 15.3

███████████

Average Annual Rates of Return from Filter Rules, 1957–1962

Value of Filter X	Return with Trading Strategy (%)	Total Transactions with Trading Strategy	Return with Trading Strategy after Commissions (%)
0.5	11.5	12,500	−103.6
1.0	5.5	8,700	−74.9
2.0	0.2	4,800	−45.2
4.0	0.1	2,000	−19.5
6.0	1.3	1,100	−9.4
8.0	1.7	700	−5.0
10.0	3.0	400	−1.4
20.0	4.3	100	3.0

Source: Eugene F. Fama and M. E. Blume, "Filter Rules and Stock Market Trading," *Journal of Business*, January 1966, pp. 226–241.

Different filter rules can be specified by choosing different values for the filter X. Fama and Blume, among others, have examined this kind of rule.[12] Table 15.3 presents some key results from their paper. Testing filters of different sizes, ranging from .5 percent to 20 percent, Fama and Blume found that the filter rules could generate positive returns on a consistent basis, if transaction costs were ignored. These returns ranged from .1 to 11.5 percent per year. One problem with this technique is that it calls for very frequent trading. The third column of Table 15.3 shows the number of transactions required to follow the filter strategy. The final column shows the total returns after considering transactions costs. Even assuming very low transaction costs of .001, the apparent profits are turned to losses in almost every case. Only the 20 percent rule generates a positive return after commissions, but it is only 3 percent, and the investor could beat that return with a risk–free bond.

Summary. These three kinds of tests of technical trading rules agree in finding no workable technical trading rules. There are many more such tests with findings broadly consistent with those presented here. In general, researchers have been unable to find any compelling evidence that technical analysis works. This does not mean that technical analysis has been proven worthless. There are many possible kinds of technical trading strategies and to make the case against technical analysis airtight requires testing all of them. However, while technical trading rules have not been proven not to work, there is very little reason to believe that they do work.

---

[12]See Eugene F. Fama and M. E. Blume, "Filter Rules and Stock Market Trading," *Journal of Business*, January 1966, pp. 226–241.

In a way, testing technical trading rules is like looking for a needle in a haystack. If we look for the needle for a long time without success, it does not mean that there is no needle. Similarly, looking without finding a successful rule does not mean that no such rule exists. However, after continued diligent and unsuccessful searching, it becomes reasonable to doubt that there is a needle in the hay. Likewise, the continued absence of evidence in favor of technical trading rules justifies a skepticism about the value of technical analysis.

Tests of the Semi–Strong Form of Market Efficiency

The semi–strong form of the market efficiency hypothesis maintains that security prices always reflect all publicly available information. Therefore, the semi–strong version implies it is impossible to use any public information to direct a trading strategy earning more than the equilibrium risk–adjusted rate of return. Usually, that risk–adjusted rate of return is the rate of return stipulated by the CAPM. This section examines three types of tests, whose results are consistent with the semi–strong EMH. It then goes on to consider some new types of evidence that appear to be inconsistent with the EMH.

Stock Splits—The Fama, Fisher, Jensen, Roll Study. One implication of the semi–strong version of the EMH is that it should be impossible to earn supernormal returns by responding very quickly to new public information. In effect, the public announcement of information should be so well anticipated by the market that security prices will have adjusted to their new equilibrium level before the announcement has even been made.

Occasionally, firms change the number of shares outstanding by a stock split or a stock dividend. A stock split occurs when a firm gives new shares for the previously outstanding shares, thereby increasing the total number of shares outstanding by 25 percent or more. If new shares are given which increase the total number of shares outstanding less than 25 percent, the event is called a stock dividend. For example, if the investor owns 100 shares and receives 150 new shares for the old shares, there has a been a stock split, because his or her holdings have been increased by 50 percent. Notice that a stock split or stock dividend involves no cash flow to the investor but simply adjusts the total number of shares outstanding. Because stock dividends and stock splits differ only in their accounting treatment and have the same economic significance, we use the terms interchangeably in the discussion that follows.

However, stock splits do tend to follow periods of unusually good performance by stocks, and this good performance seems to be a predictor of greater expected future earnings and dividends. Apparently, firms use stock dividends to signal improved circumstances to the marketplace and stock splits are often quickly followed by increases in cash dividends as well. Based on a study of 940 stock splits, Figure 15.8 shows the risk–adjusted relative performance of the sample of

Figure 15.8

Relative Performance for 940 Firms with Stock Splits

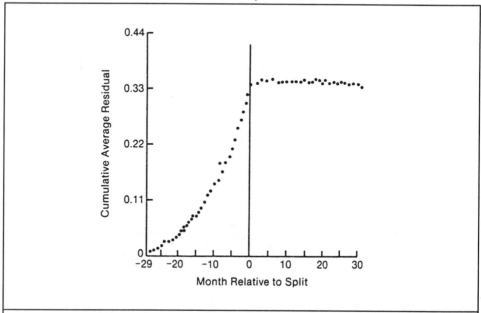

Source: E. F. Fama, L. Fisher, M. C. Jensen, and R. Roll, "The Adjustment of Stock Prices to New Information," *International Economic Review*, February 1969, pp. 1–21.

stocks taken together relative to the market as a whole.[13] The sample period consists of 30 months preceding and 30 months following the stock split. The rising line prior to the announcement of the split, which is indicated as month zero, shows that these firms, on average, did 33 percent better than other securities of comparable risk. However, by the time of the stock split, all of the relatively superior performance had been achieved, as revealed by the fact that the line is almost flat after the announcement date. The flatness of the line after the announcement indicates that the announcement of the split had no effect on the market. To the extent that the split was good news, or was associated with good news, the market had anticipated the good news and gave no reaction to the announcement itself.

While the stock split itself may not be important to investors, the fact that it does tend to accompany announcements of changing cash dividends is important. When the sample of 940 firms was divided into those firms that had increases and

---

[13] See Eugene F. Fama, Lawrence Fisher, Michael C. Jensen, and Richard Roll, "The Adjustment of Stock Prices to New Information," *International Economic Review*, February 1969, pp. 1–21.

Figure 15.9

Relative Performance for Firms with Stock Splits Which Also Increased Cash Dividends

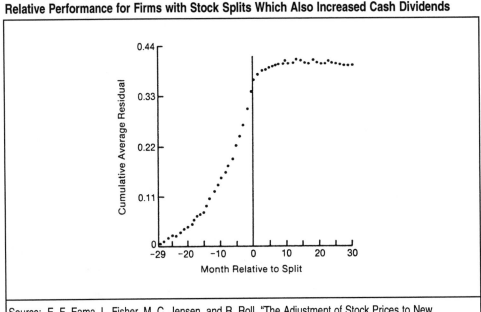

Source: E. F. Fama, L. Fisher, M. C. Jensen, and R. Roll, "The Adjustment of Stock Prices to New Information," *International Economic Review*, February 1969, pp. 1–21.

those that had decreases in cash dividends after the stock split, relative to the market, the market's expectation about increases in cash dividends was revealed. Figure 15.9 shows the relative performance for the firms that increased dividends. Notice the very slight increase in relative performance after the split announcement. This is consistent with the view that the dividend increase was almost fully anticipated. Actually increasing the cash dividend did very little to help the stock's performance. By contrast, having a dividend decrease (or a dividend increase smaller than the average dividend increase in the market) had a deleterious effect on relative performance, as shown in Figure 15.10. For those firms that announced a stock split, but had a dividend decrease, stock price performance was well under the market norm.

The results of this study have important implications for the market efficiency hypothesis. An investor who bought every stock that announced a stock split would not enjoy any performance better than the market norm (as Figure 15.8 shows). The market appears to be efficient with respect to the public information embodied in the stock split announcement. If the investor could find out in advance about the stock split, superior returns could be earned by using privileged information. This finding has implications for the strong form of the EMH which will be discussed later. Finally, if an investor could tell which of the splitting stocks would have cash dividend increases, it would be possible to buy only those, and he or she

Figure 15.10

Relative Performance for Firms with Stock Splits Which Also Decreased Cash Dividends

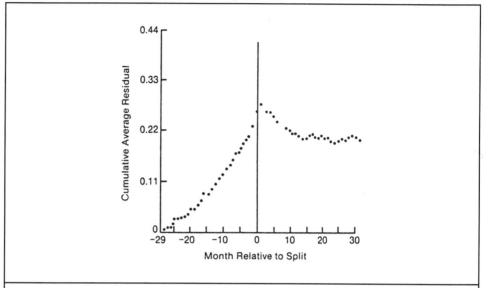

Source: E. F. Fama, L. Fisher, M. C. Jensen, and R. Roll, "The Adjustment of Stock Prices to New Information," *International Economic Review*, February 1969, pp. 1–21.

could earn a superior return. In other words, the early detection of cash dividend increases would be very useful. However, evidence suggests such predictions cannot be made on a consistently successful basis.

The Sharpe–Cooper Study. The central claim of the CAPM is that stocks with higher betas are expected to have higher returns. If that prediction did not hold true in actual practice, then such a finding would be strong evidence against the CAPM. William Sharpe and Guy Cooper tested this central claim directly.[14]

Sharpe and Cooper estimated betas for all stocks listed on the New York Stock Exchange for each year beginning in 1931 and continuing through 1967. For each year, they divided the available securities into ten deciles, with decile 1 having the 10 percent of stocks with the lowest betas, and decile 10 having the 10 percent of stocks with the highest betas. They then evaluated the average annual return on each of these ten portfolios.

---

[14] W. Sharpe and G. Cooper, "Risk–Return Classes of New York Stock Exchange Common Stocks 1931–1967," *Financial Analysts Journal*, March/April 1972, 28:2, pp. 46–54.

Figure 15.11

The Relationship Between Beta and Returns

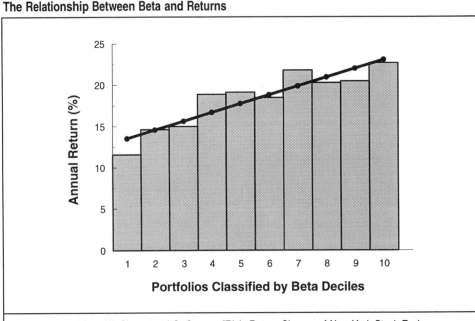

Source: Adapted from W. Sharpe and G. Cooper, "Risk–Return Classes of New York Stock Exchange Common Stocks 1931–67," *Financial Analysts Journal*, March/April 1972, 28:2, pp. 46–54.

The CAPM would predict that returns should increase as we move from decile 1 to decile 10. Further, the CAPM predicts a linear relationship between actual return and beta as well.

In evaluating the results of such a test, it is important to remember that the CAPM is a theory that relates *expected* returns to the risk–free rate, beta, and the market risk premium. Because of this focus on the future, the CAPM expresses an *ex ante* theory, because it deals with expectations. The actual results can be measured only *ex post*, or after the fact. In general, the *ex post* results will never conform exactly to the *ex ante* expectation. However, on average and in the long run, we should see a fairly close congruence between the *ex ante* theory and the *ex post* results.

Figure 15.11 presents a graph that shows the key results of the Sharpe–Cooper study. The bars represent the average annual returns earned on each portfolio over the entire period they studied. The straight line is the *ex post* SML that gives the best fit through their average returns. As the graph shows, the relationship fits very well, although not perfectly. For example, decile 7 had a higher return than decile 8, which does not match theory. Nonetheless, these results generally have been interpreted as supporting the CAPM and the EMH.

Interpretation of Early Tests.   In general, early testing generally supported the joint hypothesis of the CAPM and EMH. The study by Sharpe and Cooper was typical in many ways of the kinds of results that were reported into the early 1980s. Through approximately 1985, scholars generally believed that the empirical evidence strongly favored the CAPM and the EMH.

The general acceptance of the semi–strong version of the EMH had strong implications for fundamental analysis. Essentially, if the semi–strong form of the EMH is correct, fundamental analysis is worthless, at least as a technique for improving security returns. Under these circumstances, the investor interested only in risk–adjusted investment returns would spend nothing whatsoever for fundamental analysis. With the bulk of evidence favoring the semi–strong EMH, most scholars believed that fundamental analysis was essentially a waste of time. As we review later in this chapter, more recent evidence calls the semi–strong version of the EMH into serious question. As one scholar recently stated: ". . . the efficient market hypothesis is having a near–death experience. . ."[15]

Tests of the Strong Form of Market Efficiency

If the strong form of the EMH is true, no information is valuable for directing a securities investment program, because security prices already reflect all information. However, the best evidence clearly indicates that the strong form of the EMH is false. Access to inside or private information can be used to generate a profit in excess of the risk–adjusted norm. This section discusses two types of tests of strong form efficiency. The first looks at the investment performance of corporate insiders and the second at the returns earned by stock market specialists. It must also be emphasized that trading on the basis of inside information is generally illegal.

Corporate Insiders.   Corporate insiders often have access to potentially valuable information regarding the investment prospects of their firms before the general public gets that information. This raises the possibility that officers of corporations could use that information to earn returns in excess of the risk–adjusted norm. That appears to be exactly what occurs.

There is considerable anecdotal evidence that insiders are able to make money by trading on their privileged information. Generally, these stories only come to public attention in connection with court cases. Without too much doubt, most exciting insider trading stories never come to public attention because the illegal trading is never detected.

In addition to anecdotal evidence, there is more formal evidence as well. Corporate insiders are required to report their trading activity to the SEC within two weeks of the trade, and the SEC publishes this information in its "Official

---

[15] P. Fortune, "Stock Market Efficiency: An Autopsy?" Federal Reserve Bank of Boston *New England Economic Review*, March/April 1991, pp. 17–40.

Summary of Insider Trading." Studies of this information reveal that insiders consistently earn more than would be expected in an efficient market.[16]

Market Specialists.   As discussed in Chapter 3, the stock exchange specialist holds a book showing the orders awaiting execution at different prices. The specialist also holds an inventory in the stocks for which he or she is the specialist, and the specialist may increase or decrease this inventory at will. If the specialist sees a large number of buy orders at 50, with the current price lying at 55, he or she can be fairly confident that the price will not fall below 50, at least in the short run. This kind of privileged information is very valuable, according to studies of specialists' returns. They appear to average returns of about 100 percent on their invested capital, which is clearly above the risk–adjusted norm.[17] Almost all studies of strong form efficiency reach the same conclusion. Securities markets are not strong form efficient.

A Thought Experiment.   From the financial press, there is a clear and wide–spread belief that the Chairman of the Federal Reserve Board has a great influence on day–to–day movements in interest rates. Virtually every major securities firm has an economist poised to react to any pronouncement by the Chairman, because these firms believe that when the Chairman speaks, the market listens.

The Chairman of the Federal Reserve Board has a great deal of inside information. The Board acts to increase or decrease the money supply, and the pending actions are a closely guarded secret. They are, however, known to the Chairman. If the strong form of the efficient markets hypothesis is true, then the Chairman's inside information is not useful to direct a trading strategy. Yet, this is clearly not the case.

Assume that the Chairman is extremely anxious to buy a yacht, but this does not appear feasible on his modest salary. The Chairman decides to get his yacht money by the following strategy. Trading through a secret assistant, the Chairman buys Treasury bonds at the opening of the market. (He uses a secret assistant because the strategy is clearly illegal.) Once the bonds are securely purchased, the Chairman moves on to his 10:00 a.m. news conference. There he announces that inflation is much lower than anyone thought and predicts that interest rates will fall sharply in the next two months. The market reacts immediately to his strong speech, sending interest rates into a tail spin. From Chapter 7, we know that bond prices rise when interest rates fall. Once the market has reacted to his speech, the Chairman instructs his secret assistant to sell the bonds acquired earlier in the day.

---

[16]For two such studies, see J. Jaffe, "Special Information and Insider Trading," *Journal of Business*, July 1974, and James H. Lorie and Victor Niederhoffer, "Predictive and Statistical Properties of Insider Trading," *Journal of Law and Economics*, April 1968, pp. 35–51.

[17]See United States House Committee on Interstate and Foreign Commerce, subcommittee on Commerce and Finance, *Securities Industry Study: Report and Hearings*, 92nd Congress, 1st and 2nd sessions, 1972, Chapter 12.

Having accomplished so much in a morning, the Chairman awards himself an extended lunch for a little yacht shopping.

This thought experiment is aimed at showing that some individuals do possess inside information that is very valuable. In virtue of his position, the Chairman of the Federal Reserve Board not only has relevant inside information, but he even has the power to use it in the way shown. In the strictest sense, the strong–form EMH claims that no such person has inside information that would help to develop a trading strategy. (This thought experiment, we stress, is only that; there is no implication that any member of the Federal Reserve Board has ever acted in the way this thought experiment imagines.)

Summary

Early studies seemed to lead to fairly stable conclusions about the validity of all three versions of the EMH. Regarding the weak form, the evidence clearly supported market efficiency. Just as clearly, the early evidence also supported the view that the market is not efficient in the strong version. There is good evidence that investors with private information are able to use that information to guide a market–beating trading strategy.

The weight of early evidence also supported the semi–strong version of the EMH. Nonetheless, the conclusion was never so clear for the semi–strong version as it was for the weak form and the strong form. While the weight of evidence generally supports semi–strong efficiency, some scholars always gave voice to nagging doubts about the validity of the semi–strong version of the EMH. As we now review, those early nagging doubts have risen to a chorus and a full–blown attack against the semi–strong version is now under way.

Recent Evidence on Market Efficiency and the CAPM

In this section, we turn to a brief review of recent evidence on the efficiency of capital markets and the adequacy of the CAPM. Active research is under way on a variety of issues, and this section focuses on four major strands: market anomalies, excess volatility, mean reversion and overreaction, and noise trading. First, we consider market anomalies. A market anomaly is a well–established empirical fact that does not fit accepted theories. However, the contradiction may be resolved by future research. Whether these types of market anomalies can finally be resolved or not, they are currently important in the development of capital market theory.

Market Anomalies

In this section, we consider four important market anomalies. First, we examine the **weekend** or the **day–of–the–week** effect—the fact that securities have different levels of returns on different days of the week. Second, we consider the **January** effect—the tendency for security returns in January to be too large relative to returns in other months. Third, we consider the **earnings report** anomaly—the apparent opportunity to earn above–normal stock returns by trading on the public information provided by quarterly earnings announcements. Finally, we consider the **small firm** effect—the tendency of firms with small capitalization to earn higher returns than larger, well–established firms.

The Weekend Effect. Considerable recent attention has been devoted to the difference in daily returns on many securities, depending on which day of the week is under examination. The return for a particular day is the return from the close of business on one day through the close of business on another day. So Tuesday's return, for example, covers the period from the close of trading on Monday through the close on Tuesday.

Nothing in the CAPM or the EMH explains why returns on Thursday should be different from returns on Tuesday or Wednesday, for example. Nonetheless, a great deal of evidence shows that returns differ depending on the day of the week. These return differences are substantial, and it may be possible for investors to enhance their returns by timing their purchases to take advantage of these persistent differences. If so, the day–of–the–week effect would show either that the semi–strong EMH was not true, the CAPM was not true, or both. If the CAPM is the correct pricing relationship in the market, then the EMH must be false, because it appears that prices do not adjust correctly to reflect all available information. If the EMH is true, it seems that the CAPM must be false, because there must be additional risk factors not recognized by the CAPM to explain the differential returns depending on the day of the week.

The pattern of returns is quite peculiar. In particular, Friday returns are significantly larger than those for other days. By contrast, returns from the Friday close to the Monday close are generally negative. The unusually small returns over the weekend earns this anomaly the name of the **weekend effect**. The small return over the weekend is especially peculiar since returns from Friday to Monday should be three times as great as the returns from one trading day to the next, because funds are committed for three days instead of one. Returns on Tuesday, Wednesday, and Thursday are neither particularly large nor small. Further investigation has shown that the negative returns on Mondays are largely due to the extremely bad period at the open of Monday trading.

As an example of the findings on the day–of–the–week effect, we consider the key results of a study by Donald Keim and Robert Stambaugh, who investigated the daily returns for the S&P 500 Index for 1928–1982. Figure 15.12 shows the results from their study in which they computed the daily return for the index separately for each day–of–the–week. The value for Monday is –.1859 percent. This means that over the average weekend from 1928 to 1982, the index lost about one–fifth of 1 percent of its value. By contrast, all other days had positive average returns. Considering all days together, the index increased by .0207 percent per day

Figure 15.12

Stock Returns by the Day–of–the–Week

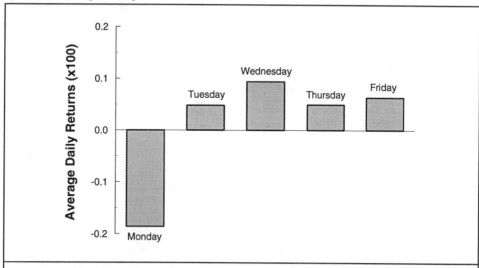

Source: Donald B. Keim and Robert F. Stambaugh, "A Further Investigation of the Weekend Effect in Stock Returns," *Journal of Finance*, July 1984, 39:3, pp. 819–835.

on average. In their study, Keim and Stambaugh found that Wednesday returns were the highest of any weekday.[18]

While the persistent differences in daily returns are not large enough to allow one to trade and to cover all transaction costs, they are sufficiently large to affect the wise timing of trading decisions. For example, if one is considering selling a stock, it would be wise to sell on Friday afternoon rather than Monday morning. Conversely, if a trader contemplates a purchase, it might be advisable to delay the purchase until mid–day on Monday rather than trading at the Monday open.[19]

The January Effect. Another peculiarity is some unusual behavior in returns in the month of January. Therefore, this anomaly has become known as the **January effect**

---

[18]Donald B. Keim and Robert F. Stambaugh, "A Further Investigation of the Weekend Effect in Stock Returns," *Journal of Finance*, July 1984, 39:3, pp. 819–835. Omitted here are their results for Saturday trading from the early period when the market was open on Saturdays.

[19]For studies of the day–of–the–week effect, see F. Cross, "The Behavior of Stock Prices on Fridays and Mondays," *Financial Analysts Journal*, November/December 1973, pp. 67–69; K. French, "Stock Returns and the Weekend Effect," *Journal of Financial Economics*, March 1980, pp. 55–69; D. Keim and R. Stambaugh, "A Further Investigation of the Weekend Effect in Stock Returns," *Journal of Finance*, July 1984, pp. 819–840; and J. Lakonishok and M. Levi, "Weekend Effects on Stock Returns," *Journal of Finance*, 1982, pp. 883–889.

or the **turn–of–the–year** effect. Capital market theory implies no reason for returns in one month to differ from returns in any other. In short, the December return should equal the January return should equal the March return, and so on.

In fact, returns in January are very large relative to other months, both in the United States and abroad. This differential return in January is so large for securities in some countries that the entire year's positive return occurs in January. Examining returns for 16 countries, Gultekin and Gultekin found a January effect in 15 of those countries. In Belgium, the Netherlands, and Italy, the January return exceeded the average return for the whole year.[20]

Returns in the United States tell a similar story. For example, Rozeff and Kinney examined the years 1904–1974 and found that the average monthly return in January was 3.5 percent, while the other months averaged about 0.5 percent.[21] This effect is found for an equally weighted index of large and small firms. Large firms by themselves do not exhibit this effect, so the January effect is concentrated mainly among small firms. For the small firms, half of their excess returns (the return over the risk–free rate) for the year occurred in January. Of these January excess returns, half occurred in the first five trading days.[22]

Some researchers have tried to explain the January effect by relating the unusual pattern of returns to tax–loss trading. While there are some conceptual problems with this approach, taxes seem to be only part of the story. For example, Japan does not tax capital gains, yet Japanese security returns exhibit the January effect. Also, the tax years in Great Britain do not begin in January, yet returns in those markets exhibit a January effect. Nonetheless, tax rules appear to be relevant, because returns in Great Britain and Australia are higher at the beginning of their tax years as well.

The January effect does not appear to be large enough to allow profitable trading by an investor facing normal transaction costs. However, the effect is probably large enough to cover transaction costs of low–cost traders. For all traders, the presence of a January effect may give reason to alter timing decisions. As an example, a trader considering purchases near year–end would be advised to acquire shares in late December rather than mid–January.

---

[20] M. N. Gultekin and N. Bulent Gultekin, "Stock Market Seasonality: International Evidence," *Journal of Financial Economics*, 1983, pp. 469–481.

[21] M. S. Rozeff and W. R. Kinney, Jr., "Capital Market Seasonality: The Case of Stock Returns," *Journal of Financial Economics*, 1976, pp. 379–402.

[22] R. W. Banz, "The Relationship Between Return and Market Value of Common Stock," *Journal of Financial Economics*, 1981, pp. 3–18; D. B. Keim, "Size Related Anomalies and Stock Return Seasonality," *Journal of Financial Economics*, June 1983, pp. 13–22; and M. R. Reinganum, "The Anomalous Stock Market Behavior of Small Firms in January: Empirical Tests for Tax–Loss Selling Effects," *Journal of Financial Economics*, June 1983, pp. 18–28.

Earnings Reports. Another market anomaly concerns the market's response to announcements of quarterly earnings. Studies of this phenomenon form an estimate of the market's expected earnings, which is usually done by using a simple regression of past earnings on time. With the forecast of next period's earnings from the regression model, the studies look for large deviations in either direction from the forecast earnings. By buying those stocks with especially favorable announcements and by selling those with unfavorable announcements, several studies have shown that it is possible to beat the market, even when including transactions costs.[23]

Figure 15.13 shows the key results from a study by Richard Rendleman, Charles Jones, and Henry Latane.[24] They used a simple trend model to forecast the next quarter's earnings announcement and, after the announcement, they compared the actual earnings figure with their prediction. Firms that announced the largest earnings relative to the prediction were put into Portfolio 10. They continued down to firms that had much lower earnings than forecast, which were placed in Portfolio 1. Figure 15.13 shows the performance of each portfolio relative to a market standard for 20 days before the announcement to 90 days after the announcement.

The figure reveals two interesting points that we can see by just focusing on the extreme Portfolios 1 and 10. For both the overachievers in Portfolio 10 and the underachievers in Portfolio 1, much of the total price movement took place in the 20 days before the announcement. In other words, the stock price reacted to the impending news before it became public. This suggests that some parties traded on the inside information of the coming earnings announcement. The second point, and the major issue for the anomaly, is the stock performance after the announcement—from day 0 to day 90. As Rendleman, Jones, and Latane emphasize, a trader who heard the public announcement and then traded could still earn a substantial profit. For example, for Portfolio 10 the 90 days after the announcement yield a full 4 percent of cumulative excess return over the comparable risk–adjusted return.

If the market is efficient with respect to these announcements and the CAPM gives the correct pricing relationship for risk and return, it would be impossible to react to these announcements in a way that gave a supernormal return. Therefore, this evidence from earnings reports presents a strong and still poorly understood challenge to the CAPM and the EMH.

The Small Firm Effect. The **small firm effect** is the empirically observed regularity that small capitalization firms earn a rate of return that is higher than the risk–adjusted market standard implies. Over the period from 1926–1993, we have

---

[23]Several of these studies are summarized in O. Maurice Joy and Charles P. Jones, "Earnings Reports and Market Efficiencies: An Analysis of Contrary Evidence," *Journal of Financial Research*, 1979, pp. 51–64.

[24]R. J. Rendleman, C. P. Jones, and H. A. Latane, "Empirical Anomalies Based on Unexpected Earnings and the Importance of Risk Adjustments," *Journal of Financial Economics*, November 1982, 10:3, pp. 269–287.

Figure 15.13

Stock Performance After Earnings Announcements

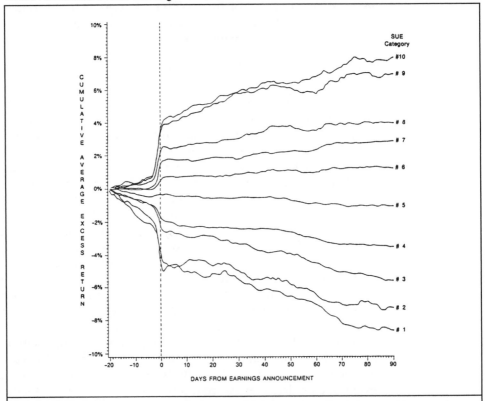

Source: R. J. Rendleman, C. P. Jones, and H. A. Latane, "Empirical Anomalies Based on Unexpected Earnings and the Importance of Risk Adjustments," *Journal of Financial Economics*, November 1982, 10:3, pp. 269–287.

already observed that small stocks outperformed large stocks by a significant degree. One dollar invested in small stocks at the beginning of 1926 would have grown to $2,757.15 by the end of 1993. By contrast, one dollar invested in the S&P 500 would have grown to $800.08 over the same period. In theory, this difference might be explained by a difference in risk between the smaller and riskier stocks versus the larger and more stable stocks in the S&P 500. However, even after making this risk adjustment in accordance with the CAPM, small stocks still earn substantially more than theory leads one to expect.

Many market observers have been aware of this small firm effect for a long period. Nonetheless, it has persisted for several decades. In the 1980s, however, the effect seemed to disappear. One dollar invested in a small stock portfolio at the end of 1979 would have grown to $3.41 by the end of 1990. By contrast, the same investment in the S&P 500 would have grown to $4.88 over the same period. In the early 1990s, however, small firms have dramatically outperformed larger firms. For the period from the end of 1980 to the end of 1990, large stock values increased by a total of 49.70 percent, while small stock values increased by a total of 69.30 percent.

Summary. In this section, we have considered four of the most important anomalies that have arisen as challenges to the CAPM and the EMH. This evidence from the weekend effect, the January effect, unexpected earnings announcements, and the small firm effect all call the ordinary understanding of risk and expected return into question. As we have pointed out, these anomalies present a challenge to the joint hypothesis of the CAPM and the EMH. They lead us to believe either that the CAPM gives an incomplete understanding of the risk/expected return relationship or that the securities markets are unable to efficiently process information.

Anomalies in the Japanese Stock Market

While U.S. markets have been studied most carefully for evidence of anomalies, recent attention has also focused on foreign stock markets, notably on the markets in Japan. In this section, we consider some recent evidence on the January effect and the weekend effect from the Japanese markets.

Kiyoshi Kato and James Schallheim studied the January effect and the small firm effect for the Tokyo Stock Exchange over the period 1964–1981. They conclude that the Japanese markets exhibit the same anomalies that we have discussed for the U.S. markets: small firms tend to earn higher returns than one would expect from the CAPM and returns in January tend to be higher than for other months. While they urge caution in interpreting their results, Kato and Schallheim conclude that the similarity in results may be evidence of well–integrated international capital markets.[25]

In the Japanese markets, J. Jaffe and R. Westerfield also found evidence of a day–of–the–week effect. The effect in the Japanese market resembles the evidence for the United States, but there are some differences. Covering the period 1970–1983, the authors computed the daily returns for the S&P 500 index in the United States, the Nikkei Dow index of 225 large capitalization stocks, and the TOPIX index, a value–weighted index of all shares on the Tokyo Stock Exchange. Table 15.4 presents their key results, with the S&P 500 from the United States included for comparison.

As in the United States, these researchers found that Monday returns were negative. However, in Japan, negative returns extended to Tuesday as well, and the Tuesday losses exceeded the Monday losses. In the United States, by contrast, Tuesday returns are positive. The Japanese markets have horrible weekends, from which they tend not to recover until Wednesday. Also, all three indexes have the

---

[25]K. Kato and J. S. Schallheim, "Seasonal and Size Anomalies in the Japanese Stock Market," in *Japanese Capital Markets*, New York: Harper & Row, 1990, pp. 225–247.

Table 15.4

▪▪▪▪▪▪▪▪

Day–of–the–Week Effect on the Tokyo Stock Exchange, 1970–1983

	Average Return by Day		
Weekday	**S&P 500 (U.S.)**	**Nikkei Dow**	**TOPIX**
Monday	−0.129	−0.020	−0.014
Tuesday	0.020	−0.090	−0.064
Wednesday	0.097	0.150	0.124
Thursday	0.032	0.026	0.026
Friday	0.078	0.063	0.057

Note: Table values are the daily percentage change in the index multiplied by 100.

Source: J. Jaffe and R. Westerfield, "The Weekend Effect in Common Stock Returns: The International Evidence," *Journal of Finance*, 1985, pp. 433–454. Reprinted with permission from the *Journal of Finance*.

highest returns on Wednesday. Alternative hypotheses have been advanced to explain why U.S. and Japanese markets differ in their weekend effects, but the mystery remains.

Excess Volatility

Volatility in the price of a security should be related to volatility in the cash flows expected to come from that security or to volatility in the valuation of those expected cash flows. For example, in the constant growth model of stock prices that we studied in Chapter 9, we have:

$$P_0 = \frac{D_1}{k - g}$$

where P_0 is the current stock price, D_1 is the dividend expected for next year, k is the discount rate, and g is the long–term growth rate for the dividends. For example, if $D_1 = \$2$, $k = .08$, and $g = .03$, then $P_0 = \$40$. Of these values, the daily published stock price is the easiest to observe. By comparison, there is not an easy way to observe k or g with such certainty.

If the model is valid, and if prices behave efficiently, volatility in the stock price must be related to volatility in D_1, k, g, or the combined volatility of all three. Assume we observe a doubling in the stock price from $40 to $80, and consider what single change in the right–hand side variables would be consistent with this price rise. First, the expected dividend could double from $2 to $4. Second, the discount rate could fall from .08 to .055. Third, the growth rate could increase from .03 to .055. These relationships open the possibility of testing the volatility of prices against the volatility of the fundamental factors of the expected dividend, the discount rate, or the growth rate.

This is essentially the approach taken by Robert Shiller.[26] Shiller first assumed that k is constant and then found the historical dividends for the S&P 500 from 1871–1979. Under this assumption of a constant discount rate, Shiller found that stock prices exhibited a volatility that was six times as great as the fundamentals would imply. In terms of the constant growth model, the left–hand side price was five to 13 times as volatile as the right–hand side fundamentals. Even allowing for k to vary with interest rates, Shiller found that the price was 50 percent too volatile compared with the fundamentals.

This evidence on volatility led Shiller to conclude that price volatility was so high that the market price of stocks could not be reacting efficiently to new information about fundamentals of expected dividends, growth rates, or discount rates. While this strand of new research is quite promising, we should note that other scholars have called the entire approach into serious question based on statistical grounds.[27]

Mean Reversion and Overreaction in Security Prices

Mean reversion is a statistical term that refers to the tendency of a variable to return to its average values. For example, assume the average growth rate for stock prices is 9 percent per year. If stocks that rise 15 percent in one year then systematically rise only 3 percent the following year, the stocks are mean reverting. After the two–year period, the average growth rate for the stocks is only the average of 9 percent. If stock prices are mean reverting, this means that they are predictable. For instance, the stocks in our example that rose 15 percent in one year should fall in the next year. Mean reversion opens the door to stock price prediction that would beat the market. Strong mean reversion also implies that the market is not efficient, because it suggests a trading strategy that would earn a return greater than the risk–adjusted return.

The example of the last paragraph ties into an interesting hypothesis of overreaction. Some scholars think that human psychology is such that investors may overreact to both good news and bad news. If so, good news might cause stock prices to rise too much relative to the real import of the news. Later, when expectations adjust, the disappointment might cause them to fall too much. The resulting path of stock prices might be rises that are too large and drops that are

---

[26]See his collection of papers, R. J. Shiller, *Market Volatility*, Cambridge, MA: The MIT Press, 1989.

[27]For two dissenting voices, see T. A. Marsh and R. C. Merton, "Dividend Variability and Variance Bounds Tests for the Rationality of Stock Prices," *The American Economic Review*, June 1986, pp. 483–498, and A. W. Kleidon, "Variance Bounds Tests and Stock Price Valuation Models," *Journal of Political Economy*, October 1986, pp. 953–1001.

Figure 15.14

The Subsequent Performance of Winners and Losers

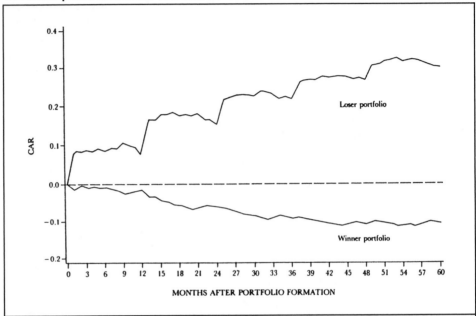

Source: W. F. M. DeBondt and R. H. Thaler, "A Mean–Reverting Walk Down Wall Street," *Journal of Economic Perspectives*, Winter 1989, 3:1, pp. 194. This copyrighted material was reproduced with permission of the American Economic Association.

too big. (In effect, this is something like Shiller's results, volatility in stock prices that is too large given the changes in fundamental information.)

Werner DeBondt and Richard Thaler investigated this overreaction hypothesis directly.[28] Using stock market data from 1926–1982, DeBondt and Thaler used five years of monthly data to form winner and loser portfolios. These portfolios consisted of the 35 stocks that did the best and the worst over the five–year period. They repeated this portfolio formation over the many years covered in their study. They then tracked the performance of these winner and loser portfolios over the next 60 months.

Figure 15.14 shows the key results of their study. Stocks that were losers in the early period were big winners in the following period. Similarly, stocks that were initially winners turned out to be losers in the test period. The figure shows the risk–adjusted excess returns, illustrating strong mean reversion in stock prices.

---

[28]W. F. M. DeBondt and R. H. Thaler, "Does the Stock Market Overreact?" *Journal of Finance*, July 1985, pp. 793–805.

Notice in Figure 15.14 that the reversal was stronger for the loser portfolios. Also, the losers' big gains occur mostly in January (the January effect!), as evidenced by the five large jumps in the values of the loser portfolios.

DeBondt and Thaler find that the stock market overreacted to bad news and to good news, but that the overreaction to bad news was even more extreme. This greater overreaction to bad news is evidenced by the bigger adjustment for the loser stocks. Notice in Figure 15.14 that the losers gain about 3 percent excess return over the five years after the portfolios are formed. This excess return is enough to cover transaction costs, so this study suggests that the market inefficiency is of a serious magnitude. As DeBondt and Thaler conclude: "If the CAPM beta is an adequate risk measure, then the difference between the winner and loser returns cannot be attributed to differences in risk."[29]

Noise Trading

Some researchers have accepted the view that prices of financial assets are not always in accordance with fundamentals. In other words, they have abandoned the efficient markets hypothesis. After all, if investor psychology is such that investors overreact and move stock prices away from fundamental values, then it is important to recognize that fact and to develop theories that accord with the presence of at least some irrational investors in the marketplace.

A **noise trader** is an investor whose demand for financial assets is affected by beliefs or sentiments that are not fully justified by the fundamentals. In other words, a noise trader has an irrational element in his or her processing of information. Noise traders contrast with rational speculators or arbitrageurs—those investors who form expectations about future values strictly on fundamentals.[30]

In standard theory, if noise traders moved prices away from fundamental values, the rational arbitrageurs would quickly take advantage of that small discrepancy and trade until the discrepancy was eliminated. For example, if irrational expectations about the prospects for cold fusion sent palladium prices too high, the arbitrageurs would sell palladium until the price of palladium again reached its fundamental values. Under this scenario, the arbitrageurs would gain at the noise traders' expense. Eventually, the noise traders would go broke and be driven from the market. In this equilibrium, prices would remain serenely in accordance with fundamentals.

---

[29] W. F. M. DeBondt and R. H. Thaler, "A Mean–Reverting Walk Down Wall Street," *Journal of Economic Perspectives*, Winter 1989, 3:1, pp. 189–202.

[30] In the signal processing literature, any transmission consists of a signal plus some noise—a random component that conveys no information. In a radio transmission, for example, there may be a song (the information) plus static (the noise). In investing, rational investors respond to the signal (information about fundamentals), while noise traders respond to noise (irrelevant static not connected to fundamentals).

However, there are limits to rational investors' abilities to conduct this arbitrage. These have been detailed by Andrei Shleifer and Lawrence H. Summers.[31] Essentially, arbitrageurs face two types of risk. First, there is the risk that their own assessment might be wrong. Even if they are rational in their forecasts, they know that they sometimes make errors, so arbitrageurs will be reluctant to trade to capture small gains. This means that prices can move some distance from their fundamental values without calling the arbitrageurs into play. Second, the arbitrageur facing prices that appear to be out of line with fundamentals must ask how much more prices can diverge from fundamentals and how long will it take for prices to return to their fundamentally justified levels? These risk factors prevent arbitrageurs from conducting their arbitrage with perfect efficiency and allow noise traders to move prices away from their fundamentally justified levels.

This noise trader approach to finance suggests that prices can diverge from fundamentals in dramatic ways and for extended periods. The potential for such price disturbances is higher when there is a herd effect, a number of noise traders following the same trading signals. While this avenue of research is very new, some scholars believe that this approach may help to bring financial theory new power in explaining the actual behavior of security prices. This approach does admit that markets are essentially inefficient, because prices can diverge from fundamental values and thereby fail to reflect relevant information.

Beta: The Debate Goes On

At present, the entire topic of market efficiency and the value of the CAPM is controversial, and it is likely that the debate will continue. In this section, we consider two diametrically opposing views from long–time defenders of market efficiency and the capital asset pricing model.

In a 1992 article in the *Journal of Finance*, Eugene F. Fama and Kenneth R. French argue that there is essentially no relationship between the beta of a stock and the returns experienced by that stock. This claim attacks the very heart of the CAPM and less directly, the efficient markets hypothesis. Figure 15.15 is drawn from Table 1 of the Fama and French paper.[32] Fama and French created ten portfolios ranging from the decile of stocks with the lowest betas (Portfolio 1) to the decile of stocks with the highest betas (Portfolio 10), as shown on the x axis of Figure 15.15. The y axis records the mean monthly return, so the symbols show the mean monthly return for each portfolio. The straight line is a simple regression showing that there is virtually no relationship between the beta of the portfolio and

---

[31]A. Shleifer and L. H. Summers, "The Noise Trader Approach to Finance," *Journal of Economic Perspectives*, Spring 1990, 4:2, pp. 19–33. This exposition of noise trading follows Shleifer and Summers.

[32]Eugene F. Fama and Kenneth R. French, "The Cross–Section of Expected Stock Returns," *Journal of Finance*, 47:2, June 1992, pp. 427–465.

Figure 15.15

Beta and Returns: The Fama and French Study

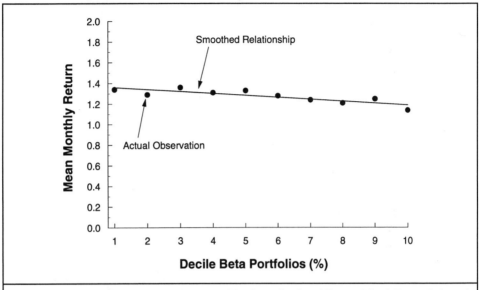

Source: Eugene F. Fama and Kenneth R. French, "The Cross–Section of Expected Stock Returns," *Journal of Finance*, 47:2, June 1992, pp. 427–465.

the returns realized by the portfolio. If anything, there is a slightly negative relationship: the high beta portfolios actually had somewhat lower returns than the low beta portfolios. As Fama and French explicitly note, these results conflict with the earlier results of a famous study by Fama and MacBeth.[33] While beta may not be related to returns in the eyes of Fama and French, they find that firm size and the ratio of the book value of equity to the market value of equity are more strongly related to returns. Clearly, if the conclusions of Fama and French are sustained, the central tenet of the CAPM—the positive relationship between beta and return—is exploded.

Not all researchers accept the conclusions of Fama and French. Fischer Black[34] argues that the central conclusions of Fama and French are most likely the result of data mining: If you look at the data hard enough, you can find some spurious relationships, such as the relationship between returns, on the one hand,

---

[33] Eugene F. Fama and James MacBeth, "Risk, Return and Equilibrium: Empirical Tests," *Journal of Political Economy*, 81, 1973, pp. 607–636.

[34] Fischer Black, "Beta and Return," *The Journal of Portfolio Management*, 20:1, Fall 1993, pp. 8–18.

Figure 15.16

Beta and Returns: The Black Study

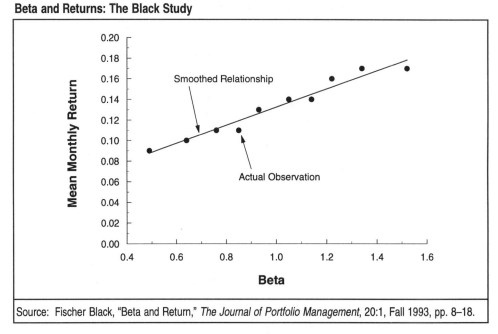

Source: Fischer Black, "Beta and Return," *The Journal of Portfolio Management*, 20:1, Fall 1993, pp. 8–18.

and size or the ratio of book to market value of equity, on the other. Black further argues that there is no theory to explain any such relationship between returns and these so–called explanatory variables.

Instead, Black says, there is a strong theory, the CAPM, to explain returns as a function of beta. Black considers excess returns, the return on a security minus the risk–free rate for a given period, and compares these excess returns to the beta of a portfolio. Similar to Fama and French, Black forms ten portfolios ranging from the decile of lowest beta stocks to the decile of highest beta stocks. Figure 15.16 is drawn from Table 3 of Black's study. It shows a consistent and persuasive positive relationship between excess returns and beta. In essence, this result contradicts one of the key findings of Fama and French.

How can these conflicting results between Fama and French and Black be reconciled? Part of the explanation rests on the different time periods examined. Fama and French consider the 1963–1990 period, while Black analyzes the 1931–1991 period. The exact selection of firms differs between the two studies, and there are other more subtle methodological differences. Because of these differences in sample periods, included firms, and econometric methodology, Fama and French and Black reach quite different conclusions. It is not obvious that the conclusions of one are correct and the other false. Instead, such conflicting results ensure that the controversy over the validity of beta will continue.

Summary

Until the last few years, it has been fairly easy to summarize the evidence on the CAPM and efficient markets. However, with the growing evidence on market anomalies and the growing attack on the CAPM, the issue is becoming more clouded. Today, however, we can still be quite confident that securities markets in the United States are efficient in the weak sense and that they are inefficient in the strong sense.

The assessment of semi–strong market efficiency is much more difficult today than it was five years ago. This chapter stressed the intimate relationship between an evaluation of a market's efficiency and reliance on a pricing model. The market anomalies mentioned in the chapter may be interpreted as calling either the pricing model or the market's efficiency into question. Today, more and more researchers believe that the anomalies constitute a severe challenge to both the CAPM and to semi–strong market efficiency. The additional evidence presented by excess volatility tests and the finding of mean reversion in asset prices strengthens the case against market efficiency. Theories of noise trading represent an abandonment of efficient markets theory and an attempt to develop a new theory of price behavior that is consistent with prices that diverge from their fundamentally justified values.

Faced with this uncertain situation, what should be the response of the investor? In some respects, evidence still favors semi–strong market efficiency. For example, the studies finding anomalies have still not provided evidence of gross or widespread inefficiencies. Further, these apparent anomalies may be due to faults in our pricing models, rather than to a failure of semi–strong efficiency. Even given the mounting evidence against efficiency, it still is not apparent how an investor can fully exploit that inefficiency.

In the light of the current state of knowledge, investors should behave as though they were confident that the market were efficient in the semi–strong sense and should follow these six rules:

1. Investors should hold a well–diversified portfolio to eliminate unsystematic risk.
2. In a market that is semi–strong efficient, investors should avoid paying needlessly for research of dubious value. (Probably it is better not to pay anything for research reports.)
3. Consistent with this approach, investors should avoid the full–fee brokerage firms and choose to trade with a discount broker. Full–fee brokerage firms "bundle" research services with brokerage services and charge for the research services by charging higher brokerage commissions.
4. If it is not really possible to analyze public information successfully, there is little reason for active trading. A policy of active trading would be appropriate if the investor believes it is possible to identify underpriced securities. In a semi–strong efficient market, this is not possible.
5. Trading should be oriented toward "buy–and–hold" strategies. When trades are made, they should generally be made for liquidity reasons.

6.   The smart investor will also trade with an eye to tax consequences. From the point of view of trading, investors should generally seek to acknowledge short–term capital losses and to avoid recognizing short–term capital gains.

Following these six rules will not help an investor beat the market. Beating the market is not a reasonable expectation no matter what advice the investor follows. Instead, these six rules should help the investor to earn a competitive return—one that earns a return that is commensurate with the risk level of the portfolio. Also, following these rules should help an investor avoid giving away profits in brokerage fees or in the form of increased taxes.

The next chapter pursues these ideas in a different context. There is an entire industry that specializes in managing securities portfolios. Firms in this industry are known as investment companies, and the mutual fund is the most important type of investment company. If accurate stock selection is possible, mutual funds, with their expert staffs, might be able to outperform the market. The performance of investment companies is perhaps surprising and gives a new dimension to the claims of the efficient markets hypothesis.

Questions and Problems

1.   What is the difference between "operational efficiency" and "informational efficiency"?
2.   What does it mean to say that prices "fully reflect" some body of information?
3.   How are the three traditional versions of the market efficiency hypothesis distinguished?
4.   Say that you have conclusive information that it is possible to beat the market by charting the past history of stock prices. Which version(s) of the efficient markets hypothesis would this evidence disprove? Why?
5.   Assume that a worker in the U. S. Patent Office learns about new products before they are publicly announced. Might this worker be able to use this information to "beat the market"? If he or she could do so, would that conflict with the efficient markets hypothesis? If so, which version(s)? Why?
6.   The weak form and semi–strong form of the efficient markets hypothesis imply that certain kinds of analysis of securities and prices are not useful. Explain these implications and their impact on the securities industry.
7.   It is often said that the CAPM and the EMH are tested together. Why is this the case? Would it be better to test each theory by itself? Why? Why aren't the two theories tested separately?
8.   Hot Stock, Inc., is trading at this moment for $6 on the NYSE and $6.75 on the Pacific Exchange. What exact transactions would you make to earn an arbitrage profit? Assume that you will trade 100 shares. How much profit would the arbitrage strategy generate?
9.   If persistent arbitrage opportunities were available, what would this imply about the CAPM? Explain.

10. Assume that an investor earned more than the S&P 500 for five years in a row. Can we conclude that this investor beat the market? Why or why not?
11. What is the relationship between the random walk hypothesis and the efficient markets hypothesis? Is the random walk hypothesis true?
12. Assume that researchers find a statistically significant tendency for price increases to be followed by price increases in stock trading. Can this information be used to generate a superior risk–adjusted return? Why or why not?
13. What is a "market anomaly" and why might it be important?
14. For the APT, assume that there is only one factor and it is the amount of systematic risk that a stock or portfolio has. What is the relationship between this version of the APT and the CAPM?

CFA Questions

All CFA examination questions are reprinted, with permission, from the Level I *1992–1994, CFA Candidate Study and Examination Program Review*. Copyright 1992–1994, Association for Investment Management and Research, Charlottesville, Va. All rights reserved.

A. An efficient market is one in which:
   a. transactions costs are low and liquidity is high.
   b. good fundamental analysis consistently produces superior portfolios.
   c. information is rapidly disseminated and reflected in prices.
   d. modern electronic communications speed trading.

B. The weak form of the efficient market hypothesis contradicts:
   a. technical analysis, but supports fundamental analysis as valid.
   b. fundamental analysis, but supports technical analysis as valid.
   c. both fundamental and technical analysis.
   d. technical analysis, but is silent on the possibility of successful fundamental analysis.

C. Two basic assumptions of technical analysis are that security prices adjust:
   a. gradually to new information, and study of the economic environment provides an indication of future market movements.
   b. rapidly to new information, and study of the economic environment provides an indication of future market movements.
   c. rapidly to new information, and market prices are determined by the interaction between supply and demand.
   d. gradually to new information, and prices are determined by the interaction between supply and demand.

D. The feature of arbitrage pricing theory (APT) that offers the greatest potential advantage over the CAPM is the:

a. identification of anticipated changes in production, inflation, and term structure of interest rates as key factors explaining the risk–return relationship.

b. superior measurement of the risk–free rate of return over historical time periods.

c. variability of coefficients of sensitivity to the APT factors for a given asset over time.

d. use of several factors instead of a single market index to explain the risk–return relationship.

E. Capital asset pricing theory asserts that portfolio returns are best explained by:

a. economic factors.

b. specific risk.

c. systematic risk.

d. diversification.

F. "Random Walk" occurs when:

a. past information is used in predicting future prices.

b. future price changes are uncorrelated with past price changes.

c. stock prices respond slowly to both new and old information.

d. stock price changes are random but predictable.

G. According to the efficient market hypothesis:

a. high–beta stocks are consistently overpriced.

b. low–beta stocks are consistently overpriced.

c. positive alphas on stocks will quickly disappear.

d. negative alpha stocks consistently yield low returns for arbitragers.

H. Assume that both X and Y are well–diversified portfolios and the risk–free rate is 8%.

Portfolio	Expected Return	Beta
X	16%	1.00
Y	12%	0.25

In this situation, you would conclude that portfolios X and Y:

a. are in equilibrium.

b. offer an arbitrage opportunity.

c. are both underpriced.

d. are both fairly priced.

I. The semi–strong form of the efficient market hypothesis asserts that stock prices:

a. fully reflect all historical price information.

b. fully reflect all publicly available information.

c. fully reflect all relevant information including insider information.

d. may be predictable.

J. Assume that a company announces an unexpectedly large cash dividend to its shareholders. In an efficient market *without* information leakage, one might expect:

    a.   an abnormal price change at the announcement.

    b.   an abnormal price increase before the announcement.

    c.   an abnormal price decrease after the announcement.

K. Which *one* of the following would provide evidence *against* the semi–strong form of the efficient market theory?

    a.   Low P/E stocks tend to have positive abnormal returns.

    b.   Trend analysis is fruitless in determining stock prices.

    c.   All investors have learned to exploit signals about future performance.

    d.   In any year, approximately 50% of pension funds outperform the market.

L. The Arbitrage Pricing Theory (APT) differs from the Capital Asset Pricing Model (CAPM) because the APT:

    a.   places more emphasis on market risk.

    b.   minimizes the importance of diversification.

    c.   recognizes multiple unsystematic risk factors.

    d.   recognizes multiple systematic risk factors.

M. Which *one* of the following is *not* a criticism of Beta?

    a.   Different calculation methods yield differing Beta numbers.

    b.   Estimated Betas on individual stocks are unstable.

    c.   In some periods, low Beta stocks outperform high Beta stocks.

    d.   Wide–scale usage has reduced the effectiveness of the Beta measure.

N. Which statement about portfolio diversification is correct?

    a.   Proper diversification can reduce or eliminate systematic risk.

    b.   The risk–reducing benefits of diversification do not occur meaningfully until at least 10–15 individual securities have been purchased.

    c.   Because diversification reduces a portfolio's risk, it necessarily reduces the portfolio's expected return.

    d.   Typically, as more securities are added to a portfolio, total risk would be expected to fall at a decreasing rate.

O.   a.   **List** and **briefly define** the *three* forms of the Efficient Markets Hypothesis.

    b.   **Discuss** the role of a portfolio manager in a perfectly efficient market.

P. **Identify** and **briefly discuss** *three* criticisms of beta as used in the Capital Asset Pricing Model (CAPM).

Q. **Briefly explain** whether investors should expect a higher return from holding Portfolio A versus Portfolio B under the Capital Asset Pricing Model (CAPM). Assume that both portfolios are fully diversified.

	Portfolio A	Portfolio B
Systematic risk (beta)	1.0	1.0
Specific risk for each individual security	High	Low

Suggested REALDATA Exercises

The following *REALDATA* exercises explore the concepts developed in this chapter: Exercises 28, 29, 33, 34.

Suggested Readings

Alexander, J. C. and P. P. Peterson, "Profitability of a Trading Strategy Based on Unexpected Earnings," *Financial Analysts Journal*, 45:4, July/August 1989, pp. 65–71.

Ariel, R. A., "High Stock Returns before Holidays: Existence and Evidence on Possible Causes," *Journal of Finance*, 45:5, December 1990, pp. 1611–1626.

Black, Fischer, "Beta and Return," *The Journal of Portfolio Management*, 20:1, Fall 1993, pp. 8–18.

DeBondt, W. F. M. and R. Thaler, "Anomalies: A Mean–Reverting Walk Down Wall Street," *Journal of Economic Perspectives*, 3:1, Winter 1989, pp. 189–202.

DeBondt, W. F. M. and R. H. Thaler, "Further Evidence On Investor Overreaction and Stock Market Seasonality," *Journal of Finance*, 42:3, July 1987, pp. 557–581.

Dyl, E. A. and J. D. Schatzberg, "The Super Bowl Phenomenon: Does the NFL Drive the Market?" *American Association of Individual Investors*, 12:1, January 1990, pp. 7–9.

Fama Eugene F., and Kenneth R. French, "The Cross–Section of Expected Stock Returns," *Journal of Finance*, 47:2, June 1992, pp. 427–465.

Fama, Eugene F. and James MacBeth, "Risk, Return and Equilibrium: Empirical Tests," *Journal of Political Economy*, 81, 1973, pp. 607–636.

Fortune, P., "Stock Market Efficiency: An Autopsy?" Federal Reserve Bank of Boston *New England Economic Review*, March/April 1991, pp. 17–40.

Garber, P. M., "Who Put the Mania in Tulipmania?" *The Journal of Portfolio Management*, 16:1, Fall 1989, pp. 53–60.

Grinold, R., A. Rudd, and D. Stefek, "Global Factors: Fact or Fiction?" *The Journal of Portfolio Management*, 16:1, Fall 1989, pp. 79–88.

Kato, K., S. L. Schwartz, and W. T. Ziemba, "Day of the Week Effects in Japanese Stocks," *Japanese Capital Markets*, New York: Harper & Row, 1990, pp. 249–281.

Lakonishok, J. and E. Maberly, "The Weekend Effect: Trading Patterns of Individual and Institutional Investors," *Journal of Finance*, 45:1, March 1990, pp. 231–243.

Lee, C. M. C., A. Shleifer, and R. H. Thaler, "Investor Sentiment and the Close–End Fund Puzzle," *Journal of Finance*, 46:1, March 1991, pp. 75–109.

Pettengill, G. N. and B. D. Jordan, "The Overreaction Hypothesis, Firm Size, and Stock Market Seasonality," *The Journal of Portfolio Management*, 16:3, Spring 1990, pp. 60–64.

Shiller, R. J., *Market Volatility*, Cambridge, MA: The MIT Press, 1989.

Shleifer, A. and L. H. Summers, "The Noise Trader Approach to Finance," *Journal of Economic Perspectives*, 4:2, Spring 1990, pp. 19–33.

Shukla, R. and C. Trzcinka, "Research on Risk and Return: Can Measures of Risk Explain Anything?" *The Journal of Portfolio Management*, 17:3, Spring 1991, pp. 15–21.

Thaler, R. H., "Anomalies: Seasonal Movements in Security Prices II: Weekend, Holiday, Turn of the Month, and Intraday Effects," *Journal of Economic Perspectives*, 1:1, Fall 1987, pp. 169–177.

Thaler, R. H., "Anomalies: The January Effect," *Journal of Economic Perspectives*, 1:1, Summer 1987, pp. 197–201.

Thaler, R. H., "Anomalies: The Winner's Curse," *Journal of Economic Perspectives*, 2:1, Winter 1988, pp. 191–202.

Zarowin, P., "Does the Stock Market Overreact to Corporate Earnings Information?" *Journal of Finance*, 44:5, December 1989, pp. 1385–1399.

CHAPTER SIXTEEN

Investment Companies and Performance Evaluation

Overview

The prospective investor, faced with thousands of stocks and bonds to choose from, may find the task bewildering. An individual investor cannot learn about all of the different firms and the investment prospects associated with their securities. If one also wishes to consider both international securities and government securities of various types, then the task becomes even more hopeless. How can one intelligently form a portfolio faced with such information overload?

One possible answer for many investors is to place funds with an **investment company**. An investment company is a firm that collects funds from a wide group of investors. These collected funds are then invested in a portfolio of securities, and each of the investors in the fund has title to a fractional share of all of the investments in the portfolio. The staff of the investment company manages the portfolio and tries to invest the funds where they will earn a high return for the level of risk.

These investment companies come in two forms, closed–end investment companies and mutual funds, each of which will be discussed in detail. Essentially, the difference between the two forms depends on how they accept funds for investment. A **closed–end company** accepts funds only at its creation, and the funds contributed at that point form the investment base that the company has to invest throughout its life. A **mutual fund**, by contrast, is always ready to receive money from new investors. The new funds are then used to expand the portfolio. These differences in the ways in which money flows into the investment companies have far–reaching implications, which are considered in detail later in this chapter.

After explaining the institutional features of investment companies and the ways in which they are regulated and taxed, this chapter discusses performance evaluation for mutual funds. As mentioned throughout this book, there are important advantages to investing in a diversified portfolio, rather than merely committing funds to one or two favorite stocks. We have also seen evidence that markets are quite efficient in the weak and semi–strong versions of the efficient markets hypothesis.

Because investment companies constitute well–diversified and professionally managed portfolios, might it be possible for them to outperform the market for the level of risk that they bear? This might be a reasonable hope for two reasons. First, mutual funds are well–diversified, so their level of unsystematic risk should be very low. Second, investment companies hire professional security analysts. If these analysts have genuine stock selecting skills, this should be revealed by the superior performance of the investment company. These issues are examined to complete the discussion of the CAPM, the EMH, and what investors can reasonably expect from their portfolios.

General Features of Investment Companies

Investment companies are essentially a phenomenon of the twentieth century. Overall, the growth of investment companies has been very strong. During the period from 1940 to 1993, investment companies grew at an annual rate of 14.9 percent, increasing the total size of assets 1,525 times. However, as Table 16.1 indicates, the strong growth has not been shared equally between closed–end companies and mutual funds. Mutual funds have increased their size more than 3,370 times during this period, while closed–end companies have had an asset increase of fewer than 180 times. As a result, the mutual fund asset pool is almost 14 times as large as that of closed–end companies. This vast difference in growth, coupled with the fact that the closed–end companies dominated in 1940, clearly shows a marked preference for mutual funds.

This preference for mutual funds must be due to the difference in the way the funds are invested. In fact, mutual funds have the natural advantage in growth,

Table 16.1

**Investment Company Assets
($ millions)**

Year	Mutual Funds	Closed–End Companies	Total
1940	448	614	1,062
1950	2,531	872	3,403
1960	17,383	2,084	19,467
1970	50,646	4,024	54,679
1980	138,333	8,053	146,386
1990	990,177	55,272	1,045,449
1993	1,510,047	110,000	1,620,047

Source: Wiesenberger Financial Services, *Investment Companies 1994*, New York: Warren, Gorham & Lamont, 1994.

since they are open–ended. Their ability to continue to receive funds at any point makes growth substantially easier. Closed–end companies, once established, can grow in asset size only through successful investment of the originally contributed funds. The closed–end segment of the investment company industry can only grow through the creation of additional closed–end companies.

Investment companies, whether closed–end companies or mutual funds, share a number of common features in their organizational form. When soliciting funds, both closed–end and open–end companies must provide a prospectus to prospective investors. This is the same requirement faced by firms planning to issue stocks or bonds, and the investment company must face the same process described in Chapter 4. The closed–end company needs to circulate a prospectus only when it is being established. Once founded, the closed–end company will not receive any more funds from the public, so there is no further need for a prospectus. The mutual fund, by contrast, needs to revise and distribute a prospectus continually, since it is always prepared to accept new funds.

In mutual funds and closed–end companies, investors purchase shares. A share is simply a title to a fraction of the assets of the investment company. The total assets of the company, minus the liabilities, constitute the **net asset value**. The **net asset value per share** is simply the total net asset value of the company, divided by the number of shares outstanding. In the case of the closed–end company, the number of shares is constant. For a mutual fund, the number of shares may increase or decrease.

Both kinds of investment companies perform the function of investment advisers and clerical staff. The investment company must keep accurate records of ownership of shares in the company and provide reports and payments to the shareholders. The reports may consist of monthly statements of the account, along with quarterly and annual reports of the fund's performance and financial standing. Investment companies also make payments to their shareholders. These may take the form of dividends or of capital gains distributions. The dividend is essentially like a cash dividend paid on the common stock of any corporation. The capital gains distribution is made for the purposes of taxation.

Essentially, the owners of a mutual fund are the indirect owners of the securities in the mutual fund's portfolio. If a shareholder were to manage his or her own portfolio, and to trade securities, he or she would realize profits and losses on those transactions. These profits and losses would generate tax liabilities. Investment companies are typically organized so that they do not pay taxes themselves, but the shareholders pay the taxes. The capital gains distribution is a bookkeeping technique for keeping track of the tax liability of the share owners.

The management of an investment company takes on the function of the investment advisor by making all of the decisions about which securities will be held in the firm's portfolio. In committing funds to an investment company, the investor puts his faith in the investment capabilities of the firm's management. The company charges a fee for this service, which is stated as a percentage of the net asset value held by the company. Usually, this fee is 1/2 to 1 percent annually.

In addition to these common features, there are important differences between closed–end companies and mutual funds as two kinds of companies.

Further, within each category, there is a wide variety of difference as well. This is particularly true among mutual funds. Given the vastly greater size of mutual funds, the following discussion of closed–end companies is rather brief, allowing more attention to the mutual funds.

Advantages of Investment Companies

The investment company industry is clearly quite large, with large fees being earned by company managers. To justify these fees, managers must offer something of value to attract investors.

Diversification.   One of the most important benefits of investment companies is the fact that they provide a ready–made portfolio for the investor. A small investor does not have enough funds to construct his own portfolio of 20 to 30 stocks without incurring very large transaction costs on a percentage basis. If the investor wants to hold 20 stocks, and the average stock price is $50 per share, the investor would need $100,000 to avoid trading in odd lots. For many investors, this is too large an amount to commit to the stock market. Providing a diversified portfolio to very small investors is probably the main benefit that investment companies provide.

Clerical Function.   The second clear benefit provided by investment companies is the clerical and management function. Managing a portfolio of 20 stocks is a time–consuming task, with much bookkeeping. The investment company achieves important economies of scale in this function that benefit the individual investor.

Professional Management.   A third possible benefit, and one that is often claimed by investment company managers, is providing professional investment advice. One of the key rationales for using a professional money manager is to capitalize on his or her greater knowledge of the market. However, it is not clear that investment companies really succeed in providing this benefit to their clients. As a group, on a risk–adjusted basis, investment company managers are not able to substantiate their claim to having expertise in picking winning securities. While the group may not be able to demonstrate such expertise, it is still possible that particular managers may really have expertise, nonetheless. This issue is examined in greater detail later in this chapter.

Closed–End Investment Companies

The most striking fact about closed–end investment companies is their refusal to accept new funds for investment. Once the original shares are issued, no more shares can ever come into existence. Further, the investment company itself will not redeem shares for their owners. Instead, shares of closed–end companies trade in a public market for whatever price the laws of supply and demand allow.

Intrinsic Value of Closed–End Funds

Since virtually 100 percent of the company's assets are in securities, it might seem that the closed–end shares would trade in the marketplace for an amount equal to the net asset value per share. This is not the case, however. Since the shareholders cannot redeem the shares for their net asset value, the price of the shares is free to wander away from the net asset value. In particular, the share price may be more or less than the net asset value. If the share price exceeds the net asset value, it is said to be at a **premium**, while a share price below the net asset value is at a **discount**.

Discounts and Premiums on Closed–End Funds

Figure 16.1 presents quotations for closed–end companies. The net asset value per share is reported for each company, followed by the stock price. The final column of figures shows the premium, or discount, on the stock price. Shares of closed–end funds often sell at a discount to their net asset value. These discounts tend to be persistent and frequently large. At times this average discount has been as large as 25 percent. At the end of 1993, the average discount was about 4 percent. While the factors that determine discounts are not perfectly understood, they do appear to be related to taxes and past performance.[1]

Recently, new research on discounts and premiums has adopted the noise trader approach to explaining this phenomenon. Charles Lee, Andrei Shleifer, and Richard Thaler cite four disturbing facts about discounts and premiums on closed–end funds:[2]

1. New funds appear on the market at a premium and move rapidly to a discount.
2. Closed–end funds usually trade at substantial discounts relative to their net asset values.
3. Discounts (and premiums) are subject to wide variation, both over time and across funds.

---

[1]See Morris Mendelson, "Closed–End Fund Discounts Revisited," *The Financial Review*, 1978, pp. 48–72, and Hans R. Stoll, "Discounts and Premiums on Shares of Diversified Closed–End Investment Funds," Working Paper No. 11–73, The Wharton School, University of Pennsylvania, 1978.

[2]C. M. C. Lee, A. Shleifer, and R. H. Thaler, "Anomalies: Closed–End Mutual Funds," *Journal of Economic Perspectives*, 4:4, Fall 1990, pp. 153–164. See also their related paper, C. M. C. Lee, A. Shleifer, and R. H. Thaler, "Investor Sentiment and the Close–End Fund Puzzle," *Journal of Finance*, 46:1, March 1991, pp. 75–109. Finally, for an accessible treatment of these issues, see J. Bradford De Long and Andrei Shleifer, "Closed–End Fund Discounts," *The Journal of Portfolio Management*, 18:2, Winter 1992, pp. 46–53.

Figure 16.1

Quotations for Closed–End Investment Companies

CLOSED-END FUNDS

Friday, June 24, 1994

Closed-end funds sell a limited number of shares and invest the proceeds in securities. Unlike open-end funds, closed-ends generally do not buy their shares back from investors who wish to cash in their holdings. Instead, fund shares trade on a stock exchange. The following list, provided by Lipper Analytical Services, shows the exchange where each fund trades (A: American; C: Chicago; N: NYSE; O: Nasdaq; T: Toronto; z: does not trade on an exchange). The data also include the fund's most recent net asset value, its closing share price on the day NAV was calculated, and the percentage difference between the market price and the NAV (often called the premium or discount). For equity funds, the final column provides 52-week returns based on market prices plus dividends. For bond funds, the final column shows the past 12 months' income distributions as a percentage of the current market price. Footnotes appear after a fund's name. a: the NAV and market price are ex dividend. b: the NAV is fully diluted. c: NAV, market price and premium or discount are as of Thursday's close. d: NAV, market price and premium or discount are as of Wednesday's close. e: NAV assumes rights offering is fully subscribed. v: NAV is converted at the commercial Rand rate. y: NAV and market price are in Canadian dollars. All other footnotes refer to unusual circumstances; explanations for those that appear can be found at the bottom of this list. N/A signifies that the information is not available or not applicable.

Fund Name	Stock Exch	NAV	Market Price	Prem /Disc	52 week Market Return
General Equity Funds					
Adams Express	N	18.74	17¼	− 8.0	−4.0
Baker Fentress	N	19.34	16¾	−13.4	9.8
Bergstrom Cap	A	90.27	88	− 2.5	−5.5
Blue Chip Value	N	7.39	7	− 5.3	−5.5
Central Secs	A	17.92	16⅝	− 7.2	25.0
Charles Allmon	N	10.31	9⅝	− 6.6	1.1
Engex	A	10.03	8⅛	−19.0	−14.5
Equus II -c	A	19.20	13⅞	−27.7	26.6
Gabelli Equity	N	10.40	11	+ 5.8	14.2
General American	N	22.44	20⅛	−10.3	−4.7
Inefficient Mkt	A	11.62	9⅝	−17.2	−1.3
Jundt Growth	N	13.23	12¾	− 3.6	−3.4
Liberty All-Star	N	9.46	10¼	+ 8.4	5.9
Morgan Gr Sm Cap	N	10.50	9⅝	− 8.3	−1.0
NAIC Growth -c	O	10.86	9⅜	−13.7	−0.3
Royce Value	N	13.10	12⅛	− 7.4	3.7
Salomon SBF	N	13.83	12⅜	−10.5	9.8
Source Capital	N	39.00	40⅝	+ 4.2	−8.1
Spectra	O	16.76	14½	−13.5	13.8
Tri-Continental -a	N	25.79	22⅛	−14.2	−0.6
Z-Seven	O	15.94	16½	+ 3.5	2.7
Zweig	N	10.53	12⅝	+19.9	7.2
Specialized Equity Funds					
Alliance Gl Env	N	11.09	9¼	−16.6	1.4
C&S Realty	A	9.20	9⅞	+ 7.3	12.3
C&S Total Rtn	N	13.97	14⅜	+ 2.9	N/A
Counsellors Tand	N	14.51	12⅜	−14.7	−11.5
Asia Pacific	N	14.54	17⅝	+21.2	41.1
Asia Tigers	N	12.48	11¾	− 5.8	N/A
Austria	N	10.36	9	−13.1	15.5
BGR Prec Metals -cy	T	17.70	16¼	− 8.2	39.8
Brazil -c	N	21.98	22⅛	+ 0.7	35.1
Brazilian Equity -c	N	15.48	17¾	+14.7	37.1
Cdn Genl Inv -cy	T	38.07	29	−23.8	−1.0
Cdn Wrld Fd Ltd -cy	T	4.82	3¾	−22.2	N/A
Central Canada -c	A	5.00	5⅜	+ 7.5	10.5
Chile	N	46.77	43⅝	− 6.7	43.0
China	N	14.43	16⅝	+15.2	11.7
Clemente Global -c	N	11.88	10¼	−13.7	19.5
Emer Mkts Grow	z	57.91	N/A	N/A	N/A
Emerging Mexico	N	17.59	17¼	− 1.9	38.9
Emerging Tigers	N	14.26	12¾	−10.6	N/A
Europe	N	12.72	11⅝	− 8.6	14.6
European Warrant -c	N	N/A	11⅝	N/A	45.6
Fidelity Em Asia	N	14.35	12¾	−11.1	N/A
First Australia -a	A	11.18	10½	− 6.1	41.2
First Iberian	A	8.58	7⅛	−17.0	1.8
First Israel	N	10.48	12⅝	+20.5	1.3
First Philippine	N	23.31	18⅝	−20.1	47.7
France Growth	N	11.53	10	−13.3	−1.8
GT Devel Mkts	N	12.45	11⅛	−10.6	N/A
GT Gr Europe	N	14.57	13	−10.8	19.0
Germany Fund	N	12.76	11	−13.8	6.2
Germany, Emer	N	9.50	7¾	−18.4	12.7
Germany, Future	N	17.20	14½	−15.7	20.2
Germany, New	N	14.15	11⅛	−21.4	17.4
Global Small Cap	A	13.12	12¼	− 6.6	N/A
Greater China	N	17.13	17¾	+ 3.6	16.7
Growth Fd Spain	N	12.03	9⅝	−20.0	4.1
Herzfeld Caribb	O	5.00	6	+20.0	N/A
India Fund	N	14.37	12¼	−14.8	N/A
India Growth -d	N	22.45	22⅜	− 0.3	59.4
Indonesia	N	10.76	13¼	+23.1	19.1
Irish Inv	N	9.84	8⅜	−14.9	7.2
Italy	N	10.91	11	+ 0.8	12.0
Jakarta Growth	N	8.85	9⅛	+ 3.1	6.5
Japan Equity	N	15.49	16	+ 3.3	38.4
Japan OTC Equity	N	11.69	12¼	+ 4.8	40.0
Jardine Fl China	N	13.80	15⅝	+13.2	11.3
Jardine Fl India -c	N	15.41	14½	− 5.9	N/A
Korea	N	18.56	21⅞	+17.9	40.9
Korea Equity	N	10.31	10¾	+ 4.3	N/A
Korean Inv	N	13.48	14⅛	+ 4.8	16.5
Latin Amer Disc	N	19.93	19⅝	− 1.5	39.7
Latin Amer Eq	N	20.71	20⅞	+ 0.8	45.4
Latin Amer Inv	N	23.82	22	− 7.6	35.0
Malaysia	N	21.13	20½	− 3.0	26.4
Mexico -c	N	29.33	28	− 4.5	34.1
Mexico Eqty&Inc -c	N	19.11	20	+ 4.7	44.5
Morgan St Africa	N	13.09	11¼	−14.1	N/A
Morgan St Em	N	23.50	25⅞	+10.1	45.1
Morgan St India	N	15.17	13⅛	−13.5	N/A
New South Africa	N	15.10	13	−13.9	N/A

Source: *The Wall Street Journal*, June 27, 1994. Reprinted by permission of *The Wall Street Journal*, © (1994) Dow Jones & Company, Inc. All rights reserved worldwide.

4. When closed–end funds are terminated, either through merger, liquidation, or conversion to an open–end fund, prices converge to net asset values.

Lee, Shleifer, and Thaler suggest that smart money traders have limited opportunities to trade to exploit departures from net asset value. First, there is little way to arbitrage the differential. Second, the supply of investors willing to make long–term bets against prices that depart from net asset values is quite limited. These factors allow persistent and wide divergences between net asset values and the prices of closed–end fund shares.

Mutual Funds: Growth and Diversity

Since 1940, the total asset size of mutual funds has grown very rapidly. In addition to this growth in assets, the industry has grown in two other important dimensions. First, the number of mutual funds has increased dramatically, and second, there are now many more types of mutual funds. From only 68 mutual funds in 1940, the industry has grown to more than 3,100 now.

There are also different types of mutual funds. In 1940, there were principally only stock, bond, and income mutual funds. By the 1980s, mutual funds specializing in money market instruments and municipal bonds had also emerged. These differences are important, since each mutual fund must specify the kind of investment strategy that it intends to follow. Table 16.2 gives a basic classification of some of the major types of mutual funds.

In its prospectus, each mutual fund is required to state its investment objectives and to follow that plan in the management of its investment strategy. For example, the T. Rowe Price Growth and Income Fund recently stated its investment objective in the following terms:

> The fund seeks to provide investors with long–term growth of their capital, a reasonable amount of current income, and a growing level of income. To achieve these objectives, the Fund will invest primarily in income–producing equity securities which have prospects for growth of both capital and dividend income. Up to 30 percent of the assets may be invested in convertible and corporate debt securities, preferred stocks, and securities of foreign issuers when consistent with the Fund's objectives. The Fund may also, to a limited extent, lend portfolio securities. While the Fund will ordinarily remain substantially invested in equity securities, it may, for defensive purposes, establish and maintain reserves in money market instruments including repurchase agreements with banks and broker–dealers.

In addition, there are a number of other kinds of specialized mutual funds. Some focus on international securities, while others focus on stocks of emerging companies, securities in the energy field, and other specialties. The break–up of AT&T has even led to a mutual fund that holds all of the new telephone companies in the same proportions as they were valued before the break–up. This gives investors who liked the old way of holding telephone securities an easy way of doing so. Not surprisingly, this new mutual fund has been dubbed the "Humpty Dumpty Fund."

Table 16.2

Types of Mutual Funds

Aggressive Growth

A mutual fund which seeks maximum capital appreciation through the use of investment techniques involving greater than ordinary risk, such as borrowing money in order to provide leverage, short selling, hedging, options, and warrants.

Growth

A mutual fund whose primary investment objective is long–term growth of capital. It invests principally in common stocks with growth potential.

Growth and Income

A mutual fund whose aim is to provide for a degree of both income and long–term growth.

Balanced

A mutual fund which has an investment policy of "balancing" its portfolio, generally by including bonds, preferred stocks, and common stocks.

Option/Income

The investment objective of these funds is to seek a high current return by investing primarily in dividend–paying common stocks on which call options are traded on national securities exchanges. Current return generally consists of dividends, premiums from expired call options, net short–term gains from sales of portfolio securities on exercises of options or otherwise, and any profits from closing purchase transactions.

Income

A mutual fund whose primary investment objective is current income rather than growth of capital. It usually invests in stocks and bonds that normally pay higher dividends and interest.

Corporate Bond

A mutual fund whose portfolio consists primarily of bonds. The emphasis of such funds is normally on income rather than growth.

Municipal Bond

A mutual fund which invests in a broad range of tax–exempt bonds issued by states, cities, and other local governments. The interest obtained from these bonds is passed through to shareholders free of federal tax. The funds's primary objective is current tax–free income.

Short–Term Municipal Bond

These funds invest in municipal securities with relatively short maturities. They are also known as Tax–Exempt Money Market Funds.

Money Market

Also called a liquid asset or cash fund, it is a mutual fund whose primary objective is to make higher interest securities available to investors who want immediate income and high investment safety. This is accomplished through the purchase of high–yield money market instruments, such as U.S. government securities, bank certificates of deposit, and commercial paper.

Source: Investment Company Institute, *1991 Mutual Fund Fact Book*, Washington, DC: Investment Company Institute, 1991, pp. 12–13.

Table 16.3

██████████

Percentage of Funds Invested by Type of Mutual Fund

Type of Fund	1980	1990	1993
Money Market	55.3	38.8	22.2
Short–Term Municipal Bonds	1.4	7.8	5.0
Equity Funds	30.4	23.0	36.1
Bond and Income Funds	12.9	30.4	36.7

Source: Investment Company Institute, *1994 Mutual Fund Fact Book*, Washington, DC: Investment Company Institute, 1994.

Without doubt, one of the most important features in the development of mutual funds in the recent past has been the emergence of the money market mutual fund—a mutual fund that holds money market securities. From their inception in 1974, money market mutual funds have come to dominate the market. Correspondingly, money market mutual funds have come to dominate in asset size as well, even though that dominance is currently not as strong as it was in recent years. Table 16.3 shows the distribution of funds by different types of mutual funds in 1980, 1990, and 1993.

Ownership of Mutual Fund Shares

Along with the growth in money market mutual funds, the ownership mix of mutual funds has been changing dramatically as well. Mutual funds have traditionally been regarded as investment vehicles particularly well suited to small investors, usually individuals. About 50 percent of all accounts have a value less than $10,000. However, institutional investors have become very active in money market funds, even spurring the creation of money market funds designed specifically for institutional investors.

Load versus No–Load Mutual Funds

Compared with closed–end investment companies, two of the main reasons for the rapid growth of mutual funds are their open–ended character, or the readiness to accept new funds, and the ease of redemption. The owner of shares in a mutual fund may withdraw the money invested in the fund at any time by returning the shares to the mutual fund and receiving the net asset value of those shares, or at least an amount very close to the net asset value. This makes a mutual fund a very liquid form of investment.

In handling investments and redemptions, mutual funds themselves fall into two main categories, however. These are called load and no–load funds. A **load fund** imposes a sales charge to invest in the fund. Usually, this load charge is a percentage of the invested assets and is charged when the investment is made.

Some load funds charge a redemption fee as well. For example, $10,000 invested in a load mutual fund with a 7 percent sales charge would yield a net asset value of only $9,300 for the investor. The $700 load charge would go to pay for the salesperson's commission and other expenses involved in making the sale. Although the stated load is 7 percent, the effective load is really higher. In this example, one pays $700 as a sales charge and receives shares with a net asset value of $9,300. From this perspective, the load is 7.53 percent of the net asset value actually received.

By contrast, a **no–load fund** imposes no sales charge. A $10,000 investment in a no–load fund yields $10,000 worth of net asset value. Load funds charge their fee to provide compensation for salespersons, essentially. No–load funds operate only by mail and have no sales force. Since there is no persuasive evidence of a difference in performance, no–load funds seem to have a clear advantage for the investor. In spite of this fact, load funds are purchased about as frequently, due to the phenomenon cited in the adage: "Mutual funds are sold and not bought." Presumably, this applies to load mutual funds.

Costs of Investing in Mutual Funds

In addition to a load, mutual funds also charge other fees for the services they offer. The management of a mutual fund performs many tasks in the arena of record keeping and managing the portfolio. Expenses for these services must be borne ultimately by the investors in the fund. To finance these fees, each account is subject to an annual charge, which is a percentage of assets. As Table 16.4 shows, these

Table 16.4

Expense Ratios by Type of Mutual Fund

	Average Expense Ratios		
	Highest 10%	Lowest 10%	All Funds
Fund Objective			
Stock Funds	1.65%	0.47%	1.02%
Bond Funds	1.60	0.52	0.96
Municipal Bond Funds	1.37	0.44	0.79
Money Market Funds	1.08	0.39	0.68
Size of Fund			
Less than $50 million	1.71%	0.54%	1.13%
$50–250 million*	1.24	0.50	0.83
More than $250 million	0.97	0.36	0.63

*Sample excludes funds with expense ratios of 2 percent or more.

Source: "Mutual Funds," in *Encyclopedia of Investments*, Marshall E. Blume and Jack P. Friedman, (eds.), Boston: Warren, Gorham, and Lamont, 1982, p. 516.

expenses differ in size by the type and size of the mutual fund. Usually they fall in the range of 1/2 to 1 percent of the assets per year. By far, the largest percentage of these fees goes to the managers of the portfolio. This management service is often

Figure 16.2

Quotations for Mutual Funds

LIPPER INDEXES

Tuesday, July 05, 1994

Indexes	Close	Prelim. Prev.	Percentage chg. since Wk ago	Dec. 31
Capital Appreciation .	399.01	− 0.05	+ 0.40	− 7.35
Growth Fund	729.64	+ 0.11	+ 0.23	− 4.79
Small Co. Growth	401.64	− 0.26	+ 1.00	− 8.93
Growth & Income	1133.91	+ 0.11	+ 0.11	− 2.34
Equity Income Fd	768.39	+ 0.15	+ 0.14	− 2.20
Science & Tech Fd	300.96	− 0.30	+ 0.44	− 8.84
International Fund ...	473.00	+ 1.06	+ 1.56	− 0.55
Gold Fund	191.79	− 1.00	− 0.65	− 11.96
Balanced Fund	834.00	+ 0.14	− 0.13	− 3.42

Source: Lipper Analytical Services, Inc.

Tuesday, July 5, 1994

Ranges for investment companies, with daily price data supplied by the National Association of Securities Dealers and performance and cost calculations by Lipper Analytical Services Inc. The NASD requires a mutual fund to have at least 1,000 shareholders or net assets of $25 million before being listed. Detailed explanatory notes appear elsewhere on this page.

	Inv. Obj.	NAV	Offer Price	NAV Chg.	YTD	13 wks	3 yrs R
AAL Mutual:							
Bond p	BIN	9.58	10.06	+0.01	−4.6	−1.2	+7.1 D
CaGr p	GRO	14.08	14.78	+0.02	−5.9	−0.1	+6.6 D
MuBd p	GLM	10.50	11.02	...	−5.1	−0.5	+7.0 D
SmCoStk p	SML	8.89	9.33	−0.08	−18.1	−14.1	NS ..
Util	SEC	9.44	9.91	−0.02	NS	NA	NS ..
AARP Invst:							
BalS&B	S&B	14.33	NL	...	NS	+0.9	NS ..
CaGr	GRO	30.43	NL	+0.02	−11.1	−3.5	+10.0 C
GiniM	BND	14.85	NL	+0.03	−3.0	−0.6	+6.3 D
Gthinc	G&I	32.53	NL	−0.02	+0.1	+3.0	+13.3 A
HQ Bd	BND	15.29	NL	+0.02	−4.9	−1.5	+7.7 C
TxFBd	ISM	17.17	NL	+0.01	−5.1	0.0	+7.9 B
ABT Funds:							
Emrg p	CAP	12.57	13.20	−0.01	−15.2	−11.9	+16.3 A
FL HI	MFL	10.11	10.61	...	−2.6	+1.0	NS ..
FL TF	MFL	10.68	11.21	+0.01	−4.3	+0.1	+8.2 B
Gthin p	G&I	10.27	10.78	+0.02	−5.2	+0.8	+5.4 E
Utilin p	SEC	11.02	11.57	+0.01	−10.9	−3.1	+6.7 D
AHA Funds:							
Balan	S&B	11.69	11.69	+0.01	−3.3	−0.9	+9.6 C
Full	BND	9.49	NL	...	−4.1	−1.1	+8.4 B
Lim	BST	10.10	NL	+0.01	−0.1	+0.3	+6.2 C
AIM Funds:							
AdiGv p	BST	9.63	9.73	...	−0.1	−0.2	NS ..
Agrsv p	SML	23.69	25.07	−0.02	−3.1	−4.1	+26.7 A
BalB t	S&B	15.04	15.04	+0.01	−5.9	NA	NS ..
Chart p	G&I	8.62	9.12	+0.02	−3.9	−0.8	+7.9 D
Const p	CAP	16.08	17.02	−0.03	−8.1	−6.2	+18.2 A
BalA p	S&B	15.03	15.78	+0.01	−5.5	−1.7	+12.9 A
GoScA p	BND	9.32	9.78	...	−3.7	−0.8	+6.0 E
GrthA p	GRO	10.05	10.63	−0.01	−11.2	−8.3	+3.0 E
GrthB t	GRO	10.00	10.00	+0.01	−11.6	−8.4	NS ..
HYIdA p	BHI	9.47	9.94	−0.01	−1.1	−1.8	+16.5 B
HYIdB t	BHI	9.46	9.46	−0.02	−1.5	−2.0	NS ..
IncoA p	BND	7.43	7.80	+0.01	−8.7	−3.1	+8.3 B
IntlE p	ITL	12.64	13.38	+0.14	−3.1	+0.9	NS ..

	Inv. Obj.	NAV	Offer Price	NAV Chg.	YTD	13 wks	3 yrs R
LimM p	BST	9.92	10.02	...	−0.1	+0.1	+5.4 D
MuniA p	GLM	8.09	8.49	...	−3.3	+0.5	+8.4 A
Sumit	GRO	8.95	NA	+0.01	−7.7	−4.4	+8.4 C
TeCt p	SSM	10.64	11.17	...	−3.2	+0.5	+7.9 B
TF Int	IDM	10.61	10.72	...	−1.5	+0.8	+7.0 B
UtilA p	SEC	12.14	12.85	+0.01	−11.8	−4.7	+8.6 C
UtilB t	SEC	12.13	12.13	...	−12.2	−5.0	NS ..
ValuA p	GRO	20.36	21.54	+0.03	−2.2	−3.3	+18.6 A
ValuB t	GRO	20.29	20.29	+0.03	−2.5	−3.6	NS ..
Weing p	GRO	16.23	17.17	+0.02	−5.4	−3.5	+5.4 E
AMCORE Vintage Fds:							
Equity	GRO	10.14	10.59	+0.01	−1.9	+1.3	NS ..
FxIncome	BIN	9.67	10.05	...	−3.5	−1.3	NS ..
IntdtTF	IDM	9.87	10.25	+0.01	−3.8	+0.2	NS ..
AMF Funds:							
AdiMtg	BST	9.83	9.83	...	+0.5	+0.1	NS ..
IntMtg	BND	9.43	NL	+0.01	−2.2	−0.6	+7.5 C
IntlLiq	BST	10.53	NL	...	−0.4	0.0	+6.5 B
MtgSc	BND	10.42	NL	+0.02	−2.8	−0.3	+6.6 D
ARK Funds:							
CapGr	GRO	9.72	NL	...	−9.2	−4.0	NS ..
Gr&Inc	S&B	9.87	NL	+0.02	−5.0	−1.1	NS ..
Income	BND	9.50	NL	+0.01	−2.6	−0.8	..
ASM Fd	G&I	9.42	NL	+0.02	−2.0	+1.1	+7.0 E
Accessor Fd:							
IntFxIn	BIN	11.43	NL	+0.01	−4.8	−1.4	NS ..
Mortg	BND	11.62	NL	+0.02	−2.3	−1.2	NS ..
ShtIntFx	BST	11.88	NL	+0.02	−1.5	−0.2	NS ..
Acornin	ITL	15.60	15.60	+0.12	−2.1	−1.8	NS ..
AcornF	SML	12.74	12.74	+0.01	−8.7	−3.6	+21.7 A
AdsnCa p	G&I	19.63	20.24	+0.04	−5.9	−2.3	+9.1 C
AdvCapl Bal p	S&B	9.85	NL	...	−5.4	−1.7	+3.5 E
AdvCapl Ret p	BND	9.52	NL	−0.01	−6.1	−3.0	NS ..
Advest Advant:							
Govt p	BND	8.96	8.96	...	−10.5	−2.2	+8.4 B
Gwth p	GRO	15.84	15.84	+0.02	−8.4	−3.3	+8.9 C
HY Bd p	BHI	8.75	8.75	−0.02	−1.6	−3.3	+19.7 A
Inco p	S&B	12.16	12.16	+0.02	−4.1	−1.2	+10.2 B
MuBdNal	GLM	9.23	9.23	...	−7.2	−0.1	NS ..
Spcl p	SML	18.79	18.79	−0.03	−9.6	−8.2	+16.9 B
Aetna Advisor:							
Aetna t	S&B	10.32	10.32	+0.01	NS	NS	NS ..
Bond t	BND	9.70	9.70	+0.01	NS	NS	NS ..
GrIncm t	G&I	10.63	10.63	...	NS	NS	NS ..
IntlGr t	ITL	11.18	11.18	+0.12	NS	NS	NS ..
TxFr	GLM	9.23	9.23	...	NS	NS	NS ..
Aetna Select:							
Aetna	S&B	10.33	10.33	...	−3.4	−0.7	NS ..
AsianGr	ITL	8.10	8.10	−0.02	NS	NA	NS ..
Bond	BND	9.70	9.70	+0.01	−3.9	−1.5	NS ..
Grwth	GRO	9.95	9.95	+0.03	NS	NA	NS ..
GrwIncm	G&I	10.64	10.64	+0.01	−2.8	+0.6	NS ..
IntlGr	ITL	11.20	11.20	+0.12	+0.3	+1.6	NS ..
SmCoGr	SML	9.79	9.79	+0.05	NS	NA	NS ..
Alger Funds:							
Growth t	GRO	18.64	18.64	−0.23	−10.3	−7.1	+13.1 B
IncGr t	G&I	11.16	11.16	−0.05	−15.1	−6.3	+4.2 E
MidCpGr t	GRO	10.86	10.86	−0.11	−13.5	−8.2	NS ..
SmCap t	SML	19.75	19.75	−0.21	−16.1	−7.2	+8.3 E
Alliance Cap:							
Allian p	GRO	6.45	6.74	−0.03	−5.8	−2.0	+12.9 B
Balan p	S&B	13.15	13.73	...	−5.7	−0.9	+6.9 E
BalB t	S&B	13.88	13.88	−0.03	−8.9	−3.1	+8.0 D
CnstvInv	S&B	10.32	10.32	+0.01	−5.3	−2.0	NS ..
CpBdA p	BND	12.51	13.07	+0.01	−12.2	−4.7	+14.0 A
CpBdB	BND	12.50	12.50	...	−12.5	−4.8	NS ..

provided by a company external to the mutual fund; however, the management company is also often related to the mutual fund. In addition to these expenses, which are delineated in the reports of the fund, there are other expenses, such as commissions, which are not so apparent. While these commissions may be reported in the annual report, they are not normally part of the percentage levied against each account for expenses.

Mutual Fund Quotations

Figure 16.2 presents mutual funds quotations from *The Wall Street Journal*. The quotations give the name of the mutual fund, the net asset value per share, and the offering price. If the offering price differs from the net asset value, the difference is the load charge. For no–load funds, the column showing the offering price begins with "N. L." The final column shows the change in the net asset value since the close of the preceding day's trading.

Mutual Fund Families

Another feature of the mutual fund industry shown by the quotations is the existence of families of mutual funds. These families are companies that offer a number of different types of mutual funds to span the range of possible investor needs. These families generally allow an investor in one fund to switch investment from one fund in the family to another with just a phone call. This gives investors considerable flexibility to take advantage of whatever beliefs they have about the direction of the market.

The basic idea behind this strategy is to switch funds from one fund based on beliefs about market conditions. An investor anticipating substantially higher interest rates might decide to keep money in a money market mutual fund until the higher rates develop. By contrast, an investor expecting a major surge in the stock market might switch funds to an aggressive growth or growth mutual fund.

Regulation and Taxation of Investment Companies

The tendency to bring more and more dimensions of the securities business under regulation, which characterized the 1930s, continued into the 1940s. The Investment Company Act of 1940 gave the SEC control over investment companies, both closed–end companies and mutual funds.

The act has two main purposes. First, it aims at disclosure of information to prospective investors, and second, it attempts to curb some potential abuses by managers of investment companies. The investment company must provide a prospectus to any new investor, and the terms governing the prospectus are similar to those for stocks or bonds.

Many potential abuses by management are specifically restricted by the act. For example, changing the goals of the investment company without the consent of the investors is prohibited by the act. The act also stipulates the care that must be taken to protect the securities themselves. One potential area of abuse, which is controlled by the act, stems from collusion between managers of the company and brokers and underwriters. Because of this possibility, brokers and underwriters are allowed to hold only a minority interest in these companies.

Taxation of Investment Company Returns

Many investment companies, both closed–end companies and mutual funds, are exempt from federal income taxation. The rationale for this policy is that the investment company holds the securities as an agent of the investor. If investment companies were taxed, and the individual investors in the fund were also taxed, then this would amount to double taxation. The law avoids double taxation of investment companies, but not of dividends. To qualify for this treatment, the investment company must distribute at least 90 percent of its investment company taxable income to its shareholders each year. Individuals are then taxed on the proceeds they receive from the mutual fund.

Mutual Fund Performance

Having discussed the different components of mutual fund returns, now consider how those returns compare to their risk–adjusted market return. In other words, are mutual funds able to outperform the market by earning a return that is higher than the market rate of return for the fund's level of risk? In the long run, one would expect the riskier funds to pay a higher return commensurate with their greater risk. In general, this seems to be what happens. Since 1958, growth funds, the most aggressive strategy represented, have outperformed the others. Normally, one would expect these kinds of funds to rank in the following order of decreasing performance: growth funds, growth/income funds, income funds, and balanced funds. As just observed, growth funds have succeeded in providing the highest return, and they are followed by growth/income funds, as we would expect. However, growth/income funds are followed by balanced funds, with income funds bringing up the rear.

Ultimately, however, one invests in a particular mutual fund. So the principal issue is to find the mutual fund with the best performance prospects having the kind of portfolio appropriate to the investor. Unfortunately, this is not so easy. Most research shows that there is very little consistency between rankings for one year and the next.[3] This variability in performance makes it difficult to evaluate the performance of mutual funds. One technique that seems quite reasonable is to compare the performance of mutual funds to various market indexes.

---

[3]See, for example, M. C. Jensen, "Risk, the Pricing of Capital Assets, and the Evaluation of Investment Portfolios," *The Journal of Business*, April 1969, 42:2, pp. 167–247.

Table 16.5

Mutual Fund Performance

	% Annualized Total Returns for Period Ending 3/31/94		
	3 Years	**5 Years**	**10 Years**
Maximum Capital Gains	12.5	12.9	12.0
Small Company Growth	15.2	14.7	13.4
Long–Term Growth	10.7	12.1	13.0
Growth & Current Income	9.8	11.0	12.9
Balanced	9.5	10.1	12.2
Equity Income	10.7	10.1	12.2
Flexible Income	12.9	11.2	12.2
S&P 500 Index	9.1	12.1	14.7

Source: *CDA/Wiesenberger Mutual Funds Update*, March 31, 1994.

Mutual funds are managed portfolios, so if they have talented management, it would seem reasonable to expect them to outperform stock market indexes, which are essentially unmanaged portfolios. In general, mutual funds do not outperform stock market indexes of comparable risk. Risk adjustment is a necessary part of correct performance comparison, especially in those cases where performance is not consistent. Even when funds are classified by type, some high–risk types do not necessarily outperform the market indexes in each period. Table 16.5 shows the performance of a number of different types of stock mutual funds for three, five, and ten year periods ending in 1994. The table also shows how mutual fund performance compares with the S&P 500. As Table 16.5 shows, mutual funds certainly do not outperform the S&P 500 in general.

As we have seen in the preceding chapters, the CAPM has achieved a wide degree of acceptance among academics over the years since its introduction. Perhaps more importantly, it has also received considerable acceptance from market practitioners. One of the most important practical uses of the CAPM has been in the area of performance evaluation. Probably the clearest example of this application of the CAPM is in the appraisal of mutual fund performance. The performance question is this: How well does a mutual fund perform in achieving a level of returns—*given its level of risk*? The idea that performance can only be evaluated accurately when the risk level is taken into account is a central tenet of the CAPM, so this application of the theory is extremely important.

Methods of Performance Evaluation

There are three well–accepted methods for evaluating the performance of mutual funds or other managed portfolios, and all stem directly from capital market theory. Each attempts to measure the fund's performance relative to a specification of the risk–adjusted return appropriate to a portfolio of the same risk. A successful performance occurs when a portfolio earns a return greater than the market equilibrium return it should have achieved.

The Sharpe Index

Consider our familiar equation for the capital market line:

$$E(R_p) = R_f + \sigma_p/\sigma_m \left[E(R_m) - R_f\right] \qquad\qquad \textbf{16.1}$$

This equation essentially looks to the future, expressing a relationship between the expected future return of a portfolio and other parameters. In performance measurement, we want to consider how well a portfolio did in the past. Accordingly, let us transform Equation 16.1 into a historical, or *ex post*, version by simply removing the expectation operators:

$$R_p = R_f + \sigma_p/\sigma_m \left[R_m - R_f\right] \qquad\qquad \textbf{16.2}$$

Subtracting R_f, dividing by σ_p, and rearranging gives Equation 16.3:

$$\left[R_p - R_f\right]/\sigma_p = \left[R_m - R_f\right]/\sigma_m \qquad\qquad \textbf{16.3}$$

The terms in brackets are the excess returns for the portfolio and for the market. If the CML holds historically, actual data will be in exact accordance with Equation 16.3. Therefore, the Sharpe Index (SI) is given by the left side of Equation 16.3:

$$SI_p = \frac{R_p - R_f}{\sigma_p} \qquad\qquad \textbf{16.4}$$

To apply this measure, consider the following data for a given period's performance, given in the following table. These data show returns, standard deviations, and the value of the Sharpe Index for the market portfolio and for several portfolios:

Asset	Return	Standard Deviation	Sharpe Index
R_f	.0700	.00	—
Market	.1977	.31	.4119
Portfolio P	.1400	.17	.4118
Portfolio Q	.1600	.17	.5294
Portfolio R	.1800	.28	.3929

These data show the individual variation we always find in portfolio performance, so we cannot expect Equation 16.3 to hold exactly for every portfolio's historical performance. If Equation 16.3 holds for a particular portfolio, then the portfolio falls

Figure 16.3

The *Ex–Post* CML

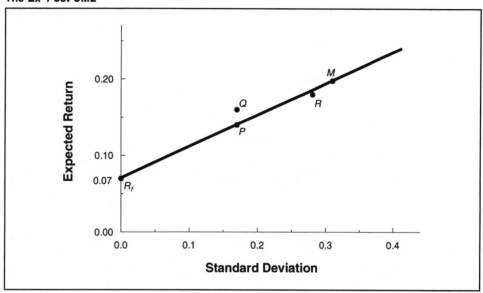

exactly on the CML as shown for Portfolio P in Figure 16.3, which is consistent with our data.

The market and any portfolio lying exactly on the CML will have an SI of .4119. If a portfolio lies above the CML, such as Q, it has an SI value greater than the market's. If a portfolio lies below the CML, such as R, its SI value is less than the market's. In Figure 16.3, it is easy to see that Portfolio Q beats R, because Q's Sharpe Index exceeds that of Portfolio R. In general, a portfolio with a higher Sharpe Index is desirable. If the Sharpe Index for a portfolio exceeds the Sharpe Index value for the market, then the portfolio has beaten the market.

The Treynor Index

Just as the Sharpe Index is drawn from the CML, the Treynor Index is the exact equivalent drawn from the *ex post* SML. By exactly the same line of reasoning, we have the Treynor Index (TI):

$$TI_p = \frac{R_p - R_f}{\beta_p} \qquad 16.5$$

For the market, the Treynor Index value always equals the market risk premium $(R_m - R_f)$ because the market's beta is always 1.0. Therefore, with the

Treynor Index, a portfolio beats the market if it has a TI value in excess of the market risk premium. Having a TI greater than the market risk premium also means that such a portfolio will lie above the security market line. In general, the greater the Treynor Index, the better the risk–adjusted performance of the portfolio.

Jensen's Alpha

According to the *ex post* SML, we have the following relationship:

$$R_j - R_f = \beta_j(R_m - R_f) \tag{16.6}$$

Equation 16.6 says that the excess return on Security or Portfolio j should equal the excess return on the market times the beta of j. We can re–cast this relationship in the form of the following regression equation:

$$(R_j - R_f)_t = \alpha_j + \beta_j(R_m - R_f)_t + \varepsilon_{jt} \tag{16.7}$$

Expressing this relationship as shown in Equation 16.7 should not have any effect on the estimated β_j. If the relationship in Equation 16.6 holds for Security or Portfolio j and we estimate Equation 16.7, we would expect to find the constant term $\alpha_j = 0$. This α_j is the constant return on Security j, after taking the beta of Security j into account.

If α_j equals zero, then Equation 16.6 holds and j's performance equals that of the market. By contrast, if α_j is significantly greater than zero, then j is outperforming the market. Likewise, if α_j is significantly less than zero, j underperforms the market. To apply Jensen's alpha, we estimate Equation 16.7 and then look for alphas significantly greater than zero to find the investment vehicles that have outperformed the market. Most studies of mutual fund performance apply one of these three methods.

Risk–Adjusted Mutual Fund Performance

Mutual funds normally employ professional security analysts to help make decisions about which stocks are worthy of investment. In addition, many large mutual funds have an enormous amount of funds under management. With a great deal of capital under management, mutual funds should be able to hold well–diversified portfolios. Further, if their professional security analysts have useful stock selection ability, they should be able to pick stocks that have a higher risk–adjusted return than the market portfolio.

Alternatively, if mutual funds underperform a portfolio made up of the risk–free asset and the market portfolio, then this would be a strong piece of evidence consistent with the semi–strong version of the EMH. If well–capitalized and well–diversified mutual funds, with the services of their professional security analysts reviewing public information, cannot outperform the equivalent risk portfolio comprised of the market portfolio and the risk–free asset, then what other group of investors could hope to?

In his classic study, Jensen reviewed the performance of 115 mutual funds over the period from 1945 to 1964.[4] In doing so, he compared the return of each mutual fund relative to a benchmark portfolio that was made up of the market portfolio and the risk–free asset in proportions that made the risk of the mutual fund and the constructed portfolio equal. In a semi–strong efficient market, the mutual funds should not be able to beat the benchmark portfolio. If the market were not semi–strong efficient and the analysts had real ability, then the mutual funds might beat the market.

Ignoring the management fees and any sales fees that the mutual funds might have, the benchmark portfolio slightly outperformed the mutual funds by .4 percent. The results are shown graphically in Figure 16.4, in which the zero point on the x axis indicates a tie between the mutual fund and the benchmark portfolio. As the figure indicates, most of the funds were beaten by the benchmark portfolio, although some mutual funds did beat the benchmark portfolio over this period.

Figure 16.4

Performance of 115 Mutual Funds Relative to an Equal Risk Benchmark Portfolio, Not Including Management Fees

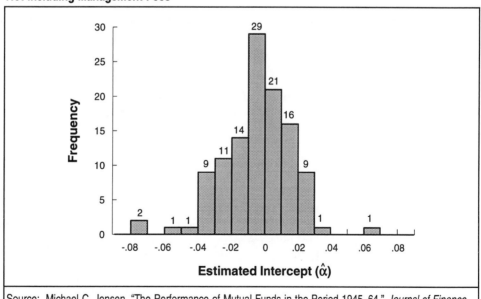

Source: Michael C. Jensen, "The Performance of Mutual Funds in the Period 1945–64," *Journal of Finance,* May 1968, pp. 389–416.

---

[4]See Michael C. Jensen, "The Performance of Mutual Funds in the Period 1945-64," *Journal of Finance,* May 1968, pp. 389–416.

Figure 16.5

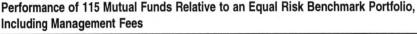

Performance of 115 Mutual Funds Relative to an Equal Risk Benchmark Portfolio, Including Management Fees

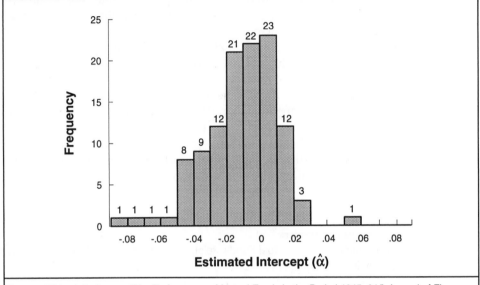

Source: Michael C. Jensen, "The Performance of Mutual Funds in the Period 1945–64," *Journal of Finance*, May 1968, pp. 389–416.

Because every mutual fund also has management fees, which go in part to pay its analysts, it is also important to evaluate mutual fund performance taking those fees into account, as shown in Figure 16.5. When management fees are considered, the benchmark portfolio beat the mutual funds by an average of 1.1 percent. This still does not include any sales fees that are charged by some mutual funds.

One possible response to these results is to acknowledge that mutual funds as a group cannot beat the benchmark portfolio. However, some funds do, in fact, beat the benchmark, and this might be due to skill rather than luck. Some market analysts may have real skill that allows them to beat the market, and it would be very difficult to be sure using statistical tests. However, Jensen's results are consistent with the view that those mutual funds that do beat the market do so by chance. In other words, the number of mutual funds that beat the market is about what one would expect to happen by chance, with no real skill being involved.

The long–term performance record of individual mutual funds also supports the view that even those mutual funds that beat the market do so by chance. True ability should lead to consistently good performance, but there appears to be very little correlation between good performance in one year by a mutual fund and its performance in the next year. While the performance of mutual funds appears to be fully consistent with the semi–strong EMH, it does not follow that mutual funds provide no useful benefit to society or that they should be avoided as an investment vehicle. While mutual funds apparently do not have the ability to beat the market, they may provide useful diversification services to many investors in a cost–effective way.

International Investment Companies

There are two essentially different ways for the U.S. investor to invest in international markets via investment companies. First, there are U.S.–based investment companies that specialize in foreign securities. Second, there is a growing mutual fund industry based outside the United States. This section considers each in turn, along with an evaluation of foreign mutual fund performance.

U.S.–Based Investment Companies

In the United States, there is a wide variety of both investment companies and mutual funds specializing in non–U.S. securities. Some closed–end funds specialize in the securities of a particular country, such as the Mexico Fund and the Korea Fund, which invest strictly in the securities of Mexico and Korea. A number of international mutual funds hold balanced portfolios of the securities from many countries.

Table 16.6

Distribution of Assets for T. Rowe Price International Stock Fund, April 30, 1994

Country	Percentage of Assets	Country	Percentage of Assets
Argentina	0.7	Malaysia	6.3
Australia	2.8	Mexico	4.6
Austria	0.1	Netherlands	6.7
Belgium	1.7	New Zealand	2.4
Brazil	0.9	Norway	1.1
Canada	0.3	Portugal	0.3
Chile	0.6	Singapore	2.3
Denmark	0.2	South Korea	0.7
Finland	0.2	Spain	1.9
France	6.2	Sweden	1.3
Germany	4.2	Switzerland	4.3
Hong Kong	4.9	Thailand	1.6
Italy	3.4	United Kingdom	13.3
Japan	20.4	Short–Term Investments	8.2

Source: T. Rowe Price, *Semi–Annual Report T. Rowe Price International Stock Fund*, April 30, 1994.

We have seen the advantage of international diversification in Chapter 13. These international mutual funds provide a form of ready–made international diversification. Mutual fund families, such as T. Rowe Price and Fidelity, offer international funds, but there are many other funds specializing in international securities. As an example of the portfolio held by international mutual funds, we consider the portfolio composition of the T. Rowe Price International Stock Fund in mid–1994. The net asset value of the fund was $5.1 billion at market value. Of this amount, 92.5 percent was invested in common stock. Virtually all of the rest of the funds were invested in short–term investments, presumably to meet withdrawals and to provide liquidity. The three industries with the largest concentration of investment were: banking (7.4 percent), building materials and components (6.3 percent) and merchandising (6.1 percent). Table 16.6 shows the distribution of the fund's investment across countries.

Foreign Mutual Funds

In addition to U.S.–based investment companies that specialize in investment abroad, foreign countries have their own mutual funds. These funds may either specialize in their own domestic markets or they can be international as well. Table 16.7 shows the assets held in foreign–based mutual funds among prominent countries. The largest amounts are in Japan and France. Together, all non–U.S. countries hold just over $2 trillion, and this almost exactly matches the $2.01 trillion held in U.S. mutual funds.

The distribution of funds in foreign countries can differ markedly from that in the United States. For example, nearly 90 percent of German holdings are concentrated in debt instruments. In France, about 75 percent are invested in debt. In the United Kingdom, the industry is organized more on the U.S. model, with equity investment being a larger portion of the whole.

Investment Performance of International Mutual Funds

We have seen that studies of U.S. mutual funds find that they are generally unable to beat the market averages. More formally, mutual funds appear unable to earn an excess risk–adjusted rate of return.

Robert Cumby and Jack Glen explored the performance of 15 international mutual funds based in the United States.[5] One of their tests utilized Jensen's alpha, which we discussed earlier in this chapter. To conduct Jensen's test requires using a proxy for the market portfolio, and Cumby and Glen used both a U.S. index and a world index of stock market performance as proxies for the market portfolio. In each case, they found that mutual funds were not able to achieve positive alphas with any regularity. That is, international mutual funds did not earn a superior

---

[5]R. E. Cumby and J. D. Glen, "Evaluating the Performance of International Mutual Funds," *Journal of Finance*, 45:2, June 1990, pp. 497–521.

Table 16.7

Assets of Foreign Mutual Funds, December 1993

Country	Assets ($ billions)
Australia	$20.7
Austria	17.8
Belgium	11.5
Canada	86.7
France	483.8
Germany	205.2
Hong Kong	24.8
Italy	56.5
Japan	448.7
Korea	67.9
Luxembourg	229.7
Mexico	16.0
Netherlands	33.6
Spain	65.5
Sweden	21.2
Switzerland	28.2
United Kingdom	141.3
Total (All Non–U.S.)	2,003.3
Total (USA)	2,011.3
Total (World)	4,014.6

Source: Investment Company Institute, *1994 Mutual Fund Fact Book,* Washington, DC: Investment Company Institute, 1994.

risk–adjusted return. Therefore, these results are broadly consistent with Jensen's classic study for domestic U.S. mutual funds.

Summary

This chapter explored the features of investment companies. Investment companies are either closed–end companies or mutual funds. Both are essentially managed portfolios in which investors own fractional shares of the entire portfolio. Closed–end companies accept funds for investment only at creation, while mutual funds accept new funds at any time. In recent years, U.S. investors have shown a preference for mutual funds. Investment companies are regulated by the SEC under the Investment Company Act of 1940. Most investment companies are not taxed directly at all, but they pass their profits to shareholders, who pay personal taxes directly.

In finance theory, diversified portfolios are especially important, because only by diversifying can an investor escape from unsystematic risk. Preceding chapters showed that investors should hold a well–diversified portfolio as their portfolio of risky assets. Investment companies fulfill this condition. Because investment companies hold professionally managed portfolios, it is also important to determine whether they beat the market by earning a supernormal risk–adjusted return. If they did so consistently, their performance would constitute evidence against semi–strong market efficiency. Based on considerable research, it appears that investment companies as a group cannot beat the market. A particular investment company might beat the market, but such a claim is not supported by the evidence.

Questions and Problems

1. What is the difference between a closed–end investment company and a mutual fund?
2. What is the "net asset value" of a share in an investment company?
3. How do mutual funds charge for their services?
4. What are some of the different kinds of investment strategies that can be observed among different mutual funds?
5. What is a "money market mutual fund"?
6. Why are there families of mutual funds?
7. For the most part, mutual funds are free of federal taxation. Why is this?
8. Respond to the following claim: "Mutual funds appear to have underperformed the market because of the necessary costs that mutual fund investment involves. However, if we consider transaction costs for both the market index and for mutual funds, then mutual funds tend to outperform the market index."
9. "To measure the performance of a mutual fund, calculate the long–term (10–year) average return earned by the mutual fund and subtract the average return earned by the S&P 500 over the same period. If the result is greater than zero, the mutual fund beat the market." Comment on this way of measuring mutual fund performance.
10. "Just as in industry, some firms perform well and others perform badly. Even if mutual funds as a group cannot outperform the market, there are some firms that can. For any five year period, there will be some mutual funds that underperform the market and some that outperform the market. This is true even on a risk–adjusted basis. Therefore, some funds do, in fact, outperform the market." Comment on the validity of this claim.

CFA Questions

All CFA examination questions are reprinted, with permission, from the Level I *1992–1994, CFA Candidate Study and Examination Program Review.* Copyright 1992–1994, Association for Investment Management and Research, Charlottesville, Va. All rights reserved.

A. The average return on a portfolio different from that predicted by the Capital Asset Pricing Model (CAPM) is measured by:

   a. reward to variability.

   b. reward to non–systematic risk.

   c. alpha.

   d. appraisal ratio.

B. Which *one* of the following methods measures the reward to volatility trade–off by dividing the average portfolio excess return over the standard deviation of returns?

   a. Sharpe's measure

   b. Treynor's measure

   c. Jensen's measure

   d. Appraisal ratio

Suggested REALDATA Exercises

The following *REALDATA* exercises explore the concepts developed in this chapter: Exercises 21, 22, 23.

Suggested Readings

Bonser–Neal, C., G. Brauer, F. Neal, and S. Wheatley, "International Investment Restrictions and Closed–End Country Fund Prices," *Journal of Finance*, 45:2, June 1990, pp. 523–547.

Brauer, G. A., "Closed–End Fund Shares' Abnormal Returns and the Information Content of Discounts and Premiums," *Journal of Finance*, 43:1, March 1988, pp. 113–127.

Cumby, R. E. and J. D. Glen, "Evaluating the Performance of International Mutual Funds," *Journal of Finance*, 45:2, June 1990, pp. 497–521.

Eun, C. S., R. Kolodny, and B. G. Resnick, "U.S.–Based International Mutual Funds: A Performance Evaluation," *The Journal of Portfolio Management*, 17:3, Spring 1991, pp. 88–94.

Ferris, S. P. and D. M. Chance, "The Effect of 12b–1 Plans on Mutual Fund Expense Ratios: A Note," *Journal of Finance*, 42:4, September 1987, pp. 1077–1082.

Fong, H. and O. A. Vasicek, "Forecast–Free International Asset Allocation," *Financial Analysts Journal*, 45:2, March/April 1989, pp. 29–33.

Fong, H. G., "Forecast–Free International Asset Allocation," *Quantitative International Investing: A Handbook of Analytical and Modeling Techniques and Strategies*, Chicago: Probus Publishing, 1990, pp. 203–209.

Fredman, A. J. and G. Scott, "An Investor's Guide to Closed–End Fund Discounts," *American Association of Individual Investors*, 13:5, May 1991, pp. 12–16.

Fredman, A. J. and G. Scott, "Fixed–Income Investing: A Look at Closed–End Bond Funds," *American Association of Individual Investors*, 13:3, March 1991, pp. 8–13.

Gibson, R. C., *Asset Allocation: Balancing Financial Risk*, Homewood, IL: Dow Jones–Irwin, 1990.

Golec, J. H., "Do Mutual Fund Managers Who Use Incentive Compensation Outperform Those Who Don't?" *Financial Analysts Journal*, 44:6, November/December 1988, pp. 75–78.

Lee, C. M. C., A. Shleifer, and R. H. Thaler, "Anomalies: Closed–End Mutual Funds," *Journal of Economic Perspectives*, 4:4, Fall 1990, pp. 153–164.

Lehmann, B. N. and D. M. Modest, "Mutual Fund Performance Evaluation: A Comparison of Benchmarks and Benchmark Comparisons," *Journal of Finance*, 42:2, June 1987, pp. 233–265.

Lynn, S. M., "Combining Active Management with Indexing," *Quantitative International Investing: A Handbook of Analytical and Modeling Techniques and Strategies*, Chicago: Probus Publishing, 1990, pp. 55–60.

Perold, A. F. and R. S. Salomon, Jr., "The Right Amount of Assets under Management," *Financial Analysts Journal*, 47:3, May/June 1991, pp. 31–39.

Samuelson, P. A., "Asset Allocation Could Be Dangerous to Your Health," *The Journal of Portfolio Management*, 16:3, Spring 1990, pp. 5–8.

Samuelson, P. A., "The Judgment of Economic Science on Rational Portfolio Management: Indexing, Timing, and Long–Horizon Effects," *The Journal of Portfolio Management*, 16:1, Fall 1989, pp. 4–12.

Sharpe, W. F., "Integrated Asset Allocation," *Financial Analysts Journal*, 43:5, September/October 1987, pp. 25–32.

Tallman, E. W., "Financial Asset Pricing Theory: A Review of Recent Developments," Federal Reserve Bank of Atlanta *Economic Review*, 70:6, November/December 1989, pp. 26–41.

Wainscott, C. B., "The Stock–Bond Correlation and Its Implications for Asset Allocation," *Financial Analysts Journal*, 46:4, July/August 1990, pp. 55–60.

Financial Derivatives and Risk Management

In the last decade, the options and futures markets have become extremely important. Chapter 17 introduces the futures market. A futures contract is a contract to buy or sell a good at a certain price, with the payment for the good and the delivery of the good taking place at a certain time in the future. For example, buying a futures contract for a T–bond commits the buyer to purchase a T–bond at a stipulated price at a certain time in the future. Futures markets originated in their present form in the United States during the nineteenth century. However, they have had a recent surge in popularity, due largely to the new kinds of futures contracts that have been introduced. Today, futures contracts are traded not only on the traditional commodities, such as agricultural goods and precious metals, but they are also traded on interest rates, currencies, oil, and stock indexes. These new financial futures have come to dominate the futures market. They give investors new speculative opportunities, but they also provide new tools for portfolio management and risk control of an existing portfolio.

In contrast with the long history of futures markets, organized options exchanges have existed in the United States only since 1973. Chapter 18 explores option pricing principles and uses of the options market. An option is a financial instrument that gives its owner the right to buy or sell a given good at a specified price for a certain period of time. For example, owning a call option on a stock gives the owner the right to purchase a share of stock for a certain price, with that right lasting until a certain date in the future. Today, options are extremely important and are traded on individual stocks, bonds, currencies, metals, and a wide variety of financial indexes. Chapter 18 explains how the options markets work and how options are priced. While options give investors rich speculative opportunities, they can also be used to control risk in a portfolio.

The swap market is the newest major derivatives market to flourish, and it is the topic of Chapter 19. In an interest rate swap agreement, two parties contract to exchange a fixed rate obligation for a floating rate obligation. Thus, the interest rate swap provides a mechanism for accepting or reducing interest rate risk. Currency swaps provide similar opportunities for accepting or reducing foreign exchange risk.

Taken together, futures, options, and swaps not only give investors new speculative opportunities, but they are also of increasing importance in other phases of investment management, notably the control of risk. As such, they round out the topics essential to an understanding of the world of investments. Chapter 20 brings together many of the threads of our study of investing by introducing the idea of financial engineering. It shows how futures and options can be used together to tailor the risk and expected return characteristics of a portfolio. Financial derivatives, such as futures, options, and swaps, can be combined to create new financial structures for the precise management of risk. Designing and building these structures is the role of financial engineering.

CHAPTER SEVENTEEN

The Futures Market

Overview

Futures markets arose in the mid–1800s in Chicago and institutionalized an ancient form of contracting, called forward contracting. A **forward contract** is an agreement reached at one point in time calling for the delivery of some commodity at a specified later date at a price established at the time of contracting. For example, an agreement made today to deliver one ton of sugar a year from today at a price of $.59 per lb., with the payment to be made upon delivery, is a typical kind of forward contract. Futures contracts are similar in many respects but have very specific features and a great deal more institutional structure than forward contracts.

This chapter explores the futures markets in the United States and the contracts traded on them. We begin with a survey of the different kinds of contracts that exist and the institutional arrangements that are common to these markets. This chapter also explores futures market quotations and pricing principles and discusses strategies for speculating with futures contracts and for using futures contracts to hedge risks.

Futures markets have a reputation for being incredibly risky. To a large extent, this reputation is justified. As we will see, however, futures contracts may also be used to manage many different kinds of risks. As such, the futures markets play a beneficial role in society by allowing the transference of risk and in helping to provide information about the future direction of prices on many commodities.

Forward Contracts

In a typical forward contract, calling for the delivery of a commodity at a future time for a payment to be made upon delivery, two parties come together and agree to terms that they believe to be mutually beneficial. Though very desirable for both parties, this kind of contract has a number of characteristics which may be drawbacks, and these can be illustrated by using our example of the forward contract for the delivery of one ton of sugar in a year.

In the sugar contract, both parties must trust each other to complete the contract as promised. The contract price was $.59 per lb., and that is the amount promised to be paid upon delivery of the sugar in one year. At the time of delivery, the price of sugar is quite likely to be different from $.59. Let us assume that the price of sugar at the time of delivery is $.69. This is the cash price or the **spot price**—the price for immediate delivery of a good. In this event, the seller is obligated to deliver the ton of sugar and to receive only $.59 per lb. for it. In the open market, however, the sugar could be sold for $.69 per lb. Obviously, the seller will be tempted to default on the forward contract obligation and to sell the ton of sugar in the open market at the spot price of $.69 per lb. The strong incentives to default on the contract are known in advance to both parties. Consequently, this kind of forward contract can reasonably take place only between two parties that know and trust each other to honor their commitments. If we restrict ourselves to doing business only with people we trust, there is likely to be very little commerce at all.

A second problem with this kind of forward contract is the difficulty of finding a trading partner. One party may wish to sell a ton of sugar for delivery in one year, but it might be difficult to find someone willing to contract now for the delivery of sugar one year from now. Not only must the timing be the same for both parties, but both parties must want to exchange the same amount of the good. These conditions can be quite restrictive and leave many potential traders unable to consummate their desired trades.

A third and related problem with this kind of forward contract is the difficulty in fulfilling an obligation without actually completing delivery. In the example of the sugar contract, imagine that one party to the transaction decides after six months that it is undesirable to complete the contract by delivery. This trader has only two ways to fulfill his or her obligation. The first is to make delivery as originally agreed. The second is to ask the trading partner to settle the contract now, by early delivery or the payment of cash, for example. This could be difficult to arrange unless the trading partner is willing to cooperate.

Because of these kinds of difficulties—establishing the contract terms, finding a trading partner, and lacking a flexible means of settling the contract—forward markets have always been restricted in size and scope.[1] Futures markets have emerged to provide an institutional framework that copes with these deficiencies of forward contracts. The organized futures exchange standardizes contract terms and guarantees performance on the contracts to both trading partners. It also provides a simple mechanism that allows any trader to complete his or her obligation at any time. In the process, however, the futures market has developed its own peculiarities that also need to be understood.

---

[1]There is a notable exception in the forward market for foreign currency, where the forward market is extremely large and overshadows the futures market.

Table 17.1

■■■■■■■■■■■■■■■■

Seat Prices for Major U.S. Futures Exchanges

Exchange	Last Sale Price
Commodity Exchange of New York	$127,500
Chicago Mercantile Exchange	725,000
Chicago Board of Trade	535,000
New York Mercantile Exchange	490,000
Coffee, Sugar and Cocoa Exchange	103,000

Source: *Futures and Options World*, June 1994, p. 69.

The Futures Exchange

A futures exchange is a nonprofit organization composed of members holding seats on the exchange. These seats are traded on an open market, so an individual wishing to become a member of the exchange can do so by buying an existing seat from a member and by meeting other exchange–imposed criteria for financial soundness and ethical reputation. Table 17.1 presents recent prices for seats on the more important exchanges. These prices fluctuate quite radically, depending largely on the level of trading activity on the exchange.

The exchange provides a setting in which futures contracts can be traded by its members and other parties who trade through an exchange member. The exchange members participate in committees that govern the exchange and also employ professional managers to execute the directives of the members. So, while the futures exchange is itself a nonprofit corporation, it is constituted to benefit its members. The futures market in the United States is regulated by the Commodity Futures Trading Commission (CFTC), an agency of the U.S. government.

Each exchange determines the kinds of goods that it will trade and the contract specifications for each of the goods. Table 17.2 lists the major world futures exchanges and the types of contracts traded by each. As we will see in more detail later, there is a great variety of goods traded, and some exchanges tend to specialize in certain segments of the industry.

Futures Contracts and Futures Trading

Each exchange provides a trading floor where all of its contracts are traded. The rules of an exchange require all of its futures contracts to be traded only on the floor of the exchange during its official hours. By specializing in a limited range of commodities, and by standardizing contract terms, the futures contract overcomes some of the difficulties noted earlier in the case of forward contracts.

Table 17.2

Futures Exchanges and the Contracts They Trade

	Date Founded	Physical	Currencies	Interest Rates	Indexes
Futures Markets in the United States					
Chicago Board of Trade (CBOT)	1848	◆		◆	◆
Chicago Mercantile Exchange (CME)	1919	◆	◆	◆	◆
Coffee, Sugar and Cocoa Exchange (New York)	1882	◆			◆
Commodity Exchange, Inc. (COMEX) (New York)	1933	◆			
Kansas City Board of Trade (KCBT)	1856	◆			◆
Mid–America Commodity Exchange (Chicago)	1880	◆	◆	◆	
Minneapolis Grain Exchange	1881	◆			
New York Cotton Exchange, Inc.	1870	◆	◆		◆
Citrus Associates of the New York Cotton Exchange	1966	◆			
Petroleum Associates of the New York Cotton Exchange	1971	◆			
New York Futures Exchange (NYFE)	1979				◆
New York Mercantile Exchange	1872	◆			
Chicago Rice and Cotton Exchange	1976	◆			
Principal Foreign Futures Markets					
International Futures Exchange (INTEX) (Bermuda)	1984	◆			◆
Bolsa de Mercadorios de Sao Paulo	1917	◆			
London International Financial Futures Exchange (LIFFE)	1982		◆	◆	◆
Baltic International Freight Futures Exchange (BIFFEX) (London)	1985				◆
Tokyo Financial Futures Exchange	1985		◆	◆	◆
Singapore International Monetary Exchange (SIMEX) (Singapore)	1984		◆	◆	◆
Hong Kong Futures Exchange	1977	◆			◆
New Zealand Futures Exchange	1985	◆	◆	◆	
Sydney Futures Exchange	1960	◆	◆	◆	◆
Toronto Futures Exchange	1984		◆	◆	◆
Kuala Lumpur Commodity Exchange	*1985	◆			

*Reorganized after default.

Source: *The Wall Street Journal, Futures Magazine, Intermarket Magazine*, various issues, and Chicago Mercantile Exchange, *1985 Annual Report*.

Typical Contract Terms

The difference between futures contracts and forward contracts can be demonstrated by examining the particular features of a futures contract. One of the oldest contracts is the wheat contract traded at the Chicago Board of Trade. This contract calls for the delivery of 5,000 bushels of wheat, with delivery taking place in one of the designated delivery months, July, September, December, March, or May. Further, only certain kinds of wheat are permitted for delivery, such as No. 2 Soft Red, No. 2 Hard Red Winter, No. 2 Dark Northern Spring, or No. 1 Northern Spring. The contract terms also control the manner of delivery. To deliver wheat under this contract, the wheat must be in a warehouse approved by the Chicago Board of Trade, and a warehouse receipt for the wheat is actually delivered to the purchaser. The warehouse receipt is a legal document of title to the wheat, which is validated by the warehouse operator. The warehouse operator certifies that the wheat actually exists and is stored in the warehouse. This standardization of the contract terms means that all of the traders will know immediately the exact characteristics of the good being traded, without negotiation or long discussion. In fact, the only feature of a futures contract that is determined at the time of the trade is the futures price.

Order Flow

Futures contracts are created when an order is executed on the floor of the exchange. The order can originate with a member of the exchange trading for his or her own account in pursuit of profit. Alternatively, it can originate with a trader outside the exchange who enters an order through a broker, who has a member of the exchange execute the trade for the client. These outside orders are transmitted electronically to the floor of the exchange, where actual trading takes place in an area called a pit. A trading **pit** is a particular area of the exchange floor designated for the trading of a particular commodity. It is called a pit because the trading area consists of an oval made up of different levels, like stairs, around a central area. Traders stand on the steps or in the central area of the pit, which allows them to see each other with relative ease.

This physical arrangement highlights a central difference between commodities exchanges and stock exchanges in the United States. In the stock market, there is a specialist for each stock, and every trade on the exchange for a particular stock must go through the specialist for that stock. In the futures market, any trader in the pit may execute a trade with any other trader. The rules of the exchange require that any offer to buy or sell must be made by **open–outcry** to all other traders in the pit. This different form of trading gives rise to the appearance of chaos on the trading floor, because each trader is struggling to gain the attention of other traders.

Once a trade is executed, the information is communicated to the exchange officials who report the transaction over a worldwide electronic communication system. Also, the trader whose order was executed will receive confirmation of the trade.

Figure 17.1

The Function of the Clearinghouse in Futures Markets

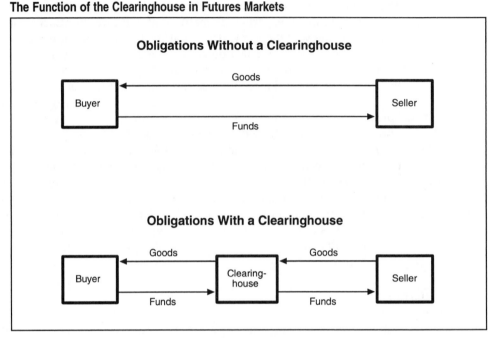

The Clearinghouse and Its Functions

The trade from an outside party must be executed through a broker, and the broker must, in turn, trade through a member of the exchange. Normally, the two parties to a transaction will be located far apart and will not even know each other. This raises the issue of trust and the question of whether the traders will perform as they have promised. We have already seen that this can be a problem with forward contracts.

To resolve this uncertainty about performance in accordance with the contract terms, each futures exchange has a clearinghouse. The **clearinghouse** is a well–capitalized financial institution that guarantees contract performance to both parties. As soon as the trade is consummated, the clearinghouse interposes itself between the buyer and seller. The clearinghouse acts as a seller to the buyer and as the buyer to the seller. At this point, the original buyer and seller have obligations to the clearinghouse and no obligations to each other. This arrangement is shown in Figure 17.1. In the top portion of the figure, the relationship between the buyer and seller is shown when there is no clearinghouse. The seller is obligated to deliver goods to the buyer, who is obligated to deliver funds to the seller. This arrangement raises the familiar problems of trust between the two parties to the trade. In the lower portion, the role of the clearinghouse is demonstrated. The clearinghouse guarantees that goods will be delivered to the buyer and that funds will be delivered to the seller.

At this point, the traders only need to trust the clearinghouse, instead of each other. Because the clearinghouse has a large supply of capital, there is little need for concern. Also, as the bottom portion of Figure 17.1 shows, the clearinghouse has no net commitment in the futures market. After all the transactions are completed, the clearinghouse will have neither funds nor goods. It only acts to guarantee performance to both parties.

The Clearinghouse and the Trader

While the clearinghouse guarantees performance on all futures contracts, it now has its own risk exposure, because the clearinghouse will suffer if traders default on their obligations. To protect the clearinghouse and the exchange, traders must deposit funds with their brokers in order to trade futures contracts. This deposit, known as **margin**, must be in the form of cash or short–term U.S. Treasury securities. This margin acts as a good–faith deposit with the broker. If the trader defaults on his or her obligations, the broker may seize the margin deposit to cover the trading losses. This provides a measure of safety to the broker, the clearing-house, and the exchange.

This margin deposit, however, is normally quite small relative to the value of the goods being traded. The margin deposit might normally have a value equal to only 5 to 10 percent of the goods represented by the futures contract. Because potential losses on the futures contract could be much larger than this margin deposit, the clearinghouse needs other protection from potential default by the trader. To give this protection, futures exchanges have adopted a system known as **daily settlement** or **marking–to–market**. The policy of daily settlement means that futures traders realize their paper gains and losses in cash on the results of each day's trading. The trader may withdraw the day's gains and must pay the day's losses.

The margin deposit remains with the broker. If the trader fails to settle the day's losses, the broker may seize the margin deposit and liquidate the trader's position, paying the losses out of the margin deposit. This practice limits the exchange's exposure to loss from a trader's default. Essentially, the exchange will lose on the default only if the loss on one day exceeds the amount of the margin. This is unlikely to happen and even if it does, the amount lost would probably be very small.

Fulfillment of Futures Contracts.   After executing a futures contract, both the buyer and seller have undertaken specific obligations to the clearinghouse. Fulfillment of those obligations can be accomplished in two basic ways. First, the trader may actually make or take delivery as contemplated in the original contract. Second, if a trader does not wish to make or take delivery, the trader can fulfill all obligations by entering a reversing or offsetting trade. In fact, more than 99 percent of all futures contracts are settled by a reversing trade.[2]

Delivery. Each futures contract will have its own very specific rules for making and taking delivery. These rules cover the time of delivery, the location of delivery, and the way in which the funds covering the goods will change hands. Some investors, who do not understand the futures market very well, imagine that one could forget about a futures position and wind up with sowbellies on the front lawn. Instead, the delivery process is more complex.

After the clearinghouse interposes itself between the original buyer and seller, each of the trading partners has no obligation to any other trader. As delivery approaches, the clearinghouse supervises the arrangements for delivery. First, the clearinghouse will pair buyers and sellers for the delivery and will identify the two parties to each other. Prior to this time, the two traders had no obligations to each other. Second, the buyer and seller will communicate the relevant information concerning the delivery process to the opposite trading partner and to the clearinghouse. Usually, the seller has the choice of exactly what features the delivered goods will have. For example, in the wheat contract, the seller has the right to choose which kind of wheat to deliver, and the buyer must be notified of these conditions. The seller must also tell the buyer the name of the bank account to which the funds are to be transmitted. Once the funds have been transmitted to the seller's account and this transaction has been confirmed by the seller's bank, the seller will deliver title to the goods to the buyer. Usually, this title is in the form of a warehouse receipt.

As long as this transaction is proceeding smoothly, which is usually the case, the clearinghouse has little to do. It acts merely as an overseer. If difficulties arise, or if disputes develop, the clearinghouse must intervene to enforce the rules of the exchange.

Reversing Trades. The delivery process can be quite cumbersome. In the case of the wheat contract, the seller may not choose to deliver the kind of wheat that the buyer really wants. Also, since the wheat must be stored in an approved warehouse, it may be inconvenient for the buyer. For example, if the buyer of the wheat is a baker in Kansas who needs winter wheat, it may be very expensive and inconvenient to receive wheat of another type, which is stored in Chicago. Because these physical commodities are bulky and difficult to transport, most futures traders fulfill their obligations by entering a **reversing trade** prior to the time of delivery. Then if they need to dispose of their supply of the good, or need to acquire the actual good, they do so in the regular spot market, outside the channels of the futures market.

Prior to the initiation of the delivery process, buyers and sellers are not associated with each other, because the clearinghouse has interposed itself between

---

[2]By contrast, more than 90 percent of foreign exchange forward contracts are completed by actual delivery.

Figure 17.2

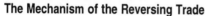

The Mechanism of the Reversing Trade

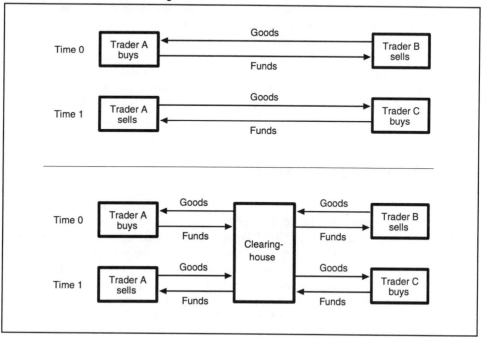

all the pairs of traders. This allows any trader a means to end his or her commitment in the futures market without actually making delivery. Figure 17.2 shows the position of three traders if there is no clearinghouse. At time = 0, Trader A buys a futures contract, and Trader B is the seller. Later, at time = 1, which is still before delivery, Trader A decides to liquidate the original position. Accordingly, he or she sells the identical contract that was purchased at time = 0 to Trader C, who buys.

In an important sense, Trader A no longer has a position in the futures contract, because he or she will just pass goods from Trader B to Trader C and will pass funds from Trader C to Trader B. After time = 1, price fluctuations will not really affect Trader A. Traders B and C, however, have a very different perspective. Both have obligations to Trader A and expect Trader A to perform on the original contracts. This means that Trader A is left with duties to perform in the delivery process. As a result, even though Trader A no longer has risk exposure, he or she still has obligations.

From the point of view of Trader A, all of this is much simpler if there is a clearinghouse, as shown in Figure 17.2. Because the clearinghouse splits the original trading partners apart as soon as the trade is consummated, Trader A can now execute a reversing trade that will take him or her out of the market altogether. After the same trades are made, the clearinghouse can recognize that Trader A has no position in the futures market, since the trader has bought and sold the identical futures contract. After time = 1, Trader C has assumed the position originally held by Trader A. As a result, Trader B's position is unaffected, and Trader A has no further obligations in the futures market.

It is important to recognize that the reversing trade must be for exactly the same futures contract as originally traded. Otherwise, the trader will have two futures positions rather than none. Also, it should be clear that any trader may execute a reversing trade at any time prior to the contract's expiration. This is exactly what most traders do. As contract expiration approaches, they execute reversing trades to eliminate their futures market commitments. In Figure 17.2, Trader C was new to the market, so there are still the same number of futures contracts outstanding. However, if Trader C had been executing a reversing trade also, the number of contracts outstanding in the marketplace would have decreased.

Futures Price Quotations

Futures price quotations are available daily in *The Wall Street Journal* and other newspapers. Figure 17.3 presents a sample of futures price quotations as they appear in *The Wall Street Journal*. The quotations are grouped by commodities and fall into four major groups: (1) agricultural and metallurgical commodities, (2) interest rate futures, (3) foreign exchange futures, and (4) stock index futures.

The agricultural and metallurgical commodities have been traded the longest and include several different grains, livestock, precious metals, and petroleum products, as well as the famous pork bellies. The other three kinds of futures—interest rate futures, foreign exchange futures, and stock index futures—are all fairly recent creations. Foreign exchange futures are the oldest of the three, having begun trading in 1972. They were followed by interest rate futures in 1975, and stock index futures began trading only in 1982.

Interest rate futures contracts exist for several kinds of U.S. government obligations, including Treasury bills, notes, and bonds. Foreign exchange futures are traded on the German mark, British pound, Japanese yen, Swiss franc, and Canadian dollar. Stock index futures are traded on several different indexes, including the S&P 500, the Value Line Composite Index, the NYSE Composite Index, and the Major Market Index, which closely tracks the Dow Jones Industrial Average.

While there are far too many different contracts to discuss each in detail, it is fortunate that their price quotations are all very similar. For illustrative purposes, we can use the corn contract traded by the Chicago Board of Trade (CBOT). The corn quotations are presented in Figure 17.4. The first line of the quotation shows the commodity, followed by the exchange where the futures contract is traded, in this case the CBOT. Next the quotations show the amount of good in a single contract. In the case of the corn contract, there are 5,000 bushels. The last item in this first line is the method of price quotation. For corn, the price is quoted in cents per bushel. While all of this is important information, it is seriously incomplete. It reveals nothing about the quality of the corn that is permitted for delivery or the places where delivery is permitted. As noted earlier, these factors are determined by the exchange, and any trader would want this information before trading.

Figure 17.3

Futures Price Quotations in *The Wall Street Journal*

FUTURES PRICES

	Open	High	Low	Settle	Change	Lifetime High	Low	Open Interest
Sept	92.00	92.25	89.05	91.25 − 1.45	134.50	89.05	11,450
Nov	94.30	94.30	91.10	93.75 − .85	134.00	91.10	2,263
Ja95	96.90	96.90	94.25	96.55 − .55	132.00	94.25	3,280
Mar	98.50	98.50	97.00	98.50 − .65	124.25	97.00	1,397

Est vol 5,000; vol Wed 1,800; open int 23,836, +150.

METALS AND PETROLEUM

COPPER-HIGH (CMX) – 25,000 lbs.; cents per lb.

	Open	High	Low	Settle	Change	Lifetime High	Low	Open Interest
June	113.70	113.70	113.10	113.10 + .15	113.70	74.10	255
July	113.20	113.80	112.30	113.05 − .15	114.35	74.20	17,299
Aug	113.80	113.80	113.30	113.30 − .10	113.80	75.30	704
Sept	113.70	114.30	112.60	113.50 − .10	114.75	74.90	30,409
Oct	113.10	113.10	113.10	112.85 + .15	113.10	75.20	276
Nov	112.80	112.80	112.80	112.35 − .15	112.80	77.75	239
Dec	112.20	112.20	111.20	111.70 − .20	112.90	75.75	7,823
Ja95	111.30	111.30	111.30	111.25 − .20	111.30	76.90	329
Feb	111.30	111.30	111.30	110.85 − .20	111.30	87.85	232
Mar	110.60	110.80	110.60	110.40 − .20	111.25	76.30	2,201
May		...		109.50 − .20	108.00	76.85	792
July		...		108.70 − .20	107.50	78.00	708
Sept	108.40	108.40	108.00	107.95 − .20	108.40	79.10	567
Dec		...		107.15 − .20	105.50	88.00	744

Est vol 12,000; vol Wed 21,480; open int 62,713, +1,107.

GOLD (CMX) – 100 troy oz.; $ per troy oz.

	Open	High	Low	Settle	Change	Lifetime High	Low	Open Interest
June	389.90	391.30	388.80	389.70 + .20	...	339.40	466
Aug	391.50	393.40	390.50	391.50 + .10	415.00	341.50	84,110
Oct	394.60	395.90	393.60	394.50 + .10	417.00	344.00	5,512
Dec	397.60	399.30	396.90	397.70 + .10	426.50	343.00	26,658
Fb95	401.70	401.70	401.30	401.20	...	411.00	363.50	6,720
Apr		...		404.70	...	425.00	385.50	6,559
June		...		408.30	...	430.00	351.00	9,743
Aug		...		412.10	...	412.50	380.50	1,533
Oct		...		416.00	...	413.30	410.20	1,052
Dec	419.70	421.00	419.70	420.00	...	439.50	358.00	4,851
Fb96		...		424.10	...	424.50	412.50	566
Apr		...		428.20	...	430.00	430.00	410
June		...		432.50	...	447.00	370.90	2,283
Dec		...		445.70	...	447.50	379.60	2,257
Ju97		...		459.50	...	441.00	436.00	988
Dec		...		473.90	...	477.00	402.00	1,337
Ju98		...		488.80 + .10	489.50	483.90	1,400
Dec		...		504.20 + .10	505.00	468.00	1,234

Est vol 31,000; vol Wed 49,155; open int 157,679, −3,704.

PLATINUM (NYM) – 50 troy oz.; $ per troy oz.

	Open	High	Low	Settle	Change	Lifetime High	Low	Open Interest
July	na	408.50	405.10	405.60 − 1.80	437.00	357.00	8,749
Oct	na	412.00	408.00	409.00 − 1.50	435.00	368.00	13,105
Ja95	na	413.00	411.50	411.50 − 1.50	429.50	374.80	1,224
Apr		...		413.90 − 1.50	428.00	390.00	1,180

Est vol 4,962; vol Wed 4,895; open int 24,258, +173.

PALLADIUM (NYM) 100 troy oz.; $ per troy oz.

	Open	High	Low	Settle	Change	Lifetime High	Low	Open Interest
June		...		139.45 + .40	142.50	114.00	46
Sept	138.50	139.00	138.50	138.95 + .40	142.00	113.00	3,769
Dec		...		139.15 + .40	141.75	122.50	831

Est vol 58; vol Wed 282; open int 4,647, −202.

GAS OIL (IPE) 100 metric tons; $ per ton

	Open	High	Low	Settle	Change	Lifetime High	Low	Open Interest
July	155.25	156.00	154.50	155.25 − 1.50	169.75	135.25	29,794
Aug	157.00	158.00	156.50	157.50 − 1.25	167.05	137.00	14,930
Sept	159.00	160.25	158.50	159.50 − 1.00	178.25	139.00	8,464
Oct	162.00	162.75	161.50	162.25 − 1.00	167.00	142.50	8,268
Nov	164.00	164.25	163.50	164.25 − 1.50	167.75	144.50	5,212
Dec	165.75	166.00	165.25	166.00 − 1.50	173.00	146.00	14,003
Ja95	166.25	166.50	165.50	166.50 − 1.75	169.50	147.25	5,295
Feb		...		164.75 − 1.25	167.75	148.00	1,456
Mar		...		163.25 − 1.25	172.00	147.25	1,849
Apr		...		161.75 − 1.25	157.75	155.00	250
June		...		157.75 − 1.50	162.00	146.00	1,169

Est vol 13,018; vol Wed 13,100; open int 90,690, +523.

INTEREST RATE

TREASURY BONDS (CBT) – $100,000; pts. 32nds of 100%

	Open	High	Low	Settle	Change	Lifetime High	Low	Open Interest
Sept	103-22	104-01	103-08	103-24 + 41	118-26	90-12	372,568
Dec	102-31	103-10	102-18	103-02 + 51	118-08	91-19	38,386
Mr95	101-31	102-18	101-31	102-12 + 41	116-20	99-14	3,051
June	101-12	101-26	101-12	101-24 + 41	113-15	98-31	1,154
Sept	100-25	101-07	100-25	101-05 + 31	112-15	99-00	184

Est vol 390,000; vol Wed 460,903; op int 417,840, +8,297.

TREASURY BONDS (MCE) – $50,000; pts. 32nds of 100%

| Sept | 103-20 | 104-01 | 103-08 | 103-23 + 31 | 15-20 | 100-10 | 11,705 |

Est vol 4,000; vol Wed 5,201; open int 11,831, +65.

TREASURY NOTES (CBT) – $100,000; pts. 32nds of 100%

| Sept | 104-19 | 104-31 | 104-14 | 104-23 + 51 | 15-01 | 101-18 | 225,159 |
| Dec | 103-23 | 104-00 | 103-18 | 103-25 + 51 | 14-21 | 100-25 | 1,953 |

Est vol 67,993; vol Wed 94,856; open int 242,566, −6,928.

5 YR TREAS NOTES (CBT) – $100,000; pts. 32nds of 100%

| Sept | 104-15 | 04-215 | 104-12 | 104-17 + 4 | 10195 | 10212 | 161,915 |

Est vol 36,500; vol Wed 42,003; open int 177,000, −2,825.

2 YR TREAS NOTES (CBT) – $200,000; pts. 32nds of 100%

| June | 03-175 | 03-205 | 03-175 | 03-195 + · 2 | 10600 | 02205 | 3,404 |
| Sept | 02-305 | 03-015 | 102-29 | 03-002 + 2¼ | 10431 | 10204 | 26,647 |

Est vol 2,500; vol 5,340; open int 30,051, +327.

30-DAY FEDERAL FUNDS (CBT)-$5 million; pts. of 100%

June	95.78	95.78	95.78	95.78	...	96.72	95.54	2,007
Jly	95.61	95.61	95.61	95.62 + .02	96.65	95.25	1,684
Aug	95.47	95.48	95.47	95.47 + .01	96.58	95.05	1,087
Sept		...		95.28 + .01	96.44	94.81	1,243
Oct		...		95.11 + .01	95.63	94.63	213
Nov		...		94.95 + .01	95.04	94.50	120

Est vol 777; vol Wed 871; open int 6,354, +70.

TREASURY BILLS (CME) – $1 mil.; pts. of 100%

	Open	High	Low	Settle	Chg	Discount Settle	Chg	Open Interest
Sept	95.29	95.31	95.28	95.31 + .03	4.69 − .03	23,531
Dec	94.72	94.75	94.68	94.74 + .05	5.26 − .05	8,327
Mr95	94.43	94.46	94.43	94.46 + .06	5.54 − .06	1,066

Est vol 5,852; vol Wed 2,974; open int 36,110, −1,176.

In the body of the quotation, there is a separate line for each contract maturity. The next contract to come due for delivery is the March contract, which is called the **nearby contract**. Other contracts, with later delivery dates, are **distant** or **deferred contracts**. For the quotations shown in Figure 17.4, there are seven

Figure 17.4

Price Quotations for Corn Futures

GRAINS AND OILSEEDS

	Open	High	Low	Settle	Change	Lifetime High	Lifetime Low	Open Interest
CORN (CBT) 5,000 bu.; cents per bu.								
July	259	260	256	257¼	− 1¾	316½	241	64,337
Sept	252	253½	249	250¼	− 2¼	292¼	240½	46,828
Dec	244½	247	242	243	− 1½	277	236½	114,843
Mr95	251½	254½	250¼	250¾	− 1¾	282½	248¾	13,577
May	256	259¼	255½	255¾	− 1¾	285	253	2,523
July	258¾	261¼	257	257¾	− 1½	285½	254	3,584
Sept	251¼	251¼	249	249	− 2	270½	249	219
Dec	244	245½	242	242	− 2½	263	242	3,460

Est vol 65,000; vol Wed 94,849; open int 249,417, −913.

different maturities of the corn contract being traded. The first three columns of figures show the "Open," "High," and "Low" prices for the day's trading.

The fourth column presents the **settlement price** for the day. In most respects, the settlement price is like a closing price, but there can be important differences. Because every trader marks to the market every day, it is important to have an official price to which the trade must be marked. That is the settlement price, and it is set by the settlement committee of the exchange. If the markets are active at the close of trading, the settlement price will normally be the closing price. However, if a particular contract has not traded for some time prior to the close of the day's trading, the settlement committee may believe that the last trade price is not representative of the actual prevailing price for the contract. In this situation, the settlement committee may establish a price that differs from the last trade price as the settlement price. The "Change" column reports the change in the contract's price from the preceding day's settlement price to the settlement price for the day being reported. The next two columns indicate the highest and lowest prices reached by a contract of a particular maturity since the contract began trading.

The last column shows the open interest at the close of the day's trading. The **open interest** is the number of contracts currently obligated for delivery. If a buyer and seller trade one contract, and neither is making a reversing trade, then the open interest is increased by one contract. For example, the transaction shown in Figure 17.1 creates one contract of open interest, since neither party has any other position in the futures market. The trades shown in Figure 17.2, however, also give rise to just one contract of open interest. When Traders A and B trade, they create one contract of open interest. When Trader A enters a reversing trade and brings Trader C into the market, there is no increase in open interest. In effect, Trader C has simply taken the place of Trader A.

Every contract begins with zero open interest and ends with zero open interest. When the exchange first permits trading in a given contract maturity, there

Figure 17.5

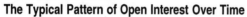

The Typical Pattern of Open Interest Over Time

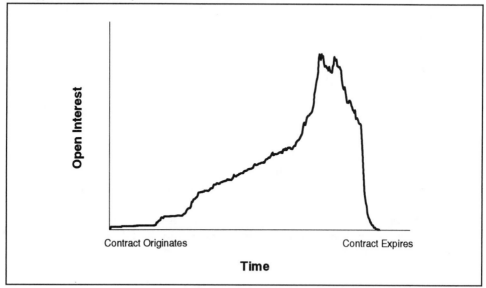

is no open interest until the first trade is made. At the end of the contract's life, all traders must fulfill their obligations by entering reversing trades or by completing delivery. After this process is complete, there is no longer any open interest. Figure 17.5 shows the typical pattern that the open interest will follow. When the contract is first opened for trading, open interest builds slowly and continues to build. In fact, the nearby contract usually has the largest open interest. As the contract nears maturity, however, the open interest falls off drastically. This is due to the fact that many traders enter reversing trades to fulfill their commitments without having to incur the expense and bother of actually making delivery. This pattern is very uniform and can be seen clearly from the quotations in Figure 17.3.

The final line of the quotations shows the number of contracts that were estimated to have traded on the day being reported and the actual volume for the preceding day's trading. This line also shows the total open interest, which is simply the sum of the open interest for all of the different contract maturities. The very last item in this line is the change in the open interest since the preceding day.

Futures Pricing

One of the most important tasks of finance is to explain why prices in a market behave as they do and to specify as clearly as possible how prices ought to behave. In the futures market, the concept of the basis plays a key role in our understanding of the factors that influence futures prices. Therefore, this section begins with a discussion of the basis. We then proceed to explore two models of futures prices. The first, and probably more important, is the cost–of–carry framework. The second, which is also important, interprets futures prices as the market's best estimate of future cash prices.

The Basis

The **basis** is defined as:

$$\text{Basis} = \text{Cash Price} - \text{Futures Price} \qquad \text{17.1}$$

Traders in the futures markets watch the basis very closely, because its behavior is governed by certain rules. Also, the various pricing theories can be stated in terms of rules about how the basis will behave.

The first rule about the behavior of the basis is that the basis must equal zero at the delivery date for the futures contract. This is necessary to rule out arbitrage possibilities. To see why the basis must be zero at this point, assume that the following prices prevail the moment prior to delivery on the corn futures contract, and assume that there are no transactions costs.

Futures Price of Corn: 300 cents per bushel

Cash Price of Corn: 295 cents per bushel

Faced with these prices and the fact that delivery is at hand, a trader could make the following transactions to earn an arbitrage profit.

Buy 5,000 bushels of corn in the spot market at 295 cents per bushel, for a total price of $14,750.

Sell 1 futures contract for the immediate delivery of corn at 300 cents per bushel, for a total futures price of $15,000.

Deliver the purchased corn against the futures contract, and collect $15,000.

These transactions, all executed simultaneously, will yield a profit of $250. In this case, there was no investment, because all of the transactions were executed simultaneously. Further, there was no risk, because the trader bought and sold the same good at the same time. If the futures price had been less than the cash price, the trader could simply have bought the futures contract, taken delivery, and sold the delivered corn for a profit in the spot market. To avoid these arbitrage opportunities, the basis must be zero at the delivery date on the futures contract. Equivalently, the cash price of a good must equal the futures price for the same good at the time of delivery, and this is also a no–arbitrage condition.

Prior to delivery, the futures price may be less than or greater than the cash price. If the cash price is greater than the futures price, the basis will be positive. Further, the futures price and cash price must converge over the life of the futures

Figure 17.6

The Convergence of Futures and Cash Prices as Futures Contracts Approach Delivery

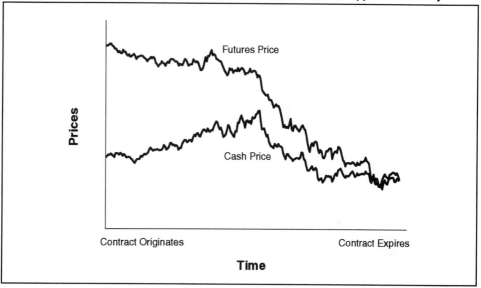

contract, because the futures and cash prices must be equal at the delivery date. Figure 17.6 illustrates this convergence.

If we can understand the factors that explain these price patterns that occur prior to delivery, we will have developed a good grasp of the key pricing principles governing futures markets. There are two basic pricing factors at work. The first, and probably more important, is known as the **cost–of–carry relationship**. The second interprets futures prices as estimates of future spot prices. Together, the two pricing relationships provide a good understanding of pricing in futures markets. We will explore each of these relationships in turn.

The Cost–of–Carry Relationship for Futures Prices

Imagine that the following prices existed for corn.

Cash Price:	250 cents per bushel
Futures Price:	300 (for delivery in three months)

Also assume that it is possible to borrow funds at a rate of 1 percent per month and that it costs $.05 per month per bushel to store corn. These storage costs include the cost of the warehousing, transportation, and insurance, for example. Faced with these facts, the following strategy appears viable.

1. Borrow $12,500 for three months at 1 percent per month.
2. Buy 5,000 bushels of corn in the cash market for 250 cents per bushel with a total outlay of $12,500.
3. Store the corn for three months at $.05 per bushel per month, with the storage cost of $750 to be paid at the end of the storage period.
4. Sell a futures contract, calling for the delivery of corn in three months at a price of 300 cents per bushel, or a total price of $15,000.

All of these transactions would be implemented at the beginning of the three–month period. At the end of the three–month period, the following transactions would be completed.

1. Deliver the 5,000 bushels of corn against the futures contract, and collect $15,000.
2. Pay the debt of $12,878.76 on the original loan, which reflects interest at 1 percent per month compounded monthly.
3. Pay the storage bill of $750.

After completing these transactions, the trader's net cash flows are as follows:

Time = 0	Time = 3 months	
$0	Collect on futures contract	$15,000.00
	Pay debt	–12,878.76
	Pay storage costs	+ –750.00
		+$1,371.24

This transaction reflects a successful arbitrage venture. The trader invested zero funds and reaped a sure profit. In a market that performs even slightly efficiently, such a transaction would be impossible. This leads to the cost–of–carry relationship:

$$\text{Futures Price} \leq \text{Cash Price} + \underbrace{\frac{\text{Storage Costs} + \text{Financing Costs}}{\text{Cost-of-Carry}}}\qquad \textbf{17.2}$$

Simply stated, the cost–of–carry relationship says that the futures price must be less than or equal to the cost of the commodity in the spot market plus the cost of carrying the commodity forward in time to deliver against the futures contract. In Equation 17.2, the cost–of–carry includes both financing and storage costs. However, holding some goods yields certain advantages. For example, if the stored good is a financial instrument, there is a financing cost for the value of the instrument, but the instrument may make interest payments that will largely offset the financing cost. Therefore, the financing cost must be interpreted as the net financing cost. If that relationship does not hold, then there will be an arbitrage opportunity.

Does the cost–of–carry relationship work the other way? In other words, is there a no–arbitrage condition that says the futures price must be equal to or greater than the cash price plus the cost–of–carry? To explore this possibility, consider prices of corn such as the following.

Cash Price: 300 cents per bushel

Futures Price: 250 (for delivery in three months)

Given these prices and unrestricted short selling, one could trade as follows:

1. Sell 5,000 bushels of corn short at 300 cents per bushel and receive $15,000. (In this transaction, the trader borrows the corn and sells it, with the obligation to return the corn to its owner later.)
2. Invest the $15,000 for three months at 1 percent per month.
3. Buy one futures contract for the delivery of corn in three months.

At the end of three months, the transactions would be completed as follows:

1. Take delivery of the 5,000 bushels of corn on the futures contract, and pay 250 cents per bushel for a total of $12,500.
2. Use the corn to cover the short position.

The trader's cash flows would be as follows:

Time = 0	Time = 3 months	
$0	Collect on investment	$15,454.52
	Pay for the delivery of the corn on the futures contract	−$12,500.00
		+$2,954.52

In this situation the trader would make a sure profit of $2954.52, again without investment. As a consequence, with unrestricted short selling the following rule must also hold:

$$\text{Futures Price} \geq \text{Cash Price} + \text{Interest}$$

Having assumed the same borrowing and investment rates, we can put these two relationships together and obtain the following rule given unrestricted short selling:

$$\text{Cash Price} + \text{Interest} \leq \text{Futures Price}$$
$$\text{Futures Price} \leq \text{Cash Price} + \text{Storage} + \text{Financing Costs}$$

For almost all commodities, however, there are restrictions on short selling. In this example, we have assumed that the trader had full use of the proceeds on the short sale. This is normally not the case. For some commodities, such as corn, it is virtually impossible to enter a short sale. For financial assets, it is possible, but there are charges to be incurred. This means that the cost–of–carry relationship implies the following:

$$\text{Futures Price} \cong \text{Cash Price} + \text{Storage Costs} + \text{Financing Costs} \qquad \textbf{17.3}$$

The relationship in Equation 17.3 does not hold as a strict equality because of the potential impact of costs for restrictions on short selling.[3]

Spreads and the Cost–of–Carry

For a single commodity, a **spread** is the difference in price between two futures contracts of differing maturities. For example, there is a price spread between different pairs of corn futures contracts in Figure 17.4. Just as the cost–of–carry implies a price relationship between the futures price and the cash price, it also implies a relationship between futures prices for contracts with differing maturities. With unrestricted short selling, it must be the case that:

$$\begin{aligned}\text{Distant Futures Price} \cong \text{Nearby Futures Price} + \text{Storage Costs} \\ + \text{Financing Costs} \qquad \textbf{17.4}\end{aligned}$$

Equation 17.4 parallels Equation 17.3 very closely in form and spirit. To rule out arbitrage, prices must adjust so that it is impossible to sell a distant futures contract, accept delivery on a nearby futures, carry the delivered good to delivery on the distant contract, and make a profit. Otherwise, there will again be arbitrage opportunities. In this case, the storage costs and financing costs are to be incurred in the future. To make the investment opportunity riskless, the prospective arbitrageur must enter a forward or futures contract to establish the storage and financing costs at the outset. So the cost–of–carry relationship, with the assumption of unrestricted short selling, determines the relationship between the cash price and any futures price, and it also determines the price relationship among all futures contracts.

Observed Futures Prices and the Cost–of–Carry Relationship

As we have seen, the cost–of–carry relationship expressed by Equation 17.3 must hold at every point in time if arbitrage opportunities are to be ruled out. Again, this relationship is predicated on the assumption that short selling is unrestricted. In

---

[3] The practical effect of restrictions on short selling is discussed in more detail later in the section of this chapter entitled Interest Rate Futures.

Table 17.3

━━━━━━━━━━━━━━━━━

Crude Oil Futures Prices Before and After the Invasion of Kuwait

	Settlement Price ($ per barrel)	
Contract Expiration	July 19, 1990	August 16, 1990
September 1990	19.86	27.36
October 1990	20.31	27.28
November 1990	20.56	26.59
December 1990	20.73	26.12

many markets, however, short selling is restricted by being costly; in some markets, short selling is almost impossible.

While the futures price generally exceeds the cash price for storable commodities, as the cost–of–carry relationship with unrestricted short selling implies, that is not always true. A search of Figure 17.3 reveals some interesting exceptions to that general rule. For most commodities, the quoted prices for the more distant futures contracts are higher than prices for the nearby contract, just as we would expect from the cost–of–carry relationship. This is certainly the case for the corn contract, as highlighted in Figure 17.4.

More distant futures contract prices do not always exceed the nearby prices. To see how normal price relationships can be dramatically upset by unexpected shifts in supply or demand, consider the effect of the Iraqi invasion of Kuwait on world oil markets. Table 17.3 shows price quotations for crude oil futures for various contract expirations. The dates are July 19, 1990, and August 16, 1990—two weeks before and two weeks after the invasion date of August 2, 1990.

These price quotations show two important features. First, there was an across–the–board jump in prices. During that four–week period, crude oil futures prices increased about 40 percent. The quotations reveal a second and equally important change in prices. In the pre–invasion period, crude oil prices follow the cost–of–carry relationship quite well. Prices for nearby contracts are below prices for more distant contracts. However, two weeks after the invasion, oil prices are inverted—nearby prices are higher than distant prices. The pre–invasion price pattern—with the deferred contract prices being greater than the nearby prices— reflects what is called a **normal market**. The pattern of crude oil prices after the invasion—with prices on deferred contracts lying below the nearby contract prices—is known as an **inverted market**.

In the post–invasion period, if unrestricted short selling were possible in the oil market, an arbitrageur could have made a fortune trading at these prices. The trader would have sold physical oil short at its higher price and purchased a distant futures contract at the lower price. The trader would maintain this position until the futures contract came due for delivery and would then accept delivery. The trader would use this oil to honor the short sale. The price difference between the cash price and the futures price would be the trader's profit, after adjusting for interest earnings and transaction costs.

From these price patterns in the post–invasion period, we may observe two things. First, there were serious barriers to short selling oil in the aftermath of the invasion of Kuwait. The invasion created a dramatic shortage of oil, especially oil for immediate delivery. A trader's ability to sell a good short depends on being able to borrow the good from someone else. After the invasion of Kuwait, oil was not available for loan, because the war had tightened supplies so dramatically. If there were no such shortages, arbitrageurs would have driven oil prices into line with the cost–of–carry relationship that we have been exploring. Second, in markets where unrestricted short selling is not possible, as was the case in the oil market after the invasion of Kuwait, the cost–of–carry relationship does not tell the whole story of futures prices. We need to account for shortages and the role of price expectations in the establishment of futures prices.

Futures Prices and Expected Future Spot Prices

Traders in futures markets have expectations about the future cash prices for various commodities. Not surprisingly, these expectations about future spot prices affect futures prices. Two questions about expected future prices and futures prices are most important. First, why and how do futures market prices adjust to expectations about future spot prices? Second, how can traders' expectations about future spot prices have an effect, given what we know about the cost–of–carry pricing relationship?

With the short selling potential of the oil market in tatters after the supply shock of the invasion, oil prices were free from cost–of–carry constraints and revealed a market expectation of higher prices in the nearby futures, followed by a gradual fall in prices over several months. The expected fall in prices was revealed by the gradual decline in futures prices for more distant maturities. This pattern of prices would be consistent with a view that supply difficulties would be reduced in the future. Such an easing of supply conditions could arise from a resolution of the Gulf crisis or the bringing of new supplies into place.

If a trader expected that the cash oil price for a particular date in the future would be greater than the current futures price for that delivery month, the trader could buy the futures. If her expectations proved correct, she would make a profit by holding the futures position and watching the price rise as the futures and cash prices converged at expiration. Similarly, if a trader believed that the cash price that would prevail in a few months would be lower than the futures price for delivery at that time, the trader could sell futures and profit from the convergence of the cash and futures prices as expiration approached. In other words, if futures prices diverge from traders' expectations about future cash prices, they will take speculative positions to profit from the difference. In effect, the traders in the crude oil futures market get to vote on the future expected price of oil, and they vote in proportion to the commitment they are willing to make by trading in the market. If the prevailing futures price does not equal the market's aggregate expectation, traders will continue to enter the market to try to capture profits. This action will drive the futures price into equality with the market's aggregate expectation of the cash price for the commodity at the time of delivery.

If there were unrestricted short selling in the oil market, the prices would have to exhibit a strictly increasing pattern, as argued earlier. On the other hand, if short selling were totally impossible in a given market, the futures prices should equal the expected future spot price of the commodity in question in order to eliminate any opportunities to earn excessive speculative profits.

The Social Function of Futures Markets

Futures markets have often come under attack from different interest groups in society and from legislative bodies. The U.S. Congress actually forbade trading in onion futures and came very close, at one point, to banning futures trading. Currently, futures markets are thriving, partially in recognition of the useful social function that they serve. There are two principal social functions of futures markets. The first is the role of price discovery, and the second is assisting in the transference of risk in society.

Price Discovery

Price discovery refers to the information that the futures market may impart about future commodity prices. In the absence of short selling, we have argued that futures prices should equal expected future spot prices. If that were the case, the futures price would be a very good forecast of future prices, because it would be aggregating the opinions of many different traders in the marketplace. In fact, there have been a number of studies testing the performance of the futures price as a predictor of subsequently observed spot prices. While the forecast embodied in the futures price often has large errors, it does seem to perform very well on average. Further, there is considerable evidence that futures prices perform better than professional forecasting services.

While futures prices may not give good forecasts in some respects, they do seem to perform better than most, if not all, alternative indicators. Because of this, the role of the futures market in price discovery is very important. Imagine, for example, a contractor preparing to bid on an important project that will require a great deal of lumber. The bid must be submitted now, but the project is not to commence for nine months. The bid the contractor submits must reflect the costs of the lumber that will be used in the project. If futures prices are a good gauge of the spot prices prevailing at the time of delivery, then it would be a mistake to submit a bid based on the current price of lumber. Instead, the bid should reflect the price of lumber that is consistent with the futures prices at the time the project is to commence.

In this case, the contractor would be using these futures prices as a guide to future spot prices. Based on a great deal of evidence, futures prices do provide better forecasts of future prices than many alternatives, so the contractor is able to acquire a quality estimate at a very cheap price. Some researchers regard the function of price discovery as the most important social function that the market serves.

Risk Transference

The second major social function of the futures market is the opportunity that it provides for risk transference. As we have seen in our discussion of the CAPM, the bearing of risk can be a very important function in the capital markets, a function that can be richly rewarded. However, as we have also seen, different investors will have different degrees of risk tolerance. Therefore, a market that allows investors to modify the amount of risk that they bear can be very useful. The futures market allows great latitude in the transference of risk from one trader unwilling to bear it to others who will accept the bearing of risk in the hope of profit.

Assume that the contractor who used the lumber futures price to formulate his or her bid receives the building contract in February. The contractor knows that he or she will need a great deal of lumber in November. However, the price of that lumber is uncertain. This means that the contractor has a considerable degree of risk. If lumber prices rise unexpectedly, the lumber must be purchased anyway, and the price increase will come directly out of the profits for the project.

In this circumstance, the contractor has a choice. The contractor may do nothing, hoping that prices do not rise. In this case, the contractor bears the risk of the price fluctuation. Alternatively, the contractor could enter the lumber futures market to reduce the risk. Assume that the current futures prices are as shown in Table 17.4 and the contractor needs 1.3 million board feet of 2–by–4s for the project.[4] If the contractor wanted to reduce the risk exposure for lumber, he or she

Table 17.4

Lumber Futures Prices in February

Expiration Month	Settlement Price
March	$134.30
May	148.20
July	160.50
September	169.50
November	176.50

Note: Each contract represents 130,000 board feet, and the contract price is the price per 1,000 board feet.

---

[4]A board foot is a square foot of lumber one inch thick, or its equivalent in volume. The lumber contract calls for the delivery of 130,000 board feet of 2–by–4s, so the contractor needs 10 contracts worth of lumber.

could buy 10 lumber contracts for November delivery at the current futures price of $176.50 per 1,000 board feet.

This transaction would guarantee the price that must be paid for the lumber. By entering this transaction, the contractor has transferred the unwanted risk to some other party in the futures market. Possibly the trader opposite the contractor is a supplier of 2–by–4s. In this case, the seller of the futures contract may be reducing his or her risk as well, because the seller would be establishing the price to be received for the 2–by–4s. In this case, there is not so much a transference of risk, but the futures market would be allowing the contractor and the 2–by–4 producer to both reduce their risks. Once the contractor enters this futures transaction, the price to be paid for lumber is fixed. If the spot price of lumber in November is $200 per 1,000 board feet, the contractor will still pay $176.50. With a position of 10 contracts, for a total of 1.3 million board feet, the contractor saved $30,550. Without the futures contract, the cost would have been $200 per 1,000 board feet for a total of 1.3 million board feet, or a total cost of $260,000. With the futures contract, the price is only $176.50 per 1,000 board feet, for a total of $229,450. The difference of $30,550 is the amount saved by having entered the futures contract. Alternatively, if the spot price for this kind of lumber is $150 per 1,000 board feet in November, the contractor will still have to pay $176.50 per 1,000 board feet. In this case, the contractor will have paid $34,450 more by being in the futures contract.

The point of this kind of transaction is not to ensure that a trader pays less for a good by entering the futures market. Instead, the goal is to reduce risk. The contractor had an initial risk position because the lumber was needed. By transacting in the futures market, the contractor hedges that risk. A **hedge** is simply a transaction that is designed to offset some existing or anticipated risk. Once the contractor has entered this hedge position, there is no more uncertainty about how much will be paid for the lumber. The price of the lumber is fixed via the futures contract and the risk is reduced.

This kind of hedge transaction is very important for society. For example, the contractor might have been so risk averse that he or she would not even have submitted a bid for the project if it were not possible to use the futures market to reduce the risk. In many cases, the physical realities of the production process involve risks, and those who carry out the production process may not be the optimal risk bearers from the point of view of society. There may be other parties in society who are better able and more willing to bear certain risks. Because the futures markets provide a means for transferring much of that risk to willing risk bearers, it provides a useful function to society.

Speculation with Futures

If there are numerous parties in the futures markets who receive an important benefit by being able to transfer their risk to other parties, who bears that risk and how are they compensated for their risk–bearing services? To some extent, it is possible for the total risk in society to be reduced in the futures market. For example, a wheat farmer might attempt to reduce his or her risk by selling the wheat crop via the futures market. Likewise, a cereal producer might reduce his or her risk, associated with the need for wheat as a cereal ingredient, by buying wheat via the futures market. In this happy circumstance, the two parties are brought together and can both reduce their risks. In this case, there is a net reduction of risk that is undertaken by society.

However, in many cases there will not be opportunities for the mutual risk reduction enjoyed by the wheat farmer and the cereal producer. In these cases, the risk that is transferred away from the hedger must be borne by a speculator. While speculators are often disparaged for their greed, they actually play a very important role in futures markets. As we will see, there are different kinds of speculators who provide different services in addition to risk–bearing.

Speculators

We can distinguish three different kinds of speculators by the length of time they usually hold a futures position. They are (1) scalpers, (2) day traders, and (3) position traders. The **scalper** has the shortest time horizon of all of the futures market speculators. It is not unusual for a scalper to make a futures trade and then to enter a reversing trade within a few minutes. Scalpers are essentially attempting to make a profit by trading on the very short–term fluctuations in futures prices. They do this by sensing the immediate direction of the market. This approach requires that the scalper actually be in the pit, so that he or she can see how the trading is progressing and can read the psychology of the other traders. Also, scalpers generate a very high number of trades. As a consequence, they must be in a position to have very low transaction costs. Even if a scalper could sense the market developments from a position out of the pit, he or she certainly could not afford the transaction costs that would be incurred in executing the transactions through a broker.

The scalper is hoping to make a profit out of a one– or two–tick fluctuation in the futures contract price. A **tick** is the minimum price movement on a contract that is permitted by the exchange. For most contracts, this will be $25 or less. For example, one tick on the Treasury–bill futures contract is $25, and one tick on the corn contract is $12.50. Obviously, if the scalper is planning to make a profit out of such small price fluctuations, he or she must be on the floor in order to have low transaction costs. For the typical scalper, a round trip transaction charge for a contract will be less than $1. A **round trip** is the purchase and sale of the contract.

Compared with the scalper, the **day trader** is a very farsighted individual. The day trader may hold a position for a long time—maybe even two or three hours. The distinguishing feature of day traders is that they never maintain a position overnight. "Taking a position home" is just too risky in most cases, because sudden changes in the economic situation can have drastic effects on futures prices. With the market closed at night, a trader has no way to abandon a losing position.[5]

To see the risk inherent in an overnight position, consider the orange juice concentrate futures contract. This contract is traded by the Citrus Associates of the New York Cotton Exchange, with 15,000 lbs. of orange juice concentrate per contract. Several times in the last decade, the orange juice market has been surprised by a sudden and unexpected freeze in the Florida orange groves. For a trader holding a short position in orange juice, this kind of development can be disastrous. For this reason, the day trader, by definition, always closes his or her position before the end of trading. This is done by reversing trades. The strategy pursued by the day trader is to follow slightly longer–term developments than those that interest the scalper.

The speculator with the longest time horizon is the **position trader**. A position trader stakes a position in the futures market, which he or she may hold for weeks or even months without adjustment. Position trades may be either outright positions or spreads. An **outright position** is simply buying or selling a given futures contract of a single maturity. Of all of the futures strategies, this is probably the riskiest, and few position traders seem to be interested in this dangerous career.

Most position traders use spreads. When the position trader trades a spread, he or she takes a position in two or more related contracts in a way that reduces the risk below that which would be encountered in an outright position. These spreads may be for different contract maturities within a single commodity. As such they are called a **time spread** or an **intracommodity spread**. Alternatively, the trader may take a position in two related, but different, commodities. This kind of trade is called an **intercommodity spread**.

For example, a trader might believe that the price of wheat is too high relative to the price of corn for a particular delivery month. A trade to capitalize on this view, if it is correct, would be to sell the wheat contract and to buy the corn contract. Since the contracts traded are for two different goods, this is an intercommodity spread. The same factors tend to affect wheat and corn, because they are substitute goods in many applications. For a transaction in two different commodities to be a spread, the price behavior of the two commodities must be related. In a spread of any type, the trader is not trading on an absolute price movement for one futures contract but is hoping that the price of one futures contract moves in a certain way relative to the price of another. Figure 17.7 shows how this kind of trade might be profitable. At the initial position, there is a relatively wide gap between the wheat and corn futures prices. Because the trader

---

[5]One interesting development in the futures market is the new tendency for markets around the world to be linked. The Chicago Mercantile Exchange and the Singapore Futures Exchange now permit dual listing of certain contracts. Since the two exchanges are on approximately opposite sides of the world, this allows trading in many more hours per day. In the not–too–distant future, futures contracts will probably be traded 24 hours per day.

Figure 17.7

Price Movements for an Intercommodity Spread Between Wheat and Corn

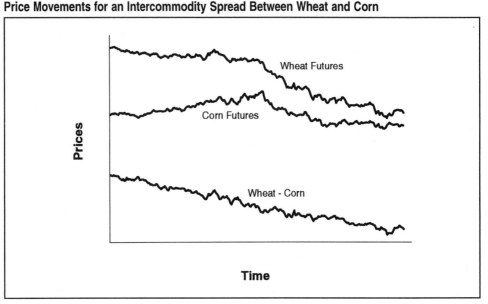

believes that the gap is too wide, he or she will sell the relatively overpriced wheat contract and buy the relatively underpriced corn contract.

As the figure shows, the prices of both goods fall, but as they do so, the gap between the two closes over time. This generates a profit for the spread position that is equal to the difference in the price gap at the initial position and the gap at the time the position is closed. Notice in this case that the purchase of the corn futures alone would have resulted in a loss, even though the trader believed that it was relatively underpriced. An outright short position in wheat would have generated a much larger profit than the spread trade, however. In spread trading, traders sacrifice the greater gains that holding just one side of the trade might generate in order to limit risk. In trading the spread, the trader was anticipating a gain on one side and a loss on the other, with the gain being more than enough to offset the loss.

In a time spread, the trader must believe that the futures prices are not correctly aligned in some sense. For example, in the lumber quotations of Table 17.4 the price for the July contract may be high relative to the May contract and low relative to the September contract, in the opinion of some speculator. One way to take advantage of this possibility, if the speculator is correct, would be to sell the July contract and buy the May contract. This position will be profitable if the July price falls relative to the May price. Because both of the contracts traded are for the same commodity, this is a time spread.

The Role of the Speculator

In our society, speculators are often regarded as evil. In the futures markets, however, they serve a very useful function. Speculative activity increases the liquidity of the market. The scalper, for example, with his or her frequent trades, makes it much easier for the hedger to transact. Without liquidity, hedgers would not be able to transact easily. A result of a lack of liquidity is typically larger bid–asked spreads and lower market efficiency. Providing liquidity to the market is one of the major social services of speculators. This is not to imply that they trade in order to provide liquidity, but their profit-seeking behavior has a beneficial side effect for the market.

The second major service to society that the speculator provides is the bearing of risk. If we think of a speculator as a trader who has no special commitment to the goods being traded, but who enters the market solely in the pursuit of profit, we have a picture of a trader who increases his or her risk in the search for profit. The willingness of the speculator to take on greater risk means that another party may be able to reduce his or her risk by transferring it to the speculator. As discussed earlier, the ability to transfer unwanted risk to someone willing to bear it makes it possible for risk–averse economic agents to undertake socially useful projects that they would be unwilling to take if they had to bear all of the risk themselves.

Speculation and the Behavior of Futures Prices

Speculators do not bear risk for free. They take on positions in the futures market that involve the bearing of risk in the hope of earning a profit. Earlier, we saw reason to believe that futures prices are good measures of future expected spot prices. If that is true, and if expectations are correct on average, that implies that speculators will not make any profit on average. However, they will be bearing risk. In other words, if futures prices equal expected future spot prices, and the expectations about future spot prices are correct, there is no way for speculators to make a profit, on average.

John Maynard Keynes and John Hicks maintain that the hedger's needs usually require speculators to be buyers of futures contracts. Speculators take on long positions by buying futures contracts at prices that are less than the expected future spot price of the commodity. If this were not the case, the speculators would be buying futures contracts without the reasonable hope of gain. If Keynes and Hicks are correct, and assuming that expectations regarding future spot prices are correct on average, this implies that futures prices should rise over time as the low futures price rises to meet the expected future spot price at the maturity of the futures contract. This process of futures prices rising over time is called **normal backwardation**.

If the hedgers' needs require speculators to be short in the aggregate, the futures price must lie above the expected future spot price if speculators are to be rewarded for their risk–bearing services. In this situation, the futures prices must

Figure 17.8

Normal Backwardation and the Contango in Futures Prices

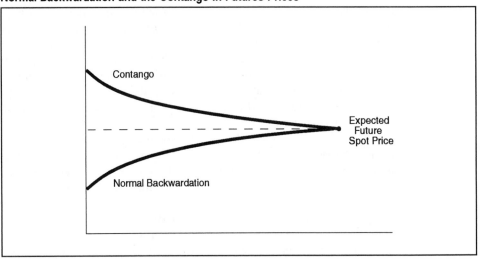

fall over time, in order for the futures price at maturity to equal the lower expected future spot price that prevailed when the hedge was entered and the speculators took a short position. This implies a pattern of falling futures prices over time, and this price pattern is called a **contango**.

Figure 17.8 illustrates these two possibilities. In this figure, the expected spot price is shown as being constant. This is done solely for the sake of convenience. If speculators are net buyers, or hold a net long position, the futures price must lie below the expected future spot price if the speculators are to be rewarded. In this situation, the futures price would rise over time, following a process of normal backwardation, until the futures price converges to the cash price at the maturity of the futures contract. Similarly, if speculators are net short, the futures price must lie above the expected future spot price, so that the speculators can earn a profit as the futures price falls to meet the cash price at the futures contract maturity.

In spite of considerable research, neither of these hypotheses has been validated. Many studies continue to show that the futures price is normally equal to the observed cash price at maturity. If that is the case, there is little opportunity for speculators to make a profit on a consistent basis. This issue is of great importance for assessing the value of the futures market, because the amount the speculators earn determines the cost of risk transference for the hedger. The evidence to date is consistent with a low, or even zero, cost of risk transference, because it does not appear that the speculators earn a consistent return.

One study explains this apparently strange result by considering the problem within the context of the CAPM. According to the CAPM, only the bearing of systematic risk is rewarded in the marketplace. Katherine Dusak advances this argument and concludes that futures contracts tend to have no systematic risk. In the CAPM framework, this finding is consistent with her observed findings that futures prices tend to equal subsequent spot prices. According to her analysis, there is no return on the risky positions the speculators assume, because they are not bearing systematic risk. This makes the speculator appear very much like a gambler. If Dusak's analysis is correct, speculators increase their risk by entering the futures market, but they do not get paid for bearing this risk on a regular basis. This is like the roulette player who increases his risk by playing, but who earns no regular return because he is not providing the service of bearing systematic risk.[6]

Interest Rate Futures

In the futures markets today, a wide variety of goods is traded, ranging from pork bellies to financial instruments. These goods are also very diverse with respect to their economic features, such as their storage characteristics and the quality of the markets for their short sale. Because of this tremendous diversity, it is impossible to cover all of the important features of these markets here.[7] Consequently, this section focuses on some key issues of financial futures. This approach illustrates how certain issues in financial futures are related to some of the other problems discussed in this book.

Interest Rate Futures and the Yield Curve

As discussed in Chapter 9, the yield curve is extremely important for bond investing and bond portfolio management. The different maturities of bonds and their commensurate yields allows investors to commit their money for different periods of time in order to take advantage of a particular shape that the yield curve might possess at any given moment. We have also seen how forward rates of interest play an important role in two theories of the term structure—the pure expectations theory and the liquidity premium theory.

In the interest rate futures markets, the exchanges have made a conscious effort to offer interest–rate futures that cover the yield curve. For example, the International Monetary Market (IMM) of the Chicago Mercantile Exchange (CME) has specialized in the shorter maturity instruments. The IMM currently offers interest rate futures contracts on Treasury bills, bank CDs, and Eurodollar deposits, all with maturities of about three months. By contrast, the Chicago Board of Trade (CBOT) has focused on the longer maturities. The CBOT trades a contract on long–term T–bonds, the most successful futures contract ever introduced. It also offers contracts on two, five, and ten year Treasury notes.

---

[6]See Katherine Dusak, "Futures Trading and Investor Returns: An Investigation of Commodity Market Risk Premiums," *Journal of Political Economy*, December 1973.

[7]For a treatment of futures markets in the United States, see R. Kolb, *Understanding Futures Markets*, 4e, Miami: Kolb Publishing, 1994.

To illustrate the connection between the yield curve and interest rate futures, we will focus on the IMM's T–bill contract. This contract calls for the delivery of T–bills with a face value of $1 million having 90 days to maturity at the time of delivery. Prices for the T–bill futures are quoted according to a system known as the IMM Index. The IMM Index is simply the discount yield on the T–bill futures subtracted from 100. So, for example, a quoted settlement value of 94.00 means that the futures yield would be 6 percent. To contract for delivery of a 90–day T–bill with a futures price of 94.00, for example, a trader would have to agree to pay a price that was commensurate with a discount yield of 6 percent.

There is an important relationship between yields implied by futures prices and the yields on spot market instruments. Essentially, interest rate futures yields may be interpreted as forward rates of interest. For example, the yield of the March 1996 T–bill futures contract is the forward rate of interest for a 90–day T–bill to run from March to June, 1996. In other words, if we calculated from the spot market the forward rate for the same period as that covered by the March 1996 T–bill futures contract, we should find a result that almost exactly matches the yield on the T–bill futures.

If that were not the case, and markets were perfect, it would be possible to generate arbitrage profits. This would be accomplished by buying and selling spot market T–bills and T–bill futures to take advantage of the yield discrepancy. In fact, if markets were perfect, and included in this is the opportunity for unrestricted short selling, the forward rates of interest and the yield on the futures contract would have to be exactly equal. Actual markets, however, are not perfect, so the relationship would not have to hold exactly. If we take into account transaction costs, though, the difference between the forward rate of interest calculated from the spot market and the rate of interest implied by the futures contract would still have to be very close.

This issue has been examined in great detail by a number of authors, but the definitive study was conducted by Rendleman and Carabini.[8] They attempted to determine if there were arbitrage opportunities between spot and futures market T–bills, given the fact that traders would have to pay transaction costs. One of these costs is the fact that short selling is constrained. In their study, they found that it cost about one–half of a percentage point, or 50 basis points, to sell a T–bill short.[9] This meant that futures yields and forward rates of interest could differ by this amount without giving rise to any arbitrage opportunities.

Using daily data for two years from 1976 to 1978, which gave a total of 1,606 observations, Rendleman and Carabini tested for the presence of arbitrage opportunities, given the 50 basis point cost of short selling in the T–bill futures

---

[8] See R. Rendleman and C. Carabini, "The Efficiency of the Treasury Bill Futures Market," *Journal of Finance*, September 1979. Rendleman and Carabini also review much of the previous research on this topic.

[9] Remember that short selling involves borrowing the good that is to be sold short. In this case, the 50 basis points is the charge imposed by the owner for lending the security.

Figure 17.9

Observed Yield Differentials Between Forward and Futures Yields in the T–Bill Market

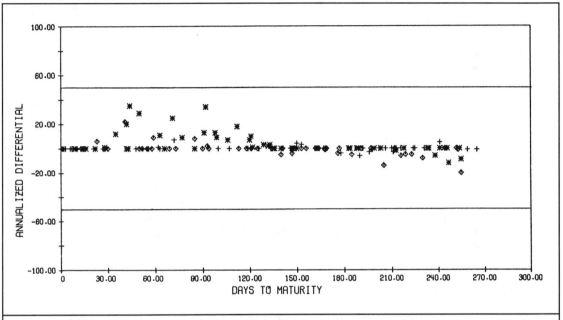

Source: R. Rendleman and C. Carabini, "The Efficiency of the Treasury Bill Futures Market," *Journal of Finance*, 34, 1979, pp. 907. Reprinted with permission from the *Journal of Finance*.

markets. Figure 17.9 depicts their results graphically. For all 1,606 observations, a random sample of which are shown in Figure 17.9, they found that the difference in yields between the forward rate and the futures rate fell within 50 basis points from perfect equality. In other words, there were no arbitrage opportunities, given the existence of transaction costs and the 50 basis point cost of short selling. This is reflected by the fact that all of the plotted points fall within a distance of 50 basis points from perfect equality. Also, as the figure shows, most of their observations fell exactly on the line of perfect equality between the forward rate and the futures rate. For these cases, this would mean that there were no arbitrage opportunities even if there were no cost to short selling.

Rendleman and Carabini's results tie in very closely with the other themes that we have been developing regarding the yield curve and the interpretation of futures prices. First, it is appropriate to treat yields on interest rate futures as forward rates, because the two are virtually identical. Second, we can be sure that they are virtually identical, because if they were not, there would be arbitrage opportunities. Third, we know from Chapter 9 that forward rates of interest have been among the very best estimates of future spot rates of interest. This is consistent with the reasons we have developed in this chapter for thinking that futures prices are good estimates of future spot prices. Finally, the results of Rendleman and Carabini are consistent with the cost–of–carry framework, because it is only in the presence of costs for short selling that there are divergences between the forward rate and the futures rate of interest.

Stock Index Futures

In recent years, stock index futures trading has flourished and received a great deal of attention from a concerned public. The most important stock index futures contracts are based on the S&P 500 stock index and on the Major Market Index (MMI). The MMI is an index of 20 stocks designed to mimic the Dow Jones Industrial Average. For both of these futures contracts, the futures price represents the current value of the stocks adjusted for the cost–of–carry. The cost–of–carry is essentially the financing cost of holding the stocks, adjusted for the dividends the stocks are expected to pay between the current date and the expiration of the futures. Because of the high liquidity and ease of trading financial assets, such as stocks, stock index futures obey the cost–of–carry model.

Stock Index Arbitrage

From time to time, slight discrepancies arise between the futures price and the value of the stocks comprising the index. For example, it may sometimes be the case that a trader could sell a futures contract for a price that exceeded the cost of buying the stocks in the index and carrying them forward to delivery. As we have seen for other commodities, such a discrepancy can lead to arbitrage activity. Efforts to exploit discrepancies between stock index futures prices and the prices of the underlying stocks are known as **stock index arbitrage**.

Traders use computers to monitor futures prices and stock prices constantly, always searching for arbitrage opportunities. When such an opportunity arises, the trader will either buy or sell the futures contract and simultaneously sell or buy the stocks that constitute the index. For the S&P 500 contract, this means selling or buying 500 different stocks. Exploiting any arbitrage opportunity depends critically on speed in responding to a momentary opportunity. The trader must execute orders for the stocks very quickly, being sure to trade the right number of each share. This is the perfect job for a computer.

Program trading is the use of computer programs to initiate orders to buy or sell stocks, and program trading plays a key role in stock index arbitrage. When an arbitrage opportunity develops, the trader can use a program trading strategy to immediately initiate orders to buy or sell the stocks that underlie the index.

Program Trading and Stock Market Volatility

Program trading strategies can lead to massive orders to buy or sell stocks, and some observers have maintained that program trading may have led to increasing stock market volatility and may even have played a role in market disruptions, such as the crash of October 1987. These issues are highly controversial and the subject of continuing investigation. Therefore, the following summary of current thinking must be regarded as provisional.

General Stock Market Volatility.   There has been a general impression of increased volatility in the stock market. This view has been strengthened by occurrences such as the October 1987 crash and the frequency of days with 50–point swings in the Dow. However, most studies conclude that stock market volatility in the 1980s (the period of stock index futures trading) has not been noticeably larger than during other periods. Thus, there does not seem to be a general increase in the overall volatility in the stock market.

Episodic Volatility.   While overall volatility may not have increased, some scholars have been concerned that short–term volatility may be higher due to stock index futures trading. For example, the massive orders associated with program trading might lead to temporary episodes of extremely high volatility, even though the month–to–month volatility shows no real change. This concern focuses on the volatility for a period of a day or even an hour and these bursts of volatility have become known as **episodic volatility** or **jump volatility**. The bulk of evidence suggests a connection between stock index futures trading and jump volatility. However, the evidence does not suggest that the temporary increase in volatility associated with futures trading impairs the functioning of the stock market.[10] As we noted at the beginning of this discussion, these issues of stock market volatility and the role of futures markets in contributing to volatility remain very controversial.

Summary

This chapter attempted to give a general introduction to futures markets. It distinguished futures and forward contracts by noting the differences in their cash flow commitments. We then examined the institutional features of futures markets, including the flow of orders, the role of the clearinghouse, and the fulfillment of commitments in the futures market.

Futures pricing was also explored in this chapter, and the importance of the basis was noted. Essentially, two models of the relationship between futures and spot prices have wide acceptance. One model views futures prices as being equal to expected future spot prices. The second model uses arbitrage concepts to express a cost–of–carry relationship. If this cost–of–carry relationship is violated, arbitrage opportunities will exist.

---

[10] For a discussion of stock index futures and stock market volatility with references to many specific studies, see R. Kolb, *Understanding Futures Markets*, 4e, Miami: Kolb Publishing, 1994, pp. 431–445.

If futures prices equal expected future spot prices, market observers can use the futures market as a valuable information source. This informational role of futures markets is known as price discovery, and this is an important social function of the futures markets. Additionally, the existence of futures markets helps society by providing a mechanism to allow hedgers to transfer unwanted risk to speculators. Speculators play an important role in the futures market because their trading activity generates liquidity for the market and because speculators are willing to bear risk that is too great for the hedgers.

Although there are many different kinds of futures contracts, including those on agricultural commodities and metals, the chapter emphasized financial futures—particularly interest rate and stock index futures.

Questions and Problems

1. What are the two major cash flow differences between futures and forward contracts?
2. What problems with forward contracts are resolved by futures contracts?
3. What are the two most important functions of the clearinghouse of a futures exchange?
4. What is the investment for a trader who buys a futures contract? Justify your answer.
5. What are the two ways to fulfill a futures contract commitment? Which is used more frequently? Why?
6. What is the difference between "open interest" and "trading volume"?
7. What is the "basis" and why is it important?
8. Explain why the futures price might reasonably be thought to equal the expected future spot price.
9. Assume that you believe the futures prices for corn are too low relative to wheat prices. Explain how you could take advantage of this belief.
10. Which is likely to have a greater variance—the basis or the cash price of a good? Why?
11. When hedgers transfer risk away to other traders, what group of traders accepts the risk? Is the risk merely transferred, leaving the total amount of risk unchanged across all traders, or can the amount of risk be reduced? Explain.
12. In previous chapters, we noted that an upward–sloping yield curve generally implied that spot interest rates were expected to rise. If this is so, does it also imply that futures prices are expected to rise? Does this suggest a trading strategy? Explain.
13. Assume that you are a bond portfolio manager and that you anticipate an infusion of investable funds in three months. How could you use the futures market to hedge against unexpected changes in interest rates?
14. Assume that the spot corn price is $3.50, that it costs $.017 cents to store a bushel of corn for one month, and that the relevant cost of financing is 1 percent per month. If a corn futures contract matures in six months and the

current futures price for this contract is $3.65 per bushel, explain how you would respond. Explain your transactions for one contract, assuming 5,000 bushels per contract, all storage costs must be paid at the outset of the transaction, and borrowing and lending rates are equal.

CFA Questions

All CFA examination questions are reprinted, with permission, from the Level I *1992–1994, CFA Candidate Study and Examination Program Review*. Copyright 1992–1994, Association for Investment Management and Research, Charlottesville, Va. All rights reserved.

    A. Futures contracts *differ* from forward contracts in the following ways:
- I. Futures contracts are standardized.
- II. For Futures, performance of each party is guaranteed by a clearinghouse.
- III. Futures contracts require a daily settling of any gains or losses.
- a. I and II only
- b. I and III only
- c. II and III only
- d. I, II, and III

    B. On the maturity date, stock index futures contracts require delivery of:
- a. common stock.
- b. common stock plus accrued dividends.
- c. Treasury bills.
- d. cash.

Suggested Readings

Baecher, E., "Spread Trading in Financial Futures," *The Handbook of Derivative Instruments*, Chicago: Probus Publishing, 1991, pp. 565–577.

Brenner, M., M. G. Subrahmanyam, and J. Uno, "The Japanese Stock Index Futures Markets: The Early Experience," *Japanese Capital Markets*, New York: Harper & Row, 1990, pp. 301–334.

Chance, D. M., "The Effect of Margins on the Volatility of Stock and Derivative Markets: A Review of the Evidence," 2, *Monograph Series in Finance and Economics*, 1990.

Clark, T. and M. Gibson, "Program Trading," *Quantitative International Investing: A Handbook of Analytical and Modeling Techniques and Strategies*, Chicago: Probus Publishing, 1990, pp. 61–74.

Dattatreya, R. E., "Asset Allocation Using Futures and Options," *The Handbook of Fixed Income Securities*, 3e, Homewood, IL: Business Irwin One, 1991.

Edwards, F. R., "Does Futures Trading Increase Stock Market Volatility?" *Financial Analysts Journal*, 44:1, January/February 1988, pp. 63–69.

Gastineau, G. L., "Arbitrage, Program Trading, and the Tail of the Dog," *The Institutional Investor Focus on Investment Management*, Cambridge, MA: Ballinger, 1989, pp. 101–113.

Hsieh, D. A. and M. H. Miller, "Margin Regulation and Stock Market Volatility," *Margins and Market Integrity*, Chicago: Probus Publishing, 1991, pp. 319–364.

Kawaller, I. G. and T. W. Koch, "Managing Cash Flow Risk in Stock Index Futures: The Tail Hedge," *The Handbook of Derivative Instruments*, Chicago: Probus Publishing, 1991, pp. 257–266.

Koenigsberg, M., "A Delivery Option Model For Treasury Bond Futures," *The Journal of Fixed Income*, 1:1, June 1991, pp. 75–88.

Kolb, R. *The Financial Derivatives Reader*, Miami: Kolb Publishing, 1992.

Kolb, R., *Understanding Futures Markets*, 4e, Miami: Kolb Publishing, 1994.

Koomar, S., "Delivery Options for Bond Futures Contracts," *The Handbook of Derivative Instruments*, Chicago: Probus Publishing, 1991, pp. 77–91.

Morris, C. S., "Coordinating Circuit Breakers In Stock and Futures Markets," Federal Reserve Bank of Kansas City *Economic Review*, March/April 1990, pp. 35–48.

Rendleman, R., and C. Carabini, "The Efficiency of the Treasury Bill Futures Market," *Journal of Finance*, 34:4, September 1979, pp. 895–914.

Tompkins, R. G., "International Portfolio Diversification with Stock Index Derivatives," *Quantitative International Investing: A Handbook of Analytical and Modeling Techniques and Strategies*, Chicago: Probus Publishing, 1990, pp. 35–54.

Tosini, P. A., "Stock Index Futures and Stock Market Activity in October 1987," *Financial Analysts Journal*, 44:1, January/February 1988, pp. 28–37.

Zurack, M., "Establishing an Arbitrage Program: Stock Index Arbitrage," *The Institutional Investor Focus on Investment Management*, Cambridge, MA: Ballinger Publishing Company, 1989, pp. 115–132.

CHAPTER EIGHTEEN

The Options Market

Overview

As the name implies, an **option** is the right to buy or sell, for a limited time, a particular good at a specified price. Such options have obvious value. For example, if IBM is selling at $120 and an investor has the option to buy a share at $100, this option must be worth at least $20, the difference between the price at which you can buy IBM ($100) and the price at which you could sell it in the open market ($120).

This chapter explores the options markets as they exist in the United States and abroad. Prior to 1973, options of various kinds were traded over the counter. But in 1973, the Chicago Board Options Exchange (CBOE) began trading options on individual stocks. Since that time, the options market has experienced rapid growth, with the creation of new exchanges and many different kinds of new option contracts. These exchanges trade options on goods ranging from individual stocks and bonds, to foreign currencies, to stock indexes, to options on futures contracts.

Options markets are very diverse and have their own particular jargon. As a consequence, understanding options requires a grasp of the institutional details and terminology employed in the market. The chapter begins with a discussion of the institutional background of options markets, including the kinds of contracts traded and the price quotations for various options.

The successful option trader must also understand the pricing relationships that prevail in the options market. For example, how much should an option to buy IBM at $100 be worth if IBM is selling at $120? With IBM trading at $120, how much more would an option be worth if it required a payment of only $90 instead of $100? Similarly, how much would an option to sell IBM for $115 be worth if IBM is trading at $120? These are the kinds of questions that prospective option investors need to have answered. Fortunately, the pricing principles for options are well developed. While the particular answers to these questions may sometimes be surprising, they are very logical upon reflection.

For a potential speculator in options, these pricing relationships are of the greatest importance. As in the futures market, much option speculation relies on techniques of **spreading**, which involves trading two or more related options to create a single position. This chapter examines some of the speculative strategies that investors might utilize. However, options are also important for hedging, and the use of options for risk control is a well–defined area of study that is also very important for understanding and utilizing options markets. For example, options contracts on stock indexes have gained wide acceptance among portfolio managers as a potential tool for controlling the risk of their equity portfolios.

One of the more recent developments in options is the trading of options on futures contracts. For example, a trader can buy an option that allows him or her to enter the futures contract at a particular price, no matter what the market of the futures contract might be. Obviously, this kind of instrument involving both options and futures contracts is more complicated than an option or futures alone. Nonetheless, these options on futures have already received a wide acceptance for some contracts.

As a result of the proliferation of these contracts, there are many ways to contract for the same good. This is very clear in the case of foreign currencies. For example, there are futures contracts on foreign currencies, such as the deutsche–mark. There are also options on marks, and even an option on the mark futures contract. The chapter concludes by exploring foreign currencies and examining the relationship among futures, options, and options on futures.

Call and Put Options

There are two major classes of options, call options and put options. Ownership of a **call option** gives the owner the right to buy a particular good at a certain price, with that right lasting until a particular date. Ownership of a **put option** gives the owner the right to sell a particular good at a specified price, with that right lasting until a particular date. For every option, there is both a buyer and a seller. In the case of a call option, the seller receives a payment from the buyer and gives the buyer the option of buying a particular good from the seller at a certain price, with that right lasting until a particular date. Similarly, the seller of a put option receives a payment from the buyer. The buyer then has the right to sell a particular good to the seller at a certain price for a specified period of time.

In all cases, ownership of an option involves the right, but not the obligation, to make a certain transaction. The owner of a call option may, for example, buy the good at the contracted price during the life of the option, but there is no obligation to do so. Likewise, the owner of a put option may sell the good under the terms of the option contract, but there is no obligation to do so. Selling an option does commit the seller to specific obligations. The seller of a call option receives a payment from the buyer, and in exchange for this payment, the seller of the call option (or simply, the call) must be ready to sell the given good to the owner of the call, if the owner of the call wishes. The discretion to engage in further transactions always lies with the owner or buyer of an option. Option sellers have no such discretion. They have obligated themselves to perform in certain ways if the owners of the options so desire. Later in this chapter we will see the conditions under which buyers and sellers find it reasonable to act in different ways.

Option Terminology

There is a great deal of special terminology associated with the options market. The seller of an option is also known as the **writer** of an option, and the act of selling an option is called **writing an option**. If the owner of the call takes advantage of the option, he or she is said to **exercise** the option. An owner would exercise a call option by buying a good under the terms of an option contract. Each option contract stipulates a price that will be paid if the option is exercised, and this price is known as the **exercise price**, **strike price**, or the **striking price**. In our first example of the call option to buy IBM at $100, when it is selling at $120, the exercise price would be $100, because this is the amount that must be paid at exercise.

Every option involves a payment from the buyer to the seller. This payment is simply the price of the option, but it is also called the **option premium**. Also, every option traded on an exchange is valid for only a limited period of time. For example, an option on IBM might be valid only through August of the present year. The option has no validity after its **expiration date** or **maturity**. This special terminology is used widely in the options market and throughout the rest of this chapter.

Option Exchanges

As shown in Table 18.1, there are quite a few options exchanges in the United States trading a variety of goods. This list can be expected to expand in the future. The present is a time of expansion and experimentation in the options market, and there will be a continuing process of maturation.

In many respects, options exchanges and futures exchanges are organized similarly. In the options market, as in the futures market, there is a seller for every buyer, and both markets allow offsetting trades. To buy an option, a trader simply needs to have an account with a brokerage firm holding a membership on the options exchange. The trade can be executed through the broker with the same ease as executing a trade to buy a stock. The buyer of an option will pay for the option at the time of the trade, so there is no more worry about cash flows associated with the purchase. For the seller of an option, the matter is somewhat more complicated. In selling a call option, the seller is agreeing to deliver the stock for a set price if the owner of the call so chooses. This means that the seller may need large financial resources to fulfill his or her obligations. The broker is representing the trader to the exchange, and is, therefore, obligated to be sure that the trader has the necessary financial resources to fulfill all obligations. For the seller, the full extent of these obligations is not known when the option is sold. Accordingly, the broker

Table 18.1

U.S. Options Exchanges and Goods Traded

Chicago Board Options Exchange
    Individual Stocks
    Long–Term Options on Individual Stocks
    Stock Indexes
    Interest Rates
American Exchange
    Individual Stocks
    Long–Term Options on Individual Stocks
    Stock Indexes
Philadelphia Exchange
    Individual Stocks
    Long–Term Options on Individual Stocks
    Stock Indexes
    Foreign Currency
    Precious Metals Index
Pacific Exchange
    Individual Stocks
    Long–Term Options on Individual Stocks
    Stock Indexes
New York Stock Exchange
    Individual Stocks
    Long–Term Options on Individual Stocks
    Stock Indexes

Note: This listing does not include options on futures contracts.

needs financial guarantees from option writers. In the case of a call, the writer of an option may already own the shares of stock and deposit these with the broker. Writing call options against stock that the writer owns is called writing a **covered call**. This gives the broker complete protection, because the shares that are obligated for delivery are in the possession of the broker. If the writer of the call does not own the underlying stocks, he or she has written a **naked option**, in this case a naked call. In such cases, the broker may require substantial deposits of cash or securities to ensure that the trader has the financial resources necessary to fulfill all obligations.

The Option Clearing Corporation (OCC) oversees the conduct of the market and assists in making an orderly market. As in the futures market, the buyer and seller of an option have no obligations to a specific individual, but are obligated to the OCC. Later, if an option is exercised, the OCC matches buyers and sellers, and oversees the completion of the exercise process, including the delivery of funds and securities.

This management of the exercise process and the standardization of contract terms are the largest contributions of the OCC. Standardized contract terms have made it possible for traders to focus on their trading strategies without having to learn the intricacies of many different option contracts. The benefits of the OCC in the marketplace are perhaps clearest in considering option quotations.

Option Quotations

No matter what the exchange or the good underlying the option, the quotations are similar. Because the market for individual stocks is the oldest and has the most overall trading activity, we will use the quotations for IBM to illustrate the basic features of the prices. Figure 18.1 shows the quotations for call and put options on individual stocks from *The Wall Street Journal*, and Figure 18.2 focuses on the quotations for options on IBM in particular. Options on IBM trade on the Chicago Board Options Exchange (CBOE) and the quotations pertain to the close of trading on the previous trading day.

Beneath the identifier "IBM," the quotations list the closing price of IBM stock for the day, while the second column lists the various striking prices or exercise prices are that available for IBM. The striking prices are kept fairly near the prevailing price of the stock. As the stock price fluctuates, new striking prices are opened for trading, at intervals of $5. As a consequence, volatile stocks are likely to have a greater range of striking prices available for trading at any one time. Each contract is written on 100 shares, but the prices quoted are on a per–share basis. Upon payment, the owner of the call would have the right to purchase 100 shares of IBM for the exercise price of, we assume, $100 per share, and this right would last until the expiration date. For the purchaser of the option, the total price to acquire a share of IBM would be the option premium plus the exercise price. The option writer would receive the premium as soon as the contract is initiated, and this amount belongs to the option writer no matter what develops. However, the option writer is obligated to sell 100 shares of IBM to the call purchaser for $100 per share, if the option purchaser chooses to exercise the option. However, the purchaser must exercise the option before it expires.

Obviously, the right to buy IBM at $100 per share, when the market price of IBM is above $100, is very valuable. By contrast, there is also a put option traded on IBM, which allows the owner to sell a share of IBM for, we assume, $100. Investors are not willing to pay very much for the right to sell IBM at $100 via an options contract if it could be sold for more than $100 in the marketplace.[1]

There are a number of important features about options that can be illustrated from the price quotations, such as those shown in Figure 18.1. First, for any given expiration, the lower the striking price for a call, the greater will be the price. Similarly, the longer the time to expiration, the higher will be the price of an option. The same relationship holds true for put options. As we will see in the

---

[1] In the place of some prices, the letters "r" and "s" appear. An *r* indicates that a particular option was not traded on the day being reported. An *s* indicates that no option with those characteristics is being made available for trading by the exchange.

Figure 18.1

Quotations for Options on Individual Stocks

LISTED OPTIONS QUOTATIONS

Thursday, June 23, 1994

Composite volume and close for actively traded equity and LEAPS, or long-term options, with results for the corresponding put or call contract. Volume figures are unofficial. Open interest is total outstanding for all exchanges and reflects previous trading day. Close when possible is shown for the underlying stock on primary market. **CB**-Chicago Board Options Exchange. **AM**-American Stock Exchange. **PB**-Philadelphia Stock Exchange. **PC**-Pacific Stock Exchange. **NY**-New York Stock Exchange. **XC**-Composite. **p**-Put.

MOST ACTIVE CONTRACTS

Option/Strike				Vol	Exch	Last	Net Chg	a-Close	Open Int
Kemper	Jul	65		7,609	PB	1/2	+ 5/16	62 5/8	5,713
Kemper	Jul	55		5,866	PB	8	+ 2 7/8	62 5/8	3,508
Oracle	Jul	35		5,530	CB	2 3/16	− 9/16	34 5/8	5,538
Kemper	Jul	60		5,400	PB	3 3/8	+ 2 1/2	62 5/8	9,988
Micsft	Jul	50	p	5,374	PC	1 3/8	+ 5/16	50 1/8	6,051
Kemper	Aug	65		4,749	PB	13/16	+ 3/8	62 5/8	50
Ph Mor	Jul	50	p	4,028	AM	3/4	+ 7/16	51 1/8	6,940
Oracle	Jul	35	p	3,785	CB	1 11/16	+ 7/16	34 5/8	2,476
TelMex	Aug	55	p	3,465	XC	2 5/8	+ 1/2	55 3/8	9,225
Kemper	Oct	65		3,297	PB	1 7/16	+ 7/8	62 5/8	5,726
TelMex	Aug	60		3,278	XC	1 3/8	− 1/2	55 3/8	16,153
PhilPt	Jul	35		2,966	AM	7/16	...	33	8,389
TelMex	Jul	55	p	2,949	XC	1 11/16	+ 9/16	55 3/8	6,192
I B M	Jul	65		2,766	CB	3/8	− 3/16	61	24,914
Kemper	Jul	60	p	2,656	PB	5/8	− 1 1/8	62 5/8	2,088
ElfAqu	Jul	30		2,510	XC	6 3/4	+ 3/4	36 5/8	90
ElfAqu	Jul	40		2,510	XC	1/8	− 1/16	36 5/8	370
ElfAqu	Jul	40	p	2,510	XC	4 3/8	− 1/2	36 5/8	12
Compaq	Aug	35		2,461	PC	1 3/8	− 5/16	32 1/8	997
Micsft	Aug	50		2,450	PC	3	− 7/8	50 1/8	1,206

Option/Strike				Vol	Exch	Last	Net Chg	a-Close	Open Int
Micsft	Jul	52 1/2		2,414	PC	5/8	− 1/2	50 1/8	3,690
Cisco	Jul	25		2,397	XC	3/16	− 3/8	21	6,527
Micsft	Jul	52 1/2	p	2,311	PC	2 3/4	+ 5/8	50 1/8	2,921
Intel	Jul	55	p	2,290	AM	11/16	+ 3/16	58 3/8	9,321
BakrHu	Jan	20	p	1,975	PC	1 3/16	− 3/16	21 5/8	267
Sybase	Sep	40	p	1,823	PC	2 1/4	+ 3/4	46 1/8	188
Ph Mor	Jul	50		1,735	AM	2	− 3/4	51 1/8	11,077
Cisco	Jul	20		1,733	XC	1 15/16	−1 13/16	21	354
Strbck	Oct	35	p	1,723	CB	9 1/4	+ 2 1/8	26 3/4	72
AMedHI	Jul	25		1,714	PB	1 5/16	−1 3/16	23 7/8	12,845
NewbNk	Jul	30		1,713	PC	1 15/16	− 15/16	28 7/8	1,144
TelMex	Jul	60		1,677	XC	3/8	− 1/4	55 3/8	15,756
HK Tel	Jul	20		1,653	XC	3/8	...	19 1/2	6,225
TelMex	Aug	50	p	1,641	XC	1	+ 1/4	55 3/8	4,880
Sybase	Jul	55		1,603	PC	7/16	− 7/16	46 1/8	2,662
Oracle	Jul	40		1,546	CB	9/16	− 3/16	34 5/8	4,581
RJR Nb	Aug	7 1/2		1,540	XC	1/8	...	5 7/8	751
IGame	Jul	17 1/2		1,496	AM	1	− 1/4	17 3/8	195
AppleC	Jul	25	p	1,448	AM	1	+ 3/8	25 1/8	5,733
TelMex	Jul	55		1,385	XC	2 1/8	− 7/8	55 3/8	2,355

Option/Strike		Exp.	−Call− Vol.	Last	−Put− Vol.	Last
ADC Tel	45	Jul	28	3/8	...	...
38 1/2	45	Nov	50	2 1/2	...	...
ALC Cm	35	Dec	158	1 9/16	...	...
A M R	60	Jul	75	1	10	2 1/2
58 3/8	65	Jul	60	1/8	...	...
A S A	40	Aug	34	6 3/4	86	1/4
46 1/8	40	Nov	50	7 1/2	10	15/16
46 1/8	45	Jul	162	1 5/8	20	1/2
46 1/8	45	Aug	23	2 3/4	45	1 3/8
46 1/8	45	Nov	56	4	5	2 1/2
46 1/8	50	Aug	47	3/4	...	...
46 1/8	50	Nov	34	1 7/8	...	...
46 1/8	50	Feb	34	2 5/8	...	...
AST Rs	12 1/2	Jul	110	1	61	1/2
13	12 1/2	Aug	5	1 1/2	30	7/8
13	12 1/2	Nov	224	2 1/2	...	...
13	15	Jul	26	3/16	45	2
13	15	Aug	24	3/4	...	...
13	17 1/2	Feb	5	1 1/8	50	5
AT&T	40	Jan	70	16 1/8	...	...
55 3/8	45	Jul	900	10 3/8	...	...
55 3/8	45	Jan	421	10 7/8	...	...
55 3/8	50	Jul	1144	5 3/8	300	1/8
55 3/8	50	Oct	545	6 1/4	...	...

Option/Strike		Exp.	−Call− Vol.	Last	−Put− Vol.	Last
27 1/4	32 1/2	Sep	118	1 3/16	...	...
Beth S	22 1/2	Jul	50	1/16	2	3
19 3/8	22 1/2	Oct	30	11/16	...	...
19 3/8	22 1/2	Jan	35	1 1/4	...	...
Bevrly	12 1/2	Jul	25	11/16	...	...
Biogen	25	Jul	40	3 1/8	100	3/4
27 1/4	25	Aug	10	5	80	1 1/16
27 1/4	30	Jul	290	7/8	40	2 3/8
27 1/4	30	Oct	23	2 1/4	30	4
27 1/4	35	Jul	101	1/4	3	5 3/4
27 1/4	35	Oct	65	1	...	...
Biomet	10	Oct	42	1 1/8	...	...
10 3/16	12 1/2	Oct	50	5/16	3	2 3/8
10 3/16	12 1/2	Jan	38	7/16	...	...
Blk Dk	17 1/2	Aug	29	1 3/16	...	...
Block	40	Jul	239	1 1/8	60	1 7/16
40 3/8	40	Aug	27	1 3/4	10	1 11/16
40 3/8	40	Jan	50	3	...	...
40 3/8	45	Jul	106	1/16	205	7
40 3/8	45	Jan	50	1 7/16	...	...
Blkbst	25	Jul	108	2 3/8	25	1/4
27	25	Aug	50	3 1/8	...	...
27	30	Jul	25	1/4	1	2 3/4
27	30	Aug	70	11/16	...	...

Option/Strike		Exp.	−Call− Vol.	Last	−Put− Vol.	Last
ChileT	90	Jul	...	...	110	3 1/4
Compaq	21 5/8	Jul	27	11	...	...
32 1/8	26 5/8	Jul	...	...	146	1/8
32 1/8	28 3/8	Jul	...	...	50	1/4
32 1/8	30	Jul	1297	2 7/8	1148	3/4
32 1/8	30	Aug	40	4 1/8	341	1 1/2
32 1/8	30	Oct	60	4 5/8	36	2 3/16
32 1/8	30	Jan	32	6	...	...
32 1/8	31 5/8	Jul	108	1 7/8	101	1 1/4
32 1/8	31 5/8	Oct	...	...	34	2 3/4
32 1/8	33 3/8	Jul	177	1	48	2 1/8
32 1/8	33 3/8	Oct	29	2 3/4	...	...
32 1/8	35	Jul	781	9/16	697	3 1/2
32 1/8	35	Aug	2461	1 3/8	...	...
32 1/8	35	Oct	116	2 3/16	49	4 3/4
32 1/8	35	Jan	147	3 3/8	12	5 1/4
32 1/8	36 5/8	Jul	443	1/4	13	4 3/4
32 1/8	36 5/8	Oct	105	1 11/16	...	...
32 1/8	36 5/8	Jan	100	2 7/8	...	...
32 1/8	38 3/8	Jul	380	1/8	13	6 1/4
32 1/8	38 3/8	Oct	24	1 5/8	3	6
32 1/8	40	Jul	253	1/16	905	7 7/8
32 1/8	40	Oct	28	7/8	...	...
32 1/8	41 5/8	Oct	52	11/16	...	...

Source: *The Wall Street Journal*, June 24, 1994, p. C11. Reprinted by permission of *The Wall Street Journal*,

section on option pricing, there are very clear reasons why these kinds of pricing relationships must obtain in the marketplace.

Figure 18.2

Quotations for Options on IBM Stock

Option/Strike		Exp.	Call Vol.	Call Last	Put Vol.	Put Last
I B M	45	Jan	24	16⅞	172	3/16
61	50	Jul	106	11¼	...	...
61	50	Jan	...	...	100	9/16
61	55	Jul	42	6¾	248	⅛
61	55	Aug	15	6¾	258	½
61	55	Oct	20	7¾	95	1⅛
61	55	Jan	28	8¾	80	1¾
61	60	Jul	1127	2⅛	946	1 1/16
61	60	Aug	268	3¼	356	1 15/16
61	60	Oct	180	4½	275	2 13/16
61	60	Jan	239	5⅝	91	3⅝
61	65	Jul	2766	⅜	455	4¼
61	65	Aug	513	1⅛	54	4¾
61	65	Oct	409	2¼	1258	5¾
61	65	Jan	112	3½	30	6
61	70	Jul	261	1/16	4	8⅛
61	70	Aug	47	⅜	...	...
61	70	Oct	32	1	...	...
61	70	Jan	116	2	1	9⅝

Source: *The Wall Street Journal*, June 24, 1994, p. C11. Reprinted by permission of *The Wall Street Journal*, © (1994) Dow Jones & Company, Inc. All rights reserved worldwide.

Option Pricing

Option pricing affords one of the showcase results of research in modern finance. The pricing models that have been developed for options perform very well, and a study of these models is very useful for the trader. In fact, traders on the options exchanges have immediate access to the information provided by option pricing models through machines located on the floors of the exchanges.

Prices of options on stocks without cash dividends depend upon five factors:

Stock Price	S
Exercise Price	E
Time until Expiration	T
Volatility of the Underlying Stock	σ
Risk–Free Interest Rate	R_f

Initially, it will be very useful to consider the effects of just the first three factors, the stock price (S), the exercise price (E), and the time until expiration (T). Later, we will consider the more complicated situations that arise from taking into account different interest rate environments and different risk levels.

For a call option, we can express the call price as a function of the stock price, the exercise price, and the time until expiration using this compact notation:

$$C(S, E, T)$$

For example, the equation:

$$C(\$120, \$100, .25) = \$22.75$$

says that a call option on a share trading at $120, with an exercise price of $100, and one quarter of a year to expiration has a price of $22.75.

The Pricing of Call Options at Expiration

The term **at expiration** refers to the moment just prior to expiration. If the option is not exercised at this time, it will expire immediately and have no value. The value of options at expiration is an important topic because many of the complications that ordinarily affect option prices disappear when the option is about to expire. With this terminology in mind, let us consider the value of a call option at expiration, where $T = 0$. In this case, only two possibilities may arise regarding the relationship between the exercise price (E) and the stock price (S). Either $S > E$ or $S \leq E$. If the stock price is less than or equal to the exercise price $(S \leq E)$, the call option will have no value. To see why this is the case, consider a call option with an exercise price of $80 on a stock trading at $70. Since the option is about to expire, the owner of the option has only two alternatives. The option may be exercised, or it may be allowed to expire.[2] If the option is exercised in this situation, the holder of the option must pay the exercise price of $80 and receive a stock trading in the market for only $70. In this situation, it does not pay to exercise the option and the owner will allow it to expire worthless. Accordingly, this option has no value and its market price will be zero. Employing our notation, we can say:

$$\text{If } S \leq E, \quad C(S, E, 0) = 0 \qquad\qquad \textbf{18.1}$$

If an option is at expiration and the stock price is less than or equal to the exercise price, the call option has no value. This equation simply summarizes the conclusion we have already reached.

The second possible relationship that could obtain between the stock price and the exercise price at expiration is for the stock price to exceed the exercise price $(S > E)$. Again, in our notation:

$$\text{If } S > E, \quad C(S, E, 0) = S - E \qquad\qquad \textbf{18.2}$$

If the stock price is greater than the exercise price, the call option must have a price equal to the difference between the stock price and the exercise price.

If this relationship did not hold, there would be arbitrage opportunities. Assume for the moment that the stock price is $50 and the exercise price is $40. If the option were selling for $5, an arbitrageur would make the following trades.

---

[2] We are assuming that it is too late to sell the option, because expiration is imminent.

Transaction	Cash Flow
Buy a call option	–$5
Exercise the option	–40
Sell the stock	50
Net Cash Flow	$5

As these transactions indicate, if the call price is less than the difference between the stock price and the exercise price, there will be an arbitrage opportunity.

What if the price of the call option is greater than the difference between the stock price and the exercise price? Continuing to use our example of a stock priced at $50 and the exercise price of the option being $40, assume now that the call price is $15. Faced with these prices, an arbitrageur would make the following transactions.

Transaction	Cash Flow
Sell a call option	+$15
Buy the stock	–50
Initial Cash Flow	–$35

The owner of this call option must then immediately exercise the option or allow it to expire. If the option is exercised, the seller of the call has these additional transactions.

Transaction	Cash Flow
Deliver stock	0
Collect exercise price	+$40
Total Cash Flow	$5

In this case, there is still a profit of $5. Alternatively, the owner of the option may allow the option to expire. In that event, the arbitrageur would simply sell the stock as soon as the option expires and receive $50. In this case the profit would be $15, since the arbitrageur simply keeps the option premium. In this second situation, in which the call price is greater than the stock price minus the exercise price, the holder of the call option would exercise the option. The important point is to see that the arbitrageur would make a profit no matter what the holder of the call might do.

At expiration, if the stock price exceeds the exercise price, the price of the call must equal the difference between the stock price and the exercise price. Combining these two relationships allows us to state the first basic principle of option pricing:

$$C(S, E, 0) = \max(0, S - E) \qquad \textbf{18.3}$$

Figure 18.3

━━━━━━━━━━

Values of Call and Put Options at Expirations when the Striking Price Equals $100

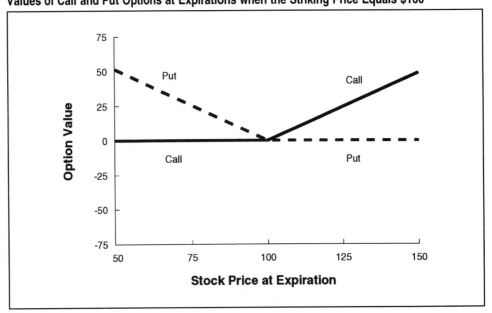

At expiration, a call option must have a value that is equal to zero or to the difference between the stock price and the exercise price, whichever is greater. This condition must hold, otherwise there will be arbitrage opportunities awaiting exploitation.[3]

Option Values and Profits at Expiration

In this discussion, it is important to keep separate the option's value or price and the profit or loss that a trader might experience. The value of options at expiration can be shown very easily by considering a concrete example. Consider both a call and a put option, with each having a striking price of $100. Figure 18.3 shows the value of these options at expiration for various stock prices. The graph shows the value of call and put options at expiration on the vertical axis as a function of the stock price, which is shown on the horizontal axis. The call price is shown as a solid line, and the put price is shown as a dotted line.

If the stock price is less than or equal to the exercise price of $100, the value of the call must be zero, as is shown in Figure 18.3. For stock prices above the

_____

[3]Most of the principles indicated here were originally proven rigorously by Robert C. Merton, "Theory of Rational Option Pricing," *Bell Journal of Economics and Management Science,* 1973, pp. 141–183.

exercise price, the call price equals the difference between the stock price and the exercise price. This is reflected by the fact that the graph of the call option's value rises at a 45 degree angle for stock prices above $100. The graph presents a similar analysis for a put option. Although we have not discussed the pricing of put options in any detail, the reader can reach the conclusion that this is the correct graph by the same kind of argument that was given earlier for call options.

Now consider the same situation, with put and call options each having an exercise price of $100, but assume that trades had taken place for the options with a premium of $5 on both the put and the call options. Knowing the price that was paid allows us to calculate the profits and losses at expiration for the sellers and buyers of both the put and call options. Alternative outcomes for all of these trading parties are shown in Figure 18.4. The top panel shows the profit and loss positions for the call option. The solid line pertains to the buyer of the call, and the dotted line to the seller.[4] For any stock price less than or equal to the exercise price of $100, the option will expire worthless and the purchaser of the call will lose the full purchase price. If the stock price exceeds $100, reaching $105 say, the owner of the call will exercise the call, paying $100 for the share and receiving a share worth $105. With a share price of $105, the call owner breaks even exactly. The entire cash flow has been the $5 for the option plus the $100 exercise price. This total outflow of $105 is exactly matched by the receipt of the share that is worth $105. For the call owner, any stock price less than $100 results in the loss of the total amount paid for the option. For stock prices greater than the exercise price, the call owner will exercise the option. The call owner may still lose money even with exercise. In this example, the stock price must be greater than $105 to generate any net profit for the call owner.

For the writer of the call, the profit picture is exactly opposite that of the call owner's. The best situation for the writer of the call is for the stock price to stay at or below $100. In this situation, the call writer keeps the entire option premium and the call option will not be exercised. If the stock price is $105, the option may be exercised and the writer of the call must deliver shares now worth $105 and receive only $100 for them. At this point, the loss on the exercise exactly equals the premium that was already received, so the call writer breaks even. If the stock price is greater than $105, the call writer will have a net loss. Notice that the buyer's profits exactly mirror the seller's losses and vice versa. This emphasizes that the options market is a **zero–sum game**. That is, the buyer's gains are the seller's losses and vice versa. If we add up all of the gains and losses in the options market, ignoring transaction costs, the total will equal zero.

The second panel of Figure 18.4 shows the profit and loss positions for the put traders. If the put buyer pays $5 for a put with an exercise price of $100, he or she will break even at $95. The writer of a put also breaks even at $95. These graphs indicate the wide variety of possible profit–and–loss patterns that traders

---

[4]Throughout this chapter, solid lines are used to indicate long positions and dashed lines are used to indicate short positions.

Figure 18.4

**Profits for Call and Put Options at Expiration when
the Striking Price Equals $100 and the Premium is $5**

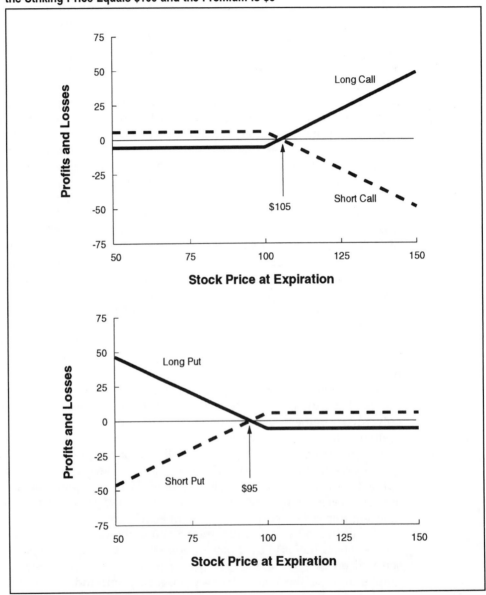

may create by using the options market. This kind of graph is useful for analyzing a wide variety of market strategies.

The Pricing of a Call Option with a Zero Exercise Price and Infinite Time until Expiration

It may appear unimportant to consider an option with a zero exercise price and an infinite time until expiration, because such options are not traded in the options market. However, this kind of option represents an extreme situation, and, as such, it can be used to set boundaries on possible option prices. An option on a stock that has a zero exercise price and an infinite time to maturity can be surrendered at any time, without any cost, for the stock itself. Since such an option can be transformed into the stock without cost, it must have a value as great as the stock itself. Similarly, an option on a good can never be worth more than the good itself. This allows us to state a second principle of option pricing.

$$C(S, 0, \infty) = S \qquad\qquad \textbf{18.4}$$

A call option with a zero exercise price and an infinite time to maturity must sell for the same price as the stock. Together, these first two principles allow us to specify the upper and lower possible bounds for the price of a call option as a function of the stock price, the exercise price, and the time to expiration. These boundaries are shown in Figure 18.5. If the call has a zero exercise price and an infinite maturity, the call price must equal the stock price, and this situation is

Figure 18.5

Boundaries for Call Option Prices

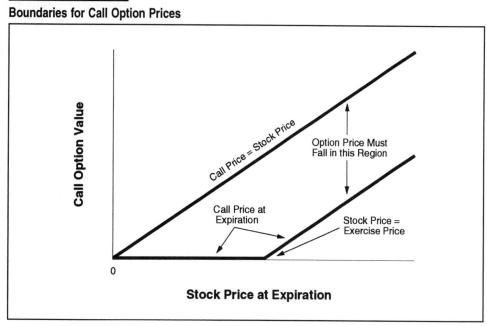

shown as the 45 degree line from the origin. This represents the upper bound for an option's price. Alternatively, if the option is at expiration, the price of the option must lie along the horizontal axis from the origin to the point at which the stock price equals the exercise price ($S = E$), and then upward at a 45 degree angle. If the stock price is less than or equal to the exercise price, the call price must be zero, as shown in the graph. If the stock price exceeds the exercise price, the option must trade for a price that is equal to the difference between the stock price and the exercise price. Other options such as those with some time remaining until expiration and with positive exercise prices would have to lie in the interior region between these two extremes. To further our understanding of option pricing, we need to consider other factors that put tighter restrictions on the permissible values of option prices.

Relationships Between Option Prices

There are numerous striking prices and expiration dates available for options on the same stock. Not surprisingly, there are definite relationships that must be maintained between these different kinds of options, if there are not to be arbitrage opportunities:

$$\text{If } E_1 < E_2, \quad C(S, E_1, T) \geq C(S, E_2, T) \qquad \textbf{18.5}$$

If two call options are alike, except that the exercise price of the first is less than that of the second, then the option with the lower exercise price must have a price that is equal to or greater than the price of the option with the higher exercise price.

In this situation, both options allow the owner of the option to acquire the same share of stock for the same period of time. However, the option with the lower exercise price allows the owner of that option to acquire the stock for a lower price. Therefore, the option with the lower exercise price should have a greater value. To see why this rule must hold, imagine a situation in which there are two options that are just alike, except the first has an exercise price of $100 and sells for $10. The second option has an exercise price of $90 and a premium of $5. The profit–and–loss graphs for both options are shown in Figure 18.6. The option with the $90 exercise price has a much better profit–and–loss profile than the option with the $100 exercise price. No matter what the stock price might be at expiration, the option with the $90 exercise price will perform better.

This is already an impossible pricing situation, because it represents a disequilibrium result. With these prices, all participants in the market would want the option with the exercise price of $90. This would cause the price of the option with the $100 exercise price to fall until investors were willing to hold it, too. But this could only occur if it were not inferior to the option with the $90 exercise price.

The same point can be made in the following context, because the profit–and–loss opportunities shown in the first panel of Figure 18.6 create an arbitrage opportunity. Faced with these prices, the arbitrageur would simply transact as follows.

Figure 18.6

**Why Options with Lower Exercise Prices Cannot Have Lower Prices
than Options with Higher Exercise Prices**

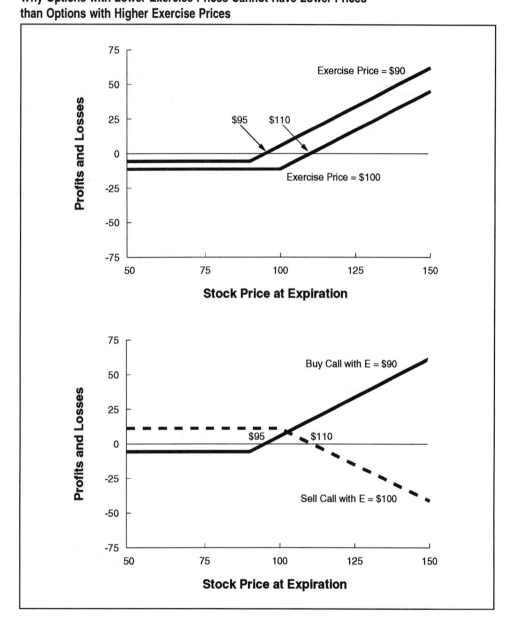

Transaction	Cash Flow
Sell the option with the $100 exercise price	$10
Buy the option with the $90 exercise price	− 5
Net Cash Flow	$5

This gives a combined position that is graphed in the second panel of Figure 18.6. Here, the sale of the option with the $100 striking price is shown as the dotted line. To see why this is a good transaction to make, consider the profit and loss position on each option and the overall position for alternative stock prices that might prevail at expiration.

	Profit or Loss on the Option Position		
Stock Price at Expiration	**For E = $90**	**For E = $100**	**For Both**
80	−$5	+$10	+$5
90	−5	+10	+5
95	0	+10	+10
100	+5	+10	+15
105	+10	+5	+15
110	+15	0	+15
115	+20	−5	+15

For any stock price, there will be some profit. If the stock price is $90 or less, the profit will be $5 from the options position, plus the net cash inflow of $5 that was received when the position was initiated. As the stock price at expiration goes from $90 to $100, the profit goes up, until the maximum profit of $15 on the options position is achieved at a stock price of $100. When stock prices at expiration are greater than $100, the profit on the options position remains at $15.

With the prices in the example, it is possible to trade to guarantee a total profit of at least $10 (the $5 inflow from initiating the position plus the minimum option value of $5) and perhaps as much as $20 (the $5 inflow from initiating the position plus the maximum option value of $15). This was accomplished without risk or investment, so it is an example of arbitrage. If option prices are to be rational, they cannot allow arbitrage. In order to eliminate the arbitrage opportunity, the price of the option with a striking price of $90 must be at least as large as the price of the option with the striking price of $100.[5]

---

[5]There is still an interesting result to be noted here. If the prices are equal, a trader could buy the option with the lower striking price and sell the one with the higher striking price. This strategy would not guarantee a profit, but it could not lose. Further, there would be some situations in which it would pay off. For this reason, options with lower exercise prices almost always sell for higher, not just equal, prices, as the quotations from The Wall Street Journal make clear.

A similar principle refers to the expiration date:

$$\text{If } T_1 > T_2, \quad C(S, T_1, E) \geq C(S, T_2, E) \qquad \textbf{18.6}$$

If there are two options that are otherwise alike, the option with the longer time to expiration must sell for an amount equal to or greater than the option that expires earlier.

Intuitively, this principle must hold, because the option with the longer time until expiration gives the investor all of the advantages that the one with a shorter time to expiration offers. But the option with the longer time to expiration also gives the investor the chance to wait longer before exercising the option or before the option expires. In some circumstances, the extra time for the option to run will have positive value.[6]

If the option with the longer period to expiration sold for less than the option with the shorter time to expiration, there would also be an arbitrage opportunity. To conduct the arbitrage, assume that two options are written on the same stock with a striking price of $100. Let the first option have a time to expiration of six months and assume it trades for $8, while the second option has three months to expiration and trades for $10. In this situation, the arbitrageur would make the following transactions.

Transaction	Cash Flow
Buy the six–month option for $8	–$8
Sell the three–month option for $10	+$10
Net Cash Flow	$2

By buying the longer maturity option and selling the shorter maturity option, the option trader receives a net cash flow of $2. However, there might appear to be some risk, because the option that was sold might be exercised. To see that the trader's position is secure, consider that if the option that is sold is exercised against the arbitrageur, he or she can simply exercise the six–month option that was purchased and use the stock that is received to deliver on the three–month option. This will guarantee that the $2 can be kept, so there will be a $2 profit no matter what happens to the stock price. Since this profit is certain and was earned without investment, it is an arbitrage profit.[7] The option with the longer time to expiration

---

[6]Strictly speaking, this argument holds for **American options**. An American option allows exercise at any time until maturity. By contrast, a **European option** allows exercise only at maturity. Thus, an American option gives all the advantages of the European option, plus it allows the possibility of early exercise. For this reason, an American option must always have a value at least as great as a European option, other factors being equal.

[7]This result requires that the six–month option be an American option so that it could be exercised at will prior to expiration.

cannot be worth less than the option with the shorter time to expiration. Otherwise, there will be arbitrage opportunities.

Generally, the option with the longer time to expiration will actually be worth more than the option with the shorter time to expiration. We have already seen that any option must be worth at least the difference between the stock price and the exercise price $(S - E)$ at expiration. If the stock price is greater than the exercise price $(S > E)$, the option is said to be **in–the–money**, but if the stock price is less than the exercise price $(S < E)$, the option is **out of–the–money**. If the stock price equals, or nearly equals, the exercise price $(S = E)$, the option is **at–the–money**. Prior to expiration, an in–the–money option will normally be worth more than $S - E$. This difference $(S - E)$ is known as the **intrinsic value** of the option, which is simply the value of the option if it were exercised immediately. An in–the–money option prior to expiration can be worth more than $S - E$, because the value of being able to wait to exercise normally has value. If the option is exercised prior to expiration, the trader will receive only the amount $S - E$ for the option. By selling the option in the market, the trader will get the market price of the option, which normally exceeds $S - E$. So it generally will not pay to exercise an option early.[8]

Figure 18.7

Bounds on Option Prices and Permissible Relationships Between Pairs of Option Prices

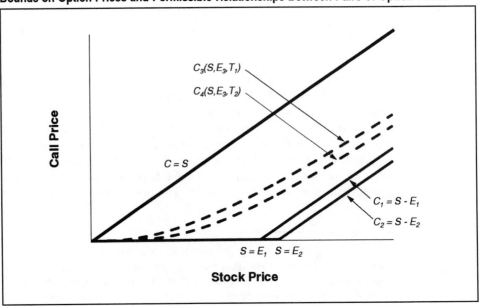

---

[8]In the case of a dividend–paying stock, this will not always be true.

Thus far, we have set bounds for option prices and we have established relationships between pairs of options, as shown in Figure 18.7. There, the two options, C_1 and C_2, are alike except that option C_1 has a lower exercise price. Accordingly, the price C_1 is more tightly bounded than that of option C_2. The two options in the second pair, C_3 and C_4, differ only by the time to expiration. Consistent with this fact, the price of the option with the longer time to expiration, C_4, has a higher price. While we can now put bounds on the overall price of options and establish which of two options should have the higher price, we need to be able to put further restrictions on the price of a call option. To do this, we need to consider the impact of interest rates.

Call Option Prices and Interest Rates

Assume that a stock now sells for $100 in the marketplace and that over the next year its value can change by 10 percent in either direction. For a round lot of 100 shares, the value one year from now will be either $9,000 or $11,000. Assume also that the risk–free rate of interest is 12 percent and that a call option exists on this stock with a striking price of $100 per share and an expiration date one year from now. With these facts in mind, imagine two portfolios constructed in the following way.

Portfolio A	100 shares of stock, current value $10,000.
Portfolio B	A $10,000 pure discount bond maturing in one year, with a current value of $8,929, which is consistent with the 12 percent interest rate. One option contract, with an exercise price of $100 per share, or $10,000 for the entire contract.

Which portfolio is more valuable, and what does this tell us about the price of the call option? In one year, the stock price for the round lot will be either $11,000 if the price goes up by 10 percent, or $9,000 if the price goes down by 10 percent. This result is shown for Portfolio A in Table 18.2. For Portfolio B, there are both bonds and the call option to consider. As is also shown in Table 18.2, the bonds will mature in one year and will be worth $10,000 no matter what happens to the stock price. The stock price will have a strong effect on the value of the call option, however. If the stock price goes up by 10 percent, the call option will be worth exactly $1,000, the difference between the stock price and the exercise price $(S - E)$. If the stock price goes down by 10 percent, the option will expire worthless. So, if the stock price goes down, Portfolio B will be worth $10,000, while if the stock price goes up, Portfolio B will be worth $11,000.

In this situation, Portfolio B is clearly the better portfolio to hold. If the stock price goes down, Portfolio B is worth $1,000 more than Portfolio A. But if the stock price goes up, Portfolios A and B have the same value. An investor could never do worse by holding Portfolio B, and there is some chance that he or she could do better. Therefore, the value of Portfolio B must be at least as great as the value of Portfolio A.

Table 18.2

━━━━━━━━━

Portfolio Values in One Year

	Stock Price:	
	Rises 10%	Falls 10%
Portfolio A		
Stock	$11,000	$9,000
Portfolio B		
Maturing Bond	10,000	10,000
Call Option	1,000	0

This tells us something very important about the price of the option. Since Portfolio B is sure to perform at least as well as Portfolio A, it must cost at least as much. Further, we know that the value of Portfolio A is $10,000, so the price of Portfolio B must be at least $10,000. The bonds in Portfolio B cost $8,929, so the option must cost at least $1,071. This means that the value of the call must be worth at least as much as the stock price minus the present value of the exercise price. If the call did not meet this condition, any investor would prefer to purchase Portfolio B in the example, rather than Portfolio A. Further, there would be an arbitrage opportunity.[9] Previously, we were able to say only that the price of the call must be either zero or $S - E$ at expiration. Based on the reasoning from the example, we can now say the following:

$$C \geq S - \text{Present Value}(E) \qquad\qquad \textbf{18.7}$$

The call price must be greater than or equal to the stock price minus the present value of the exercise price. This substantially tightens the bounds that we can put on the value of a call option.

As the next example indicates, it must also be true that the higher the interest rate, the higher will be the value of call option, if everything else is held constant. In the previous example, the interest rate was 12 percent, and we were able to conclude that the price of the call option must be at least $1,071, because:

$$C \geq \$10,000 - \frac{\$10,000}{(1.12)} = \$1,071$$

---

[9] The arbitrage transactions would involve buying Portfolio B and selling Portfolio A short. Assume that the price of the call option is $1,000 and try to work out the transactions and the arbitrage profit that must result.

For the same portfolio, imagine that the interest rate had been 20 percent rather than 12 percent. In that case, the value of the call option must have been at least $1,667, as is shown by the following equation:

$$C \geq \$10,000 - \frac{\$10,000}{(1.20)} = \$1,667$$

From this line of reasoning, we can assert the following principle:

$$\text{If } R_{f1} > R_{f2}, \qquad C(S, E, T, R_{f1}) \geq C(S, E, T, R_{f2}) \qquad \textbf{18.8}$$

Other things being equal, the higher the risk–free rate of interest, the greater must be the price of a call option.

Prices of Call Options and the Riskiness of Stocks

Surprisingly enough, the riskier the stock on which an option is written, the greater will be the value of the call option. This principle can also be illustrated by an example. Consider a stock trading at $10,000 that will experience either a 10 percent price rise or a 10 percent price decline over the next year. As in our earlier example of Table 18.2, a call option on such a stock with an exercise price of $10,000 and a risk–free interest rate of 12 percent would be worth at least $1,071. Now consider

Table 18.3

Portfolio Values in One Year

	Stock Price:	
	Rises 10%	Falls 10%
Portfolio B		
Maturing Bond	$10,000	$10,000
Call Option	1,000	0

	Stock Price:	
	Rises 20%	Falls 20%
Portfolio A		
Stock	$12,000	$8,000
Portfolio B		
Maturing Bond	10,000	10,000
Call Option	2,000	0

a new stock, which trades at $10,000, but that will experience either a 20 percent price increase or a 20 percent price decrease over the next year. If we hold the other factors constant, by assuming that interest rates are 12 percent per year, and focus on an option with a striking price of $10,000, what can we say about the value of the call option?

As Table 18.3 shows, the call option on the stock that will go up or down by 10 percent must be worth at least $1,071. If the stock price goes down, the call will be worth zero. If the stock price goes up, the call will be worth $1,000. In the bottom panel of Table 18.3, the stock will go up or down by 20 percent. If the stock price goes down, the call in this case will be worth zero. This is the same result as the call in the top panel. If prices go up, the call in the bottom panel will be worth $2,000, which is the difference between the exercise price and the stock price.

In this scenario, any investor would prefer the option in the bottom panel, because it cannot perform worse than the call in the top panel, and it might perform better if the stock price goes up. This means that the value of the call in the bottom panel must be at least as much as the value of the call in the top panel, but it will probably be worth more. The only difference between the two cases is the risk level of the stock. In the top panel, the stock will move up or down by 10 percent, but the stock in the bottom panel is riskier, because it will move 20 percent. By reflecting on this example, we can derive the following principle:

$$\text{If } \sigma_1 > \sigma_2, \quad C(S, E, T, R_f, \sigma_1) \geq C(S, E, T, R_f, \sigma_2) \qquad \textbf{18.9}$$

Other things being equal, a call option on a riskier good will be worth at least as much as a call option on a less risky good.

Call Options as Insurance Policies

In Table 18.2, the call option will be worth either $1,000 or zero in one year, and the value of that option must be at least $1,071. At first glance, it is a terrible investment to pay $1,071 or more for something that will be worth either zero or $1,000 in a year. However, the option offers more than a simple investment opportunity; it also involves an insurance policy. The insurance character of the option can be seen by comparing the payoffs from Portfolio A and Portfolio B. If the stock price goes down by 10 percent, Portfolio A will be worth $9,000 and Portfolio B will be worth $10,000. If the stock price goes up by 10 percent, both portfolios will be worth $11,000. Holding the option insures that the worst outcome from the investment will be $10,000. This is considerably safer than holding the stock alone. Under these circumstances, it would make sense to pay $1,071 or more for an option that has a maximum payoff of $1,000. Part of the benefit from holding the option portfolio is the insurance that the total payoff from the portfolio will be at least $10,000. This also makes sense of the fact that the riskier the stock, the more the option will be worth. This relationship results, because the riskier the stock, the more valuable will be an insurance policy against particularly bad outcomes.

option values according to their model, and we can understand the relationship between the OPM and the conclusions we have reached in previous sections.

The formula for the Black–Scholes OPM is given by:

$$C = SN(d_1) - Ee^{-R_fT}N(d_2)$$ 18.11

where $d_1 = \dfrac{\ln(S/E) + [R_f + (1/2)\sigma^2]T}{\sigma\sqrt{T}}$

$d_2 = d_1 - \sigma\sqrt{T}$

$N(d_1), N(d_2)$ = cumulative normal probability values of d_1 and d_2, respectively

S = stock price

E = exercise price

R_f = the risk-free rate of interest

σ = the instantaneous standard deviation of the stock's returns

T = time to expiration of the option

The most difficult part of this formula to understand is the use of the normal cumulative probability function. However, this is exactly the part of the OPM that takes account of the risk and allows the model to give such good results for option prices. The best way to understand the application of the model is with an example. Let us assume values for the five parameters and calculate the Black–Scholes value for an option. For purposes of the example, assume the following:

S = \$100
E = \$100
T = 1 year
R_f = 12%
σ = 10%

These values make it possible to calculate the Black–Scholes theoretical option value, and the first task is to calculate values for d_1 and d_2.

$$d_1 = \frac{\ln(S/E) + [R_f + (1/2)\sigma^2]T}{\sigma\sqrt{T}}$$

$$= \frac{\ln(100/100) + [.12 + 1/2(.01)]1}{(.1)(1)} = \frac{0 + .1250}{.1}$$

$$= 1.25$$

$$d_2 = d_1 - \sigma\sqrt{T}$$

$$= 1.25 - (.1)(1) = 1.15$$

Having calculated the values of d_1 and d_2, the next step is to calculate the cumulative normal probability values of these two results. Essentially, these two values are simply z–scores from the normal probability function, such as the one shown in Figure 18.9. In this graph the two values of interest, 1.15 and 1.25, are shown. In calculating the cumulative normal probability values of $d_1 = 1.25$ and $d_2 = 1.15$, we simply need to determine the proportion of the area under the curve that lies to the left of the value in question. For example, if we were interested in a z–score of 0.00, we would know that 50 percent of the area under the curve lies to the left of a z–score of 0.00. This is because the normal probability distribution is symmetrical about its mean, and we know that the z–scores are standardized so that they have a mean of 0.00.

Figure 18.9

The Normal Probability Function

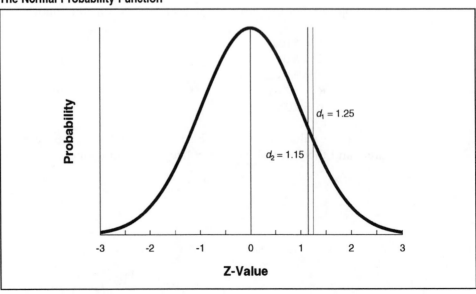

Table 18.4

Cumulative Distribution Function for the Standard Normal Random Variable

	.00	.01	.02	.03	.04	.05	.06	.07	.08	.09
0.0	.5000	.5040	.5080	.5120	.5160	.5199	.5239	.5279	.5319	.5359
0.1	.5398	.5438	.5478	.5517	.5557	.5596	.5636	.5675	.5714	.5753
0.2	.5793	.5832	.5871	.5910	.5948	.5987	.6026	.6064	.6103	.6141
0.3	.6179	.6217	.6255	.6293	.6331	.6368	.6406	.6443	.6480	.6517
0.4	.6554	.6591	.6628	.6664	.6700	.6736	.6772	.6808	.6844	.6879
0.5	.6915	.6950	.6985	.7019	.7054	.7088	.7123	.7157	.7190	.7224
0.6	.7257	.7291	.7324	.7357	.7389	.7422	.7454	.7486	.7517	.7549
0.7	.7580	.7611	.7642	.7673	.7704	.7734	.7764	.7794	.7823	.7852
0.8	.7881	.7910	.7939	.7967	.7995	.8023	.8051	.8078	.8106	.8133
0.9	.8159	.8186	.8212	.8238	.8264	.8289	.8315	.8340	.8365	.8389
1.0	.8413	.8438	.8461	.8485	.8508	.8531	.8554	.8577	.8599	.8621
1.1	8643	.8665	.8686	.8708	.8729	.8749	.8770	.8790	.8810	.8830
1.2	.8849	.8869	.8888	.8907	.8925	.8944	.8962	.8980	.8997	.9015
1.3	.9032	.9049	.9066	.9082	.9099	.9115	.9131	.9147	.9162	.9177
1.4	.9192	.9207	.9222	.9236	.9251	.9265	.9279	.9292	.9306	.9319
1.5	.9332	.9345	.9357	.9370	.9382	.9394	.9406	.9418	.9429	.9441
1.6	.9452	.9463	.9474	.9484	.9495	.9505	.9515	.9525	.9535	.9545
1.7	.9554	.9564	.9573	.9582	.9591	.9599	.9608	.9616	.9625	.9633
1.8	.9641	.9649	.9656	.9664	.9671	.9678	.9686	.9693	.9699	.9706
1.9	.9713	.9719	.9726	.9732	.9738	.9744	.9750	.9756	.9761	.9767
2.0	.9772	.9778	.9783	.9788	.9793	.9798	.9803	.9808	.9812	.9817
2.1	.9821	.9826	.9830	.9834	.9838	.9842	.9846	.9850	.9854	.9857
2.2	.9861	.9864	.9868	.9871	.9875	.9878	.9881	.9884	.9887	.9890
2.3	.9893	.9896	.9898	.9901	.9904	.9906	.9909	.9911	.9913	.9916
2.4	.9918	.9920	.9922	.9925	.9927	.9929	.9931	.9932	.9934	.9936
2.5	.9938	.9940	.9941	.9943	.9945	.9946	.9948	.9949	.9951	.9952
2.6	.9953	.9955	.9956	.9957	.9959	.9960	.9961	.9962	.9963	.9964
2.7	.9965	.9966	.9967	.9968	.9969	.9970	.9971	.9972	.9973	.9974
2.8	.9974	.9975	.9976	.9977	.9977	.9978	.9979	.9979	.9980	.9981
2.9	.9981	.9982	.9982	.9983	.9984	.9984	.9985	.9985	.9986	.9986
3.0	.9987	.9987	.9987	.9988	.9988	.9989	.9989	.9989	.9990	.9990
3.1	.9990	.9991	.9991	.9991	.9992	.9992	.9992	.9992	.9993	.9993
3.2	.9993	.9993	.9994	.9994	.9994	.9994	.9994	.9995	.9995	.9995
3.3	.9995	.9995	.9995	.9996	.9996	.9996	.9996	.9996	.9996	.9997
3.4	.9997	.9997	.9997	.9997	.9997	.9997	.9997	.9997	.9997	.9998

Because the standardized normal probability distribution is so important and so widely used, tables of its values are included in virtually every statistics textbook. Table 18.4 shows a typical table. As we can see, the probability of drawing a value from this distribution that is less than or equal to $d_1 = 1.25$ is .8944. So, the two values we seek are:

$$N(d_1) = N(1.25) = .8944$$
$$N(d_2) = N(1.15) = .8749$$

Returning to the OPM, we can now make the final calculation:

$$C = S\ N(d_1) - E\ e^{-R_f T}\ N(d_2)$$
$$C = \$100(.8944) - \$100e^{-(.12)(1)}(.8749)$$
$$= \$89.44 - \$100(.8869)(.8749)$$
$$= \$89.44 - \$77.60$$
$$= \$11.84$$

In this calculation, the term $e^{-R_f T} = .8869$ is simply the discounting factor for continuous time with an interest rate of 12 percent and a period of one year. So, according to the OPM, the call option should be worth \$11.84.

This calculation of the value of this option by the OPM corresponds very closely to our earlier example from Table 18.2. There we concluded that an option with similar characteristics must be worth at least \$10.71. The result from the OPM is consistent with our earlier analysis, but it is much more exact. The difference between the OPM value of \$11.84 and the minimum value of \$10.71 is due to the value of the insurance policy that we were unable to capture without the sophisticated approach of the OPM.[12]

Also, it should be clear that the OPM result is very close to the result that we reached by just a process of reasoning. We were able to conclude that:

$$C = S - \text{Present Value}(E) + I \qquad \textbf{18.12}$$

and the OPM says that:

$$C = S\ N(d_1) - E\ e^{-R_f T}\ N(d_2)$$

The term $Ee^{-R_f T}$ is simply the present value of the exercise price when continuous discounting is used. This means that the OPM is saying:

---

[12]Actually, part of the difference is due to the discounting method. Had our example used continuous discounting at 12 percent, we would have found that the value of the option had to be at least as great as \$100 − \$100 (.8869) = \$11.31. This is much closer to the OPM value of \$11.84.

$$C = S\,N(d_1) - \text{Present Value}(E)\,N(d_2)$$

The terms involving the cumulative probability function are the terms that take account of risk. Coupled with the rest of the formula, they capture the value of the insurance policy. If the stock involved no risk, the calculated values for d_1 and d_2 would be very large and the subsequent calculated cumulative functions would both approach a value of 1. If $N(d_1)$ and $N(d_2)$ both equal 1, the OPM could be simplified to:

$$C = S - \text{Present Value}(E)$$

which is very close to the result we were able to reach without the OPM. This expression simply does not reflect the value of the option as an insurance policy, a value we know it has and that we can measure by using the OPM.

Upon first acquaintance with the OPM, many people think that it is too complicated to be useful. Nothing could be further from the truth. Of all of the models in finance, the OPM is among those receiving the widest acceptance by actual investors. For example, there are machines on the floor of the CBOE that give traders OPM prices for all options using instantaneously updated information on all of the parameters in the model. Further, most investment banking houses have staffs that specialize in options and which use the OPM on a daily basis. Finally, the OPM has achieved such widespread acceptance that some calculator manufacturers have even made special modules to allow their calculators to calculate OPM values automatically.

This widespread acceptance is due in large part to the very good results of the OPM. The Black–Scholes theoretical model price is usually very close to the market price of the option. Without doubt, the OPM has contributed greatly to our understanding of option pricing and many traders use it as a key tool in their trading strategies.

The Valuation of Put Options

Although the OPM pertains specifically to call options, it can also be used to price put options, through the principle of **put–call parity**.[13] Assume that an investor makes the following transactions:

> Buy one share of stock $S = \$100$
> Buy one put option with price $P = ?$, $E = \$100$, and $T = 1$ year
> Sell one call option with price $C = \$11.84$, $E = \$100$, and $T = 1$ year

Assume also that the put and call options are on the same stock.

---

[13] The put–call parity relationship was first derived by Hans Stoll, "The Relationship Between Put and Call Option Prices," *The Journal of Finance*, December 1969, pp. 802–824.

Table 18.5

Possible Outcomes for Put–Call Parity Portfolio

Stock Price	Call Value	Put Value	Portfolio Value
$ 80	$0	$20	$100
90	0	10	100
100	0	0	100
110	−10	0	100
120	−20	0	100

At expiration, the stock price could have many different values, some of which are shown in Table 18.5. The interesting feature about this portfolio is that its value will be the same, $100 = E$, no matter what the stock price is at expiration. Consistent with Table 18.5, no matter what the stock price at expiration might be, the value of the entire portfolio will be $100 = E$. Holding these three instruments in the way indicated gives a risk–free investment that will pay $100 = E$ at expiration, so the value of the whole portfolio must equal the present value of the riskless payoff at expiration. This means that we can write:

$$S - C + P = \frac{E}{(1 + R_f)^T} \qquad \textbf{18.13}$$

The value of the put–call portfolio equals the present value of the exercise price discounted at the risk–free rate.

Since it is possible to know all of the other values, except for the price of the put P, we can use this put–call parity relationship to calculate P. To see how this is done, let us assume, as before, that $R_f = 12$ percent and that the call value is $11.84, as was calculated according to the OPM. Rearranging the put–call parity formula gives a put value of $1.13.

$$P = \frac{E}{(1 + R_f)^T} - S + C$$

$$P = \frac{\$100}{(1.12)} - \$100 + \$11.84 = \$1.13$$

Speculating with Options

Many option traders are attracted to the market by the exciting speculative opportunities that options offer. Relative to stocks, options offer a great deal of leverage. A given percentage change in the stock price will cause a much greater percentage change in the price of the option.

Using the example of the option worth $11.84, consider the effect of a sudden 10 percent change in the price of the stock. If the stock price changes by 1 percent, the option price will change by 7.52 percent in the same direction. The following call values were calculated from the Black–Scholes formula, assuming only that the stock price had changed as indicated.

Original Values	1% Stock Price Increase	1% Stock Price Decrease
$S = \$100$	$S = \$101$	$S = \$99$
$C = \$11.84$	$C = \$12.73$	$C = \$10.95$

This leverage means that trading options can give investors much more price action for a given investment than simply holding the stock. It also means that options can be much riskier than holding stock. While options can be risky as investments, they need not be. In fact, options can be used to take very low risk speculative positions by using options in combinations. The combinations are virtually endless, including strips, straps, spreads, and straddles. We discuss these in Chapter 20.

Hedging with Options

As we have seen with futures, very risky financial instruments can be used to control risk. One of the most important applications of options is their use as a hedging vehicle. Once again, the OPM gives important insights into this process.

To illustrate the idea of hedging with options, let us use our original example of a stock selling at $100 and having a standard deviation of 10 percent. Recall that a call option with an exercise price of $100 and a time to expiration of one year would sell for $11.84. Recall, too, that a sudden 1 percent price rise in the stock from $100 to $101 would drive the option price to $12.73. If the stock price and the option price are so intimately related, it should be possible to use options to offset risk inherent in the stock. This possibility is shown in Table 18.6.

Consider an original portfolio comprised of 8,944 shares of stock selling at $100 per share and assume that a trader sells 100 call option contracts, or options on 10,000 shares, at $11.84. In the table, this short position in the option is indicated by a minus sign. That entire portfolio would have a value of $776,000. Now consider the effect of a 1 percent change in the price of the stock. If the stock price increases by 1 percent to $101, the shares will be worth $903,344. The option price will increase from $11.84 to $12.73. But this portfolio involves a short position in

Table 18.6

A Hedged Portfolio

Original Portfolio	S = $100	C = $11.84	
8,944 shares of stock			$894,400
A short position for options on 10,000 shares (100 contracts)			−$118,400
		Total Value	$776,000
Stock Price Rises by 1%	**S = $101**	**C = $12.73**	
8,944 shares of stock			$903,344
A short position for options on 10,000 shares (100 contracts)			−$127,300
		Total Value	$776,044
Stock Price Falls by 1%	**S = $99**	**C − $10.95**	
8,944 shares of stock			$885,456
A short position for options on 10,000 shares (100 contracts)			−$109,500
		Total Value	$775,956

10,000 options, so this creates a loss of $8,900. After these two effects are taken into account, the value of the whole portfolio will be $776,044. This is virtually identical to the original value.

On the other hand, if the stock price falls by 1 percent, there will be a loss on the stock of $8,944. The price of the option will fall from $11.84 to $10.95, and this means that the entire drop in price for the 10,000 options will be $8,900. Taking both of these effects into account, the portfolio will then be worth $775,956. As this example indicates, the overall value of the portfolio will not change no matter what happens to the stock price. If the stock price increases, there is an offsetting loss on the option. Likewise, if the stock price falls, there will be an offsetting gain on the option.

In this example, holding .8944 shares of stock for each option sold short will give a perfect hedge. The value of the entire portfolio will be insensitive to any change in the stock price. How can we know exactly the right number of options to trade to give this result? The careful reader might recall the number .8944. When the value of this call option was calculated, we saw that $N(d_1) = .8944$. This value gives the appropriate hedge ratio to construct a perfect hedge, and the principle can be summarized by the following rule.

> A portfolio comprised of a short position of one option and a long position of $N(d_1)$ shares of the stock will have a total value that will not fluctuate as the share price fluctuates.

Alternatively, to hedge a long position of one share in a stock, sell a number of options equal to $1/N(d_1)$. This hedge will hold for infinitesimal changes in the stock price. In the preceding example, the hedge was not quite perfect because the change in the stock price was discrete. Actually, the value of the portfolio fluctuates by only .00057. Also, a change in the stock price will change the value of $N(d_1)$, because the value of d_1 will change. This means that the hedge must be adjusted periodically as the stock price changes if it is to be kept perfect.

Foreign Currency Options

The many different kinds of futures and options come together in the foreign currency market, because it is only in foreign exchange that all four kinds of speculative contracts discussed in the last two chapters are traded. In this section, we focus on the German mark, where we find:

♦ an option on the German mark itself,
♦ a forward contract on the German mark,
♦ a German mark futures contract, and
♦ an option on the German mark futures contract.

Figure 18.10 presents quotations for all four instruments. To see how to read these quotations, note the following facts. In the quotations, the spot price of the German mark is shown in the first column for the Philadelphia Exchange options. The German mark option trades on the Philadelphia Exchange and the contract size is 62,500 marks, with the quotations being shown in one–hundredths of a cent per mark. The striking prices are shown in half–cent intervals. The figure also shows prices for options on the futures contract. These instruments act as a combination of the option and the futures. When a futures option is exercised, the exercising party receives a futures position and a cash payment from the original seller of the futures option.

By now the reader will suspect that there are likely to be law–like relationships among the prices of these diverse instruments. In fact, we observed the relationships between futures and forward prices. For the sake of convenience, assume that the futures and options contracts are all written for 1,000,000 marks and that all prices are quoted in U.S. dollars per mark. We also assume that both options and the futures contract expire in four months and we assume that the risk–free interest rate is 1 percent per month.

To illustrate the pricing relationships between futures and options, consider a portfolio constructed by buying one call option and selling one put option, each with an exercise price of $.31 and the same expiration date in four months. The value of this option portfolio at expiration depends on the value of the German mark at the time of expiration. If the mark is worth $.31 or less at expiration, the call expires worthless. For values of the mark above $.31, the call option increases in value. However, for each cent the mark falls below $.31 at expiration, there is an additional one cent contribution loss on the short put position. Considering the

Figure 18.10

Quotations for Currency Futures, Options, and Futures Options

FUTURES OPTIONS

JAPAN YEN (CME)–12.5 million yen; $ per yen (.00)

	Open	High	Low	Settle	Change	Lifetime High	Lifetime Low	Open Interest
Sept	.9969	.9983	.9898	.9945	– .0038	1.0090	.8942	61,084
Dec	1.0000	1.0047	.9950	1.0016	– .0038	1.0140	.9525	2,945
Mr95	1.0075	1.0090	1.0075	1.0094	– .0038	1.0200	.9680	443

Est vol 24,331; vol Wed 38,851; open int 64,559, +1,485.

DEUTSCHEMARK (CME)–125,000 marks; $ per mark

	Open	High	Low	Settle	Change	Lifetime High	Lifetime Low	Open Interest
Sept	.6223	.6248	.6200	.6236	+ .0010	.6295	.5600	78,329
Dec	.6215	.6246	.6215	.6240	+ .0010	.6297	.5590	2,172
Mr95	....	....	....	.6250	+ .0010	.6250	.5798	710

Est vol 39,246; vol Wed 47,994; open int 81,227, –4,408.

CANADIAN DOLLAR (CME)–100,000 dlrs.; $ per Can $

	Open	High	Low	Settle	Change	Lifetime High	Lifetime Low	Open Interest
Sept	.7187	.7194	.7176	.7186	– .0001	.7740	.7068	36,491
Dec	.7140	.7145	.7138	.7141	– .0001	.7670	.7038	2,711
Mr95	.7100	.7100	.7100	.7101	– .0001	.7605	.7020	647
June	....	....	....	.7057	– .0001	.7600	.6990	169

Est vol 3,740; vol Wed 4,035; open int 40,076, –371.

BRITISH POUND (CME)–62,500 pds.; $ per pound

	Open	High	Low	Settle	Change	Lifetime High	Lifetime Low	Open Interest
Sept	1.5284	1.5406	1.5272	1.5380	+ .0076	1.5456	1.4440	38,127
Dec	1.5330	1.5390	1.5330	1.5362	+ .0076	1.5440	1.4400	413

Est vol 10,869; vol Wed 13,827; open int 38,557, –1,594.

SWISS FRANC (CME)–125,000 francs; $ per franc

	Open	High	Low	Settle	Change	Lifetime High	Lifetime Low	Open Interest
Sept	.7403	.7436	.7380	.7422	+ .0010	.7490	.6590	46,955
Dec	.7440	.7447	.7422	.7436	+ .0010	.7505	.6885	944

Est vol 17,223; vol Wed 19,845; open int 47,911, –1,237.

AUSTRALIAN DOLLAR (CME)–100,000 dlrs.; $ per A.$

	Open	High	Low	Settle	Change	Lifetime High	Lifetime Low	Open Interest
Sept	.7320	.7352	.7300	.7308	– .0046	.7467	.6645	8,287

Est vol 791; vol Wed 1,833; open int 8,315, –140.

U.S. DOLLAR INDEX (FINEX)–1,000 times USDX

	Open	High	Low	Settle	Change	Lifetime High	Lifetime Low	Open Interest
Sept	90.95	91.00	90.54	90.69	– .06	98.55	89.98	12,424
Dec	91.29	91.12	91.02	91.01	– .12	99.00	90.58	3,041

Est vol 2,000; vol Wed 2,276; open int 15,469, +937.
The index: High 90.78; Low 90.27; Close 90.36 –.13

FUTURES

JAPANESE YEN (CME)
12,500,000 yen; cents per 100 yen

Strike Price	Calls–Settle Jly	Calls–Settle Aug	Calls–Settle Sep	Puts–Settle Jly	Puts–Settle Aug	Puts–Settle Sep
9850	1.53	2.14	2.69	0.58	1.20	1.75
9900	1.25	1.87	2.44	0.80	1.42	1.99
9950	0.99	1.63	2.20	1.04	1.68	2.25
1000	0.78	1.41	1.98	1.33	1.96	2.53
1050	0.60	1.21	1.77	1.65	2.25	2.81
1100	0.46	1.03	1.58	2.01	2.57	3.12

Est vol 7,047 Wed 5,912 calls 8,706 puts
Op int Wed 56,696 calls 62,263 puts

DEUTSCHEMARK (CME)
125,000 marks; cents per mark

Strike Price	Calls–Settle Jly	Calls–Settle Aug	Calls–Settle Sep	Puts–Settle Jly	Puts–Settle Aug	Puts–Settle Sep
6150	1.12	1.41	1.71	0.26	0.55	0.86
6200	0.78	1.11	1.42	0.42	0.75	1.06
6250	0.52	0.86	1.16	0.66	1.00	1.30
6300	0.34	0.66	0.97	0.98	1.30	1.60
6350	0.20	0.49	0.78	1.34	1.63	....
6400	0.11	0.36	0.63	....	....	2.25

Est vol 11,778 Wed 5,702 calls 12,-164 puts
Op int Wed 108,123 calls 112,563 puts

CANADIAN DOLLAR (CME)
100,000 Can.$, cents per Can.$

Strike Price	Calls–Settle Jly	Calls–Settle Aug	Calls–Settle Sep	Puts–Settle Jly	Puts–Settle Aug	Puts–Settle Sep
7100	0.90	....	1.22	0.04	0.19	0.37
7150	0.51	....	0.92	0.15	0.35	0.56
7200	0.23	0.43	0.65	0.37	0.57	0.79
7250	0.07	0.25	0.44	0.71	0.89	1.07
7300	0.03	0.14	0.30	1.17	1.27	1.43
7350	0.01	0.08	0.20	1.65	....	1.83

Est vol 293 Wed 580 calls 91 puts
Op int Wed 9,346 calls 5,174 puts

BRITISH POUND (CME)
62,500 pounds; cents per pound

Strike Price	Calls–Settle Jly	Calls–Settle Aug	Calls–Settle Sep	Puts–Settle Jly	Puts–Settle Aug	Puts–Settle Sep
1500	3.96	4.38	4.86	0.16	0.60	1.10
1525	1.96	2.64	3.26	0.66	1.34	1.98
1550	0.66	1.40	2.06	1.86	2.60	3.24
1575	0.18	0.64	1.20	....	....	4.86
1600	0.06	0.32	0.66	....	....	6.80
1625	0.02	....	0.36	....	....	8.98

Est vol 4,098 Wed 805 calls 7,652 puts
Op int Wed 11,325 calls 29,788 puts

SWISS FRANC (CME)
125,000 francs; cents per franc

Strike Price	Calls–Settle Jly	Calls–Settle Aug	Calls–Settle Sep	Puts–Settle Jly	Puts–Settle Aug	Puts–Settle Sep
7300	1.48	1.85	2.20	0.26	0.64	0.99
7350	1.12	1.55	1.90	0.40	....	1.19
7400	0.82	1.27	1.64	0.60	1.05	1.42
7450	0.57	1.02	1.40	0.85	0.30	1.68

EXCHANGE RATES

Thursday, June 23, 1994

The New York foreign exchange selling rates below apply to trading among banks in amounts of $1 million and more, as quoted at 3 p.m. Eastern time by Bankers Trust Co., Dow Jones Telerate Inc. and other sources. Retail transactions provide fewer units of foreign currency per dollar.

Country	U.S. $ equiv. Thurs.	U.S. $ equiv. Wed.	Currency per U.S. $ Thurs.	Currency per U.S. $ Wed.
Argentina (Peso)	1.01	1.01	.99	.99
Australia (Dollar)	.7330	.7365	1.3643	1.3578
Austria (Schilling)	.08870	.08850	11.27	11.30
Bahrain (Dinar)	2.6522	2.6522	.3771	.3771
Belgium (Franc)	.03030	.03024	33.00	33.07
Brazil (Cruzeiro real)	.0004080	.0004080	2451.04	2451.00
Britain (Pound)	1.5390	1.5305	.6498	.6534
30-Day Forward	1.5382	1.5297	.6501	.6537
90-Day Forward	1.5370	1.5282	.6506	.6544
180-Day Forward	1.5355	1.5265	.6513	.6551
Canada (Dollar)	.7202	.7222	1.3885	1.3847
30-Day Forward	.7192	.7210	1.3904	1.3869
90-Day Forward	.7166	.7178	1.3955	1.3931
180-Day Forward	.7120	.7131	1.4045	1.4023
Czech. Rep. (Koruna)				
Commercial rate	.0350557	.0350557	28.5260	28.5260
Chile (Peso)	.002438	.002438	410.24	410.24
China (Renminbi)	.115221	.115221	8.6790	8.6790
Colombia (Peso)	.001212	.001212	825.20	825.20
Denmark (Krone)	.1589	.1586	6.2949	6.3067
Ecuador (Sucre)				
Floating rate	.000463	.000463	2160.00	2160.00
Finland (Markka)	.18761	.18761	5.3302	5.3302
France (Franc)	.18240	.18213	5.4825	5.4905
30-Day Forward	.18223	.18195	5.4876	5.4960
90-Day Forward	.18197	.18164	5.4954	5.5054
180-Day Forward	.18173	.18131	5.5027	5.5155
Germany (Mark)	.6234	.6226	1.6040	1.6062
30-Day Forward	.6232	.6222	1.6047	1.6072
90-Day Forward	.6229	.6219	1.6055	1.6080
180-Day Forward	.6231	.6221	1.6050	1.6075
Greece (Drachma)	.004131	.004120	242.07	242.70
Hong Kong (Dollar)	.12937	.12938	7.7298	7.7290
Hungary (Forint)	.0097733	.0098078	102.3200	101.9600
India (Rupee)	.03212	.03212	31.13	31.13
Indonesia (Rupiah)	.0004613	.0004613	2168.00	2168.00
Ireland (Punt)	1.5110	1.5051	.6618	.6644
Israel (Shekel)	.3281	.3281	3.0480	3.0480
Italy (Lira)	.0006353	.0006346	1574.00	1575.68
Japan (Yen)	.009860	.009906	101.42	100.95
30-Day Forward	.009880	.009924	101.21	100.77
90-Day Forward	.009930	.009967	100.70	100.33
180-Day Forward	.009990	.010036	100.10	99.64
Jordan (Dinar)	1.4767	1.4767	.6772	.6772
Kuwait (Dinar)	3.3695	3.3695	.2968	.2968
Lebanon (Pound)	.000595	.000595	1682.00	1682.00
Malaysia (Ringgit)	.3864	.3864	2.5880	2.5880
Malta (Lira)	2.6846	2.6846	.3725	.3725
Mexico (Peso)				
Floating rate	.2959018	.2964280	3.3795	3.3735
Netherland (Guilder)	.5565	.5556	1.7970	1.7998
New Zealand (Dollar)	.5900	.5925	1.6949	1.6878
Norway (Krone)	.1434	.1432	6.9725	6.9838
Pakistan (Rupee)	.0327	.0327	30.61	30.61
Peru (New Sol)	.4705	.4705	2.13	2.13
Philippines (Peso)	.03774	.03774	26.50	26.50
Poland (Zloty)	.00004448	.00004447	22480.00	22485.00
Portugal (Escudo)	.006044	.006011	165.45	166.35
Saudi Arabia (Riyal)	.26667	.26667	3.7500	3.7500
Singapore (Dollar)	.6545	.6540	1.5280	1.5290
Slovak Rep. (Koruna)	.0307220	.0307220	32.5500	32.5500
South Africa (Rand)				
Commercial rate	.2769	.2737	3.6108	3.6543
Financial rate	.2117	.2116	4.7247	4.7250
South Korea (Won)	.0012403	.0012403	806.28	806.28
Spain (Peseta)	.007530	.007480	132.80	133.68
Sweden (Krona)	.1297	.1299	7.7101	7.6961
Switzerland (Franc)	.7402	.7399	1.3510	1.3515
30-Day Forward	.7403	.7399	1.3508	1.3515
90-Day Forward	.7407	.7402	1.3500	1.3509
180-Day Forward	.7424	.7413	1.3470	1.3489
Taiwan (Dollar)	.036969	.036969	27.05	27.05
Thailand (Baht)	.03981	.03981	25.12	25.12
Turkey (Lira)	.0000314	.0000320	31829.14	31222.75
United Arab (Dirham)	.2723	.2723	3.6725	3.6725
Uruguay (New Peso)				
Financial	.201613	.201613	4.96	4.96
Venezuela (Bolivar)				
Floating rate	.00583	.00583	171.50	171.50
SDR	1.43754	1.44241	.69563	.69328
ECU	1.19500	1.19410	....	....

Special Drawing Rights (SDR) are based on exchange rates for the U.S., German, British, French and Japanese currencies. Source: International Monetary Fund.

European Currency Unit (ECU) is based on a basket of community currencies.

OPTIONS
PHILADELPHIA EXCHANGE

		Calls Vol.	Calls Last	Puts Vol.	Puts Last
FFranc					**182.53**
250,000 French Franc EOM-European style.					
18¼	Jul	5545	1.96	...	...
18½	Jul	5545	1.10	...	...
BPound					**153.99**
31,250 British Pound EOM-European					
152½	Jun	32	1.40	...	...
DMark					**62.40**
62,500 German Mark EOM-European style.					
63	Jun	500	0.06	...	...
62,500 German Marks EOM-European style.					
45	Jul	25	0.10	...	...
58½	Jul	...	...	50	0.04
61½	Jun	...	...	500	0.03
62½	Jun	100	0.21	...	...
66½	Jul	50	0.04	...	...
SFranc					**74.14**
62,500 Swiss Franc EOM-European style.					
71½	Jun	4	2.72	...	...
62,500 Swiss Francs-European style.					
71	Jun	5	3.12	...	...
72	Jul	4	2.50	...	...
Australian Dollar					**73.21**
50,000 Australian Dollars-European Style.					
73	Jul	80	0.86	...	...
50,000 Australian Dollars-cents per unit.					
71	Sep	1	2.66	50	0.44
72	Sep	1	1.95	...	...
British Pound					**153.99**
31,250 British Pound EOM-cents per unit.					
155	Jun	6	0.15	...	...
31,250 British Pounds-European Style.					
150	Aug	...	...	32	0.62
155	Jul	130	1.00	...	...
157½	Jul	130	0.32	...	...
157½	Sep	32	1.14	...	...
31,250 British Pounds-European units.					
147½	Sep	...	...	32	0.61
31,250 British Pounds-cents per unit.					
140	Sep	...	...	160	0.12
147½	Sep	...	...	60	0.59
150	Jul	...	...	3	0.45
150	Aug	...	...	32	0.88
152½	Jul	3	1.67	...	...
155	Jul	30	0.95	...	...
157½	Sep	750	1.43	...	...
British Pound-GMark					**246.26**
31,250 British Pound-German Mark cross.					
244	Jul	...	...	10	0.78
248	Jul	10	0.78	...	...
31,250 British Pound-German mark EOM.					
246	Jun	4	0.34	...	...
110	Sep	...	...	96	0.20
114	Jul	...	...	80	0.10
114	Aug	...	...	224	0.35
French Franc					**182.53**
250,000 French Francs-European Style.					
17	Jul	...	...	6595	0.04
18¼	Sep	5	3.30	...	...
German Mark					**62.40**
62,500 German Marks EOM-cents per unit.					
60	Jun	2	2.42	...	...
61½	Jun	...	...	400	0.04
62	Jun	150	0.50	100	0.10
62½	Jun	3610	0.21	2	0.30
62,500 German Marks-European Style.					
57½	Jul	200	4.74	...	...
57½	Sep	200	4.82	...	...
59½	Jul	...	...	50	0.04
60	Jul	...	...	50	0.08
60	Sep	...	...	200	0.56
60½	Sep	...	...	26	0.53
63	Jul	213	0.43	...	...
63	Aug	10	0.72	...	...
64½	Jul	25	0.11	...	...
65½	Jul	200	0.04	...	...
62,500 German Marks-cents per unit.					
57	Sep	...	...	56	0.09
58	Sep	...	...	128	0.15
59	Aug	...	...	260	0.12
59	Sep	...	...	344	0.24
59½	Jul	...	...	355	0.04
60	Aug	...	...	140	0.24
60	Sep	...	...	2	0.42
60½	Jul	...	...	200	0.12
61	Jul	110	1.60	...	...
61½	Jul	5	1.01	405	0.32
61½	Aug	80	1.54	10	0.64
61½	Sep	...	...	37	0.93
62	Jul	5	0.88	10	0.60
62	Sep	130	1.50	23	1.14
62½	Jul	...	...	300	0.74
62½	Sep	160	1.25	2	1.39
63	Jul	105	0.41	...	...
63	Aug	65	0.77	...	...
63	Sep	141	1.04	10	1.80
63½	Sep	130	0.85	...	...
Japanese Yen					**98.88**
6,250,000 Japanese Yen EOM-100ths of a cent per unit.					
94	Jun	6	4.90	...	...
99½	Jun	...	...	10	0.89
100½	Jun	200	0.06	...	...
6,250,000 Japanese Yen-100ths of a cent per unit.					
90½	Jul	5	8.50	...	...
93	Sep	...	...	6	0.34
93½	Jul	...	...	100	0.07
94	Jul	6	5.10	...	...
94½	Aug	...	...	10	0.41
95	Sep	...	...	7	0.70
95½	Jul	...	...	100	0.19
96	Jul	30	3.12	20	0.29
96	Sep	...	...	30	1.06
96½	Sep	...	...	6	1.18
97	Jul	...	...	5	0.50
97	Aug	...	...	11	0.83
97	Sep	...	...	79	1.39
98	Jul	...	...	8	0.81
98½	Jul	...	...	20	1.00
99	Jul	805	1.22	20	1.24
99	Aug	800	1.90	10	1.74
99	Sep	...	...	5	2.24
99½	Jul	6	1.07	...	...
100	Jul	...	...	12	1.73
100	Aug	...	...	25	2.26
100	Sep	...	...	3	2.74
100½	Jul	300	0.75	...	...
101½	Jul	10	0.54	...	...
104	Sep	23	0.88	...	...
6,250,000 Japanese Yen-European Style.					
94	Aug	...	...	8	0.30
95	Jul	...	...	10	0.15
96	Aug	...	...	8	0.68
98	Sep	...	...	10	1.60
99	Sep	...	...	5	2.00
100½	Aug	16	1.40	...	...
Swiss Franc					**74.14**
62,500 Swiss Francs-European Style.					
67	Jul	60	7.00	...	...
67	Sep	60	7.02	...	...
71	Sep	...	...	60	0.58
72	Jul	5	2.26	...	...
74	Jul	100	0.88	...	...
76	Jul	100	0.23	...	...
62,500 Swiss Francs-cents per unit.					
67	Sep	...	...	20	0.06
67½	Sep	...	...	20	0.08
69	Jul	10	5.12	...	...
69	Sep	...	...	40	0.18
70½	Jul	...	...	20	0.05
71½	Aug	...	...	10	0.33
73	Jul	10	1.21	2	0.48
73½	Jul	2	1.15	8	0.53

Source: *The Wall Street Journal*, June 24, 1994, p. C15. Reprinted by permission of *The Wall Street Journal*,

Figure 18.11

Currency Futures and Option Portfolios Profits and Losses

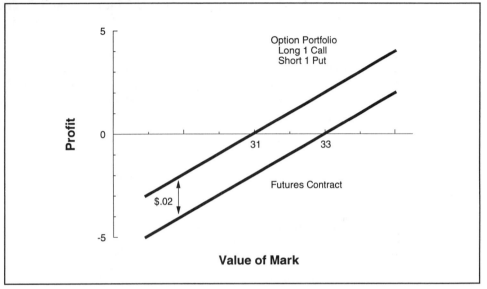

entire portfolio, there will be a positive value to the long call/short put portfolio if the mark lies above $.31 when the options expire. If the spot price of the mark is less than $.31 at expiration, the portfolio will have a negative value. Notice that we have focused on the value of the portfolio so far, and we have ignored the cost of the combined call and put portfolio.

Now we need to compare the value of this two–option portfolio with the futures contract. In Figure 18.11 we assume that a futures contract is available at a price of $.33. There is no cost for entering a futures contract, except for the transaction costs that we ignore. Therefore, the line for the futures contract in Figure 18.11 shows the profit or loss that will be realized on the futures at its expiration, which we assume is the same expiration date that prevailed for the options.

As the graph shows, no matter what the value of the mark might be at expiration, the option portfolio will have a value that exceeds the profit or loss for the futures. For example, if the mark is at $.33 at expiration, the futures contract will have no value, but the option portfolio will be worth $.02 per mark. If the mark is worth $.31 at the expiration date in March, the options portfolio will be worthless, but the futures contract will show a loss of $.02 per mark. No matter what the mark is worth at expiration, the options portfolio will perform $.02 better than the futures contract.

Since the options portfolio will always perform better, it must be priced higher than the futures contract. Otherwise, all traders would prefer the options portfolio. In fact, since we know exactly how much better the options portfolio will perform at expiration, we can calculate how much more the options portfolio will be worth than the futures contract. If the current price of the futures contract is $.33, it costs nothing to enter the futures contract at that price. The options portfolio is certain to pay off $.02 per mark better than the futures contract at expiration, so it has a positive value. This must be the case since the futures contract costs nothing to enter.

How much will the options portfolio be worth? Using our assumption of the contract size being 1,000,000 marks, what will be the difference in the dollar payoffs between the futures position and the options portfolio at maturity? With a payoff difference of $.02 per mark, the difference in the payoffs between the futures and options portfolio must be a total of $20,000, because we are assuming a contract size of one million marks. In mathematical terms, the difference in the payoffs can be represented as:

$$F - E = \$20,000$$

where:

    E = $310,000, the exercise price for a contract on 1,000,000 marks
    F = $330,000, the total futures price for 1,000,000 marks

By acquiring the options portfolio rather than the futures contract, the investor is certain to receive $20,000 more at expiration than the futures contract holder will receive. Because this $20,000 incremental payoff is certain, and because the price of the futures contract is zero, the holder of the options portfolio must be willing to pay the present value of that future payoff. In other words, the options portfolio must be worth the present value of the $20,000 that will be received in June. That means the price of the options portfolio must equal the present value of the difference between the futures price and the exercise price on the options:

$$C - P = \frac{F - E}{(1 + R_f)^T} \qquad \qquad \textbf{18.14}$$

In our example, the difference $F - E$ is $20,000, so the cost of the options portfolio must be the present value of $20,000 discounted at the risk–free rate. Assuming that the interest rate is 1 percent per month and that the expiration is four months away, the total cost of the options portfolio should be $20,000/ $(1.01)^4$ or $19,220. This gives us a technique for establishing a relationship between futures and option prices.[14]

Another way to see the same point is to assume that a trader makes the following transactions:

---

[14]For more on the relationships between options and futures on foreign currencies, see I. Giddy, "Foreign Exchange Options," *The Journal of Futures Markets*, 1983, pp. 143–166.

Buy 1 call
Sell 1 put
Sell 1 futures

We now consider the payoffs on this three–asset portfolio for different values of the German mark at the expiration of the three instruments. First, if the mark is worth $.31, the two options are both worthless and a short futures position is worth $.02, so the total portfolio is worth $.02. If the mark is worth $.33 at expiration, the futures profit is zero, the short put expires worthless, and the long call is worth $.02, for a total portfolio value of $.02. In fact, for any value of the German mark, the portfolio is worth $.02. Therefore, we see that a long call/short put/short futures simulates a risk–free pure discount instrument that pays the futures contract price less the common option exercise price. It may seem surprising that options and futures, instruments known for their riskiness, can be combined to create a risk–free investment. However, Chapter 20 explores the combinations of different instruments that can be created to tailor risk positions in an amazing variety of ways.

Summary

This chapter presented an overview of the options market in the United States. Option trading on organized exchanges began in 1973 with the introduction of options on individual stocks. Since that time, option markets in the United States have expanded greatly with options on metals, stock and other indexes, foreign currencies, and options on futures contracts.

Options can be classified as put or call options, each of which may be bought or sold. Ownership of a call option confers the right to buy a given good at a specified price for a specified period of time. Selling a call option confers those same rights to the owner of a call option in exchange for a payment from the call option purchaser. Ownership of a put option permits the sale of a good at a specified price for a specified period of time. Selling a put option gives those rights to the buyer in exchange for a payment from the buyer.

The theory of option pricing is very well developed. Starting merely from the assumption that options should be priced in a way that allows no arbitrage opportunities, it is possible to bound option prices very closely. Essentially, it can be shown using the no–arbitrage condition that call option prices are a function of the stock price, the exercise price of the option, the time to expiration, the interest rate, and the risk level of the good underlying the option. Additionally, Black and Scholes developed an option pricing model that gives an exact price for a call option as a function of the same five variables. While their model is a theoretical model, it has been shown to accord very well with option prices that are actually observed in the market.

Options are useful financial instruments for both speculation and hedging. For example, an investor expecting a stock price to increase can profit from being correct by buying a call option or selling a put option on that stock. By speculating with options, it is possible to achieve more leverage than by merely trading the stock itself. Options are useful for controlling risk as well, because the careful combination of options and positions in the underlying good can provide virtually any degree of risk that is desired. Further, combinations of options themselves widen the range of payoff possibilities available to the investor.

Questions and Problems

1. Respond to the following claim: "Buying a call option is very dangerous because it commits the owner to purchasing a stock at a later date. At that time the stock may be undesirable. Therefore, owning a call option is a risky position."

2. "I bought a call option with an exercise price of $110 on IBM when IBM was at $108 and I paid $6 per share for the option. Now the option is about to expire and IBM is trading at $112. There's no point in exercising the option, because I will wind up paying a total of $116 for the shares—$6 I already spent for the option plus the $110 exercise price." Is this line of reasoning correct? Explain.

3. What is the value of a call option on a share of stock if the exercise price of the call is $0 and its expiration date is infinite? Explain.

4. Why is the value of a call option at expiration equal to the maximum of zero or the stock price minus the exercise price?

5. Two call options on the same stock have the following features. The first has an exercise price of $60, a time to expiration of 3 months, and a premium of $5. The second has an exercise price of $60, a time to expiration of 6 months, and a premium of $4. What should you do in this situation? Explain exactly, assuming that you transact for just one option. What is your profit or loss at the expiration of the nearby option if the stock is at $55, $60, or $65?

6. Two call options are identical except that they are written on two different stocks with different risk levels. Which will be worth more? Why?

7. Explain why owning a bond is like a short position in a put option.

8. Why does ownership of a convertible bond have features of a call option?

9. Assume the following: a stock is selling for $100, a call option with an exercise price of $90 is trading for $6 and matures in one month, and that the interest rate is 1 percent per month. What should you do? Explain your transactions.

10. Consider a German mark futures contract with a current price of $.35 per mark. There are also put and call options on the mark with the same expiration date in 3 months that happen to have a striking price of $.35. You buy a call and sell a put. How much should your combined option position cost? Explain. What if the interest rate were 1 percent per month and the striking prices were $.40? How much should the option position be worth then?

11. Two call options on the same stock expire in 2 months. One has an exercise price of $55 and a price of $5. The other has an exercise price of $50 and a price of $4. What transactions would you make to exploit this situation?

CFA Questions

All CFA examination questions are reprinted, with permission, from the Level I *1992–1994, CFA Candidate Study and Examination Program Review.* Copyright 1992–1994, Association for Investment Management and Research, Charlottesville, Va. All rights reserved.

A. In the Black–Scholes option valuation formula, an increase in a stock's volatility:
   a. increases the associated call option value.
   b. decreases the associated put option value.
   c. increases or decreases the option value, depending on the level of interest rates.
   d. does not change either the put or call option value because put–call parity holds.

B. An American option is more valuable than a European option on the same dividend paying stock with the same terms because the:
   a. European option contract is not adjusted for stock splits and stock dividends.
   b. American option can be exercised from date of purchase until expiration, but the European option can be exercised only at expiration.
   c. European option does not conform to the Black–Scholes model and is often mispriced.
   d. American options are traded on U.S. exchanges, which offer much more volume and liquidity.

C. In the options markets, the purpose of the clearinghouse is to:
   I.   issue certificates of ownership.
   II. ensure contract performance.
   III. match up the option buyer who exercises with the original option writer.
   a. II only
   b. II and III only
   c. III only
   d. I, II, and III

D. You can create a strap by buying two calls and one put on ABC stock, all with a strike price of $45. The calls cost $5 each, and the put costs $4. If you close your position when ABC is priced at $55, your *per share* gain or loss is a:
   a. $4 loss.
   b. $6 gain.
   c. $10 gain.
   d. $20 gain.

E. A put on XYZ stock with a strike price of $40 is priced at $2.00 per share, while a call with a strike price of $40 is priced at $3.50. What is the maximum per share *loss* to the *writer* of the uncovered put and the maximum per share *gain* to the *writer* of the uncovered call?

	Maximum Loss to Put Writer	Maximum Gain to Call Writer
a.	$38.00	$ 3.50
b.	$38.00	$36.50
c.	$40.00	$ 3.50
d.	$40.00	$40.00

F. Which *one* of the following will *increase* the value of a call option?
   a. An increase in interest rates
   b. A decrease in time to expiration of the call
   c. A decrease in the volatility of the underlying stock
   d. An increase in the dividend rate of the underlying stock

G. A client will move his investment account unless you earn at least a 10% rate of return on the account. The rate of return for the portfolio you have chosen has a normal probability distribution with an expected return of 19% and a standard deviation of 4.5%. What is the probability you will keep this account?
   a. 0.475
   b. 0.95
   c. 0.975
   d. 1.00

H. A protected put position (stock plus put) has more positive skewness than the stock alone. This added skewness implies:
   a. the protected put position is truncated.
   b. the mean of the protected put position is higher than the mean of the stock alone.
   c. when compared to the stock alone, the protected put position has a greater probability of higher returns.
   d. when compared to the stock alone, the protected put position has a higher variance.

Suggested Readings

Abken, P. A., "Interest–Rate Caps, Collars, and Floors," Federal Reserve Bank of Atlanta *Economic Review*, November/December 1989, pp. 2–23.

Black, F., "Fact and Fantasy in the Use of Options," *Financial Analysts Journal*, 31:4, July/August 1975, pp. 36–72.

Black, F., "How to Use the Holes in Black–Scholes," *Journal of Applied Corporate Finance*, 1:4, Winter 1989, pp. 67–73.

Black, F. and E. Hakanoglu, "Simplifying Portfolio Insurance for the Seller," *The Institutional Investor Focus on Investment Management*, Cambridge, MA: Ballinger Publishing, 1989, pp. 709–726.

Black, F. and R. Rouhani, "Constant Proportion Portfolio Insurance and the Synthetic Put Option: A Comparison," *The Institutional Investor Focus on Investment Management*, Cambridge, MA: Ballinger Publishing, 1989, pp. 695–708.

Black, F. and M. Scholes., "The Pricing of Options and Corporate Liabilities," *Journal of Political Economy*, 1973, pp. 637–654.

Black, F., E. Derman, and W. Toy, "A One–Factor Model of Interest Rates and Its Application to Treasury Bond Options," *The Handbook of Derivative Instruments*, Chicago: Probus Publishing, 1991, pp. 93–111.

Fried, S., "Americus Trust Scores," *The Handbook of Derivative Instruments*, Chicago: Probus Publishing, 1991, pp. 335–347.

Fried, S., "Equity Warrants," *The Handbook of Derivative Instruments*, Chicago: Probus Publishing, 1991, pp. 315–334.

Giddy, I., "Foreign Exchange Options," *Journal of Futures Markets*, 3:2, 1983, pp. 143–166.

Hill, J. M., A. Jain, and R. A. Wood, Jr., "Portfolio Insurance: Volatility Risk and Futures Mispricing," *The Institutional Investor Focus on Investment Management*, Cambridge, MA: Ballinger Publishing, 1989, pp. 727–753.

Jarrow, R. A. and A. Rudd, *Option Pricing*, Homewood, IL: Richard D. Irwin, 1983.

Jonas, S., "Rolling Down the Vol Curve," *The Handbook of Derivative Instruments*, Chicago: Probus Publishing, 1991, pp. 499–507.

Kolb, R., *The Financial Derivatives Reader*, Miami: Kolb Publishing, 1992.

Kolb, R., *Options: An Introduction*, 2e, Miami: Kolb Publishing, 1994.

Kolb, R., W. and G. D. Gay, *Interest Rate and Stock Index Futures and Options: Characteristics, Valuation and Portfolio Strategies*, Charlottesville, VA: Financial Analysts Research Foundation, 1985, Monograph No. 18.

Kritzman, M., "What's Wrong with Portfolio Insurance?" *The Institutional Investor Focus on Investment Management*, Cambridge, MA: Ballinger Publishing, 1989, pp. 755–761.

Leong, K. S., "Volatility and Option Pricing," *The Handbook of Derivative Instruments*, Chicago: Probus Publishing, 1991, pp. 113–127.

Merton, R. C., "Theory of Rational Option Pricing," *Bell Journal of Economics and Management Science*, 1973, pp. 141–183.

O'Brien, T. J., "How Option Replicating Portfolio Insurance Works: Expanded Details," *Monograph Series in Finance and Economics*, Vol. 4, 1988.

Rubinstein, M., "Portfolio Insurance and the Market Crash," *Financial Analysts Journal*, 44:1, January/February 1988, pp. 38–47.

CHAPTER NINETEEN

The Swap Market

Overview

A **swap** is an agreement between two or more parties to exchange sets of cash flows over a period in the future. For example, Party A might agree to pay a fixed rate of interest on $1 million each year for five years to Party B. In return, Party B might pay a floating rate of interest on $1 million each year for five years. The parties that agree to the swap are known as **counterparties**. The cash flows that the counterparties make are generally tied to the value of debt instruments or to the value of foreign currencies. Therefore, the two basic kinds of swaps are **interest rate swaps** and **currency swaps**.

This chapter provides a basic introduction to the swap market. As we will see, the swap market has grown rapidly in the last few years, because it provides firms that face financial risks with a flexible way to manage that risk. We will explore the risk management motivation that has led to this phenomenal growth in some detail.

A significant industry has arisen to facilitate swap transactions. This chapter considers the role of **swap facilitators**—economic agents who help counterparties identify each other and help the counterparties consummate swap transactions. Swap facilitators, who are either brokers or dealers, may function as agents that identify and bring prospective counterparties into contact with each other. Alternatively, swap dealers may actually transact for their own account to help complete the swap.

By taking part in swap transactions, swap dealers expose themselves to financial risk. This risk can be serious, because it is exactly the risk that the swap counterparties are trying to avoid. Therefore, the swap dealer has two key problems. First, the swap dealer must price the swap to provide a reward for his services in bearing risk. Second, the swap dealer essentially has a portfolio of swaps that results from his numerous transactions in the swap market. Therefore, the swap dealer has the problem of managing a swap portfolio. We explore how swap dealers price their swap transactions and how swap dealers manage the risk inherent in their swap portfolios.

The Swap Market

In this section, we consider the special features of the swap market. For purposes of comparison, we begin by summarizing some of the key features of futures and options markets. Against this background, we focus on the most important features of the swap product. The section concludes with a brief summary of the development of the swap market.

Review of Futures and Options Market Features

In Chapters 17 and 18 we explored the futures and options markets. In Chapter 17 we observed that futures contracts trade exclusively in markets operated by futures exchanges and regulated by the Commodity Futures Trading Commission. Chapter 18 focused on exchange–traded options. Again, this portion of the options market is highly formalized with the options exchanges playing a major role in the market, and the options exchanges are regulated by the Securities Exchange Commission.

Futures markets trade highly standardized contracts, and the options traded on exchanges also have highly specified contract terms that cannot be altered. For example, the S&P 500 futures contract is based on a particular set of stocks, for a particular dollar amount, with only four fixed maturity dates per year. In addition, futures and exchange–traded options generally have a fairly short horizon. In many cases, futures contracts are listed only about one to two years before they expire. Even when it is possible to trade futures for expiration in three years or more, the markets do not become liquid until the contract comes much closer to expiration. For exchange–traded stock options, the longest time to maturity is generally less than one year. These futures and options cannot provide a means of dealing with risks that extend farther into the future than the expiration of the contracts that are traded. For example, if a firm faces interest rate risk for a ten–year horizon associated with a major building project, the futures market allows risk management only for the horizon of futures contracts currently being traded, which is about three years.

In summary, the futures and options markets that we have explored are regulated markets, and they are dominated by the exchanges where trading takes place. The futures and options contracts are highly standardized, they are limited to relatively few goods, and they have a few fixed expirations per year. In addition, the horizon over which they trade is often much shorter than the risk horizon that businesses face.

Characteristics of the Swap Market

In large part, the swap market has emerged because swaps escape many of the limitations inherent in futures and exchange–traded options markets. Swaps, of course, have some limitations of their own.

Swaps are custom tailored to the needs of the counterparties. If they wish, the potential counterparties can start with a blank sheet of paper and develop a contract that is completely dedicated to meeting their particular needs. Thus, swap agreements are more likely to meet the specific needs of the counterparties than exchange–traded instruments. The counterparties can select the dollar amount that they wish to swap, without regard to some fixed contract terms, such as those that prevail in exchange–traded instruments. Similarly, the swap counterparties choose the exact maturity that they need, rather than having to fit their needs to the offerings available on an exchange. This is very important in the swap market, because this flexibility allows the counterparties to deal with much longer horizons than can be addressed through exchange–traded instruments.

On futures and options exchanges, major financial institutions are readily identifiable. For example, in a futures pit, traders will be able to discern the activity of particular firms, because traders know who represents which firm. Therefore, exchange trading necessarily involves a certain loss of privacy. In the swap market, by contrast, only the counterparties know that the swap takes place. Thus, the swap market affords a privacy that cannot be obtained in exchange trading.[1]

We have noted that the futures and options exchanges are subject to considerable government regulation. By contrast, the swap market has virtually no government regulation. As we will see later, swaps are similar to futures. The swap market feared that the Commodity Futures Trading Commission might attempt to assert regulatory authority over the swap market on the grounds that swaps are really futures. However, the Commodity Futures Trading Commission has formally announced that it will not seek jurisdiction over the swap market. This means that the swap market is likely to remain free of federal regulation for the foreseeable future. For the most part, participants in the swap market are thankful to avoid regulation.

The swap market also has some inherent limitations. First, to consummate a swap transaction, one potential counterparty must find a counterparty that is willing to take the opposite side of a transaction. If one party needs a specific maturity, or a certain pattern of cash flows, it can be very difficult to find a willing counterparty. Second, because a swap agreement is a contract between two counterparties, the swap cannot be altered or terminated early without the agreement of both parties. Third, for futures and exchange–traded options, the exchanges effectively guarantee performance on the contracts for all parties. By its very nature, the swap market has no such guarantor. As a consequence, parties to the swap must be certain of the creditworthiness of their counterparties.

As we will see later in this chapter, the swap market has developed mechanisms to deal with these three limitations. The problem of potential default

---

[1]This does not mean to imply that exchange trading sacrifices all anonymity. However, traders watch the activities of major institutions. When these institutions initiate major transactions, it is not possible to maintain complete privacy. It is somewhat ironic that individual traders can trade on futures and options markets with a discretion that is not available to multi–billion dollar financial institutions.

is perhaps the most important. Assessing the financial credibility of a counterparty is difficult and expensive. Therefore, participation in the swap market is effectively limited to firms and institutions that either engage in frequent swap transactions or have access to major swap facilitators that can advise on creditworthiness. In effect, the swap market is virtually limited to firms and financial institutions, and there are few or no individual transactors in the market.

The Emergence of the Swap Market

The origins of the swap market can be traced to the late 1970s, when currency traders developed currency swaps as a technique to evade British controls on the movement of foreign currency. The first interest rate swap occurred in 1981 in an agreement between IBM and the World Bank. Since that time, the market has grown rapidly. Table 19.1 shows the amount of swaps outstanding at year–end for 1987–1992. By the end of 1992, interest rate swaps with $3.85 trillion in underlying value were outstanding, and currency swaps totaled another $860 billion. The total swaps market approached a principal amount of $5 trillion, with about 80 percent of the swaps being interest rate swaps and the remaining 20 percent being currency swaps. Of these swaps, about 45 percent involved the U.S. dollar.

Table 19.1 presents the stock of interest rate and currency swaps outstanding at particular dates, but it does not reflect swaps that were initiated and completed or terminated before 1994. Table 19.2 details the intiation of interest rate and currency swaps during the year ending on June 30, 1993. The U.S. dollar is clearly the currency of choice for both interest rate and currency swaps. Not surprisingly, the Japanese yen is the second most favored currency.

Table 19.1

Value of Outstanding Swaps
($ billions of principal)

Year	Total Interest Rate Swaps	Total Currency Swaps
1987	$ 682.9	$182.8
1988	1,010.2	316.8
1989	1,539.3	434.8
1990	2,311.5	577.5
1991	3,065.1	807.2
1992	3,850.8	860.4

Source: International Swap Dealers Association.

Table 19.2

Swaps Initiated from July 1992 through June 1993
($ billions of principal)

Currency	Interest Rate Swaps	Currency Swaps
U.S. Dollar	$1,437.7	$111.7
Japanese Yen	575.2	41.7
French Franc	336.4	9.0
Deutschemark	331.8	26.2
British Sterling	249.5	16.8
Other Currencies	512.2	97.3
Total of All Currencies	3,442.8	302.7

Source: International Swap Dealers Association.

Plain Vanilla Swaps

In this section, we analyze the different kinds of swaps that are available, and we show how swaps can help corporations manage various types of risk exposure. We begin by considering the mechanics of the simplest kinds of swaps. A **plain vanilla swap**, the simplest kind, can be an interest rate swap or a foreign currency swap.

Interest Rate Swaps

In a plain vanilla interest rate swap, one counterparty has an initial position in a fixed rate debt instrument, while the other counterparty has an initial position in a floating rate obligation. In this initial position, the party with the floating rate obligation is exposed to changes in interest rates. By swapping this floating rate obligation, this counterparty eliminates exposure to changing interest rates. For the party with a fixed rate obligation, the interest rate swap increases the interest rate sensitivity. (Later, we explore the motivation that these counterparties might have for taking their respective positions. First, however, we need to understand the transactions.)

To see the nature of the plain vanilla interest rate swap most clearly, we use an example. We assume that the swap covers a five–year period and involves annual payments on a $1 million principal amount. Let us assume that Party A agrees to pay a fixed rate of 12 percent to Party B. In return, Party B agrees to pay a floating rate of LIBOR + 3 percent to Party A. As we saw in Chapter 2, LIBOR stands for "London Interbank Offered Rate," and it is a base rate at which large international banks lend funds to each other. Floating rates in the swap market are most often set as equaling LIBOR plus some additional amount. Figure 19.1 shows the basic features of this transaction. Party A pays 12 percent of $1 million, or

Figure 19.1

A Plain Vanilla Interest Rate Swap

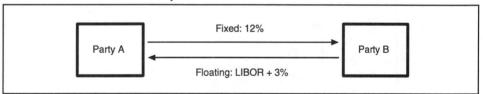

$120,000 each year to Party B. Party B makes a payment to Party A in return, but the actual amount of the payments depends on movement in LIBOR.

Conceptually, the two parties also exchange the principal amount of $1 million. However, actually making the transaction of sending each other $1 million would not make practical sense. As a consequence, principal amounts are generally not exchanged. Instead, the principal plays a conceptual role in determining the amount of the interest payments. Because the principal is not actually exchanged, it is called a **notional principal**, an amount used as a base for computations, but not an amount that is actually transferred from one party to another. In our example, the notional principal is $1 million, and knowing that amount lets us compute the actual dollar amount of the cash flows that the two parties make to each other each year.

Let us assume that the LIBOR is 10 percent at the time of the first payment. This means that Party A will be obligated to pay $120,000 to Party B. Party B will owe $130,000 to Party A. Offsetting the two mutual obligations, Party B owes $10,000 to Party A. Generally, only the **net payment**, the difference between the two obligations, actually takes place. Again, this practice avoids unnecessary payments.[2]

Foreign Currency Swaps

In a currency swap, one party holds one currency and desires a different currency. The swap arises when one party provides a certain principal in one currency to its counterparty in exchange for an equivalent amount of a different currency. For example, Party C may have German marks and be anxious to swap those marks for U.S. dollars. Similarly, Party D may hold U.S. dollars and be willing to exchange those dollars for German marks. With these needs, Parties C and D may be able to engage in a currency swap.

---

[2]The practice of net payments and not actually exchanging principal also protects each counterparty from default by the other. For example, it would be very unpleasant for Party A if it paid the principal amount of $1 million in our example and Party B failed to make its payment to Party A. Making only net payments greatly reduces the potential impact of default.

Figure 19.2

A Plain Vanilla Currency Swap (Initial Cash Flow)

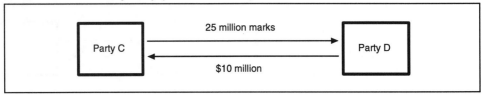

A plain vanilla currency swap involves three different sets of cash flows. First, at the initiation of the swap, the two parties actually do exchange cash. The entire motivation for the currency swap is the actual need for funds denominated in a different currency. This differs from the interest rate swap in which both parties deal in dollars and can pay the net amount. Second, the parties make periodic interest payments to each other during the life of the swap agreement. Third, at the termination of the swap, the parties again exchange the principal.

As an example, let us assume that the current spot exchange rate between German marks and U.S. dollars is 2.5 marks per dollar. Thus, the mark is worth $.40. We assume that the U.S. interest rate is 10 percent and the German interest rate is 8 percent. Party C holds 25 million marks and wishes to exchange those marks for dollars. In return for the marks, Party D would pay $10 million to Party C at the initiation of the swap. We also assume that the term of the swap is seven years and the parties will make annual interest payments. With the interest rates in our example, Party D will pay 8 percent interest on the 25 million marks it received, so the annual payment from Party D to Party C will be 2 million marks. Party C received $10 million dollars and will pay interest at 10 percent, so Party C will pay $1 million each year to Party D.

In actual practice, the parties will make only net payments. For example, assume that at year 1 the spot exchange rate between the dollar and mark is 2.2222 marks per dollar, so the mark is worth $.45. Valuing the obligations in dollars at this exchange rate, Party C owes $1 million and Party D owes $900,000 (2 million marks times $.45). Thus, Party C would pay the $100,000 difference. At other times,

Figure 19.3

A Plain Vanilla Currency Swap (Annual Interest Payment)

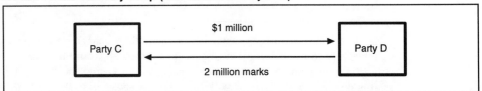

Figure 19.4

A Plain Vanilla Currency Swap (Repayment of Principal)

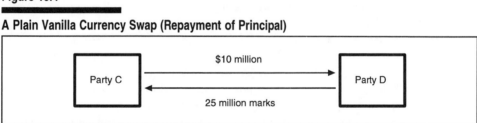

the exchange rate could be different, and the net payment would reflect that different exchange rate.

At the end of seven years, the two parties again exchange principal. In our example, Party C would pay $10 million and Party D would pay 25 million marks. This final payment terminates the currency swap. Figure 19.2 shows the first element of the swap, which is the initial exchange of principal. Figure 19.3 represents the payment of interest, and in our example there would be seven of these payments, one for each year of the swap. Finally, Figure 19.4 shows the second exchange of principal that completes the swap.

Summary

In this section we considered the transactions involved in plain vanilla interest rate and currency swaps. As we saw for an interest rate swap, the essential feature is the transformation of a fixed rate obligation to a floating rate obligation for one party, and a complementary transformation of a floating rate obligation to a fixed rate obligation for the other party. In a currency swap, the two parties exchange currencies to obtain access to a foreign currency that better meets their business needs. To this point, we have only focused on the elementary transactions involved in simple swaps, but we have not considered the motivation that leads to swap agreements.

Motivations for Swaps

In our example of a plain vanilla swap, we saw that one party begins with a fixed rate obligation and seeks a floating rate obligation. The second party exchanges a floating rate for a fixed rate obligation. For this swap to occur, the two parties have to be seeking exactly the opposite goals.

There are two basic motivations that we consider in this section. First, the normal commercial operations of some firms naturally lead to interest rate and currency risk positions of a certain type. Second, some firms may have certain advantages in acquiring specific types of financing. Firms can borrow in the form that is cheapest and use swaps to change the characteristics of the borrowing to one that meets the firm's specific needs. In this section, we consider several simple examples of motivations for swaps.

Commercial Needs

As an example of a prime candidate for an interest rate swap, consider a typical savings and loan association. Savings and loan associations accept deposits and lend those funds for long–term mortgages. Because depositors can withdraw their funds on short notice, deposit rates must adjust to changing interest rate conditions. Most mortgagors wish to borrow at a fixed rate for a long time. As a result, the savings and loan association can be left with floating rate liabilities and fixed rate assets. This means that the savings and loan is vulnerable to rising rates. If rates rise, the savings and loan will be forced to increase the rate it pays on deposits, but it cannot increase the interest rate it charges on the mortgages that have already been issued.

To escape this interest rate risk, the savings and loan might use the swap market to transform its fixed rate assets into floating rate assets or transform its floating rate liabilities into fixed rate liabilities. Let us assume that the savings and loan wishes to transform a fixed rate mortgage into an asset that pays a floating rate of interest. In terms of our interest rate swap example, the savings and loan association is like Party A—in exchange for the fixed rate mortgage that it holds, it wants to pay a fixed rate of interest and receive a floating rate of interest. Engaging in a swap as Party A did will help the association to resolve its interest rate risk.

Figure 19.5

Motivation for the Plain Vanilla Interest Rate Swap

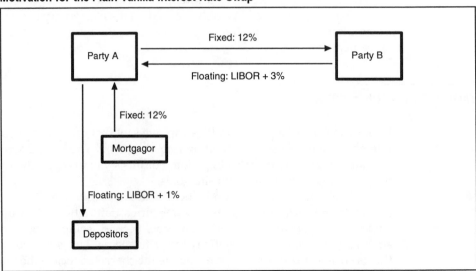

To make the discussion more concrete, we extend our example of the plain vanilla interest rate swap. We assume that the savings and loan association has just loaned $1 million for five years at 12 percent with annual payments, and we assume that the savings and loan pays a deposit rate that equals LIBOR plus 1 percent. With these rates, the association will lose money if LIBOR exceeds 11 percent, and it is this danger that prompts the association to consider an interest rate swap.

Figure 19.5 shows our original plain vanilla interest rate swap with the additional information about the savings and loan that we have just elaborated. In the figure, Party A is the savings and loan association, and it receives payments at a fixed rate of 12 percent on the mortgage. After it enters the swap, the association also pays 12 percent on a notional principal of $1 million. In effect, it receives mortgage payments and passes them through to Party B under the swap agreement. Under the swap agreement, Party A receives a floating rate of LIBOR plus 3 percent. From this cash inflow, the association pays its depositors LIBOR plus 1 percent. This leaves a periodic inflow to the association of 2 percent, which is the spread that it makes on the loan.

In our example, the association now has a fixed rate inflow of 2 percent, and it has succeeded in avoiding its exposure to interest rate risk. No matter what happens to the level of interest rates, the association will enjoy a net cash inflow of 2 percent on $1 million. This example clarifies how the savings association has a strong motivation to enter the swap market. From the very nature of the savings and loan industry, the association finds itself with a risk exposure to rising interest rates. However, by engaging in an interest rate swap, the association can secure a fixed rate position.

Comparative Advantage

In many situations, one firm may have better access to the capital market than another firm.[3] For example, a U.S. firm may be able to borrow easily in the United States, but it might not have such favorable access to the capital market in Germany. Similarly, a German firm may have good borrowing opportunities domestically but poor opportunities in the United States.

Table 19.3 presents borrowing rates for Parties C and D, the firms of our plain vanilla currency swap example. In the plain vanilla example, we assumed that, for each currency, both parties faced the same rate. We now assume that Party C is a German firm with access to marks at a rate of 7 percent, while the U.S. firm, Party D, must pay 8 percent to borrow marks. On the other hand, Party D can borrow dollars at 9 percent, while the German Party C must pay 10 percent for its dollar borrowings.

As the table shows, Party C enjoys a comparative advantage in borrowing marks, and Party D has a comparative advantage in borrowing dollars. These rates

---

[3] This discussion of comparative advantage draws on the excellent analysis by K. Kapner and J. Marshall in *The Swaps Handbook*, New York: New York Institute of Finance, 1990.

Table 19.3

Borrowing Rates for Two Firms in Two Currencies

Firm	U.S. Dollar Rate	German Mark Rate
Party C	10%	7%
Party D	9%	8%

raise the possibility that each firm can exploit its comparative advantage and share the gains by reducing overall borrowing costs. This possibility is shown in Figures 19.6–19.8, which parallel Figures 19.2–19.4.

Figure 19.6 resembles Figure 19.2, but it provides more information. In Figure 19.6, Party C borrows 25 million marks from a third party lender at its borrowing rate of 7 percent, while Party D borrows $10 million from a fourth party at 9 percent. After these borrowings, both parties have the funds to engage in the plain vanilla currency swap that we have already analyzed. To initiate the swap, Party C forwards the 25 million marks it has just borrowed to Party D, which reciprocates with the $10 million it has borrowed. In effect, the two parties have made independent borrowings and then exchanged the proceeds. For this reason, currency swaps are also known as an **exchange of borrowings**.

Figure 19.7 shows the same swap terms we have already analyzed. Party C pays interest payments at a rate of 10 percent on the $10 million it received from Party D, and Party D pays 2 million marks interest per year on the 25 million marks

Figure 19.6

A Plain Vanilla Currency Swap (Initial Cash Flow with Lenders)

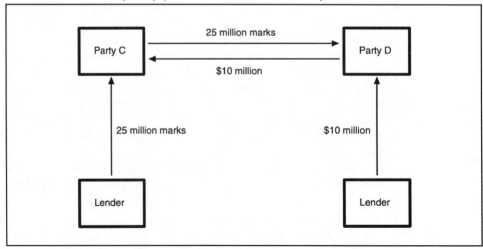

Figure 19.7

A Plain Vanilla Currency Swap (Interest Payments with Lenders)

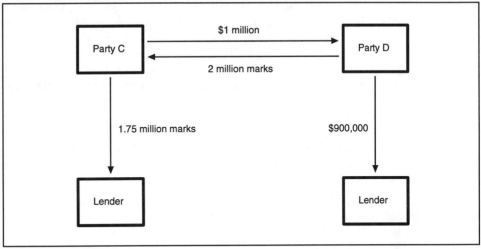

it received from Party C. Notice that these rates are the same ones that the two firms could obtain from other sources. However, Figure 19.7 also shows the interest payments that Parties C and D must make on their borrowings. Party C pays 1.75 million marks interest annually, but it receives 2 million marks from Party D. For

Figure 19.8

A Plain Vanilla Currency Swap (Repayment of Principal with Lenders)

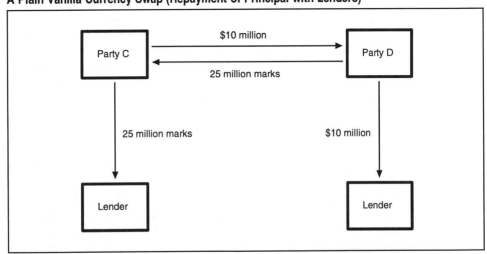

its part, Party D receives $1 million from Party C, from which it pays interest of $900,000.

Now we can clearly see how the swap benefits both parties. Party C gets the use of $10 million and pays out 1.75 million marks. Had it borrowed dollars on its own, it would have paid a full 10 percent, or $1 million per year. At current exchange rates of 2.5 marks per dollar, Party C is effectively paying $700,000 annual interest on the use of $10 million. This is an effective rate of 7 percent. Party D pays $900,000 interest each year and receives the use of 25 million marks. This is equivalent to paying 2,250,000 marks annual interest ($900,000 times 2.5 marks per dollar) for the use of 25 million marks, or a rate of 9 percent. By using the swap, both parties achieve an effective borrowing rate that is much lower than they could have obtained by borrowing the currency they needed directly. By engaging in the swap, both firms can use the comparative advantage of the other to reduce their borrowing costs. Figure 19.8 shows the termination cash flows for the swap, when both parties repay the principal.

Summary

In this section, we have explored two motivations for engaging in swaps—commercial needs, and comparative borrowing advantages. The first led to an interest rate swap, while the second motivated a currency swap. Both swaps that we have analyzed are plain vanilla swaps. While swaps can become much more complex, they are generally motivated by the considerations that we have explored in this section.

Swap Facilitators

As we mentioned earlier, a swap facilitator is a third party who assists in the completion of a swap. When a swap facilitator acts strictly as an agent, without taking any financial position in the swap transaction, the facilitator acts as a **swap broker**. In some instances, a swap facilitator may actually transact for its own account to help complete the swap. In this case, the swap facilitator acts as a **swap dealer**. Both swap brokers and swap dealers are known as **swap banks,** so a swap bank is equivalent to a swap facilitator. This section explores the role of swap brokers and dealers.

Swap Brokers

For a swap transaction to occur, two counterparties with matching needs must find each other. As we have seen, a firm with a short–term and fairly standard risk exposure might use futures or exchange–traded options to manage that risk. Special risk exposures often lead firms to look beyond futures and exchange–traded options to the swap market for the management of that special exposure. For example, even with the plain vanilla interest rate and currency swaps examples that we considered, the risks faced by the parties could not be managed completely with futures or exchange–traded options. As the risk exposure goes beyond the plain vanilla variety, futures and exchange–traded options are even less adequate for managing these more complex risks.

For a potential swap participant with a specific need, finding a counterparty can be very difficult. For example, in the previous example of a plain vanilla currency swap, Party C must find another firm that meets a number of conditions. The firm that will act as a counterparty to Party C must have: preferential borrowing access to $10 million, a need for German marks, a requirement that matches Party C in size ($10 million versus 25 million marks), a time horizon of seven years, a willingness to transact at the time desired by Party C, and an acceptable credit standing. For Party C to find this potential counterparty is a daunting task.

The difficulty of finding counterparties creates an opportunity for a swap broker. A swap broker has a number of firms in her client base and stands ready to search for swap counterparties upon demand. In the example of the plain vanilla currency swap, Party C might approach a swap broker and seek assistance in finding a counterparty. In effect, Party C would rely on the swap broker's specialized knowledge of the swap needs of many firms.

After Party C solicits the assistance of a swap broker, the broker contacts potential counterparties. Generally, a firm like Party C will desire privacy, so the broker will not identify Party C until she finds a very likely counterparty. (This is another reason that firms use swap brokers. By having a swap broker conduct the search, Party C in our example can preserve its anonymity.) Once the swap broker finds a suitable counterparty, which turns out to be Party D in our plain vanilla currency swap example, the broker brings the two parties together. The broker then helps to negotiate and complete the swap contract. For her services, the swap broker receives a fee from each of the counterparties.

In summary, the swap broker serves as an information intermediary. The broker uses her superior knowledge of potential swap participants to find the right counterparty. The broker exercises discretion by protecting the identity of the potential counterparties until the swap partners are found. Notice that the swap broker is not a party to the swap contract. As a broker, the swap facilitator does not bear financial risk, but merely assists the two counterparties in completing the swap transaction.

Swap Dealers

A swap dealer fulfills all of the functions of a swap broker. In addition, a swap dealer also takes a risk position in the swap transaction by becoming an actual party to the transaction. Just because the swap dealer may take a risk position to complete a swap transaction does not mean that the swap dealer is a speculator. Instead, the swap dealer accepts a risk position in order to complete the transaction for the initial counterparty. The swap transaction may leave the swap dealer with a risk position, but the swap dealer will then try to offset that risk. The swap dealer functions as a financial intermediary, earning profits by helping to complete swap transactions. If completing a swap results in a risk position for the swap dealer, the dealer will then try to minimize that risk by its own further transactions.

To explore the functions served by the swap dealer, we assume that the dealer begins with its optimal set of investments. In other words, the swap dealer has financial assets, but they are invested in a way that the swap dealer finds optimal. Therefore, if the swap dealer takes part in a swap transaction and has his financial position altered as a result of that transaction, we assume that the change in the swap dealer's position represents an unwanted risk that the dealer accepted only to help complete the swap transaction and to earn profits thereby. Against this background, we return to our example of a plain vanilla interest rate swap to explore the additional role performed by the swap dealer.

In the plain vanilla interest rate swap example, we noted that Party A was a savings and loan association that paid a floating rate of LIBOR + 1 percent to its depositors and made a five–year fixed rate mortgage loan at 12 percent. This initial business position left Party A exposed to rising interest rates, and Party A wanted to avoid this risk by converting the fixed rate it received on its mortgage loan to a floating rate. Party A's ability to complete this swap depended on finding a suitable counterparty with a matching need, such as Party B in our example.

If a firm like Party B cannot be found, Party A is left unable to complete the swap. Often a swap broker will be unable to find a suitable counterparty, or the swap broker can find only a partial match. In many instances, the swap broker may be able to find a potential counterparty that will take only a portion of the swap that the initial counterparty wants to complete, or the potential counterparty does not want to transact at the time the initial counterparty desires.

Figure 19.9

A Plain Vanilla Interest Rate Swap with a Swap Dealer

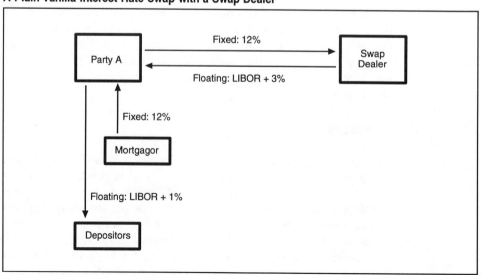

To complete the swap transaction for Party A, the swap dealer may act as a counterparty. Figure 19.9 shows the plain vanilla interest rate swap example as before, except the swap dealer acts as the counterparty to Party A. As a result, we see that the swap gives the swap dealer the same cash flows that Party B had in Figure 19.5.

As a result of this transaction, the swap dealer now has an undesired risk position. Over the next five years the dealer is obligated to pay a floating rate of LIBOR + 3 percent and to receive a fixed rate of 12 percent on a notional amount of $10 million. The swap dealer must believe that he can make money by acting as a counterparty to Party A. To do so, the swap dealer wants to offset the risk that he has undertaken, but he needs to offset that risk on better terms than he undertook as a counterparty to Party A.

Let us assume that the dealer knew of a potential party in the swap market, Party E, that was willing to pay a floating rate of LIBOR + 3.1 percent in exchange for a fixed rate of 12 percent on a notional amount of $10 million. However, Party E is willing to accept a term of only three years, not the five years that Party A desires. Given a knowledge of this client, the swap dealer decides to act as a counterparty to Party A. By also transacting with Party E, the swap dealer is able to offset a substantial portion of the risk he accepts by transacting with Party A. Figure 19.10 shows the transactions involving Parties A and E, along with the swap dealer. After completing these transactions, we see that the swap dealer has some profits to show for his efforts. Specifically, the dealer is making 10 basis points on the floating rate side of the transaction because he receives LIBOR + 3.1 percent and

Figure 19.10

The Swap Dealer as Intermediary in a Plain Vanilla Interest Rate Swap

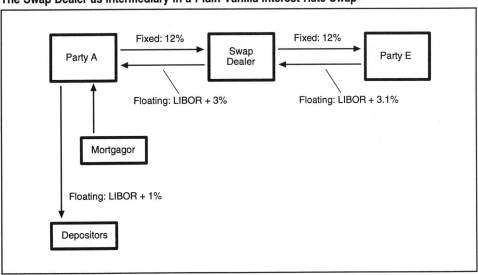

Table 19.4

The Swap Dealer's Cash Flows

Year	From Party A	To Party A	From Party E	To Party E	Dealer's Net Cash Flow
1	$1,200,000	LIBOR + 3%	LIBOR + 3.1%	$1,200,000	$10,000
2	1,200,000	LIBOR + 3%	LIBOR + 3.1%	1,200,000	10,000
3	1,200,000	LIBOR + 3%	LIBOR + 3.1%	1,200,000	10,000
4	1,200,000	LIBOR + 3%	0	0	$1,200,000 - LIBOR + 3%
5	1,200,000	LIBOR + 3%	0	0	1,200,000 - LIBOR + 3%

pays LIBOR + 3 percent. However, the swap dealer still has considerable risk as a result of the transaction.

Table 19.4 shows the swap dealer's cash flows resulting from the swap. The first two columns of Table 19.4 show the cash flows that result from the swap dealer's transactions with Party A. To serve the needs of Party A, the swap dealer has agreed to receive a 12 percent fixed rate payment in exchange for paying LIBOR + 3 percent on a $10 million notional amount. Based on the portion of the transaction with Party A, the swap dealer will receive $1.2 million each year and pay LIBOR + 3 percent on $10 million each year. Which set of cash flows is better is uncertain because the future course of interest rates is not known. For example, if LIBOR stays constant at 8 percent over the five years, the swap dealer will profit handsomely, making 1 percent per year for five years on $10 million. However, if LIBOR jumps to 11 percent and remains constant, the swap dealer will be paying 14 percent on $10 million each year. As a result, the swap dealer will receive $1.2 million but must pay $1.4 million each year, for an annual net loss of $200,000. Thus, the riskiness of acting as a counterparty to Party A is clear.

Table 19.4 also shows the swap dealer's cash flows that result from transacting with Party E. For each of the first three years, the dealer will pay a fixed interest rate of 12 percent on $10,000,000, which is $1,200,000. In addition, the dealer will receive a rate of LIBOR + 3.1 percent on a notional amount of $10,000,000.

The final column of the table shows the swap dealer's net cash flows. For the first three years, the swap dealer has achieved a perfect match in cash flows, receiving $1.2 million from Party A and paying it to Party E. The dealer has a net zero cash flow on this part of the transaction. During the first three years, the dealer also receives LIBOR + 3.1 percent from Party E and pays LIBOR + 3 percent to Party A, both on notional amounts of $10 million. On this portion of the transaction, the dealer receives a net spread of 10 basis points on a $10 million notional amount. Taking all of the dealer's cash flows during the first three years into account, we see that the dealer has a net cash inflow of $10,000 per year.

Even after transacting with both Parties A and E, the swap dealer has a residual risk that is evident in Table 19.4. In years four and five, the dealer will receive $1.2 million from Party A, but he must pay LIBOR + 3 percent. Whether this will create a profit or loss for the dealer depends on future interest rates. However, in Table 19.4 we can see that the dealer has substantially reduced his risk position by trading with Party E.

Swap Dealers as Financial Intermediaries

Table 19.4 also shows that the swap dealer is making a profit as a financial intermediary. Because of his superior knowledge of the market, the dealer was able to find Party E. By transacting with Party E, instead of just transacting with Party A, the swap dealer secures a 10 basis point spread on the notional amount for three years. In addition to earning a profit on the spread, the dealer's transaction with Party E offsets a substantial portion of the risk inherent in acting as a counterparty to Party A in the initial swap transaction.

In our example of the swap dealer's transactions, we assumed that the swap dealer had an initial portfolio of assets that met his needs in terms of risk and diversification. By acting as a counterparty to Party A, the swap dealer assumed a risk in pursuit of profit. The dealer could have taken this position as a speculation on interest rates. However, the swap dealer prefers to act as a financial intermediary, making a profit by providing informational services. In our example, the swap dealer is able to capture a spread of 10 basis points and reduce risk by transacting with Party E. Ideally, the swap dealer acting as a financial intermediary would also like to avoid the remaining risk exposure in years 4 and 5. Being able to do so requires that the dealer find another swap partner. We explore the ways in which swap dealers manage the risks associated with acting as counterparties later in this chapter.

Summary

In this section, we have seen that swap facilitators or swap banks may act as either brokers or dealers. A swap broker facilitates swap transactions by bringing potential counterparties together, but the broker does not take a risk position in the swap. By contrast, a swap dealer acts as a counterparty in the swap, in addition to providing the informational assistance provided by a broker. Notice that the same firm can act as a swap broker in some transactions and as a swap dealer in others. Calling a firm a swap broker or swap dealer refers to the function that the firm fulfills in a particular transaction.

By taking a position in a swap transaction, a swap dealer accepts a risk position. The firm that accepts this risk position could approach the transaction as a speculator or as a swap dealer. Functioning as a swap dealer, the firm accepts the position with the idea of avoiding as much of the risk exposure as possible. Specifically, the firm acting as a financial intermediary will attempt to offset the initial risk and will be satisfied to make a profit by acting as a conduit between other swap parties. When the swap dealer acts as a counterparty, the dealer intends to be only a temporary substitute for an unavailable counterparty.

Pricing of Swaps

In this section, we explore the principles that underlie swap pricing. To simplify the discussion, we focus on plain vanilla interest rate swaps, and we assume that the swap dealer wishes to act as a pure financial intermediary. That is, the swap dealer does not want to assume a risk position with respect to interest rates. The principles apply, however, to swaps of all types.

Factors that Affect Swap Pricing

The swap dealer must price swaps to reflect a number of factors. These include the creditworthiness of the potential swap partner, the availability of other swap opportunities that will allow the swap dealer to offset the risk of an initial swap, and the term structure of interest rates.[4] We discuss each of these in turn.

Creditworthiness. The swap dealer must appraise the creditworthiness of the swap partner. As we have seen earlier in this chapter, there is no clearinghouse in the swap market to guarantee performance on a contract if one of the counterparties defaults. If the swap dealer suffers a default by one of its counterparties, the dealer must either absorb the loss or institute a lawsuit to seek recovery on the defaulted obligation.

In most swaps, the timings of cash flows between the counterparties are matched fairly closely. For example, in the plain vanilla interest rate swap of Figure 19.10, the fixed and floating cash flows occur at similar times, and we noted that only the net amount is actually exchanged. Thus, default on a swap seldom could involve failure to pay the notional amount or even an entire periodic payment. In this sense, default on a swap is not as critical as default on a corporate bond, in which an investor might lose the entire principal. Instead, a swap default would generally imply a loss of the change in value due to shifting interest rates. While this amount can be quite significant, such a default would not be as catastrophic as a bond default in which the entire principal could be lost.

As we saw in Figure 19.10 and as we explore in more detail later in this chapter, the swap dealer seeks to build a swap portfolio in which the risks of individual swaps offset each other. In Figure 19.10, the risks in the swap with Party A are largely offset by the risks in the swap with Party E. When a swap dealer suffers a default, the elaborate structure of offsetting risks can be upset. This leaves the swap dealer in a riskier position, and the dealer must struggle to re-establish the risk control that was upset by the default.

---

[4]The swap dealer will also consider some other issues in setting final pricing terms. If the swap is very complicated, the swap dealer may charge a higher price than otherwise. Similarly, if the swap is to involve cross-border currency flows, the dealer may be concerned with regulatory constraints that might impede the flow of funds.

Because of the potential costs associated with default, the swap dealer will adjust the pricing on swaps to reflect the risk of default. Parties that have a high risk of default are likely to be excluded from the market. For example, airlines under bankruptcy protection probably have very limited access to the swap market. As we noted earlier, the swap market is mainly a market for financial institutions and corporations due to the importance of default considerations and the need for one party to be able to confirm the creditworthiness of a prospective counterparty.

Availability of Additional Counterparties. Because we are assuming that the swap dealer wishes to act only as a financial intermediary, the swap dealer will be very concerned about how the risk involved in a prospective swap can be offset by participating in other swaps. For example, in the dealer's swap of Figure 19.10, the willingness of the swap dealer to enter the transaction with Party A may well depend on the dealer's knowledge of Party E. If the dealer considers transacting with Party A and does not know of Party E, the dealer may require more favorable terms to transact with Party A. However, if the dealer knows about Parties A and E from the outset, the dealer may accept less favorable terms because he knows he can offset some of the risk of acting as Party A's counterparty by engaging in a second swap with Party E.

As we noted, the swap dealer faces the net cash flows in the last column of Table 19.4 after engaging in the two interest rate swaps with Parties A and E. Assume now that another potential swap participant, Party F, is available to swap the cash flows in years 4 and 5. In other words, Party F would be willing to pay a floating rate on a $10 million notional amount for years 4 and 5 and to receive a fixed rate of 12 percent. The swap dealer would find Party F to be a very attractive counterparty. The dealer might be quite willing to swap with Party F on even terms ($1,200,000 versus LIBOR + 3%) just to offset the risk that remained after swapping with Parties A and E. In sum, the swap dealer will be very pleased to create a structure of swaps that leaves no interest rate risk and still provides a decent profit.

The Term Structure of Interest Rates. As we have seen in Chapter 8, the term structure of interest rates is an important feature in bond pricing. Not surprisingly, the market for interest rate swaps must reflect the term structure that prevails in the bond market. If the swap market did not reflect the term structure, traders would find ready arbitrage opportunities, and they could quickly discipline swap traders to pay attention to the term structure. For example, if the term structure is rising, the swap dealer must charge a higher yield on swaps of longer maturity. The next section illustrates these considerations from the term structure.

The Indication Swap Pricing Schedule

In the early to mid–1980s, swap banks were often able to charge a **front–end** fee for arranging a swap. As the market has matured, that ability has been competed away. (For some very complicated swaps that require substantial analysis, front–end fees are still charged, however.) Therefore, the swap dealer today generally receives his total compensation by charging a spread between the rates he is willing to pay and

Table 19.5

Sample Swap Indication Pricing

Maturity (years)	Bank's Fixed Rates: (T–Note Rate Plus Indicated Basis Points)		T–Note Yields
	Bank Pays	Bank Receives	
2	18	28	7.40
3	34	45	7.66
4	52	68	7.84
5	70	89	8.05
7	82	102	8.14
10	88	110	8.20

Source: Adapted from J. Marshall and K. Kapner, *Understanding Swap Finance*, Cincinnati: South–Western Publishing, 1990, p. 61.

the rate he demands on swap transactions. With a maturing market, this spread has also narrowed. Whereas in the mid–1980s spreads might have been 50 basis points, a 10 basis point spread is much more common today. This tightening spread reflects the increasing liquidity, sophistication, and pricing efficiency of a maturing financial market.

Table 19.5 shows a sample indication pricing schedule for an interest rate swap. The table assumes that the customer of the swap bank will offer LIBOR flat, that is, a rate exactly equal to LIBOR without any yield adjustment. There are two important features of Table 19.5. First, the rate the bank pays or receives increases with the maturity in question. This increase reflects the upward–sloping term structure revealed by the column of current T–note yields. Second, the swap bank makes a gross profit that equals the spread between what the bank pays and what it receives. Consequently, the spread ranges from 10 basis points for a two–year horizon to 22 basis points for a ten–year horizon. This increasing spread for more distant maturities reflects the lower liquidity of longer–term instruments.

As an example of how the pricing schedule in Table 19.5 functions, assume that the customer wishes to pay a floating rate and receive a fixed rate for seven years. Based on the pricing schedule of Table 19.5, the customer would pay the LIBOR rate on the notional amount in each period and would receive a fixed rate from the swap bank that equals the seven–year T–note rate of 8.14 percent plus 82 basis points for a total rate of 8.96 percent. By contrast, if the customer wishes to pay a fixed rate for a seven–year horizon, the customer would pay the seven–year

T–note rate of 8.14 percent plus 102 basis points for a rate of 9.16 percent. In return, the bank would pay the customer the LIBOR rate in each period.[5]

Swap Portfolios

In this section, we briefly consider the principal risks that a swap dealer faces in managing a swap portfolio. These risks range from default risk to interest rate risk. We then illustrate how the swap dealer can manage some of these risks.

Risks in Managing a Swap Portfolio

In managing a portfolio of many swaps, the swap dealer faces a number of different risks. First, there is the risk that one of its counterparties might default, as we discussed earlier. Second, the bank faces **basis risk**—the risk that the normal relationship between two prices might change. To illustrate this risk, assume that a bank engages in an interest rate swap agreeing to receive the T–note rate plus some basis points and to pay LIBOR. After this agreement is reached, assume that market disturbances in Europe cause LIBOR to rise relative to the T–note rate. The swap dealer must still pay LIBOR, but this rate is now higher than the swap dealer anticipated when it initiated the swap. Therefore, the swap dealer suffers a loss due to basis risk as the normal relationship between LIBOR and the T–note rate has changed.

The swap dealer also faces mis–match risk. When he acts as a counterparty in a swap, the swap dealer accepts a risk position that he is anxious to offset by engaging in other swaps. Mis–match risk refers to the risk that the swap dealer will be left in a position that he cannot offset easily through another swap. This arises if there is a mis–match in the needs between the swap dealer and other participants. In Table 19.4, for example, the two swaps with Parties A and E left the swap dealer with a residual risk position, due to the mis–match between the needs of Parties A and E.

One of the most serious risks that the swap dealer faces is interest rate risk. For example, the swap dealer may have promised to pay a floating rate and to receive a fixed rate. If the general level of interest rates rises, the swap dealer's cash outflows will rise as well. However, the dealer continues to receive the stipulated fixed rate. The swap dealer incurs a loss due to a shift in interest rates. In Table 19.4, for example, the swap dealer is left to receive $1.2 million annually and to pay LIBOR + 3% on a notional principal of $10 million in years four and five. If rates rise, the payments that the dealer must make will increase, while its cash inflows will remain the same. Such a rise in interest rates would generate a loss for the swap dealer, so the dealer faces interest rate risk.

---

[5]In actual market practice, the participants must carefully consider the actual way in which yields are calculated on Treasury securities versus the money market computations that govern LIBOR. We abstract from these technicalities.

Managing Mis–Match and Interest Rate Risk in a Swap

We illustrate how swap dealers can manage mis–match and interest rate risk by considering the swap dealer's transactions with Parties A and E, as shown in Table 19.4. We have already noted that the swap dealer accepts a risk position by acting as a counterparty in a swap. Because we assume that the swap dealer wishes to function strictly as a financial intermediary and not as a speculator, the dealer is anxious to avoid any risk that it might have temporarily undertaken to complete the swap.

In our discussion of Table 19.4, for example, we saw that the dealer participated in a swap with Party A and was able to offset part of the risk by engaging in another swap with Party E. As Table 19.4 shows, however, some residual risk remains. Specifically, the swap bank is still committed to receiving $1.2 million and paying LIBOR + 3% on a notional amount of $10 million in years four and five.

This residual risk position reflects both mis–match risk and interest rate risk. The mis–match risk occurs because the dealer was unable to offset the risks associated with the swap with Party A. The transaction with Party E offset most of the risk arising from the swap with Party A, but some risk remains due to the mismatch between the needs of Parties A and E. The transactions of Table 19.4 also reflect a continuing interest rate risk. As we noted, if rates rise, the dealer suffers a loss as it must pay the higher floating rates that result.

As a consequence, the swap dealer will be anxious to avoid these two remaining risks associated with his commitments in periods four and five in Table 19.4. Ideally, the dealer would arrange a third swap, in addition to those with Parties A and E, to offset this risk. For example, the dealer would like to swap to receive floating and pay fixed for years four and five. Such a transaction would avoid both the mis–match and the interest rate risk. However, such swaps are not always immediately available to the dealer. As a consequence, the swap dealer will seek other means to control this risk.

When the swap dealer faces a risk such as that in Table 19.4, he can use the futures market as a temporary means of offsetting the risk. For example, the swap dealer might sell Eurodollar futures with a distant expiration. Eurodollar rates are highly correlated with LIBOR. With this transaction, the swap dealer offsets a considerable portion of the risk that remains in Table 19.4. When the swap dealer executes the futures transaction properly, he will be left only with an obligation to pay a fixed amount.

However, even after this transaction, some risk remains. Eurodollar futures may be a close substitute for the unavailable swap, but they are unlikely to provided a perfect substitute. In our example, the dealer will probably not be able to match the futures expiration with the four and five year cash flows, there is likely to be some imperfection in setting the quantity of futures to trade, and there is still some basis risk between the LIBOR rate of the cash flows in years four and five and the rate on the Eurodollars.

Because of these imperfections in substituting for the unavailable swap, the swap dealer will likely continue to seek a swap that meets his risk needs exactly.

However, until that is available, the Eurodollar futures position can act as an effective risk–reducing position.

Summary

This chapter introduced the swap market. From origins in the late 1970s and early 1980s, the swap market has grown to enormous proportions, with notionals approaching $5 trillion. Most of the market is concentrated in interest rate swaps, but there are also billions of dollars of foreign currency swaps outstanding as well. Of all swaps, about 40 to 50 percent involve the U.S. dollar.

In contrast with futures and exchange–traded options, we noted that swap agreements are extremely flexible in amount, maturity, and other contract terms. As further points of difference between futures and exchange–traded options versus swaps, the swap market does not utilize an exchange and is virtually free of governmental regulation.

The chapter also analyzed plain vanilla interest rate and currency swaps. We saw that an interest rate swap essentially involves a commitment by two parties to exchange cash flows tied to some principal, or notional, amount. One party pays a fixed rate, while the second party pays a floating rate. In a foreign currency swap, both parties acquire funds in different currencies and exchange those principal amounts. Each party pays interest to the other in the currency that was acquired, with these interest payments taking place over the term of the swap agreement. To terminate the agreement, the parties again exchange foreign currency. Motivations for swaps arise from a desire to avoid financial risk or a chance to exploit some borrowing advantage.

Swap brokers and dealers are two kinds of swap facilitators. A swap broker helps counterparties complete swaps by providing introduction and guidance in the negotiation of the swap, but the swap broker does not take a risk position in the swap. By contrast, a swap dealer provides the services of the swap broker, but also will act as a counterparty in a swap. For the swap dealer, we considered the factors that influence pricing, and we discussed the techniques that swap dealers use to manage the risk associated with their portfolios of swaps.

Questions and Problems

1. Explain the differences between a plain vanilla interest rate swap and a plain vanilla currency swap.
2. What are the two major kinds of swap facilitators? What is the key difference between the roles they play?
3. Assume that you are a financial manager for a large commercial bank and that you expect short–term interest rates to rise more than the yield curve would suggest. Would you rather pay a fixed long–term rate and receive a floating short rate, or the other way around? Explain your reasoning.

4. Explain the role that the notional principal plays in understanding swap transactions. Why is this principal amount regarded as only notional? (Hint: What is the dictionary definition of "notional"?)

5. Consider a plain vanilla interest rate swap. Explain how the practice of net payments works.

6. Assume that the yield curve is flat, that the swap market is efficient, and that two equally creditworthy counterparties engage in an interest rate swap. Who should pay the higher rate, the party that pays a floating short–term rate or the party that pays a fixed long–term rate? Explain.

7. In a currency swap, counterparties exchange the same sums at the beginning and the end of the swap period. Explain how this practice relates to the custom of making interest payments during the life of the swap agreement.

8. Explain why a currency swap is also called an "exchange of borrowings."

9. Assume that LIBOR stands today at 9 percent and the seven–year T–note rate is 10 percent. Establish an indication pricing schedule for a seven–year interest rate swap, assuming that the swap dealer must make a gross spread of 40 basis points.

10. Explain how basis risk affects a swap dealer. Does it affect a swap broker the same way? Explain.

11. Assume a swap dealer attempts to function as a pure financial intermediary avoiding all interest rate risk. Explain how such a dealer may yet come to bear interest rate risk.

Suggested Readings

Abken, P. A., "Beyond Plain Vanilla: A Taxonomy of Swaps," Federal Reserve Bank of Atlanta *Economic Review*, 76:2, March/April 1991, pp. 12–29.

Apsel, D., J. Cogen, and M. Rabin, "Hedging Long–Term Commodity Swaps with Futures," *The Handbook of Derivative Instruments*, Chicago: Probus Publishing, 1991, pp. 413–433.

Bhattacharya, A. K. and J. Breit, "Customized Interest–Rate Agreements and Their Applications," *The Handbook of Fixed Income Securities*, 3e, Homewood, IL: Business Irwin One, 1991.

Brown, K. C. and D. J. Smith, "Forward Swaps, Swap Options, and the Management of Callable Debt," *Journal of Applied Corporate Finance*, 2:4, Winter 1990, pp. 59–71.

Einzig, R. and B. Lange, "Swaps at Transamerica Analysis and Applications," *Journal of Applied Corporate Finance*, 2:4, Winter 1990, pp. 48–58.

Goodman, L. S., "The Use of Interest Rate Swaps in Managing Corporate Liabilities," *Journal of Applied Corporate Finance*, 2:4, Winter 1990, pp. 35–47.

Kapner, K. R. and J. F. Marshall, *The Swaps Handbook: Swaps and Related Risk Management Instruments*, New York: New York Institute of Finance Corp., 1990.

Kopprasch, R. W., J. Macfarlane, J. Showers, and D. Ross, "The Interest–Rate Swap Market: Yield Mathematics, Terminology, and Conventions," *The Handbook of Fixed Income Securities*, 3e, Homewood, IL: Business Irwin One, 1991.

Marshall, J. F. and K. R. Kapner, *Understanding Swap Finance*, Cincinnati, OH: South–Western Publishing, 1990.

Nadler, D., "Eurodollar Futures/Interest Rate Swap Arbitrage," *The Handbook of Fixed Income Securities*, 3e, Homewood, IL: Business Irwin One, 1991.

Smith, C. W. Jr., C. W. Smithson, and L. M. Wakeman, "The Market for Interest Rate Swaps," *The Handbook of Financial Engineering*, New York: Harper Business, 1990, pp. 212–229.

Venkatesh, R. E. S., V. Venkatesh, and R. E. Dattatreya, "Introduction to Interest Rate Swaps," *The Handbook of Derivative Instruments*, Chicago: Probus Publishing, 1991, pp. 129–159.

CHAPTER TWENTY

Financial Engineering

Overview

The idea of financial engineering is fairly new, and the concepts of financial engineering extend the basic ideas of risk management in finance. The engineering metaphor highlights the specialized nature of the financial structures that can be created to manage particular risks. Any building project requires materials. The three previous chapters, covering futures, options, and swaps, described the building blocks that financial engineers use to create specialized financial structures for the management of risk.

This chapter has three main purposes. First, we explore techniques for combining options to generate profit profiles that are not available with positions in single options. These include strategies with rather colorful names: straddles, strangles, bull and bear spreads, and butterfly spreads. Second, the chapter analyzes the relationship among underlying securities, futures, forwards, swaps, and options. As we explore in some detail, each of these building blocks can be simulated by a combination of others. Therefore, we will explore how to create a **synthetic instrument**—a financial structure that has the same value as another identifiable instrument. For example, we will show how investment in options and a risk–free bond can create a synthetic stock position. Third, we show how to alter the risk and return characteristics of an existing position by using derivative instruments.

Financial engineering is application oriented. With a financial engineering approach, the investment manager can tailor a given risk position in a variety of ways. Thus, given some initial position, financial engineering can create a less risky position, a riskier position, or a position with a very specialized risk exposure. We will explore this issue in the context of the equity market. Specifically, we begin with an equity portfolio and show how its risk characteristics can be altered in a variety of ways by holding futures and options in conjunction with the stock portfolio itself.

Option Combinations

The reader of the popular financial press would almost surely receive the impression that options are very risky instruments. This is partially correct, because option positions can be extremely risky. However, options are complex instruments. By combining options in certain ways, it is possible to create a position that has almost any desired level of risk exposure. In this section, we explore techniques for combining options to create new payoff profiles.

Straddles

A **straddle** is an option position involving a put and a call option on the same stock. To buy a straddle, an investor will buy both a put and a call that have the same expiration and the same striking price. To sell a straddle, a trader sells both the call and the put. Consider a put and a call option and assume that both have an exercise price of $100. Assume further that the call sells for $10 and that the put trades at $7. Table 20.1 shows the profits and losses for the call, the put, and the straddle as a function of the stock price at expiration. If the stock price equals the exercise price at expiration, both the put and the call expire worthless, and the loss on the straddle is $17, the entire premium paid for the position.

Table 20.1

Profits and Losses for a Call, Put, and Straddle

Stock Price at Expiration	Elements of a Straddle		Straddle $P = \$17$
	Call $E = \$100; P = \$10$	Put $E = \$100; P = \$7$	
$50	-$10	$43	$33
80	-10	13	3
83	-10	10	0
85	-10	8	-2
90	-10	3	-7
95	-10	-2	-12
100	-10	-7	-17
105	-5	-7	-12
110	0	-7	-7
115	5	-7	-2
117	7	-7	0
120	10	-7	3
150	40	-7	33

Figure 20.1

Profits and Losses on a Straddle

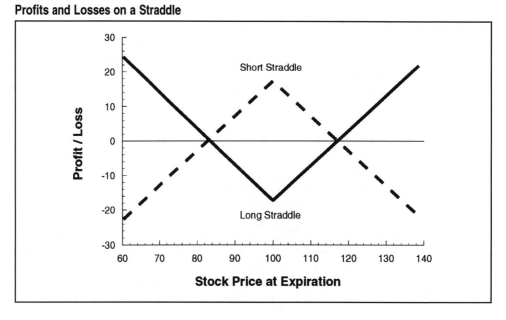

Any movement in the stock price away from $100 at expiration gives a better result. In fact, the value of the straddle increases $1 for every $1 movement in the stock price at expiration away from $100. The straddle position breaks even if the stock price either rises to $117 or falls to $83. In other words, a $17 price movement away from the exercise price at expiration will cover the initial investment of $17. If the price of the stock differs greatly from the exercise price, there is an opportunity for substantial profit. These possible results are shown graphically in Figure 20.1, which shows the profit and losses for the long and short straddle positions.

The graph shows the profits and losses for buying the straddle position with a solid line. As this graph makes clear, the purchaser of a straddle is betting that the price of the stock will move dramatically away from the exercise price of $100. The owner of the straddle will profit if the stock price goes above $117 or below $83. Figure 20.1 shows the profit–and–loss position for the seller of a straddle with the dotted lines. The seller of the straddle will profit if the stock price at expiration lies between $83 and $117. Obviously, the purchaser of this straddle would be making a bet on a large movement in the stock price in some direction, while the seller of a straddle would be betting that the stock price remains reasonably close to the exercise price of $100.

Strangles

A strangle is similar to a straddle. As we have seen, buying a straddle involves buying a call and buying a put option with the same striking price and the same term to expiration. A long position in a **strangle** consists of a long position in a call and a long position in a put on the same underlying good with the same term to expiration, with the call having a higher exercise price than the put. For example, consider the same put option of the previous example, which had an exercise price of $100 and a premium of $7. A call option on the same good with the same term to expiration has a striking price of $110 and sells for $3.

To buy a strangle with these options, a trader buys both the put and the call, for a total outlay of $10. Table 20.2 shows the profits and losses at expiration for the call and put individually and on the strangle position as well. Figure 20.2 shows the profit profile for the long and short strangle. As the table and figure show, the put and the call cannot both have value at expiration. If the stock price rises above $110, the call has a value, while a stock price below $100 allows the put to finish in the money. For the long strangle to show a profit, the call or the put must be worth more than the $10 total cost of the strangle. This means that the stock price must exceed $120 or fall below $90 for the strangle to show a net profit.

The figure shows that a wide range of stock prices will give a loss, even a total loss of the $10 investment for some prices. For example, if the stock price is

Table 20.2

Profits and Losses for a Call, Put, and Strangle

Stock Price at Expiration	Elements of a Strangle		Strangle P = $10
	Call E = $110; P = $3	Put E = $100; P = $7	
$50	-$3	$43	$40
80	-3	13	10
83	-3	10	7
85	-3	8	5
90	-3	3	0
95	-3	-2	-5
100	-3	-7	-10
105	-3	-7	-10
110	-3	-7	-10
115	2	-7	-5
117	5	-7	-2
120	7	-7	0
125	12	-7	5
150	37	-7	30

Figure 20.2

Profits and Losses on a Strangle

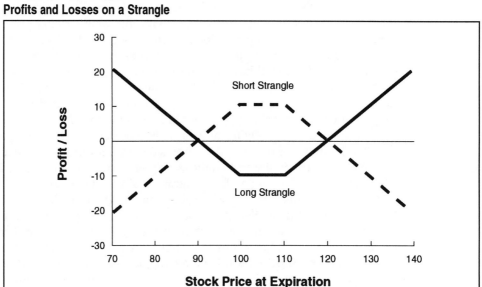

between $100 and $110 at expiration, both the put and the call will expire worthless, giving a net loss of $10.

Bull and Bear Spreads

A **bull spread** in the options market is a combination of call options designed to profit if the price of the underlying good rises.[1] Both calls in a bull spread have the same expiration, but they have different exercise prices. The buyer of a bull spread buys a call with an exercise price below the stock price and sells a call option with an exercise price above the stock price. The spread is a "bull" spread because the trader hopes to profit from a price rise in the stock. The trade is a "spread" because it involves buying one option and selling a related option. Compared to buying the stock itself, the bull spread with call options limits the trader's risk. However, it also limits the profit potential compared to the stock itself.

To illustrate this spread, assume that the stock trades at $100. One call option has an exercise price of $95 and costs $7. The other call has an exercise price of $105 and costs $3. To buy the bull spread, the trader buys the call with the $95 exercise

---

[1]The reader should note that the use of terms such as **bear spread** and **bull spread** is not standardized. While this book uses these terms in familiar ways, other traders may use them differently.

Figure 20.3

The Two Call Options for a Bull Spread

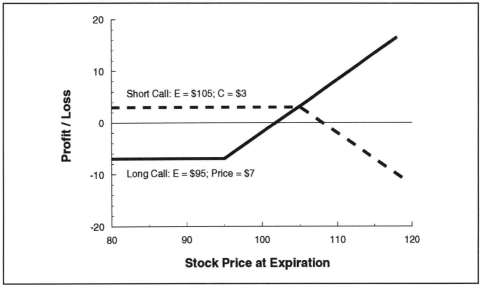

price, and sells the other. The total outlay for the bull spread is $4. Figure 20.3 graphs the profits and losses for the two call positions individually. The long position profits if the stock price moves above $102. The short position profits if the stock price does not exceed $108. As the graph shows, low stock prices result in an overall loss on the position, because the cost of the long position outweighs the amount received from the short position. It is also interesting to consider prices at $105 and above. For every dollar by which the stock price exceeds $105, the long position has an extra dollar of profit. However, at prices above $105, the short position starts to lose money. Thus, for stock prices above $105, the additional gains on the long position match the losses on the short position. Therefore, no matter how high the stock price goes, the bull spread can never give a greater profit than it does for a stock price of $105.

Figure 20.4 graphs the bull spread as the solid line. For any stock price at expiration of $95 or below, the bull spread loses $4. This $4 is the difference between the cash inflow for selling one call and buying the other. The bull spread breaks even for a stock price of $99. The highest possible profit on the bull spread comes when the stock sells for $105. Then the bull spread gives a $6 profit. For any stock price above $105, the profit on the bull spread remains at $6. Therefore, the trader of a bull spread bets that the stock price goes up, but he hedges his bet. We can see that the bull spread protects the trader from losing any more than $4. However, the trader cannot make more than a $6 profit. We can compare the bull spread with a position in the stock itself in Figure 20.4. Comparing the bull spread

Figure 20.4

Profits and Losses on Bull and Bear Spreads

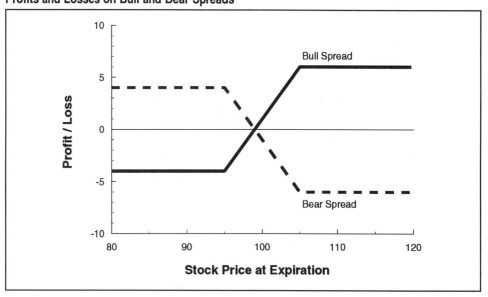

and the stock, we find that the stock offers the chance for bigger profits, but it also has greater risk of a serious loss.

Figure 20.4 also shows the profit and loss profile for a bear spread with the same options. A **bear spread** is a combination of options designed to profit from a drop in the stock price. In our example, the bear spread is just the short positions that match the bull spread. In other words, the short position in the bull spread is a bear spread. The dotted line shows how profit and losses vary if a trader sells the call with the $95 strike price and buys the call with the $105 strike price. This position exactly mirrors the bull spread we have considered. In a bear spread, the trader bets that the stock price will fall. However, the bear spread also limits the profit opportunity and the risk of loss compared to a short position in the stock itself. We can compare the profit and loss profiles of the bear spread in Figure 20.4 with the short position in the stock.

Butterfly Spreads

To buy a **butterfly spread**, a trader buys one call with a low exercise price and buys one call with a high exercise price, while selling two calls with a medium exercise price. The spread profits most when the stock price is near the medium exercise price at expiration. In essence, the butterfly spread gives a payoff pattern similar to a straddle. Compared to a straddle, however, a butterfly spread offers lower risk at the expense of reduced profit potential.

Figure 20.5

Individual Options for a Butterfly Spread

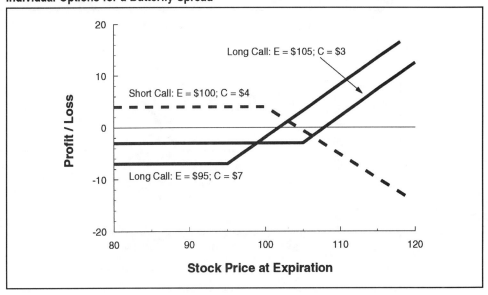

As an example of a butterfly spread, assume that a stock trades at $100 and a trader buys a spread by trading options with the following prices. As the table shows, the buyer of a butterfly spread sells two calls with a striking price near the stock price and buys one each of the calls above and below the stock price.

	Exercise Price	Option Premium
Long 1 Call	$105	$3
Short 2 Calls	$100	$4
Long 1 Call	$95	$7

Figure 20.5 graphs the profits and losses from each of these three option positions. (This is the most complicated option position we consider.) To understand the profits and losses from the butterfly spread, we need to combine these profits and losses, remembering that the spread involves selling two options and buying two.

Let us consider a few critical stock prices to see how the butterfly spread profits respond. The critical stock prices always include the exercise prices for the options. First, if the stock price is $95, the call with an exercise price of $95 is worth zero and a long position in this call loses $7. The long call with the $105 exercise price also cannot be exercised, so it is worthless, giving a loss of the $3 purchase price. The short call position gives a profit of $4 per option and the spread trader sold two of these options, for an $8 profit. Adding these values gives a net loss on the spread of $2, if the stock price is $95. Second, if the stock price is $100, the long call with a striking price of $95 loses $2 (the $5 stock profit minus the $7 purchase

Figure 20.6

Profits and Losses on a Butterfly Spread

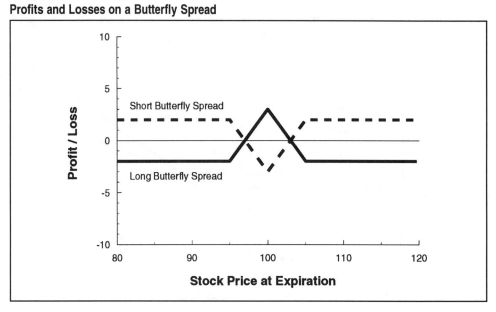

price). The long call with an exercise price of $105 loses its full purchase price of $3. Together, the long calls lose $5. The short call still shows a profit of $4 per option, for a profit of $8 on the two options. This gives a net profit of $3 if the stock price is $100. Third, if the stock price is $105 at expiration, the long call with an exercise price of $95 has a profit of $3. The long call with an exercise price of $105 loses $3. Also, the short call position loses $1 per option for a loss on two positions of $2. This gives a net loss on the butterfly spread of $2. In summary, we have: a $2 loss for a $95 stock price, a $3 profit for a $100 stock price, and a $2 loss for a $105 stock price.

Figure 20.6 shows the entire profit and loss graph for the butterfly spread. At a stock price of $100, we noted a profit of $3. This is the highest profit available from the spread. At stock prices of $95 and $105, the spread loses $2. For stock prices below $95 or above $105, the loss is still $2. As the graph shows, the butterfly spread has a zero profit for stock prices of $97 and $103. The buyer of the butterfly spread essentially bets that stock prices will hover near $100. Any large move away from $100 gives a loss on the butterfly spread. However, the loss can never exceed $2. Comparing the butterfly spread with the straddle in Figure 20.1, we see that the butterfly spread resembles a short position in the straddle. Compared to the straddle, the butterfly spread reduces the risk of a very large loss. However, the reduction in risk necessarily comes at the expense of a chance for a big profit.

Summary

In this section, we saw how to combine options to create new payoff profiles. Although options are typically regarded as very risky instruments, we saw that it is possible to create option positions that have substantially lower risk than an outright position in an option.

If we compare the payoff profiles for a straddle and a strangle, we see that a straddle is a riskier position than a strangle, other factors being equal. The straddle offers a speculation with a more varied outcome. It has a chance of losing all of the investment, but it also holds a promise of substantial reward if prices move radically away from the striking price.

Compared to a straddle, a strangle has a bigger chance of incurring some loss. However, the maximum possible loss will usually be lower with a strangle than with a straddle. Of course, the likely payoffs are also smaller for a strangle. For a butterfly spread, there is a higher probability of some loss, but it will likely be a small one, if it occurs. The maximum loss on a butterfly spread is relatively low because the position involves purchasing and selling some calls. The receipts from selling calls helps to finance the purchase of the other calls.

Synthetic Instruments

In this section, we show how to create synthetic financial instruments. For example, it is possible to create a portfolio of options that will have the same profits and losses as the underlying asset at the expiration date of the options. To understand how to create synthetic instruments, we begin by reviewing the put–call parity relationship first introduced in Chapter 18. We then proceed to illustrate specific synthetic instruments.

Put–Call Parity and Synthetic Instruments

In Chapter 18, we used the principal of put–call parity to find the price of a put option, given knowledge of the price of a call option on the same underlying good. To apply put–call parity, we need a call option with the same striking price and the same term to expiration as the put we are attempting to price. Subject to those conditions, we saw that the put–call parity maintains that:

$$P = C - S + \frac{E}{(1 + R_f)^T}$$

20.1

where:

S = stock price
P = put price
C = call price

E = common exercise price for the call and put
R_f = risk–free rate
T = common term to expiration for the call and put

This put–call relationship provides the basic blueprint for creating synthetic securities. By rearranging Equation 20.1 to isolate individual instruments on the left–hand side of the equation, we see what combination of other instruments will simulate a particular instrument of interest. We now show how to create synthetic equity, synthetic puts, synthetic call options, and a synthetic T–bill.

Synthetic Equity

Rearranging Equation 20.1 to isolate the stock (S), we have:

$$S = C - P + \frac{E}{(1 + R_f)^T} \qquad \textbf{20.2}$$

Equation 20.2 shows that a position in the stock is equivalent to a long call plus a short put, coupled with an investment at the risk–free rate. The investment at the risk–free rate is an amount that will pay the common exercise price on the call and the put at the time of expiration. Thus, **synthetic equity** consists of a long call, short put, and an investment of the present value of the exercise price at the risk–free rate.

To illustrate this equivalence, consider the following example. Assume a call and a put have an exercise price of $80 and expire in one year. The risk–free rate of interest is 7 percent per annum. With this interest rate, an investment of $74.77 will pay the exercise price of $80 in one year. Table 20.3 presents several alternative stock prices that might arise in one year, and it shows the value of the call, put, bond, and the synthetic equity as well.

As Table 20.3 shows, the synthetic equity will have the same value as the stock in one year, no matter what the stock price might be. To see this equivalence, consider a stock price in one year of $95. With this stock price, the put will be worthless and the call will be worth $15. The risk–free bond will pay $80, so the synthetic equity position will be worth $95 as well ($15 from the call and $80 from the risk–free bond). Given the purchase of the synthetic equity, it is also possible to convert the synthetic position into the underlying equity, if the trader wishes. For example, the trader could exercise the call option and use the bond proceeds to pay the exercise price.

To complete the example, consider a terminal stock price below $80. If the stock is worth $65 at expiration, for example, then the call expires worthless, and the risk–free bond is worth $80. However, the synthetic equity involves a short position in a put option which can be exercised against the writer. The short put is a liability of $15 for the synthetic equity holder. Considering the long call, the short

Table 20.3

Synthetic Equity

Stock Price at Expiration	Elements of Synthetic Equity			Synthetic Equity
	Call $E = \$80$	Short Put $E = \$80$	Risk–Free Investment	
$60	$ 0	-$20	$80	60
65	0	-15	$80	65
70	0	-10	$80	70
75	0	-5	$80	75
80	0	0	$80	80
85	5	0	$80	85
90	10	0	$80	90
95	15	0	$80	95
100	20	0	$80	100

put, and the bond together, the synthetic equity position is worth $65, the same as the stock itself.

Synthetic Put Options

The put–call parity relationship of Equation 20.1 shows that a **synthetic put** consists of a long call and short stock position, coupled with investing the present value of

Table 20.4

A Synthetic Put

Stock Price at Expiration	Put $E = \$80$	Elements of a Synthetic Put			Synthetic Put
		Call $E = \$80$	Short Stock	Risk–Free Investment	
$60	$20	$ 0	-$60	$80	$20
65	15	0	-65	$80	15
70	10	0	-70	$80	10
75	5	0	-75	$80	5
80	0	0	-80	$80	0
85	0	5	-85	$80	0
90	0	10	-90	$80	0
95	0	15	-95	$80	0
100	0	20	-100	$80	0

the exercise price in a risk–free instrument. Table 20.4 shows the values of an actual put and the synthetic put for alternative stock prices at expiration. The value of the synthetic put equals the sum of a long call, plus a short stock position, plus an investment in the risk–free bond.

Synthetic Call Options

As the put–call parity relationship indicates, a **synthetic call** consists of a long position in both the stock and the put option, and a short position in a risk–free bond that will pay the exercise price at the expiration of the option. To create the synthetic call, a trader borrows the present value of the exercise price and uses these funds to help finance the purchase of the put and the stock. Table 20.5 shows the values at expirations for the constituent elements and for a synthetic call. The table also shows that the synthetic call and the actual call have the same values at expiration for every terminal stock price.

Synthetic T–Bills

A synthetic T–bill can also be created by the proper combination of a long put, short call, and a long position in the stock. The resulting position is a synthetic T–bill, because the synthetic instrument will pay the exercise price at the expiration date of the options no matter what the stock price might be. In a sense, it is ironic that "risky" instruments such as a call, put, and stock can be combined to simulate a T–bill. Table 20.6 shows the value of the constituent elements and the resulting synthetic T–bill.

Table 20.5

A Synthetic Call

Stock Price at Expiration	Call E = $80	Elements of a Synthetic Call			Synthetic Call
		Put E = $80	Stock	Short Risk–Free Investment	
$60	$ 0	$20	$60	-$80	$0
65	0	15	65	-$80	0
70	0	10	70	-$80	0
75	0	5	75	-$80	0
80	0	0	80	-$80	0
85	5	0	85	-$80	5
90	10	0	90	-$80	10
95	15	0	95	-$80	15
100	20	0	100	-$80	20

Table 20.6

A Synthetic T–Bill

Stock Price at Expiration	Risk–Free Investment	Elements of a Synthetic T–Bill			Synthetic T–Bill
		Short Call $E = \$80$	Put $E = \$80$	Stock	
$60	$80	$ 0	$20	$60	$80
65	$80	0	15	65	$80
70	$80	0	10	70	$80
75	$80	0	5	75	$80
80	$80	0	0	80	$80
85	$80	-5	0	85	$80
90	$80	-10	0	90	$80
95	$80	-15	0	95	$80
100	$80	-20	0	100	$80

Synthetic Futures and Forwards and Put–Call Parity

In our discussion of forwards and futures in Chapter 17, we saw that the futures price sometimes conforms to the cost–of–carry relationship. This relationship holds almost exactly in some markets, notably the financial futures markets. However, the cost–of–carry relationship provides a less complete understanding of markets for traditional commodities, such as foodstuffs. We now consider the special case in which the cost–of–carry relationship holds exactly, and we assume that the cost–of–carry equals the risk–free rate. Most financial futures closely approximate these assumptions.

Under these assumptions, the futures price will equal the spot price times one plus the cost of carry:

$$F = S(1 + R_f) \qquad\qquad 20.3$$

where:

F = futures price
S = spot price
R_f = the risk–free rate, assumed to be the cost–of–carry for the good

We now want to integrate the cost–of–carry model with the put–call parity relationship and with the analysis of synthetic securities. Rearranging the terms of the put–call parity relationship gives:

$$C - P = S - \frac{E}{(1 + R_f)^T} \tag{20.4}$$

Combining Equations 20.3 and 20.4 gives:

$$C - P = \frac{F - E}{(1 + R_f)^T} \tag{20.5}$$

Equation 20.5 says that the difference between the call and put price equals the present value of the difference between the futures price and the exercise price of the options. For example, if the exercise price is $100, the futures price is $120, the risk–free rate is 10 percent, and the options expire in one year, we have:

$$
\begin{aligned}
C - P &= \frac{F - E}{(1 + R_f)^T} \\
&= \frac{\$120 - \$100}{1.10} \\
&= \$18.18
\end{aligned}
$$

In this example, the call price must exceed the put price by $18.18. While this equation gives only the relative value of the call and put, we know that the call option must be worth at least $20, because the call is $20 in–the–money. For its part, the put will have relatively little value because it is so far out–of–the–money.

For the special case in which the current futures price equals the exercise price, then the quantity $F - E$ equals zero. This implies that $C - P$ also equals zero, which means that the call and put must have the same price. If the futures price is less than the exercise price, the quantity $F - E$ is negative. This implies that the put will be more valuable than the call. For the same instruments of the example in the last paragraph, if the futures price is $90, the quantity $F - E = -\$10$, and the value of $C - P$ must be –$9.09.

The Swap as a Portfolio of Forwards

In this section, we indicate how interest rate swaps are related to forward and futures contracts. We present the analysis in terms of forwards to avoid the complications with margin cash flows on futures. However, if we ignore the daily settlement cash flows characteristic of futures, the analysis holds equally well for both futures and forwards.

In an interest rate swap, two parties agree to make interest payments on the same underlying principal or notional amount over a specified period. One party agrees to pay a fixed interest rate, while the second party promises to pay a floating rate. Upon contracting, the fixed payor knows exactly the cash flows that it is obligated to make, but the floating payor's cash flows depend on the course of interest rates during the life of the agreement. For example, an interest rate swap might have a notional amount of $1 million and the fixed rate payor might promise to pay 10 percent annually for ten years. Thus, the fixed payor promises to make ten annual payments of $100,000. For its part, the floating rate payor might promise to pay LIBOR plus 2 percent. If LIBOR is 8 percent at the time a particular payment is made, the floating rate payor will also pay 10 percent of $1 million or $100,000. If LIBOR is less than 8 percent, the floating rate payor will pay less than it receives; if LIBOR exceeds 8 percent, the floating rate payor will pay more than it receives. (Generally, only the difference is paid on any particular payment date.)

Let us consider just one of the ten payments in this example of an interest rate swap. The fixed rate payor has promised to pay $100,000 in return for a payment that depends on LIBOR. We may analyze this payment as a forward contract to pay $100,000 at a future date in return for a value that is to be determined by the value of LIBOR on that future date. In essence, this forward contract has the same structure as any interest rate forward or futures contract.

We can see this equivalence by considering a T–bill futures contract. The purchaser of a futures contract promises to pay a certain amount on a future date in return for a 90–day T–bill to be delivered at that time. At the time of contracting, the buyer of the futures knows what payment it will be required to make, but it does not know the value of the T–bill it will receive. The value of the bill depends upon future interest rates. Similarly, in the swap agreement, the fixed rate payor knows what payment it will make on a future date, but it does not know what payment it will receive.

An interest rate swap generally includes a series of payments. In our example, the swap had ten annual payments. We saw that each of these payments can be analyzed as an interest rate forward contract. Because the swap agreement includes a sequence of ten such arrangements, the swap is a portfolio of forward contracts.

Portfolio Insurance

Chapter 18 has already explored the basic features of speculating and hedging with options. As we discussed in this chapter, prices of futures options behave similarly to options on physicals. Therefore, essentially similar speculative and hedging strategies are available for users of both options on physicals and options on futures. This section considers some uses of options on futures that were not directly considered in Chapters 17 and 18. We approach the subject through an extended example or case study.

Background for the Case Analysis

In this section, we consider how to use options on the physical or options on futures to tailor the risk of an investment. For convenience, we focus on payoffs at option expirations, so we can ignore the difference between American and European options. Because the analysis focuses on European options, the conclusions we reach apply to both futures options and options on the physical.

We present the case analysis for a stock index, although the conclusions we reach apply to many different instruments. Consider a stock index that is currently at $100. Stocks in the index pay no dividends, and the expected return on the index is 10 percent, with a standard deviation of 20 percent. A put option on the index with an exercise price of $100 is available and costs $4. We consider three investment strategies:

Portfolio A:	Buy the index; total investment $100.
Portfolio B:	Buy the index and one–half of a put; total investment $102.
Portfolio C:	Buy the index and one put; total investment $104.

At expiration in one year, the profits and losses associated with these three portfolios depend entirely on the value of the index, because the value of the put at expiration also depends strictly on the index value. For the put, the value at expiration equals the maximum of either zero, or the exercise price minus the index value.

At expiration, the three portfolios will have profits and losses computed according to the following equations:

Portfolio A:	Index Value – $100
Portfolio B:	Index Value + .5 MAX{0, Index Value – $100} – $102
Portfolio C:	Index Value + MAX{0, Index Value – $100} – $104

The value of Portfolio A at expiration is just the index value, and the profit or loss is the value of the portfolio at expiration less the investment of $100. The terminal value of Portfolio C is the index value plus the value of the put. The profit or loss is the terminal value less the investment of $104. Portfolio B consists of the index plus one–half of a put. This gives a total investment of $102, and the terminal value of Portfolio B consists of the index value plus the value of the half put. Figure 20.7 graphs the profits and losses of these three portfolios for different terminal index values.

Portfolio Insurance

Of particular interest in Figure 20.7 is the profit and loss graph for Portfolio C, consisting of the index plus a put on the index. The worst possible loss on Portfolio C is $4. This loss occurs if the terminal index value is $100 or below. With a terminal index value of $100, the portfolio is worth $100, because the put expires

Figure 20.7

Profits and Losses on Three Portfolios

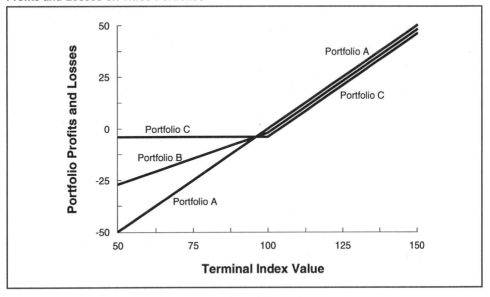

worthless. This is the worst possible loss, however. For instance, if the terminal index value is $95, the put is worth $5 and the index investment is worth $95, for a total of $100. Portfolio C must always be worth at least $100.

Portfolio C is an insured portfolio. In **portfolio insurance**, a trader transacts to ensure that the value of a portfolio cannot fall below a given amount. In the case of Portfolio C, the value cannot fall below $100. Further, this example is the classic case of portfolio insurance: buying a good at a given price and buying a put on the same good with an exercise price equal to the purchase price of the good. To create Portfolio C, a trader bought the index at $100 and bought an index put with an exercise price of $100.

Synthetic Portfolio Insurance and Put–Call Parity

Figure 20.7 shows that the insured portfolio's profit and loss profile is exactly the profile for a call option on the stock index. This should not be surprising. Earlier we saw that a long position in the underlying good plus a long put would have the same profits and losses as a call. Applying the put–call parity equation to our index example, we have:

$$C = \text{INDEX} + P - \frac{E}{(1 + R_f)^T} \qquad \textbf{20.6}$$

The put–call parity equation shows that an instrument with the same value and profits and losses as a call can be created by holding a long put, long index, and borrowing the present value of the exercise price. The portfolio on the right–hand side of Equation 20.6 will have the same value and same profits and losses as the call. By contrast, the long index plus long put merely has the same profits and losses as the call. At expiration, the value of the put plus the index will exceed the value of the call.

Therefore, we now see that an insured portfolio is the long put/long index position that has the same profits and losses as a call. From put–call parity, there is another way to create a portfolio that exactly mimics the insured portfolio's value at expiration. We can hold a long call plus invest the present value of the exercise price in the risk–free asset. From the put–call parity relationship, we see:

$$ C + \frac{E}{(1 + R_f)^T} = P + \text{INDEX} \qquad\qquad 20.7 $$

The long call plus investment in the risk–free asset creates the same insured portfolio as the long index plus long put. Both positions have the same value and the same profits and losses at expiration.

This also shows why the put plus index portfolio that has the same profits and losses as a call does not have the same value as the call. The put plus index portfolio requires considerable investment to purchase the underlying index.

Tailoring Risk and Return Characteristics with Futures and Options

To this point we have not explicitly considered Portfolio B as defined above. Portfolio B consists of buying the index and buying one–half a put. In essence, Portfolio B is half–insured. Expressed differently, Portfolio B consists of two equal portions: $50 in an insured portfolio, plus $50 in an outright position in the index. As Figure 20.7 shows, Portfolio B has profits and losses that fall between the totally insured and completely uninsured portfolios.

The partially insured Portfolio B has less risk than the uninsured Portfolio A, but it has more risk than the fully insured Portfolio C. Figure 20.7 shows this intermediate risk position by showing that the losses for the half–insured Portfolio B are less than the losses for the uninsured Portfolio A, but more than the losses for the fully insured Portfolio C. This example suggests that traders can use futures and options to tailor the risk characteristics of the portfolio to individual taste. With the variety of futures and option instruments available, the financial engineer can create almost any feasible combination of risk and return.

One of the dominant lessons of modern finance concerns the risk/expected return trade–off. In well–functioning markets, finding the chance for higher returns always means accepting higher risk. In comparing the fully and partially insured portfolios with the uninsured portfolio, we have seen that portfolio insurance reduces risk. However, there must be a reduction in expected return that accompanies the reduction in risk.

Risk and Return in Insured Portfolios

We now explore the risk and expected return characteristics for Portfolios A–C. The portfolios have different probabilities of achieving given terminal values that depend on the price of the index at expiration. Likewise, the probability of achieving a given return on the portfolios depends on the index value at expiration. We explore these issues by assuming that returns on the index follow a normal distribution with a mean of 10 percent and a standard deviation of 20 percent.

Terminal Values for Portfolios A–C. The portfolio values at expiration depend on the price of the index at expiration. For each, the terminal value is:

Portfolio A = Index
Portfolio B = Index + MAX{0, .5(100.00 − Index)}
Portfolio C = Index + MAX{0, 100.00 − Index}

We can now answer questions such as: What is the probability that Portfolio C will have a terminal value equal to or less than $100? Portfolio C will have a terminal value of at least $100 no matter what the value of the underlying index. In fact, there is a 30.85 percent probability that Portfolio C will have a terminal value of exactly $100. Portfolio C is worth $100 at expiration if the index is $100 or less at expiration, and there is a 30.85 percent chance that the index value will be $100 or less. What is the probability that Portfolio A will have a terminal value less than $90? The probability that the terminal value of Portfolio A will lie below $90 is the probability that the terminal index value will fall more than 1.0 standard deviation below its expected value. Because we assume the returns on the index are normally distributed, there is a 15.87 percent chance that Portfolio A's value will be less than $90 at expiration. Table 20.7 shows some portfolio values and the probabilities that each portfolio will be equal to or less than the given terminal value at the expiration date.

In Table 20.7, the uninsured Portfolio A has the largest chance of an extremely low terminal value. For example, the chance that Portfolio A will be worth $80 or less is 6.68 percent. For Portfolio B, the chance of such an unhappy outcome is less than 1 percent, and there is no chance that Portfolio C could be worth $80 or less. (We already know that Portfolio C has to be worth at least $100.) It is interesting to note in Table 20.7 that the chance of each portfolio being worth $100 or less is the same—30.85 percent. Likewise, there is a 50 percent chance for each portfolio that the portfolio's value will be $110 or less. In fact, for terminal portfolio values at or above $100, the three portfolios have exactly the same probabilities. This makes sense, because if the terminal index value is $100 or more, the put option has zero value, and the remaining portion of each portfolio is the same.

Figure 20.8 graphs terminal portfolio values from $50 to $170 and shows the probability for each portfolio that the terminal portfolio value will be below or

Table 20.7

Probability that the Terminal Portfolio Value Will Be Equal to or Less than a Specified Value

Terminal Portfolio Value	Probabilities		
	Uninsured Portfolio A	Half–Insured Portfolio B	Fully Insured Portfolio C
50.00	0.0014	0.0000	0.0000
60.00	0.0062	0.0000	0.0000
70.00	0.0228	0.0002	0.0000
80.00	0.0668	0.0062	0.0000
90.00	0.1587	0.0668	0.0000
100.00	0.3085	0.3085	0.3085
110.00	0.5000	0.5000	0.5000
120.00	0.6915	0.6915	0.6915
130.00	0.8413	0.8413	0.8413
140.00	0.9332	0.9332	0.9332
150.00	0.9773	0.9773	0.9773
160.00	0.9938	0.9938	0.9938
170.00	0.9987	0.9987	0.9987

Figure 20.8

**Probabilities that Terminal Values of Portfolios A–C
Will Be Equal to or Less than a Given Amount**

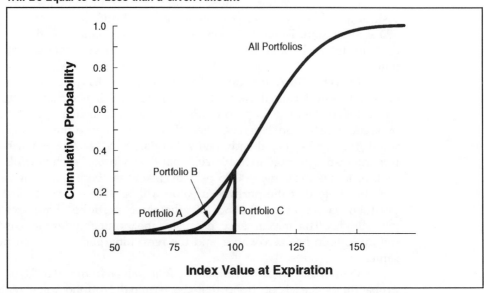

equal to the given amount. The three probability graphs differ for terminal portfolio values below $100. However, for all terminal portfolio values at or above $100, the graphs are identical. This matches the values we already saw in Table 20.7.

Concentrating only on terminal values, and neglecting the different investments required to obtain each portfolio, Figure 20.8 shows that the fully insured portfolio is the most desirable, followed by the half–insured portfolio, and then the uninsured portfolio. If we could choose one of these three portfolios as a gift, the fully insured portfolio is the clear choice. No matter what the terminal index value is, the fully insured Portfolio C will pay at least as much as either Portfolio A or B. If the terminal index value is less than $100, the insured portfolio still pays $100, which is more than either Portfolio A or B. However, this conclusion neglects the different investment costs. Portfolio A costs only $100, while Portfolio B costs $102, and Portfolio C costs $104. We now consider the returns on each portfolio.

Returns on Portfolios A–C. Because Portfolios A–C have different costs, we need to compare the returns on each portfolio to make them more directly comparable. As we saw, Portfolio C is preferable to Portfolios A or B if we neglect cost. Once we consider cost, the answer is much less clear. Instead of having a clear choice, the investor faces the risk/expected return trade–off in portfolio insurance.

For each portfolio, we can evaluate the chance of a given return. For example, the lowest possible terminal value for the fully insured portfolio is $100, which implies a return of $(100/104) - 1 = -0.0385$. The chance of a return on Portfolio C below –0.0385 is zero. However, the chance of Portfolio C having a return of exactly –0.0385 is 30.85 percent, the chance that Portfolio C is worth $100 at expiration.

Table 20.8 shows the probability that each portfolio will achieve a return greater than a specified return. For example, there is an 84.13 percent probability that the uninsured Portfolio A will do better than –10 percent. The half–insured Portfolio B has a 90.66 percent chance of returning at least –10 percent. For fully insured Portfolio C, there is no chance the return could be as bad as –10 percent.

So far, everything still looks good for the insured portfolios. The greater the level of insurance, it seems, the better the portfolio performs. However, we must now consider other possible returns. For example, what is the probability of no gain or a loss? For the uninsured Portfolio A, there is a 30.85 percent chance of a loss. The fully insured Portfolio C, however, stands 38.21 percent chance of a zero gain or a loss. Similarly, let us consider the chances of gaining more than 10 percent. The uninsured Portfolio A has a 50 percent chance, because there is a 50 percent chance the terminal index value will exceed the expected value of $110. The insured Portfolio C has only a 41.29 percent chance of beating a 10 percent return.

Now we can see the risk/expected return trade–off implied by portfolio insurance strategies. Portfolio insurance protects against large losses by sacrificing the chance for large gains. Thus, portfolio insurance is aptly named. With any insurance contract, the insured pays the insurance premium to insure against some unpleasant event. By paying the insurance, the insured knows that the expected return on the portfolio will be less than it would be without insurance, but the insured hopes to avoid the extreme loss.

Table 20.8

Probability of Achieving a Return Equal to or Greater than a Specified Return

	Probabilities		
Portfolio Return	Uninsured Portfolio A	Half–Insured Portfolio B	Fully Insured Portfolio C
-0.5000	0.9987	1.0000	1.0000
-0.4000	0.9938	1.0000	1.0000
-0.3000	0.9773	0.9996	1.0000
-0.2000	0.9332	0.9904	1.0000
-0.1000	0.8413	0.9066	1.0000
0.0000	0.6915	0.6554	0.6179
0.1000	0.5000	0.4562	0.4129
0.2000	0.3085	0.2676	0.2297
0.3000	0.1587	0.1292	0.1038
0.4000	0.0668	0.0505	0.0375
0.5000	0.0228	0.0158	0.0107

Figure 20.9

Cumulative Probability of Returns for Portfolios A–C Exceeding a Given Value

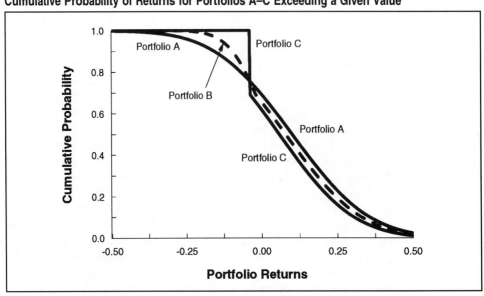

Figure 20.9 graphs the probabilities for each portfolio for the range of returns from –50 percent to 50 percent. Each point in the graph shows the probability that a portfolio will have returns greater than the return specified on the x–axis. For example, consider the returns in the range of –15 percent. There is a 100 percent chance that the fully insured Portfolio C will beat a –15 percent return. Also, Portfolio C has a 100 percent chance of beating any return up to –3.846 percent. The chance of doing better than –3.846 percent, however, is only 61.15 percent. Similarly, the half–insured Portfolio B has a very good chance of beating –15 percent. Portfolio A has the lowest chance of beating –15 percent.

As we noted from Table 20.8, however, the fortunes of the portfolios turn when we consider the probability of particularly favorable outcomes. For instance, the probability of exceeding a 20 percent return is 30.85 percent for Portfolio A, but only 26.76 percent for Portfolio B and only 22.97 percent for Portfolio C. Thus, the uninsured Portfolio A has the biggest chance of big gains and big losses. By comparison, the fully insured Portfolio C gives up the chance for big gains to avoid the chance of large losses. The half–insured Portfolio B occupies the middle ground.

Summary.   In this section we have seen that holding a stock index in conjunction with a put option creates an insured portfolio. By increasing the degree of insurance, the trader can avoid more and more risk. However, this risk avoidance has a price—the sacrifice of the chance for high returns. Thus, the concepts of portfolio insurance constitute one more example of the perennial trade–off between risk and expected return.

Summary

In this chapter, we have seen how the financial engineer can use single instruments as building blocks to create new financial structures with new risk and return characteristics. First, we saw how options can be combined to create positions with risk and return profiles that differ markedly from the position attainable with a single option. For example, we saw that a butterfly spread can be created that has very limited potential for large gains or losses.

We also used the put–call parity relationship to explore the creation of synthetic securities. If we considered an underlying instrument, a call, a put, and investment in a risk–free instrument, we saw that any of the four could be created synthetically by a combination of the other three instruments. We also analyzed an interest rate swap as a portfolio of interest rate forward contracts.

As the last topic, we considered portfolio insurance. There we saw that the financial engineer could take an existing stock portfolio and purchase accompanying put options to make the stock plus put portfolio behave like a call option. We went on to show how slightly different commitments to the put option could dramatically affect the risk and return profile of the resulting stock plus put portfolio.

Questions and Problems

1. Is a call option a synthetic instrument? Explain what makes a financial instrument synthetic.

2. Explain the difference between a straddle and a strangle.

3. A stock trades at $100 per share. A call option on the stock has an exercise price of $100, costs $16, and expires in six months. A put on the stock also has an exercise price of $100, costs $10, and expires in six months. The annual risk–free rate of interest is 10 percent. State exactly what instruments to buy and sell to create a synthetic equity position in the stock.

4. For the preceding question, make a table showing the profits and losses at expiration from the option portion of the synthetic equity as a function of the stock price in six months.

5. A stock trades for $40 and a call on the stock with an expiration date in three months and a $40 strike price sells for $5. The risk–free rate of interest is 12 percent. State exactly how you would trade to create a synthetic put with a strike price of $40. Make a table showing the terminal values of your synthetic put and the actual put at expiration as a function of the stock price.

6. A stock sells for $75 and a call with an exercise price of $75 sells for $7 and expires in six months. The risk–free rate of interest is 10 percent. What is the price of a put with a striking price of $75 and the same term to expiration?

7. How much would you pay for a portfolio consisting of a short stock, short put, and a long call? Assume that the options have a striking price equal to the current price of the stock and that both options expire in one year.

8. For the same underlying stock, a call and put both expire in one year, and their exercise price equals the current market price of the stock. Assume that you sell the stock short and can use 100 percent of the proceeds. You buy the call option and sell the put. You invest all remaining funds in the risk–free asset for one year. How much will this entire portfolio (stock, put, call, and bond) be worth in one year? Explain.

Use this information for the remaining questions. Assume a stock portfolio manager believes that her portfolio has an expected return of 12 percent and a standard deviation of 20 percent. Also, assume that the portfolio mimics an index on which call and put options trade. Assume that the index value is now 100 and the portfolio is worth $100. The risk–free rate of interest is 8 percent. Calls and puts on the index trade with a $100 strike price and are one year away from expiration. The call costs $11.40. The focus is on the value of the portfolio in one year.

9. How much should the put cost? Explain.

10. The manager asks you to devise a strategy to keep the value of the portfolio no less than $96. How would you transact? Explain.

11. The manager asks you to devise a strategy that will provide a terminal portfolio value of $112. How would you transact? Explain.

12. The manager asks you to devise a strategy that will dramatically increase the expected return on the portfolio. Give a qualitative description of how you would transact to achieve this goal.

13. The manager is determined not to trade any stocks to avoid transaction costs. Nonetheless, she desires a risk–free portfolio. How would you transact to meet her wishes? Explain.

CFA Questions

All CFA examination questions are reprinted, with permission, from the Level I *1992–1994, CFA Candidate Study and Examination Program Review.* Copyright 1992–1994, Association for Investment Management and Research, Charlottesville, Va. All rights reserved.

  A. Assume you purchase 100 shares of Company X common stock on the New York Stock Exchange for $50 per share. Which of the following transactions would you combine with that transaction in order to engage in risk–free arbitrage?

    a. Purchase one call option on Company X common stock having an exercise price exceeding $50.

    b. Purchase one put option on Company X common stock having an exercise price below $50.

    c. Sell 100 shares of Company X common stock in the over–the–counter market at $51 per share.

    d. Sell 100 shares of Company X common stock on the New Year Stock Exchange at $49 per share.

  B. Robert Chen, CFA, is reviewing the characteristics of derivative securities and their use in portfolios.

    a. Chen is considering the addition of either a short position in stock index options to an existing well–diversified portfolio of equity securities. **Contrast** the way in which *each* of these *two* alternatives would affect the risk and return of the resulting combined portfolios.

    b. Four factors affect the value of a futures contract on a stock index. Three of these factors are: the current price of the stock index, the time remaining until the contract maturity (delivery) date, and the dividends on the stock index. **Identify** the *fourth* factor and **explain** *how and why* changes in this factor affect the value of the futures contract.

    c. Six factors affect the value of call options on stocks. Three of these factors are: the current price of the stock, the time remaining until the option expires, and the dividend on the stock. **Identify** the other *three* factors and **explain** *how and why* changes in *each* of these three factors affect the value of call options.

Suggested Readings

Bullen, H. G., R. C. Wilkins, and C. C. Woods III, "The Fundamental Financial Instrument Approach: Identifying the Building Blocks," *The Handbook of Financial Engineering*, New York: Harper Business, 1990, pp. 579–586.

Chen, A. H. and J. W. Kensinger, "Putable Stock: A New Innovation in Equity Financing," *The Handbook of Financial Engineering*, New York: Harper Business, 1990, pp. 514–532.

Eckl, S., J. N. Robinson, and D. C. Thomas, *Financial Engineering: A Handbook of Derivative Products*, Cambridge, MA: Basil Blackwell, Inc., 1990.

Finnerty, J. D., "The Case for Issuing Synthetic Convertible Bonds," *The Handbook of Financial Engineering*, New York: Harper Business, 1990, pp. 461–477.

Finnerty, J. D., "Financial Engineering in Corporate Finance: An Overview," *The Handbook of Financial Engineering*, New York: Harper Business, 1990, pp. 69–108.

Markese, J., "Asset Allocation Strategies: Portfolio Balancing Acts," *American Association of Individual Investors*, 12:6, July 1990, pp. 31–34.

O'Brien, T. J., "How Option Replicating Portfolio Insurance Works: Expanded Details," *Monograph Series in Finance and Economics*, Vol. 4, 1988.

Rubinstein, M., "Derivative Assets Analysis," *Journal of Economic Perspectives*, 1:2, Fall 1987, pp. 73–93.

Smith, C. W., Jr. and C. W. Smithson, "Financial Engineering: An Overview," *The Handbook of Financial Engineering*, New York: Harper Business, 1990, pp. 3–29.

Smith, C. W., Jr., C. W. Smithson, and D. S. Wilford, *Managing Financial Risk*, New York: Harper & Row, Ballinger Division, 1990.

Smith, D. J., "The Arithmetic of Financial Engineering," *Journal of Applied Corporate Finance*, 1:4, Winter 1989, pp. 49–58.

Smith, D. J., "The Pricing of Bull and Bear Floating Rate Notes: An Application of Financial Engineering," *The Handbook of Financial Engineering*, New York: Harper Business, 1990, pp. 444–460.

Appendix

Cumulative Distribution Function
for the Standard Normal Random Variable

	.00	.01	.02	.03	.04	.05	.06	.07	.08	.09
0.0	.5000	.5040	.5080	.5120	.5160	.5199	.5239	.5279	.5319	.5359
0.1	.5398	.5438	.5478	.5517	.5557	.5596	.5636	.5675	.5714	.5753
0.2	.5793	.5832	.5871	.5910	.5948	.5987	.6026	.6064	.6103	.6141
0.3	.6179	.6217	.6255	.6293	.6331	.6368	.6406	.6443	.6480	.6517
0.4	.6554	.6591	.6628	.6664	.6700	.6736	.6772	.6808	.6844	.6879
0.5	.6915	.6950	.6985	.7019	.7054	.7088	.7123	.7157	.7190	.7224
0.6	.7257	.7291	.7324	.7357	.7389	.7422	.7454	.7486	.7517	.7549
0.7	.7580	.7611	.7642	.7673	.7704	.7734	.7764	.7794	.7823	.7852
0.8	.7881	.7910	.7939	.7967	.7995	.8023	.8051	.8078	.8106	.8133
0.9	.8159	.8186	.8212	.8238	.8264	.8289	.8315	.8340	.8365	.8389
1.0	.8413	.8438	.8461	.8485	.8508	.8531	.8554	.8577	.8599	.8621
1.1	8643	.8665	.8686	.8708	.8729	.8749	.8770	.8790	.8810	.8830
1.2	.8849	.8869	.8888	.8907	.8925	.8944	.8962	.8980	.8997	.9015
1.3	.9032	.9049	.9066	.9082	.9099	.9115	.9131	.9147	.9162	.9177
1.4	.9192	.9207	.9222	.9236	.9251	.9265	.9279	.9292	.9306	.9319
1.5	.9332	.9345	.9357	.9370	.9382	.9394	.9406	.9418	.9429	.9441
1.6	.9452	.9463	.9474	.9484	.9495	.9505	.9515	.9525	.9535	.9545
1.7	.9554	.9564	.9573	.9582	.9591	.9599	.9608	.9616	.9625	.9633
1.8	.9641	.9649	.9656	.9664	.9671	.9678	.9686	.9693	.9699	.9706
1.9	.9713	.9719	.9726	.9732	.9738	.9744	.9750	.9756	.9761	.9767
2.0	.9772	.9778	.9783	.9788	.9793	.9798	.9803	.9808	.9812	.9817
2.1	.9821	.9826	.9830	.9834	.9838	.9842	.9846	.9850	.9854	.9857
2.2	.9861	.9864	.9868	.9871	.9875	.9878	.9881	.9884	.9887	.9890
2.3	.9893	.9896	.9898	.9901	.9904	.9906	.9909	.9911	.9913	.9916
2.4	.9918	.9920	.9922	.9925	.9927	.9929	.9931	.9932	.9934	.9936
2.5	.9938	.9940	.9941	.9943	.9945	.9946	.9948	.9949	.9951	.9952
2.6	.9953	.9955	.9956	.9957	.9959	.9960	.9961	.9962	.9963	.9964
2.7	.9965	.9966	.9967	.9968	.9969	.9970	.9971	.9972	.9973	.9974
2.8	.9974	.9975	.9976	.9977	.9977	.9978	.9979	.9979	.9980	.9981
2.9	.9981	.9982	.9982	.9983	.9984	.9984	.9985	.9985	.9986	.9986
3.0	.9987	.9987	.9987	.9988	.9988	.9989	.9989	.9989	.9990	.9990
3.1	.9990	.9991	.9991	.9991	.9992	.9992	.9992	.9992	.9993	.9993
3.2	.9993	.9993	.9994	.9994	.9994	.9994	.9994	.9995	.9995	.9995
3.3	.9995	.9995	.9995	.9996	.9996	.9996	.9996	.9996	.9996	.9997
3.4	.9997	.9997	.9997	.9997	.9997	.9997	.9997	.9997	.9997	.9998

Index

Name

A

Allen, D. S., 155n
Altman, E. I., 56n
Aridas, Tina, 345n

B

Babcock, G. C., 219n
Baier, Jerome R., 269n
Banz, R. W., 52n
Barnes, A., 188n, 189n
Baruch, Bernard, 24
Bierwag, G. O., 223n, 278n
Black, Fischer, 390n, 625
Blume, Marshall E., 54n, 56n, 475, 511
Boardman, Calvin M., 260n, 261n
Boschan, Charlotte, 336n
Box, G. E. P., 338
Bradbury, Katharine L., 356n, 357n, 358n
Brealey, Richard, 500n, 509n
Breasley, R. A., 510n
Brenner, Menachem, 475n
Briloff, Abraham, 390n
Brooks, R., 219n

C

Carabini, C. 596—58
Carter, R., 154n
Chua, J. H., 219n
Cook, Timothy Q., 68, 259
Cooper, Guy, 515—16, 517n
Cross, F., 52n
Cumby, Robert, 560

D

DeBond, Werner F. M., 528, 529
DeFina, Robert H., 327n
De Long, J. Bradford, 544n
Dickey, D. A., 339n
Donnel, J., 189n
Dubofsky, D. A., 90n
Dusak, Katherine, 594, 595n

E

Echols, M. E., 258n
Elliot, J. W., 258n
Elliot, Walter, 269n
Emery, Kenneth M., 337n

F

Fabozzi, Frank J., 55n, 268n, 475n
Fabozzi, T. D., 55n, 268n
Fama, Eugene F., 22n, 89n, 491, 500n, 507n,
    508n, 509, 510, 511, 512—15, 530, 531,
    532
Farnsworth, Clyde, 335n
Fisher, Black, 531, 532
Fisher, Irving, 225
Fisher, Lawrence, 89n, 261n, 512—15
Fomby, Thomas B., 344
Fons, J. S., 262n, 263n, 264n
Ford, Henry, 362
Fortin, R. D., 118
Fortune, P., 517
Foster, F. D., 155n
Francis, Jack Clark, 475n

Subject

A